Byzantine Court Culture
from 829 to 1204

Byzantine Court Culture from 829 to 1204

edited by Henry Maguire

Dumbarton Oaks Research Library and Collection
Washington, D.C.

Distributed by Harvard University Press

Paperback Edition, 2004
ISBN-13: 978-0-88402-308-1

Printed in the United States of America
Fourth Printing, 2020

LIBRARY OF CONGRESS CATALOGING-IN-PUBLICATION DATA
Byzantine court culture from 829 to 1204 / edited by Henry Maguire.
    p.   cm.
    English and French.
Papers from a symposium held in April, 1994.
    Includes bibliographical references and index.
    ISBN-10: 0-88402-308-7 (alk. paper)
1. Byzantine Empire—Civilization—Congresses.
2. Byzantine Empire—Court and courtiers—History—Congresses.
3. Byzantine Empire—Foreign relations—Congresses.
I. Maguire, Henry, 1943-.
II. Dumbarton Oaks.
    DF521.B934   1997
    949.5'02—dc21
                    96-47558

Cover illustration: Emperor Alexander mosaic, Hagia Sophia, Istanbul, Turkey, ca. 1960s. Byzantine Institute, MS.BZ.004-BF.S.HS140, The Byzantine Institute and Dumbarton Oaks Fieldwork Records and Papers, ca. late 1920s–2000s, Image Collections and Fieldwork Archives, Dumbarton Oaks, Trustees for Harvard University, Washington, D.C.

www.doaks.org/publications

Contents

Introduction

In 1950 a symposium was held at Dumbarton Oaks on the topic of "The Emperor and the Palace," with a roster of speakers that included Andreas Alföldi, Francis Dvornik, André Grabar, Ernst H. Kantorowicz, Hans P. L'Orange, and Paul A. Underwood. Forty-four years later, in April 1994, this subject was revisited by a new generation of scholars in another Dumbarton Oaks symposium held in the same room but with a different title, "Byzantine Court Culture from 829 to 1204." The limiting dates, which reflect the increasing specialization of Byzantine studies in the intervening years, were chosen to encompass the golden age of Byzantine court life. This period began with the reign of Theophilos, the "lover of adornment" who was responsible for the revival of palace construction and for automata such as the fabled golden tree with its singing birds; it ended with the Fourth Crusade and the destruction of the court in Constantinople. For the most part, the same chronological limits are observed in this publication of the symposium, which thus records the Byzantine court at its apogee.

The subject of this book is both old and new. Ever since the Middle Ages, the imperial court in Constantinople has been central to the outsider's vision of Byzantium. However, in spite of its fame in literature and scholarship, there have been relatively few attempts to analyze the Byzantine court in its entirety as a phenomenon. While there have been important studies of different aspects of court life, such as its art or its ceremonial, these aspects have seldom been integrated into a composite/picture. The studies gathered together in this volume aim to provide such a unified composition by presenting Byzantine courtly life in all of its interconnected facets. The authors discuss the imperial palaces, gardens and parks, the ceremonials and liturgies, the costumes and regalia, the relics kept in the palace, the court icons, the courtly rhetoric, the intellectual life of courtiers, the social composition of the court, the hierarchy of titles, including the incomes of the title holders, and the iconography and ideology of court art. At the same time, attention is paid to the relationships between the court of the Byzantine emperors and those of other medieval rulers, Islamic, Armenian, and Norman. Finally, consideration is given to the interaction of the imperial court on earth with the supreme court in heaven, especially as expressed in panegyric and art.

Without attempting to summarize the papers collected here, which need no amplification as an account of the rich and complex mechanisms of Byzantine court culture, I would like to draw attention to one important theme that runs through a majority of the discussions. As many of the authors show, a fundamental change took place in the character and role of the court in the course of the eleventh century. This change affected all levels and all aspects of palace life. It had its basis in the social makeup of the court. In the Macedonian period, the emperor selected his top administrators without paying great attention to their birth, but under the Komnenian emperors the elite posts were given to members of a hereditary aristocracy or, in the case of the highest positions, to the emperor's own relatives. Consequently there was more vertical mobility in the tenth and early eleventh centuries than in the later part of our time frame. However, the courtiers of the Macedonian period, promoted and salaried by the emperor, were more dependent on him, whereas by the twelfth century the ethos of the court had changed. Under the Komnenoi, the individual courtiers had acquired a more detached and individualistic attitude toward their roles with respect to the monarch, a shift that is detectable even in the literary productions of the intellectuals. Moreover, the formal segregation of women at court that is revealed by sources such as the tenth-century *Book of Ceremonies* seems to have been to some extent abandoned by the twelfth century.

These social changes within the Byzantine court were also reflected in the spheres of art and architecture. The change is best symbolized by the relocation of the court from the pavilions, gardens, and terraces of the Great Palace to the castlelike environment of the Blachernai at the city walls, overlooking the hunting grounds of the Philopation. In the realm of small objects, the tightly choreographed high-level exchanges of gifts between courts, characteristic of the tenth and eleventh centuries, were replaced in the twelfth century by a much broader and more decentralized distribution of similar but more commercially produced items for a wider clientele of aristocratic and mercantile purchasers. These changes in the social composition, mentality, and material culture of the court demonstrate that, as in so many other aspects of Byzantine civilization, the image of permanence and immutability projected by the forms of palace life was more apparent than real. Behind the golden facade of ceremonial, rhetoric, and art, there was constant development and renewal.

In conclusion, I would like to thank the speakers who agreed to participate in the symposium and who contributed their papers for inclusion here. I am also grateful to Hedy Schiller and to Allison Sobke, who helped in various ways to prepare this book for publication, and to the staff of the Publications Office at Dumbarton Oaks, who saw the book through the press.

Henry Maguire
University of Illinois, Urbana-Champaign

List of Abbreviations

ActaIRNorv	*Acta ad archaeologiam et artium historiam pertinentia*, Institutum Romanum Norvegiae
ActaSS	*Acta sanctorum Bollandiana*
AJA	*American Journal of Archaeology*
AnalBoll	*Analecta Bollandiana*
ArtB	*Art Bulletin*
BHG	*Bibliotheca hagiographica graeca*, 3d ed., ed. F. Halkin, 3 vols. (Brussels, 1957)
BMGS	*Byzantine and Modern Greek Studies*
BollGrott	*Bollettino della Badia greca di Grottaferrata*
Bonn ed.	Corpus scriptorum historiae byzantinae, ed. B. G. Niebuhr et al. (Bonn, 1828–97)
BSCAbstr	*Byzantine Studies Conference, Abstracts of Papers*
ByzF	*Byzantinische Forschungen*
BZ	*Byzantinische Zeitschrift*
CahArch	*Cahiers archéologiques*
CCSG	Corpus christianorum, Series graeca
CCSL	Corpus christianorum, Series latina
CFHB	Corpus fontium historiae byzantinae
CSEL	Corpus scriptorum ecclesiasticorum latinorum
CSHB	Corpus scriptorum historiae byzantinae (*see* Bonn ed.)
De cer.	*De ceremoniis aulae byzantinae*, ed. J. J. Reiske, 2 vols. (Bonn, 1829–30); *Le livre des cérémonies*, ed. and trans. A. Vogt, 2 vols. (Paris, 1935–39)
Δελτ.Χριστ.'Αρχ.'Ετ.	Δελτίον τῆς Χριστιανικῆς 'Αρχαιολογικῆς 'Εταιρείας
DOP	*Dumbarton Oaks Papers*
DOS	Dumbarton Oaks Studies
EO	*Échos d'Orient*
'Επ.'Ετ.Βυζ.Σπ.	'Επετερὶς 'Εταιρείας Βυζαντινῶν Σπουδῶν
GBA	*Gazette des beaux-arts*
GCS	Die griechischen christlichen Schriftsteller der ersten [drei] Jahrhunderte (1897–)
GRBS	*Greek, Roman and Byzantine Studies*
ILS	*Inscriptiones latinae selectae*, ed. H. Dessau, 3 vols. (Berlin, 1892–1916)
JbKSWien	*Jahrbuch der Kunsthistorischen Sammlungen in Wien*
JÖB	*Jahrbuch der Österreichischen Byzantinistik*

JÖBG	*Jahrbuch der Österreichischen Byzantinischen Gesellschaft*
JTS	*Journal of Theological Studies*
Mansi	J. D. Mansi, ed., *Sacrorum conciliorum nova et amplissima collectio* (Paris-Leipzig, 1901–27)
MGH	Monumenta Germaniae historica (Hannover, Berlin, etc., 1826–)
———, *ScriptRerGerm*	*Scriptores rerum Germanicarum*
———, *SS*	*Scriptores*
MünchJb	*Münchner Jahrbuch der bildenden Kunst*
Νεος Ἑλλ.	*Νέος Ἑλληνομνήμων*
ODB	*The Oxford Dictionary of Byzantium*, ed. A. P. Kazhdan et al., 3 vols. (New York-Oxford, 1991)
OCA	Orientalia christiana analecta
OCP	*Orientalia christiana periodica*
OKS	*Ostkirchliche Studien*
PG	Patrologiae cursus completus, Series graeca, ed. J. P. Migne (Paris, 1857–66)
PO	Patrologia orientalis
RB	*Reallexikon der Byzantinistik*, ed. P. Wirth, 6 fascs. (Amsterdam, 1968–76)
RBK	*Reallexikon zur byzantinischen Kunst*, ed. K. Wessel (Stuttgart, 1963–)
REArm	*Revue des études arméniennes*
REB	*Revue des études byzantines*
REG	*Revue des études grecques*
SC	Sources chrétiennes
SemKond	*Seminarium Kondakovianum*
ST	Studi e testi
SubsHag	Subsidia hagiographica, Société des Bollandistes
Synaxarium CP	*Synaxarium ecclesiae Constantinopolitanae. Propylaeum ad ActaSS Novembris*, ed. H. Delehaye (Brussels, 1902)
TAPS	*Transactions of the American Philosophical Society*
TM	*Travaux et mémoires*
VizVrem	*Vizantijskij vremennik*
Zepos, *Jus*	J. and P. Zepos, eds., *Jus graecoromanum*, 8 vols. (Athens, 1931; repr. Aalen, 1962)
ZRVI	*Zbornik radova Vizantološkog instituta*
ZKunstg	*Zeitschrift für Kunstgeschichte*

The Emperor in His Church:
Imperial Ritual in the Church of St. Sophia

George P. Majeska

That the Byzantine emperor is a "sacred" figure is as commonplace in modern scholarship as in ancient sources. The basic texts involved in this question, beginning with Constantine the Great's reputed claims to be "bishop of those outside" and "general bishop," to Leo III's claim that he is "priest and emperor" (a statement that the pope, at least, found shocking), are well known.[1] Exactly what is meant by the emperor's "sacred nature" is a question that has generated volumes of scholarship, and will continue to do so; the topic is fundamental to understanding Byzantium.[2] The present study joins the ongoing discussion of Byzantine political theory by analyzing the ritual behavior of the Middle Byzantine emperor in his "official" public church, namely, the great cathedral of St. Sophia in Constantinople. The focus is not merely on what the emperor does in certain regularly recurring ceremonial situations in the Great Church, but also on what these elements of ritual behavior mean to those who witness them or hear about them. This study, then, is intended to be an analysis of the significance of the ritualized behavior patterns of an emperor, particularly in the liturgical context of worship at sacred functions in St. Sophia.

Although there are many occasions during which the emperor publicly participates in services at the Great Church, three seem to be especially useful for an analysis of the significance of the emperor's participation in liturgical activity: the coronation of the emperor; the solemn patriarchal liturgy on dominical festivals; and an unusual once-a-year Holy Saturday rite of censing the sacred vessels of the church's treasury. Studying the emperor's behavior in these three specific contexts provides some insight into the "liturgical" character of his sacred charisma and suggests how an emperor is perceived to combine *sacerdotium* and *imperium*.[3]

---

[1] ἐπίσκοπος τῶν ἐκτός, Eusebios, *Vita Constantinae*, IV.24; κοινὸς ἐπίσκοπος, ibid., I.44; βασιλεὺς καὶ ἱερεύς, Pope Gregory II, "De sacris imaginibus," Mansi, XII, 975.

[2] The fundamental study of this topic is now G. Dagron, *Empereur et prêtre: étude sur le "césaropapisme" byzantin* (Paris, 1995), unfortunately unavailable to me when this paper was written. A good recent summary treatment, with useful bibliographies, is D. M. Nicol, "Byzantine Political Thought," in *The Cambridge History of Medieval Political Thought c. 350–c. 450*, ed. J. H. Burns (Cambridge, 1988), 51–79, 696–703.

[3] The basic sources for this study are Constantine VII's *De cerimoniis* and the *Euchologion* of the Great Church; see Constantine VII Porphyrogennetos, *Le livre des cérémonies*, ed. A. Vogt, 2 vols. in 4 parts (Paris, 1935–40)

Coronation by the patriarch is obviously the appropriate place to begin. It was by his coronation, one would assume, that the emperor acquired his special liturgical charisma.[4]

The emperor, with his entourage, arrives for his coronation at the southwest portal of St. Sophia (**1** on Fig. 1) much as he does on major feasts (see below), and is met by the patriarch at the entrance to the inner narthex (**2**). From there they enter the nave together through the central ("imperial") doors (**3**) and go onto the *solea* (**4**), the raised balustraded pathway leading from the ambo, the great pulpit in the center of the church, to the chancel barrier.[5] When they arrive at the central gates to the sanctuary (**5**), the emperor, with a lighted candle in his hand, prays with the patriarch before the holy doors of the sanctuary but does not enter the sanctuary precincts.[6] Rather, he and the patriarch turn and walk back to mount the ambo (**6**), where the coronation paraphernalia, the crown and the *chlamys* and *fibula,* lay ready on a small table (ἀντιμίνσιον).[7] After a litany intoned by the deacon, the patriarch reads a special prayer over the imperial *chlamys* and *fibula* and then hands them to courtiers, who vest the emperor in them.[8]

(hereafter *Le livre des cérémonies*), and *Euchologion sive rituale graecorum,* ed. J. Goar (Venice, 1730; Graz, 1960) (hereafter Goar, *Euchologion*). Among older treatments of the emperor as a religious-liturgical figure, O. Treitinger, *Die Oströmische Kaiser- und Reichsidee* (Jena, 1938; Darmstadt, 1956) and L. Bréhier,ʹΙερεὺς καὶ βασιλεύς, *Mémorial Louis Petit,* Archives de l'Orient chrétien 1 (Bucharest, 1948), 41–45; cf. also J. Ebersolt, "Études sur la vie publique et privée de la cour byzantine," in his *Mélanges d'histoire et d'archéologie byzantines* (Paris, 1917), 91–101.

[4] The following description of a Middle Byzantine imperial coronation is based on *De cerimoniis* 47 (38), *Le livre des cérémonies,* vol. II, 1, pp. 1–3, and Goar, *Euchologion,* 726–30. The latter reflects two manuscripts, one datable to about 795, the other coming from the 12th century. The insignificance of the variations between the two *euchologion* texts suggests that the ceremony, at least from the point of view of the officiating clergy for whom the texts were copied, remained quite stable for the period in question. This paper does not discuss the secular elements of elevation to imperial status. On the elevation of emperors in Byzantium, see Ai. Christophilopoulou, Ἐκλογή, ἀναγόρευσις καὶ στέψις τοῦ Βυζαντινοῦ αὐτοκράτορος, in Πραγματεῖαι τῆς Ἀκαδημίας Ἀθηνῶν 22.2 (Athens, 1956); on the evolution of the Byzantine coronation ritual, see F. E. Brightman, "Byzantine Imperial Coronations," *JTS* 2 (1901), 359–92; see also the recent liturgically oriented study, M. Arranz, "Couronnement royal et autres promotions de cour. Les sacrements de l'institution de l'ancien Euchologe constantinopolitain," *OCP* 56 (1990), 83–133.

[5] On the internal arrangements of the Great Church, see Fig. 1 and R. J. Mainstone, *Hagia Sophia: Architecture, Structure and Liturgy of Justinian's Great Church* (London, 1988), particularly 219–35.

[6] Up to this point we have the normal ceremonial arrival of the emperor at St. Sophia and his entrance into the church with the patriarch as prescribed for major festivals (see below). He is, thus, in a certain sense, acting as emperor even before his coronation. This pre-coronation imperial behavior might be seen as reflecting the theory recently put forward by P. Yannopoulos, "Le couronnement de l'empereur à Byzance: rituel et fond institutionnel," *Byzantion* 61 (1991), 73–89, that the man to be crowned is already emperor, not only de facto but also de jure, by dint of his control of the palace, the army, and the Senate; it is this control that allows him to arrange the ecclesiastical coronation, which adds the charismatic seal to the political reality. Note, however, that the emperor does not exercise any genuinely liturgical functions (such as entering the sanctuary, kissing the altar, or censing, which he does at this point in similar ceremonies) until he has been raised to "sacred" imperial status by his coronation.

[7] Or ἀντιμήσιον, ἀντιμίσιον (*antimension*), a small table normally used in the distribution of communion, not the modern "corporal" of the same name; on the meaning of this word in the present context, see R. F. Taft, "The Pontifical Liturgy of the Great Church according to a Twelfth-Century Diataxis in Codex *British Museum Add. 34060,*" *OCP* 45 (1979), 302–3, notes. The *chlamys* (χλανίς?) was a ceremonial cloak worn by emperors; cf. Arranz, "Couronnement royal," 90 note 13.

[8] Texts of this prayer and of the subsequent prayer over the crown, along with rubrics, in Goar, *Euchologion,* 726–27; English translation of the prayers in Brightman, "Coronations," 380–81. In the 12th century, the cus-

The patriarch then reads a prayer over the imperial crown and, making the sign of the cross with it, places it on the emperor's head, saying, "In the name of the Father, and of the Son, and of the Holy Ghost," and then intoning "Worthy!" The congregation repeats the patriarch's chant of the word "Worthy" three times.[9] The ritual here would strike a Byzantine as quite familiar. Except for the lack of actual "laying on of hands" (a quite fundamental element, of course), its form is that of ordination to holy orders, the sacramental act that distinguishes clergy from laity:[10] the ceremony is assigned to a specific moment in the eucharistic liturgy, the first or "little entrance" (ἡ μικρὰ εἴσοδος),[11] and a specific place in the church, the clerical territory of the ambo;[12] it is performed by a bishop, who, after specified prayers, makes the sign of the cross over the ordinand and invests him with the robe or robes peculiar to his office to the accompaniment of an exclamation of "Worthy!" repeated three times by the congregation to signify its agreement in the consecration of the candidate.[13] Later in the liturgy during which the ordination is performed, the newly ordained clergyman performs for the first time a task specific to his new rank. Perhaps in the case at hand we should note several actions performed by the emperor during the liturgy at which he is crowned that would seem to be specific to the new ecclesiastical (clerical?) rank of the emperor, actions he will perform with some regularity once crowned: he participates in the procession of the

---

tom of anointing the new emperor with chrism was introduced, doubtless in imitation of the western custom; see Brightman, 383–89, and D. M. Nicol, "*Kaisersalbung:* The Unction of Emperors in Late Byzantine Coronation Ritual," *BMGS* 2 (1976), 37–52; cf. John Kantakouzenos, *Historiarum,* vol. I (Bonn, 1828), 197–98; Pseudo-Kodinus, *Traité des offices,* ed. J. Verpeaux (Paris, 1966), 258. The prayer that accompanied the imperial anointing was based on the two prayers just noted (text and French translation published in Pseudo-Kodinus, *Traité des offices,* 353–54).

[9] I here combine the two texts dealing with the coronation of emperors and co-emperors recorded in *De cerimoniis,* chap. 47 (38). The first text, which describes the coronation of an independent emperor by the patriarch, does not mention the patriarch's exclamation "Worthy!" repeated by the congregation, but skips to the longer congregational chant, "Holy, holy, holy, Glory to God in the highest and on earth peace!" which follows the patriarchal intoning of "Worthy!" and its repetition by the congregation in the immediately following description of the parallel ritual of the coronation of a co-emperor (*Le livre des cérémonies,* vol. II, 1, pp. 2–3). Note that the later Byzantine coronation descriptions testify to the patriarchal chant of "Worthy!" at this point in the service, and the congregation taking it up; see Kantakouzenos, *Historiarum,* 198; Pseudo-Kodinus, *Traité des offices,* 259, etc. I suspect that the copyist in the first coronation description in *De cerimoniis,* in a kind of homœoarchon, skipped over Ἄξιος! (Worthy!) and rather picked up the Ἅγιος! (Holy!) from the immediately following acclamation by the congregation, "Holy, holy, holy . . ." On the nature and role of such public acclamations in Byzantine life, see R. F. Taft, "The Dialogue before the Anaphora in the Byzantine Eucharistic Liturgy III: 'Let us give thanks to the Lord. It is fitting and right," *OCP* 55 (1989), 69–72, and the literature cited there.

[10] On clerical ordination in this period, see Goar, *Euchologion,* 194–261, and P. de Meester, *Studi sui sacramenti amministrati secondo il rito bizantino* (Rome, [1947]), 243–74, especially 243–44 on characteristics of ordination rites; cf. also Symeon of Thessalonica, *De sacris ordinationibus,* PG 155:361–470. I am grateful to Merlin Packard for his insistence on the importance of the "laying on of hands" in clerical ordination.

[11] Imperial coronations can also, probably when the need for a new emperor is pressing, be performed outside of the liturgy, but that would seem to be an exceptional circumstance. In such cases the newly crowned ruler is communicated from the reserved sacrament (κοινωνεῖ προηγιασμένα); see Goar, *Euchologion,* 727, 729.

[12] On the liturgical functions of the ambo, see R. F. Taft, *The Great Entrance: A History of the Transfer of Gifts and other Preanaphoral Rites of the Liturgy of St. John Chrysostom,* OCA 200 (Rome, 1975), 312–13; see also P. H. Jakobs, *Die frühchristlichen Ambone Griechenlands* (Bonn, 1987).

[13] See above, notes 8, 9.

"great entrance" (ἡ μεγάλη εἴσοδος) in the liturgy; he is commemorated by the clergy as they enter the sanctuary in the same way they commemorate the celebrating bishop or patriarch; he exchanges the kiss of peace with the patriarch; and he partakes of the eucharist, not like a layman with the consecrated bread and wine together in a spoon, but like a priest or deacon, receiving the consecrated bread in his hand from the patriarch and drinking the consecrated wine from the chalice held by the patriarch (the once universal custom, but now restricted to higher clergy and emperors).[14] It is, however, precisely in the reception of communion that the ambiguity of this "imperial ordination" manifests itself. Unlike bishops, priests, and deacons, the newly crowned emperor does not communicate inside the sanctuary at the holy table itself, but rather at a special small table set before the central entrance to the sanctuary.[15] His "ecclesiastical" rank, then, would seem to be below that of higher clergy (bishops, priests, and deacons—all ordained inside the sanctuary), who take the bread and wine of communion separately at the altar itself, but above the traditional ranks of the lower clergy ("ordained," like the emperor, outside the sanctuary), who take communion outside the sanctuary but in both forms together (like lay people).

To summarize here what members of the congregation in St. Sophia would have seen at a normal imperial coronation and how they would have interpreted what they saw: the imposition of ceremonial regalia (the *chlamys* and crown) by the patriarch to the chant of "Worthy!" would have been perceived as an ordination to sacred clerical office, an interpretation that would have been confirmed by the newly crowned emperor's taking part in the great entrance procession, being commemorated at that moment like a priest or bishop, sharing the kiss of peace with the celebrating clergy, and then taking communion as the higher clergy do. The emperor's ritually programmed actions are those of a clergyman (albeit a clergyman of indeterminate rank).[16]

Many of these symbolically powerful ritual acts were performed by emperors as part of their traditional behavior when they made major ceremonial appearances in St. Sophia, particularly on the major dominical feasts. It would be very useful to describe the emper-

---

[14] See sources cited in note 3 above. It is also possible, of course, that the emperor's reception of communion in this manner is simply an anachronistic custom preserved, as is often the case, in rare services on special occasions.

[15] Cf. Symeon of Thessalonica, *De sacro templo*, PG 155:351, and ibid., *De sacris ordinationibus*, cols. 361–64, 463–65. However, as a special exception, in the post-1204 period, the emperor was apparently allowed to take communion at the high altar with the clergy, but only on his actual day of coronation; see the discussion in G. Majeska, *Russian Travelers to Constantinople in the Fourteenth and Fifteenth Centuries*, DOS 19 (Washington, D.C., 1984), 433. See also below on the emperor's communion.

[16] Note that in Palaiologan times the emperor's ecclesiastical rank is that of *deputatus*, a certain official of St. Sophia in minor orders, a sort of verger whose staff he, in fact, often carries in religious ceremonies; see Taft, *The Great Entrance*, 27 note 65, and Majeska, *Russian Travelers to Constantinople*, 428.

It is interesting to compare the ritual of crowning an emperor or co-emperor who will have a special sacred charisma (investing by the patriarch with the crown to the chant of "Worthy!" in the ambo of St. Sophia) with the coronation of an empress who will have no clear liturgical function (investing by the emperor with the crown in the Augusteus, a ceremonial room in the palace, with no ordination-like chant of "Worthy!"); see *Le livre des cérémonies*, vol. II, pp. 6–23, and Goar, *Euchologion*, 727.

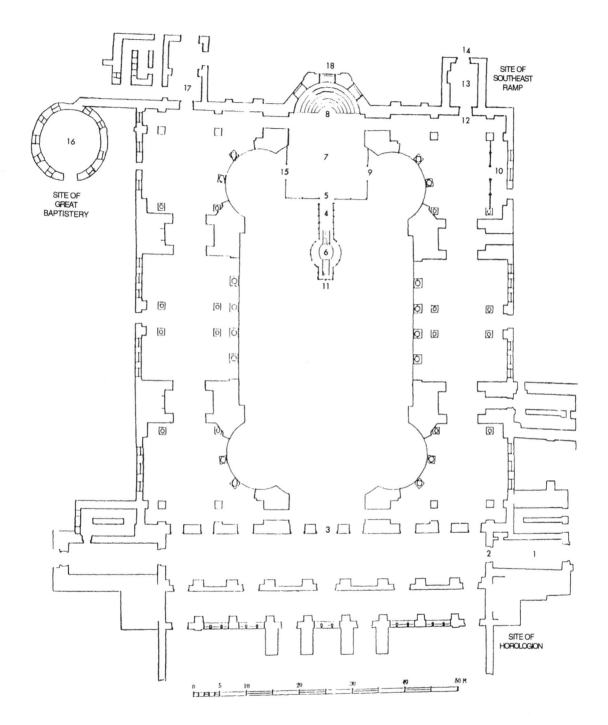

SITE OF
SOUTHEAST
RAMP

SITE OF
GREAT
BAPTISTERY

SITE OF
HOROLOGION

0   5   10   20   30   40   50 M

1   St. Sophia in Constantinople

or's actions in conjunction with the patriarchal liturgy on these great holidays in St. Sophia.[17]

Having crossed from the palace through the Augusteon square to the accompaniment of stylized acclamations (sung at least on solemn occasions in ecclesiastical liturgical "tones," according to the *Book of Ceremonies*)[18] from representatives of the demes gathered specifically for this purpose, the emperor arrives at the south entrance to the inner narthex of St. Sophia, at the so-called beautiful door (ἡ ὡραία πύλη) (**1** on Fig. 1), near the *horologion*. There he is divested of his crown in a draped booth (a *metatorion*)[19] in the southwest vestibule (**1**) (the emperor apparently wears his imperial crown inside St. Sophia only at his coronation).[20] Bareheaded, he enters through the south door of the inner narthex (walking beneath the famous mosaic of Constantine and Justinian on the two sides of the enthroned Mother of God with the Christ Child) (**2**), and is greeted by the patriarch and clergy. The emperor kisses the Gospel book and cross[21] presented by attending clergy, and then he and the patriarch kiss each other on the cheek and go hand in hand to the imperial doors (αἱ βασιλικαὶ πύλαι), the central doors leading from the narthex into the nave (**3**).

There the emperor receives a lit candle from the *praipositos*[22] and prays and bows three times before the doors (above which is depicted, of course, an emperor in the act of bowing in *proskynesis* before the throne of Christ). Meanwhile the patriarch reads the prayer of the little entrance of the liturgy. When the prayer is over, the emperor returns the candle to the *praipositos*, again kisses the Gospel book carried by the archdeacon,[23] and the emperor and patriarch enter the body of the church. Together they go around the ambo (**6**) and enter the *solea* (**4**), the low-walled walkway connecting the ambo to the area immediately before the chancel barrier. They follow it to the holy doors (τὰ

---

[17] The following is a distillation of the regularly repeated elements of imperial ritual during patriarchal liturgies at the Great Church as recorded in the *Book of Ceremonies*, particularly chaps. 1 and 32 (23) (*Le livre des cérémonies*, vol. I, pp. 3–20, 119–26), but with material also drawn from chaps. 9 and 37 (28) (*Le livre des cérémonies*, vol. I, pp. 58–62, 145–48); cf. also D. F. Beljaev, *Ežednevnye i voskresnye priemy vizantijskih carej i prazdničnye vyhody ih v hram Sv. Sofii v IX-X vv.* = *Byzantina*, vol. II (St. Petersburg, 1893), 150–96, and Ieromonah Ioann, *Obrjadnik vizantijskogo dvora kak cerkovno-istoričeskij istočnik* (Moscow, 1895), 144–47. The emperor attended the liturgy with full ceremony in St. Sophia on Easter, Pentecost, Transfiguration, Christmas, and Epiphany; see *Le livre des cérémonies*, vol. I, p. 17 et al., but also occasionally less formally, as on the Sunday of Orthodoxy (ibid., 145–47 et al.) and at the start of processions to other stational churches (ibid., 21–22, 66–67 et al.); see J. F. Baldovin, *The Urban Character of Christian Worship*, OCA 228 (Rome, 1987), and Ioann, *Obrjadnik*, 106–12, and 138–41, on imperial religious processions in Constantinople.

[18] Cf. *Le livre des cérémonies*, vol. I, p. 54; cf. Beljaev, *Ežednevnye i voskresnye priemy*, 86.

[19] *Le livre des cérémonies*, vol. I, p. 58. On these imperial "changing rooms," see J. B. Papadopoulos, "Le mutatorium des églises byzantines," *Mémorial Louis Petit*, Archives de l'Orient chrétien 1 (Bucharest, 1948), 366–68, and T. Mathews, *The Early Churches of Constantinople: Architecture and Liturgy* (University Park, Pa., 1971), 134.

There is some dispute about the location of the "beautiful door"; see C. Strube, *Die westliche Eingangsseite der Kirchen von Konstantinopel in justinianischer Zeit* (Wiesbaden, 1973), 50 et al.

[20] See Constantinus VII Porphyrogenitus, *De cerimoniis aulae byzantinae*, ed. J. J. Reiske (Bonn, 1829–30), vol. II, pp. 93–95 (commentary) (hereafter Reiske).

[21] *Le livre des cérémonies*, vol. I, p. 58.

[22] The *praipositos* was an extremely high court official; see R. Guilland, "Le Préposite," *Byzantinoslavica* 22 (1961), 241–301, repr. in his *Recherches sur les institutions byzantines*, vol. I, Berliner Byzantinische Arbeiten 35 (Berlin, 1967), 333–80.

[23] And the cross, according to *Le livre des cérémonies*, vol. I, p. 59.

ἄγια θύρια) (**5**) leading into the sanctuary, where once again they pray; the emperor, who stands on a porphyry disk set in the floor before the central doors of the chancel barrier,[24] again takes a candle from the *praipositos* and returns it to him after his prayer is completed. Then the patriarch enters through the holy doors and kisses the altar table (**7**). He is followed by the emperor, who does the same,[25] with the patriarch lifting the altar cloth (ἡ ἄγια ἐνδυτή) so that the emperor may kiss it more easily.[26] The emperor then takes from the hands of the *praipositos* two white altar covers (εἰλιτά)[27] and places them on the altar along with an *apokombion,* that is, a bag of gold coins. These are his regular gifts to the church. On certain holidays (notably on Pentecost), he also lays on the altar one or more chalices and patens that he is contributing to the Great Church.[28] He then kisses the two chalices and patens on the altar, and then the "swaddling clothes of Christ" (τὰ ἄγια σπάργανα), which the patriarch presents to his lips.[29] He then accompanies the patriarch, who circles the altar censing it, and they go together into the apse (**8**), where, again with a candle in his hand, the emperor prays before the large cross.[30] He kisses it and then takes the censer from the patriarch and himself censes the cross. The patriarch then escorts the emperor to the south door of the sanctuary (**9**), where they kiss each other. Following this exchange of kisses, the emperor goes to his *metatorion* (a combination imperial box and private oratory attached to a reception room) in the southeast corner of the nave (**10**), which will be his normal station for the rest of the service.[31]

This ceremony of imperial arrival looks very much like the ritualized arrival of higher clergy at church to prepare for the liturgy: the officiating higher clergy enter the church through the main door and go to the holy doors of the altar screen, where, after praying, they enter the sanctuary and kiss the altar. Laymen, of course, do not enter the sanctuary, and only those who "serve the altar" are allowed to kiss it: the emperor here clearly behaves as a clergyman serving the altar. Particularly telling is the emperor's kissing the

---

[24] *Le livre des cérémonies,* vol. I, p. 11. On the porphyry disk, see P. Schreiner, "Omphalion und Rota Porphyretica. Zum Kaiserzeremoniell in Konstantinopel und Rom," *Byzance et les Slaves: Études de Civilisation, Mélanges Ivan Dujčev* (Paris, n.d.), 401–10.

[25] The emperor is the only layman admitted to the clerical precincts of the sanctuary in Byzantine tradition; see the sources and discussion in Taft, *The Great Entrance,* 27; cf. ibid., 29–30.

[26] *Le livre des cérémonies,* vol. I, p. 11.

[27] On these altar covers see P. Speck, "Die Ἐνδυτή," *JÖB* 15 (1966), 323–75.

[28] *Le livre des cérémonies,* vol. I, p. 59; cf. ibid., p. 11; Reiske, vol. II, pp. 162–63 (commentary).

[29] This relic is normally kept on the high altar of the Great Church; see *Le livre des cérémonies,* vol. I, p. 11; cf. ibid., vol. I, 2, p. 61 (commentary).

[30] On some holidays it might be the emperor who censes around the altar at this point; see the description of the emperor censing the altar of St. Sophia at the beginning of the procession for the stational liturgy on the holiday of the Nativity of the Mother of God: *Le livre des cérémonies,* vol. I, p. 22. On censing at this point in the liturgy by clerics or an emperor, see R. F. Taft, "The Pontifical Liturgy of the Great Church," *OCP* 45 (1979), 288–89, and *OCP* 46 (1980), 106–10; cf. Reiske, vol. II, p. 110 (commentary), and Goar, *Euchologion,* 47–48, 51, 70, 79, where the censing actually follows the clergy's vesting and preparing the eucharistic elements, which they do after entering the sanctuary and kissing the altar; the censing is immediately preliminary to the beginning of the public part of the service.

[31] Outside the *metatorion* he kisses a cross with the Passion relics depicted on it; *Le livre des cérémonies,* vol. I, p. 12. On the imperial *metatorion* in St. Sophia, see Mainstone, *Hagia Sophia,* 223–26; cf. also below, note 38.

altar cloth held up for him by the patriarch in exactly the same way the patriarch kisses the altar cloth held up for him by a church dignitary when he celebrates in St. Sophia.[32] Censing in the sanctuary is, of course, also a clerical prerogative. Once again the emperor publicly does things normally reserved to higher clergy. Indeed the ceremonial entrance of the emperor and the patriarch into the nave together after kissing each other on the cheek (as equals greet each other) would have been perceived as demonstrating a relationship of equality: clergy of the same rank walk together in pairs on liturgical occasions.[33] Still, it should be noted, the emperor's normal place during the liturgy will be in the imperial box in the nave of the church, the area open to laity, not in the sanctuary.

When the emperor is summoned by the *referendarius,* a clergy aide to the patriarch,[34] to participate in the ceremony of the great entrance, that is, the transferral of the bread and wine from the place of preparation to the high altar, the emperor resumes the *chlamys,* the ceremonial robe he had removed when he went to the *metatorion,* and, accompanied by his banners, bodyguards, and courtiers, goes to the center of the church, before the ambo (**11**), where he meets the clergy procession bringing the bread and wine to the altar. Carrying a lamp (λαμπάς or κηρίον) that was waiting for him at the ambo, he leads the procession as it moves into the *solea* (**4**) and up to the holy doors of the sanctuary barrier (**5**), where the patriarch waits. The civil officials follow along on either side of the *solea* as far as the chancel screen. Here the emperor stops and steps aside to allow first the archdeacon carrying the paten and then the priest carrying the chalice to enter the holy doors. As he passes, the archdeacon censes the emperor and the patriarch and then he censes the altar. As he passes the emperor, each clergyman says, "May the Lord God remember your majesty in his kingdom, now and ever and ever more." After the bread and wine have been set on the altar, the emperor and the patriarch bow to each other, and the emperor returns to the *metatorion* (**10**). The liturgical prerogatives of the emperor displayed in these moments send mixed messages. Although leading the great entrance procession with a candle is a function often performed by someone in minor orders, being commemorated during the transferral of the gifts just as the patriarch and officiating clergy are commemorated at this moment is extraordinary,[35] as is being censed by the deacon in the same way the patriarch and the altar are censed.

The ritual connected with the ceremony of the kiss of peace is also significant. Once more summoned by the patriarch's *referendarius,* the emperor again puts on his *chlamys* and then goes with his entourage to the central entrance to the sanctuary (**5**), where he

---

[32] Cf. Taft, "The Pontifical Liturgy," 286–87.

[33] An exception occurs, actually, at ordinations, when the person to be ordained is brought forward by two members of the clergy in the rank to which he is being raised, one on each side; see above, note 10.

[34] The *referendarius* also serves as regular liaison between the patriarch and the emperor outside the liturgy; see J. Darrouzès, *Recherches sur les ὀφφίκια de l'Église byzantine,* Archives de l'Orient chrétien 11 (Paris, 1970), 373–74.

[35] On the formula by which the clergy commemorate one another as they enter the sanctuary at this point, see Taft, *The Great Entrance,* 241–42; cf. also ibid., 195–96, on the emperor's role in this part of the liturgy.

stands just to the right.[36] At the edge of the sanctuary, actually through the doorway, he exchanges the kiss of peace, first with the patriarch, and then one by one with all the higher clergy taking part in the liturgy as they are led up to him by the *referendarius*. The emperor exchanges the kiss of peace once more with the patriarch, and then, stepping down to the level of the nave from the level of the sanctuary, again he gives the kiss of peace, now to the members of the Senate and a number of other important officials in attendance as they are presented to him in turn by the master of ceremonies (ὁ τῆς καταστάσεως).[37] The perceived symbolism here is on many levels. Standing literally in the doorway between the sanctuary and the body of the church—symbolically, then, between heaven and earth—the emperor, this clerical-lay figure, mediates between the two worlds, bringing the *pax* of the altar to the lay world of the empire.

Once more the emperor returns to his *metatorion* (**10**), where he remains until he is summoned to communion. Then he again puts on his ceremonial robe and goes to the holy doors of the chancel (**5**), in front and to the right of which has been prepared a small table (*antimension*), at which he stops.[38] The patriarch brings the consecrated bread and wine out through the holy doors and places them on the small table and then puts a particle of the consecrated bread into the hand of the emperor, who steps down one step and eats it. The emperor then mounts the steps again, and the patriarch holds the chalice for him as he drinks some of the sacred wine while two *ostiarii*[39] hold a napkin. The emperor here takes communion as deacons and priests do, receiving the bread in his hand and drinking from the chalice held by the bishop, not in the sanctuary, be it noted, but just outside it, where laymen do—although he receives the two species separately, whereas lay folk are communicated with the bread and wine together on a spoon.[40] Once again we have an unclear set of symbols of the emperor's status, or, perhaps better, an ambiguity that all could interpret in their own fashion. The emperor's treatment is neither wholly that of a clergyman nor wholly that of a layman.[41]

---

[36] *Le livre des cérémonies*, vol. I, pp. 60–61, makes it clear that the ceremony of the imperial kiss of peace was performed to the right of the holy doors in the middle of the front of the chancel barrier, where the emperor's small table (*antimension*) was.

[37] And sometimes, at least, to three newly baptized Christians; *Le livre des cérémonies*, vol. I, p. 124 (Christmas). On the emperor's kiss of peace, see Taft, *The Great Entrance*, 395–96, and Ebersolt, "Études sur la vie publique," 95–97.

[38] Mathews, *The Early Churches of Constantinople*, 172–73, would have the emperor come to the sanctuary through the *solea* (4 on Fig. 1). This woud be an appropriate route only if the emperor were coming from a throne such as Mathews locates at the west side of the southeast pier (ibid., 96, 133–34), not from the *metatorion* in the southeast exedra (10 on Fig. 1); see *Le livre des cérémonies*, vol. I, pp. 13, 124.

[39] There were both court and ecclesiastical officials called *ostiarii*; see R. Guilland, "L'Ostiaire (ὀστιάριος)," *REB* 13 (1955), 79–84, repr. in his *Recherches sur les institutions byzantines*, 286–89, 296–99, and Darrouzès, *Recherches sur les ὀφφίκια*, index, s.v.

[40] "Excursus: The Emperor's Communion," R. F. Taft, *A History of the Liturgy of St. John Chrysostom 5: The Communion and Final Rites* (forthcoming), with references to the scholarship; I am very grateful to Professor Taft for allowing me to read this chapter of his book in typescript. Mathews, *Early Churches of Constantinople*, 172–73, is incorrect in his assertion that the emperor regularly takes communion at the high altar; see Taft, "The Emperor's Communion," and above, notes 15, 36.

[41] As in the emperor's entrance into the church at the moment of the little entrance, the emperor's participation in the passing of the kiss of peace, and his reception of the eucharist in both kinds separately, we have here a

After receiving the eucharist, the emperor returns to his *metatorion* (**10**) (actually, probably to the adjoining reception rooms), where he breakfasts with important officials. At the end of the service, the patriarch comes to join the emperor; they kiss, and then they proceed, together with their respective entourages, through the door at the south side of the east end of the church (**12**) into the shrine of the Holy Well (**13**).[42] Here the emperor presents bags of money (*apokombia*) to the archdeacon and to various officials of the church as well as to representatives of the poor as their names are announced by the imperial almoner (ὁ ἄργυρος). The emperor and the patriarch then enter the small draped chamber in the shrine, where the patriarch places the crown on the emperor's head and gives him some of the blessed bread (*antidoron*) from which the eucharistic matter had been cut and some perfumed oil. In return, the emperor gifts the patriarch with *apokombia* containing ten pounds of gold coins. They exchange kisses and part, the patriarch returning to his residence through the church, the emperor returning to the palace via the short route (**14**), accompanied by acclamations from the assembled representatives of the demes, as when he arrived.

The leave-taking ceremony in the private and restricted space of the shrine of the Holy Well is pregnant with symbolic meaning. The gift of money to the ecclesiastical functionaries and the poor depicts the emperor as supporter and patron of the church. In return, the patriarch gives the emperor what laymen receive at the end of the liturgy, a *eulogia* (a token; literally, "a blessing") of *antidoron* along with fragrant oil. The roles are clearer here than perhaps at any other time in the service. The emperor is a lay patron of the church. How he received that position is symbolized by the patriarch's crowning the emperor anew as he leaves the church building for the world where he wears the crown.

The final ceremonial appearance of the emperor in St. Sophia to be discussed is seemingly quite private, and the larger population is probably unaware of its occurrence. It comes on the morning of Holy Saturday and is connected with the tradition of stripping and washing the altar in connection with Good Friday.[43] At the third hour (that is, about nine in the morning), the emperor comes to the southeast entrance to the Great Church (**14**), the entrance connected to the Holy Well shrine (**13**), where he lights a candle and prays. He is met there by the patriarch, who, after the usual exchange of kisses, goes with the emperor through the so-called door of the poor (**12**) to the main or holy doors of the chancel barrier (**5**). Both pray there, the emperor with a candle in his hand. The patriarch then enters through the holy doors, as does the emperor after giving the candle back to the *praipositos*. The emperor covers the altar table (**7**) with a new cloth cover or

---

reminder of an ancient custom that had fallen into disuse under normal circumstances but was followed on certain special occasions; cf. Taft, *The Great Entrance*, 395–96.

[42] On the shrine of the Holy Well, see Cyril Mango, *The Brazen House: A Study of the Vestibule of the Imperial Palace of Constantinople* (Copenhagen, 1959), 60–72 and fig. 1.

[43] The ceremony is described twice in the *Book of Ceremonies*, more fully in chap. 44 (35) and somewhat summarily in chap. 1; *Le livre des cérémonies*, vol. I, pp. 169–71, 27–28; cf. 167–68. See also Beljaev, *Ežednevnye i voskresnye priemy*, 224–29, and Ioann, *Obrjadnik*, 119–21.

covers (quite likely that he has contributed) and then takes a large bag of gold coins (a hundred pounds!) from the *praipositos* and lays it on the step before the altar. He also takes another bag of gold (smaller) and places it on the altar table as an offering. He then takes the censer from the patriarch and circles the altar three times, censing it in the form of a cross.[44]

The patriarch and emperor then leave the sanctuary through the north door of the chancel screen (**15**) and go to the *skeuophylakion*, the freestanding treasury building on the north side of the church, which functioned as the church's sacristy (**16**).[45] There, candle in hand, the emperor prays, and then, taking the censer from the patriarch, he censes the holy vessels and relics in the cases, which have been opened for this purpose. The patriarch and the emperor then sit down on the thrones set up for them there. During this time the patriarch gives the emperor vessels of nard oil and pieces of cinnamon, apparently used to make the sacred chrism during Holy Week. The *chartoularios* of the *skeuophylakion*, who had given these things to the patriarch to give to the emperor, now asks the patriarch's blessing to distribute nard to the emperor's entourage, first to those who accompanied him into the building and then to the officials waiting outside.[46] After the nard has been distributed, the patriarch and the emperor leave the building and go through the north part of the church, through the women's narthex, where the deaconesses of the Great Church have their station (**17**),[47] and through the corridor behind the apse (the "passage [διαβατικά] of St. Nicholas") (**18**),[48] until they come to the Holy Well Shrine (**13**). There the patriarch gives the emperor a *eulogia* of blessed bread, as he had done when they entered the passage of St. Nicholas; they kiss and say good-bye. The patriarch returns to the church, and the emperor goes to the palace through the porticoes (**14**) as representatives of the demes acclaim him in a special fashion.

What is the nature of the role the emperor plays in this liturgical drama performed on Holy Saturday morning in company with the leading members of the imperial court? Certainly he is functioning here as patron of the Great Church: he lays a very significant gift at the foot of the altar and another gift on the altar table itself, and probably provides new altar coverings. One might also think that there the emperor also fulfills the role of a minor official of the church, a sort of sexton assisting at washing and covering the holy altar; he is, after all, in the rank of *deputatus*, at least according to fourteenth-century

---

[44] The "informal" entrance of the emperor into the church and the sanctuary and the censing of the altar follow the format for beginning imperial liturgical processions that go from St. Sophia to other major shrines of the city, particularly on holidays devoted to the Mother of God; see, for example, the description of the emperor's participation in the start of the procession from St. Sophia to the shrine of the Mother of God at Chalkoprateia on the Nativity of the Mother of God (8 September): *Le livre des cérémonies*, vol. I, pp. 20–22 ff. See also above, note 17.

[45] On this building, see Taft, *Great Entrance*, 185–91, 199, and G. Majeska, "Notes on the Skeuophylakion of St. Sophia," *VizVrem* (forthcoming).

[46] The *chartoularios* of the *skeuophylakion* was a clergy assistant to the *skeuophylax* of the Great Church who managed, among other things, the church's collection of sacred vessels and vestments; see Darrouzès, *Recherches sur les* ὀφφίκια, 85 note 3, 175, 314–18. On the nard and holy oil (*myron*), see Beljaev, *Ežednevnye i voskresnye priemy*, 226–27 note 1.

[47] The location of the narthex of the deaconesses is clear from the itinerary suggested in *De cerimoniis*.

[48] On the passage of St. Nicholas, see Mango, *The Brazen House*, 66–72.

sources.[49] But the sanctuary is the preserve of higher clergy, not of vergers like the *deputatus,* and indeed the emperor also fulfills the role of higher clergy by censing the altar, normally the prerogative of deacons, priests, and bishops. Is it, then, as clergyman that the emperor censes not only the altar but also the holy vessels used in the liturgy while he is in the *skeuophylakion?* The Holy Saturday services are dedicated to renewal of life, the message of the resurrection of Christ. It is for this renewal that the altar, unused on Good Friday, is washed and revested in order to be revivified on Easter. It would seem that the emperor's censing of the altar and the sacred vessels is a reconsecration ritual of the newly cleansed holy materials and that he is, by his censing, reconsecrating, as it were, these things, just as his predecessor Justinian actively participated in the original consecration of St. Sophia.

The answer to the question originally posed about the nature of the emperor's clerical charisma is far from clear. Indeed it would seem that the exact nature of the role the emperor is seen to play in liturgical functions in St. Sophia is purposely ambiguous. The symbols are not meant to be decoded easily. The emperor's clerical status is demonstrated by his active participation in the ritual with the clergy. Still, although the exact nature of his clerical status is never spelled out, there are sacramental limits beyond which he clearly does not go. He does not, for example, take communion himself but receives it; although he enters the sacred precincts of the sanctuary regularly, his normal place in the church is in the nave with the lay people. He is certainly a consecrated "holy emperor," but, to judge from his participation in the liturgical life of the first church of Byzantine Christianity, he is no priest-king. His ritualized actions, in fact, can almost serve as a metaphor for the tensions inherent in the peculiar nature of the relations between church and state in Byzantium in the Middle Ages. The emperor is, perhaps, priest and king, but he is not priest-king.

University of Maryland at College Park

---

[49] Pseudo-Kodinus, *Traité des offices,* 264; Symeon of Thessalonica, *De sacro templo,* col. 352 (δεποτάτου for δεσποτάτου; cf. Goar, *Euchologion,* 198, 230). The *deputatus* seems to have been equivalent to an acolyte (κηροφόρος) in terms of status; cf. Darrouzès, *Recherches sur les* ὀφφίκια, 231, 272 (chart).

Gardens of the Palaces

A. R. Littlewood

Realization of the fact that soil, when once it has been disturbed, frequently retains interpretable evidence of that disturbance has been utilized for many years by archaeologists in such things as the tracing of postholes in long-rotted wooden buildings, but only recently, mainly through the pioneering work of Wilhelmina Jashemski,[1] has it been applied to any appreciable extent in the discovery of ancient gardens; and even now little has been done outside Campania. Byzantine archaeologists have, furthermore, usually been handicapped by the superimposition of later buildings, often still in use today, over former gardens.[2] Indeed there is to date only a single piece of firm archaeological evidence for the nature of Byzantine palatial gardens: in the Great Palace at Constantinople the famous early mosaic pavement showing scenes of hunting, gardens, and everyday

[1] In especially *The Gardens of Pompeii, Herculaneum and the Villas destroyed by Vesuvius* (New Rochelle, N.Y., 1979–93); "The Gardens of Pompeii, Herculaneum and the Villas Destroyed by Vesuvius," *Journal of Garden History* 12.2 (1992), 102–25; "The Contribution of Archaeology to the Study of Ancient Roman Gardens," in *Garden History: Issues, Approaches, Methods,* ed. J. D. Hunt, Dumbarton Oaks Colloquium on the History of Landscape Architecture 13 (Washington, D.C., 1992), 5–30. See also K. L. Gleason, *Towards an Archaeology of Landscape Architecture in the Ancient Roman World,* D. Phil. thesis (Oxford, 1989) and, in general, C. Taylor, *The Archaeology of Gardens* (Princes Risborough, 1983). It is unfortunate that archaeologists have tended to interpret all marks of disturbance in soil that has not been built upon as agricultural rather than possibly horticultural.

[2] Little research has been done on Byzantine gardens. For many years the lengthiest overall treatment was the scanty and sometimes unreliable section in M. L. Gothein, *Geschichte der Gartenkunst,* vol. I (Jena, 1914), 143–48, although O. Schissel made a fine study of the garden in the Byzantine romances (*Der byzantinische Garten,* Akademie der Wissenschaften in Wien, Phil.-hist. Klasse, Sitzungsberichte 221.1 [1942], to which may now be added A. R. Littlewood, "Romantic Paradises: The Rôle of the Garden in the Byzantine Romance," *BMGS* 5 [1979], 95–114 and C. Barber, "Reading the Garden in Byzantium: Nature and Sexuality," *BMGS* 16 [1992], 1–19). The subject was dealt with very perfunctorily in Ph. I. Koukoules, Βυζαντινῶν βίος καὶ πολιτισμός, vol. IV (Athens, 1951), 315–17. More recently there have appeared A. R. Littlewood, "Gardens of Byzantium," *Journal of Garden History* 12.2 (1992), 126–53 and L. Brubaker and A. R. Littlewood, "Byzantinische Gärten," in *Der Garten von der Antike bis zum Mittelalter,* ed. M. Carroll-Spillecke (Mainz am Rhein, 1992), 213–48 (containing an extensive bibliography, 247–48), both of which include sections on palatial gardens that have been mined for the present paper. Some provocative questions have also been asked by J. Wolschke-Bulmahn, "Zwischen Kepos und Paradeisos: Fragen zur byzantinischen Gartenkultur," *Das Gartenamt* 4 (1992), 221–28 (with some useful bibliography), some of which with our present evidence unfortunately do not admit of answers. H. Maguire has recently discussed palatial gardens specifically ("Imperial Gardens and the Rhetoric of Renewal," in P. Magdalino, ed., *New Constantines: The Rhythm of Imperial Renewal in Byzantium, 4th-13th Centuries* [Aldershot, 1994], 181–97), but, apart from a brief summary of their physical characteristics (181–87), his purpose is to examine them as "receptacles of political ideas" that "sometimes even had a role to play in diplomacy" (181).

rural life once enclosed a bed of garden soil, but even this was thrown away by the workmen before its vegetal contents could be analyzed.[3]

Byzantine art, in pavements and miniatures, provides many instances of a stylized paradise,[4] but of secular gardens only glimpses as details in larger compositions which, though usually of biblical scenes, tend anachronistically to show what was familiar to the artist. The outstanding example of this is codex Paris. gr. 74, an eleventh-century *tetraevangelion*. Out of its 361 miniatures[5] no fewer than 209 contain both trees and flowers, which are often disposed in gardens on ground level, and perhaps adorned with a balustrade or a fountain (Fig. 1),[6] but on occasion also take the form of tiny rooftop gardens (Fig. 2).[7] The book indeed indicates a very popular Byzantine enthusiasm in that only twenty miniatures are completely devoid of vegetation, which occurs in lush and even bizarre form in the most unlikely situations such as Moses lifting the serpent in the wilderness.[8] However, Byzantine artists have bequeathed to us no known attempt to depict any specific garden, never mind a palatial one, with the single possible exception of a miniature in a twelfth-century manuscript of the Homilies of Gregory of Nazianzos now at Mount Sinai that offers a stylized, shorthand indication of gardens that could conceivably indicate those around the Nea Ekklesia in the Great Palace (see below, p. 27 and Fig. 3).[9] There do exist, it is true, several frescoes and miniatures that include

[3] Communication from Tamara Talbot Rice. Evidence does survive of marble canalization at the crossroads of Altıyol in Kadiköy that could have been associated with the palace of Chalkedon (R. Janin, *Constantinople byzantine: développement urbain et répertoire topographique,* 2d ed. [Paris, 1964], 494). Villehardouin's comment that the area around the palace there of Alexios III "fu bele et riche et plantëürose de toz biens" (*La conquête de Constantinople,* 135, ed. E. Faral [Paris, 1961], I, 136) may refer to agricultural land separate from or attached to the palace, but the remark of Niketas Choniates that ἄμιλλαι ἵππων and θέατρα were performed at the palace (ed. I. A. van Dieten, CFHB 11.1 [Berlin-New York, 1975], 530.50–51) implies nonagricultural palatial grounds and perhaps gardens.

[4] See especially H.Maguire, *Earth and Ocean: The Terrestrial World in Early Byzantine Art* (University Park, Pa.-London, 1987).

[5] All are illustrated in H. O(mont), *Évangiles avec peintures byzantines du XIe siècle,* 2 vols. (Paris, 1908).

[6] Fol. 52r showing Priests and Scribes before Caiaphas (Omont, vol. 1, pl. 42), illustrated also in Littlewood, "Gardens of Byzantium," 147, fig. 28.

[7] Fol. 149v showing Zacchaeus in sycamore espying Christ (right) and entertaining him at his home in Jericho (left) (Omont, vol. 2, pl. 129), illustrated also in Littlewood, "Gardens of Byzantium," 148, fig. 30. Perhaps the best and most famous miniature including a roof garden is that in the late 12th-century icon at Sinai of the Annunciation that has been frequently reproduced (e.g., K. Weitzmann et al., *Frühe Ikonen* [Vienna-Munich, 1965], pl. 30; Littlewood, "Gardens of Byzantium," 144, fig. 25; Brubaker and Littlewood, "Byzantinische Gärten," 242, fig. 85). Figure 7 below probably also shows roof gardens. They first appear, though in an unusual form, in Cicero's reference to "sollertiam eam quae posset vel in tegulis proseminare ostreas" (*Hort.,* frag. 78 apud Non. 216.14). Following the lead of his father's contemptuous "in summis culminibus mentita nemora" (*Contr.* 5.5), the Younger Seneca comments disapprovatively on the craze in Rome of the 1st century A.D.: "Non vivunt contra naturam qui pomaria in summis turribus serunt? Quorum silvae in tectis domuum ac fastigiis nutant, inde ortis radicibus quo inprobe cacumina egissent?" (*Ep.* 122.8: cf. id. *Ira* 1.21.1; *Thy.* 464–65). The standard term may have been "horti pensiles" (Quintus Curtius 5.1.32 [of the "Hanging Gardens of Babylon"]; Pliny, *N.H.* 19.23.64, 36.20.94).

[8] Fol. 171r (Omont, vol. 2, pl. 148; Littlewood, "Gardens of Byzantium," 132, 134, fig. 11).

[9] Cod. Sinaiticus 339, fol. 4v (*The Monastery of St. Catherine on Mount Sinai* [St. Catherine's, 1985], pl. 153; K. Weitzmann and G. Galavaris, *The Monastery of St. Catherine at Mount Sinai: The Illuminated Greek Manuscripts,* vol. I [Princeton, 1990], 140–53, fig. 472; Littlewood, "Gardens of Byzantium," 145, fig. 26; Maguire, "Imperial Gardens," 182–84, fig. 1).

1   Cod. Paris. gr. 74, fol. 52r, detail (after O[mont], *Évangiles,* I, pl. 42)

2   Cod. Paris. gr. 74, fol. 149v, detail (after O[mont], *Évangiles,* II, pl. 129)

3　Cod. Sinaiticus 339, fol. 4v (after *The Monastery of St. Catherine*, pl. 153)

4   Cod. Ath. Iviron 463, fol. 53v, detail (after Pelekanidis et al., *Treasures of Mount Athos,* II, 70, pl. 81)

5   Baradā panel, Great Mosque of Damascus, detail (after Creswell, *Early Muslim Architecture,* I.2, pl. 57c; by permission of the Oxford University Press)

6 Cod. Ath. Panteleimon 6, fol. 37v, detail (after Pelekanidis et al., *Treasures of Mount Athos,* I, 175, pl. 300)

7 Cod. Ath. Pantocrator 234, fol. 23v, detail (after Pelekanidis et al., *Treasures of Mount Athos,* III, 154, pl. 242)

8 Cod. Ath. Iviron 463, fol. 100r, detail (after Pelekanidis et al., *Treasures of Mount Athos,* II, 79, pl. 106)

vegetation in a palatial context. This, however, is usually little more than the row of cypresses behind a wall in the scene of Saint Nicholas of Myra speaking in a dream to Emperor Constantine asleep in his palace that is part of the cycle of the saint's life on the walls of the prothesis in the early fourteenth-century church of the Dormition at Gračanica.[10] A little more revealing is an illustration in a twelfth- or thirteenth-century manuscript of the Romance of Barlaam and Joasaph on Mount Athos (cod. Iviron 463, fol. 53v) of a tiny swimming pool between pruned trees enclosed by a fence and palatial buildings (Fig. 4).[11] However, the nearest that we can probably get to a realistic visual representation of a Byzantine palatial garden is probably the pair of garden pavilions set on a beflowered terrace in the eighth-century mosaic known as the Baradā panel in the Great Mosque at Damascus (Fig. 5) that probably both was made by Egyptian work-men[12] familiar with the Byzantine tradition and reflects contemporary Byzantine pala-tial design.[13]

Byzantine literature affords numerous references to gardens. Some of the more sub-stantial of these, however, are tralatitious: for instance Nikephoros Kallistos Xantho-poulos repeats verbatim some eight hundred years later Prokopios' description of the

[10] Illustrated in N. P. Ševčenko, *The Life of Saint Nicholas in Byzantine Art* (Turin, 1983), 258, pl. 22.6. See ibid., 119 note 13 for *similia* (I am indebted to Dr. Ševčenko for this information).

[11] S. Der Nersessian, *L'illustration du roman de Barlaam et Joasaph* (Paris, 1937), 169, pl. VIII, fig. 27; S. M. Pele-kanidis et al., *The Treasures of Mount Athos,* vol. II (Athens, 1975), 70, pl. 81; Maguire, "Imperial Gardens," 184–85, fig. 2.

[12] There survive on papyrus letters in Greek and mainly from Kurra ibn Sharīk, governor of Egypt (709–714), to Basileios, pagarch (prefect) of the District of Aphrodito, concerning the sending of workmen, wages, and ma-terials from Aphrodito for various building projects in the caliphate. One of these involves the supply for the Great Mosque at Damascus of copper chains or plates and another, backed by a separate requisition, the wages and expenses for a sawyer, probably sent earlier from Aphrodito (*PLond.* 1368, 1341, 1411 respectively, in *Greek Papyri in the British Museum,* IV: The Aphrodito Papyri, ed. H. I. Bell [London, 1910], 42–43, 12–13, 80). A Cop-tic letter from Aphrodito also relates to building expenses in Damascus, probably at the Great Mosque (*PLond.* 1515; ibid., 449–50). Further similar Greek letters relate to the construction of mosques and palaces at Damascus (*PLond.* 1342, ibid., 13–14), Fusṭāṭ (*PLond.* 1362, 1378; ibid., 36–38, 51) and Jerusalem (*PLond.* 1366, 1403; ibid., 40–41, 74–75), and one in Coptic concerns workmen and building materials for the caliph's riverside pal-ace at Babylon, which is probably to be interpreted here as Fusṭāṭ (*PLond.* 1517; ibid., 450). Employment of "Byzantine" workmen by the Arabs may go back even before the Hijra, for there is a tale told by Azraqī (d. A.D. 858) that in 608, when a Byzantine merchant ship was wrecked at Shuʿaibīya, the port of Mekka at that time, the Quraysh ordered a rescued Greek (Copt) carpenter to rebuild the dilapidated *kaʿaba,* and, if his further story is true that the interior decoration of the *kaʿaba* included a painting of Christ with his Mother and angels, we can suspect the involvement of a "Byzantine" painter too (*Die Chroniken der Stadt Mekka,* vol. I, ed. H. F. Wüstenfeld [Leipzig, 1857], 104–5, 107, 111, 114). There is a further tradition in Balādhurī from 868 that in 707–709 Ca-liph al-Walīd sent money, materials and eighty workmen from Syria and Egypt to Madīna for the reconstruction of the mosque (*Futuḥ al-Buldān,* ed. de Goeje, 6–7). According to Yaʿqūbī, writing six years later, Justinian II sent money, materials, and one hundred workmen for this purpose (*Taʾrīkh* 2.340). In certain skills the Muslims continued to rely on Christians living in their territory: e.g., in 1313 the "Palace of Felicity" (*Dar as-Saʿada*) in Cairo was constructed by Christian marble workers sent for the purpose from Damascus (al-Mufaḍḍal ibn Abīʾl-Faḍaʾil, *al-Nahdj al-Sadīd,* ed. and trans. E. Blochet, *Histoire des Sultans Mamlouks,* PO 20 [1929], 236–37 [742–43]). "Byzantine" involvement in the Great Mosque at Damascus itself can be extended to as recently as 1893 when after the fire in October of that year "two old Christian workmen . . . were the only men capable of executing certain of the repairs" (M. Ḥabīb Zayyāt quoted from a letter by M. Gautier-van Berchem in K.A.C. Creswell, *Early Muslim Architecture,* 2d ed. [Oxford, 1969], vol. I, pt. 1, 241 note 2. In general on this subject see ibid., 1–2, 143, 229–45).

[13] See further below, pp. 26–27.

gardens around the shrine of the Zoodochos Pege (modern Balıklı Kilesi) just outside the walls of Constantinople,[14] and, far more misleading because it properly portrays a different garden, Nicholas Mesarites, sacristan of the churches in the Great Palace, in his own eulogy, written sometime between 1198 and 1203, of the gardens around the church of the Holy Apostles[15] quotes extensively from Libanios' *Antiochikos* in praise of the famous pagan sanctuary at Daphne. In the more original compositions, with the passing of time, generic trees tend to replace specific (just as happens also in art), and the height of precision usually vouchsafed by our Byzantine servants of literary artistry is an expression such as "bosky fecundity." We do, however, possess one highly ornate poetic *ekphrasis* of an imperial suburban park which probably contains sufficient clues for it to be identified[16] and many brief allusions to various other palatial gardens for whose general appearance we can with caution use the often lengthy and detailed descriptions in the romances.[17]

The classical Roman belief that agriculture and horticulture were gentlemanly pursuits, so clearly shown from the time of Marcus Terentius Varro onwards, was held also by the Byzantines,[18] for instance by no less a man than Photios, who tells us that he tried out on his own estate precepts from an agricultural manual by Vindanios that is related to the *Geoponika*.[19] Unlike the ancient Romans, however, the Byzantines had also specific biblical exhortation, for, in addition to the frequent agricultural scenes of the parables, Psalm 128:2 specifically enjoins the eating of "the fruit of the labour of your hands" which, it claims, will bring happiness, while in Jeremiah's blunt injunction (29:5 = 29:28) to "plant gardens and eat their produce," the word "gardens" is most significantly a Greek addition to the Hebrew.

Byzantine emperors themselves, like their Roman predecessors,[20] did not disdain such interests. Julian boasts of having planted with his own hands a vineyard on his grand-

---

[14] Xanthopoulos, *Eccl. Hist.* 15.25; Prokopios, *Aed.* 1.3.6.

[15] G. Downey, ed. and trans., "Nikolaos Mesarites: Description of the Church of the Holy Apostles at Constantinople," *TAPS*, n.s., 47 (1957), secs. 3–5, pp. 897–98 (trans. 862–65). Mesarites' omissions, however, suggest that he does not borrow phrases entirely inapposite to his theme (see below, note 100).

[16] See below, p. 37.

[17] For a list of these see Littlewood, "Romantic Paradises," 110–14. They range from formal gardens to rural parks.

[18] See J. L. Teall, "The Byzantine Agricultural Tradition," *DOP* 25 (1971), 35–59; Littlewood, "Gardens of Byzantium," 128–29; Brubaker and Littlewood, "Byzantinische Gärten," 216–20.

[19] *Bibliotheca* 163. On the *Geoponika*, its origins and medieval translations, see Teall, "Agricultural Tradition," 39–42; J.A.C. Greppin, "The Armenians and the Greek *Geoponika*," *Byzantion* 57 (1987), 46–55.

[20] Hadrian is for the modern world the outstanding example with his grandiose villa at Tivoli, but other emperors had, if we may believe the sources, some odd notions of landscape gardening: Augustus adorned his gardens not only with statues, terraces, and groves, but also with "colossal bones of monstrous sea creatures and wild beasts" and "weapons of heroes" (Suet. *Aug.* 72.2–3); Caligula built a dining-room for fifteen guests with servants in a plane tree at his villa at Velitrae (Plin. *H.N.* 12.5.10) and transformed ships into floating gardens (Suet. *Calig.* 37.2), and Elagabalus created temporary hills out of snow and introduced a flower garden into his dining room in the form of a reversible ceiling that smothered his guests (*S.H.A., Heliog.* 22.5, 23.8). Moreover, one would-be emperor, Decimus Claudius Albinus, is known to have composed a book of *Georgics* (idd. *Clod.* 11.7). For further instances of imperial interest see A. R. Littlewood, "Ancient Literary Evidence for the Pleasure Gardens of Roman Country Villas," in *Ancient Roman Villa Gardens*, ed. E. B. MacDougall, Dumbarton Oaks Colloquium on the History of Landscape Architecture 10 (Washington, D.C., 1987), 7–30, especially 17–26.

mother's old estate;[21] Herakleios created vegetable gardens and parks;[22] Theophilos encouraged not only the building of palace complexes involving gardens at Hiereia and Bryas and in the city itself but also the creation of wall mosaics with gardenly scenes;[23] Basil I laid out the garden called the Mesokepion in the Great Palace;[24] Constantine VII ordered the compilation of the *Geoponika,* while gardens are frequently mentioned in historical works written by him or under his supervision; Michael IV, in rebuilding the church of the Anargyroi (Saints Kosmas and Damian), known as the Kosmidion, just outside the walls of the city at the modern Eyüp, oversaw, Psellos implies, the construction of the adjoining "beauteous baths, numerous fountains, lovely lawns, and whatever else can delight the eye and attract the senses to their proper objects";[25] Constantine IX Monomachos had a passion for landscape architecture and horticultural legerdemain;[26] Andronikos I had himself portrayed at the church of the Forty Martyrs not in imperial vestments but as a laborer holding a reaping hook;[27] John III Vatatzes gained a reputation at Nicaea for agricultural innovation;[28] and two deposed emperors, Romanos I Lekapenos[29] and Michael VII Parapinakes,[30] ended their lives as monks working in the gardens and fields (Alexander's revival in the Hippodrome, during his short reign, of the pagan flower festival called the Anthesteria[31] is, however, ambiguous evidence of a horticultural interest on his part). It is also noteworthy that when, shortly after A.D. 512, the citizens of Honoratae wished to thank that very grand imperial lady, Anicia Juliana, they chose to have made for her that most splendid of illustrated Byzantine manuscripts, the Vienna Dioscorides, for a gift of a later copy of which herbal there survives from 948 a letter of thanks from the Cordoban caliph Abd al-Rahman III to Romanos II.[32] A further indication that emperors and gardens were not regarded as incompatible may perhaps be seen in arboricultural imagery for imperial activities. Thus the library of Leo III is described as a gracious orchard of book-bearing trees in which an Adam tended everlastingly unfading plants;[33] when Romanos III married to his niece the future emperor Constantine IX, whose "blooming countenance" was "like fruit in springtime," he "grafted this fine young cutting onto his own rich, fertile olive";[34] and, rather gro-

[21] *Ep.* 25, 427D.

[22] Theophanes Continuatus, *Vita Basilii* 92, Bonn ed. (1838), 338.

[23] See below, pp. 24–25 and 33.

[24] Theoph. Cont., *Vita Theophili* 43, Bonn ed., 144; *Vita Basilii* 68, ibid., 328–29.

[25] *Chronographia* 4.31.

[26] See below, pp. 28 and 29.

[27] Niketas Choniates, *Hist.,* ed. van Dieten, I, 332.22–34 (as above, note 3).

[28] Theodore Skutariotes (Akropolites 1, 286–87, ed. Heisenberg); Nikephoros Gregoras 2.6, Bonn ed. (1829–35), I, 42.

[29] Liutprand of Cremona, *Antapodosis* 5.25.

[30] *Excerpta Scylitzae,* in Kedrenos, Bonn ed., 2 vols. (1838–39), II, 738.

[31] Arethas, *Funeral Oration on Patriarch Euthymios,* in *Arethae Scripta minora,* ed. L. G. Westerink (Leipzig, 1968), I, 91.7–8.

[32] F. Dölger, *Regesten der Kaiserurkunden des Oströmischen Reiches von 565–1453,* vol. I (Munich-Berlin, 1924), 82, no. 657. See further M. M. Sadek, *The Arabic Materia Medica of Dioscorides* (Québec, 1983), 9. In 951 a monk named Nicholas who was conversant with Arabic was also sent to Cordoba to translate the book. For Arabic plant lists from Moorish Spain, see below, note 108.

[33] Constantine Manasses, *Chron.* 4257–69, Bonn ed. (1837), 182–83.

[34] Psellos, *Chron.* 6.15–16.

tesquely, after taking Prusa Andronikos I "clipped the fingers" of some of the citizens "as if they were branches of vines," while their real vines "he left weighed down with the bodies of those hanged there like other clusters of grapes" as those whom he had impaled "swayed in the wind like scarecrows hung up by the garden watchers in cucumber beds."[35]

Did the Byzantine emperors regard the possession of ornate gardens as an overt symbol of their power and greatness? Magnates in late Republican Rome certainly did, and Cicero makes the revealing comment that he had proved that it was legitimate to borrow money from friends in order to buy villas, which of course included ornate gardens, "in order to reach a certain position" in society.[36] Gardens and associated porticoes and temples in Rome, aided by their specifying decoration, served to emphasize to the public the military conquests and political power of both generals, such as Pompey, and emperors.[37] The assertion of imperial might demonstrated by the complex of buildings and gardens on the Palatine was imitated by native rulers in the Roman world, most notably, in the present state of archaeological evidence, at Fishbourne in southern England where at the late first-century A.D. palace (usually credited to King Cogidubnus) to the eight published gardens recent excavation has now added a ninth,[38] and also, on the evidence of the poems of Luxurius in the early sixth century, in North Africa where the Vandal rulers rapidly absorbed Roman ways.[39] Although the continuation of this form of imperial and regal propaganda into the early Byzantine form of the Roman Empire cannot be asserted unequivocally,[40] it has a lengthy history in the Near East that one would

---

[35] Niketas Choniates, *Hist.*, ed. van Dieten, I, 289.74–75, 84–89. See further Littlewood, "Gardens of Byzantium," 130 and Maguire, "Imperial Gardens," 190.

[36] *Att.* 1.13.6.

[37] On Pompey's garden see now Gleason, *Towards an Archaeology*, 161–214. The Forma Urbis Romae, a marble plan of Rome created shortly after A.D. 210 and displayed in the Temple of Peace, shows nine portico gardens associated with public buildings (E. Rodríguez-Almeida, *Forma Urbis Marmorea: Aggiornamento generale 1980* [Rome, 1981]; R. B. Lloyd, "Three Monumental Gardens on the Marble Plan," *AJA* 86 [1982], 91–100). In general see further Gleason, op. cit., 37–58, 260.

[38] For the formal garden in the central court, the five peristyle gardens of the north and east wings, and the kitchen garden in the northwest corner, see B. W. Cunliffe, *Excavations at Fishbourne*, I: *The Site* (London, 1971) and, more conveniently, idem, "Roman Gardens in Britain: A Review of the Evidence," in *Ancient Roman Gardens*, ed. E. B. MacDougall and W. F. Jashemski, Dumbarton Oaks Colloquium on the History of Landscape Architecture 7 (Washington, D.C., 1981), 101–8. More extensive work has been subsequently done to the south of the palace revealing "a massive programme of land levelling . . . to create an extensive . . . terrace extending for more than 100 m south to the contemporary shoreline," while in 1985/6 "elements of an extensive and long-lived garden" were discovered to the east of the palace (to be published in *Chichester Excavations* IX, ed. B. W. Cunliffe, A. G. Down, and D. J. Rudkin. I am grateful to Professor Cunliffe for letting me see a typescript of the relevant portions).

[39] Luxurius 5, 6, 18, 34, 46, ed. Rosenblum (= *Anth. Lat.* 1.291, 292, 304, 320, 332). The Vandal pleasure gardens are mentioned also by Prokopios in his account (*Vand.* 2.6.9) of Belisarios' campaign in 533.

[40] It is a pity that there has not yet been sufficient excavation at the vast estate owned by the Constantinian dynasty at Mediana, east of Naissus, to reveal whether there were formal gardens in addition to agricultural land. Certainly, especially in the western part of the empire, increasing lawlessness from the middle of the 3rd century and later also barbarian military threat demanded a more defensive style of villa and palace, particularly in the countryside, that discouraged extensive gardens. At, for instance, Gamzigrad, which may well have been an imperial estate in the early 4th century, substantial excavation has revealed little in the way of gardens. For the country estates of the later Roman Empire see Littlewood, "Ancient Literary Evidence," 26–30; idem, "Gardens of

expect to have had an effect upon an increasingly eastern-looking Byzantine world,[41] especially when there is evidence of rivalry between imperial and caliphal courts from at least the time of Theophilos. Since we are told that Theophilos accepted the suggestion of John Synkellos,[42] his ambassador in probably 829/30 to Caliph al-Ma'mūn in Baghdad, that he build the palace of Bryas exactly in the style of the Abbasid palaces,[43] a dominant feature of which was gardens, it is pertinent to look briefly at the lengthy eastern tradition.

The most striking surviving evidence is an inscription that the Assyrian king Ashurnasirpal II (883–859 B.C.) had engraved on a sandstone block near the doorway to the throne room of his palace at Calah. It concerns his building of the palace, his construction of the royal garden, and the festival in celebration of the inauguration of the complex. After an immense catalogue of "trees (and plants raised from) seeds from wherever I discovered (them)" in "the countries through which I marched and the mountains which I crossed," it continues: "they vied with each other in fragrance; the paths . . . [were well *kept*], the irrigation weirs [distributed the water *evenly*]; its pomegranates glow in the pleasure garden like the stars in the sky, they are interwoven like grapes on the vine . . . in the pleasure garden . . . in the garden of happiness."[44] Destruction of an opponent's symbol was also, therefore, an assertion of superiority. As early as ca. 1458 B.C. the Egyptian king Thutmose III boasted on a granite stele set up at Gebel Barkal near the Fourth Cataract that "I . . . felled all their groves and all their pleasant trees . . . it became a [. . .] upon which there are no trees,"[45] while the Assyrian king Shalmaneser III (858–824 B.C.) thought fit to record that in his eighteenth year he crossed the Euphrates for the sixteenth time and at the royal residence of Hazael at Damascus "I cut down his gardens."[46] The Achaemenid Persians are primarily responsible for bringing *paradeisoi* as far west as the Levant,[47] pleasure gardens being regular features of both the

---

Byzantium," 126–28; J. J. Rossiter, "The Roman Villas of the Greek East and the Villa in Gregory of Nyssa, *Ep. 20," Journal of Roman Archaeology* 2 (1989), 101–10.

[41] It should not be forgotten that in both conception and appearance Roman palatial gardens themselves owe a debt to ancient Oriental models through the intermediation of the Hellenistic kingdoms (see P. Grimal, *Les jardins romains,* 3d ed. [Paris, 1984], 78–86).

[42] Later the patriarch of Constantinople, John VII (Grammatikos).

[43] Theoph. Cont., *Vita Theophili* 9, Bonn ed., 98; Zonaras 15.26.31–32, Bonn ed., III (1897), 363. Barber warns ("Reading the Garden," 3–4) that this assertion could be mere calumniation against the Iconoclasts Theophilos and John, whose reputations would be further besmirched by any reference to consorting with or being influenced by heretical foreigners. See further below, pp. 24–25.

[44] J. B. Pritchard, *Ancient Near Eastern Texts Relating to the Old Testament,* 3d ed. (Princeton, 1969), 559. The catalogue includes many trees that were grown also in Byzantine gardens (see below, pp. 28–29), e.g., cedar, cypress, fir, oak, willow, terebinth, juniper, nut trees, olive, apple, pear, plum, fig, pomegranate, and grape vines.

[45] Ibid., 240.

[46] Ibid., 280.

[47] The single piece of evidence for an earlier *paradeisos* in the Levant is the Damascene toponym Ḥayr Sarjūn , i.e., the *ḥayr* of the Assyrian Sargon II who had a palace there in the 8th century B.C. A *ḥayr* seems to have been at first an enclosed hunting park (from the *ḥāsir* ["tank"] that watered it) and later a pleasure garden, analogous to the *paradeisos* (from the Old Persian *pairidaeza* ["wall around"]). See Creswell, *Early Muslim Architecture,* vol. I, pt. 2, 536; J. Dickie, "The Hispano-Arab Garden: Notes towards a Typology," in *The Legacy of Muslim Spain,* ed. Salma Khadra Jayyusi, Handbook of Oriental Studies 1, The Near and Middle East 12 [Leiden, 1992], 1018–21).

Great King's and his satraps' palaces that asserted their owners' status. Xenophon tells us that the Elder Cyrus, wherever he lived or even visited, had *paradeisoi* created which he filled with "all the good and beautiful things that the earth wishes to put forth, and in these he himself spends most of his time except when the season of the year prevents it."[48] Even more revealingly he relates the conversation of the Spartan Lysander on his visit to the palace of the Younger Cyrus at Sardis where, having admired the orderly rows of fragrant trees, he added that he was most impressed by the man who had designed it all, to which the delighted Cyrus replied, "I myself did all the measuring and the arranging and some of the planting."[49] According to Xenophon, the Younger Cyrus took as much pride in such matters as he did in warfare,[50] and he too understood their symbolism for he deliberately destroyed the palace and "a very large and beautiful *paradeisos* with all the products of the seasons" belonging to the Syrian ruler Belesys.[51] Under this eastern influence Sicilian tyrants followed suit, Hieron II of Syracuse distinguishing himself by ordering the Corinthian architect Archias, with the help of Archimedes, to design a stupendously elaborate pleasure boat with garden beds and bowers of ivy and vines, the whole the subject of a treatise by a certain Moschion.[52] In the East itself, whatever "Persian" dynasty ruled, a garden persisted in being a necessary appurtenance of a palace. Of Byzantium's early foes, the Sassanians, undoubtedly the most famous and influential garden was that made for the palace of Khosro II Parviz (591–628) at Qasr-i Shirin on the road to Kirmanshah, which from a high terrace overlooked a great pool in a garden and, beyond a wall, a park containing rare animals.[53]

For the Arabs, coming largely from one of the most arid parts of the Near East, an umbrageous and well-watered garden with abundant fruits was not only their heavenly reward, its delights far more emphatically proposed than in the Christian world, but also a much appreciated earthly boon and, in many places, an expression of mastery over an hostile environment. The proliferation of gardens in the Muslim world was vastly greater than in any previous civilization, even if we treat with caution the assertions of Yāqūt and al-Dimashqī that there were, respectively, 40,000 gardens with fruit trees in

---

[48] *Oec.* 4.13.

[49] Ibid., 4.20–24.

[50] Ibid., 4.17.

[51] Id., *Anab.* 1.4.10. For further references to Achaemenid gardens, see id., *Oec.* 4.13–16; *Cyr.* 1.3.14; *Anab.* 1.2.7, 1.2.9; *Hell.* 4.1.15–16; Plut. *Alc.* 24.5 (in an unusual variation on the theme of prestige, the satrap Tissaphernes named his most beautiful garden in honor of his guest Alkibiades).

[52] Athenaeus (5.206d–209e) quotes extensively from it (Caligula later had a similar, though less elaborate, floating garden for his musical cruises along the Campanian coast [Suet. *Calig.* 37.2]). Hieron used to hold audience in a garden called "Mythos," Gelon of Gela constructed a place called "The Horn of Amaltheia" in a well-watered grove (both in Athenaeus 12.542a), and Dionysios of Syracuse transported planes to adorn his palace at Reggio (Plin. *H.N.* 12.3.7). Nevertheless, on the whole Persia had little effect upon the Greek gardens of even the Sicilian tyrants (see R. Osborne, "Classical Greek Gardens," in Hunt, *Garden History* [as above, note 1], 389–90. For surveys of Greek gardens see M. Carroll-Spillecke, Κῆπος: *Der antike griechische Garten*, Wohnen in der klassischen Polis 3 [Munich, 1989]; idem, "Griechische Gärten," in *Der Garten von der Antike* [as above, note 1], 153–75; idem, "The Gardens of Greece from Homeric to Roman Times," *Journal of Garden History* 12.2 [1992], 84–101; Osborne, op. cit., 373–91, where [373 note 2] further bibliographical material may be found).

[53] See R. Pinder-Wilson, "The Persian Garden: *Bagh* and *Chahar Bagh*," in *The Islamic Garden*, ed. E. B. MacDougall and R. Ettinghausen, Dumbarton Oaks Colloquium on the History of Landscape Architecture 4 (Washington, D.C., 1976), 72–73.

thirteenth-century Nisibin and no fewer than 110,000 in fourteenth-century Damascus.[54] Thus the caliphs, sultans, and other rulers strove to assert their superiority with increasingly magnificent gardens, and, unlike the Byzantines who tended to consider their paradises but reflections of the heavenly one, they vied in claiming that their garden was as good or even better than that to which in their piety they aspired.[55] This claim is perhaps best shown not by one of the famous instances but by a poem on the achievements of Humāyūn, the second Mughal ruler (1530–56), which makes him assert that "Even the garden of Paradise is not (the) equal" of his "wonderful garden," which was in fact nothing more than four barges linked together with pavilions in each corner and a central octagonal courtyard, a setting for theological discussion as he floated on the river at Agra.[56]

It would be strange if the Byzantine emperors had been completely unaffected by these attitudes of their Roman forerunners and their eastern rivals, and Henry Maguire's recent study of the ideology of imperial gardens[57] shows that they did indeed accept them, but, in true Byzantine fashion, with slight modifications. From the tenth century an imperial garden may be described as a "new second creation" or, more often, a "new Eden," and thus, with frequent reference to its vernal character, may lay emphasis upon the act of renewal of the emperor who, as vicegerent on earth of God, becomes the terrestrial Creator; but the garden could be regarded too as "an embodiment of the virtues of the emperor,"[58] whether these were pacific as in John Geometres' claim that the emperor "is himself the greatest beauty of the place. . . . a beauty to the beauties of the place,"[59] or militant as in the emperor's successful hunting in the game parks of animals that symbolize barbarian enemies.[60]

What Byzantine palatial gardens are known to us today? It is unlikely that any palace, urban or suburban, imperial or private, was completely devoid of gardens. This is emphasized by the effrontery of a Byzantine ambassador to Baghdad who reportedly ex-

---

[54] For these and other figures see A. M. Watson, *Agricultural Innovation in the Early Islamic World* (Cambridge, 1983), 117–19.

[55] See especially D. N. Wilber, *Persian Gardens and Garden Pavilions* (Rutland, Vt.-Tokyo, 1962; 2d ed., Washington, D.C., 1979); MacDougall and Ettinghausen, *The Islamic Garden*; E. B. Moynihan, *Paradise as a Garden in Persia and Mughal India* (New York, 1979); J. Lehrman, *Earthly Paradise: Garden and Courtyard in Islam* (London, 1980); J. Brookes, *Gardens of Paradise: The History and Design of the Great Islamic Gardens* (London, 1987); Y. Tabaa, "The Medieval Islamic Garden: Typology and Hydraulics," in Hunt, *Garden History,* 303–29; J. Dickie, "Granada: A Case Study of Arab Urbanism in Muslim Spain," in Jayyusi, *The Legacy of Muslim Spain* (as above, note 47), 88–111; idem, "The Hispano-Arab Garden: Notes towards a Typology," ibid., 1016–35.

[56] Quoted by J. L. Wescoat Jr., "Gardens of Invention and Exile: The Precarious Context of Mughal Garden Design during the Reign of Humayun (1530–1556)," *Journal of Garden History* 10.2 (1990), 108, from Muḥammad Khwāndamīr, *Qānūn-i-Humāyūnī, Bibliotheca Indica* 263 (260?) (Calcutta: Royal Asiatic Society of Bengal, 1940), 37–41, 56.

[57] "Imperial Gardens."

[58] Ibid., 190. One imperial park was indeed named "Aretai" (see below, p. 37), which Maguire takes to refer to the virtues not only of park but also of emperor (ibid., 189).

[59] Ibid., 190. The whole poem is given by J. A. Cramer in *Anecdota e Codd. Manuscriptis Bibliothecae Regiae Parisiniensis,* vol. IV (Oxford, 1841), 278, and again, with translation and discussion, by H. Maguire in "A Description of the Aretai Palace and Its Garden," *Journal of Garden History* 10 (1990), 209–13.

[60] Maguire, "Imperial Gardens," 191–97. Maguire rightly points out that successful hunting may symbolize also successful suppression of internal passions (ibid., 192).

claimed to Caliph al-Mansur, "the eye is green and yearns for green foliage, yet there is no garden in this palace of yours."[61] Specific evidence, and even this frustratingly imprecise, exists, however, only for the Great Palace, that vast complex of public reception and banqueting halls, residential quarters, churches, chapels, baths, pavilions, sports grounds, pleasure and vegetable gardens, orchards and fishponds that spread down terraces, often adorned with statues,[62] from the Hippodrome and the Baths of Zeuxippos to the Sea of Marmara and served as the emperor's official residence for more than eight hundred years until, having suffered under the "sanctified bandits" of the Fourth Crusade, it fell into ruins, providing shelter for monks and a latrine for the populace. Of its gardens we know the names of two. The Mesokepion[63] was a well-watered and variously planted garden bounded on the north and south by porticoes, on the east by a polo field, and on the west by the Nea Ekklesia; but the Anadendradion was probably no more than an arbor of vines attached to the Magnaura palace.[64] There were, however, others, some built on terraces extended for the purpose by Theophilos and, still within the complex, separate gardens belonging to a palace of the logothete Theoktistos,[65] minister of Theodora and tutor of Michael III, and to the church and monastery of Saint George of Mangana.[66] In addition we may note that, adjoining the Great Palace, Hagia Sophia was approached from the west through a porticoed atrium enclosing a fountain surrounded by trees[67] and that the patriarchal palace boasted an orchard.[68]

Suburban palaces (or sometimes merely villas) were built by emperors, in continuation of a lengthy tradition, from the time of Constantine to the Komnenoi in both Europe and Asia and frequently on the shores of the Sea of Marmara and the Bosporos,[69]

---

[61] Al-Mansur is reported to have replied that "we were not created for frivolity and play." The Byzantine ambassador further complained that there was insufficient water for the populace, which the caliph denied but promptly had remedied (al-Khaṭīb al-Baghdādī, *Ta'rīkh Baghdad* [Cairo, 1931], vol. I, 78–79, trans. J. Lassner, *The Topography of Baghdad in the Early Middle Ages* [Detroit, 1970], 58. See further ibid., 246 note 50). Urban Muslim palatial gardens consisted of little more than courts planted with flowers until the building of the complex of Jawsaq al-Khāqānī at Samarra by Caliph al-Mu'taṣim (833–842) where 172 of 432 acres were devoted to gardens and their pavilions (Pinder-Wilson, "The Persian Garden," 74).

[62] E.g., in 596 Maurice placed his statue on the circular terrace that he built around the Magnaura palace (Theophanes, Bonn ed., I [1839], 423; Kedrenos, Bonn ed., I, 198), while soon after Phokas thought fit to put a statute of himself there (*Scriptores originum constantinopolitanarum* I.68, ed. T. Preger [Leipzig, 1901–7], I, 74.4–5). In the 10th century, Constantine VII embellished the Bukoleon complex with statues "that he brought in from different places" (Theoph. Cont., *Vita Constantini* 15, Bonn ed., 447).

[63] See above, note 24.

[64] Constantine VII, *De cer.* 1.39, 1.41, Bonn ed. (1829), 201, 215 = 48, 50 ed. A. Vogt, vol. II, 1 (Paris, 1939), 9, 22; op. cit. 2.15, Bonn ed., 580. On the third day of her wedding the *augusta* would pass the organs of the factions in the Anadendradion when she proceeded to her ceremonial bath.

[65] George Monachos, *Vita Michaelis cum matre Theodora* 6, apud Theoph. Cont., Bonn ed., 815–16.

[66] See below, p. 26.

[67] Either cypresses or laurels. See G. P. Majeska, *Russian Travelers to Constantinople in the Fourteenth and Fifteenth Centuries*, DOS 19 (Washington, D.C., 1984), 201.

[68] Dobrinja Jadrejković (the future archbishop Antony of Novgorod), ed. C. Loparev, in *Pravoslavnij palestinskij sbornik* 51 (1899), 23.

[69] For convenient lists, with sources and notable historical events that took place in them, see R. Janin, *Constantinople byzantine*, 138–53; S. Runciman, "The Country and Suburban Palaces of the Emperors," in *Charanis Studies*, ed. A. E. Laiou-Thomadakis (New Brunswick, N.J., 1980), 219–28.

in order to provide a retreat from the bustle and heat of the city.[70] There is here definitely unbroken tradition from the Republican period of Rome, in which Lucullus once, retorting to Pompey's criticism that his villa was highly unsuitable for winter, claimed that he was not "more stupid than the cranes and storks [in] that I do not change my residences with the seasons,"[71] a tradition at which Julian in his time saw fit to complain;[72] however, it is perhaps significant that in the early thirteenth century Niketas Choniates finds an eastern rather than a Roman parallel for the imperial desire to spend summers around the Sea of Marmara.[73] Although the name Jucundianae for one such palace of Justinian I[74] is supremely apposite, even if it is only an eponym,[75] they were considered also to be healthier than urban residences. Indeed, according to Patriarch Nikephoros,[76] Constantine III built a palace at Chalcedon ca. 680 in the hope that its fresh air would improve his health, while the hopeful Theophilos had an edifice constructed of great beauty and size and named after himself to house erstwhile prostitutes, whose "baneful lusts would be washed away" by the fresh air and lovely views.[77] The *Geoponika* is more specific in its recommendation that the healthiest site for a dwelling place, which should itself face the east, is one near the sea or on a hill or a slope inclining to the north, while it warns that a house facing west or built in a depression or marshy area is particularly bad.[78] The garden should be close "so that not only may the view be pleasant for those indoors, but also that the surrounding air, because it is infected by the exhalations of the plants, may make the house salubrious," and, again, it will not only be good for general health and "recuperation from diseases" but also offer the delight of its appearance and in particular its fragrance.[79]

[70] This could be the purpose even of a palace within the area of the city but away from the main center, for we are told that the palace of Bonos was built by Romanos I Lekapenos to obtain relief from the heat of summer (Kedrenos, Bonn ed., II, 343). Unfortunately, it cannot be accurately placed: it was presumably near the eponymous cistern that may have been in the area of the church of the Holy Apostles, and therefore the palace could have been above the general level of the city (see Janin, *Constantinople byzantine*, 128–29, 206–7). Liutprand avers (*Antapodosis* 6.5) that the name of the Magnaura palace within the complex of the Great Palace means "strong breeze" (*magna aura*), which would suggest that it could have been at times more than just refreshing, but unfortunately the name is rather a corruption of *magna aula* (Bryas is, however, probably a corruption of Εὖρος [Janin, *Constantinople byzantine*, 492]).

[71] Plut. *Luc.* 39.4–5.

[72] *Or.* 1.13D, 2.101D. Eunapios (*Vitae Sophist.* 464) and Kallinikos (*Vita Hypatii* 4.4, 37.3) mention Constantinopolitan senators owning estates in Bithynia to avoid the summer's heat, and Libanios (*Ep.* 419) rich Antiochians similarly owning villas at Daphne.

[73] Although he must, as a writer in the *Hochsprache,* refer to the Persians at Susa and Ecbatana (ed. van Dieten, I, 206.52–56).

[74] At Hebdomon, on the coastline of the Sea of Marmara, some seven miles west of the city (Prokopios, *Aed.* 1.11.16).

[75] See Janin, *Constantinople byzantine*, 140.

[76] *Epit. Hist.,* ed. C. de Boor (Leipzig, 1880), 28.19–21.

[77] Theoph. Cont., *Vita Theophili* 8, Bonn ed., 95.

[78] Although it admits that some people prefer the house to face the south in order to gain more sunshine, it fears the south wind that is wet, fitful, and noxious (2.3.1–5).

[79] Ibid., 10.1.1, 12.2. A little-known poem on the Pantokrator complex in Constantinople, that included the hospital famous today because of the monastery's detailed *typikon,* claims more specifically that its surrounding gardens with their soft breezes were conducive to the health of those suffering from convulsions (or possibly just depression?): ἀντιπνεόντων ἡδέως τῶν πνευμάτων, / αὔραις πραείαις καταθέλγον εἰς κόρον / καὶ τῶν νοσούντων ῥωννύον τοὺς σπωμένους (R. Volk, *Gesundheitswesen und Wohltätigkeit im Spiegel der byzantinischen Klost-*

It is inconceivable that all such imperial suburban villas and palaces did not possess gardens, but our brief references rarely allude to them, a fact that should not cause surprise since our sources are mainly the historians. Apart from hunting lodgings and palaces associated with game parks,[80] the only imperial suburban or country palaces for which vegetation is specifically mentioned are Makellon, the palace at Hiereia, and the Bryas palace, although we may assume that the beauteous gardens around the shrine of the Zoodochos Pege[81] were at least accessible to the neighboring palace and thus made Justinian's devotions there the more comfortable. Makellon was the name of the royal estate at the foot of Mount Argaios near Caesarea where Julian and Gallus were held as boys: it boasted fine gardens which, to judge from the name of the estate, were probably surrounded by a wall.[82] Hiereia, on the peninsula of Fenerbahçe, was the site of a palace with baths, harbor, park, and church that Justinian built for Theodora to spend the summers and that Prokopios maliciously reports was hated by her courtiers because on their journeys there they were frightened of both seasickness and the attacks of a monstrous whale.[83] It may be the subject of some poems in the *Palatine Anthology,* one of which reads: "The sea washes the abode of the earth, and the navigable expanse of the dry land blooms with marine groves. How skilled was he who mingled the deep with the land, seaweed with gardens, the floods of the Nereids with the streams of the Naiads."[84] If this identification is correct, the palace was built out into the sea, like many ancient Roman villas,[85] a style that seems not to be recorded later in Byzantium. It underwent various changes: Herakleios filled in its cisterns and created vegetable gardens and parks, while Basil I reversed the process by "changing the meadow, recently flowering with plants, back to its earlier state and making a reservoir of plentiful, flowing water in place of the park," but Constantine VII could still appreciate the fresh air and the fragrance presumably of its gardens, and in his time it was the starting point of the annual procession in honor of the vintage.[86] The palace of Bryas on the shore of the Sea of Marmara opposite the Princes' Islands was originally built by Tiberios II and Maurice,[87] but by 832 Theophilos had a completely new complex built by his architect Patrikios, which, apart from an oratory and a church dedicated respectively to the

---

ertypika [Munich, 1983], 190. I am indebted to Professor Timothy S. Miller for bringing this poem to my attention).

[80] On which see below, pp. 35–38.

[81] See above, note 14. We may note also the palace that Philippikos built near his monastery at Chrysopolis and where he entertained his wife's brother, Emperor Maurice, and his children. This palace had fish ponds and gardens (Niketas Choniates, ed. C. de Boor, vol. I [Leipzig, 1883], 272.22–26).

[82] Sozomenos 5.2.9.

[83] *Anecd.* 15.37. For Prokopios' account of this 30-cubit monster, named Porphyrio, see *Goth.* 7.29.9–16.

[84] 9.663. Cf. ibid., 9.664, 820.

[85] The earliest instance recorded is of a villa on the Bay of Naples belonging to Lucullus, "a Xerxes in a toga" who "surrounded his buildings with circuits of the sea . . . and constructed residences in the sea" (Plut. *Luc.* 39.3).This became a *topos* for those carping at the extravagance of resorts like Baiae where Horace wryly observed that the maritime extensions of the villas were making the fish feel cramped for space (*Carm.* 2.18.20–22, 3.1.33–37).

[86] Theoph. Cont., *Vita Basilii* 92, *Vita Constantini* 26, Bonn ed., 338, 451–52; Constantine VII, *De cer.* 1.78, Bonn ed., 373 = 87 ed. Vogt, II, 1.175.

[87] *Script. orig. const.* 3.170, ed. Preger, II, 268.10–269.2.

Mother of God and Saint Michael, was all in the style of an Arab palace with vast gardens and abundant canals of water.[88] Theophilos was responsible also for some pavilions in the Great Palace that have certain features in common with their Arab counterparts.[89]

Before we try to glean what information there may be on the appearance and contents of Byzantine palatial gardens, a general point must be made. They seem to have been designed largely to be viewed and delighted in from indoors, or at least from the shade of a colonnade, as is regular in near eastern palaces. Nevertheless, there is some evidence that in Byzantium actual exploration of the gardens was encouraged, for Theodore Metochites wistfully tells us that at his private palace, which was pillaged by Andronikos III in 1328, he had been especially fond of a circular, shaded path paved with stone and sprinkled with lime dust to produce a surface admirably suited for both walking and riding.[90] Julian claims that as a boy he enjoyed lying on the ground at his grandmother's estate amid the fragrant flowers, reading a book and gazing out at the Sea of Marmara,[91] but this was a partly agricultural estate[92] and not truly imperial. The semi-public gardens around churches[93] were, of course, intended to be enjoyed by those walking in them

[88] Theoph. Cont., *Vita Theophili* 9, Bonn ed., 98–99; Zonaras 15.26.30–32, Bonn ed., III, 363 (cf. Theoph. Cont., *Vita Leonis* 10, Bonn ed., 21; Georg. Mon., *Vita Theophili* 14, ibid., 798; Leo Gramm., Bonn ed. [1842], 221). Excavation of the site at Küçükyalı (between Bostancı and Maltepe) reveals an Abbasid layout, but is barren for the gardens themselves (S. Eyice, "Quatre édifices inédits ou mal connus," *CahArch* 10 [1959], 245–58; idem, "Un palais construit d'après les plans des palais Abbasides: le palais de Bryas," *Belleten* 23 [1959], 79–99). For Arab influence see also above, note 43.

[89] See A. Grabar, *Iconoclasme byzantin,* 2d ed. (Paris, 1984), 167–210. We must, however, as Barber warns ("Reading the Garden," 4–5), be wary of assuming that the influence in palaces and their gardens was always from east to west, since we are told that in 859 Caliph al-Mutawakkil copied at huge expense one of Theophilos' additions to the Great Palace in the 830s. Byzantium rather engaged in an artistic and technological rivalry with Muslim courts (see also below, pp. 32–33), a rivalry that was at its height in the 9th century but that extended to at least the mid-12th century when there was constructed to the west of the Chrysotriklinos of the Great Palace a building known as the Mouchroutas or "Persian House," which according to the description of Nicholas Mesarites was clearly in the Seljuk stalactitic style (ed. A. Heisenberg, *Die Palastrevolution des Johannes Komnenos* [Würzburg, 1907], 44–45. For the dating of the building, see C. Mango, *The Art of the Byzantine Empire, 312–1453* [Englewood Cliffs, N.J., 1972; repr. Toronto, 1986], 229 note 235).

[90] R. Guilland, ed., "Le palais de Théodore Métochite," *REG* 35 (1922), 82–95. The palace was probably within the city. It is noteworthy that in the second and shorter Latin version of the apocryphal Acts of Saint Thomas, the ideal palace that the apostle designed for the local Indian king Gundaforus contained as its twelfth and final feature "ypodromum et per gyrum arcus deambulatorii" (*Acta Thomae,* ed. M. Bonnet [Leipzig, 1883], 140): the *arcus deambulatorii* were probably true paths in a court or garden rather than mere curving colonnades, while *hippodromus* in Latin does not necessarily mean a riding place, but can signify a path for walking in the shape of a traditional hippodrome (see A. N. Sherwin-White, *The Letters of Pliny* [Oxford, 1960], 327–28). Exercise in the garden was a Roman fashion: the Younger Pliny, for example, describes his daily habit of taking four separate walks and one ride either in a carriage or on horseback (*Ep.* 9.36.5), and admires the seventy-seven-year-old Vestricius Spurinna who every day took three walks, one of three miles, and a carriage ride of seven miles at his estate (ibid., 3.1.4, 7). Circuits were measured to give a standard "constitutional" (e.g., "in hoc pomario gestationis per circuitum itum et reditum quinquiens efficit passus mille" [H. Dessau, *ILS,* II, 1.478, no. 6030: cf. ibid., no. 6031]).

[91] *Ep.* 25, 427B–C.

[92] See above, pp. 16–17.

[93] To some extent these replaced the great public parks of antiquity. For an early Byzantine description of one of these, see the poem by Marianos Scholastikos which invites the wearied traveler to rest his limbs under the shade of plane trees by streams amid violets and roses in a park named Eros at Amaseia (*Anth. Pal.* 9.669: cf. ibid., 663–68).

even when they were within the bounds of the Great Palace, as Michael Psellos makes clear in noting that the overall harmony of design in Constantine IX Monomachos' gardens around his rebuilt church of Saint George of Mangana continually offered strollers a new detail of delectation as they wandered around, and, as at Metochites' private palace, the grounds were suitable for riding too.[94]

For their general appearance and contents we may perhaps first summarize the features most often mentioned and expatiated upon in the idealizing romances (including the epic of Basil Digenis Akritas) whose *ekphraseis*[95] were clearly based upon real palatial gardens. These features are trees that whisper in the wind, their branches intertwined to form shady arbors; fragrant flowers, frequently vernal or unfading; a gentle wind that sways branches and leaves of trees and wafts the scents of flowers; melodiously warbling birds;[96] statues, usually pagan in origin; garden pavilions of delicate and consummate workmanship that may house mosaics and paintings, sometimes vegetal and often the most important item in the *ekphrasis;* a fountain either exquisitely wrought with mosaics or decorated with cunningly contrived automata; an altar, shrine, or chapel; a surrounding wall of elaborate structure often so carefully constructed that its joins are invisible.

How much of this can be said with certainty about real palatial gardens? In their general layout rural and suburban palaces were set in expansive gardens often enclosed by a wall, while the Great Palace (and probably to a lesser extent other urban palaces) was a complex of buildings—some substantial, others mere pavilions—and open spaces that were usually gardens with numerous watercourses and fountains. Specific description is sadly lacking, although a continuator of Theophanes does say that the Mesokepion near the polo field was well watered and "blooming with all manner of plants."[97] However, we should probably not err excessively in extrapolating to the Great Palace from the huge early eighth-century Baradā panel of the great Umayyad mosque at Da-

---

[94] *Chron.* 6.186–87. It is evident from John Geometres that even a tiny courtyard garden need not be enjoyed only from within as he expatiates on the delights it presents as one enters it (A. R. Littlewood, *The Progymnasmata of Ioannes Geometres* [Amsterdam, 1972], 11, line 16; 13, line 25. Geometres wrote two *enkomia* [ibid., 7–13] of his own walled garden in the center of Constantinople, probably near the church of the Holy Apostles).

[95] See above, note 17.

[96] The brief surviving descriptions of palatial gardens do not mention real birds, but they feature in the gardenly artwork of the pavilions (see below, p. 34) and in miniatures that include gardens (most frequently in stylized foliate headpieces and canon tables), while the *Geoponika* gives advice (14.18) on the rearing of peacocks that graced gardens as exquisite expressions of God's creation and one of which Basil I had depicted in the Kainourgion of the Great Palace (Theoph. Cont., *Vita Basilii* 89, Bonn ed., 333). Peacocks and other birds do, however, appear in a capitulary of Charlemagne *de villis imperialibus* dating to 812: "[Volumus] ut unusquisque iudex per villas nostras singulares etlehas, pavones, fasianos, enecas, columbas[,] perdices, turtures, pro dignitatis causa omnimodis semper habeant" (MGH, *Legum Tomus,* I [Hannover, 1835], 184, no. 40). The Grottaferrata version of the Romance of Basil Digenis Akritas specifically mentions tame peacocks, parrots, and swans as well as nightingales and other songbirds in the wondrous meadow that the hero improved with horticulture of his own for the delectation of himself and his wife. Wild birds and those that "obtain their food by flattering humans," songbirds and brightly colored birds, join the peacocks, parrots, and swans (described with only minor changes of wording) in the garden around Basil's new palace by the Euphrates, where, perhaps significantly, the garden is the first element presented to the reader or auditor (6.21–28, 44; 7.31–41, ed. J. Mavrogordato [Oxford, 1956], 162–64; 218).

[97] Theoph. Cont., *Vita Basilii* 86, Bonn ed., 328–29.

mascus.[98] There, set amid green lawns and "gracefully shaped trees" on the bank of the river, are "two graceful pavilions . . . flanked by two similar and symmetrical palaces, with which they are connected by terraces bordered by elegant, open-work balustrades. . . . Between the two pavilions rises up the trunk of a tree . . . , its foot embedded in a kind of wharf overhanging the river . . . while the part covered with ornaments probably indicates a mosaic pavement" (Fig. 5).[99] For gardens around churches within the Great Palace we learn from Psellos that those around Constantine IX Monomachos' rebuilt church of Saint George of Mangana had numerous beflowered lawns, hanging gardens, copses of shady trees on different levels, baths, watercourses, and fountains,[100] while that part of the Mesokepion that adjoined the Nea Ekklesia may just possibly be represented, albeit in shorthand, in the "inside-outside" miniature of the twelfth-century Homilies of Gregory of Nazianzos at Mount Sinai (Fig. 3)[101] that depicts the saint writing within the church in whose atrium are shown two fountains[102] flanked by two tiny gardens containing brightly colored flowers and trees, one in each garden pruned in topiarian manner, behind elaborate marble balustrades. The church, as Maguire points out, may not be the Nea Ekklesia, but it is similarly multidomed and is similarly associated with gardens and two fountains, while the manuscript, despite its present location, was made for the abbot of the Constantinopolitan monastery of the Pantokrator.[103]

Trees were often planted in straight rows when water channels were necessary, as is well shown in a twelfth-century copy of the Homilies of Gregory of Nazianzos at the

[98] Measuring 113 feet by 24 feet, it covers the wall of the western portico facing the courtyard. For its probable "Byzantine" workmanship, see above, note 12.

[99] Van Berchem in Creswell, *Early Muslim Architecture,* I, pt. 1, 342–43. The main mosaic of the Great Palace at Constantinople portrays a building through two arches of whose lower storey water pours into a pool, while, above, a tower supports an overhanging, conical roof and two further structures flank a large and luxurious tree; but the whole ensemble bears close similarities with Roman mural paintings and is unlikely to represent contemporary palatial design (illustrations in *The Great Palace of the Byzantine Emperors: Second Report,* ed. D. T. Rice [Edinburgh, 1958], frontispiece and pl. 46A).

[100] *Chon.* 6.186–87. This description may be compared with that by Psellos of the church of the Anargyroi (the Kosmidion) when it was restored in the mid-11th century by Michael IV Paphlagon (quoted above, p. 17). As mentioned earlier (p. 16 and note 15), Nicholas Mesarites copied often verbatim from Libanios' description of the pagan sanctuary at Daphne for his own *enkomion* of the church of the Holy Apostles in Constantinople written sometime between 1198 and 1203. Since, however, his omission of certain details suggests that what he did include applies, even if in a somewhat vague manner, to his subject, it may be worthwhile to quote him in part, although it must be remembered that there seems to have been more open ground around this church than around those in the Great Palace. It was situated in fertile land equally good for vineyards and fruit trees: "one may see saffron growing . . . , balsam and lilies, fresh clover and hyacinth, roses and oleanders and everything sweet-smelling. . . . There are different gardens there, pleasant aqueducts, numerous springs, houses hidden in trees, a theater of every view, choruses of musical birds, a moderate breeze, sweet odors of spices . . . , a source of every contentment, vines and fig trees and pomegranates. . . . Who could not love the manmade springs of water around the church, the pools, the colonnades . . . ?" A poem on the Pantokrator monastic complex in Constantinople lauds the surrounding sward with its profusion of colorful flowers, cypresses, watercourses, fountains, and gentle breezes (Volk, *Gesundheitswesen,* 189–90). Archaeology confirms one aspect here, for traces of canalization have been found to the west of the church (Majeska, *Russian Travelers,* 291).

[101] Above, note 9.

[102] See below, p. 31.

[103] "Imperial Gardens," 182–84.

Athonite monastery of Saint Panteleimon (Fig. 6).[104] Nevertheless, we do hear of Saint Theodore of Stoudion on his estate at Boskytion deliberately planting new trees between those already standing to create a crescent;[105] and vistas could be altered even more drastically by landscape architecture. The *Geoponika* recommends that in the absence of a naturally forested hill a copse should be grown, and it proceeds to recommend specific trees for specific soils.[106] Happily we are vouchsafed by Michael Psellos a description, albeit with tongue in cheek, of the impatient expertise of the greatest imperial landscape architect, Constantine IX Monomachos: "If ever he wished to create a grove or put a wall around a park or widen a racetrack, not only did he carry out his original intention but other ideas came to him at once, and while some meadows were covered with soil, others were straightway fenced about, while some vines were uprooted others were spontaneously created together with their fruits. How was this done? Suppose the emperor wished to convert a barren field into a fertile meadow: his wish was immediately carried out, for trees growing elsewhere were transported thither together with their fruit and planted firmly in the earth while soil from mountain groves was heaped to cover the plain entirely. Unless without delay cicadas were chirring on his spontaneously created trees and nightingales singing about his grove, the emperor was very upset. . . . He performed miracles to the disbelief of most people who on the third day saw a field where on the day before there had been a plain and the day before that a hill."[107]

Although few species of trees are specified in descriptions of palatial gardens, the Baradā panel[108] supplies poplar,[109] cypress, olive, apricot, walnut, fig, plum, and apple or pear, while in the *ekphraseis* of the gardens of the romances[110] we find also elm, plane, alder, willow, bay, myrtle, pine, fig, box, and of course the ubiquitous vine which was usually trained up trellises or growing trees. To these lists the *Geoponika* can add oak, ash, beech, maple, fir, cedar, mastich, terebinth, arbutus, tamarisk, juniper, sorb, peach, citron, quince, damson, cherry, pomegranate, date palm, jujube, medlar, carob, mul-

---

[104] Cod. 6, fol. 37v (Pelekanidis et al., *Treasures of Mount Athos,* vol. II [Athens, 1975], 175, pl. 300; Littlewood, "Gardens of Byzantium," 136, fig. 15). Beneath the farmer tending trees the miniaturist has depicted a fowler with his traps. On watercourses see further below, note 127.

[105] *Vita S. Theodori Studitae* 6, PG 99:121B-C.

[106] 2.8. Archaeological evidence shows that in the Roman world natural preexisting features were rarely employed in the creation of gardens, for which the first tasks were customarily the clearing and leveling of the ground. The evidence at present is, however, largely from urban and suburban sites, and we can reasonably assume that the same was generally true of Byzantine urban palaces if not the rural estates.

[107] *Chron.* 6.173–75. A similar exploit is recorded in Baghdad when the Būyid amir 'Aḍud ad-Dawlah (977–983) used elephants to destroy some houses and compact the soil in order to create a garden with two great hillocks within the complex of al-Mukharrim (al-Khaṭīb Baghdādī, *Ta'rīkh* 106, trans. Lassner, *Topography of Baghdad,* 93–94). Psellos describes groves on "high ground" and "sloping down towards level areas" in gardens around the church of Saint George of Mangana (*Chron.* 6.186).

[108] The slightly earlier mosaics in the Qubbat as Sakhra (Dome of the Rock) in Jerusalem, that also may have been created by Christian workmen, show among identifiable fruit apple, pear, pomegranate, plum, quince, lemon, cherry, fig, grape, date, and olive. A comparison may be made with lists of trees, flowers, and other plants from Islamic Spain in the 11th and 12th centuries, although it is not known how many of these actually appeared in the palatial gardens (J. H. Harvey, "Gardening Books and Plant Lists of Moorish Spain," *Garden History* 3.2 [1975], 10–21).

[109] The romances and the *Geoponika* specify both black and white poplar.

[110] See above, note 17.

berry, hazel, almond, pistachio, and sweet chestnut.[111] Since gardens were the natural home of Byzantine arboricultural and horticultural experiment, it is no surprise that Psellos ironically extols Constantine IX for "vanquishing the seasons and producing from nothing, as it were, plants with their proper characteristics,"[112] but there is no evidence that Constantine's attempts to improve upon nature in his palace gardens extended to attempts to change the taste or color of fruit, by grafting them onto alien trees, or even their shape, by enclosing them in molds in the form of birds, animals, and human heads, all of which together with other bizarre experiments are described to gardeners' ultimate frustration in the *Geoponika*.[113] Clearly, however, the enhancing of the color of fruit and of fragrance was an important aim of the Byzantine gardener. Pruning was done for reasons both practical and aesthetic, the mosaic of the Great Palace in Constantinople and the Baradā panel (Fig. 5) both showing good examples of the stumps of lopped-off lower branches, a feature commonly seen also in miniatures (Figs. 1, 2). Topiarian work is more problematical: this art, supposedly invented by a certain Caius Matius in the time of Augustus,[114] became all the rage in the first century A.D. when cypress and box in particular were carved into hunting scenes, fleets of ships, names of the gardeners, and other perversities,[115] but in Byzantium the only evidence, and it is extensive, is from art where it is quite impossible to distinguish between topiarists' fashion and artists' imagination, which the occasionally bizarre choice of colors such as pink and blue for foliage shows was not greatly restrained.[116] The standard topiarian convention shown in art is of two strata of outstretched branches, one at the crown of the tree and one beneath, separated by bare trunk (Figs. 1, 2, 3).[117]

Flowers were highly appreciated for color and fragrance,[118] but problems with watering made them more difficult to grow than trees and bushes, and for this reason they were often to be found in the spaces between trees where they had the benefit of shade and water channels (Fig. 6). In this arrangement the *Geoponika* recommends roses, lilies, violets and crocuses, which please the eye and benefit bees; and art shows that these and other flowers were so used in alternation. Although the manual itself admits that diver-

---

[111] Passim. The *Porikologos* adds orange, lemon, and sloe. The main mosaic of the Great Palace portrays cypress, pine, date palm, oak, olive, pear, plum, citrus, and pomegranate, but these are not, of course, intended to be representative of trees that were actually grown in palatial gardens (see Rice, *Great Palace*, 132–34).

[112] *Chron.* 6.175. In imperial Rome the Younger Seneca had already castigated those who procured blooms out of season by employing artificial heating during the winter (*Ep.* 122.8: cf. Martial 8.14, 8.68). Constantine IX did have an imperial predecessor in this at least, for Pliny notes that Tiberius' addiction to cucumbers was such that, lest their master should be deprived of them for even a single day, his gardeners mounted cucumber beds onto wheels to facilate their exposure to the sun and in winter covered them with sheets of mica or selenite ("[lapis] specularis," *H.N.* 19.23.64).

[113] 4.4, 10.7, 10.9, 10.14–15, 10.17, 10.19, 10.24, 10.27, 10.47, 10.53, 10.60, 10.69, 10.76, 10.83.

[114] Plin. *H.N. 12.6.13*.

[115] Ibid., 16.60.140; Younger Pliny, *Ep.* 5.6.

[116] For bizarre colors associated with topiarian work see, for instance, the 12th-century illustrations of Paradise in the manuscript of the Homilies of James of Kokkinobaphos in Paris (cod. Paris. gr. 1208) reproduced in color in (fol. 47r) Brubaker and Littlewood, "Byzantinische Gärten," pl. 34 and (fol. 50r) A. Grabar, *Byzantine Painting* (Geneva, 1953), 180.

[117] The 11th-century *tetraevangelion* in Paris (above, p. 14 and note 5) exhibits a splendid range of real or imagined topiarian work.

[118] Libanios (8.482, ed. Foerster) adds touch.

sity produces charm, it nonetheless decrees that plants should not be grown "haphaz-ardly or in combination"[119] but in general the species should be separate "so that the less may not be overpowered by the greater or be deprived of their nourishment."[120] Roses, whether planted in orderly rows, spiraling up trees, in baskets and pots,[121] or trained like other trailing plants to hang down, were especially prized for both their beauty and fragrance[122] and their ability to bloom at any season of the year. The variety of flowers was, however, far more limited[123] than that of trees (or vegetables), the *Geoponika* treating only of the narcissus, pimpernel, and, for ground cover, periwinkle in addition to those just mentioned, although it should be noted that it refers also to ivy that was used for decorative effect.[124] The romances add merely the scented lotus, but the border of the peristyle mosaic in the Great Palace shows among identifiable flowers the acanthus, sunflower, peony, and possibly an orchid. Unspecified reeds also grace some of the romances' descriptions. The pleasure garden's fragrance depended upon its trees and flowers since herbs[125] were more commonly grown for practicality in a separate garden or with the vegetables.[126]

Gardens of any appreciable size were dependent upon the watercourses that some-times even dictated their arrangement[127] and not only irrigated grass, trees, and flowers but also fed ponds and fountains. Psellos once more ironically pokes fun at Constantine IX who built a pavilion near a pool in the midst of an orchard where he delighted in

---

[119] τὰ δὲ φυτὰ μὴ ἀτάκτως μηδὲ μικτὰ φυτευέσθω (10.1.2).

[120] Loc. cit.

[121] They were thus to be brought on early (ibid., 11.18.4).

[122] The *Geoponika* claims that their fragrance could be enhanced by growing them in dry soil or interspersed with garlic (11.18.1), the latter method also eliminating dung beetles (ibid., 13.16.3).

[123] See Littlewood, "Gardens of Byzantium," 137–38; Brubaker and Littlewood, "Byzantinische Gärten," 222.

[124] This is clear from the romances. Ivy was prized in gardens from at least the time of Alexander III of Macedon, for Theophrastos tells (*H.P.* 4.4.1) that it alone of Harpalos' imports from Greece failed to grow in the gardens at Babylon. Cicero has particular praise for ivy in a reference to his brother's gardener who "has so clothed everything with ivy, both the foundation wall of the villa and the spaces between the columns of the promenade, that to be sure those Greek statues seem to be landscape gardeners themselves offering their ivy for sale" (*QFr.* 3.1.5), although the Elder Pliny points out (*H.N.* 16.62.144) that it is destructive to walls.

[125] See Littlewood, "Gardens of Byzantium," 140; Brubaker and Littlewood, "Byzantinische Gärten," 223–24. Basil is, however, to be found in the romances.

[126] On vegetable gardens see Littlewood, "Gardens of Byzantium," 138, 142; Brubaker and Littlewood, "By-zantinische Gärten," 222–23 and now J. Koder, *Gemüse in Byzanz: Die Versorgung Konstantinopels mit Frischgemüse im Lichte der Geoponika*, Byzantinische Geschichtsschreiber, suppl. 3 (Vienna, 1993).

[127] The scanty and not necessarily reliable evidence of art suggests that the watercourses were usually straight, but Nonnos' gardener at least ἐξ ἀμάρης ὀχέτευε πολυσχίδες ἀγκύλον ὕδωρ εἰς φυτὸν ἄλλο μετ' ἄλλο (*D.* 3.166–67). Islamic watercourses were not infrequently curved, al-Muʿtaṣim, for instance, in the 11th century, comparing the water in a garden of his palace at Almería with a slithering and twisting snake (apud Ibn Khāqān, *Qalāʾ id al-ʿiqyān fī maḥāsin al-aʿyān*, ed. Muḥammad al-Innabi [Tunis, 1966], 55, quoted in Dickie, "The Hispano-Arab Garden," 1019). I know of no evidence, despite their imitation of paradise, that the Byzantines ever used watercourses to create the quadripartite arrangement of the *chahar-bagh*, which, if we accept the evi-dence of the Samarra bowl, can be taken back to ca. 2000 B.C. (Dickie, op. cit., 1016). John Geometres, it is true, in his ekphrastic poem of an imperial park (above, note 59) avers that "four springs flowing from the old Eden water the new Eden," but, as Maguire observes, we cannot be sure from this "whether . . . the four rivers . . . were actually evoked in the design of the garden in some way, or whether the mention of the rivers is a purely rhetorical conceit" ("Imperial Gardens," 191).

both bathing and watching would-be apple scrumpers inadvertently tumbling into the water,[128] which we can picture as "natural" with grassy banks. As Maguire notes,[129] there are echoes of this in an illustration in the twelfth- or thirteenth-century manuscript of the Romance of Barlaam and Joasaph at Iviron in which trees between buildings and behind a fence surround a pool, used here, however, not for swimming but for the baptism of Joasaph (Fig. 4). Some pools in the Great Palace contained fish, bred for giving emperors the delights of both gazing and catching.[130]

A far more spectacular use of water was afforded by the fountains, which fascinated the continuators of Theophanes far more than did the vegetation. They attribute to the time of Theophilos the Mystic Fountain of the Trikonchos palace that spouted water through the jaws of two bronze lions[131] and at receptions had its bowl filled with pistachios, almonds, and pine nuts while spiced wine flowed for participants.[132] From the time of Basil I there were two fountains in the Mesokepion near his Nea Ekklesia, at the southern one of which water poured from a perforated pinecone (a refinement of possibly Assyrian origin)[133] into a porphyry basin surrounded by two sculptured serpents; while the northern one, which had a marble basin, used as conduits for water not only a similar pinecone but also bronze cocks, goats, and rams disposed in an elevated circle, as beneath wine used to spurt up to quench the thirst of passersby for whom cups lay there already provided.[134] As has already been noted,[135] these may have been inaccurately depicted in the twelfth-century copy of Gregory of Nazianzos' Homilies at Sinai (Fig.

[128] *Chron.* 6.201. Its size must be a matter of speculation, but we do know that at al-Muʻtaṣim's Jawsaq al-Khāqānī at Samarra there was a rectangular pool ca. 110 yds. by 135 yds. (Pinder-Wilson, "The Persian Garden," 74). Pools in courts and around fountains were, of course, much smaller. There is no evidence that the Byzantines built pavilions *in* pools such as the octagonal pavilion in a square pool (18 yds. by 18 yds.) which was the focal point of the whole Umayyad palace of Khirbat al-Mafjar near Jericho (R. W. Hamilton, *Khirbat al Mafjar: An Arabian Mansion in the Jordan Valley* [Oxford, 1959], 110–21; Creswell, *Early Muslim Architecture*, vol. I, pt. 2, 559–61). Neither is there Byzantine evidence for streams of water flowing through actual rooms of the palace as in Sassanian and later Muslim architecture (Pinder-Wilson, op. cit., 75). The surviving literature, moreover, does not suggest that reflection of buildings in water was a major consideration, as it came to be in Muslim architecture, or that the pools took on the exuberant curvilinear shapes that they did later in especially Persia and India.

[129] "Imperial Gardens," 184.

[130] Theoph. Cont., *Vita Basilii* 92; *Vita Constantini* 15, Bonn ed., 338, 447. After Justinian's conquest of Italy, Cassiodorus converted his private palace at Scylacium (Squillace in Calabria) into a monastery called Viridarium where monks could enjoy the luxury of well-irrigated gardens and the Gates of Neptune, a tunnel and chamber that he had carved out of the rock so that fish could swim in, "sporting in their free captivity," and rush to accept tasty morsels from human hands before themselves becoming monastic fare (*Var.* 12.15; *Instit.* 1.29. Cf. Sidonius Apollinaris' description of a friend's estate at which the flow of water brought fish right into the dining room [*Carm.* 22.207–10]).

[131] Cf. the fountain shown in the remains of the mosaic pavement in the Great Palace where there is a "tower-like structure . . . with an arched opening in the front wall. The fountain itself, in the form of the lion's head in grey, is on the back wall; water gushes from it and is caught in a basin below, which is protected by a yellow-brown grille" (Rice, *Great Palace*, 123 and pl. 44A).

[132] Theoph. Cont., *Vita Theophili* 43, Bonn ed., 141–42.

[133] See J. Strzygowski, "Der Pinienzapfen als Wasserspeier," *Mitteilungen des kaiserlich deutschen archæologischen Instituts, ræmische Abteilung* 18 (1903), 185–206.

[134] Theoph. Cont., *Vita Basilii* 85, Bonn ed., 327–28. The former fountain was later transferred by Andronikos I to the courtyard of the church of the Forty Martyrs (Niketas Choniates, ed. van Dieten, I, 332.18–21).

[135] Above, p. 27.

3), but the specific shape of a pinecone is occasionally shown as in a scene of Saint Luke pondering over the composition of his gospel in a twelfth- to thirteenth-century *tetraevangelion* at the Pantokrator monastery on Mount Athos (Fig. 7)[136] or, with water dramatically pouring forth, in the eleventh-century *tetraevangelion* cod. Paris. gr. 74 (Fig. 1). The most grandiose fountain of all, however, appears in the twelfth-century romance of Eustathios Makrembolites, who envisages a circle of marble seats roofed over by myrtles around a fountain of multicolored stones that enhance the sparkle of the water: a gilded eagle squirts water over his outstretched wings, as below a goat drinks while being milked by a goatherd, a hare washes his chin and a swallow, peacock, pigeon, turtledove, and cock emit jets of water with appropriate songs.[137] A further miniature in the Romance of Barlaam and Joasaph at Iviron that depicts Joasaph's vision of Paradise includes, beneath a ciborium surrounded by trees, a fountain topped by an eagle, although the water, which runs out at the bottom through a spout in the form of a lion's head, appears to issue from the central column below the eagle (Fig. 8).[138]

Automata such as Makrembolites' Daedalean fountain are best represented at Byzantium by the famous golden tree with singing birds that was built for Theophilos and then melted down by his son Michael II to help provide pay for the army.[139] Although the requisite hydraulic virtuosity and even its use of singing birds are Hellenistic in origin,[140] the tree was probably another theme for imperial/caliphal rivalry. A Muslim historian, the Khaṭīb al-Baghdādī, relates that in 917 Byzantine ambassadors to Baghdad were astounded by birds of gold and silver whistling and singing as they perched upon the twigs of a silver tree weighing 500 dirhams whose eighteen boughs regularly swayed so that the multicolored leaves rustled as if in a breeze.[141] Shortly thereafter, in the reign

---

[136] Cod. 234, fol. 23v, S. M. Pelekanidis et al., *Treasures of Mount Athos,* vol. III (Athens, 1979), pl. 242.

[137] *Hysmine and Hysminias* 1.5–6. Cf. the description of a fountain surmounted by an eagle and surrounded by statues attributed to no less than Pheidias, Zeuxis, and Praxiteles in *Drosilla and Charikles* 1.77–108.

[138] Cod. 463, fol. 100r, S. Der Nersessian, *Barlaam et Joasaph,* pl. xv, fig. 53; S. M. Pelekanidis et al., *Treasures of Mount Athos,* vol. II (Athens, 1975), 79, pl. 106.

[139] Theoph. Cont., *Vita Michaelis* 21, Bonn ed., 173; Symeon Magistros, apud Theoph. Cont., 627, 659; Georg. Mon., ibid., 793; Leo Gramm., Bonn ed., 215; Kedrenos, Bonn ed., II, 160; Zonaras 16.3, ed. L. Dindorf (Leipzig, 1868–75), IV, 8–9; Michael Glykas, Bonn ed. (1836), 537, 543; Constantine Manasses 4793–4803, 5070–79, Bonn ed. (1837), 205, 216–17; Theodosios of Melitene, ed. T.F.L. Tafel, *Theodosii Meliteni qui fertur Chronographia ex Codice Graeco Regiae Bibliothecae Monacensis,* Monumenta Saecularia von der königlich bayerischen Akademie der Wissenschaften 3.1 (Munich, 1859), 148. Two further texts are given in D. Serruys, "Recherches sur l'épitomé," *BZ* 16 (1907), 15 and (with discussion and translation) J. Psichari, "L'arbre chantant," in *Mélanges offerts à M. Emile Chatelain* (Paris, 1910), 628–33. Some of these accounts specify a plane, and not all mention birds.

[140] Vitruvius describes (10.7.4) a device of Ktesibios of Alexandria, most famous as the inventor of the related hydraulic organ, in which birds sang varied songs through the pressure of water. For later classical literary and artistic evidence and for the eventual combination with the symbolic image of the tree, see G. Brett, "The Automata in the Byzantine 'Throne of Solomon,'" *Speculum* 29 (1954), 477–87.

[141] *Ta'rīkh* 102–3, trans. Lassner, *The Topography of Baghdad,* 88, 90 (for other Arab accounts see P. Jacobsthal, *Ornamente griechischer Vasen* [Berlin, 1927], 106–8 note 187). In the time of al-Muqtadir (908–932) there were two trees with artificial birds in the palace (Lassner, op. cit., 269–70 note 14). Ca. 1405 there was at Timur's court at Samarkand in the tent of his principal wife a golden tree in the form of an oak with artificial, though not warbling, gold-enameled birds picking at fruits of precious stones (R. Gonzalez de Clavijo, *Embajada a Tamorlán,* ed. F. López Estrada [Madrid, 1943], 194.34–195.17). For eastern artistic influence in general on Byzantium

of Constantine VII Porphyrogennetos, there appeared in the Magnaura palace a new tree that in 949–950 impressed even the acidulous papal ambassador Liutprand, who avers that it was of gilded bronze, its branches filled with birds of similar fashioning "that uttered the cries of different birds according to their species."[142]

Whereas the Abbasid court manifested its desire to vie with and worst nature in the creation of artificial gardenly features such as ponds and streams,[143] the Byzantines manifested the same desire not so much in their hydraulic tree, as we have just seen, as in the extension of the gardens into the pavilions by means of mosaics or frescoes, again a Roman tradition.[144] Literature far more than surviving art is of help here, although we may note that in the Baradā panel the symmetrical palaces by the garden pavilions reveal floral motifs that probably represent floral mosaics (Fig. 5). Theophilos depicted "trees and green ornamentation" with "figures picking fruit" in wall mosaics at the Kamilas pavilion and associated buildings in the Great Palace, while the floor mosaic of his Mousikos moved a historian to comment that "when you see this building you believe that it is a meadow abounding in various flowers";[145] Basil I decorated the walls of his new residential building the Kainourgion with marble representing a vine and various animals and "with multicolored plaques of glass that give the walls the appearance of blossoming with the shapes of various flowers";[146] Constantine VII covered a gilded ceiling

---

at this time see A. Grabar, "Le succès des arts orientaux à la cour byzantine sous les Macédoniens," *MünchJb* 3.2 (1951), 32–60.

[142] *Antapodosis* 6.5. Cf. Constantine VII, *De Cer.* 2.15, Bonn ed., 569. The romance *Kallimachos and Chrysorrhoë* briefly describes (317–18) a similar golden tree with precious stones for fruit but no birds.

[143] E.g., in the center of the New Kiosk, "a building situated amidst two gardens. In the center . . . was an artificial pond of white lead surrounded by a stream of white lead more lustrous than polished silver. The pond was thirty by twenty cubits and contained four fine *tayyārah* boats with gilt seats adorned with brocade work. . . . Surrounding this lake was a lawn area (*maydān*) in which there was a garden containing, it is said, four hundred palm trees, each five cubits high. Dressed in a sculptured teakwood, each tree was covered from top to bottom with rings of gilt copper, and each branch bore marvellous dates which were not quite ripe" (al-Khaṭīb, *Ta'rīkh* 103, trans. Lassner, *The Topography of Baghdad*, 89–90).

[144] For the Romans' delight in a counterfeit nature see Z. Pavlovskis, *Man in an Artificial Landscape: The Marvels of Civilization in Imperial Roman Literature,* Mnemosyne, suppl. 25 (Leiden, 1973); N. Purcell, "Town in Country and Country in Town," in MacDougall, *Ancient Roman Villa Gardens* (as above, note 20), 185–203.

[145] Theoph. Cont., *Vita Theophili* 43, Bonn ed., 144–45.

[146] Theoph. Cont., *Vita Basilii* 89, Bonn ed., 333. On the evidence of an anacreontic *ekphrasis* by Leo Choirosphaktes, P. Magdalino claims that Basil's son Leo VI decorated the bath house of the "Palace of Marina" (within the confines of the Great Palace and probably by the seawalls) with representations of, among other things, a golden-leafed tree laden with fruit and birds, aquatic scenes, banquets on islands in the water, a songbird, and Leo himself with his wife Zoe Karbonopsina ("The Bath of Leo the Wise and the 'Macedonian Renaissance' Revisited: Topography, Iconography, Ceremonial, Ideology," *DOP* 42 [1988], 116–17. For identification of the site see ibid., 99–101 and idem, "The Bath of Leo the Wise," in *Maistor: Classical, Byzantine and Renaissance Studies for Robert Browning,* ed. A. Moffatt, Byzantina Australiensia 5 (Canberra, 1984), 233. Mango has, however, strongly argued that the iconography better fits a much earlier period, that of the original construction of the palace in the early 5th century, and that the "imperial" couple is really divine, Poseidon with Amphitrite or Okeanos with Tethys ("The Palace of Marina, the Poet Palladas and the Bath of Leo VI," Ευφρόσυνον: Αφιερώμα στον Μανόλη Χατζιδάκη, vol. I [Athens, 1991], 321–30, especially 326–27). There seems to be no other surviving description of an imperial bathhouse, as opposed to pavilion, with vegetal decoration in any medium, but one does occur in the early 14th-century(?) romance *Kallimachos and Chrysorrhoë* (292–318), whose mosaics could well have been modeled on a palatial exemplar.

in the ceremonial dining chamber of the Nineteen Couches with "various sculptures resembling the tendrils and leaves of the vine and the shapes of trees," while he turned the Chrysotriklinos of the Great Palace "into a blooming and odoriferous rose garden, as tiny, variegated mosaic cubes imitated the colors of freshly opened flowers."[147] The most detailed description of a palatial representation of nature is of a painting of a garden and game park on a ceiling in an unidentified room[148] that impressed Manuel Philes in ca. 1300: he marveled at how the painter could produce so lifelike a scene of fruit trees, flowers, and birds and mammals both tame and wild. The realism of the scene is emphasized by Philes' conceit that the artist deliberately avoided swallows, nightingales, and swans as noisy birds likely to disturb the peacefulness of this imperial chamber.[149] Our faith in the realism of some of these descriptions is, however, assailed by the knowledge that panels of different colored marble, that we see so commonly in Byzantine churches, were believed to simulate natural scenes,[150] and that Prokopios could describe the surviving galleries of Hagia Sophia as "a meadow in bloom."[151] It would be similarly indicative

[147] Theoph. Cont., *Vita Constantini* 20, 33, Bonn ed., 449–50, 456.

[148] The lemma to the poem reads simply Εἰς τὸν ἐν τοῖς βασιλείοις ἐζωγραφημένον ὄροφον.

[149] *Carm.* 62, ed. E. Miller, *Manuelis Philae Carmina* (Paris, 1855–57), II, 127–31. This is worth quoting almost in its entirety: "Where has this luxurious garden been planted? Do you not see it above ground . . . ? In what manner, being as it is suspended and stretched out under the roof, does it preserve so securely its interwoven contexture, lest its bond be disrupted by the breezes and so force the fruit to drop off before its time? What moisture have the roots absorbed to have produced such delicate shoots on the plants? . . . Whence has the warmth of the vegetation crept through to put forth flowers that adorn the boughs, to make leaves with their hidden shadows? Who has gone by and painted, next to the lilies, all those colors of the beautiful grove? Do you see the white, the dark green, the hue that grows pale as if from sickness, and the one that is adorned with purple . . . ? Be mindful, O spectator, not to touch the lilies; for you are not permitted to use your knife here, lest any [plant] be stabbed and quickly fade away, and so deprive the birds of their food. See how the painter has shown himself an excellent caretaker of the grove: for he has depicted the carnivorous animals pursuing only those which by nature feed on herbs, so that the meadow should not be given over to grazing to be ravaged all too soon. And lest the fowl devour the grass, he has confined them in circular pens. And the foursome of hares . . . he has gathered in a single group lest they be parted from one another, and one of them, rushing out into the meadow, be immediately seized by the jaws of those bloodthirsty animal-stalkers. And if . . . in some parts of the garden you chance to see a bird perched in the hollow of a lily, gathering the sperm of the flower, do not be astonished at the painter: for he provides food for the humble, and he makes the garden a place of strange and soft delight; otherwise one might have thought that the green grass was devoid of moisture and unsuitable for eating. As you can see, he has painted also a female lion and given her a fixed abode that she might feed her cubs, and fenced her with a woven barrier, lest she boldly sally forth and chase away the roe with her young" (trans. Mango, *Art of the Byzantine Empire*, 248).

[150] A certain Manasses was sent to Prokonessos to cut "marble there in the likeness of earth and green marble in the likeness of rivers" (*Narratio de S. Sophia* 28, ed. Preger, 107–8), and Cassiodorus refers to marble workers able to cut and join panels to simulate nature (*Var.* 1.6), as was done successfully, according to Chorikios (*Laudatio Marciana* 2.40), at Gaza.

[151] *Aed.* 1.1.59 (for a similar seemingly far-fetched description see Paul the Silentiary, *Desc. Ambonis S. Sophiae* 224–31). Chorikios' description, written some time between 536 and 548, of a river flanked by meadows that decorated the aisle walls of the church of Saint Stephen at Gaza (*Laudatio Marciana* 2.50) may be similarly ambitious, but could equally indicate a mosaic similar to the Baradā panel. A degree of realism must have been obtained in iconoclastic decoration of churches, for an iconodule inveighs against Constantine V for adorning the walls of the church of Blachernai with mosaics of "trees and all manner of birds and beasts and swirls of ivy leaves" to render it "an orchard and an aviary" (*Vita S. Stephani Iunioris*, PG 100:1120c). For further examples and a discussion of what could and what could not be thus described, see H. Maguire, "Originality in Byzantine Art Criticism," in A. R. Littlewood, ed., *Originality in Byzantine Literature, Art and Music* (Oxford, 1995), 102–4.

of the Byzantine attitude to art if, as is likely, it is to the peristyle pavement of agricultural scenes in the Great Palace that John of Ephesos refers as "a lovely *garden* that had existed in the middle of the palace to the great delight of former emperors" when he mourns its destruction by Tiberios II in the late sixth century.[152]

Finally there should briefly be considered the game park. Near eastern kings in a never-ending tradition had kept wild animals for hunting as a symbol of royal status, the Assyrian Ashurnasirpal II claiming in the ninth century B.C. that he had "organised herds of wild bulls, lions, ostriches and . . . monkeys and had them breed like flocks."[153] This sometimes led to a separation of hunting park and menagerie, as at Cabeira, the country estate of Mithridates VI of Pontos,[154] and in the early tenth century we hear of a separate zoological garden within the confines of the caliphal residence in Baghdad where on the occasion of a Byzantine ambassadorial visit "herds of wild animals . . . were brought (to the palace) from the garden, and . . . drew near to the people sniffing them, and eating from their hands."[155] Was this also a field for imperial/caliphal rivalry? Exotic animals always held a fascination for the Byzantines and were, of course, regularly exhibited in the Hippodrome, especially in the early centuries, but from the time of Iconoclasm there is no definite mention of a menagerie until the eleventh century when Constantine IX Monomachos established one whose elephant and giraffe marvelously astonished Michael Attaleiates.[156] Nonetheless, there is an intriguing hint in the Life of Saint Basil the Younger: when in 896 the saint was being interrogated by Samonas for spying he exasperated the *parakoimomenos* by accusing him of sodomy, for which lack of tact the keeper of wild animals was summoned "since the emperor kept in the Oikonomeion (of the Great Palace) a very fearsome lion" which then refused to perform its intended rôle at the saint's expense.[157]

In the West the Roman tradition of game parks extended back to the late Republican

[152] *Eccl. Hist.* 3.23. It must be remembered that in a sense the Byzantines did consider art more "real" than nature: indeed they held "that the ideal state of nature is to approximate to that of art" (R. Beaton, *The Medieval Greek Romance* [Cambridge, 1989], 25. See further Maguire, "Truth and Convention in Byzantine Descriptions of Works of Art," *DOP* 28 [1974], 111–40; A. Kazhdan and G. Constable, *People and Power in Byzantium: An Introduction to Modern Byzantine Studies* [Washington, D.C., 1982], 61; C. Cupane, "'Natura Formatrix': Umwege eines rhetorischen Topos," in Βυζάντιος: *Festschrift für Herbert Hunger zum 70. Geburtstag*, ed. W. Hörandner, J. Koder, O. Kresten, and E. Trapp [Vienna, 1984], 37–52). The Byzantines here were merely following Romans like the Younger Pliny for whom the countryside around his Tuscan villa was rather a painted picture than real (*Ep.* 5.6.13).

[153] Pritchard, *Ancient Near Eastern Texts,* 559–60.

[154] Strabo, 12.3.30 (C 556). For Roman menageries see J. Aymard, *Essai sur les chasses romaines des origines à la fin du siècle des Antonins* (Paris, 1951), 185–89.

[155] Al-Khaṭīb, *Ta'rīkh* 103 (also 99), trans. Lassner, *The Topography of Baghdad,* 89 (also 86).

[156] Bonn ed. (1853), 48–49. Pachymeres records the gift to Michael VIII Palaiologos of a giraffe from the king of Ethiopia (Bonn ed. [1835], I, 177–78). See further G. Loisel, *Histoire des ménageries de l'antiquité à nos jours,* vol. I (Paris, 1912), 140–44; Koukoules, Βυζαντινῶν βίος, vol. III (Athens, 1949), 73–80, 247–53; J. Théodorides, "Les animaux des jeux de l'Hippodrome et des ménageries impériales à Constantinople," *Byzantinoslavica* 19 (1958), 73–84.

[157] Ed. G. Vilinskij, *Zapiski Imp. Novorossijskago Univ.* 7 (Odessa, 1911), 285–88, summarized by Mango, "Palace of Marina," 325–26.

magnates,[158] but, while they attempted to tame wild boars, stags, and other animals,[159] their hunting became increasingly effete, especially during the principate.[160] The Byzantines, like many of their eastern counterparts,[161] took hunting more seriously than their Roman predecessors: indeed no fewer than three emperors—Theodosios I, Basil I, and John II Komnenos—are reported to have lost their lives in this pursuit; Liutprand attributes Romanos I Lekapenos' rise to power to his single-handed slaying of a lion when, to the great admiration of Leo VI, he used his cloak much in the manner of a matador his *capa*;[162] John Kinnamos claims that Manuel I "had fought more wild beasts than any man of whom I have ever heard";[163] and Andronikos I had himself depicted at his residence by the church of the Forty Martyrs as a hunter, cutting up and cooking venison and boar with his own hands.[164]

Some palaces were built as bases for hunting without probably including enclosed game parks. Such was that built by Tiberios II and completed by Maurice at Damatrys, some twelve miles from the Asiatic coast of the Sea of Marmara,[165] where Manuel I Komnenos slew an animal that Kinnamos seems to find a cross between a lion and a leopard;[166] and one at Meloudion, probably at the Beylerbey of today on the Asiatic side of the Bosporos, which was associated with Andronikos I and was probably employed by him for hunting in the neighboring hills.[167] We do, however, have descriptions of three proper game parks,[168] of which two at least had associated palaces.

[158] According to the Elder Pliny (*H.N.* 8.78.211), they were introduced to the Roman world in the mid-1st century B.C. by Fulvius Lippinus, a man celebrated also for his innovation of segregated snail ponds (ibid., 9.82.173–74).

[159] For instance Varro avers (*Rust.* 3.13.2–3) that in a thirty-acre enclosure on his estate at Laurentum the orator Q. Hortensius used to dine at a table to which a huge crowd of tamed wild animals would come when summoned on lyre and horn by a slave accoutred as Orpheus.

[160] In general see Aymard, *Chasses romaines*, especially 25–196, 469–558.

[161] The most appalling "bag" of a Middle Eastern ruler seems to be one of the earliest and emphasizes the royal prerogative: Ashurnasirpal II claims that "Ninurta and Palil, who loved me as (their) high priest, handed over to me all the wild animals and ordered me to hunt (them). I killed 450 big lions; I killed 390 wild bulls from my open chariots in direct assault as befits a ruler; I cut off the heads of 200 ostriches as if they were caged birds; I caught 30 elephants in pitfalls. I caught alive 50 wild bulls, 140 ostriches (and) 20 big lions with my own (. . .) and *stave*" (Pritchard, *Ancient Near Eastern Texts*, 559).

[162] *Antapodosis* 3.25.

[163] 6.6, Bonn ed. (1836), 266.

[164] Niketas Choniates, *Hist.*, ed. van Dieten, I, 333.55–57. On imperial interest in hunting see E. Patlagean, "De la chasse et du souverain," *DOP* 46 (1992), 257–63; and on Byzantine hunting in general, Ph. I. Koukoules, Κυνηγετικὰ ἐκ τῆς ἐποχῆς τῶν Κομνηνῶν καὶ τῶν Παλαιολόγων, Ἐπ.Ἑτ.Βυζ.Σπ. 9 (1932), 3–33; idem, Βυζαντινῶν βίος καὶ πολιτισμός, vol. V (Athens, 1952), 387–423; A. Karpozilos, Βασιλείου Πεδιαδίτη: "Ἔκφρασις ἁλώσεως ἀκανθίδων," Ἠπειρωτικὰ Χρονικά 23 (1981), 284–98.

[165] *Script. orig. const.* 3.170, ed. Preger, II, 268–69.

[166] Loc. cit. (above, note 163).

[167] Niketas Choniates, *Hist.*, ed. van Dieten, I, 344.51, 346.31. The palace at Argyrolimne just outside the walls of the city may have been similarly used as a base for hunting, for imperial hunters used to leave by the eponymous city gate for hunting in the area (Nikephoros Gregoras 8.6, Bonn ed., I, 315; John Kantakouzenos 1.18, Bonn ed. [1828–32], I, 89–90).

[168] No Byzantine source gives any indication of size. For what it is worth here, we may note that the Umayyad game parks at Qaṣr al-Ḥayr ash-Sharqī (nearly 60 miles northeast of Palmyra) and Khirbat al-Mafjar were respectively ca. 1850 and ca. 150 acres in extent (Creswell, *Early Muslim Architecture*, I, pt. 2, 536, 546).

In 968 or the following year Nikephoros II Phokas invited Liutprand to visit a park containing wild asses and roe deer, but the biased ambassador disdainfully dismisses it as "fairly large, hilly and wooded, but highly displeasing" and its wild asses as no different from their domestic counterparts.[169] At about the same time the poet John Geometres rhapsodizes over an imperial estate that seems to have included a game park, a more formal pleasure garden, and a palace, even though he runs these together.[170] He finds the earth "arrayed like a bride . . . with laurels, with plants, with [young] shoots, with bushes, with vines, with ivy clusters, with fruit-bearing trees": there are "fountains, shadows, reeds, woods, streams, grasses, pastures, ravines, peaks, hollows, coppices or meadows, caves and wooded vales, all flowers, all beauties, every scent, every complexion, flaxen, purple, gold, milky-white" and "rose beds, lilies, scented violets, chrysanthemum, sweet narcissus and crocus, the sweeter purple hyacinth and the more conspicuous flame-coloured variety."[171] He mentions a "multitude of beasts, birds and fish," including hares and roe deer that were traditionally hunted by the emperors, but he does not make clear which were real and which sculptures. Maguire argues,[172] I think rightly, that this park is that at Aretai. If so, we have a second description of the same park from Anna Komnene who mentions a magnificent summer resort of Romanos IV Diogenes in the elevated district of Aretai in view of the sea a little to the west of the city's walls, a charming site with a temperate climate, although in her day it was "completely devoid of bushes so that you would say that the hill had been laid bare by woodcutters."[173] By far the most famous of these game parks, however, was the Philopation, somewhere outside the Gate of Charisios and visible from the galleries of the church of the Holy Apostles.[174] This was, we know from Zonaras, favored by Alexios I,[175] but when the actual enclosure was first made is uncertain.[176] Odo of Deuil, who visited it as chaplain of Louis VII on the Second Crusade in 1147, called it a splendid "springtime resort" of the emperors with "a beautiful and spacious enclosed area with canals and ponds" where

---

[169] *Legatio* 37–38. Wild asses were hunted regularly in the caliphate: for instance, Ya'qūbī lists the inhabitants of the outer enclosure at al-Mu'taṣim's complex at Samarra as gazelles, wild asses, deer, hares, and ostriches (Creswell, *Early Muslim Architecture*, I, pt. 2, 536), of which the middle three animals are attested for Byzantine game parks also.

[170] See above, note 59.

[171] Maguire's trans., "A Description of the Aretai Palace," 211.

[172] Ibid., 212. Maguire suggests as a parallel the surviving Zisa palace outside Palermo begun by William I in 1164/65, a pavilion with fountain set in a garden with fish ponds and surrounded by a park of wild beasts, the whole complex probably being that known as *Gennet-ol-ardh* ("Paradise of the Earth") ("Imperial Gardens," 186).

[173] *Alexiad* 2.8.5.

[174] This "Outer Philopation" is, of course, quite distinct from the "Inner Philopation" within the city that is to be identified with the Mangana palace (Niketas Choniates, *Hist.*, ed. van Dieten, I, 255.29–30; Anon. apud K. N. Sathas, Μεσαιωνικὴ Βιβλιοθήκη, vol. VII [Venice, 1894], 323.25–26, 343.5–6).

[175] 18.26.5–8, Bonn ed., III, 753.

[176] It is first known from the 9th century when the future Basil I killed a huge wolf "in the area called 'Philopation'" (Theoph. Cont., *Vita Basilii* 14, Bonn ed., 231–32) and shortly after in the "Philopation's" "gullies and hollows" Jakovitzes, who aided in the assassination of Michael III, was killed in a hunting accident (George Monachos, *Vita Basilii* 2, apud Theoph. Cont., Bonn ed., 839). That the area itself provided lairs for wild animals is suggested by the story that in the 11th century Constantine IX bade gypsies clear the area of them because they were spoiling the imperial hunting (*Vita S. Georgii Hagioritae* 33, *AnalBoll* 36 [1917], 102–3).

the emperors hunted varied game that used "hollows and caves as hiding places in the absence of woods."[177] Unless, however, the descriptions are inaccurate or of different parts of the estate, there must subsequently have been extensive planting there, for later that century John Kinnamos comments on its trees (and rich grass).[178]

Evidence for Byzantine gardens, even when existent, is frustratingly imprecise. That they were an important part of Byzantine life, not only for health and aesthetic delight but also as a microcosm of the eternal paradise, is, however, abundantly clear. Imperial gardens doubtless frequently fulfilled to Byzantine taste Geometres' claim for the suburban park that so dazzled him: "Nothing is absent that would be better present, nothing is present that ought to be absent."[179]

University of Western Ontario

[177] *De Profectione Ludovici VII in Orientem* 3.31.
[178] 2.14, Bonn ed., 74–75.
[179] Maguire's trans., "A Description of the Aretaí Palace," 211.

Middle Byzantine Court Costume

Elisabeth Piltz

Introduction

Middle Byzantine costume is a variegated theme. It deals with the visual aspect of the imperial image, the visual signs of the emperor's sanctity, and the visual expression of the power delegated to his dignitaries[1] (Fig. 1).

In the court theater of Byzantium with its strictly prescribed protocol, costumes change according to their own rhythm and logic as a consequence of the variation of festivals and the degree of intimacy at the imperial table. It is my task to put its rhythm into a system and to decipher its logic. This task is not easy, but full of obstacles. Some of them are perhaps due to repetitions and mistakes made by the copyist of the relevant manuscript, when the text is obscure and contradictory, or perhaps the simple reason is that the source is written for a contemporary audience able to fill out what is understated. Other problems are connected to the almost complete lack of descriptions of costumes and the limited repertory of pictorial representations at our disposal for this period.

All things belonging to the emperor and his officials were considered sacred.[2] Consequently, the *vestes sacrae* were kept in the seclusion of the vestiary, carefully guarded by the *vestitores,* an unbearded corps of dignitaries belonging to the most intimate entourage of the emperor.

The people of the imperial chamber formed a circle or even a double circle around the emperor when he changed dress at prescribed moments of the imperial ritual, if he did not change dress behind curtains suspended at certain intervals along the processional route. Already here we come across the taboos associated with change of costume and coronation.

The emperor was never crowned in front of bearded officials (ἔμπροσθε βαρβάτον μὴ στέφεσθαι), except when he was crowned by the patriarch. It was for this reason

---

[1] A. Grabar, *L'empereur dans l'art byzantin* (Paris, 1936), 4–23, 264–67; L. Bréhier, *Les institutions de l'empire byzantin* (Paris, 1970), 79–137.

[2] L. Bréhier and P. Batiffol, *Les survivances du culte impérial romain* (Paris, 1920), 36–73; O. Treitinger, *Die oströmische Kaiser- und Reichsidee nach ihrer Gestaltung im höfischen Zeremoniell* (Jena, 1938), 214–18.

that the unbearded officials of the *koubouklion* formed a circle.[3] In this way the eunuchs were considered to protect the emperor from the evil eye (Fig. 2).

Garments were used for making signals at court. The *praipositos* opens his hands from the interior of the *chlamys*. The caesarian insignia[4] were used for making cross-signs over the promoted caesar, and at the Hippodrome from his throne in the *kathisma* the emperor blessed the people with his folded *chlamys*.

Two sources from the Middle Byzantine period give attention to the custom of wearing costumes: the *kletorologion* of Philotheos,[5] dated 899, and the *Book of Ceremonies* by Constantine VII Porphyrogennetos from the tenth century. As Philotheos only gives some indications on costume which in general correspond to those given by Constantine, I will concentrate on the *Book of Ceremonies*. Constantine VII gives the most detailed account of Middle Byzantine palace ritual and its costumes and delights in enumerating the proper costumes for every event, but he makes the same mistake as his later author-colleague Pseudo-Kodinos[6]—he gives no detailed descriptions of the costumes, which might allow them to be identified with accuracy. Consequently for their identification one must rely on the scarce pictorial evidence. However, representations in art are stylized and do not reflect the whole variety of tunics and coats mentioned in the sources. Moreover, from whatever was left of imperial costume in 1453, not a strip has survived, so we are often left with conjectures.

Constantine VII takes for granted that the reader of his work is quite familiar with the subject: he speaks of the "usual costume" and the "costume of parade" for both dignitaries and sovereigns. Therefore, in trying to make a reconstruction of imperial costume and that of the dignitaries and priests of the Middle Byzantine period, the eventual degree of success relies on the degree of logic and reliability of the literary sources.

The crown, the *loros* costume, the *chlamys,* the *kampagia,* and the shoes and stockings can easily be identified. But what are the sovereigns and dignitaries wearing under the *loros* and the *chlamys*? Constantine described the imperial splendor in terms of rare flowers giving a perfect and luminous mirror of the court. The senators reflect the order and dignity of the delegated imperial power. "In this way the imperial power, exerted with order and measure, thus represents (εἰκονίζοι) the harmony and movement which the Creator has installed in all things. So it appears to the subjects more majestic and through the same more pleasant and more admirable."[7] The court theater of Byzantium is the mirror of the harmonious movement of the universe, and its role is to appear magnificent and beautiful and to impress the subjects.

The crown of the Middle Byzantine era was an open stemma with a large precious

---

[3] Constantine VII Porphyrogennetos, *De ceremoniis aulae byzantinae* (hereafter *De cer.*), ed. A. Vogt, *Le livre des cérémonies,* 2 vols. (Paris, 1967), vol. I, 101, vol. II, 107: Χρὴ εἰδέναι ὅτι ἐνώπιον βαρβάτων ὁ βασιλεὺς οὐδέποτε στέφεται, ἐξ αὐτῆς τῆς ἀρχῆς ταύτης τῆς παραδόσεως φυλαττομένης.

[4] E. Piltz, *Kamelaukion et mitra,* Acta Universitatis Upsaliensis, Figura, n.s., 15 (Stockholm, 1977), 50 f.

[5] "Le Klètorologion de Philothée," ed. N. Oikonomidès, in *Les listes de préséance byzantins des IXe et Xe siècles* (Paris, 1972), 165–235.

[6] Pseudo-Kodinos, *Traité des offices,* ed. J. Verpeaux (Paris, 1966).

[7] *De cer.,* I, 1–2.

1   Theodosios I and St. Gregory of Nazianzos. MS gr. 543, fol. 288v. Paris, Bibliothèque Nationale

2 The coronation of David. MS gr. 139, fol. 6v. Paris, Bibliothèque Nationale

3 Constantine VII Porphyrogennetos crowned by Christ, ivory.
State Pushkin Museum of Fine Arts, Moscow
(photo: Hirmer Photoarchiv)

4   Romanos II crowned by Christ. Cabinet des Médailles, Paris
(photo: Bibliothèque Nationale)

5   Standing emperor, relief in marble from Italy. Dumbarton Oaks Collection

6   Nikephoros III Botaneiates and Empress Mary. MS Coislin 79, fol. 2bis v.
Paris, Bibliothèque Nationale

7   The exaltation of David. MS gr. 139, fol. 7v. Paris, Bibliothèque Nationale

8 Prostrating emperor, narthex of St. Sophia (photo: Dumbarton Oaks)

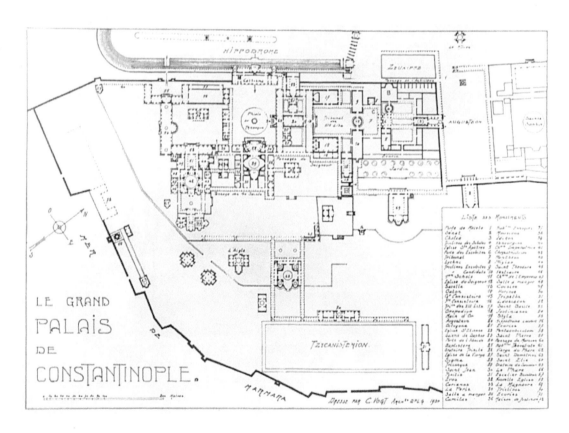

9 Reconstruction of the Great Palace in Constantinople (after Vogt, *De cer.*)

10   Constantine VII Porphyrogennetos, ivory.
Dumbarton Oaks Collection

11   Nikephoros III Botaneiates between St. John Chrysostom and St. Michael.
MS Coislin 79, fol. 2v. Paris, Bibliothèque Nationale

12 Alexios V Murtzuphlos. Vind. hist. gr. 53, fol. 291 v.
Vienna, Kunsthistorisches Museum

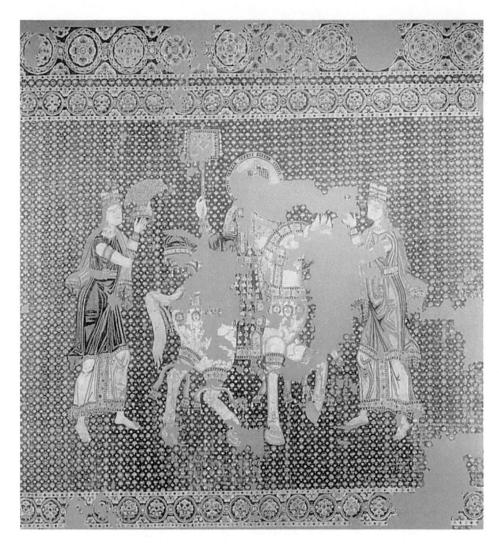

13 Emperor on horseback in triumph. The Bamberg cloth with personifications of
Constantinople. Treasury of the cathedral of Bamberg

14 Nikephoros III Botaneiates and his courtiers. MS Coislin 79, fol. 2r.
Paris, Bibliothèque Nationale

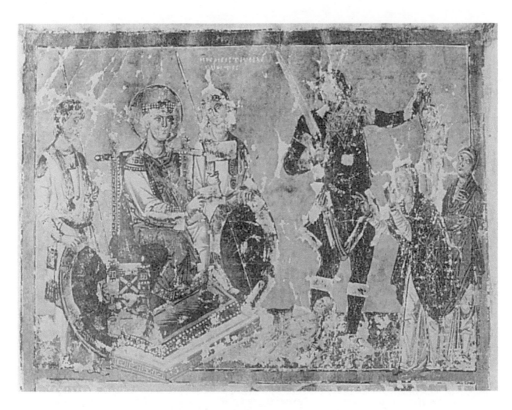

15   Solomon with *protospatharioi*. MS gr. 510, fol. 215v. Paris, Bibliothèque Nationale

16   St. Helen. MS gr. 510, fol. 440. Paris, Bibliothèque Nationale

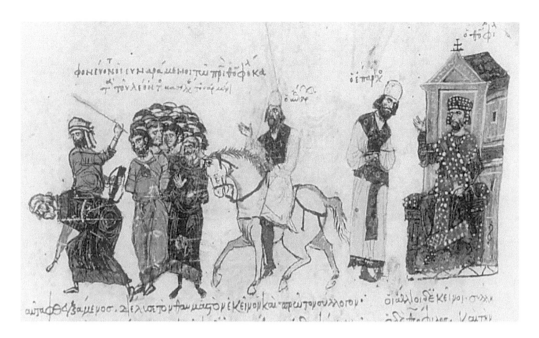

φονευοντες γναραμενοι τω πριγκιφικα
τ΄ τον λεον τ' κατα τον σφ[ε]μ[?]

αππαφθ[?]αμενος . ϛελοιτετου θαυμα[ϛο]ν εκεινον και πρωτογουσυλλογου
οιαλλιοιϛε κεινοι σ[?]
Σ΄ Απαχ[?]αει . καιτι[?]

17   Emperor Theophilos punishes participants in the assassination of Leo V: the eparchical costume. Skylitzes matritensis. MS vitr. 26–2, fol. 43r. Madrid, Biblioteca Nacional

18   The costume of a martyr in Garda, Gotland, ca. 1150: the *skaramangion* and the *chlamys* (photo: K. Brobäck)

19   Liturgical bands with Byzantine arabesque, bishop's seat
of Holar, Iceland, ca. 1200

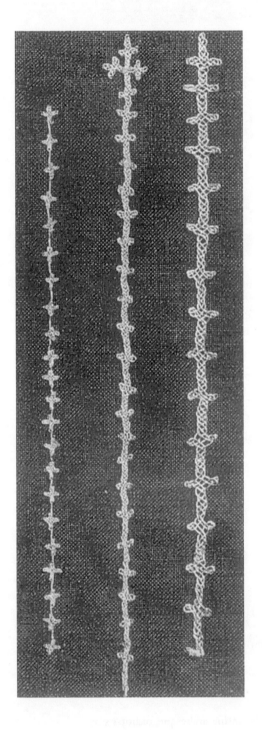

20 Golden ornaments of Byzantine type found in Birka in Sweden, tenth century

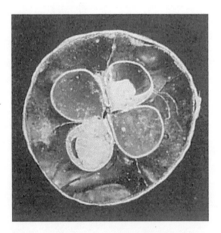

21 Ornament in gold and glass pearls, horse's attire from Byzantium found in the "black earth" in Sigtuna, eleventh century

stone on the diadem in front of the forehead in either of the four colors of the factions—red, white, blue, or green—placed over a silk calotte of the same color. During the Komnenian dynasty, the open stemma was replaced by a closed hemisphere, described by Anna Komnene.[8] Caesars and sebastokrators wore open crowns with or without crossing bands over the skull.

The *loros,* which in Constantine VII's coronation picture is a heavy band arranged freely around the body (Fig. 3), already in the tenth century becomes an all-covering apron falling from the shoulders to the feet, completely covering the body, full of precious stones and pearls (Fig. 4). No wonder that Zoe Monomachos hated to carry this burden. On a relief from Italy in the Dumbarton Oaks Collection, we see that the artist is not familiar with court dress accuracy. He puts a *chlamys* without a *fibula* over the *loros,* which was never the case (Fig. 5).

The costume of the empress is characterized by a broad necklace over the shoulders and the oval shield falling from the waist, called the *thorakion,* worn over a sumptuous tunic, the *sticharion* (Fig. 6).

The imperial *chlamys* (Fig. 7) with a *tablion* is in principle of the same type as that of the time of Justinian, but the *mandyas* is no longer mentioned. The *chlanidion* of the dignitaries is decorated all around with golden bands, as we also see on the prostrating emperor in the narthex of St. Sophia (Fig. 8).

The emperor's *kampagia* are very luxurious, with eagles, precious stones, and pearls; those of dignitaries are much simpler. An Arabic author, Harun Ibn Yahya of the ninth to tenth century, describes the red and black boots of the co-emperor.[9]

No headgear is mentioned. Still we have several pictures showing hats of different types, also turbans worn by dignitaries (Fig. 1). Liutprand of Cremona maintains that no one is allowed to wear a hat in the presence of an emperor.[10]

Let us now try to find the logic of the *Book of Ceremonies.* In the morning of each feast day, for the usual cortege or procession, the *vestitores* enter the Chrysotriklinos, and the dignitaries of the imperial chamber in charge of the imperial wardrobe (οἱ τῶν ἀλλαξίμων τοῦ κουβουκλείου), together with the *diaitarioi* who belong to their rank, take the chest in which are placed the imperial garments and the boxes containing the imperial crowns. The imperial *spatharioi* take the imperial weapons, shield, and lance, and the dignitaries in charge of the imperial wardrobe bring the imperial garments to the Octagonal chamber in the Daphne palace in front of the sanctuary of the first martyr, St. Stephen (Fig. 9).[11]

The sovereigns, dressed in the *skaramangion,* come out of the sacred apartment, put on the *sagion* decorated with gold, and pass by the Phylax. The sovereigns, with only the personnel of the chamber and the *kitonites,* go to the Octagonal chamber in front of St. Stephen, where the imperial garments have been deposited, and there the personnel

---

[8] Anne Comnène, *Alexiade,* ed. B. Leib, 3 vols. (Paris, 1967, 1945), I, bk. 3, pp. 113–14.

[9] A. A. Vasiliev, "Harun Ibn Yahya and His Description of Constantinople," *SemKond* 5 (1932), 149–63.

[10] Liutprand of Cremona, *Legatio,* 37, MGH, *ScriptRerGerm* (Hannover, 1877), 152: "fas non esse, quempiam, ubi imperator esset, pileatum, sed teristratum incedere."

[11] *De cer.,* I, 4–14.

of the imperial chamber wait to present their homage in the Daphne apartment. The *vestitores* enter, dress the sovereigns in their brilliant *chlamydes,* and leave. The *praepositos* crowns the sovereigns, who pass to the *triklinos* and the Augusteus.

The *praepositos,* having made an inclination of his head toward the sovereigns, gives a sign with his *chlamys* to the *ostiarios,* who holds in his hands the golden staff. Four *ostiarioi* in fact hold golden staffs decorated with precious stones. On a sign from the emperor the *praepositos* makes a sign to the master of ceremonies with his *chlamys* and says "Please." Then follow the entrances of the dignitaries.

During the liturgy, when the sacred gifts are brought in procession to the altar, the *praepositoi* enter and dress the sovereigns in their *chlamydes* and they stand with uncovered heads. After the communion they dine with invited senators, and after that the *praepositos* enters with the chief of the imperial wardrobe, and they dress the sovereigns in their *chlamydes.* Then the sovereigns return with the personnel of the imperial chamber to the Octagonal Hall in front of St. Stephen and take off their crowns and *chlamydes,* and they enter into the Daphne apartment wearing the *divitision.* There they take on the *sagion* decorated with gold and enter the Sacred Palace, preceded by the *praepositos* and the personnel of the imperial chamber. This ritual is repeated every feast day (Fig. 9).

Imperial Costumes Listed in the *Book of Ceremonies*

The Divitision and the Tzitzakion

At Easter[12] and on Easter Thursday for the Kissing ceremony in the Chrysotriklinos (*De cer.,* I, 84) the sovereigns wear the *divitision* and the *tzitzakion* in combination, on Easter Sunday (I, 17) only the *tzitzakion.* At the coronation of an emperor (II, 1), the *divitision* and the *tzitzakion* are worn in combination with the *sagion* at the top. Here for once Constantine comments on a costume: "You must know that the *tzitzakion* is a Khazar costume that appeared in this God-protected imperial city since the empress of Khazaria" (most likely the wife of Constantine V). The white *divitision* is worn at Ascension and Pentecost (I, 176). The coemperor wears the *tzitzakion* at the coronation and wedding ceremony of an *augusta* (II, 21). The *divitision* alone is worn at the feast of Orthodoxy (I, 148), and the purple *divitision* on the emperor's birthday (II, 86).

The Chlamys

The *divitision* is worn with the *chlamys* at Hypapante (I, 138), Pentecost (I, 176), and Palm Sunday (I, 160). The *chlamys* is the costume of parade *par préférence.* It can be white (II, 65), purple, green, blue, or golden. The scarlet *chlamys* is used at the acclamation of the demes on the promotion of a *nobelissimos* (II, 36). The golden *chlamys* is used for the funeral of the emperor when he lies on the *lit de parade* (II, 84).

---

[12] *De cer.,* I, 17; hereafter all references to this source will be given parenthetically in the text.

The Sagion

On St. Basil's feast day, 1 January (I, 128), the *divitision* and the *sagion* with golden embroidery are worn. The golden *sagion* is also worn at Easter (I, 175) and at the coronation and wedding of an *augusta* (II, 21).

The purple *sagion* is worn at the coronation of an emperor (II, 1). At Hypapante (I, 141, 143), the second day of the first week of the year, the emperor gives a sermon in the Magnaura in the *sagion*. It is also worn on the Sunday of Orthodoxy (I, 145).

The Loros

The *loros,* the imperial insignium par excellence, is worn at Easter (I, 175) and on Pentecost (I, 57). It is associated with Christ's victory over death (Fig. 10).

The Skaramangion

Another important imperial tunic, the *skaramangion,* is worn on the Feast of Orthodoxy (I, 147) and at the coronation of an emperor (II, 1). The golden *skaramangion* is worn on All Saints Day (I, 177). On Easter Sunday (I, 175) a dark red *skaramangion* with a *sagion* with golden embroidery is worn. A dark purple *skaramangion* is also used at Ascension (I, 176) and on the Feast of Orthodoxy (I, 147). At the feasts of the Presentation (I, 178) and the Dormition (I, 177), a dark purple *skaramangion* is worn, and a *skaramangion* with golden bands at the Annunciation (I, 179; Fig. 11 may show a type of *skaramangion*).

The Kolobion

A luxurious tunic used less often is the *kolobion* of various types. On the feast of the Grape Harvest (II, 175) at the Hieria, a *kolobion* is worn with a *sagion* decorated with gold, and on Easter Monday (I, 72) a *kolobion* of purple silk, called the "cluster," with golden threads, precious stones, and pearls. On the eve of Easter Monday (I, 176), a *kolobion* with figures of rams is worn (Fig. 12 may show a type of *kolobion*).

The Himation

On Easter Thursday (I, 166) and Good Friday (I, 168) no costumes of parade are used. The emperor appears in a simple *himation* as a sign of humility.

The Sticharion and the Baltidin

At the promotion of a *magistros* (II, 41), the emperor wears a simple tunic, the *sticharion,* and a girdle, the *baltidin.*

The Imperial Horse Harness

On Easter Monday (I, 72, 73), the emperor mounts a horse with a golden harness, adorned with precious stones and pearls, and with silk bands hanging down at the horse's tail and four legs (Fig. 13). On Wednesday of Middle Pentecost at the church of St. Mochios (I, 92, 93, 97), the emperor, dressed in a white *skaramangion* with golden bands and wearing a crown, mounts a horse with silk bands on its tail and legs and with a harness decorated with enamels, gems on a golden ground, and pearls. When he returns from St. Mochios he mounts a white horse with a golden harness of gems, enamels on a golden ground, and pearls.

The Costumes of Dignitaries

The Loros

The golden *loros* costume, the most prestigious imperial insignium, is also worn by the "twelve dignitaries" who are *magistroi* and proconsuls at Easter (I, 18). The *loros* is further worn by the eparch (II, 70) and the girded *patrikia* (II, 64) at their promotion.

The Chlamys

The white *chlamys* with purple *tablion* is worn by the patricians at Epiphany (I, 132) and the Annunciation (I, 151). The *chlamys* with a golden *tablion* decorated with lions is worn by the *praipositoi* on Easter Saturday (I, 169).

The so-called united *chlamys* is worn by the patricians at the Exaltation of the Holy Cross (I, 116).[13] In MS Coislin 79, three dignitaries surrounding the emperor—the *epi tou kanikleiou*, the dean, and the great *primikerios*—wear a *chlamys* arranged symmetrically which might be of this type (Fig. 14), and the fourth, the *protovestiarios*, perhaps a *sagion* with medallions. The purple *chlamys* of Tyre, a particularly luxurious silk, is worn by the *kouropalates* at his promotion (II, 37) and by the dignitaries of the imperial chamber at Easter Saturday (I, 169) and at the feast called the Vow (II, 160).

The purple *chlamys* of Tyre with green-yellow medallions is worn by the most important titularies of great offices at Christmas (I, 119), and the purple *chlamys* of Tyre with peacocks by the personnel of the imperial chamber at Christmas. At the same feast the domestic of the Schools makes a cross-sign with a colored *chlamys*. The *chlamys* of dark color is worn by patricians, domestics, and the whole Senate on Easter Saturday (I, 169) and at the feast called the Vow (II, 160).

The blue *chlamys* is worn by the demarch of the Blues on Wednesday of Middle Pentecost (I, 98) and at Christmas (I, 125), and at his promotion (II, 79) he wears the blue and purple *chlamys* of Tyre. The blue *chlamys* with golden embroidery is worn by the domestic of the Schools on Wednesday of Middle Pentecost (I, 97).

The green *chlamys* is worn by the demarch of the Greens on Wednesday of Middle Pentecost (I, 97) and at his promotion (II, 79); the green *chlamys* with golden embroidery is worn by the *democrates* on Wednesday of Middle Pentecost (I, 98); and the green *chlamys* with golden roses and golden *tablion* is worn by the *nobelissimos* (II, 34).

The Kamision

A costume worn in the first place by the *spatharokubikoularioi* on Easter Monday (I, 73) and by the *spatharokubikoularioi* and the people of the imperial chamber on Wednesday of Middle Pentecost (I, 92) is the *kamision*. It is also worn by the eparch at his promotion

---

[13] Cf. I. Spatharakis, *The Portrait in Byzantine Illuminated Manuscripts* (Leiden, 1976), 110, pl. 71; H. Omont, *Miniatures des plus anciens manuscrits grecs de la Bibliothèque nationale du VIe au XIVe siècle* (Paris, 1929), 32–34.

(II, 70). At Easter (I, 19) the proconsuls and patricians wear the *kamision* and white *chlamys*. The *kamision* is also worn by the personnel of the chamber at the Exaltation of the Holy Cross (I, 116).

The Sagion

The *sagion,* one of the most important overtunics, is worn by the *strategoi* on the emperor's birthday (II, 86) and by the factions at the promotion of a demarch (II, 75). The red *sagion* is worn by the silentiaries at the promotion of patricians, senators, and *strategoi* (II, 47–49), by the *praipositos* at the promotion of an eparch (II, 69), and by the *praipositos,* master of ceremonies, and silentiaries at the promotion of a demarch (II, 75).

The purple *sagion* is worn by the dignitaries of the imperial chamber, the *magistroi,* the patricians, and the whole Senate on Easter Monday (I, 73), by the *kouropalates* at his promotion (II, 38), by the patricians at the promotion of patricians and *strategoi* (II, 47, 48), and by the promoted *magistros* (II, 43) over his tunic. The purple *sagion* is in general more prestigious than the red.

The Skaramangion

The *skaramangion,* the Persian riding costume according to N. P. Kondakov, is worn by all dignitaries at the Exaltation of the Holy Cross (I, 116), at Ascension (I, 101), and at Hypapante (I, 137), by all invited for dinner on the Feast of Orthodoxy (I, 147), and by the Senate at the emperor's funeral (II, 84). Either a white *skaramangion* or a colored one is worn by the invited friends of the emperor for dinner on Easter Saturday (I, 172). The *skaramangion* is worn with the *chlamys* by all dignitaries at the Exaltation of the Holy Cross (I, 118), the *skaramangion* and the red *sagion* by the factions at the promotion of a demarch (II, 76), and the *skaramangion* and the purple *sagion* by the patricians at their promotion (II, 56). *Skaramangia* were given as salaries at the court according to Liutprand of Cremona.[14]

The Spekion

The *spekion* is worn exclusively by *protospatharioi* (Fig. 15), a purple one by the bearded on Wednesday of Middle Pentecost at the church of St. Mochios (I, 92), and at Hypapante (I, 137). When they ride in the cortege on Easter Monday (I, 73–74) the bearded *protospatharioi* wear a *spekion* and the unbearded a purple *spekion* with golden bands.

The Divitision

Another imperial tunic, the *divitision,* is worn by the protospatharian eunuchs at Epiphany (I, 132) and at the reception in the Great Phiales (II, 110); a *divitision* of white color is worn by the protospatharian eunuchs on Wednesday of Middle Pentecost (I, 93, 94). The red *divitision* is worn by the *nobelissimos* at his promotion (II, 34), and the purple *divitision* by the *kouropalates* at his promotion (II, 37).

---

[14] Liutprand of Cremona, *Antapodosis,* VI, 10, 123: "Quorum prius est rector domus, cui non in manibus, sed in humeris posita sunt numismata cum scaramangis quattuor."

The Sabanion

The *sabanion,* eventually a tunic of linen, is worn by the protospatharian eunuchs at the promotion of a proconsul (II, 61), on Wednesday of Middle Pentecost (I, 94), and at the reception in the Great Phiales (II, 110). Here is a case where three different costumes are said to be worn on the same occasion.

The Sticharion

A *sticharion* is said to be worn by the protospatharian eunuchs at the reception in the Great Phiales (II, 110).

The Delmatikin

The *delmatikin* is a tunic worn exclusively by the girded *patrikia* at her promotion (II, 63).

The Pelonion

The *pelonion* is exclusively worn by the eparch at the acclamation of the demes at his promotion (II, 70).

The Thorakion and the Maphorion

The oval shield, the *thorakion,* insignium of the empress, is worn by the girded *patrikia* at her promotion (II, 63). She also wears a veil, *maphorion* (identical to that of the *augusta* at her coronation), and the *propoloma,* the high hairdo.

The Abdia

The ἀβδία is a tunic (perhaps of Slavonic or Arab origin) worn by the demarch at the promotion of a patrician (II, 60).

The Paragaudion

At Epiphany (I, 132) the *ostiarioi* wear the *paragaudion,* another imperial overtunic, and hold staffs.

The Fiblatorion

The *vestitor* wears a *fiblatorion* with a *fibula,* according to Philotheos.[15]

The Omophorion

The *omophorion* (I, 72 and II, 175), the band around the shoulders (Fig. 1), is worn by the patriarch and corresponds to the imperial *sagion.* It is taken off for dinner with the emperor at great festivals and put on again afterwards. In Figure 1 the Middle Byzantine division of the two earthly hierarchies, the imperial and the ecclesiastical, is illustrated.

---

[15] Philotheos, ed. Oikonomidès, 89–90.

The Phelonion

Under the *omophorion* the patriarch wears the chasuble, the *phelonion* (II, 175). The patriarch's staff is not mentioned but is seen in Figure 1. In this image the patriarch wears a *sakkos,* the short-sleeved vestment with crosses all over, not mentioned yet in the sources.

The Staff

Golden staffs are carried by *ostiarioi* at the feast of St. Basil (I, 128), 1 January, on Palm Sunday, decorated with precious stones (I, 160), Easter (I, 18), Pentecost (I, 61), and at the reception at the Golden Hippodrome (II, 94). Golden staffs with precious stones were carried by four *silentiarioi* on Wednesday of Middle Pentecost (I, 93), and also by the *skribones* and *mandatores.*

The Maniakion

The necklace, *maniakion,* is worn by *spatharokandidatoi, spatharioi, manglavites, spatharioi* of the personal service, *spatharokubikoularioi,* the personnel of the imperial chamber at Hypapante (I, 137), by the bearded *protospatharioi* at the reception in the Great Phiales (II, 110), and by the *protospatharioi* and *spatharokandidatoi* at the reception of the Golden Hippodrome (II, 96, 99), and on Easter Monday (I, 73; Fig. 16).

Unnamed Costumes

At the promotion of a patrician (II, 60), the *praipositos* is said to wear a costume with two purple embroidered bands.

At the ballet, that is, the dinner on the emperor's birthday (II, 103), the tribunes and vicars are said to wear a dark blue and white costume with short sleeves and golden bands.

Very difficult to interpret are the general terms "usual costume" and "costume of parade." Usual costume is worn by *kandidatoi, mandatores,* and *skribones* on Wednesday of Middle Pentecost at St. Mochios (I, 92). Costume of parade is in some cases identical to the purple *sagion,* in most cases to the *chlamys.* White costume of parade is identical to the white *chlamys.*

Dignitaries' Horse Harness

In the cortege on Easter Monday (I, 73, 74) the dignitaries of the imperial chamber, the *magistroi,* the patricians, and the whole Senate participate mounted on harnessed horses with coats of mail, and they wear the purple *sagion* (cf. Fig. 17). The *spatharokandidatoi* and the *spatharioi* mount harnessed horses, carrying swords, shields, and axes, while the protospatharian eunuchs ride wearing the purple *spekion* with golden bands, armed with swords and spears on their shoulders, and riding on horses harnessed with mail coats.

The logothete of the *dromos* appears in the purple *sagion,* mounted on a harnessed horse, and the bearded protospatharians in the *spekion,* carrying spears on their shoulders and mounted on harnessed horses.

Commentary

Imperial Costumes

A particular difficulty in interpreting the *Book of Ceremonies* is to determine the combinations in which various garments were worn (i.e., which garments were worn on top of others). The following passages bear on this problem.

For dinner in the palace the *chlamys* (Fig. 18) is used by the dignitaries, while the *sagion* is worn by the emperor and the *omophorion* by the patriarch. These costumes are taken off before the meal and put on after it. The *chlamys* is also worn by the emperor for communion in the church.

At the Annunciation (I, 179) the emperor wears the *skaramangion* for the liturgy.

The costume of the Feast of Orthodoxy (I, 145–48) is full of enigmas. The sovereigns wear the *sagion,* and they are dressed like everybody else in white costumes of parade (i.e., the *chlamys*). At the dinner in the palace they wear the *skaramangion.* They enter into the *metatorion,* take off their *chlamydes,* and listen to the Gospel and the litany. In the *metatorion* of the patriarch they take off the *divitision* to dine. Have they worn the *skaramangion,* the *divitision,* the *sagion,* and on top of them the *chlamys*?

On Easter Sunday (I, 175) the sovereigns dress in a dark red *skaramangion* and a *sagion* with golden embroidery. In the Daphne apartment they put on a *thorakion,* the oval shield, and the *tzitzakion.* Here the *thorakion* is mentioned as a costume for both the emperor and empress, though in the pictorial representations it appears only on the empress and the *patrikia.* After the Kiss of Peace they take off the *tzitzakion* and put on the *loros* and white and red crowns. Do the *skaramangion* and the *sagion* remain under the *loros*? It is most likely that they do.

During Easter week (I, 176) the sovereigns dress in a white *divitision* and the *tzitzakion* for the procession at church. On the Sunday of Orthodoxy (I, 178) the sovereigns leave the palace in the dark purple *skaramangion* and the *sagion* with golden embroidery and proceed to the *catechumena* of St. Sophia. There they dress in the purple *divitision* and *chlamys.* Are these on top of the first-mentioned costumes, or have the latter been taken off?

At the promotion of patricians (II, 51), the emperor is dressed by the vestitors in his *chlamys* behind the curtain in the vaulted chamber oriented toward the sanctuary of St. Theodore. Again, in complete seclusion, the *praipositos* takes off the emperor's crown and the *vestitor* his *chlamys.*

For dinner on Palm Sunday (I, 164), after the litany the emperor wears the *skaramangion.* In conclusion, it seems that the *skaramangion* is the tunic usually worn under the *sagion* or the *divitision* by the emperor.

Costumes of Parade

Many passages in the *Book of Ceremonies* concern costumes of parade.

At the Annunciation (I, 155, 157) the dignitaries of the imperial chamber, the master of ceremonies, and four silentiaries wear the purple *sagion* in the procession and for dinner. On this day the costume of parade implies a purple *sagion.*

For dinner in the palace on Easter Saturday (I, 169–72), all take off their costumes of parade, and the emperor's invited friends wear the white or the colored *skaramangion.* Consequently the *skaramangion* is not counted as a costume of parade.

Another obscure passage concerns Easter Sunday (II, 48). On this day the Senate is asked to bring their white *chlamys* and the *chlamys* of dark color, because before the sovereigns go to church, the court receives them in the Chrysotriklinos, where the promotion takes place, wearing the white *chlamys.* In the consistory the whole Senate dresses in the dark-colored *chlamys* according to custom on Easter Sunday. This is on the occasion of the promotion of patricians, senators, and *strategoi.* The eparchal costume (II, 70) of the Middle Byzantine period consists of the *kamision* and *pelonion,* the *loros,* and shoes (Fig. 17). From this passage the conclusion could be drawn that luxurious tunics are worn under the *loros.*

Several passages indicate that costumes of parade are put on in ranked order: the colors and the different sorts of *tablion,* or perhaps the lack of a *tablion,* indicated rank position.

At the emperor's birthday, the differentiation of costume according to rank is manifested. It is said that all enter in costumes of parade, patricians wearing the *chlamys* with a golden *tablion,* *strategoi* the *sagion,* *protospatharioi* and other dignitaries their own costume, each according to his proper dignity.

At the banquet they take off their *chlamys* and the *sagion.* Thus most likely the *protospatharioi* and the other dignitaries wear a simple type of *chlamys,* perhaps without a *tablion.* On the emperor's birthday, if it is a Sunday, the dignitaries of the chamber form a double circle in costumes of parade.

At the reception of the Golden Hippodrome (II, 94–96), all arrive in costumes of parade with the white *chlamys:* patricians with the *chlamys* with a golden *tablion,* the others each according to his dignity, *ostiarioi* carrying their staffs, the protospatharian eunuchs their *sticharia* and *sabania,* the *spatharokandidatoi* wearing their necklaces and swords with shields and battle-axes (so Harold Hardraada was dressed when he served at the court of Zoe Monomachos).[16]

At the promotion of two demarchs at the same time (II, 79), that of the Blues and that of the Greens, it is said that the Blue demarch wears the blue and purple *chlamys* of Tyre and the Green the green *chlamys,* because they are imperial. Does it mean that these types of *chlamydes* are identical to imperial ones in order to emphasize the delegated power exerted by the demarchs?

At the reception at the Secret Phiale in the Triconch (in winter) (II, 105), the patricians, the *strategoi,* and the whole Senate arrive at night each in his proper costume. Again the differentiation of costume according to rank is emphasized.

Several passages refer to the folding of the *chlamys* and to its roles in ceremonial. The master of ceremonies, having folded the *chlamys* according to his habit, gives it to the emperor. The representatives of the factions hold the folded *chlamys* of the demarch (II, 107–9) and receive gifts from the emperor.

In the Golden Hippodrome (II, 96), the master of ceremonies takes the outer border of the *chlamys* of the emperor and having folded it, gives it to the emperor, who from his throne blesses the people with this fold according to custom. The same ceremony is

---

[16] E. Piltz, "De la Scandinavie à Byzance," *Toutes les routes mènent à Byzance,* Médiévales 12 (1987), 11–18.

repeated on 11 May at the horse race in honor of the anniversary of the city of Constantinople (II, 145) and at the horse race on the carnival called Lupercalia (II, 165).

At the promotion of a *magistros* (II, 40, 41), the emperor places himself at the Golden Hand in front of a curtain decorated with hens. The *praipositos* makes a sign with his *chlamys.*

At Hypapante (I, 137–38) only the protospatharian eunuchs wear the so-called complete costume of parade, that is, the *kamision* and the white *chlamys*. On the same feast day the master of ceremonies opens his hands from the interior of his *chlamys* and says to the emperor "Advance, O Lord." At the promotion of a *kouropalates* (II, 37–38), it is shown that the sovereigns take an active part in the ritual of putting on the costumes. The sovereigns give the purple *chlamys* to the *kouropalates,* and they attach the *fibula* with their own hands. Patricians, consuls, and silentiaries form a consistory (a circle), and two silentiaries hold a staff. They escort the *kouropalates* during three days while he is dressed in the purple *sagion.*

Five colors are imperial. Gold appears in combination with the colors of the factions. White is associated with Easter, purple with coronations, funerals, and promotions, and blue and green with two of the demes.

The constant change of costumes, the incessant variation of the mosaic screen, the sparkling colors, and the sumptuous use of gold, precious stones, and pearls all preach the divine character of the legitimate dynasty and its hierarchy, always appearing with new effects, overwhelming and never boring to the beholder. The splendor of the delegated power of the officials helped keep the empire from falling apart during more than a thousand years.

What remains of Middle Byzantine costume, and what are the prospects for new finds? Comparatively little research has been undertaken on Byzantine costume. Kondakov wrote about the *skaramangion,* Braun, Papas, and myself about ecclesiastical vestments.[17] Irina Andreescu has written about costume in art,[18] and my own research has focused on the *loros,* the *sakkos,* and the costume of the dignitaries of the Palaiologan era.[19]

Archaeological excavations in the periphery of the former Byzantine territory have brought forth new and interesting fragments of costume in Scandinavia—on Iceland[20]

---

[17] N. P. Kondakov, "Les costumes orientaux à la cour byzantine," *Byzantion* 1 (1924), 7–49; cf. *ODB,* s.v. costume, I, 538–40; J. Braun, *Die liturgische Gewandung im Occident und Orient* (Freiburg, 1907), 302 f, 487 f, 550 f, 601 f, 669–73, 707–9, 753; T. Papas, *Geschichte der Messgewänder,* Miscellanea Byzantina Monacensia 3 (Munich, 1965); E. Piltz, "Liturgische Gewänder im byzantinischen Ritus," *Byzantinorussica* (forthcoming).

[18] I. Andreescu, "Torcello IV," in *III. Colloquio Internazionale sul Mosaico Antico* (Ravenna, 1980–84), 535–51.

[19] E. Piltz, "Loros—ett bysantinskt insignium," *RBK,* III, 428–44; *Konsthistorisk tidskrift* 55 (1972), 1–8; *Byzantina—Nordisk tidskrift för bysantinologi* 1 (1972), 8–15; *Trois sakkoi byzantins,* Figura, n.s., 17 (Stockholm, 1976) and supplement, Figura, n.s., 19 (Stockholm, 1981), 469–76; *Le costume officiel des dignitaires byzantins à l'époque Paléologue,* Figura, n.s., 26 (Uppsala, 1994); "Costume in Life and Death," in *Bysans och Norden,* Figura, n.s., 23 (Stockholm, 1989), 153–65.

[20] *Les Vikings* (Uddevalla, 1992), 56: liturgical embroidery from the cathedral of Holar, northern Iceland, ca. 1200, with the same Byzantine arabesque as is found in Garde church on Gotland. Cf. *Corpus de la peinture monumentale byzantine: La Suède* (Uppsala, 1989); golden thread from Byzantium. It is held that the king of Birka appeared in Byzantine ornaments.

and in Birka and Sigtuna in Sweden[21] (Figs. 19–21)—testifying to intense contacts with Byzantium during the Viking period. These findings from the outermost periphery may help to illuminate the court culture of the center of the empire.

University of Copenhagen

---

[21] I. Hägg, "Birkas orientaliska praktplagg," *Fornvännen* 78 (1983), 204–23; accoutrement for horse attire from Constantinople, of gold and glass pearls, found in Sigtuna.

Helping Hands for the Empire:
Imperial Ceremonies and the Cult of Relics at the Byzantine Court

Ioli Kalavrezou

The existing information on saints' relics in Constantinople, although meager, is suffi-cient to give a sense of the great number of relics accumulated over the centuries in its churches and shrines. The number is staggering; it has been calculated that there were more than 3,600 relics for about 476 different saints.[1] Relics were brought to the city since the time of its foundation; however, for the vast majority of these we know neither the date nor the events and circumstances of their arrival in Constantinople. Visual evi-dence concerning their finding, translation, or veneration is even poorer considering their large numbers.[2] Few are the images attesting to their cults, and most are from the few surviving illustrated *menologia* and *synaxaria* of the Middle Byzantine period.[3]

Many of the relics in the city owe their presence to imperial interest and initiative. A great number of relics were housed in the palace in specially built churches that became the repositories of the greatest treasures of Christendom. These relics, amassed at the center of political power, also gave the city itself a special and privileged place in relation to the rest of the Christian world. After the rise and expansion of Islam, Constantinople saw itself as the guardian of Christianity, especially in the East. Certainly in terms of its relics, Constantinople surpassed all other Christian cities, especially after the loss of Jeru-salem, whence many relics were brought.

This study is an expanded version of my symposium paper, incorporating textual and visual evidence mainly relevant to the relic of the right arm of St. John the Baptist. I hope to devote a more detailed study to this im-portant relic and to discuss and analyze further the complete text of the *logos* (speech) that Daphnopates gave on the anniversary of the arrival of this relic in Constantinople.

[1] O. Meinardus, "A Study of the Relics of Saints of the Greek Church," *Oriens Christianus* 54 (1970), 130–33; H. Delehaye, *Les origines du culte des martyrs*, SubsHag 20 (Brussels, 1933).

[2] For the ceremonies, processions, and terms used in connection with the cult of relics, see K. Holum and G. Vikan, "The Trier Ivory, *Adventus* Ceremonial, and the Relics of St. Stephen," *DOP* 33 (1979), 115–33; R. Taft, "Byzantine Liturgical Evidence in the *Life of St. Marcian the Oeconomos*: Concelebration of the Preanapho-ral Rites," *OCP* 48 (1982), 159–70.

[3] For example, *Il Menologio di Basilio II,* Codices e vaticanis selecti 8 (Turin, 1907), vol. II, 121, 324, 344, 353. Further illustrated examples in C. Walters, *Art and Ritual of the Byzantine Church* (London, 1982), pls. XVI, XVIII–XXII.

Relics at the Court

The special angle of interest I bring to the topic of relics in the context of a discussion of the Byzantine court derives from my broader preoccupation with imperial iconography, especially how the court created and used symbols and images for imperial self-definition and presentation. The Byzantine predilection for signs and symbols is well known, and some of the most important symbols for the empire were its saints and their relics. The court used these relics not only to define the Byzantine notion of orthodox Christianity but also, perhaps even more important, the Byzantine notion of empire.[4]

An example from legendary accounts points to the direction of this analysis. According to legend, after the finding of the True Cross, Helena, Constantine I's mother, sent a piece of it together with two nails to her son in Constantinople. Depending on which version of the legend one reads, Constantine incorporated the nails into either his helmet or his diadem.[5] Both versions of the incorporation of the nails into imperial insignia could be valid, each signaling the role and power of these relics for the good of the empire. Worn by the emperor in war (helmet) or state affairs (diadem), they served as defenders, protectors, and guides in the emperor's actions and decisions. They empowered the ruler with God's grace and power and supported the idea that the empire and Christianity had a symbiotic relationship. This study, then, examines more closely the imperial component in ceremonies in which relics featured: why were certain relics kept at the court, in shrines and churches within the Great Palace, and what was their role in relation to the emperor? These relics not only gave the Byzantine ruler who possessed them a privileged position in the Christian world but also provided a special construct for the Byzantine emperor to exercise the power of his imperial office. At certain politically stressed periods throughout Byzantine history, emperors sought to secure their position of power or establish the dynasty's legitimate claim to the throne: turning to Christian actions—building churches promoting religious cult objects such as icons and procuring relics—were some of the means to these ends.[6]

The discussion here focuses on two objects of unusual character; they have remained unnoticed, although they carried a heavy ideological weight. These objects are the relic of the arm of St. Stephen, which was brought to Constantinople in the first half of the fifth century, and the arm of St. John the Baptist (or Prodromos), which arrived in the

---

[4] Although this paper was part of the art historical contributions to the symposium, it has partly extended its borders into the related disciplines of history and anthropology.

[5] For the various accounts of the legend of Helena and the discovery of the True Cross (Gelasius of Caesarea, Rufinus, Sozomen, Theodoret, Ambrose, Paulinus of Nola, etc.), see J. W. Drijvers, *Helena Augusta* (Leiden, 1992), 95–96. See also A. Kazhdan, "'Constantin imaginaire': Byzantine Legends of the Ninth Century about Constantine the Great," *Byzantion* 57 (1987), 196–250.

[6] For example, in the early 5th century, with the Theodosian succession, and later in the 9th century, with Basil I's taking the imperial throne and establishing the Macedonian dynasty, we have two periods in Byzantine history where major changes are instituted in court life and court ceremonial, and in both cases what lay behind all the developments was the insistence on dynastic succession. See K. Holum, *Theodosian Empresses* (Berkeley, 1982); G. Moravcsik, "Sagen und Legenden über Kaiser Basileios I," *DOP* 15 (1961), 59–126; I. Kalavrezou-Maxeiner, "The Portraits of Basil I in Paris gr. 510," *JÖB* 27 (1978), 19–24; P. Magdalino, "Basil I, Leo VI, and the Feast of the Prophet Elijah," *JÖB* 38 (1988), 193–96.

city and was placed in the Pharos church in the middle of the tenth century. Both are associated with individuals from the biblical past who were guided by the Holy Spirit and who were exemplary to Christian and imperial thought. Here I argue that their relics functioned as instruments of power, investiture, and leadership, guaranteeing political authority and displaying divine approval to those who possessed them.[7]

Among the various buildings that housed relics within the walls of the Great Palace, two were the most famous not only because of the relics they contained but because of the special place they occupied in the ceremonial life of the court. One, the older structure of the two, was the church of St. Stephen of Daphne, built in the fifth century; here emperors and empresses were married, and empresses and co-emperors were crowned. The other was the church of the Virgin of the Pharos, the repository of the most important relics of Christendom, those of Christ's Passion.[8]

The Church of the Virgin of the Pharos

The church of the Virgin of the Pharos, τῆς Θεοτόκου τοῦ Φάρου, is known from textual evidence to have existed already as an important church of the palace in the eighth century. It is mentioned first by Theophanes for the year 769. It is the church where Patriarch Niketas officiated at the betrothal of Irene of Athens to the future Leo IV shortly after her arrival in Constantinople.[9] The church was much rebuilt by Michael III as one of the first buildings to be restored after Iconoclasm. A homily was delivered by Patriarch Photios on the day of its rededication, most likely in 864.[10] This is the famous tenth homily of Photios in which he also provides a description of the building and its mosaics, the first figural decoration after the period of Iconoclasm.[11] That of Hagia Sophia would follow soon after.

---

[7] Of the many Christian relics, the most important place was given to the True Cross. In the palace itself there were two major fragments kept at different locations. One was placed in the church of St. Stephen, the other, at least from the 9th century until the Fourth Crusade of 1204, in the church of the Theotokos or Virgin of the Pharos. Although the True Cross has received many studies, there is still much to be learned about its role in the ceremonies of the court. I hope to continue this research in the near future.

[8] According to C. Mango, the church of St. Stephen and that of the Virgin of the Pharos were the two palace chapels par excellence: "The Church of Saints Sergius and Bacchus at Constantinople and the Alleged Tradition of Octagonal Palatine Churches," *Studies on Constantinople* (Brookfield, Vt., 1993), art. XIII, 193. One might possibly add the church of Christ, the oldest in the Daphne palace, but this church and its role in the palace need further study.

[9] Leo and Irene's marriage, however, a month and a half later on 17 December, took place in the chapel of St. Stephen and her coronation in the *triklinion* of the Augusteus. Theophanes, *Theophanis chronographia*, ed. C. de Boor (Leipzig, 1885), vol. II, p. 444; trans. H. Turtledove, *The Chronicle of Theophanes* (Philadelphia, 1982), 132.

[10] R.J.H. Jenkins and C. Mango, "The Date and Significance of the Tenth Homily of Photius," *DOP* 9–10 (1955–56), 130 and note 38. C. Mango, *The Homilies of Photius Patriarch of Constantinople* (Cambridge, Mass., 1958), 177–90.

[11] Michael also restored the Chrysotriklinos, the throne room of the Daphne palace located a few yards away. These two buildings became for the following centuries the central or pivotal points of imperial presentation and ceremonial within the palace. For the Chrysotriklinos see *Anthologia graeca* I, 106, in C. Mango, *The Art of the Byzantine Empire, 312–1453* (Englewood Cliffs, N.J., 1972), 184.

The church of the Virgin of the Pharos was located close to the imperial apartments and the Chrysotriklinos, the throne room of the Daphne palace complex. It was a small building with a central ribbed dome, three apses, a narthex, and a beautiful atrium. According to Photios, the church was of such great beauty that it could leave the spectator petrified with wonder. The revetment of its exterior facade, completely of white marble, was so well joined that it seemed to be of one piece. The interior was lavishly covered with colorful marbles and gold mosaic tesserae. Gilding and silver sheathing decorated the church furnishings, and the altar table was encrusted with precious stones and enamels. When entering, one had the feeling that one had entered heaven itself, a divine and venerable second palace for the Mother of God on earth.[12] Although not a large church, it must have been a jewel of a building which over the centuries increased in importance since it became the repository of the most valued relics of Christendom. Already in the tenth century, as we learn from the *Book of Ceremonies,* in the treasury of this church was kept the great cross of Constantine, newly refashioned by the Christ-loving Constantine Porphyrogennetos.[13] By the end of the twelfth century, when we have a full account of its treasures by Anthony of Novgorod, the most prominent are those relics associated with Christ's Passion: the cross, the crown of thorns, the nails, the sponge, and the lance that pierced his side.[14] Over the centuries, emperors added to this collection, usually relics brought back from campaigns, as, for example, a sandal of Christ added by John Tzimiskes after his campaign of 975.[15] One of the more important relics in this treasury was brought back by Romanos I in 944. This was the holy Mandylion of Edessa with the imprint of Christ's face. This relic arrived in Constantinople with great pomp and was then deposited in the church of the Pharos.[16] The following year, during the reign of Constantine VII Porphyrogennetos, the relic of the right arm of John the Baptist was also placed in the same treasury.[17]

---

[12] Mango, *Homilies,* 185–86.

[13] εἰς τὸν ναὸν τῆς ὑπεραγίας Θεοτόκου τοῦ Φάρου τοῦ μεγάλου παλατίου· ὁ νεοκατασκεύαστος μέγας σταυρὸς Κωνσταντίνου τοῦ φιλοχρίστου καὶ πορφυρογεννήτου βασιλέως: J. J. Reiske, ed., *Constantini Porphyrogeniti imperatoris De cerimoniis aulae byzantinae,* 2 vols. (Bonn, 1829–30), II, 40, p. 640. See the article of J. Koder for a possible identification of this cross with the True Cross in the staurotheque of Limburg: "Ὁ Κωνσταντίνος Πορφυρογέννητος καὶ ἡ σταυροθήκη τοῦ Λίμπουργκ," in *Constantine VII Porphyrogenitus and His Age,* ed. A. Markopoulos (Athens, 1989), 171.

[14] M. Ehrhard, "Le livre du pèlerin, d'Antoine de Novgorod," *Romania* 58 (1932), 44–65, esp. 57. See also Robert of Clari's description of these relics: *Historiens et chroniques du Moyen Age,* ed. A. Panphilet (Paris, 1979), 63; *The Conquest of Constantinople,* trans. E. H. McNeal (New York, 1969), 103. In the French text, the Pharos church is referred to as "la Sainte Chapele," exactly what the royal chapel in Paris came to be called (ca. 1250), into which most of the Pharos relics relating to Christ's Passion were deposited after the looting of the Fourth Crusade.

[15] J. Ebersolt, *Sanctuaires de Byzance* (Paris, 1921), 20. Together with the sandal he also brought back some of St. John the Baptist's long locks, which he deposited in the church of the Chalke gate which he had newly enlarged. *Leonis Diaconi Caloënsis Historiae,* ed. C. B. Hase (Bonn, 1828), X, 4, 165–66.

[16] *Ioannis Scylitzae Synopsis Historiarum,* ed. I. Thurn (Berlin, 1973), 231–232.58–62. A. Grabar and M. Manoussacas, *L'illustration du manuscrit de Skylitzès de la Bibliothèque Nationale de Madrid* (Venice, 1979), fol. 131a, fig. 158, p. 77. K. Weitzmann, "The Mandylion and Constantine Porphyrogenitus," *CahArch* 11 (1960), 163–84, Av. Cameron, "The History of the Image of Edessa: The Telling of a Story," *Okeanos: Essays Presented to Ihor Ševčenko on His Sixtieth Birthday,* ed. C. Mango and O. Pritsak (Cambridge, Mass., 1984), 80–94.

[17] Skylitzes, ed. Thurn, 245.27–32. Grabar and Manoussacas, *L'illustration,* fol. 138r, fig. 169, p. 81. For a list of the relics in the church of the Pharos in 1201 by its *skeuophylax* Nicholas Mesarites, see A. Heisenberg, *Nikolaos Mesarites, Die Palastrevolution des Johannes Comnenos* (Würzburg, 1907), 29–31.

The rare two-sided icon of the twelfth century now in the Tretiakov Gallery is almost an illustration of the precious contents of the church of the Pharos (Fig. 1a).[18] On its two sides it depicts the most important relics relating to Christ and his Passion. On one side is the face of Christ as it usually appears on the Mandylion, but here it is represented against a golden background. Christ's eyes are more strongly turned toward the side, almost hinting at the image on the reverse. There the True Cross is depicted in plain dark wood with the crown of thorns hung at its crossing (Fig. 1b). Below the arms of the cross the two archangels Michael and Gabriel hold in a raised position the other two important relics, the sponge and the lance, in a manner strongly reminiscent of their actual use in the Crucifixion. Above, seraphim and cherubim attend to the cross. When looking at this icon with its golden and white backgrounds, one cannot but recall the church itself where these relics were housed. The gold reflects its interior surfaces, and the whiteness its marble exterior, so emphatically expressed by Photios in his homily. These colors, for the Byzantines, at the same time bring to mind the image of paradise.

It is well known that a large number of these relics, especially those relating to the Passion of Christ, were acquired by King Louis IX of France and with great ceremonial were brought to Paris and placed in a setting very similar in concept to that of the Byzantine palace church of the Pharos. The consecration of Louis IX's palace chapel, the famous Sainte Chapelle, took place in 1248. It was especially built to house the newly arrived relics, had the form of a large Gothic reliquary, and was directly connected to the royal palace of the Louvre. The church of the Virgin of the Pharos, on the other hand, sadly did not survive the Latin occupation of Constantinople.

The Church of St. Stephen and Its Surroundings

The church of St. Stephen (Hagios Stephanos) was the older structure of the two palace chapels, built already in the fifth century. We do not know its architectural form, but it probably was a small building, smaller than the Pharos church, since it is often referred to as εὐκτήριον (oratory).[19] This chapel was built specifically to house the relic of the right arm of St. Stephen. It was added to the palace complex of Daphne by Pulcheria Augusta, the sister of Emperor Theodosios II, about the year 421.[20]

This event is recorded in Theophanes the Confessor when narrating the reign of Theodosios II: "under the influence of the blessed Pulcheria, Theodosios sent much money to the archbishop of Jerusalem for distribution to the needy and a golden cross studded with stones to be erected on Golgotha. In exchange for these gifts the arch-

[18] V. I. Antonova and N. E. Mneva, *Gosudarstvennaia Tret'iakovskaia Gallereia: Katalog drevnerusskoi zhivopisi XI–nachala XVIII v.v.,* 2 vols. (Moscow, 1963), I, no. 7, pp. 66–68, figs. 26, 27.

[19] J. Ebersolt, *Le Grand Palais de Constantinople et le Livre des cérémonies* (Paris, 1910), 52; R. Janin, *La géographie ecclésiastique de l'Empire byzantin,* III: *Les églises et les monastères* (Paris, 1953), 490.

[20] K. Holum, "Pulcheria's Crusade A.D. 421–422 and the Ideology of Imperial Victory," *GRBS* 18 (1977), 163 note 46. St. Stephen became one of the most popular saints in the East, as well as in the West. During the 5th century more of his relics were acquired and brought to the city, especially as the result of the efforts of Eudokia, the wife of Theodosios II. In Rome we have the early Christian church of San Stefano Rotondo, a circular building making through its architecture reference to his name, *stephanos* (wreath).

bishop dispatched the relic of the right arm of Stephen the Protomartyr, in the care of St. Passarion. . . . receiving it into the palace, she [Pulcheria] built a notable (ἔνδοξον) house for the holy Protomartyr and in it she deposited the holy relic."[21]

In their study of the Trier ivory plaque, Kenneth Holum and Gary Vikan identified the scene on the ivory as the representation of the translation and arrival of the relics of St. Stephen in Constantinople and the ivory plaque itself as probably a side panel of a reliquary (Fig. 2).[22] This interpretation of the scene as the historical event of the arrival of the relics of St. Stephen in Constantinople, and more precisely as the deposition of the relics inside the imperial palace, is based on a number of iconographic details that are quite convincing. Without repeating the arguments of Holum and Vikan in full, I would point out several details that are unique and thus significant for the interpretation. At the same time they are consistent with the historical circumstances and ideological needs of the time. Significant is the court atmosphere, felt not only through the impressive background architecture and the monumental gate, probably the Chalke, but also through the orderly arrangement of the accompanying crowd as part of imperial ceremonial. The arrangement of the figures on the second story is not part of a spontaneous gathering of townsmen who come to watch and celebrate the arrival of holy relics in their town but a well-staged part of a ritual. I may add here in support of their argument a fact that has not been associated with St. Stephen before. Although censing was part of Byzantine ritual, in this case the repetitive censing and its prominence in this image make a direct reference to St. Stephen whose relic is being translated: St. Stephen as deacon is always depicted censing.

Of importance in this composition is also the singling out of the empress. As the instigator of the event and the patron of the church that was to house the relic, she is appropriately placed at the entrance of the church and is shown as the only one to receive the approaching procession of the holy relic.[23] The new construction of this church is made visually clear by showing workers still putting the final touches on its roof. All this takes place directly behind her. I would also like to add that the size of the reliquary carried by the two deacons is small and quite appropriate for an arm. In contrast, when the complete relics of a saint are translated, as, for example, those of John Chrysostom in the Menologion of Basil II, a full-length sarcophagus is depicted, suggesting that the entire body of the saint is being carried.[24] Thus in the Trier ivory we

---

[21] Theophanes, *Chron.*, ed. de Boor, I, 86.26–87.5: Τούτῳ τῷ ἔτει Θεοδόσιος ὁ εὐσεβὴς κατὰ μίμησιν τῆς μακαρίας Πουλχερίας πολλὰ χρήματα τῷ ἀρχιεπισκόπῳ Ἱεροσολύμων ἀπέστειλεν εἰς διάδοσιν τῶν χρείαν ἐχόντων, καὶ σταυρὸν χρυσοῦν διάλιθον πρὸς τὸ παγῆναι ἐν τῷ ἁγίῳ κρανίῳ. ὁ δὲ ἀρχιεπίσκοπος ἀντίδωρον ἀποστέλλει λείψανα τῆς δεξιᾶς χειρὸς τοῦ πρωτομάρτυρος Στεφάνου διὰ τοῦ ἐν ἁγίοις Πασσαρίωνος. . . . ἡ (Πουλχερία) δὲ ἀναστᾶσα καὶ τὸν ἀδελφὸν αὐτῆς λαβοῦσα ἐξῆλθεν εἰς συνάτησιν τῶν ἁγίων λειψάνων, καὶ ταῦτα εἰς τὸ παλάτιον λαβοῦσα κτίζει οἶκον ἔνδοξον τῷ ἁγίῳ πρωτομάρτυρι κἀκεῖ τὰ ἅγια κατέθετο λείψανα. My translation is based on Holum and Vikan, "Trier Ivory," 127.

[22] Holum and Vikan, "Trier Ivory," 121–27, 130.

[23] Pulcheria rather prominently extends her *right arm* to receive the relic of the *right arm* of St. Stephen. I cannot believe that the Byzantines looking at this image did not see some connection between the two, or that on the day of the event itself they did not comment on her association with the arm, especially since the name Πουλχερία contains in part the stem of the word χείρ.

[24] The translation of the body of St. John Chrysostom to Constantinople took place in the year 438, and was brought about by the initiative of Proklos. It is illustrated in *Il Menologio*, 353; see also the other translations or de-

1b   Instruments of Christ's Passion, two-sided icon, twelfth century, Moscow, Tretiakov Gallery

1a   The Mandylion, two-sided icon, twelfth century, Moscow, Tretiakov Gallery

2　The translation of the relics of the arm of St. Stephen, ivory, sixth century, Trier, Rheinisches Landesmuseum

3a Gold coin of Eudoxia,
Dumbarton Oaks Collection
48.17.1118

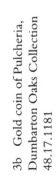

3b Gold coin of Pulcheria,
Dumbarton Oaks Collection
48.17.1181

4 Icon of St. Stephen, St. Petersburg,
Hermitage, tenth–eleventh century
(after Banck, *Byzantine Art*, pl. 221)

5b Mosaic of St. Lawrence, Kiev, Hagia Sophia, south side of apse, eleventh century (photo: Dumbarton Oaks)

5a Mosaic of St. Stephen, Kiev, Hagia Sophia, north side of apse, eleventh century (photo: Dumbarton Oaks)

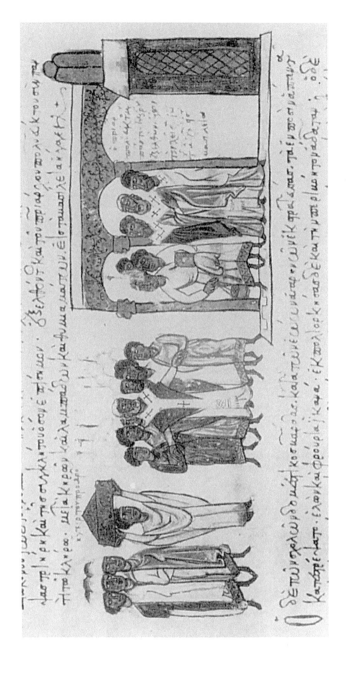

7 Illustration of the translation of the arm of St. John into the palace, Madrid, Biblioteca Nacional, vitr. 26–2, fol. 106v (after Grabar and Manoussacas, *L'illustration du manuscrit de Skylitzès*, fig. 169)

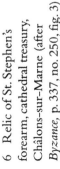

6 Relic of St. Stephen's forearm, cathedral treasury, Châlons–sur–Marne (after *Byzance*, p. 337, no. 250, fig. 3)

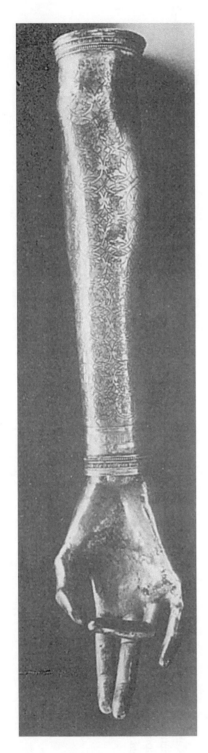

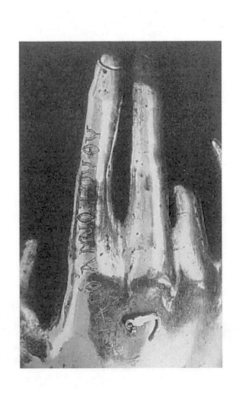

8a Arm of St. John the Baptist, Istanbul, Topkapi Museum (whole) (after Bayraktar, "Topkapi Sarayi Müzesi'nde Hagios Ioannes Prodromos'a (Vaftizei Yahya) Ait Rölikler," fig. 1)

8c–d Details of wrist with Venetian stamp (photo: after Bayraktar, "Topkapi Sarayi Müzesi'nde Hagios Ioannes Prodromos'a (Vaftizei Yahya) Ait Rölikler," figs. 4–5)

8b Detail of hand (photo: after Bayraktar, "Topkapi Sarayi Müzesi'nde Hagios Ioannes Prodromos'a (Vaftizei Yahya) Ait Rölikler," fig. 3)

9   Icon of John the Baptist with scenes of his life, twelfth century, Mount Sinai
(photo: Michigan–Princeton–Alexandria expedition to Mount Sinai)

10 Baptism of Christ, northwest squinch, Hosios Loukas, eleventh century
(photo: Dumbarton Oaks)

12 Gold coin of Alexander
(812–813) proclaimed
emperor by John the Baptist
(photo: Dumbarton Oaks)

11   Ivory plaque with Constantine Porphyrogennetos proclaimed
emperor by Christ, State Pushkin Museum of Fine Arts, Moscow
(photo: Victoria and Albert Museum)

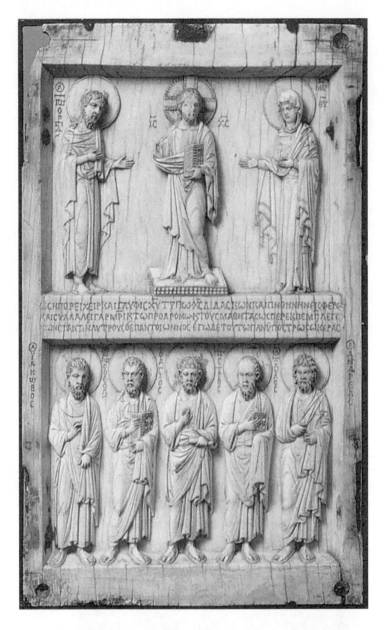

13   Deesis, ivory triptych, detail, Palazzio Venezia, Rome, mid-tenth century (photo: Victoria and Albert Museum)

have the rare case of the survival of an accurate representation of the historical circumstances as they have come down to us in the sources.

It is also believed that at this period Pulcheria and Theodosios II brought to the palace a cross containing a particle of the True Cross, which in the fourth century was kept in the Helenianai palace outside Constantinople.[25] This cross probably is the one that, in the tenth century at least, was kept in the treasury of the church of St. Stephen and is called in the *Book of Ceremonies* the "large cross of Constantine." Possibly it was kept there since its transfer to the Great Palace in the fifth century. Although originally the church of St. Stephen was built specifically to house the relic of his right arm, we learn that other important "relics" were to be found within this treasury, objects that hint at the function of this church: the large cross of Constantine mentioned above, three scepters, seven *ptychia* (insignia or banners), and golden *kandidatikia,* which were fancy and probably rather valuable chains worn around the neck and down the chest. These last objects were used by or given to officials on the day of their promotion to a high office and were considered decorations and marks of distinction; however, although presented to the courtiers on that day, remained in the treasury of the church.[26] In contrast to the church of the Virgin of the Pharos, the objects of this treasury were more secular or political in nature, as opposed to ecclesiastical—even the large cross—and were meant to be used in imperial ceremonies and court promotions. The point of my argument in this paper is to establish that the arm of St. Stephen should be seen as having a similar function within this ceremonial context.

We know that the church of St. Stephen was built adjacent to the Augusteus (Αὐγουστεύς or Αὐγουσταῖος or Τρίκλινος of the Αὐγουστέως), which is not to be confused with the Augustaion, the open space or court between the palace and Hagia Sophia. This building was one of the oldest large ceremonial halls in the palace used for receptions of foreign ambassadors and other important ceremonial events such as coronations and promotions. It certainly predated the church of St. Stephen since it was part of the oldest palace building complex, that of the Constantinian palace of Daphne with which it communicated.

The shape of this hall is not known, but from some directional words used in the *Book of Ceremonies* it seems to have been more of an elongated hall than a centralized

---

positions on pp. 121, 344. In contrast to holy figures, the unearthed and moved bones of lay people (including emperors) were carried in a *lamax,* a wooden box of small dimensions, as were those, for example, of Michael III; see Grabar and Manoussacas, *L'illustration,* fol. 106v, p. 65, fig. 120. It is probably not appropriate to call these remains relics as in Vikan and Holum, "Trier Ivory," fig. 6. This word is misleading and could suggest the remains of a saint, which Michael III was not.

[25] Holum and Vikan, "Trier Ivory," 130 note 89; *De cer.,* ed. Reiske, I, 91, p. 414: ἐκεῖ δὲ αὐτῷ ἀπαντᾷ καὶ ὁ σταυρὸς ἐκ δεξιῶν αὐτοῦ ἱστάμενοπ ἐπ᾽ ἐδάφους καὶ κρατούμενος ὑπὸ τῶν βεστητόρων.

[26] *De cer.,* ed. Reiske, II, 40, p. 640: εἰς τὸν ναὸν τοῦ ἁγίου Στεφάνου τῆς Δάφνης ὁ μέγας σταυρὸς τοῦ ἁγίου καὶ μεγάλου Κωνσταντίνου. σκῆπτρα γ. πτυχεία ζ. κανδιδατίκια χρυσᾶ. N. Oikonomidès, *Les listes de préséance byzantines des IXe et Xe siècles* (Paris, 1972), 88 note 28. The crowns and nuptial crowns used for the coronation and marriage ceremonies were kept in a different location and brought to the church for the occasion; e.g., the nuptial crowns were hung inside the *pentapyrgion,* the large piece of furniture where imperial insignia were stored in the great hall of the Magnaura palace. *De cer.,* ed. Reiske, I, 39, p. 200; Constantin VII Porphyrogenete, *Le livre des ceremonies,* ed. A. Vogt, 2 vols. (Paris, 1935–39), II, 48, p. 8.

building.[27] It had an apse where the emperors sometimes sat, and it had a side entrance probably on the side of the church of St. Stephen. The Augusteus is also known as the Στέψιμον, a name used several times in the *Patria* and meaning something like "coronation hall," since *stepsimon* means coronation.[28] Liutprand of Cremona in his *Legatio*, describing his visit to Constantinople, also mentions that Emperor Nikephoros received him "in a structure called *Stephana* which means Crown."[29] In any case, both names, Augusteus and Stepsimon, identify this room as a coronation hall or a hall of the Augousti. We know also from the *Book of Ceremonies* that, even after the construction under Justin II of the Chrysotriklinos, which was to become the throne room and ceremonial center of the palace, the Augusteus remained for a long time the hall where actual coronations, more precisely coronations of empresses, took place. Ceremonies related to coronations and weddings that took place in the adjacent church of St. Stephen also extended into this hall.[30] We read often that when leaving the church of St. Stephen, as, for example, after the marriage ceremony, the couple passes through the Octagon, which was located in front of the church, and enters into the Augusteus.[31] There is also the διαβατικόν, a passage, that leads from St. Stephen to the Augusteus. This is mentioned when the future empress is brought into the Augusteus for her coronation and wedding. She is mentioned as waiting in the chamber of the Octagon before she is brought in. This suggests a more private entrance probably close to the apse, where the emperor and patriarch were waiting for the ceremony.[32]

What exactly determined the choice of location for the coronation of an empress is not so obvious, especially when we have cases where, within a few years, both the church of St. Stephen and the Augusteus are chosen. The cases in the family of Herakleios are particularly telling. For example, Herakleios himself was crowned emperor by Patriarch Sergios in the oratory of St. Stephen upon his entering Constantinople in 610. On the same day he married Eudokia, who also was crowned augusta there.[33] His daughter Epiphaneia was crowned augusta in 613 in the church of St. Stephen, but his second wife Martina in 614 was crowned in the Augusteus.[34]

---

[27] R. Guilland, *Études de topographie de Constantinople byzantine*, 2 vols. (Berlin, 1969), I, 82.

[28] Theodor Preger, *Beiträge zur Textgeschichte der Patria Konstantinoupoleos* (Munich, 1895), 2, p. 144. Ebersolt, *Le Grand Palais*, 52 note 1.

[29] Liutprand of Cremona, *Relatio de Legatione Constantinopolitana*, ed. B. Scott (London, 1993), *Legatio* 3, p. 2: "In domo quae Stephana, id est Coronaria." Ebersolt, *Grand Palais*, 52 note 1.

[30] The following examples of empresses who were crowned in this hall are mentioned in Guilland, *Études*, 82, 91, and Theophanes, *Chron.*, ed. de Boor, 300, 400, 444, 494: Martina, the wife of Herakleios in 614, Maria, the wife of Leo III the Isaurian on 25 December 718, Irene the Athenian in 769, Prokopia, the wife of Michael I Rangabe at the beginning of the 9th century, etc. Examples of marriages in the church of St. Stephen are those of Herakleios and Eudokia in 610, Leo IV with Irene the Athenian in 769, Michael III and Eudokia, and so on.

[31] For example, at the wedding of an emperor, *De cer.*, ed. Reiske, I, 39, p. 197; ed. Vogt, II, 48, p. 6. This has to be a side entrance since they do not enter the building through the main door, which would have meant passing through the area of the Golden Hand just in front of its entrance. This occurs only after the coronation or wedding ceremony, since there the emperors receive acclamations.

[32] *De cer.*, ed. Reiske, I, 41, p. 208; ed. Vogt, II, 50, pp. 16–17; Guilland, *Études*, 81–82.

[33] Theophanes, *Chron.*, ed. de Boor, 299; trans. Turtledove, p. 9.

[34] Theophanes, *Chron.*, ed. de Boor, 300; trans. Turtledove, p. 10.

Thus the church of St. Stephen by its location developed into a building with an important place in palace ritual. It became directly associated with coronation ceremonies.[35] It also became the preeminent chapel for the marriages of the emperors, the *Stephanoma* (τὸ στεφάνωμα) during which, in the Orthodox rite, the couple is crowned by joined crowns or wreaths. Thus again Stephanos made his presence felt. Until and during the ninth century, all marriages took place there. It was not until the tenth that they began to be celebrated in the church of the Pharos, a custom most likely introduced by Leo VI.[36]

The Relic of the Arm of St. Stephen

It is already becoming clear that the choice of location for the building of the church of St. Stephen adjacent to this coronation hall is not accidental. Nor does it seem to be mere coincidence that the relic chosen for the church is the right arm of a saint called Stephanos ("crown," "wreath").[37] The "discovery" of the body of this saint might have been a lucky find, but bringing this most important body part to Constantinople and specifically to the palace was a clever move that served a clear and specific purpose: the association of heavenly victory with the imperial office and in particular with the Theodosian dynasty. Proklos, who was patriarch of Constantinople from 434 to 437 under Theodosios II, in his *enkomion* of St. Stephen, delivered on St. Stephen's day (27 December, just after Christmas), makes a few very relevant statements concerning St. Stephen and the effect his name had on anyone who heard it. Speaking about Christ's Nativity that had just been celebrated, he says: "yesterday He was born and today Stephanos [a crown] is brought to Him; Stephanos, the martyr wearing the name itself [here he makes reference to the crown of martyrdom], Stephanos, the living *stephanos* [wreath]; Stephanos, the self-braided diadem; Stephanos, the self-forged crown visible all around; Stephanos, the one crown, self-grown from his own head."[38] All this sounds rather awk-

---

[35] Another related ceremony that was connected with St. Stephen was the elevation to the throne of the co-emperor. In view of these ceremonies, it is not surprising that the churches of St. Stephen, St. Michael (another 5th-century building), as also the Nea and the Chalke, all located within the palace complex, were exempt from patriarchal and episcopal jurisdiction (see *Cupido Legum,* ed. L. Burgmann, M. T. Fögen, and A. Schminck [Frankfurt am Main, 1985], 20, for the legislation concerning this exemption).

[36] It is mentioned in the *Book of Ceremonies* as a change made in recent years: *De cer.,* ed. Reiske, I, 39, p. 201; ed. Vogt, II, 48, 10. P. Magdalino, "Basil I, Leo VI, and the Feast of the Prophet Elijah," *JÖB* 38 (1988), 196, suggests that it was Leo VI since he mints a coin with the Virgin orant iconographically similar to that of the Pharos' apse. I believe that Leo's choice of the Virgin as patron saint was connected to his concerns for the continuation of the dynasty as he was childless at the time. The Virgin is the obvious intercessor where there is want of an heir, and he is the first male to adopt her officially.

[37] On the similar notion of the victor's crown in relation to St. Stephen and his intercession for Pulcheria, see Holum, *Theodosian Empresses,* 107–8.

[38] Proklos, *Orat.* 17.2, PG 65:809–12: Χθὲς ἐτέχθη, καὶ σήμερον αὐτῷ Στέφανος προσηνέχθη· Στέφανος, ὁ φερώνυμος μάρτυς· Στέφανος, ὁ ἔμψυχος στέφανος· Στέφανος, τὸ αὐτόπλεκτον διάδημα· Στέφανος, τὸ αὐτοχάλκευτον περίθεμα· Στέφανος, τὸ αὐτοφυὲς τῆς ἰδίας κορυφῆς στεφάνωμα· Στέφανος, τὸ πολυανθὲς τῆς πίστεως βλάστημα . . . See also M. Aubineau, "Ps.-Chrysostome, *in S. Stephanum* (PG 63, 933–934): Proclus de Constantinople, l'impératrice Pulchérie et saint Etienne," in A.A.R. Bastiaensen, A. Hillhorst, and C. H.

ward in translation, but it is an example of the rhetoric of the time and the wordplay that the name of this saint encouraged.

Stephen is the first martyr of the Christian church and is commemorated for the martyrdom he suffered by stoning. "A man full of faith and the Holy Spirit," he was chosen together with seven other brothers and appointed first deacon by the apostles who laid their hands on them.[39] And in this office "Stephen, full of faith and power, did great wonders and miracles among the people." He bested his opponents in the synagogue, and, according to the Acts of the Apostles, "they could not withstand his wisdom and the Spirit that prompted his speaking." Once arrested and brought before the council, Stephen in his defense gives a long speech in which he presents the succession of prophetic authority from Abraham to Moses. He expands most on the story of Moses and how Moses presents a pattern that Christ fulfills; he concludes his narration of those chosen by God with David the king who found favor before God, and Solomon who finally built God's house. Then he turns to the people and accuses them of being stubborn and having always resisted the Holy Spirit: "Can you name a single prophet your ancestors have not persecuted? In the past they killed those who foretold the coming of the Just One, and now you have become his betrayers, his murderers. You who had the Law brought to you by angels are the very ones who have not kept it."

Understanding Stephen's place in the history of those enlightened by God, those who have received the Holy Spirit and are the guardians of the Law,[40] one can see the appropriateness of a relic of this saint being in the possession of the Byzantine emperor. The emperor, like Stephen, was chosen by God; he was another apostle who, like them, was enlightened through the Holy Spirit and was the keeper and defender of God's Law.[41] In addition, what better coincidence than to obtain the relic of such a martyr with the name of Stephanos ("crown") and to associate this relic with two ceremonies: the coronation *stepsimon,* the most important ritual of kingship, and the marriage ceremony, the *stephanoma.* This play on words, but also symbols, falls easily into the pattern of the Byzantine love for such uses of the Greek language. It must have been carefully planned to have the church that was to house Stephen's right arm set up in proximity to the ceremonial hall where coronations took place and to have the church itself made into the marriage chapel of the imperial court.

Kreepkens, eds., *Fructus Centesimus: Mélanges offerts à Gérard J. M. Bartelink à l'occasion de son soixante-cinquième anniversaire,* Instrumenta Patristica 19 (Steenbrugis, 1989), 1–16.

[39] All quotations in this section are from the Acts of the Apostles relating to the story of St. Stephen. They are quoted or paraphrased from *The Jerusalem Bible,* ed. A. Jones (New York, 1968).

[40] Basil the Great discussing the apostolic role of St. Thekla ranks Stephen and Thekla as following behind the apostles, as the New Adam and Eve of the martyrdom family; see Gilbert Dagron, ed., *Vie et miracles de Sainte Thècle* (Brussels, 1978), 172.

[41] I venture at this point to suggest that the choice of name Stefan for the Serbian dynasty is not incidental and is a direct reference to the concepts just discussed. It accompanies all family names. Starting with Stefan Nemanja and then Stefan the First-Crowned (1196–1228) there are, alphabetically, Stefan Dragutin, Stefan Dusan, Stefan Uroš, Stefan Uroš Milutin, Stefan Voislav, etc. The same can also be said in connection with the Hungarian royal dynasty. There is in the 11th century Stephen Géza, and then the line continues with Stefan I to Stefan V. In addition, there is the Hungarian crown itself, the so-called St. Stephen's crown. I believe that all this needs to be studied more closely in relation to the Byzantine tradition and the role of St. Stephen for the imperial court.

The Golden Hand

There is further evidence that adds significance and special meaning to this whole complex of buildings and underlines the importance given to names and symbols by the Byzantines, whenever presentation and ceremonial were at stake. All elements discussed can be tied together: the rituals of the ceremonial hall of Αὐγουστεύς or Στέψιμον, the church of St. Stephen, St. Stephen the first martyr and deacon, the *stephanos*/crown, his right arm, and contemporary imperial iconography. In this case the evidence is a portico, or better said, the name of an area in the portico that led into the hall of Augusteus at its main facade. According to the *Book of Ceremonies*, this portico, or the area of the portico directly before the central door, had the name of Χρυσῆ Χείρ ("Golden Hand"). It was a very important location, since it was the place where the emperor and the empress would show themselves to the courtiers and dignitaries after the coronation, and where the adoration and acclamations would take place.[42] It seems also to have been a pivotal point in the processional entries and exits of the emperor from and to the palace, and also the place where he would be awaited and acclaimed on the major feast days, as, for example, on Christmas day at the ceremony of adoration that took place there.[43]

In the absence of textual data informing us why the name Golden Hand came about, we must proceed cautiously with an interpretation. However, it cannot be too far-fetched to suggest, as have J. Ebersolt and R. Guilland, that the name derives from some possible representation of a golden hand, either painted or even suspended from above.[44] What form this hand might have had is hard to say. Ebersolt thought of a blessing hand, blessing those entering or symbolizing the protective power of Christ.

To imagine its possible form, one might recall representations of the *manus dei* often found in images in early Christian art where it appears above as the sign of God's approval or the manifestation of God's power. However, I would like to suggest a different iconographic representation for this hand. On the coinage of the Theodosian dynasty, specifically of the women, there reappears a motif that had not been seen on coins since the earlier years of Arcadius' reign (383–386): a *manus dei* holding a crown made of pearls(?) over the ruler's head.[45] His wife, Eudoxia, reintroduces it in 402 in the form of a wreath, and it remains an iconographic motif associated with the coinage of the empresses (Fig. 3a).[46] For example, the solidi struck in the name of Pulcheria Augusta during the reign of her brother Theodosios II from 414 to 453 all depict a hand suspended from above holding a wreath over the augusta's head and crowning her (Fig.

---

[42] *De cer.*, ed. Reiske, I, 1, p. 9; I, 40, p. 204; I, 41, pp. 207, 210, 212, 214; I, 46, p. 231; II, 15, pp. 537, 584; ed. Vogt, I, 1, p. 6; II, 49, p. 12; II, 50, pp. 16, 18, 20, 21. Guilland, *Études*, II, 82–93.

[43] *De cer.*, ed. Reiske, I, 1, p. 9; ed. Vogt, I, 1 p. 6.

[44] Ebersolt, *Grand Palais*, II, 45 and note 6; Guilland, *Études*, II, 82. The golden hands of a saint that can heal and perform miracles are also well known, as, for example, those of St. Demetrios represented in a mosaic of the north aisle of his church in Thessaloniki; see H. Belting, *Bild und Kult* (Munich, 1990), 51; trans. *Likeness and Presence: A History of the Image before the Era of Art* (Chicago, 1994).

[45] P. Grierson and M. Mays, *Catalogue of Late Roman Coins in the Dumbarton Oaks Collection and in the Whittemore Collection* (Washington, D.C., 1992), pls. 1–3.

[46] Grierson and Mays, *Late Roman Coins*, 133–35, pl. 11.

3b). The smaller denominations show Pulcheria only in profile without the crowning hand with the wreath; instead she introduces the wreath with the cross at its center on the obverse.[47] The crowning motif is found on the coins of Galla Placidia (425–430); Eudocia, the wife of Theodosios II (423–460); Justa Grata Honoria (426–450); and Licinia Eudoxia (439).[48] Does this iconographic motif, so distinct on the women's coinage, relate to the ceremonial hall of the Augusteus and its portico of the Golden Hand, the Χρυσῆ Χείρ? In this hall the women were crowned, and after the coronation they made their appearance as augustae in the Golden Hand where they were also adored.

Nothing should be taken as coincidental. When rituals and ceremonies are concerned, actions and symbols invariably convey a specific message. Building upon tradition with subtle change and innovation was the Byzantines' approach to expressing their most important concerns in a powerful way. Changes were so gradual that to some critics they never took place. It can be safely said that the creation of lasting images, either in ceremonial or in art, was the outcome of this type of Byzantinism. Ceremonies were meant to be dramatic, as if everything in some fateful way had come together in that moment to exalt the emperor. Obviously careful planning and long experience in the staging and presentation of the imperial image contributed to this effect.

In the case of the arm/hand of Stephanos "who wears the name itself," the relic participates in combining word (*stephanos*) and symbolic act to intensify the one matter of importance: imperial greatness manifested through god-sent power by the holy hand presenting the crown of kingship. It contributes to the symbolism of the blessing hand and at the same time it becomes part of the *stepsis* and the *stephanoma* (crowning and marriage), which now can take place jointly between the Augusteus and the church of St. Stephen set up specifically for those rituals.

St. Stephen the Deacon and Protomartyr

St. Stephen became one of the most popular saints in the early Christian world. The iconic image of St. Stephen, the one that became the standard type in Byzantium throughout the centuries, is that of Stephen as deacon, the office given to him by the apostles. His martyrdom and death through stoning, the first to have come about in defense of a follower's belief in Christ, is, on the other hand, remembered by the epithet that almost always accompanies him, that of "Protomartyr." One of the earliest icons is a tenth- to eleventh-century icon of St. Stephen in the Hermitage (Fig. 4).[49] There he is depicted as a youth standing, wearing a deacon's white tunic, with his left hand holding a container with incense and his right hand in the process of censing. What is unusual

---

[47] Grierson and Mays, *Late Roman Coins,* 152–54, pl. 17, 436–43; for the *semissi*, pl. 17, 444–47. The solidi have in one type of reverse a victory figure holding the studded cross. For the importance of the cross and its meaning in the coinage of Pulcheria, see Holum, *Theodosian Empresses,* 108–9, and J. Gagé, "Σταυρὸς Νικοποιός: La victoire impériale dans l'Empire chrétien," *Revue d'histoire et de philosophie religieuses* 13 (1933), 370–400.

[48] Grierson and Mays, *Late Roman Coins,* pl. 32, 824–28, 834; pl. 34, 844–46, 866.

[49] A Bank, *Byzantine Art in the Collections of Soviet Museums* (New York–Leningrad, 1977), fig. 233, p. 315.

in his representation, and has become characteristic of all depictions of St. Stephen, is the exaggerated right arm holding the censer, which is not only large but is always held away from the body in an outward curve emphasizing the movement of censing. Without wishing to claim that this iconographic detail has anything to do with the relic of that arm in Constantinople, it is hard to suppress the thought, especially when we look at other representations of St. Stephen in comparison to other deacons. For example, another well-known representation of St. Stephen is found in the church of Hagia Sophia in Kiev (Fig. 5a). In the eleventh-century mosaic program of the apse, below the Communion of the Apostles, St. Stephen stands at the right side, at the level of the bishops and church fathers. Here, too, we see the exaggerated and extended right arm that holds the censer (lower part restored). In the exact symmetrical position at the left of the same row of bishops, there is the figure of St. Lawrence, another early Christian deacon and martyr of the church (Fig. 5b). In contrast to St. Stephen, although he is also represented censing, his arm is held close to the body with no visible distinction to emphasize his action. This is also the case with other deacons.[50] I do not want to make too much of this iconographic peculiarity with St. Stephen, but it is worth observing, remembering its possible associations to which I would like to add one more.

There is another aspect of St. Stephen which brought the deacon into a symbolic association with the emperor. On the great feast days—Easter, Pentecost, the Transfiguration, Christmas, and Epiphany—the emperor went to Hagia Sophia and participated in the liturgy in conjunction with the patriarch.[51] Although for the most part he attends the liturgy as a layman, there are a few moments when he acts in part like the clergy. For example, he enters the church together with the patriarch, and with him he enters the sanctuary where he kisses the altar cloth.[52] He receives and gives the kiss of peace, and he is also asked to participate in the great entrance, although only up to the holy doors. Clearly he does not co-officiate with the patriarch. The only time he is asked to perform a clerical task is when, having entered the sanctuary through the holy doors at the beginning of the liturgy and having kissed and venerated the altar cloth and the holy vessels, he is then handed the holy censer by the patriarch and is asked to cense the golden Crucifixion. This image was located in the κυκλίν, the space behind the altar in the circular area of the apse, into which the patriarch and the emperor enter together through the right side of the bema.[53]

This act of censing within the sanctuary is a prerogative of the clergy and is associated

---

[50] L. Hadermann-Misguich, *Kurbinovo: Les fresques de Saint-Georges et la peinture byzantine du XIIe siècle* (Brussels, 1975), 68 with further references.

[51] On this topic and the emperor's role within ecclesiastical ceremonies, see George Majeska, "The Emperor in His Church," in this volume.

[52] *De cer.,* ed. Reiske I, 1, p. 15; ed. Vogt, I, 1, p. 11.

[53] *De cer.,* ed. Reiske, I, 1, pp. 15–16; ed. Vogt, I, 1, p. 12. Anthony of Novgorod, who gave a detailed record of all relics, miraculous images, and objects he saw when visiting Constantinople a few years before the Latin conquest, states that in the passage behind the apse of St. Sophia there was a painted image of St. Stephen, the protomartyr, above and over the doors, in front of which they censed; Erhard, "Antoine de Novgorod," 56. It could be a mere coincidence that such an image was located in that area, but considering the Byzantine tradition of finding associations and connections in words and gestures, it is unlikely, and the image must have had a specific function.

with one of the duties of a deacon and other priests. I see this action as quite significant, marking the role or place of the emperor between layman and clergy, a place never clearly defined either through texts or ceremonial, but left ambiguous. The emperor receives this layman–clergyman status already at his coronation, which at various points has the appearance of an ordination, especially at the moment when he is acclaimed ἄξιος ("worthy") three times, a familiar formula from an ordination to clerical office.[54] I would argue that the act of censing marks the emperor's status within the ecclesiastical hierarchy close to that of a deacon, whose office is the lowest of the high clergy and who assists the priest and bishop in the celebration of the liturgy, but cannot celebrate the mystery of the liturgy alone. A mark of the lower nature of the deacon's office is the act of censing, which in iconographic terms is represented through the censer, the attribute the deacon always holds. The emperor has very similar restrictions and converts to the status of a layman during the high moments of the liturgy.[55] The office of the deacon, we should not forget, has apostolic connections which also are related to the notions of the imperial office (see above), and thus make it from that point of view the most appropriate one for the emperor.[56]

The relic of the right arm of St. Stephen was still to be seen by the year 1200 when the last to see and remark on it was again Anthony of Novgorod, who says that unfortunately the front of it, that is, the fingers, was damaged.[57] There is still the possibility that the arm of St. Stephen, or at least the major bone of that arm, has not totally been lost, for in the cathedral of Châlons-sur-Marne there is a relic identified as the *cubitus* (i.e., elbow) of St. Stephen with a Byzantine silver mount at one end of it (Fig. 6).[58]

What I have presented concerning the relic of St. Stephen is an accumulation of evidence which, however disparate, when brought together provides a complete picture. The importance of this particular relic is difficult to conceive without this synthesis of detailed information. While moderns may have difficulties in grasping the intrinsic value and use of the relic, this was not so for the Byzantines, who had the mentality to draw out subtle symbolisms rarely recognized today. From its arrival in Constantinople, a place for the relic of the arm of St. Stephen within the imperial palace was inevitable, considering the possibilities it offered in enriching imperial ceremonial and strengthening the

---

[54] Majeska, "Emperor," pp. 3–4.

[55] Majeska, "Emperor," p. 6.

[56] There are a few other occasions on feast days when the emperor censes, for example, on the feast of the Birth of the Virgin, *De cer.*, ed. Reiske, I, 1, p. 28; ed. Vogt, I, 1, p. 22. Another is on the feast of Sts. Constantine and Helena when he goes to the church of the Holy Apostles. When the emperor enters the area where the tombs of the emperors are located, he is received by the patriarch. After having bowed three times while carrying lit candles, the patriarch hands him the censer and the emperor censes the imperial tombs, especially that of Constantine the Great: *De cer.*, ed. Reiske, II, 5, p. 533. Another occasion is when on the day of the Beheading of John the Baptist (29 August) he goes to the Stoudios monastery, where the relic of the head was kept, and censes at the beginning of the liturgy, and then he goes to the right of the bema, where the head is kept, and lights candles: *De cer.*, ed. Reiske, II, 13, p. 563.

[57] Ehrhard, "Antoine de Novgorod," 56.

[58] *Byzance: L'art byzantin dans les collections publiques françaises* (exh. cat., Musée du Louvre, Paris, 1992), 337, fig. 3. There is also a text by Michael Italikos in the 12th century that has an icon or a reliquary of St. Stephen speak, complaining of the cupidity of the sacristan who sold him to the Venetians: P. Gautier, *Michel Italikos, lettres et discours* (Paris, 1972), 234–36.

position of the emperor. It seems plausible to suggest that St. Stephen's right arm set in motion a chain of ideologically loaded architectural and iconographic events which in an indirect way demonstrate the value of that rather humble historical event of the translation of that relic from Jerusalem to Constantinople and into the imperial palace.

The Relic of the Arm of St. John the Baptist

The arm of John the Baptist was brought to Constantinople from Antioch in 956 by Emperor Constantine VII Porphyrogennetos specifically to be deposited in the Great Palace. Skylitzes reports: "In this period the holy arm of Prodromos arrived also in the capital, having been stolen from Antioch by a certain deacon, Job by name. When it reached Chalcedon the emperor sent out the royal barge, and while the Senate at its most splendid and Patriarch Polyeuktos came out (to greet it) with the whole clergy with candles, torches, and incense, he carried it into the palace."[59]

The miniature that accompanies this text in the illustrated copy of Skylitzes in Madrid (Fig. 7) depicts a youth, most likely the deacon Job, who is carrying a box with a pyramidal cover on his head. This container, the reliquary where the arm of St. John is being kept, is decorated with a fine pattern commonly found on metalwork. The inscription reads: ἡ χεὶρ τοῦ προδρόμου ("the arm of Prodromos"). The deacon is followed by a group of high officials, all with their hands covered in reverence to the relic. Just before the deacon, Patriarch Polyeuktos, with both his arms outstretched, is holding back the crowd which has eagerly come to see the arrival and translation of the arm to the palace. Soldiers or the imperial guard are included in the crowd, their spears visible in the background. Within the palace on the right of the miniature a deacon with a censer is censing at the entrance. A second deacon, a guard, and three bishops await the procession. The emperor is not represented. Next to the group of figures within the palace is the following inscription rephrasing the Skylitzes text: ὁ πατριάρχης Πολύευκτος μετὰ παντὸς τοῦ κλήρου ἐξελθών, ἄγων τὴν χεῖρα Ἰωάννου τοῦ Προδρόμου εἰς τὰ βασίλεια ("Patriarch Polyeuktos, with the whole clergy having come out, leads the arm of John Prodromos into the palace"). It is interesting to note that, although the text makes clear that it was the emperor who brought the relic to Constantinople, he has been excluded from the illustration, and the accompanying text is slanted in a way to benefit the patriarch.[60]

Although a specific church is not mentioned in the text, when Anthony of Novgorod saw the arm of St. John the Baptist in 1200, it was kept among the important relics of

---

[59] Skylitzes, ed. Thurn, 245.27–32: Ἤχθη δὲ κατὰ τὸν αὐτὸν καιρὸν καὶ ἡ τιμία χεὶρ τοῦ Προδρόμου εἰς τὴν βασιλίδα ἐξ Ἀντιοχείας, ἀποκλαπεῖσα παρά τινος διακόνου Ἰὼβ τὸ ὄνομα· ἣν καταλαβοῦσαν τὴν χαλκηδόνα ὁ βασιλεὺς τὴν βασιλικὴν ἐκπέμψας τριήρη, καὶ τῆς συγκλήτου ὅσον ἐπίσημον ἐξελθόντος καὶ τοῦ πατριάρχου Πολυεύκτου σὺν παντὶ τῷ κλήρῳ μετὰ κηρῶν καὶ λαμπάδων καὶ θυμιαμάτων, εἰς τὰ βασίλεια ἤγαγεν.

[60] It would be worthwhile to check throughout the manuscript for other cases of this type where the emperor has been left out of the illustrative material and the church is credited with the events; e.g., the reburial of Michael by Leo VI: Grabar and Manoussacas, *L'illustration*, fol. 131a, fig. 158, p. 77.

Christ and the Virgin in the palace chapel of the Virgin of the Pharos. Thus we should assume that it was housed there from the time of its arrival. In addition to the arm, Anthony lists an iron rod topped by a cross, also belonging to St. John.[61]

While it cannot be fully ascertained that this arm of St. John is extant, there is a relic that is identified as the right arm of St. John the Baptist in the Topkapi Museum in Istanbul.[62] This relic can be traced back to the period immediately after the conquest of Constantinople. It had an interesting history which can be followed in part through some defters that survive in the archives of the Topkapi and the Prime Ministry. The most important event took place in 1484 when the arm was sent to the Hospitalers on Rhodes, specifically to Pierre d'Aubusson, by Bayezid II. Sometime during the last decade of the sixteenth century, the arm returned to Ottoman hands.[63] Until some years ago it was kept in the Emanet Hazine Treasury together with the holiest relics, including Mohammed's mantle.[64] Today it is displayed in a case together with the upper section of the cranium of the head of the same John, which we know was separated into two pieces in the Byzantine period.[65] The face or lower part of the head had found its way to France through the Fourth Crusade when it arrived in Amiens in 1206 where it is still to be seen in the treasury of the cathedral.[66]

The arm relic as we see it today is not in its original state (Fig. 8a,b). What we see is a western medieval type of encasement which creates the shape of an arm and its hand in realistic terms. This way of encasing a relic does not follow Byzantine tradition, or at least it would have been rather unusual. Most likely this form which recreates the arm and hand was avoided as, I believe, it was thought to be too realistic or too much like a three-dimensional piece of sculpture to be accepted by the church, while at the same time the relic remained almost invisible to the viewer. The Byzantines preferred to leave the bones exposed (what better proof for their existence) and apply a silver or gold band

---

[61] Ehrhard, "Antoine de Novgorod," 57.

[62] There is mention of the right arm of St. John the Baptist being presented to the monastery of Citeaux in 1263 by Eudes de Cicons, seigneur de Charistos, who had it from Emperor Baldwin II. This relic was kept in a gilded silver reliquary with an inscription in verse explaining that this arm of Prodromos, once held by the barbarians, was ripped from their hands by Emperor Constantine, who deposited it in a treasury "where it protects the empire and brings (gives) him augmented power." He probably had this reliquary fashioned after the relic had arrived in the city. Du Cange, *Traité historique du chef de S. Jean-Baptiste* (Paris, 1665), 183; Ebersolt, *Sanctuaires,* 134–36. This is very good evidence for the relic of the right arm having been taken to France, since the inscription is relevant to Constantine and makes good sense in terms of its use for the empire and for the emperor personally.

[63] For the history of this relic after the conquest of Constantinople see N. Bayraktar, "Topkapi Sarayi Müzesi'nde Hagios Ioannes Prodromos'a (Vaftizei Yahya) Ait Rölikler," *Topkapi Saray Müzesi* 1 (1985), 9–20, esp. 11–12. I would like to thank my colleagues Gülru Necipoğlu and Cemal Kafadar for translating the Turkish text for me.

[64] The history of this relic points out its importance and its intrinsic value throughout the centuries for various religious groups. For the Knights of St. John the arm is clearly of great importance; for the Ottoman Empire it seems it was just as important since until recently it was placed among its most holy relics.

[65] Anthony of Novgorod saw the upper part of the head of St. John in the Blachernai where there was also some of his hair enclosed and sealed in an icon with the imperial seal; the face he saw in the Stoudios: Ehrhard, "Antoine de Novgorod," 58. For the history of the head of St. John the Baptist, see Du Cange, *Traité historique;* Ebersolt, *Sanctuaires,* 134–36; C. Walter, "The Invention of John the Baptist's Head at Gračanica," *Zbornik za likovnje umetnosti* 16 (1980), 71–83.

[66] Ebersolt, *Sanctuaires,* 80–81; *Byzance,* no. 240, pp. 325–26, fig. 1, with earlier bibliography.

on their ends or joints, often with an inscription identifying the relic (e.g., Fig. 6). The relic then would have been kept in a rectangular box of varying materials and decoration.

This was also the case with the arm of St. John. When the Spanish ambassador Clavijo saw the relic in the church of the Virgin Peribleptos in 1404, the relic was exposed. It was well preserved and was encased in thin bands of gold, but the thumb was missing. A second arm he saw he described in a similar way, saying that the arm extended only from the shoulder down to the hand (no fingers) and had golden ring-bands with precious stones at the joints of the elbow and wrist.[67] His description of the first relic identifies it as the right arm of St. John since the fact that the thumb was missing is in accord with the legend that the thumb was taken from the hand and used to kill a dragon when the arm was still in Antioch.[68] That this and other relics were no longer in their original location after the Latin occupation has to do with either the destruction of the church they were housed in before, like the church of the Pharos, or the need to move them for safekeeping. Thus, through the textual sources written after 1204, we discover a number of known relics to be in new locations.

The metalwork now covering the arm in the Topkapi Museum is recognizable as Italian. It covers the whole surface of the arm in low relief in a continuous vine-and-leaf pattern creating medallions as if it were a silk sleeve over the arm. The work can be identified more specifically as Venetian, made most likely when this relic was in the hands of the Hospitalers on Rhodes, since it has two silver stamps repeated twice: the Venetian lion with its wings and a crown, and next to it the Maltese cross (Fig. 8c,d). One stamp is on the hand at the level of the wrist, and the other around the top of the sleeve over the name of John on the inscription.[69] There are altogether three inscriptions on the object: the inscription around the wrist reads: ΑΥΤΗ Η ΧΕΙΡ ΕCΤΙ ΙΩΑΝΝΟΥ ΤΟΥ ΒΑΠΤΙCΤΟΥ ("this is the hand of John the Baptist"); the other is incised on the index finger and is a quotation from John 1:36: ΙΔΕ Ο ΑΜΝΟC ΤΟΥ ΘΕΟΥ ("this is the Lamb of God"). The third is at the level of the elbow around the flat end, the lid of the encasement: + ΔΕΥCΗC (ΔΕΗCΙC) ΤΟΥ ΔΟΥΛΟΥ ΤΟΥ ΘΕΟΥ ΔΑΝΙΥΛ (ΔΑΝΙΗΛ) ΜΟΝΑΧΟΥ ("Prayer of the servant of God Daniel the monk"). At this point we do not know who Daniel the monk was. There are misspellings in the inscription, specifically

---

[67] Clavijo actually saw two arms which he identifies as being relics of St. John the Baptist, one in the Peribleptos, the other at the monastery at Petra. The one in the Peribleptos was the right arm of the Baptist since it is also described by Russian travelers as being there. The text for the right arm is as follows: "du coude en bas avec la main; il était tout à fait bien conservé et intact; il était enchassé dans de minces baguettes en or, mais il lui manquait le pouce." The description for the other is the following: "il n'y avait que la partie entre l'épaule et la main; les jointures du coude et de la main étaient ornées en or, avec des pierres précieuses": P. Bruun, *Constantinople, ses sanctuaires et ses reliques au commencement du XVe siècle: Fragment de l'Itinerario de Clavijo* (Odessa, 1883), 5, in Ebersolt, *Sanctuaires,* 80–81 note 4. As Ebersolt has argued, the left arm was never in Constantinople and remained at Sebaste, and Clavijo must have confused another relic with it. The left arm was from 1323 until sometime between 1981 and 1983 in the cathedral of Saint-Jean-Baptiste at Perpignan, where it was brought and deposited by a stranger before going on pilgrimage: *Byzance,* no. 367, p. 477.

[68] Theodore Daphnopates, ed. V. V. Latyshev, Θεοδώρου τοῦ Δαφνοπάτου λόγοι Δύο, *Pravoslavnyi palestinskij sbornik* 59 (St. Petersburg, 1910), sections 13–14, pp. 26–27 (hereafter Δύο λόγοι). Anthony of Novgorod saw the thumb of St. John in the church of the Stoudios monastery: Ehrhard, "Antoine de Novgorod," 58.

[69] The silver gilt encasement consists of two parts, the hand and the arm. Its total length is 50 cm, the hand being 20 cm and the arm 32 cm: Bayraktar, "Topkapi Sarayi," 13.

with the letter H written as Y. This does not necessarily mean much, since misspellings occur often enough on Byzantine objects with inscriptions, but it is surprising for someone who is a monk to have also misspelled his own name. Perhaps the craftsman was Italian and knew little Greek.

The fingers of the hand are shaped in the well-known gesture appropriate to John. It is much like the blessing gesture often seen in Byzantine art, but it is also the gesture used by John when he is pointing at Christ as the lamb in the early tradition or at Christ himself in art after the late seventh century.[70] There is a rectangular opening in the encasement on the hand to let the bones be visible to the pious; it has now lost its cover. It is not clear how many of the fingers are still present.

John the Baptist, the Prophet and Forerunner

St. John the Baptist or Prodromos is a pivotal figure in the Bible and became one of the most popular saints of the Byzantines. Because of his having lived in the desert, he is also regarded in monastic literature as the ideal monk, which explains his great popularity as the patron saint of monastic foundations such as the famous Stoudios monastery in Constantinople, that of Lips, or that of Petra. In Constantinople alone he was venerated in at least thirty-six churches that were dedicated to him, eight of which were monasteries.[71] John's importance lies in his relation to Christ. John's primary role in the Gospels is to bear witness to Christ and to be his precursor, a role that already within the Gospel text defines Christ's theological direction. Except for the Virgin Mary, there is no other figure closer to Christ.

The "Forerunner of Christ" was the son of the priest Zacharias and Elizabeth, a relative of Mary. John's birth was announced by an angel who also told Zacharias to give him the name of John (Luke 1:13–20). According to belief, John was endowed with grace by God at the Visitation, before his birth: "Now as soon as Elizabeth heard Mary's greetings, the child leapt in her womb and Elizabeth was filled with the Holy Spirit" (Luke 1:41).[72] John appeared around A.D. 27 as a mission preacher on the banks of the Jordan asking repentance and baptism from his followers, preparing them for the approach of the "Kingdom of God." In general, in his actions, teachings, and appearance, he was reminiscent of and followed in the tradition of the Old Testament prophets; he was taken, even in his own time, to be the prophet Elijah himself and was called the New Elijah (Matt. 11:14). At the same time he is the contemporary of Christ, thus spanning the Old and New Testaments. In iconographic terms he is also dressed like Elijah, whose pallium and fur mantle he wears. He foreshadowed Christ, however, mainly through his preachings. He is also the one who recognized Jesus as the promised Messiah by pointing him out to those being baptized in the Jordan (Ἰδοὺ ὁ ἀμνὸς τοῦ

[70] K. Corrigan, "The Witness of John the Baptist on an Early Byzantine Icon in Kiev," *DOP* 42 (1988), 1–11.

[71] R. Janin, "Les églises byzantines du Précurseur à Constantinople," *EO* 37 (1938), 312–51; *ODB*, II, 1068–69.

[72] *Oxford Dictionary of the Christian Church* (London, 1958), 733–34; *ODB*, II, 1068–69.

Θεοῦ). Later he denounced Herod Antipas for his marriage to the wife of his brother Philip, Herodias, and this led to his imprisonment and beheading.

In Christian thought three episodes from John's life hold special significance: his prophecies concerning the role of the Savior, his baptism of Christ, and his arrest by Herod and beheading. He is commemorated several times during the year.[73] His Nativity (24 June) and Beheading (29 August) are two major feasts, but in connection with the relic of the right arm the most relevant and appropriate feast is Epiphany (6 January), the day when in the Orthodox church Christ's Baptism is celebrated, the day of Enlightenment (τὰ ἅγια Θεοφάνεια, τῶν ἁγίων Φώτων). In addition, there is 7 January, an extension of Epiphany dedicated to John and the relic of his right arm and celebrated with his *synaxis*.[74]

The right arm of St. John plays an important role in two of the three most important events of his life: first, when he points to Jesus as the Savior at the bank of the Jordan River, and secondly, a theologically even more important moment, when he baptizes Christ.

Iconographically, too, St. John's right arm had become an important element in images of the standard iconic type already in the early Christian centuries. There are a number of early examples in which John is shown with his raised arm pointing toward the Savior either as a lamb or as a bust. I mention here, however, only one icon as an example of the traditional iconographic features. This icon is in the monastery of Mount Sinai and dates from the late twelfth century (Fig. 9). John is standing frontally in the center of the icon. Next to him is the axe leaning at the root of the tree ready to cut down all those who do not bring forth good fruit (Matt. 2:10). John is holding in his left hand the open scroll with the text from John 1:29, for all to read and remember his prophecy and recognition of the Savior. He also holds a long staff topped with a cross. His right hand is raised with the hand turned outward and slightly tilted toward his right. The first two fingers are held together, and the middle finger is bent to touch the thumb. This gesturing hand, although reminiscent of a blessing hand, is pointing upward as is common for John when pointing to a bust of Christ. Here, however, he points to the image that is within the frame at precisely that level. The scene represents exactly the moment when John meets Christ and gestures toward him, the moment of his saying "this is the Lamb of God." It is part of a cycle of narrative scenes from his life arranged in a sequence in such a way as to create a visually interpretive reading of the whole composition. The scene of the Visitation, for example, also falls at a critical place on the icon. It is at the center top of the frame exactly at a point where one expects the Holy

---

[73] The feast of his Nativity is on 24 June, and 29 August is the commemoration of his beheading (Mark 6:14–29). At the Stoudios monastery the second day was celebrated from the 10th century in connection with the relic of his head, which came to the monastery at that time; in Jerusalem, however, it was celebrated since the 5th century: *De cer.*, ed. Reiske, II, 13, pp. 562–63; Janin, *Églises et monastères*, 433.

[74] The seventh of January, the day following Epiphany, is the only day that does not commemorate a specific event associated with his life. In the *Synaxarion* this day is dedicated to the right arm of St. John: *Synaxarium CP* 375–76. I thank Ihor Ševčenko for reminding me of this text. It is clear that the commemoration of this important relic had to be connected with the day of the Baptism, but could not be placed on such an important christological feast. Thus the following day extends the celebration and brings the relic itself into association with it.

Spirit to make its appearance. Depicted is the moment when John was endowed with prenatal grace and recognized Christ's divinity by leaping in his mother's womb.

Epiphany and Baptism

The arm plays the most important role in the scene of the Baptism. The feast icon of the day is the established scene of John baptizing Christ in the Jordan, which iconographically goes back to the early Christian period.[75] A good Middle Byzantine example is the mosaic of this scene in the *katholikon* of the monastery of Hosios Loukas (Fig. 10). The event itself is one of the two moments during Christ's life on earth when his divine nature manifested itself. The entire Trinity was revealed. In one single moment the voice of God was heard, the Holy Spirit flew down over the head of Christ, and Christ was present himself. The act of baptism in art is represented by the placing of the hand over the head of the one to be baptized. The imposition of a hand in symbolic terms signals that something supernatural, or something the individual did not possess previously, a virtue or even a blessing, has been passed to that person.[76] In the case of Christ's Baptism, it was important to stress the descent of the Holy Spirit and the emphatic gesture of John as he stretches his hand over the head of Christ.[77] The same can be said of the actual rite of baptism. Through baptism one's sins are erased, and the individual receives God's grace through enlightenment. It is a moment of transition and change from an old state to a new one.

At this point we need to enter the mentality of the Byzantines, first to recall their notion of the imperial office in Byzantine society and then to realize why the day of Christ's baptism was a day of primary importance for the Byzantine emperor. Since the foundation of the Christian imperial office came about through divine revelation—that is, simply put, the emperor was chosen by God for this office—the day of Epiphany provided a valid opportunity for the ritualistic renewal of this concept. On the day of Epiphany, the day of divine revelation, in *mimesis* of Christ, the emperor would symbolically receive the Holy Spirit in affirmation of his selection and legitimate elevation to the imperial office.[78]

---

[75] C. Walter, "Baptism in Byzantine Iconography," *Sobornost* 2.2 (1980), 1–18.

[76] L. de Bruyne, "L'imposition des mains dans l'art chrétien romain," *Rivista dell'archeologia cristiana* 20 (1943), 216. C. Walter, *Art and Ritual of the Byzantine Church* (London, 1982), 125–30. Since the early centuries it had become customary for imperial baptisms to take place on one of the three great feasts of the year, Easter, Pentecost and Epiphany: see P. Grierson, "The Date of the Dumbarton Oaks Epiphany Medallion," *DOP* 15 (1961), 222.

[77] The composition of this mosaic scene of the Baptism is quite rare since it is reversed. This is due to its location in the northwestern squinch within the naos of Hosios Loukas, which requires the figures in action to move toward the center of that space. Thus this mosaic shows John the Baptist on the right side and Christ to his left, so that his stretched right arm moves from right to left. Most of the scenes of the Baptism are illustrations in manuscripts, and there, because of the direction in which we move our eyes to read, John is placed on the left stretching his arm toward Christ to his right. This is also the case in most decorative programs in churches.

[78] Of similar importance for the office of the emperor and probably already well established by the 9th century was the day of Pentecost, the day when the Holy Spirit descended upon the apostles: see K. Corrigan, "The Ivory Scepter of Leo VI: A Statement of Post-Iconoclastic Imperial Ideology," *ArtB* 60 (1978), 407–16. On the

To celebrate the feast of Epiphany the emperor went twice to church, a rare occurrence, the other feast day on which this occurred being that of Christmas. On the eve of Epiphany he stayed within the palace complex. The patriarch came to the palace, and the ceremony of the Blessing of the Waters took place in the church of St. Stephen.[79] The next day, the day of Epiphany, he first appointed and promoted individuals to the position of magistrates. This took place in the Konsistorion, one of the throne rooms of the palace, where promotions and government appointments often were handed out by the emperor.[80] Then, after having completed this ceremony, he went with great pomp to Hagia Sophia. The procession to the church and the festivities of this day were of the highest order and equal to those of Christmas, Easter, and Pentecost.[81] At various points during the procession from the palace to Hagia Sophia and back, acclamations to the emperor were chanted by the Blues and the Greens. These are meticulously recorded in the *Book of Ceremonies*. They are explicit testimonies to the Byzantine ideology and perception of the imperial office and make clear the appropriateness of the day to restate them. For example, at the fourth reception the Greens chant: "He who today was baptized through the hand of the Prodromos, proclaims you today emperor with his awesome hand, god-crowned benefactors, and points you out worthy throughout the universe."[82] These words draw on the image of the Baptism to present the emperor in the place of Christ. John's hand baptized Christ, and Christ's hand now proclaims the emperor.[83] While this parallel position of Christ-emperor is expressed through the action of the hands, the divine selection of the emperor is confirmed by having Christ place his hand over the head of the emperor.

Thus, when we turn to the ivory plaque with the representation of Constantine Porphyrogennetos being proclaimed by Christ, made to commemorate his elevation to the throne as main emperor in 945, it becomes immediately clear that what is expressed here in visual terms is what was said in words in the acclamation (Fig. 11). First, there is the confirmation of the selection of the emperor through God, and secondly, the emperor takes on a Christlike position. Not only visually but symbolically and ideologically the parallel between Christ's baptism and imperial proclamation becomes obvious. The well-known Byzantine images representing the emperor's right to rule through the laying of a hand on the emperor's head by Christ or a saint are in imitation of the baptism of Christ. I am quite convinced that this iconography develops in connection with the propaganda that disseminated from the court of Basil I and does not exist before

---

mimesis of God in Byzantium, see H. Hunger, *Prooimion: Elemente der byzantinischen Kaiseridee in den Anreden der Urkunden* (Vienna, 1964), 58–63.

[79] *De cer.*, ed. Reiske, I, 25; ed. Vogt, I, 39.

[80] *De cer.*, ed. Reiske, I, 25, pp. 143–44; ed. Vogt, I, 39, pp. 133–34.

[81] *De cer.*, ed. Reiske, I, 1, pp. 5–35, esp. 22 and I, 26; ed. Vogt, I, 1, pp. 2–28, esp. 17 and I, 35.

[82] *De cer.*, ed. Reiske, I, 3, p. 43; ed. Vogt, I, 3, p. 36: ὁ Τῇ παλάμῃ βαπτισθεὶς σήμερον τοῦ Προδρόμου τῇ φρικτῇ αὐτοῦ παλάμῃ βασιλεῖς ὑμᾶς κηρύττῃ, θεόστεπτοι εὐεργέται, καὶ χρηστοὺς ὑμᾶς δεικνύῃ πάσῃ τῇ οἰκουμένῃ.

[83] We should keep in mind that the verb used here to describe Christ's gesture is κηρύσσω,–ττω, which means "to proclaim," "to announce"; it is a much stronger statement about the meaning of this act than the term "blessing an emperor's rule," which we commonly use when describing these images.

the late ninth century. The earliest representations of the symbolic placing of the hand over the head of an emperor are from his reign.[84]

The first emperor to use this iconography on his coinage was Alexander. After the death of his brother Leo VI in 912, after thirty years of waiting as co-emperor, he finally rules the empire as the divinely chosen and sole *autokrator*. Immediately upon his accession he issues a solidus which represents literally, or more appropriately graphically, what was until then only expressed through allusion and parallel compositional symbolism (Fig. 12). On his gold issues, Alexander introduces a saint who with his right hand is proclaiming his rule. Catherine Jolivet-Lévy has pointed out that, from the garments he wears, the pallium and fur mantle, he should be identified as John the Baptist.[85] More critical than his garments for the identification is, I believe, the staff he holds which is topped by a cross, by this period a standard attribute only of John.[86] This is the first representation of a coronation scene of this type on Byzantine coinage. Alexander was also the first to use on his miliaresia the title of *autokrator*.[87]

Anthony of Novgorod, when listing the relics in the palace chapel of the Virgin of the Pharos, says: "There is the right hand of John the Baptist, with which the emperor is consecrated, and there is also a staff of John the Baptist made of iron and mounted by a cross, with which the newly appointed emperor is blessed at the moment of the coronation."[88] His remarks are very important for understanding these relics and their role in Byzantine tradition and thought. Even if the arm itself, as I believe, was not physically used to crown the emperor, as Anthony tells us (this would go too far and not be an appropriate act in the simple and solemn liturgical ceremony of the Byzantine imperial coronation ritual), the relic might have been a prominent feature and its presence in the ceremonies would have clearly recalled God's selection of an individual

---

[84] The first images are those of Basil I in the Gregory manuscript in Paris. gr. 510, where the Prophet Elijah together with the Archangel Gabriel are represented crowning Basil on one rejected folio and Gabriel alone on the final version of this illustration: I. Kalavrezou-Maxeiner, "The Portraits of Basil I," 19–24. The other is on the Palazzo Venezia ivory box with Christ placing his hands over the heads of the imperial couple. For the identification see H. Maguire, "The Art of Comparing in Byzantium," *ArtB* 70 (1988), 88–103; and I. Kalavrezou, "A New Type of Icon: Ivories and Steatites," in *Constantine Porphyrogenitus and His Age*, ed. A. Markopoulos (Athens, 1989), 391–96. For a different date for the ivory box, see A. Cutler and N. Oikonomides, "An Imperial Byzantine Casket and Its Fate at a Humanist's Hands," *ArtB* 70 (1988), 77–87; on the general topic of the divine power of the emperor, see C. Jolivet-Lévy, "L'image du pouvoir dans l'art byzantin à l'époque de la dynastie Macédonienne (867–1056)," *Byzantion* 57 (1987), 441–70.

[85] Jolivet-Lévy, "L'image du pouvoir," 442–43. N. Thierry, "Le Baptiste sur le solidus d'Alexandre (912–913)," *Revue numismatique* 34 (1992), 237–41.

[86] There are a number of saints that could be chosen for the identification since the type of dress is not enough to justify one or another. For example, there is Elijah with whom John had great similarities and who was the patron saint of Basil I, that is, a familiar figure; then St. Alexios, of whom there is a 10th-century ivory plaque in Verona (A. Goldschmidt and K. Weitzmann, *Byzantinische Elfenbeinskulpturen*, vol. II [Berlin, 1934], no. 8) showing him very much like John; in the past he has been seen as the figure on Alexander's coin. Actually the saint is usually referred to as Alexander, on the assumption that he is Emperor Alexander's namesake: P. Grierson, *Byzantine Coins* (Berkeley, 1982), 179. However, it is the staff that distinguishes and identifies John from all others.

[87] Grierson, *Byzantine Coins,* 179, pl. 43, fig. 778.

[88] Ehrhard, "Antoine de Novgorod," 57. My translation is based on the French translation by B. de Khitrovo published and amended by Ehrhard. Whether both these relics were actually physically used or not, we do not know. However, as long as this is what was being believed and told, their symbolism and power remain the same.

for the Byzantine throne through John's mediation and the emperor's Christlike role on earth.

Saints and Dynasties

With the reign of Basil I we see that the day of Epiphany and St. John the Baptist as intercessor are chosen for important family events concerned with establishing the future of the Macedonian dynasty and confirming its legitimacy. Basil I in the year 870 raised his son Leo VI to the throne on 6 January, the day of Christ's baptism, the day of Epiphany. Leo VI in turn has his son, the illegitimate Constantine, baptized on Epiphany of the year 906 by Patriarch Nicholas Mystikos, who had agreed to perform the baptism, not, however, within the church of Hagia Sophia proper but rather in the *metatorion*.[89] For Constantine VII Porphyrogennetos this was the day of his legitimation and acceptance by the church as the rightful heir to the throne, as the rightful *porphyrogennetos*. Later, in 912, Leo VI's brother Alexander chose to depict John the Baptist on the main coinage of his reign in order to state visually his right to rule.[90] Even Romanos Lekapenos, who usurped the throne from the young Constantine VII, followed in the steps of the Macedonian family by choosing the day of Christ's baptism to crown his wife Theodora as augusta in 921 after his own coronation a month earlier.[91]

Constantine VII Porphyrogennetos had to wait about thirty years to get his throne back in the year 945, and 6 January had become for him the most important day in his claim to legitimacy. Constantine VII seems never to have forgotten this, and he always recognized John the Baptist's intercession for him. I say this because there are a few works of art that can be associated with him where, in the scene of the Deesis, John the Baptist holds an unusual position, but the interpretation of this iconographic feature has so far left much to be desired. For example, in the Palazzo Venezia ivory triptych depicting the Great Deesis and in the Limburg Staurotheque, which also has on its cover a representation of the Deesis, John the Baptist is standing on the right-hand side of

---

[89] Skylitzes, ed. Thurn, 184–85.16–25. See also the illustration in Grabar and Manoussacas, *L'illustration,* fol. 112b, fig. 134, p. 67. In the miniature the child is being held by the patriarch, who is about to immerse him in the font. The child's arms are both raised upward in an orant position as if praying and thanking God. The emperor is not present, only a group of figures who are receiving him. On the tetragamy of Leo VI and the illegitimate birth of his son Constantine, see N. Oikonomides, "Leo VI and the Narthex Mosaic in St. Sophia," *DOP* 30 (1976), 151–72. There is a gold medallion at Dumbarton Oaks, the so-called Epiphany Medallion, which on one side has the Nativity of Christ and on the other the Baptism. It seems to date from the year 584 when on 6 January Theodosios, the son of Maurice, was baptized. It was to commemorate the great event of the birth of a *porphyrogennetos,* a successor to establish a dynasty, something that had not taken place for almost two hundred years. A parallel can be drawn with the case of Constantine Porphyrogennetos. For a discussion of these issues, see Grierson, "Epiphany Medallion," 221–24.

[90] P. Grierson, *Catalogue of the Byzantine Coins in the Dumbarton Oaks Collection,* vol. III, pt. 2 (Washington, D.C., 1973), p. 528. Romanos I Lekapenos was the first to issue gold coins with Christ proclaiming his rule; see Grierson, op. cit., pp. 544–45, pl. xxxvi.

[91] Romanos Lekapenos' coronation was on 17 December 920: Theoph. Cont., 397–98. Obviouly this must have been an opportune moment for him to act successfully, otherwise there are several important feast days in this time period that he could have chosen. Probably the most favored day to be crowned emperor in Byzantium, if one had the chance or privilege to choose a date, was Easter day.

Christ, that is, he has been placed on the more important side of Christ traditionally given to the Virgin (Fig. 13). It used to be said that since these objects were made for an emperor, that is, a male individual, prominence was given to John since he was the male figure of the Deesis. Johannes Koder has gone even further to suggest that at least in the Limburg Staurotheque we have possibly the figure of Constantine Porphyrogennetos himself in the guise of John the Baptist.[92] Now, however, I believe it becomes evident why Constantine Porphyrogennetos preferred John the Baptist for his personal intercession in prayer.

Constantine went even further: as mentioned above, he had the right arm of St. John, a relic barely remembered and in Arab hands, brought from Antioch to Constantinople in 956, even though it meant stealing it. The arrival of the relic on Epiphany was celebrated with great pomp and ceremony. Placed in a reliquary, it was brought to the palace (Fig. 7).[93] It was an important event for Constantinople but most specifically for the ruling Macedonian dynasty and Constantine in particular. He had already been on the throne ten years, and this must have been one of the most important religious events of his reign.[94] We shall recall that the other great relic, the holy cloth with the face of Christ, the Mandylion, had arrived in the city in 944 shortly before Constantine reestablished his rule and is to be credited to the reign of Romanos I Lekapenos.[95]

On the first anniversary of the relic's arrival, Theodore Daphnopates, a speech and letter writer of the emperor, was asked to write and deliver a commemorative speech in praise of John the Baptist's right arm.[96] This panegyrical speech has been preserved. It is a lengthy text that narrates the story of John to his beheading, emphasizing the moments

---

[92] Th. von Bogyay, "Deesis," *RBK,* I (1966), 1178–86; idem, "Deesis," *Lexikon der christlichen Ikonographie,* I (1968), 494–99. Koder, "Ὁ Κωνσταντίνος Πορφυρογέννητος καὶ ἡ σταυροθήκη τοῦ Λίμπουργκ," 165–84. There is in Berlin the center piece of an ivory Deesis triptych which also has John the Baptist on the right side of Christ. The left wing of this icon is in Verona and represents St. Alexios. St. Alexios in type and dress is close to the Prophet Elijah and John the Baptist, who incidentally in the Deesis compositions does not wear his tunic and mantle. This triptych in Berlin, which has a carving style different from the Palazzo Venezia Triptych (Goldschmidt and Weitzmann, *Elfenbeinskulpturen,* II, nos. 8 and 31), should be seen as one of the earliest pieces of the 10th century with a date after 906, the baptism of Constantine VII and his later sole rule (Kalavrezou, "A New Type of Icon," 386–89 note 19, 396). A possible reconstruction for the right triptych wing might be a plaque with the prophet Elijah, the other patron saint of the Macedonian dynasty. See above, notes 6, 86, and below, note 94.

[93] Daphnopates, ed. Latyshev, Δύο λόγοι, sections 17–18, pp. 31–32; for the discussion of the reliquary, see above, note 62.

[94] We should recall Basil I's efforts to establish the cult of the prophet Elijah in the palace and throughout the city, Elijah being his patron saint; see Theophanes Continuatus (Bonn, 1838), pp. 308, 319, 325, 329, 337; G. Moravcsik, "Sagen und Legenden über Kaiser Basileios I," *DOP* 15 (1961), 59–126; Kalavrezou, "Portraits," 22–24; Magdalino, "Basil I," 193–96.

[95] Skylitzes, ed. Thurn, 231–32.66–72.

[96] Theodore Daphnopates came as a young man in the service of the palace as imperial secretary sometime between 925 and 933. He served under Romanos I and seems to have continued his service under Constantine VII. He held the title of *protoasekretis.* Under Romanos II ca. 960 he was made eparch; see J. Darrouzès and L. G. Westerink, *Théodore Daphnopatès Correspondance* (Paris, 1978), 2–4. Not much is known about his life, but we can be certain that he could not have been Armenian or half-Armenian as Darrouzès and Westerink argue. Their contention is based on his command of the Armenian language drawn from letter 10, where he states: "we have received your letter, we have translated it from the Armenian into Greek; we have read and understood the content." Surely a native speaker would not need to translate a text before understanding it. Darrouzès and Westerink, op. cit., pp. 1–2.

when the hand acted in wisdom. Then we hear of his body, which had been buried at Sebaste, and the separation of his right arm, the miracles it performed, and how it had been forgotten until the great emperor Constantine brought it to Constantinople and deposited it in the palace.[97] From the text it is clear that the speech was delivered within a church where the relic was also present, but the church itself is not mentioned by name. I would like to believe that it was the church of the Virgin of the Pharos where the relic was kept and that the emperors who are mentioned in the text, Constantine and Romanos, were also present on that occasion.[98] The *Synaxarion of Constantinople* says that on the seventh of January, when the arm of John the Baptist is also commemorated, the *synaxis* takes place in the church of John in the Sphorakion (an area of Constantinople close to the Milion).[99] I do not see this statement as a contradiction of my position, since the text of the *Synaxarion* speaks of the annual celebration of the established feast in the city. The day Daphnopates gave his speech was a special one-time event. It was the occasion when, through official channels, the commemoration of this relic became established, and the secretary of the emperor was asked to present the argument for the importance of this arm relic for the empire and the emperor himself. It is a highly rhetorical text full of wordplay, especially on words such as φῶς and χείρ, similar to the way wordplays were made and meanings were suggested with the name of Stephanos.[100] I give here a somewhat pedestrian translation of the last section of this speech, where Daphnopates draws the relationship of the arm to the imperial family:[101]

Section 23.

But, oh Baptist, voice of the Logos, sun's dawn and seal of the law, origin of grace, protector and provider of every highest and heavenly gift, be present invisibly among us today, present through your miracle-working and holy hand appearing entire to the worthy, appearing fully visible to the pure of mind and being fully present at all times in this holy sanctuary. Bear witness to the faith of the most faithful emperor who trusts in you, measure the fervor of desire he has for you, behold with what festivals he welcomes you, with what displays of light he honors you, and with what high spiritual melodies and bright beaming torches he illuminates the entry of your hand.

[97] Daphnopates, ed. Latyshev, Δύο, λόγοι Greek text, pp. 17–38.

[98] These are Constantine VII and his son Romanos II; both emperors are mentioned by name once, and another time Constantine is mentioned alone: Daphnopates, ed. Latyshev, Δύο λόγοι, p. 29, section 15, and p. 31, section 17.

[99] *Synaxarium CP* 376. For 29 August, the day of John's beheading, the *Synaxarion* also says that the *synaxis* takes place in the church of John in the Sphorakion. We do know, however, that since the head was transferred to the Stoudios monastery in the 10th century, the *synaxis* took place there and the imperial court attended with great ceremony: *De cer.*, ed. Reiske, II, 13, pp. 562–63, Janin, *Églises et monastères*, 450, 456. For the date of the *Synaxarion* during the reign of Constantine VII Porphyrogennetos, see Ihor Ševčenko, "Re-reading Constantine Porphyrogenitus," in *Byzantine Diplomacy* (Aldershot, 1992), 188 and note 52. The text of the *Synaxarion* on the hand of St. John is based on the speech by Daphnopates, as is immediately recognizable in the choice and sequence of words and phrases, and thus it dates after 957 or close to it.

[100] For example, in section 22 toward the end of his speech he mentions the word φῶς (light) and its compounds eleven times within seven lines. Daphnopates, ed. Latyshev, Δύο λόγοι, p. 37.

[101] My thanks to those who helped me improve the translation of this highly rhetorical text: Sarolta Takacs, Paul Magdalino, and John Duffy.

Him (Constantine VII) whom from the womb you have protected by your mediations, him to whom you have granted imperial rule as a paternal inheritance (reference to his legitimation on Epiphany 906), and whom you do not fail to make ever more victorious with the trophies and the victories over his enemies, this man we beseech you to be blessed with Christian perfection for the long passage of time, and that you grant both those born and those still to be born from the fruit of the womb of his line, that they sit now and in the future on the throne of the empire (of kingship).

And may you bestow on us to be ruled well by them and that we maintain our service and obedience pure, that we may lead a peaceful and quiet life, glorifying him through whom emperors rule and through whom every man coming to this world is enlightened (baptized); for he is the enlightenment and the mercy of mankind, and to him is especially due glory, honor, and worship together with the One without beginning and *homoousios* Father and the likewise without beginning and coeternal Holy Spirit, now and for the ages of ages. Amen.[102]

These concluding paragraphs make clear the association of the relic of John the Baptist with the well-being of the empire and its ruling dynasty, not only for that day but also for the generations to come. John the Baptist is the intercessor to the One through whom emperors rule and the provider and bestower of that heavenly gift, the power to rule, to the emperors.

I believe that Constantine VII, by transferring the relic to the city and more directly into the palace, acted much like Pulcheria in the fifth century in securing his dynasty on the throne. Already under Basil I, his grandfather, great efforts were undertaken to establish the place of the new emperor on the throne as a legitimate ruler by turning to propagandistic stories of prophecies concerning his predestined role and by associating himself with the prophet Elijah.[103] Constantine saw to it that, whatever theoretical or ideological structure and imagery had developed since Basil, physical proof was provided for its justification. Now the arm and hand of John were physically present in the palace itself, in the hands of the Byzantine emperor. It functioned much like the arm of St. Stephen in earlier centuries, as an instrument of power, investiture, and leadership, guaranteeing political authority and divine approval to the one who possessed it.[104]

Constantine also solidified what were perceivable changes concerning the place and role of the imperial figures in Byzantine political and cultural ideology, that is, their place as rulers in relation to God on the one hand and to their subjects on the other. One critical shift had occurred in the role or representation of the emperor as the divinely chosen individual to rule God's empire on earth. This shift from the emperor as an apostlelike figure of the early centuries of Byzantium—a concept that went back to Constantine the Great—to the Christlike figure of the tenth century took centuries to develop and institute itself, but by this period it was well established; one only needs

---

[102] Daphnopates, ed. Latyshev, Δύο λόγοι, p. 38, section 23.

[103] See note 36 above.

[104] The reliquary box that is recorded to have arrived in Citeaux had an inscription that represented Constantine's opinion on the relic's function and importance; see note 62 above.

to look at the acclamations to the emperor in the *Book of Ceremonies*. These two different notions of the role of the emperor are manifested in the two arm relics discussed in this paper. Each clearly served the needs and ideologies of its time, five hundred years apart.

This study focused on two relics that had ritualistic presence at important ceremonial moments at the court and on the nexus between the two arm relics and imperial ceremony.[105] It also pointed out the making of imperial images and concepts and the subtle and indirect visual language that developed alongside the political needs and that left its mark in the artistic production of Byzantine images. These are some of the symbols with which the Byzantine court operated. The two arm relics, through their presence and association with the emperor and the court, provided directives and "support" in the developing concepts of the emperor as the ruler of a Christian empire.

Harvard University

[105] Another important relic at the court, for which I am preparing a separate publication, was the staff or rod of Moses. It has to be seen as the Ur-relic, and the Byzantines treated it as such. I recently discovered that it is not lost, as previously assumed, and is today in the Topkapi Museum in the holy treasury together with relics such as the mantle of Mohammed.

Court Culture and Cult Icons in Middle Byzantine Constantinople

Annemarie Weyl Carr

Constantin Stanislavsky's production of *Hamlet* in 1911 at the Moscow Arts Theatre presented the court engulfed in a single, vast cloth-of-gold mantle, falling from Claudius' shoulders over the entire assembly, whose heads emerged from holes in its flood of gold.[1] Gripping as it is, Stanislavsky's conceit sits oddly on Shakespeare's shoulders, a reminder of the degree to which our conceptions of courts are molded by our own vantage points. The Dumbarton Oaks symposium on the Byzantine court invited us to unpack our preconceptions of this court. This paper treats icons and the Byzantine court, a subject shaped for us by Byzantinists who grew up in the empires of the early twentieth century. André Grabar wrote of it:[2]

> C'était l'Empire d'*Orient* dans le vrai sens du mot, où le latin avait justement cessé d'être la langue officielle de la chancellerie impériale, qui venait d'abandonner l'organisation romaine de l'administration des provinces et où les empereurs ayant pris le titre officiel de *basileus,* faisaient une politique "orientale", tandis que les influences de l'Orient s'accentuaient dans les différents domaines de la civilisation byzantine; l'Empire *orthodoxe* qui, pour la première fois au VIIIe siècle, introduisait des passages de la Bible dans la rédaction de ses lois et où les empereurs vouaient un culte officiel empressé aux reliques et aux icones miraculeuses, en faisant de la Sainte Croix, du *Mandylion* et d'une image de la Vierge comme des *palladia* de l'Empire.

Grabar here conjures up a court consolidated around symbols of power that took the form of icons. As they were courtly images, membership of their cults presumably defined membership of the court, and like Old Glory they represented the "republic"— or in this case the court—"for which they stood." Certainly this paradigm has shaped the way in which we have constructed the stories of the great politically laden icons of post-Byzantine history. The Vladimirskaya has been seen as the "dynastic icon" of the

---

[1] Constantin Stanislavsky, *My Life in Art* (Boston, 1927), 514–15. It was designed by Gordon Craig during a winter in Rome.

[2] André Grabar, *L'empereur dans l'art byzantin* (Strasbourg, 1936), 164–65.

Kievan court, its presence standing for the state it defended.[3] Hans Belting has conjured up the ceremonies of the Mesopanditissa in Venice as imitating the Byzantine ones, with the doge playing the role of the emperor.[4] The nationalistic charge carried by Cyprus' Kykkotissa has been projected deep into the island's history, casting her as a gift from the Constantinopolitan emperor that carried with it allegiance to the Greek and Orthodox court for which it stood.[5]

But is this paradigm a Byzantine one? Is it a Middle Byzantine one? That someone arriving in Constantinople from afar—as we do—should view the Byzantine court in terms of sacred objects is readily explained, for the court used these objects to present its city as a Hagiopolis, a New Jerusalem. The relics in the Great Palace are presented as a virtual Holy Land pilgrimage by Nicholas Mesarites, who falls into his cicerone's script as he inventories the items in the wake of John the Fat's palace revolution, making of them a reenactive passage through the events of the Gospel story.[6] The anonymous English pilgrim of the early twelfth century opens his description of the imperial city inside the Great Palace in front of these objects, especially the Mandylion, and as he proceeds, the city's topography opens out along the paths of icon processions honoring miracle-working images of the Mother of God.[7] In war, too, the Byzantine standards carried images of Christ, the archangels, and the Mother of God.[8] But if we approach the city from the inside and ask how the court defined itself vis-à-vis the other groups in the city, icons assume a different and more differentiated role.

Icons, for the purposes of this paper, are portable devotional panels. This is less an artistic than a functional definition.[9] Rather than aesthetic dimensions of icons, it is their

---

[3] See particularly pointedly Konrad Onasch, "Die Ikone der Gottesmutter von Vladimir," *OKS* 5 (1956), 56–66.

[4] Hans Belting, *Bild und Kult: Eine Geschichte des Bildes vor dem Zeitalter der Kunst* (Munich, 1990), 228–29.

[5] I am preparing a study of this icon; meanwhile see George Soteriou, Ἡ Κυκκιώτισσα, *Νέα Ἑστία* (Christmas 1939), 3–6.

[6] Franz Grabler, *Die Kreuzfahrer erobern Konstantinopel,* Byzantinische Geschichtsschreiber 9 (Graz, 1958), 287–90.

[7] Krijnie N. Ciggaar, "Une description de Constantinople traduite par un pèlerin anglais," *REB* 34 (1976), 211–68. Though R. Janin dates this account to the 1190s, Ciggaar (212–27) argues that the text was written in the early 12th century on the basis of an earlier Byzantine pilgrim guide from the last decade of the 11th century.

[8] J. F. Haldon, *Constantine Porphyrogenitus: Three Treatises on Imperial Military Expeditions,* CFHB 28 (Vienna, 1990), 272, 274. Niketas Choniates includes in his description of John II's triumph in 1136 "images of Christ and the saints fashioned by the weaver's hand"—presumably standards bearing the image of Christ. That these were understood as sacred images is indicated by his report that the clergy assigned the earthquake during Manuel I's triumph of 1161 to divine retribution for Manuel's having permitted his Muslim brother-in-law, Alexios Axouch, to "show himself and participate in a triumph embellished by the likenesses of the saints and sanctified by the image of Christ." See Jan-Louis van Dieten, ed., *Nicetae Choniatae Historia,* 2 vols., CFHB 11 (Berlin, 1975), 18.80–84, 119.47–52 (translations from Nicetas Choniates, *O City of Byzantium,* trans. Harry Magoulias [Detroit, 1984], 12, 67).

[9] While I am perfectly sure that the court circle had developed—by the mid-11th century at least—an attitude that deplored piety devoid of aesthetic taste, and created an aesthetic and eventually stylistic boundary around itself, I have not been able in any meaningful way to use such boundaries to define who belonged to the court and how. As evidence of the attitude I cite, see Michael Psellos' acute pleasure in icons as objects of aesthetic—indeed, synaesthetic—response (Alexander P. Kazhdan and Ann Wharton Epstein, *Change in Byzantine Culture in the Eleventh and Twelfth Centuries* [Berkeley, 1985], 199; Elizabeth A. Fisher, "Image and Ekphrasis in Michael Psellos," *Byzantinoslavica* 55.1 [1994], 44–55), but his disgust with Empress Zoe's showy devotional response to her icon of Christ Antiphonites (Emile Renauld, ed. and trans, *Michel Psellos. Chronographie ou histoire*

functions that are at issue here: who used particular kinds of icons and how. The quest is to find icons whose use defined the Byzantine court.

Portable devotional panels obviously existed at court—the Madrid Skylitzes includes miniatures of Theophilos' five daughters learning icon veneration from their grand-mother, Theopiste, and of Leo VI venerating an icon of Christ (Figs. 1, 2)[10]—and icon stories surface in many histories. Basil I laid before an icon of the Virgin a challenge from the emir of Tarsus, thus sanctifying his hostile response to it.[11] Leo VI's wife, Zoe, became pregnant after encircling her body with a cord that had been measured around the perimeter of an icon of the Virgin at the church of the Pege.[12] Nikephoros II Phokas was murdered as he slept on a panther skin in his closet before icons of Christ, the Mother of God, and John the Baptist.[13] Romanos III dissolved in tears when he found his icon of Mary unharmed in the debris of defeat.[14] Empress Zoe adored her dichroic icon of Christ Antiphonites.[15] Anna Dalassena, facing partisan judges, whipped an icon of Christ from under her robes and confronted them with it.[16] Her son Alexios I was cured of serious illness by being covered with the veil that hung before the icon of the Christ Chalkites.[17] Andronikos I had a favored icon of Paul that wept as his end ap-

---

d'un siècle de Byzance (976–1077), 2 vols. [Paris, 1926], I, 194.xvi, 1–18; E.R.A. Sewter, trans., *Fourteen Byzantine Rulers: The* Chronographia *of Michael Psellus* [Harmondsworth, 1953], 188). Or see John Tzetzes' complaint that "the chains and fetters of bogus holy men were more highly prized in aristocratic chapels than 'icons of saintly men by the hand of some first-rate artist' " (quoted from Paul Magdalino, *The Empire of Manuel I Komnenos, 1143–1180* [Cambridge, 1993], 397).

[10] André Grabar and M. Manoussacas, *L'illustration du manuscrit de Skylitzès de la Bibliothèque nationale de Madrid*, Bibliothèque de l'Institut hellénique d'études byzantines et post-byzantines de Venise 10 (Venice, 1979), fol. 44v, pl. xi; fol. 115v, fig. 142.

[11] Immanuel Bekker, *Theophanes Continuatus* (Bonn, 1838), 285; Leopold Breyer, trans., *Von Bauernhof auf den Kaiserthron: Leben des Kaisers Basileios I., beschrieben von seinem Enkel, dem Kaiser Konstantinos VII. Porphyrogennetos*, Byzantinische Geschichtsschreiber 14 (Graz, 1981), 98 P50.

[12] "Anonymous Miracula of Theotokos tes Peges," *ActaSS*, November III, 885E. For this reference, as for so many things, I am indebted to Alice-Mary Talbot.

[13] Charles Benedict Hasius, ed., *Leonis Diaconi Caloënsis Historiae libri decem* (Bonn, 1828), 86.20–24; Franz Loretto, trans., *Leon Diakonos, Nikephoros Phokas "Der bleiche Tod der Sarazenen" und Johannes Tzimiskes*, Byzantinische Geschichtsschreiber 10 (Graz, 1961), 83.

[14] Renauld, *Michel Psellos*, I, 39.x, 21–27; Sewter, *Fourteen Byzantine Rulers*, 69–70.

[15] See note 9 above.

[16] Nikephoros Bryennios, *Nicéphore Bryennios Histoire*, ed. and trans. Paul Gautier, CFHB 9 (Brussels, 1975), 130–31.5–10. Icons appear recurrently in judicial contexts. It was in conjunction with an effort to settle a legal battle by referring it to an icon that Michael Psellos wrote his description of the "usual miracle" at Blachernai (Venance Grumel, "Le 'miracle habituel' de Notre-Dame des Blachernes," *EO* 34 [1931], 129–46); Michael Atta-leiates' reference to the Blachernitissa in Romanos IV's camp occurs in conjunction with his narrative of a judg-ment passed by the emperor (Immanuel Bekker, ed., *Michael Attaleiota*, CSHB 50 [Bonn, 1853], 153); Alexios I Komnenos seems to have placed an admonitory picture of the Last Judgment in a hall where one of the judicial tribunals sat and could see it (Paul Magdalino and Robert Nelson, "The Emperor in Byzantine Art of the Twelfth Century," *ByzF* 8 [1982], 125).

[17] B. G. Niebuhr, gen. ed., *Ioannis Zonarae Epitomae Historiarum*, 3 vols., CSHB (Bonn, 1897), vol. III, ed. Theodor Büttner-Wobst, 751.9–15; Erich Trapp, trans., *Johannes Zonaras. Militärs und Höflinge im Ringen um das Kaisertum: Byzantinische Geschichte von 969 bis 1118 nach der Chronik des Johannes Zonaras*, Byzantinische Ge-schichtsschreiber 16 (Graz, 1986), 173. Later Alexios, the son of Andronikos the *sebastokrator* and Irene *sebasto-kratorissa*, was similarly healed by the veil of the Christ Chalkites: Valerie Nunn, "The Encheirion as Adjunct to the Icon in the Middle Byzantine Period," *BMGS* 10 (1986), 85. Just what icon this was is ambiguous. Choni-ates (van Dieten, ed., *Nicetae Choniatae Historia*, 332.15–18) says of Emperor Andronikos I: "The icon of our Savior Christ, through which, it is reported, Christ spoke so long ago with the Emperor Maurice, he covered over with precious adornment" (trans. Magoulias, *O City of Byzantium*, 183). The story of Maurice was linked

1   Madrid, Biblioteca Nacional, vitr. 26–2, fol. 44v. The five daughters of Theophilos and Theophano learning about icons from their grandmother, Theopiste

2   Madrid, Biblioteca Nacional, vitr. 26–2, fol. 114r. Leo VI with an icon of the Mother of God

3   Madrid, Biblioteca Nacional, vitr. 26–2, fol. 12v. Leo V proclaimed emperor

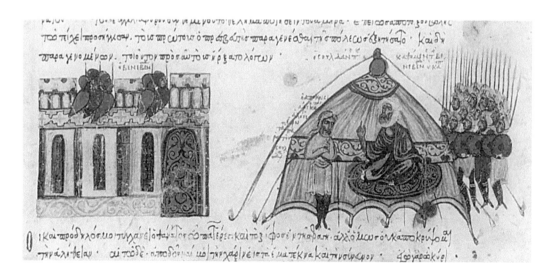

4   Madrid, Biblioteca Nacional, vitr. 26–2, fol. 97r. Emir Souldan before the town of Capua

5 Washington, D.C., Dumbarton Oaks.
Gold histamenon of Michael IV

6 Washington, D.C., Dumbarton Oaks.
Gold hyperpyron of Manuel I
(photo: Whittemore Collection)

7 Moscow, State Pushkin Museum of
Fine Arts. Ivory plaque with
Constantine VII and Christ
(photo: Dumbarton Oaks)

8 Madrid, Biblioteca Nacional, vitr. 26–2, fol. 114v. Coronation of Constantine VII

9   Vatican, gr. 666, fol. 1v. Church fathers presenting their writings
(photo: Biblioteca Apostolica Vaticana)

10 Vatican, gr. 666, fol. 2r. Emperor (Alexios I?) receiving the writings of the church fathers (photo: Biblioteca Apostolica Vaticana)

11 Venice, Biblioteca Marciana, gr. Z 540, fol. 12v. Christ receiving the evangelists' Gospels

12 Vatican, gr. 666, fol. 2v. Emperor presenting *Panoplia Dogmatica* to Christ
(photo: Biblioteca Apostolica Vaticana)

13   Washington, D.C., Dumbarton Oaks.
Silver miliaresion of Basil II
(photo: Whittemore Collection)

14   Washington, D.C., Dumbarton Oaks.
Silver two-thirds miliaresion of
Constantine IX with the Mother of God
Blachernitissa

15   Bern, Zacos Collection. Lead seal of John,
πρωτοπρόεδρος καὶ ἐπὶ τῆς βασιλικῆς
σακέλλες, with the Mother of God Blachernitissa
(after Zacos, *Byzantine Lead Seals,* II, no. 522)

16 Vienna, Kunsthistorisches Museum. Münzkabinett. Lead seal of Nicholas Skleros, πρωτοπρόεδρος μεγάλος σκευοφύλακι τῶν Βλαχερνῶν καὶ πρῶτος τῆς πρεσβείας, with the Mother of God Hodegetria

17 Bern, Zacos Collection. Lead seal of the Monastery of the Hodegon (after Zacos, *Byzantine Lead Seals,* II, no. 765)

18 Bern, Zacos Collection. Lead seal of Michael VIII showing him holding icon of the Mother of God (after Zacos and Veglery, *Byzantine Lead Seals,* I.3, no. 2756 bis)

proached.[18] Isaac II Angelos collected icons in great numbers and adorned them extrava-
gantly, installing many richly sheathed panels of Mary in the more heavily frequented
churches of the capital.[19]

Some of these stories treat public icons; others were private. Consistently, however,
the contexts of the events are personal. The episodes multiply as the historical narratives
themselves become more personally specific. One suspects that these stories differed
little from icons' intervention in the lives of more ordinary folk. The courtly chroniclers
who tell them often color them, in fact, with a thinly veiled disgust as reflections of
popular credulity. Nonetheless, it is courtiers like Psellos and Choniates who tell them,
and the stories serve a purpose in their narratives. They displace the emperors to the
supernatural realm of fatal events in which great deeds and deep inadequacies stand out
starkly and the rulers' often horrible ends assume an aura of fatality. What the stories do
not in any case exhibit is an icon that interacts with an emperor as a symbol of the state.
No icon summons an emperor to his duties, clarifies his insight as a ruler, urges him on
to enlightened judgment, or confirms his right to office by a miraculous gesture. No
icon, in short, functions as a symbol for the state.

The icon stories serve to assimilate the emperors to the realm of the sacred and supernatural. This is something that imperial art and rhetoric had been doing consistently.
Visually, the image-language of icons was a basic instrument of imperial art. No one
reading the Madrid Skylitzes could fail to see that the Greek emperor sat as Christ sat,
while the Arabic emir sat quite outside the Christian order (Figs. 3, 4).[20] Currency
presented the emperor and Christ as two sides of the same coin. In contrast to verbal
rhetoric, however, which assimilated the emperor to sacred figures, especially Christ,
visual rhetoric never showed the emperor as Christ. In the case of coins, their costumes
and faces are distinct, and a Hand of God above Michael IV in Figure 5 demonstrates a
process not of identification but of transmission.[21] The distinction is especially clear in
the case of Manuel I: "my Christ" to his panegyrists,[22] he is clearly not Christ on his
coins (Fig. 6). The pun on his name, Emmanuel, is left to the realm of words. Rather

---

after Iconoclasm to the icon placed on the Chalke gate. An icon placed outdoors would scarcely be swathed in
veils of precious fabric like those in the stories of Alexios I and his later homonym, however, and Cyril Mango
has suggested that the icon in question was one inside the church of Christ at the Chalke gate: *The Brazen House:
A Study of the Vestibule of the Imperial Palace of Constantinople* (Copenhagen, 1959), 133. It may well be that this is
the same icon cited in Andronikos I's case: an outdoor icon is equally unlikely to have been sheathed in gems
and gold. The identity of the icon gifted by Andronikos is of interest because Choniates' association of it with
Maurice suggests that it had a particular bond with the emperors and so approached the status of a "court icon."

[18] Van Dieten, ed., *Nicetae Choniatae Historia*, 353.11–14; Magoulias, trans., *O City of Byzantium*, 194.

[19] Van Dieten, ed., *Nicetae Choniatae Historia*, 444.14–18; Magoulias, trans., *O City of Byzantium*, 244.

[20] Grabar and Manoussacas, *L'illustration*, fols. 12v, 97r, pls. II, XVI.

[21] Philip Grierson, *Catalogue of the Byzantine Coins in the Dumbarton Oaks Collection and in the Whittemore Collection*, 3: *Leo III to Nicephorus III, 717–1081*, 2: *Basil I to Nicephorus III (867–1081)* (Washington, D.C., 1973), 724,
pl. LVII, 1.a.3–1f.

[22] On the panegyrists of Manuel, see especially Magdalino, *The Empire*, chap. 6 and passim; Wolfram Hörandner, *Theodorus Prodromos. Historische Gedichte*, Wiener byzantinische Studien 11 (Vienna, 1974), especially poems
30 and 31 on Manuel's triumphs. Verbally, the Komnenian emperors were compared not only to Christ but to
Christ's icons, icons that emitted wondrous corporal effluvia: Magdalino, 433, quoting Nikephoros Basilakes;
Hörandner, poem 11.

than by assimilation, visual rhetoric operated by association: the emperor was shown with Christ, or interacting with sacred figures in any of a range of substitution devices.[23]

The most usual of the substitution devices entailed replacing the people around the emperor with sacred figures. Grabar has paralleled the ivory image of Constantine VII being crowned by Christ with the miniature of the patriarch crowning him in the Madrid Skylitzes (Figs. 7, 8).[24] This is not to say that the ivory therefore records the event of Constantine's coronation, but rather that it presents Constantine as crowned by divine rather than human agency. The human patriarch becomes invisible, and it is Christ himself who interacts with the ruler.[25]

A viewer conversant in turn with pages like those in Venice, Marciana Z 540 (see Fig. 11), or Vatican, gr. 756, showing Christ receiving the writings of the evangelists, might link him visually with the emperor in the frontispieces of the *Panoplia Dogmatica*, who is receiving the writings of the assembled church fathers (Figs. 9, 10).[26] Here, however, Christ is included in an arc above the emperor, precluding the direct substitution of the emperor for Christ. On the following page, then, the two appear together (Fig. 12). In contrast to Constantine's ivory, where Constantine is clearly himself and Christ acts a role, translating the human activities around the emperor into divine ones, here in the *Panoplia Dogmatica* it is Christ who is himself, while the emperor is elevated to the role of a rather uppity sacred father in his heavenly court.

A similar effect may have been achieved in military parades, for the imperial standards were painted with images of holy figures and surrounded the emperor with a sacred army, a heavenly host.[27] Certainly the most literal of the substitution devices occurred in the triumphs of John II and Manuel I Komnenos, when an icon of Mary replaced the emperor in his triumphal chariot.[28]

Like the icon stories, the substitution devices have the effect of elevating the emperor

---

[23] For a more subtle analysis of this phenomenon, see Henry Maguire's paper in this volume.

[24] Grabar, *L'empereur*, 117, pl. xxvii, 2.

[25] This image could be variously exploited, as is illustrated in the *Epanagogues* attributed to Patriarch Photios, where the patriarch is exalted over the emperor by being cast in the role of Christ: Paul Magdalino, "The Bath of Leo the Wise and the 'Macedonian Renaissance' Revisited: Topography, Iconography, Ceremonial, Ideology," *DOP* 42 (1988), 114.

[26] On the identity of the emperor in the portraits prefacing Vatican, gr. 666, see Magdalino and Nelson, "The Emperor," 149–51. For Vatican, gr. 756, see Hugo Buchthal, *Miniature Painting in the Latin Kingdom of Jerusalem* (Oxford, 1957), pls. 142a, b.

[27] On the standards with holy figures, see note 8 above. It is surely significant in this context that the word σίγνον was used for both military standards and processional icons. On this word, see Nancy Patterson Ševčenko, "Icons in the Liturgy," *DOP* 45 (1991), 46 note 7; Haldon, *Constantine Porphyrogenitus*, 271–72.

[28] Van Dieten, ed., *Nicetae Choniatae Historia*, 19.80–84, 158.66–72; Magoulias, trans., *O City of Byzantium*, 12, 90; Hörandner, *Theodoros Prodromos*, poems 3, 6, 31, 32. As Hörandner, 196, points out, in his description of John II's triumph, Theodore Prodromos plays upon the precedent offered by the previous emperor John, John I Tzimiskes, who was offered wreaths and a chariot with white horses by the Senate and demarchs of Constantinople when he returned in triumph from Bulgaria, but who loaded the chariot with Bulgarian booty surmounted by an icon of the Mother of God, instead, and followed it on a white horse (Niebuhr, ed., *Ioannis Zonarae Epitomae*, vol. III, 535.12–536.1; Trapp, trans., *Johannes Zonaras*, 40). Prodromos nowhere says what icon was in John II's chariot; John I's icon is equally elusive. Belting's conclusion, *Bild und Kult*, 209, that it was a Bulgarian icon taken as booty is not clearly indicated in Zonaras' text. The association of the icon with the booty does, nonetheless, distinguish it from the Komnenian emperors' icon of the Virgin, which clearly appeared in their stead as the head of the army.

to a sacred and extraordinary realm. This occurred not only in imagery but also in affect. There is fair evidence that imperial images had a charismatic power of their own. One sees this in the power that portraits of the emperor were expected to exercise, bringing his presence to the very ends of his domain;[29] one sees it in the frequent appearance of portraits of the Komnenoi over portals, a characteristic place for apotropaic images.[30]

This said, however, only one imperial icon is known actually to have been assimilated to the rank of a holy image with a liturgically realized ritual of veneration. This is the image of Basil I in the women's side of the Nea Ekklesia.[31] Its ritual veneration seems to have been short-lived, and its cult in essence failed. Thus we see that the relation of the imperial and the sacred was accomplished not through actual sanctification but through iconic substitution devices. The assimilation was—and was understood to be—rhetorical.

The rhetoric yields two insights. First, it curtails the depiction of the emperor together with his own court. Images like that of Michael VII in Paris, Bibliothèque Nationale, Coislin 79 showing the emperor with human courtiers are, in fact, notably rare.[32] Displaced by sacred actors or abandoned in favor of the court of heaven, the courtiers of Byzantium are conspicuously absent in imperial art. This suggests that this art was created as a tool for use within the court, stating the emperor's authority in the face of the court. It spoke to the court: the court was the audience, not the subject, of state portraits. The emperor imaged the state.

In the second place, such images are intriguing for us in that they almost never show the emperor with an identifiable icon. They show him with Christ or Mary and saints themselves. Ordinary people might appear in paintings in the company of icons, as Theodore Gabras and his wife, Irene Gabraba, do in the dedicatory miniatures of St. Petersburg, Public Library, gr. 291, where they stand outside the frames containing the figures of Christ and Mary to whom they relate.[33] But emperors did not. Their contact with the realm of the sacred was imaged as being immediate. The mediation of icons was not part of this rhetoric. Until the Interregnum period, when the Laskarid emperors Theodore I and John III Vatatzes depicted themselves on the reverse of coins and seals showing on their obverse the Christ Chalkites,[34] only two equivocal cases present themselves

---

[29] See Euthemios Malakes comparing the image of the emperor to that of Christ, quoted by Henry Maguire, "The Mosaics of Nea Moni: An Imperial Reading," *DOP* 46 (1992), 208: "in the same way, my emperor, the imitation of my Christ, is one and [yet] shared over all the earth."

[30] See Magdalino and Nelson, "The Emperor," 135–36.

[31] Constantina Mentzou-Meimare, "Ο Αυτοκράτωρ Βασίλειος Α΄ και η Νέα Εκκλησία: Αυτοκρατορική ιδεολογία και εικονογραφία," *Βυζαντιακά* 13 (1993), 47–94. I find it hard to agree that this was a portable icon. Mentzou-Meimare does not inquire into the significance of the icon's being on the women's side of the church; on gendered spaces see William C. Young, "The Ka'ba, Gender, and the Rites of Pilgrimage," *International Journal of Middle Eastern Studies* 25 (1993), 285–300.

[32] Fol. 2r. See Ioannes Spatharakis, *The Portrait in Byzantine Illuminated Manuscripts* (Leiden, 1976), 107–18, fig. 71. The miniature is reproduced in color in the *Encyclopedia of World Art*, rev. ed. (New York, 1972), vol. II, pl. 489, s.v. Byzantine art. Another example would be the scene of John VI Kantakouzenos at the Council of 1351 in Paris, B.N., gr. 1242, fol. 5v: *Byzance: L'art byzantin dans les collections publiques françaises* (exh. cat., Musée du Louvre, Paris, 1992), 419, where lay figures cluster behind the clerics.

[33] Spatharakis, *The Portrait*, 59–60, 244, pls. 27–28.

[34] Philip Grierson, *Byzantine Coins* (London, 1982), 241–42, 253, 332, nos. 1150, 1151, pl. 69 (Theodore I Laskaris); Mango, *The Brazen House*, 136–37, fig. 21 (John III Vatatzes).

in which emperors are portrayed with an actual icon. There is the icon on Mount Sinai in which Constantine VII assumes the role of Abgar carrying the Mandylion;[35] and there are rare coin issues of the mid-eleventh century showing rulers on the reverse and Mary on the obverse with the toponymic Blachernitissa, possibly indicating a particular icon (see Fig. 14).[36] Their rarity seems to prove the rule. Emperors might stand with crosses and flags; they did not stand with symbols of their state or court that took the form of icons.

The absence of icons in imperial images may merely be a matter of genre: something that visual art did not do or that we do not recognize. One turns, accordingly, to the descriptions of imperial ceremonial, to watch how icons function in the rituals of state.

Constantine VII's *Book of Ceremonies* does, indeed, cite several icons: there is the cluster of icons in the bath at Blachernai; there is the enameled icon of Mary at the church of St. Demetrios; there is the icon of Basil I in the Nea; and Hans Georg Thümmel points out that reference to the Abraamite monastery near the Golden Gate as the monastery of the Acheiropoietos implicitly recognizes that monastery's miraculous icon.[37] But these are the only ones. The great name icons are missing: the Hodegetria, the Blachernitissa, the Hagiosoritissa, the Christ Antiphonites, the Christ Chalkites. Moreover, the ones that are cited figure almost purely chorographically, as place-markers in the rituals. They are neither the goal of the processions nor the focus of the ceremonies; at most, as in the icons of the Virgin at Blachernai and of Basil I at the Nea, the emperor lights a candle as he makes his way past them.[38] By the same token, it is clear that no icon played a role in the marriage, coronation, or burial ceremonies of the emperors. When Theophanes Continuatus spoke of Michael III's destroying the things that most gave distinction to the court of Constantinople, he listed not icons but secular objects: golden trees, lions, griffins, and the golden organ.[39]

---

[35] Kurt Weitzmann, *The Monastery of Saint Catherine at Mount Sinai. The Icons*, I: *From the Sixth to the Tenth Century* (Princeton, 1976), 94–98, no. B58, pls. xxxvi–xxxvii, xliii–xlvi; idem, "The Mandylion and Constantine Porphyrogenitus," *CahArch* 11 (1960), 163–84. There are, of course, generic images of the emperor with icons of the Virgin in the representations of the Akathistos and the Feast of Orthodoxy: see Ševčenko, "Icons in the Liturgy," pls. 8, 9.

[36] Grierson, *Catalogue* (as in note 21 above), 747, pl. lix, 8.a.1 (two-thirds miliaresion of Constantine IX with orante Virgin *en buste*) and 8.a.5 (the same with Mary flanked by globules); 753, pl. lxii, AR 3 (two-thirds miliaresion of Theodora with orante Virgin); 758, pl. lxii, AR 3 (the same, of Michael VI); David R. Sear, *Byzantine Coins and Their Value*, 2d ed. (London, 1987), 356, no. 1834 (silver miliaresion of Constantine IX with standing orante Virgin).

[37] See Hans Georg Thümmel, "Kreuze, Reliquien und Bilder im Zeremonienbuch des Konstantinos Porphyrogennetos," *ByzF* 18 (1992), 125 and passim; Albert Vogt, trans., *Constantine VII Porphyrogénète. Le livre des cérémonies*, 2d ed., 2 vols. in 4 pts. (Paris, 1967), vol. I, pp. 109, 112 (Basil I's icon), 158 (enamel icon); Constantinus Porphyrogenitus, *De cerimoniis aulae byzantinae*, PG 112:1021 (bath at Blachernai). On the icon at the Abraamite monastery, see note 41 below.

[38] Thus on the feast of Elijah (Vogt, trans., *Constantine VII*, vol. I, p. 109) and again on the anniversary of the dedication of the Nea (ibid., 112): Καὶ διερχόμενοι διὰ τοῦ αὐτοῦ γυναικίτου, ἅπτουσι κηροὺς εἰς τὴν εἰκόνα Βασιλείου, τοῦ φιλοχρίστου Δεσπότου, καὶ εὐθέως ἀποχαιρετίζοντες τὸν πατριάρχην, εἰσέρχονται ἐν τῷ ἐκεῖσε προσευχαδίῳ. . . . Or again at the bath at Blachernai (PG 112:1021): καὶ ἐξέρχονται τοῦ βήματος, καὶ ἀπέρχονται ἀπὸ δεξιᾶς εἰς τὴν ἐπίσκεψιν, καὶ ἅπτουσιν κἀκεῖσε κηροὺς καὶ προσκυνοῦσιν. Καὶ ἀπὸ τῶν ἐκεῖσε ἀπέρχονται ἔξω τοῦ μητατωρικίου, ἐν ᾧ ἡ εἰκὼν τῆς Θεοτόκου καὶ ὁ ἀργυροῦς ἵδρυται σταυρός, καὶ ἅπτουσιν κἀκεῖσε κηροὺς, καὶ εἰσέρχονται εἰς τὸ μητατώριον.

[39] Ioannes Thurn, ed., *Ioannis Scylitzae Synopsis Historiarum*, CFHB 5 (Berlin, 1973), 111.73–77; Hans Thurn, trans., *Byzanz wieder ein Weltreich*, Byzantinische Geschichtsschreiber 15 (Graz, 1983), 131.

Thümmel suggested that icons do not figure in Constantine VII's *Book of Ceremonies* because the icon cults of Constantinople were not yet developed.[40] But this cannot be the whole truth. Not only were many cults well attested by the mid-tenth century,[41] but the same dearth of icons characterizes the Palaiologan ceremonies described by Pseudo-Kodinos.[42] Apparently icons—and above all the great cult icons—did not find a place in the court ceremonies. Rather than in the fragility of the icons' cults, an explanation for their absence must be sought in the ceremonies themselves and the things they were designed to accomplish. Both Averil Cameron and Paul Magdalino have concluded that the ceremonies were designed as a way of defining and consolidating the court as an enclave around the emperor.[43] If this is so, if the ceremonies were essentially about the court, then it becomes apparent that icons were not among the means by which emperor and court negotiated their relationship.

This would seem to be confirmed by the great icons that did get swept into courtly settings. One after another, they vanish.[44] This is shown above all by the Mandylion.[45] The Mandylion was brought to Constantinople with tremendous fanfare by Romanos I and celebrated a year later by Constantine VII with an anniversary sermon that still survives.[46] Yet it is mentioned only once—in a scholion—in the *Book of Ceremonies*,[47] and it vanishes with astonishing promptitude from all imperial activities. Basil II used on a coin the inscription that Constantine VII recorded as being on the Mandylion's case (Fig. 13), but he associated it with an image of the Virgin rather than with the Mandylion.[48] The object surfaces again—under the name of "Mandylion" for the first time—in Kedrenos' account of the reign of Zoe and Michael IV, but now thoroughly

[40] Thümmel, "Kreuze, Reliquien und Bilder," 120.

[41] One can cite the cult at the church of the Virgin Pege, to which Zoe Karbonopsina had recourse (see note 12 above). Likewise, the Abraamite church, where both Basil I and Nikephoros II Phokas made a station on their triumphal entries into the capital, was distinguished by its icon: Raymond Janin, *La géographie ecclésiastique de l'Empire byzantin*, I: *Le siège de Constantinople et le patriarchat oecuménique*, 3: *Les églises et les monastères* (Paris, 1969), 4–6; Michael McCormick, *Eternal Victory: Triumphal Rulership in Late Antiquity, Byzantium, and the Early Medieval West* (Cambridge, 1986), 155–56.

[42] Jean Verpeaux, ed., *Pseudo-Kodinos, Traité des offices* (Paris, 1966).

[43] Averil Cameron, "The Construction of Court Ritual: The Byzantine *Book of Ceremonies*," in *Rituals of Royalty: Power and Ceremonial in Traditional Societies*, ed. David Cannadine and Simon Price (New York-London, 1987), 106–36; Paul Magdalino, "Basil I, Leo VI, and the Feast of the Prophet Elijah," *JÖB* 38 (1988), 194.

[44] Though the Mandylion is the example of choice here, one might equally well point to the bleeding icon of the Crucifixion from Beirut that was installed in the chapel of Christ Chalkites by John I Tzimiskes. Cited already in the Letter of the Oriental Patriarchs and among the icons whose stories are found most often in both Greek and Latin miracle collections, this icon is not described by the English Pilgrim (see note 7 above) and seems in time to have become lost: Mango, *The Brazen House*, 151–52. Certainly this icon—like the Maria Romaia and the icon wounded by an Arab on Cyprus, which also were featured in the recurrent core collection of stories about miraculous icons—does not seem to have had a recognized visual form that was replicated in art. Only later in the West does the story get attached to a great visual object, the *Volto Santo* of Lucca, but this is a sculpture: Belting, *Bild und Kult*, 343.

[45] See Ernst von Dobschütz, *Christusbilder: Untersuchungen zur christlichen Legende*, Texte und Untersuchungen zur Geschichte der altchristlichen Literatur 18 (Leipzig, 1899), 146–77, and most recently Averil Cameron, "The History of the Image of Edessa: The Telling of a Story," in *Okeanos: Festschrift for I. Ševčenko, Harvard Ukrainian Studies* 7 (1983), 80–94.

[46] Constantinus Porphyrogenitus, *Narratio de imagine Edessena*, PG 113:423–51.

[47] Vogt, trans., *Constantine VII* (as in note 37 above), vol. I, p. 5.

[48] See note 55 below.

trivialized.[49] And when Leo of Chalcedon adopted it as the focal example in his very seriously argued case against Emperor Alexios I's "iconoclastic" appropriation of the historiated doors at the Chalkoprateia church, Alexios countered him without any suggestion that he found in Leo's choice of example a particularly pointed attack upon the state and its symbols.[50] Other references to it arise from its status as a pilgrimage object. It was not an image of state. And in fact, though the version in the Vatican remains mysterious, study of the Genoese Mandylion has revealed no imperial connections.[51]

My impression in the end is that the linkage of court and icon is due very largely to one icon, an icon that is an exception to almost every rule. This is the Hodegetria. The Hodegetria clearly was a portable panel; her name labeled an object rather than a site. Her assumption of a state function was a process, not a premise, and a process that was accomplished at the expense of, not in accord with, the other icons of Constantinople.

The Hodegetria points up the fact that the great icons of Constantinople were icons of the Mother of God. Mary's churches gathered at points of tension: the Abraamite monastery, the Pege, and the church of Blachernai guarded the gates in the Theodosian walls, while the Chalkoprateia and the Hodegon watched over the city's center.[52] One after another, they acquired icons. The emperors associated with these icons in times not of courtly panoply but of war. The first of them to figure in the post-Iconoclastic period is the Acheiropoietos icon at the Abraamite monastery by the Golden Gate, where first Basil I and then Nikephoros II Phokas made a station in his triumphal progress into the city.[53] It was near this same point that the demes and senators of the city offered John I Tzimiskes the triumphal chariot which he loaded with Bulgarian booty and an icon of Mary, but it is impossible to know what icon this was. Basil II actually took an icon of Mary into battle with him against the usurper Bardas Phokas; Psellos says that he held it in his left hand—apparently it was small enough to be carried in this way.[54] This icon has been linked with the figure of Mary on a silver miliaresion (Fig. 13).[55] The coin's attribution to Basil has been challenged,[56] but the inscription on the reverse inclines me to support its association with an event like the victory over Bardas, for it repeats the inscription that Constantine VII said was on the Mandylion: ὁ εἰς σὲ ἐλπίζων οὐκ ἀποτυγχάνει.[57] It must have derived special potency from this source.

---

[49] Dobschütz, *Christusbilder,* 176: at the time of their marriage, Empress Zoe sent the Mandylion, the wood of the True Cross, the letter of Christ to Abgar, and an icon of the Virgin as a guarantee of safe passage to the patrician Constantine Dalassenos in order to induce him to return to the city, but she broke her oath to him as soon as he complied; later in the same year (1036/37) Michael himself carried the Mandylion in procession to Blachernai to plead for rain, but again with demeaning results, for a hailstorm broke out.

[50] Venance Grumel, "Léon de Chalcédoine et le canon de la fête du Saint Mandilion," *AnalBoll* 58 (1950), 135–52.

[51] Colette Dufour Bozzo, *Il "Sacro Volto" di Genova,* Istituto nazionale d'archeologia e storia dell'arte, Monografie 1 (Rome, 1974), 64–65 and passim.

[52] Anthony Cutler, *Transfigurations: Studies in the Dynamics of Byzantine Iconography* (University Park, Pa., 1975), devotes his last chapter, 111–41, to a study of the Virgin's symbolic associations with city and walls.

[53] See note 41 above.

[54] Renauld, *Michel Psellos* (as in note 9 above), I, 10.xvi, 2–5; Sewter, *Fourteen Byzantine Rulers,* 36.

[55] Philip Grierson, "A Misattributed Miliaresion of Basil II," *Zbornik radova* 8 (1963), 111–16.

[56] Werner Seibt, "Der Bildtypus der Theotokos Nikopoios," *Βυζαντινά* 13.1 (1985), 552–53.

[57] PG 113:437A. On the coin it is in the feminine, adapted to the Virgin.

Nonetheless, its use here would seem to show that the Virgin, not the Mandylion, was judged the appropriate protector of the emperor.

The image on this coin has been linked with various named icons: the Nikopoia, the Blachernitissa, the icon that Psellos said the emperors "usually" took into battle.[58] Much of the scholarly interest in the image has arisen from the hope of finding in it one of those great icons presumed to be icons of the state, above all the Blachernitissa. Since the year 626 the Virgin's church on the walls at Blachernai had been associated with Constantinople's defense. Thus, among the city's great icons, the icon of Blachernai is the one most often sought as a symbol in the rituals of the state's divine protection. It is to the Blachernitissa that we turn now.

That the emperors before Basil had used icons in battle is altogether likely. George Dennis has drawn attention to the religious intensity especially of the armies of Nikephoros II Phokas and John I Tzimiskes;[59] Gustav Schlumberger has recounted the vivid Mariolatry with which Nikephoros' troops were harangued;[60] and one of John Tzimiskes' battles was even accompanied by a vision of the Virgin, a vision that recurred in remarkably similar form in the twelfth century under Manuel I.[61] Both the visions and the harangue focus on Mary, but not on Mary as shown on the coin. Now standing, now striding, now enthroned, she appears surrounded by a host of helpers who include first and most visibly the warrior saints; when named, they are Theodore and George. This image of Mary, flanked by warriors whose help she invokes, was deeply ingrained in the Byzantine imagination, and it was especially current in the century before Basil II. It must have been somewhere visualized. If this was the Mary of the battlefield, though, she has not survived in any known icons from our period. In any period, in fact, Mary surrounded by warrior saints is exceptional in art.[62] The accounts recall, if anything, the early icon of the Virgin flanked by saints and angels from Sinai, whose military saints are generally identified as Theodore and George.[63]

---

[58] Renauld, *Michel Psellos,* I, 39.x, 26; Sewter, *Fourteen Byzantine Rulers,* 70.

[59] George Dennis, "Religious Services in the Byzantine Army," in *ΕΥΛΟΓΗΜΑ: Studies in Honor of Robert Taft, S.J., Studia Anselmiana* 110 (1993), 107–17.

[60] Gustav Schlumberger, *Un empereur byzantin au dixième siècle: Nicéphore Phocas* (Paris, 1890), 91.

[61] Niebuhr, ed., *Ioannis Zonarae Epitomae,* III, 533.6–534.7; Trapp, trans., *Johannes Zonaras,* 39. In this case a woman in Constantinople had a dream of the Mother of God accompanied by many people and striding forward. She said to one who preceded her: "Lord Theodore, your John and mine faces dangerous battles; hurry and stand by him." In the 12th century Choniates tells of a man named Mavropoulos, who had a dream before the battle of Myriokephalon in which the icon of the Virgin Kyriotissa cried out: "The emperor is now in the utmost danger. Who will go forth in my name to assist him?" One after the other—beginning with George and then Theodore—the military saints were named, but in this case none would go to his aid. See van Dieten, ed., *Nicetae Choniatae Historia,* 190.92–191.8; Magoulias, trans., *O City of Byzantium,* 197.

[62] See Maguire, "The Mosaics of Nea Moni," 212, on the narthex dome at Nea Moni with its rare composition of the Virgin surrounded by martyrs and warrior saints, and a surviving description of an icon that may have shown the Virgin, the emperor, and warrior saints. The rarity of this combination makes all the more striking the two icons from the Crusader period that link Mary with a warrior: the diptych on Mount Sinai with the Virgin and St. Prokopios, and the double-sided icon in Paphos with the same Virgin and an unnamed saint, perhaps Merkourios. See Constantine Manaphes, gen. ed., *Sinai: Treasures of the Monastery* (Athens, 1990), pl. 65; Athanasios Papageorghiou, *Icons of Cyprus* (Nicosia, 1993), pls. 15A, 15B.

[63] Weitzmann, *The Monastery of Saint Catherine,* 18–21 and especially 20, no. B3, pls. IV–V, XLIII–XLVI.

The Virgin's church at Blachernai had relics of both Theodore and George;[64] it was closely associated with the defense of the city; and the Virgin appeared in visions there accompanied by hosts of people.[65] Thus one wonders if the militant Mary with her warrior saints might reflect the Blachernitissa. The church at Blachernai certainly contained many icons. But there is no evidence that it had a great name icon in the tenth century, much less a name icon that formed the focus of the kind of high courtly veneration that we are seeking. Not only can the image on the coin of Basil II not be linked with Blachernai; it is very hard to link any one icon with Blachernai.

Legend, of course, assigned a great icon to seventh-century Blachernai; the Letter of the Oriental Patriarchs said that this icon had been hidden or destroyed by Constantine V.[66] Its removal does not seem to have diminished the church as a focus of the cult of Mary—we read, for instance, of the Iconoclast emperor Theophilos going there every week on horseback to venerate the Virgin[67]—and we hear nothing of a post-Iconoclastic replacement of the icon. It was, instead, Blachernai's relic, the *maphorion*, that Photios dipped in the sea in 864, and when Romanos I went to Blachernai to fortify himself against Tsar Symeon, it was the *maphorion* he rode off with.[68]

It is likely that Theophilos went to Blachernai on Fridays. Kedrenos, writing in the twelfth century, reports that ever since the time of Emperor Maurice, a *presbeia* or procession set out each Friday from Blachernai, crossing the whole city to the church of the Mother of God at Chalkoprateia.[69] Certainly it was on Friday that St. Basil told Irene of Chrysobalanton to go to Blachernai to see Mary when she came.[70] She came in Irene's vision with a host of fine people; her face, however, was invisible because of the radiant light that shone from it. In contrast to St. Basil, who had appeared to Irene the night before "looking such as the icons represent him,"[71] the Virgin eluded specific form; certainly she did not appear in the form of a particular icon.

Now the court, too, made visits to Blachernai on Fridays. Constantine VII's *Book of Ceremonies* describes an elaborate Friday ritual at the bath at Blachernai.[72] Perhaps it was this event that lent such splendor to the crowds seen in the visions there. If so, however, it must be noted that we have no concrete evidence whatever that the court so much as acknowledged the procession to Chalkoprateia, or gave any recognition to such icon or icons as might have been involved in it. The *Book of Ceremonies* mentions neither. Even

[64] Janin, *La géographie*, 169, notes that Anthony of Novgorod speaks of the body of Theodore Stratelates there, and that the Latins are supposed to have taken away the arm of St. George.

[65] See the visions of Andrew Salos and Irene of Chrysobalanton: Lennart Rydén, "The Vision of the Virgin at Blachernae and the Feast of the Pokrov," *AnalBoll* 94 (1976), 63–82; Jan Olof Rosenqvist, *The Life of St. Irene Abbess of Chrysobalanton* (Uppsala, 1986), 58–59.

[66] John of Damascus, Ἐπιστολὴ πρὸς τὸν Βασιλέα Θεόφιλον," PG 95:361D–364A.

[67] Immanuel Bekker, ed., *Georgius Cedrenus*, 2 vols., CSHB 34–35 (Bonn, 1838–39), vol. II, p. 101; Michael Glykas, "Annales," PG 158:537B.

[68] Thurn, ed., *Ioannis Scylitzae Synopsis*, 219.31–35; Thurn, trans., *Byzanz wieder ein Weltreich*, 257.

[69] Bekker, ed., *Georgius Cedrenus*, I, 694.21–23; Ševčenko, "Icons in the Liturgy," 51.

[70] See note 65 above.

[71] Rosenqvist, *The Life of St. Irene*, 56–57.

[72] See notes 37–38 above.

in the eleventh century when Psellos came to describe the "usual miracle" before the veiled image at Blachernai—yet a third event that eventually took place there on Friday evenings—he offered no indication that the emperor felt himself obliged to be present in person.[73]

The *presbeia*, the imperial bath, the "usual miracle" yield a very busy picture of Blachernai on Fridays. But they do *not* yield either a single icon symbolizing the distinctive presence of Mary at this site or any evidence of official courtly engagement with such an icon. Appealing as Hans Belting's statement is that the people of Constantinople saw their rulers when they went to visit the icons,[74] Blachernai offers us no concrete evidence that the imperial processions were either conceived or perceived by their courtly participants as being focused on the veneration of icons. The emperors seem to have had their own agenda with Mary at Blachernai.

In 1031, in the reign of the pious emperor Romanos III, an ancient icon of Mary was discovered at Blachernai.[75] In view of the fact that an icon was known to have been hidden there, it may not have been entirely fortuitous that one was recovered, and one is entitled to ponder whether something might not have made it expedient to find an icon there in the 1030s. The decades between 1030 and about 1080 saw the church's most consistent use for imperial occasions.[76] These are also the decades that saw the emergence of multiple toponymics for the Virgin Mary, among them the name Blachernitissa. The toponymics appear in conjunction with the multiplication of privately endowed monasteries in Constantinople,[77] and they presumably served to tie the Virgin's grace and the benefices it earned to their particular sites. The process was facilitated by giving the toponymics also to the icons that benefactors venerated. Blachernai, too, may have found it expedient to assemble one or several portable icons to which such appellations could be addressed. This said, however, it must be emphasized that the name Blachernitissa appears not with one but with any of several iconographic types: we see it applied to the orante full-length Virgin, the orante half-length Virgin, and the Virgin with a medallion of Christ on her breast (Figs. 14, 15).[78] Thus it cannot be understood to label any one icon or be traced by following any one iconographic type. The name confounds visual pursuit.

However, the name offers a different avenue of pursuit, for it assumes a particular

---

[73] Grumel, "Le 'miracle habituel,'" 129–46.

[74] Belting, *Bild und Kult,* 208.

[75] Thurn, ed., *Ioannes Scylitzae Synopsis,* 384.

[76] See the synopsis of events recorded as occurring at the Virgin's church at Blachernai by Janin, *La géographie,* 162–64.

[77] On this process see Cyril Mango, "The Development of Constantinople as an Urban Centre," in *The Seventeenth International Byzantine Congress, Main Papers* (New Rochelle, N.Y., 1986), 131–32; Ioanna Tognazzi Zervou, "L'iconographie e la 'Vita' delle miracolosi icone della Theotokos Brefokratousa: Blachernitissa e Odegetria," *BollGrott* 40 (1986), 229.

[78] For the coins, on which the Blachernitissa is shown as a standing or bust-length orante, see note 36 above. An 11th-century seal of John, *protoproedros* of the imperial *sakelles,* with orante Virgin labeled "Blachernitissa" bearing the medallion bust of Christ on her breast, is published by G. Zacos, *Byzantine Lead Seals,* 2: *Numbers 1–1089,* ed. John Nesbitt (Bern, 1984), 272 no. 522. I owe John Cotsonis my sincerest gratitude for help in negotiating the ocean of seals and their research.

functional profile. It appears, of course, on seals, the home ground of toponymics.[79] But it appears also in two further contexts in which other toponymics do not appear. One of these, though rare, is coins. It appears on two issues of Constantine IX Monomachos (Fig. 14), on one of Zoe and Theodora, and one of Michael VI.[80] Uniquely among the toponymics, then, the Blachernitissa appears in the most public of imperial contexts. It appears in a second imperial context as well: it is the name given by Michael Attaleiates to the icon that Romanos IV took into battle.[81]

Attaleiates cites the Blachernitissa in a squalid little story in which Romanos demonstrates his resolute sense of justice by slitting the nose of a soldier who had stolen a mule; the story takes place in the presence of the icon. It gives no hint as to what the icon in question was or what relation—if any—it had to any icon or icon type housed at Blachernai. Nonetheless, the story is useful in showing us the emperor being associated with an icon—this is not the icon of the army but the icon the emperor took into war—and it gives us a context for such an association. The context is military, not civic or civilian. The icon brings with it the legendary charisma of Blachernai—the icon found in 1031 may have been an effort to reactivate this charisma—and the emperor is fortified by it rather than lending it the glamour of his office. In a military if not in a civilian and courtly context, then, the eleventh century does seem to yield an association of the emperors and a great, name icon of Blachernai.

The same association has often been seen in the well-known story of Alexios I Komnenos' precipitous return to Constantinople from his campaign against Bohemond in 1107 because the "usual miracle" had failed to occur on the Friday of his departure.[82] That Blachernai had a special significance to Alexios when he went to war seems clear, for Anna Komnene tells us that her father carried with him into battle in 1089 the relic of the Virgin's *maphorion*;[83] Romanos I had done the same centuries earlier when fighting Tsar Symeon.[84] On this occasion, then, and perhaps even customarily, Alexios seems to have made a ceremonial visit to Blachernai to venerate the Virgin and get the relic before leading his army on campaign. Certainly the caesar Bardas and John I Tzimiskes are both known to have made visits to shrines of Mary before leaving Constantinople for battle, and John went specifically to Blachernai.[85] Such a ceremonial reception of the *maphorion* and sanctification of the campaign would have created a strong bond between Blachernai and the emperor's battles, and would explain the immediate linkage of a failure of the "usual miracle" with his military moves. The emperor's interaction, however, was with the relic, not an icon. The story offers no indication of any recurrent courtly involvement with either the icon processions across the city or the "usual mira-

---

[79] See Zacos, *Byzantine Lead Seals*, 272 no. 522.

[80] See Grierson, *Catalogue*, and Sear, *Byzantine Coins*, in note 36 above.

[81] Bekker, ed., *Michael Attaleiota*, 153.

[82] Bernard Leib, ed., *Anne Comnène, Alexiade*, 3 vols. (Paris, 1967), vol. III, 87.15–23; E.R.A. Sewter, trans., *The Alexiad of Anna Comnena* (Harmondsworth, 1969), 395.

[83] Leib, ed., *Anne Comnène*, II, 98.23–29; Sewter, trans., *Anna Comnena*, 225. The relic's fate was scarcely edifying, for Alexios was forced to stuff it into a tree and abandon it when he fled the battlefield.

[84] See note 68 above.

[85] On Bardas see note 94 below; on John I see McCormick, *Eternal Victory*, 249.

cle." Nancy Ševčenko is surely right that Alexios had felt no obligation to be at Blachernai on the Friday night of his departure,[86] but was forced to return there by the powerful
hold that the institution had upon the city's imagination. It is an awkward incident and
the last of its kind. Once the Komnenoi took up residence at the palace of Blachernai,
imperial engagement with its holy objects vanishes from the records.[87] While Blachernai
clearly played a sustained symbolic role in the rituals of war, then, it is a role that engaged
the emperor and his army more than it did the emperor and his court, and the role of
an identifiable icon known as the Blachernitissa is elusive.

Attaleiates' use of the term *Blachernitissa* is military, but the word's fleeting appearance
on coins is not, and one wonders if this might not testify at last to the kind of civilian
identification of emperor, court, and icons around which we have built our picture of
the Byzantine court, enacting itself to itself by participating with the emperor in icon
rituals. Certainly the processions to and from Blachernai were flourishing, as one gathers
from a spate of seals bearing the inscription πρῶτος τῆς πρεσβείας τῶν Βλαχερνῶν.[88]
The finest of them belonged to one Nicholas Skleros, a layman and courtier who held
a number of offices in Alexios I's government (Fig. 16).[89] His office, as πρωτοπρόεδρος
μεγάλος σκευοφύλακι τῶν Βλαχερνῶν καὶ πρῶτος τῆς πρεσβείας, was interpreted
by Laurent as a kind of Byzantine counterpart to Louis XIV's Office de l'Administration
de l'Argenterie, Menus-Plaisirs et Affaires de la Chambre du Roi.[90] This interpretation
of it as an official post, overseeing imperial ceremonial and managing the state exchequer
to meet its great expense, implied precisely the sort of conjoining of ecclesiastical and
state in the celebration of the processions that Grabar had conjured up. It is not clear,
however, that Nicholas' offices were so eminent as to warrant such an interpretation.[91]
More recently, Nancy Ševčenko has suggested that the office of *protos* was not a court
position, but was rather the presidency of a brotherhood dedicated to an icon.[92] With
this, the imperial bond loosens again. The seal tells us that court figures participated in
Blachernai's cult, but it does not imply that this was an official cult or that membership
of it identified one as a courtier. In fact, no evidence has emerged of icon brotherhoods
whose membership carried with it the connotation of court membership, as did the high
knightly orders in the West. Thus the bond of court and cult loosens, and it remains
unclear whether the coins bearing the Blachernitissa signal a recurrent courtly ritual
or—as in the case of Theophilos—the personal devotion of the rulers involved.

Since his seal identifies him with Blachernai, one presumes that Nicholas was attached

---

[86] Ševčenko, "Icons and the Liturgy," 51.

[87] Anna Komnene's reference to the cape *maphorion* of the Virgin is the last instance of such an association
that I know (see note 82 above). John II certainly carried an icon of the Virgin with him into battle, for Choniates describes with completely cynical detachment how he exploited it with shows of piety to incite his soldiers:
van Dieten, ed., *Nicetae Choniatae Historia*, 15.86–93; Magoulias, trans., *O City of Byzantium*, 10. We do not
know what icon it was, though.

[88] V. Laurent, *Le corpus des sceaux de l'Empire byzantin*, 2 vols. in 5 pts. (Paris, 1963–81), 118–23, nos.
1199–1204.

[89] Ibid., 120–22, no. 1202.

[90] Ibid., 121; Alain-Charles Gruber, *Les grandes fêtes et leurs décors à l'époque de Louis XIV* (Geneva, 1972), 7 and
passim.

[91] *ODB*, III, 1910, s.v. Skleros.

[92] Ševčenko, "Icons and the Liturgy," 55 note 72.

to an icon of Blachernai. But the image on his seal challenges this. It is identified clearly not as ἡ Βλαχερνίτισσα but as ἡ Ὁδηγητρία. It is among the earliest instances of the Hodegetria's name.

The Hodegetria is associated with the Hodegon, a monastery built or perhaps rebuilt by Emperor Michael III in the ninth century not far from the imperial palace.[93] The caesar Bardas is known to have made a private visit to the church of the Virgin at the Hodegon on the eve of his Cretan campaign,[94] and it is usually assumed—though without textual support—that he went to visit the icon. An eleventh-century book of miracle stories, Paris, B.N., gr. 1474, speaks of the icon's public processions on Tuesdays.[95] Otherwise, however, we hear nothing of the Hodegetria until the twelfth century. At this point she appears in a variety of courtly contexts. Her church was restored in the reign of Manuel I by George Palaiologos Komnenos Doukas with portraits of seven emperors and scenes of Manuel's *res gestae*.[96] Members of the Komnenian family made showy donations to her. These donations were both rich and of self-conscious aesthetic excellence, and consistently took the same form, as splendidly embroidered veils.[97] Thus they emerge as an exercise in competitive clique membership. To be such a donor was presumably to be a member of the courtly elite. Significantly, the gifts involved veiling and thus controlling—making arcane—the image at issue.

Under John II Komnenos, the Hodegetria was made to take part in the liturgical commemorations of the imperial dead: ceremoniously brought to the funeral heroon of the Komnenoi at the Pantokrator monastery on the anniversaries of the deaths of John and his family, she was left overnight to incubate the tombs.[98] At the end of the century, Anthony of Novgorod saw the icon in the palace itself.[99] As he was in Constantinople at Easter time, this very probably indicates that the Palaiologan custom of taking the Hodegetria to the palace during Easter was in origin a Komnenian one, linking her once again with the emperors.[100] It may be that the Hodegetria had always had this courtly character. She was never circulated on coins, and the posture that we identify as hers

[93] Janin, *La géographie* (as in note 41 above), 199–206; also the monumental article of Zervou, "L'iconographie e la 'Vita,'" 233–62. The association of the name Hodegetria with the monastery of the Hodegon can be traced as far back as the 12th century; when it is found in both the English pilgrim and Choniates: Ciggaar, "Une description de Constantinople" (as in note 7 above), 249; van Dieten, ed., *Nicetae Choniatae Historia*, 382.53–61; Magoulias, trans., *O City of Byzantium*, 209–10. It is generally preferred today over the explanation that bases the name on the Virgin's gesture, "showing the way." This accords with the current preference for toponymic explanations over aesthetic ones rooted in the way the images look. Another example of the triumph of the toponymic is offered by the epithet Kyriotissa, long explained as designating the frontal, "lordly" Virgin but now explained by reference to the Constantinopolitan monastery of the Virgin τῶν Κύρου: Janin, *La géographie*, 193–94. Nonetheless, it is important to remember that the Hodegetria's association with the Hodegon, and above all its association with a presumed single, long-lived icon at the Hodegon, is very probably a historical artifact—a Byzantine one, but an artifact nonetheless.

[94] Thurn, ed., *Ioannis Scylitzes Synopsis*, 111.73–77; Thurn, trans., *Byzanz wieder ein Weltreich*, 147.

[95] Ernst von Dobschütz, "Maria Romaia. Zwei unbekannte Texte," *BZ* 12 (1903), 211.

[96] Cyril Mango, *The Art of the Byzantine Empire, 312–1453: Sources and Documents in the History of Art* (Englewood Cliffs, N.J., 1972), 227, from Venice, Marciana, gr. 524, fol. 108r.

[97] Nunn, "The Encheirion as Adjunct to the Icon" (as in note 17 above), 74–76 and passim; Hörandner, *Theodoros Prodromos* (as in note 22 above), 525–26.

[98] Paul Gautier, "Le Typikon du Christ Sauveur Pantocrator," *REB* 32 (1974), 80–83.

[99] Janin, *La géographie*, 204.

[100] Verpeaux, ed., *Pseudo-Kodinos*, 231.

appears in the overwhelming majority of tenth- and eleventh-century devotional ivories, a medium likely to have been shaped by an extremely elite patron group.[101] It is dangerous to identify her too closely with this posture, however, for the seals of the Hodegon monastery use a variety of iconographic forms, including the orante (Fig. 17).[102] Her history is thus elusive without her name. Her name, however, like that of the Blachernitissa, does designate certain functions. These are courtly functions, and they become visible, significantly, in the era of the court's aristocratization under the Komnenoi.

Among these functions was the Hodegetria's appearance on anniversaries among the tombs of John II and his family. She was not the only icon to visit their tombs, however. John had also prescribed a weekly visitation of the tombs on Fridays by the Eleousa, name icon of the Pantokrator monastery's Eleousa church, and "all the other icons."[103] Nancy Ševčenko associated this event with the weekly Friday procession from Blachernai.[104] The Friday procession, presumably, made a station at the Pantokrator. It may well have made other stations, too, for the terminology of John II's *typikon* suggests that the procession had come to incorporate many icons. The seal of Nicholas Skleros implies that the Hodegetria, too, was among them. The Blachernai procession went from the Theodosian walls to the church of the Chalkoprateia, thus traversing most of the breadth of Constantinople. The monastery of the Hodegon lay beyond Chalkoprateia by the sea; drawing the Hodegetria into the procession would have extended it implicitly to embrace virtually the entirety of the city. The Hodegetria may thus literally—as well as figuratively in Nicholas' seal—have come to form Blachernai's counterpart, bracketing between them both city and procession. The Pantokrator *typikon* suggests that by mid-century yet another potent element had entered the mix. It suggests that, with the heroon as its nexus, the imperial family had become a meeting ground for the pageantry and the power of Constantinople's icons.

The Hodegetria's own processions were on Tuesdays, as we learn from Paris. gr. 1474 and the English Pilgrim.[105] Neither of these sources says anything further of them. Anthony of Novgorod, however, at the end of the twelfth century, says that the Hodegetria

---

[101] The posture we call the Hodegetria's does contrast with the various orante postures that are usually associated with Blachernai in the fact that it recurs in certain very defined contexts. I have not yet deciphered the message of this pattern of distribution. One of these contexts is the ivories: see Adolf Goldschmidt and Kurt Weitzmann, *Die byzantinischen Elfenbeinskulpturen*, 2 vols., 2d ed. (Berlin, 1979), where the Virgin appears set apart as the central figure in thirty-nine ivories, in thirty-five of which she exhibits the "Hodegetria" pose. The other is the seals of the patriarchs of Constantinople from the late 9th through the mid-11th century: Zacos, *Byzantine Lead Seals*, 2, nos. 7b–12, 14c–15; Nicolas Oikonomides, *A Collection of Dated Byzantine Lead Seals* (Washington, D.C., 1986), nos. 54, 74, 84, 88. Photios first takes up the pose (Zacos, no. 7b; Oikonomides, no. 54), with the Virgin touching the Child's feet in a variant used already before Iconoclasm by the emperors from Justinian II through Leo III and again in 813–815. This is replaced in the mid-11th century by a "true" Hodegetria, seen especially clearly on the seals of Michael Keroularios (Zacos, no. 15; Oikonomides, no. 88). The latter pose appears once and only once in coinage, on a silver miliaresion of Romanos III: Philip Grierson, *Catalogue* (as in note 21 above), pl. LVII, 3a.1–3a.4. Grierson, 713 note 11, suggests aptly that this figure may refer to the Peribleptos, to whom Romanos III dedicated an opulent church.

[102] Zacos, *Byzantine Lead Seals*, 357, no. 765.

[103] Gautier, "Le Typikon," 74–75.

[104] Ševčenko, "Icons and the Liturgy," 52.

[105] Ciggaar, "Une description de Constantinople," 249.

went on Tuesdays from her church to the church of Blachernai, and that the Holy Spirit descended upon her.[106] The phrase is the one used about the "usual miracle," and one wonders if this was not the Hodegetria's response to Blachernai's "hyped-up" spectacle. In the Palaiologan period, the Hodegetria went to the palace over Easter; then on Easter Monday, a day on which the emperors traditionally went to Blachernai, the Hodegetria was returned by the imperial guard to the "Hypsila," identified by R. Janin as being at Blachernai,[107] presumably in readiness for her Tuesday procession from Blachernai to the Hodegon the next day. By the Komnenian era if not earlier, then, the Hodegetria had apparently become associated with Blachernai and its ceremonies.

The processions were not the only ground on which the two traditions met. The Hodegetria also became—or became the name for—the great defensive icon of the emperors. We meet it in action in Choniates' account of the rebellion of 1186, in which he specifies that the icon of the Hodegetria was taken onto the walls by Isaac II.[108] But the idea was far more widespread. Eustathios of Thessalonica, acerbic reporter of metropolitan events, remarks at one point that the Constantinopolitans shrug off imperial weakness with the claim that "the Hodegetria, the protectress of our city, will be enough, without anyone else, to secure our welfare."[109] His own metropolitan city of Thessalonica had an icon known as the Hodegetria, too, with a brotherhood that oversaw processions. The Thessalonian Hodegetria surely was known by this name because, as Eustathios tells us, she was the one who looked out for the city's protection: whatever her aesthetic or iconographic character, she shared the functional profile implied in the name.[110]

---

[106] Janin, *La géographie*, 204.

[107] Ibid., 214. On this ceremony, see also Laurent, *Corpus*, 121; Verpeaux, *Pseudo-Kodinos*, 231. Tognazzi Zervou, "L'iconografia," 246, identifies the "Hypsila" with the chapel of the Nikopoios cited by Pseudo-Kodinos (Verpeaux, 228) as the place where the Orthros of Palm Sunday ended. Laurent, 231, who places it at Blachernai, identifies it with the place where Anthony of Novgorod saw the Hodegetria.

[108] Van Dieten, ed., *Nicetae Choniatae Historia*, 382.53–61; Magoulias, trans., *O City of Byzantium*, 209–10.

[109] J. R. Melville Jones, trans., *Eustathios of Thessalonike: The Capture of Thessalonike* (Canberra, 1988), 42–43.11–12.

[110] Ibid., 142–43.3–4. I am struck by the dearth of foundations dedicated to the Hodegetria in Janin's inventory of churches and monasteries outside of Constantinople: Raymond Janin, *Les églises et les monastères des grandes centres byzantins: Bithynie, Hellespont, Latros, Galésios, Trébizonde, Athènes, Thessalonique* (Paris, 1975). He cites only the church in Thessalonica (p. 382). A church of the Hodegetria was dedicated around 1150 in Monemvasia: see Haris Kalligas, *Byzantine Monemvasia: The Sources* (Monemvasia, 1990), 68; Konstantine Em. Kalogeras, Μονεμβασία, ἡ Βενετία τῆς Πελοποννήσου, Texte und Forschungen zur byzantinisch-neugriechischen Philologie 46 (Athens, 1955), 22–24. And Peter Schreiner, "Das Hodegetria-Kloster auf Leukas im 11. Jahrhundert: Bemerkungen zu einer Notiz im Vatican gr. 2561," *ByzF* 12 (1987), 57–62, cites a monastery of the Hodegetria on Leukas, mentioned in a colophon which he believes should be attributed to 1025. Schreiner's monastery is known by the name Hodegetria for certain only as of the 15th century, however. Both Thessalonica and Monemvasia were notable in the 12th century for their urban development, and my inclination would be to see in this inventory the message that the Hodegetria was above all an urban protectress, and that this role became articulated in the 12th century. It was probably fully crystallized only with the events of 1261. This suggests that the role of urban protectress associated with the huge Hodegetrias of Dugento Tuscany was a very contemporary product, associated as much with Byzantium's formation as a city-state as with Tuscany's cities: see Rebecca W. Corrie, "Coppo di Marcovaldo's Madonna del Bordone and the Meaning of the Bare-Legged Christ Child in Siena and the East," *Gesta* 35.1 (1996), 55–58. It is to be noted in this connection that the sermon on the Akathistos Hymn associated with George Pisides (PG 92:1335–72, especially 1351D) is now assigned to Nikephoros Kallistos (Ševčenko, "Icons in the Liturgy," 49 note 31).

Thus the Hodegetria seems to have gathered and amalgamated functions that other icons represented singly, succeeding one by one as she did so in displacing those others. She became the most formidable of the additions to the processions from Blachernai, perhaps displacing the Chalkoprateia, home of the Hagiosoritissa, as their symbolic end. She brought the courtly devotion of the imperial circle into the urban and ecclesiastical processions of Blachernai. A panel and portable, she negotiated these journeys easily, becoming a star in the city's most grandiose religious spectacles. She assumed the defensive role associated with Blachernai, and she bound it firmly to the person of the emperor. Once the Hodegetria had produced this compound persona, the Blachernitissa drops from view.

Whether or not the icon placed by John II and Manuel in their triumphal chariot was the Hodegetria we will never know.[111] We do know that the icon placed by Emperor Michael VIII in his triumphal chariot in 1261 was called the Hodegetria.[112] Just what this meant visually is considerably complicated by a seal of the emperor himself. Associating him as the "New Constantine" with the triumphant reconquest of 1261, it shows him holding aloft an icon, but it is an icon not of the Hodegetria as we conceive it, but of the orante Mother of God (Fig. 18).[113] It does indicate that functionally, however, the complex of ideas that this icon stood for was known by the name Hodegetria. At this point, the Hodegetria surely did stand for a kind of ruler and, through him, for the state as well. It is she alone, and she only slowly, who could answer in any way to the expectation elicited by Grabar's image of the Byzantine court as crystallized around symbols of the state that took the form of icons. And even she was identified with the state less through the court than through the person of the emperor in his role as defender. At the very beginning, this paper cited the Cretan icon of the Mesopanditissa, offered as a kind of miraculous healer of the body politic, an image in Venetian terms of Byzantine rituals that bound ruler to ruled by means of an icon. In fact, it is remarkable how little evidence we have of any civilian context in which a recurrent procession honored an icon as the sign of a courtly contract, between court and city, or between court and emperor.

The Mesopanditissa turns our attention to one final variety of evidence, and this is the body of post-Byzantine icon stories, for these, too, have belied earlier expectations.[114] I

---

[111] The process of carrying the Hodegetria may be a relevant consideration. Palaiologan accounts emphasize the special ability of the members of the icon's brotherhood of keepers to manage its exceptional cumbersomeness; already John II makes special provision for these men in his *typikon*. One wonders whether this jealously guarded "union labor" could be displaced. See Ševčenko, "Icons in the Liturgy," 48 note 24, and her article, "'Servants of the Holy Icon,'" in *Byzantine East, Latin West: Art-Historical Studies in Honor of Kurt Weitzmann*, ed. D. Mouriki et al. (Princeton, 1995), 547–51.

[112] Nikephoros Gregoras, *Byzantinae Historiae Libri XXXVII*, PG 148:217c; Tognazzi Zervou, "L'iconographie e la 'Vita,' " 259–60.

[113] G. Zacos and A. Veglery, *Byzantine Lead Seals*, I.3: *Nos. 2672–3231* (Basel, 1972), 1579–81, no. 2756bis.

[114] I rely largely on two compendia: Timotheos of Jerusalem, Αἱ ἐπωνυμίαι τῆς Παναγίας, *Νέα Σιών* 47 (1952), 177–92, 225–70; 48 (1953), 1–32, 71–102; 49 (1954), 1–32; Andreas Ebbinghaus, *Die altrussischen Marienikonen-Legenden*, Osteuropa-Institut an der freien Universität Berlin, Slavistische Veröffentlichungen 70 (Berlin, 1990). Among the Russian icons, the icon of Tikhvin is the major exception, preserving in many variants the story of the Vladimirskaya with its Constantinopolitan origin. Even the Tikhvin icon's story is less specially aulic than that of the Kykkotissa, however, throwing the latter into sharper relief.

had expected to find in them icons that conjured up the imperial state that they had presumably once validated. In fact, however, Constantinople and its radiant living icon of the imperial court barely figure in them at all. Of the legion Lukan icons, only the icon of Kykko retains an aulic character in her story, and this serves very particular ends.[115] More telling may be the Vladimirskaya. Traveling from Constantinople to the royal family of Kiev, she behaved as most icons in the Byzantine court did: that is, her activity was personal, her miracles private ones.[116] Only far later, in a different place and state, did she begin to assume the public role for which she is famous. But that was the artifact of a different time. It suggests that the role of icons as a symbol of the court was not so central to Byzantium's legacy as we have believed. Perhaps the most vividly informative picture of cult, court, and icon is offered by the legend of the now vanished Monemvasiotissa,[117] for it is linked not with the court as such but with the emperor himself: it is an icon given by the emperor to stand in his stead as a protector of the city in times of war, clothed as he was in precious jewels, and housed in a shrine of the Hodegetria.

Southern Methodist University

---

[115] See note 5 above.

[116] David V. Miller, "Legends of the Icon of Our Lady of Vladimir: A Study of the Development of Moskovite National Consciousness," *Speculum* 43 (1968), 657–63.

[117] Kalogeras, *Μονεμβασία*, 24.

Byzantine Court Culture
from the Point of View of Norman Sicily:
The Case of the Cappella Palatina in Palermo

William Tronzo

This study focuses on the royal chapel of Palermo, the Cappella Palatina (Figs. 1, 2).[1] Not only is the chapel the best-preserved building from twelfth-century Sicily, it is one of the most comprehensive ensembles of architecture and decoration to have come down to us anywhere from the Middle Ages as a whole. It bears today probably much the same relationship to its context that it did in the twelfth century. It forms the center of the most famous "monument" in Palermo, the Palazzo Normanno, or the Norman royal palace, whose origins also go back to the twelfth century (Figs. 3, 4).[2] Palace and chapel dominate Palermo in a topographic sense, being located on the highest point of the city within the walls.[3] But perhaps most significantly, the chapel, as indeed the palace

[1] I would like to thank Ernst Kitzinger and Henry Maguire for their generosity in reading this paper and offering useful comments and suggestions. The present argument depends upon a detailed examination of the Cappella Palatina that will appear in my forthcoming monograph on the chapel, an overview of which I have published in *Word and Image* 9 (1993), 197 ff, "The Medieval Object-Enigma and the Problem of the Cappella Palatina in Palermo." For views of the chapel, see Otto Demus, *The Mosaics of Norman Sicily* (London, 1950), 25 ff, and the essential study of Ernst Kitzinger, "The Mosaics of the Cappella Palatina in Palermo: An Essay on the Choice and Arrangement of Subjects," *ArtB* 31 (1949), 269 ff. See also Wolfgang Krönig, *Il Duomo di Monreale e l'architettura normanna in Sicilia* (Palermo, 1965), 167 ff; Guido di Stefano, *Monumenti della Sicilia normanna,* 2d ed. with additions of Wolfgang Krönig (Palermo, 1979), 37 ff; Benedetto Rocco, "La Cappella Palatina di Palermo: Lettura teologica (Parte prima/parte seconda)," *B.C.A. Bollettino d'informazione per la divulgazione dell'attività degli organi dell'Amministrazione dei Beni culturali e ambientali della Regione Siciliana* 4–5 (1983–84), 21 ff and 31 ff; Slobodan Ćurčić, "Some Palatine Aspects of the Cappella Palatina in Palermo," *DOP* 41 (1987), 125 ff; Ernst Kitzinger, "Mosaic Decoration in Sicily under Roger II and the Classical Byzantine System of Church Decoration," in *Italian Church Decoration of the Middle Ages and Early Renaissance: Functions, Forms and Regional Traditions,* ed. W. Tronzo (Bologna, 1989), 147 ff; Beat Brenk, "La parete occidentale della Cappella Palatina a Palermo," *Arte medievale,* 2d ser., 4.2 (1990), 135 ff; Eve Borsook, *Messages in Mosaic: The Royal Programmes of Norman Sicily, 1130–1187* (Oxford, 1990), 17 ff. On the restoration of the chapel, see Lucio Trizzino, *"La Palatina" di Palermo: Dalle opere funzionali al restauro, dal ripristino alla tutela* (Palermo, 1983), but with caution.

[2] On the Norman palace, see Francesco Valenti, "Il palazzo reale di Palermo," *Bollettino d'arte* 4 (1924–25), 512–28; M. Guiotto, *Palazzo ex-reale di Palermo: Recenti restauri e ritrovimenti* (Palermo, 1947); G. Giacomazzi, *Il palazzo che fu dei re: Divagazione storico-artistica sul palazzo dei normanni* (Palermo, 1959); R. Delogu and V. Scuderi, *La reggia dei normanni e la Cappella Palatina* (Florence, 1969); di Stefano, *Monumenti della Sicilia normanna,* 92–95. See also Trizzino, *"La Palatina,"* passim.

[3] The urban development of Palermo in the Middle Ages is discussed in Cesare DeSeta and Leonardo di Mauro, *Palermo* (Bari, 1981), 15 ff.

around it, was a project of the first of the Norman kings, Roger II, who cast a longer and more intent gaze on the art of Byzantium than almost any other western prince before or after him. Nowhere is this interest more in evidence than in the royal chapel. In fact, the use of Byzantine models in the Cappella Palatina has earned the chapel some quite derogatory labels such as "derivative" or "unoriginal," with the implication that the edifice has little to tell us beyond the story of the Norman misuse of Byzantine art.[4] This paper is offered with a modest counterproposal in mind, namely, that a better understanding of the Cappella Palatina may sharpen our picture of contemporary Byzantine practice. This is a counterproposal that I would like to explore selectively, and I have chosen to do so under two rubrics: Christomimesis and style.

The Cappella Palatina was founded by royal charter on 28 April 1140, and, although the building of it has often been thought to have been begun in the early 1130s, in conjunction with the creation of a parish in the palace precinct, there is no reason to date it much earlier than the charter itself.[5] This chronology is confirmed by an inscription at the base of the dome of the sanctuary which yields a date of 1143.[6] King Roger at this point was at the height of his power. Having had his crown recently reaffirmed by the leader of western Christendom, Innocent II, who had opposed him all his life, Roger was ready to bring his new kingdom visually into focus.[7] The choice of Palermo as his capital city formed an important part of his program. In the words of his chronicler, Alexander of Telese, Roger chose a city that had been a capital of the island in the days of old, thus lending the new regime the patina of prestige.[8] Here, on the city's highest point, Roger built his royal residence and the chapel that formed its centerpiece.

Briefly put, the Cappella Palatina consists of two parts: a sanctuary, which is composed of three apses with an altar in each, opening from a domed choir and two barrel-vaulted transept arms, and a nave flanked by two aisles, which are covered with wooden ceilings.[9] The distinction between sanctuary and nave carries over into the decoration. Scenes from Christ's life, for instance, are located in the sanctuary.[10] The nave contains an Old Testament cycle, from the Creation through the story of Jacob, and stories from the lives of Peter and Paul on the aisle walls.[11] The nave ceiling is most remarkable. It consists

---

[4] An extreme formulation of this view is that of Ćurčić, "Some Palatine Aspects," esp. 144. Borsook, on the other hand, overly stresses the Norman contribution; see *Messages in Mosaic*, xxxi ff ("Introduction"), 17 ff.

[5] For the charter, see Aloysius Garofalo, *Tabularium Regiae ac Imperialis Capellae Collegiate Divi Petri in Regio Panormitano Palatio* (Palermo, 1835), 7; Carlrichard Brühl, *Urkunden und Kanzlei König Rogers II. von Sizilien*, Studien zur normannisch-staufischen Herrscherurkunden Siziliens 2 (Cologne-Vienna, 1978), 89 f.

[6] On the significance of the inscription for the decoration of the chapel, see Ernst Kitzinger, *I mosaici del periodo normanno in Sicilia*, fasc. 1, *La Cappella Palatina di Palermo: I mosaici del Presbiterio* (Palermo, 1992), 11 f.

[7] Erich Caspar, *Roger II (1101–1154) und die Gründung der normannisch-sizilischen Monarchie* (Innsbruck, 1904), 89 ff; Ferdinand Chalandon, *Histoire de la Domination Normande en Italie et en Sicile* (Paris, 1907), II, 1 ff; Reinhard Elze, "Ruggero II e i papi del suo tempo," in *Società, potere e popolo nell'età di Ruggero II: Atti delle terze giornate normanno-sveve, Bari, 1977* (Bari, 1979), 27 ff.

[8] *De rebus gestis Rogerii Siciliae regis libri IV*, ed. Giuseppe del Re (Naples, 1845), chap. 2, I, 101–102.

[9] Pseudo-transept is perhaps a better term. The lateral spaces flanking the choir to the north and south are not true transept arms because their vaults run parallel to the main axis of the chapel rather than at right angles to it.

[10] Kitzinger, *I mosaici*, fasc. 1, with numerous illustrations and a discussion of the condition of the sanctuary mosaics.

[11] Ernst Kitzinger, *I mosaici del periodo normanno in Sicilia*, fasc. 2, *La Cappella Palatina di Palermo: I mosaici delle Navate* (Palermo, 1993).

1 Palermo, Cappella Palatina, view to west

2   Palermo, Cappella Palatina, dome

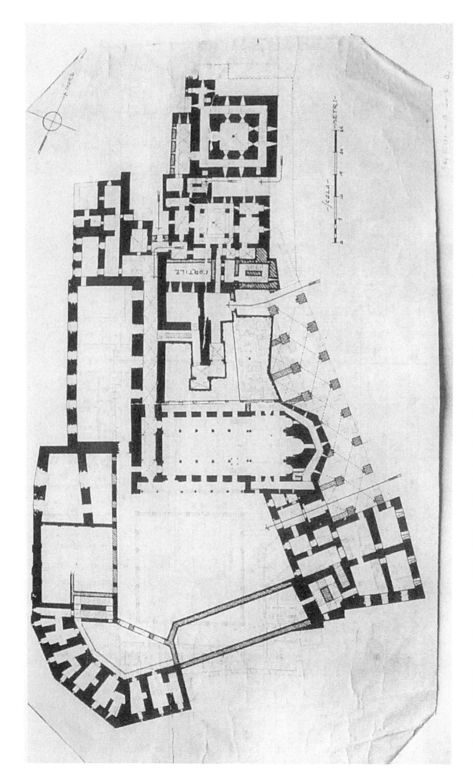

3 Palermo, Biblioteca Comunale, 5Qq 188 no. 17, pl. 5a, plan of Norman Palace showing location of the Cappella Palatina

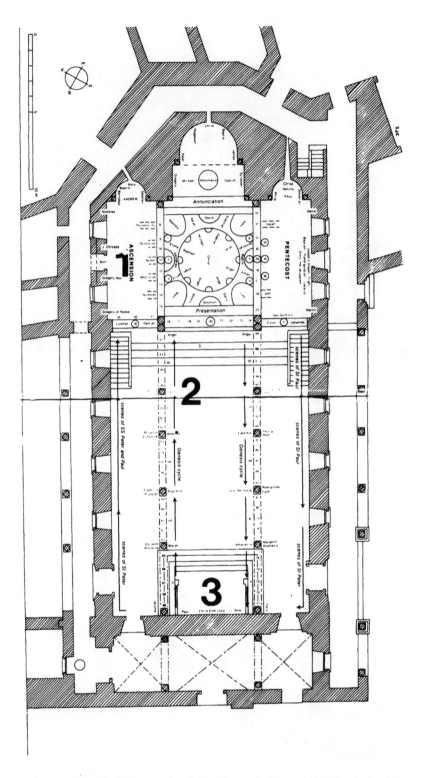

4   Palermo, Cappella Palatina, plan (after Borsook, *Messages in Mosaic,* fig. 16, with additions showing location of: 1. Royal balcony in northern transept arm; 2. Nave balcony; 3. Royal throne platform)

5 Palermo, Cappella Palatina, east wall of the southern transept arm, Nativity

6   Pskov, cathedral of the Transfiguration, east wall of southern cross arm, Nativity

7   Pskov, cathedral of the Transfiguration, view of southern cross arm

8   Palermo, Cappella Palatina, view of south wall of southern transept arm

9   Palermo, Cappella Palatina, view of north wall of northern transept arm

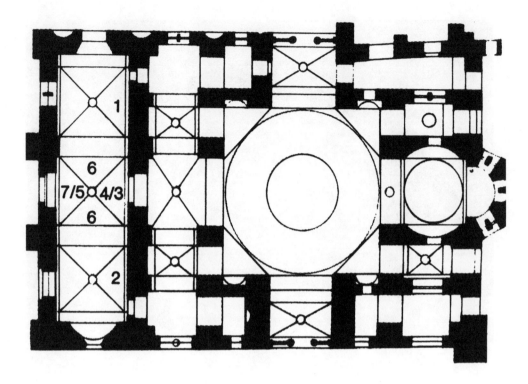

10   Phokis, Hosios Loukas, plan showing location of: 1. Crucifixion; 2. Anastasis; 3. Pantokrator
(after Kartsonis, *Anastasis,* fig. 84)

11 Palermo, St. Mary's of the Admiral, portrait of Roger II

12 Rome, Biblioteca Vaticana, gr. 666, fol. 2v, Euthymios Zygabenos, *Panoplia Dogmatica*, portrait of Alexios I

13 Palermo, Cappella Palatina, plan of chapel showing design of opus sectile pavement (after Domenico Lo Faso Pietrasanta Duca di Serradifalco, *Del duomo di Monreale e di altre chiese siculo normanne ragionamenti tre* [Palermo, 1838], pl. xv)

14   Palermo, Cappella Palatina, ceiling of nave

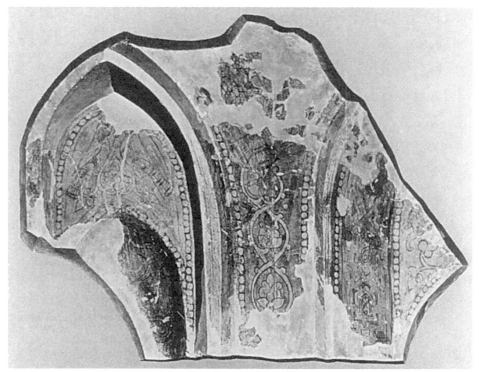

15 Cairo, Islamic Museum, fragments of *muqarnas* from Bath of Abu'l-Su'ud
(after Sourdel-Thomine and Spuler, *Kunst des Islam,* pl. 34)

16   Cefalù, cathedral, main apse

17   Palermo, Zisa, fountain room

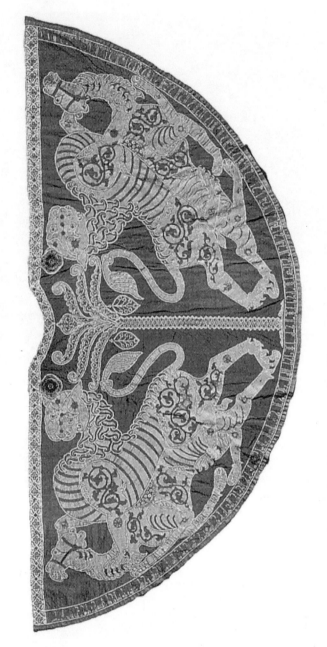

18 Vienna, Kunsthistorisches Museum, mantle of Roger II

19   Palermo, Cappella Palatina, ceiling of nave, detail

20   Monreale, cathedral, choir and main apse

of a central panel of twenty eight-pointed stars surrounded by a frame in the *muqarnas* (stalactite) technique, whose roots are probably to be sought in Fatimid Egypt.[12]

Christomimesis

It is useful to begin with the issue of derivation to which reference has already been made. The essential lines of at least one major component of the problem were spelled out in the study of Ernst Kitzinger published in the *Art Bulletin* in 1949.[13] The focus of this study was the mosaic decoration of the sanctuary of the chapel, which Kitzinger showed was based on the Middle Byzantine program for the domed, centrally planned church to an amazingly precise degree: from the Pantokrator in the apex of the dome, through the rings of angels, evangelists, scenes from Christ's life and saints that descended downward and outward from it.[14] Kitzinger spoke about this program in the abstract, but it may be possible now to be more specific. In this regard, an important case is the cathedral of the Transfiguration in Pskov, which has a *terminus post quem* of 1156 and is thus a near contemporary of the Cappella Palatina.[15] The fully painted interior of the cathedral presents several rather striking analogies to the Cappella Palatina: in terms of individual scenes, for instance, like the scene of the Nativity, which is such a complicated iconographic construction in itself and so closely mirrored in the version in the chapel (Figs. 5, 6); in terms of the choice of narrative subjects—eleven of the presumed thirteen christological events depicted in the chapel find parallels in Pskov;

---

[12] The ceiling in the nave of the Cappella Palatina is now undergoing restoration, and it is to be hoped that a preliminary report on its condition will soon appear. For the most complete photographic survey of the ceiling to date, see the monograph of Ugo Monneret de Villard, *Le pitture musulmane al soffitto della Cappella Palatina in Palermo* (Rome, 1930), with a discussion of *muqarnas*. On the ceiling of the Cappella Palatina, see in addition A. A. Pavlovskij, *Zhivopis' Palatinskoi Kapelly v Palermo* (St. Petersburg, 1890); idem, "Decoration du plafond de la Chapelle Palatine," *BZ* 2 (1893), 361 ff; Richard Ettinghausen, "Painting of the Fatimid Period: A Reconstruction," *Ars Islamica* 9 (1942), 112 ff; André Grabar, "Image d'une église chrétienne parmi des peintures musulmanes de la Chapelle Palatine à Palerme," *Aus der Welt der islamischen Kunst: Festschrift für Ernst Kühnel* (Berlin, 1959), 100 ff; R. Ettinghausen, *Arab Painting* (Lausanne, 1962), 44 ff; Dalu Jones, "The Cappella Palatina, Problems of Attribution," *Art and Archaeology Research Papers* 2 (1972), 41 ff; Annabelle Simon Cahn, *Some Cosmological Imagery in the Decoration of the Ceiling of the Palatine Chapel in Palermo*, Ph.D. diss. (Columbia University, 1978); Francesco Gabrieli and Umberto Scerrato, *Gli Arabi in Italia* (Milan, 1985), 359 ff; David Gramit, "The Music Paintings of the Cappella Palatina in Palermo," *Imago Musicae: International Yearbook of Musical Iconography*, ed. Tilman Seebass, vol. II (Durham, N.C., 1985), 9 ff; Staale Sinding-Larsen, "*Plura ordinantur ad unum*: Some Perspectives regarding the 'Arab-Islamic' Ceiling of the Cappella Palatina at Palermo (1132–1143)," *ActaIRNorv* 7 (1989), 55 ff. On the origins and development of *muqarnas*, see Ernst Herzfeld, "Damascus: Studies in Architecture I," *Ars Islamica* 9 (1942), 1 ff; Lucien Golvin, *Recherche archéologiques à la Qal'a des Banu Hammad* (Paris, 1965), 124 ff; Jonathan M. Bloom, "The Introduction of the Muqarnas into Egypt," *Muqarnas* 5 (1988), 21 ff. On the derivation of the design of the ceiling, see below.

[13] Kitzinger, "Choice and Arrangement," *passim*, esp. 271 ff.

[14] Kitzinger, "Mosaic Decoration," 147 ff.

[15] Viktor Lazarev, *Old Russian Murals and Mosaics from the XIth to the XVIth Century*, trans. B. Roniger and N. Dunn (London, 1966), 99 ff, 247 ff; M. N. Soboleva, "Stenopis Spaso-Preobraženskogo sobora Mirožskogo monastyrja v Pskove," *Drevne-russkoe iskusstvo: khudožestvennaja kul'tura Pskova*, ed. V. N. Lazarev (Moscow, 1968), 7 ff; Hubert Faensen and Wladimir Iwanow, *Altrussische Baukunst* (Vienna, 1972), 283 f, and 283 plan, figs. 122–27.

but also in terms of the disposition of scenes.[16] The Nativity finds a similar place to the southeast in both chapel and church, and, in both cases, too, side walls flanking the central domed space are decorated with multiple tiers of narrative scenes (Figs. 7, 8).

These resemblances are more than merely circumstantial. They suggest that some kind of directive, perhaps in the form of a model book, and perhaps also promulgated from some central point, was available to the designers who worked in both places, who then adapted these prescriptions to their own individual architectural contexts, which bore a certain similarity to one another in any case.[17] But to my mind the more important point is the light that this relationship may shed on one unusual feature of the chapel. Ernst Kitzinger has argued that the bunching up of the narrative scenes from Christ's life on the south wall of the southern transept arm of the chapel was effected primarily in order to create a view for the king, who must have occupied what was, in all likelihood, a balcony to the north, on the north wall of the northern transept arm (Figs. 8, 9).[18] This is almost a cinematographic concept, and Kitzinger implied, furthermore, that it was unique. What Pskov raises, however, is the possibility of formulating two additional hypotheses: that the designer of the chapel program may have been adapting a format that was in use in other places, and that the real departure of the chapel may have been in inserting into this narrative structure the figure of the king. It is to the latter proposition that I would now like to turn.

It is important to understand that the king's balcony in the chapel, though demonstrated beyond any reasonable doubt by archaeology and documents, no longer exists, nor does the original surface of the wall that must have immediately surrounded it.[19]

---

[16] See Soboleva, esp. figs. on pp. 12–15, for overall arrangement of subjects. On the relationship between the scene of the Nativity in the Cappella Palatina and that of Pskov, see Ernst Kitzinger, *I mosaici di Santa Maria dell'Ammiraglio a Palermo* (Palermo, 1990), 175 ff.

[17] On the role of model books in the creation of the Norman mosaic programs, see Ernst Kitzinger, *The Mosaics of Monreale* (Palermo, 1960), 43 ff, and idem, *Santa Maria dell'Ammiraglio*, 180 f; see also Hugo Buchthal, *The "Musterbuch" of Wolfenbüttel and Its Position in the Art of the Thirteenth Century* (Vienna, 1979); Otto Demus, *Byzantine Art and the West* (New York, 1970), 31 ff; Claudine Dauphin, "Byzantine Pattern Books: A Reexamination of the Problem in the Light of the 'Inhabited Scroll,' " *Art History* 1 (1978), 400 ff.

[18] Kitzinger, "Choice and Arrangement," 283 ff.

[19] Trizzino, *"La Palatina,"* 35, dissents, adducing the report of Valenti regarding the discovery of fragments of two window frames embedded in the upper zone of the north wall, essentially corresponding in size to the two windows in the same zone on the wall opposite (south wall of the southern transept arm). In the opinion of the architect, these frames exclude the possibility of a royal loge on the north wall in Norman times because they were broken into by the larger opening between them. For the Valenti report, see Palermo, Biblioteca Comunale, 5 Qq E146, nos. 36 (18 October 1928), 441' (and 1"), and 5Qq E146, no. 28, photo no. 10 ("muro nord del presbiterio con le finestre antiche vandalicamente deturbate ed ostrutto con fabbriche moderne"). The upper portions of the two window frames are still visible on the exterior of the north wall of the northern transept arm, the surface of which, however, has been entirely restored. Both Valenti and Trizzino appear to be unaware of Cesare Pasca's report cited in note 23 below, and of the fact that the present opening on the north wall was created in 1838. The opening that Pasca described, however, was considerably narrower: 11 palmi = 2.83 m. As such it would have been fully compatible with the two windows of Norman date. In any case, such window frames in and of themselves could never be taken as proof of Trizzino's conclusion; see, for example, Maria Andaloro et al., *I mosaici di Monreale: Restauri e scoperte (1965–1982). XIII Catalogo di opere d'arte restaurate* (Palermo, 1986), esp. 47 ff, regarding changes in the windows of the cathedral between the time the walls were constructed and the mosaic decoration was put up. The issue is also discussed by Ingamaj Beck, "The First Mosaics of the Cappella Palatina in Palermo," *Byzantion* 40 (1970), 127 ff.

This surface is covered today with modern mosaics showing John the Baptist preaching and a landscape.[20] But how would it have been decorated in the twelfth century? The most plausible explanation is Kitzinger's. Kitzinger observed that the sanctuary program, like that of the classical Middle Byzantine system as a whole, possessed a christological cycle that was a true cycle, that is, complete, with a beginning, a middle, and an end, and with all of the major events—or feasts—of Christ's life depicted, save two: the Crucifixion and the Anastasis, the feast scenes for Good Friday and Easter Sunday respectively.[21] Now especially in twelfth-century Byzantium or the Byzantine-influenced Mediterranean world, such a cycle is unthinkable without these most important subjects.[22] The only place they could have gone is on the two pieces of wall flanking the balcony. That there was space enough for the scenes we know almost as a fact. The same text that mentions the balcony also records its width—that is, 11 palmi ("largo 11 palmi alto 10")—which would have left ample sections of wall vacant on either side of the structure for the two scenes.[23] Placing them there—which would seem to be the only viable solution to the problem of the original decoration of the sanctuary—however, does more than simply complete the cycle: it creates a pairing around the balcony of the king which had a distinct resonance in Byzantine tradition.

One finds such a pairing, for instance, in the narthex of Hosios Loukas, where scenes of the Crucifixion and the Anastasis are significantly singled out for placement in the two large lunettes over the side doors leading into the nave (Fig. 10).[24] These scenes flank a figure of the Pantokrator in the lunette over the main door, who holds an open book proclaiming "I am the light of the world. He that follows me will not walk in darkness but will have the light of life" (John 8:12). Similarly, in the monastery church of Daphni, the Crucifixion and the Anastasis are also pendants, on the eastern faces of the north and south cross arms of the nave, although in this case what they flank may

---

[20] Demus, *Norman Mosaics*, 36; Kitzinger, "Cappella Palatina," 276 note 38.

[21] Kitzinger, "Cappella Palatina," 275 f.

[22] See the discussion of Ernst Kitzinger, "Reflections on the Feast Cycle in Byzantine Art," *CahArch* 36 (1988), 51 ff, esp. 53 note 27, with bibliography.

[23] Cesare Pasca, *Descrizione della Imperiale e Regale Cappella Palatina di Palermo* (Palermo, 1841), 29 ff, 100: "Furono inoltre rimossi dall'interno della regia cappella per ridurla alla sua primitiva semplicità, due palchi di disgustosa apparenza, uno più piccolo nella metà superiore del muro della Cappella del Sacramento, che servia per gli antichi vicerè, e inferiormente un altro più grande per uso della regale corte. Quest'ultimo era tutto di legno ricoperto di velluto rosso con frange d'oro, era attaccato alla parete ove sono rappresentate le figure di alcuni santi della chiesa, e protraevasi fino al muro, che forma spalliera agli stalli del coro. *Nel palchetto superiore ch'era tutto di legno fu ritrovato un arco acuto, era largo undici palmi, ed alto dieci; essendo stato riconosciuto quest'arco di epoca primitiva per alcuni segni non fallaci, si congettura che potea essere un arco d'ingresso al palchetto da servire alla regale corte normanna, quando volea intervenire alle sacre funzioni del tempio, tanto più che non troviamo alcun luogo in esso che ci possa far credere d'essere stato adatto a tal uso.* Fu ordinato da S.M. d'ingrandirsi quest'arco per servir come palco per la regal corte. Al lato sinistra dell'arco medesimo è stato poco fa portato a compimento un quadro a musaico, che rappresenta la predicazione di S. Giovanni nel deserto esequito sopra il cartone del sig. Rosario Riolo; forma continuazione al rimanente del musaico del lato opposto fatto ai tempi del Cardini, ove vedesi una boscaglia col bastone di S. Giovanni con lo scritto ecce Agnus Dei. Si pretese dagli artisti con somma imperizia di rappresentate in questo musaico il deserto, e vi fecero appartenere un'antica figura è in nessuna maniera adatta per quella rappresentazione" (italics mine).

[24] Ernst Diez and Otto Demus, *Byzantine Mosaics of Greece* (Cambridge, Mass., 1931), 67 ff, 119 (plan of church), fig. 12 (Pantokrator), pls. XIII (Crucifixion) and XIV (Anastasis); Anna D. Kartsonis, *Anastasis: The Making of an Image* (Princeton, 1986), 217 f, figs. 83 (Anastasis) and 84 (plan of church).

be construed in two terms: as the Pantokrator in the central dome on the one hand, or as the altar below, which is another kind of image of Christ, being tomb and table where he is materially present, on the other.[25] Anna Kartsonis, who has studied these pairings, has concluded that they were intensely meaningful. She has called them an "incantation for salvation," that is, an "expression of . . . a sacramental, liturgical, theological and historical *synopsis* of Christ and his church as the means and ends of redemption."[26] It should also be mentioned that although both of these examples are earlier in date than the Cappella Palatina, there are later cases, and the practice that they indicate seems to have been more widely known.[27]

These cases would appear to have certain features in common, which, in the present context, may be defined as three: first, the two scenes, although clearly paired, also form a part, and a critical part, of the christological cycle as a whole—they are not entirely isolated and independent units; second, although the scenes flank fields in several different formats—a lunette, a dome, and an altar—all of these fields may be understood in terms of an image of the Lord; and third, these scenes are also situated in relationship to an opening—a door—which may be construed as a passage *into* the ruler's realm, either from the narthex into the nave of the church or from the nave into the bema. In a certain sense, therefore, the pair of scenes, together with their centerpiece, may be thought of as a building block—individual and coherent, albeit one of many of which the classical Middle Byzantine system of church decoration was composed; but one, too, that was capable of inflection in terms of siting and form that lent it a great deal of flexibility, and opened the door to a variety of opportunities for its use. All these conditions may also be fulfilled in the Cappella Palatina: if present, the scenes of the Crucifixion and the Anastasis would clearly have formed part of the christological cycle, which was constructed around the chapel in essentially the same zone; they would also have clearly flanked an opening, the king's balcony, which was also nothing less than the passage into the ruler's space.[28] The question is, could the designer of the sanctuary program have intentionally varied this apparent composition of three elements, to embrace, instead of the image of the Byzantine Pantokrator, the real presence of the Norman king? To the best of my knowledge, such a variation involving the emperor had never been attempted in the monumental arts of Byzantium, and to imagine it here, in the Cappella Palatina, would be to posit a bold move.[29]

---

[25] Diez and Demus, *Byzantine Mosaics*, 67 ff, 121 (plan of church), frontispiece (Pantokrator in dome), figs. 99 (Crucifixion) and 100 (Anastasis); Kartsonis, *Anastasis*, 219 ff, figs. 85 (Anastasis) and 86 (plan).

[26] Kartsonis, *Anastasis*, 219 and 221.

[27] See, for instance, the decoration in the church of Christos in Veroia by Kalliergis (1315): Stylianos Pelekanidis, Καλλιέργης: Ὅλης Θετταλίας ἄριστος ζωγράφος (Athens, 1973), 14, pls. 5, 8 f; Kartsonis, *Anastasis*, 220 f, figs. 87 (Anastasis) and 88 (layout).

[28] The area immediately behind the northern transept arm has been rebuilt in modern times; see Francesco Valenti, "L'arte nell'era normanna," in *Il Regno normanno* (Milan, 1932), 220; Trizzino, *"La Palatina,"* passim, esp. 21 ff.

[29] Carmen Laura Dumitrescu points out what may in fact be a related phenomenon: the distinct echo, in the portrait of Emperor Michael VII Doukas in Coislin 79, fol. 2, of the composition of the Deesis, in which the emperor himself appears as the center of a group of three (between St. John Chrysostom [left] and the Archangel Michael "Chonaiates" [right]), as if he had been substituted for and in turn was meant to evoke in the memory of the viewer the figure of Christ; C. L. Dumitrescu, "Remarques en marge du *Coislin 79*: Les trois eu-

Such a move may find an analogy, and a rationale, in the single most famous image of King Roger to have come down to us from his own lifetime. This image is the mosaic panel made for the church of St. Mary's of the Admiral in Palermo around the time the Cappella Palatina was being decorated in the 1140s (Fig. 11).[30] It was once probably situated in the narthex of the church. The image was based on a Byzantine prototype, as embodied, for instance, in the ivory plaque showing the emperor Constantine VII crowned by Christ.[31] The Norman mosaic copies the Byzantine image down to the details of Roger's garb, which are taken directly from the emperor's costume. But in this relationship the Norman image also seems to embody a kind of paradox in the following sense. Although close to the Byzantine visual prototype, the Norman mosaic also differs from it, markedly, in one important respect, namely, in the degree to which the face of the king has been assimilated to that of Christ. Roger, with his long hair and beard and idealized features, looks very much like Christ, as has been repeatedly pointed out— which is something the Byzantines never seemed to have attempted.[32] When the emperor was depicted in the presence of the Allruler in Byzantium, there was always a basic physiognomic distinction between the two, as witness Constantine VII, or any of the relevant images from the twelfth century (Fig. 12).[33] On the other hand, Byzantine rhetoric, and especially as it developed in the twelfth century, came increasingly to stress this important similarity.[34] It suffices to quote a short passage from an encomium of Manuel I (1143–80) by Michael Italikos, composed sometime after August or November 1143, in which the emperor is compared to his father, John, and God in terms that have been described as extreme: "You dwell here below as a living and moving statue of the king who made you king, O Emperor, and I don't know of anyone else on earth more like him. For bearing his name is an indication of your strong resemblance to him. For think: Emanuel is the theological name from above; Manuel is the name acclaimed here below. . . . If God is expressed in both names, he is the first and heavenly God, while you are the second and earthly one."[35] The paradox is that the Norman image expresses the extremity of the Christomimetic theme especially as it developed in Byzantium in

nuques et le problème du donateur," *Byzantion* 57 (1987), 32 ff, esp. 40 f, fig. 4. I would like to thank Henry Maguire for drawing this reference to my attention.

[30] Kitzinger, *Santa Maria dell'Ammiraglio*, 191 ff, 315 ff (catalogue); pl. xxiii, figs. 120 ff.

[31] Adolph Goldschmidt and Kurt Weitzmann, *Die byzantinischen Elfenbeinskulpturen des X.–XIII. Jahrhunderts* (Berlin, 1934), vol. II (reliefs), 35 f, fig. 35.

[32] Ernst Kitzinger, "On the Portrait of Roger II in the Martorana in Palermo," *Proporzioni* 3 (1950), 30 ff.

[33] See, for example, the portrait of Alexios I in the *Panoplia Dogmatica* of Euthymios Zygabenos, Vat. gr. 666 (early 12th century); Ioannes Spatharakis, *The Portrait in Byzantine Illuminated Manuscripts* (Leiden, 1976), 122 ff, fig. 80. Robin Cormack's argument, apropos of the mosaic of Christ with Constantine IX Monomachos and Zoe in the south gallery of St. Sophia, that the head of Christ was changed when the head of the emperor was changed, because the head of Christ was originally made to resemble the first emperor represented in the mosaic (Zoe's first husband, Romanos III), is unconvincing; see R. Cormack, "Interpreting the Mosaics of S. Sophia at Istanbul," *Art History* 4 (1981), 131 ff, esp. 141 f, fig. 6.

[34] Alexander Kazhdan, in collaboration with Simon Franklin, *Studies on Byzantine Literature of the Eleventh and Twelfth Centuries* (Cambridge, 1984), 110 f; Henry Maguire, "Style and Ideology in Byzantine Art," *Gesta* 28 (1989), 299; idem, "The Mosaics of Nea Moni: An Imperial Reading," *DOP* 46 (1992), 205 ff.

[35] Michael Italikos, ed. Paul Gautier, *Michel Italikos, lettres et discours*, Archives de l'Orient chrétien 14 (Paris, 1972), 294; trans. Paul Magdalino, *The Empire of Manuel I Komnenos, 1143–1180* (Cambridge, 1993), 437.

the twelfth century *better* than any work of art that we know from Byzantium, and the question is why?

A critical consideration may be in the function of these words—as in the passage just quoted. Clearly they did not set out simply to repeat what images of the emperor must have already shown.[36] They provided an alternate set of information that complemented, elaborated, or focused on selected aspects of these images, and this must have been the heart of the relationship between images and words in the Byzantine court. Images and words existed in a symbiotic relationship to one another. They explained one another, while not at the same time merely repeating the explanation. They amplified and elaborated one another, thus conspiring to fill the most important sensory dimensions through which a Byzantine courtier could expect to construct a worldview. In the context of the Byzantine court of the twelfth century, with its dramatic revival of the rhetorical arts, recently and brilliantly exposed by Paul Magdalino, we have to understand this relationship as having been brought to a new height.[37]

Such a tradition, however, did not pass to Sicily. The Italo-Greek homilary, with its sermons scattered somewhat enigmatically throughout the liturgical year and only very rarely attested by its author, Philagathos, as having been recited in the presence of the king, is a poor substitute for the works of Michael Italikos, Theodore Prodromos, and the "Manganeios Prodromos" as he has been differentiated by Magdalino.[38] But such a project could hardly have succeeded in any case. With its multiple languages, and insistence on maintaining these differences, the Norman court could hardly have sought to follow a single path in the rhetorical arts.[39] What was incumbent on the Normans to create was an image that could stand on its own, that was not embedded in or dependent upon a single rhetorical tradition for explanation, that did not need or benefit excessively from verbal commentary—that was, in a word, visually self-sufficient. This, I would argue, is what they created in their portrait of Christ and the king: an image that explained the derivation of Roger's power—not from pope or emperor but from God

---

[36] See the discussion of Henry Maguire, *Art and Eloquence in Byzantium* (Princeton, 1981), with bibliography.

[37] Magdalino, *Manuel I Komnenos*, 413 ff.

[38] For the sermons of Philagathos, see PG 132; Filagato da Cerami, *Omelie per i vangeli domenicali e le feste di tutto l'anno*, ed. Giuseppe Rossi Taibbi (Palermo, 1969). In addition, Stefano Caruso, "Le tre omelie inedite 'Per la Domenica delle Palme' di Filagato da Cerami (LI, LII, LIII Rossi-Taibbi)," *Ἐπ.Ἑτ.Βυζ.Σπ.* 41 (1974), 109 ff; Bruno Lavagnini, "Filippo-Filagato promotore degli studi di greco in Calabria," *BollGrott*, n.s., 28 (1974), 3 ff; idem, *Profilo di Filagato da Cerami, con traduzione della omelia XXVII pronunziata dal pulpito della Cappella Palatina in Palermo* (Palermo, 1992). For the "Manganeios Prodromos," see Magdalino, *Manuel I Komnenos*, 494 ff.

[39] A case in point is the inscription in three languages that formed a part of a water clock erected by Roger II in the Norman Palace; see Michele Amari, *Le epigrafi arabiche in Sicilia*, ed. F. Gabrieli (Palermo, 1971), 29 ff, pl. I, fig. 3. Of interest in this context is also the quadrilingual epitaph (Greek, Latin, Arabic, and Hebrew) of Anna, mother of the priest Grisandus; Amari, *Epigrafi*, 201 ff, pl. IX, fig. 2.

On the relationship of ethnic groups, linguistic and otherwise, see Vera von Falkenhausen, "I gruppi etnici nel regno di Ruggero II e la loro participazione al potere," in *Società, potere e popolo nell'età di Ruggero II* (as in note 7 above), 133 ff; also V. DiGiovanni, "Divisione etnografica della popolazione di Palermo nei secoli XI, XII, XIII," *Archivio storico siciliano*, n.s., 13 (1888), 1 ff; Antonio de Stefano, *La cultura in Sicilia nel periodo normanno* (Palermo, 1938); Giuseppe Galasso, "Social and Political Developments in the Eleventh and Twelfth Centuries," in *The Normans in Sicily and Southern Italy* (Oxford, 1977), 47 ff.

alone—and at the same time demonstrated the fact of *similitudo*—his essential Christo-mimetic nature—*in purely visual terms*. Such an image could thus be understood by any-one—Arab, Norman, Greek, or Latin.[40]

Returning to the sanctuary of the Cappella Palatina, I would argue that a similar point was being made here also: that the Norman king was intended to have a place in this Byzantine-derived triadic scheme, as the divinely appointed ruler on earth, whose nature was essentially Christomimetic. This interpretation is supported by two other features of the chapel's east end. The first is the balcony itself. This structure defined the place of the king in God's realm, the sanctuary, as clearly above that of other mortal men. But perhaps more important in this most hierarchical scheme, it placed the king on the level with and integrated into Christ's life, which he, in an important sense, completed. In the downward and outward progression from the image of the Pantokrator in the sanctuary of the Cappella Palatina, the king took up his place in the stratum of Christ's life, where a portrait of the ruler might have been expected to have been placed.[41]

The other point concerns the south wall to which we should now return (Fig. 8). It has been noted that on his balcony the king must have stood directly across from the scene of the Transfiguration. This relationship has been understood primarily in terms of the king's view: that he was here meant to be the direct witness of the glorification of Christ.[42] But the configuration changes if we imagine that this relationship was also appreciated from a different point of view—from the point of view of those standing below who would have understood the two images—the king and Christ—as pendants, parallel glories of divine and divinely appointed rulers, and, in them, the necessary balance of the composition.[43]

Style

Since we have focused on the sanctuary of the chapel, it is important also to consider the nave. The very fact that the chapel lends itself to treatment in two parts is interesting

---

[40] It is interesting to observe that the church of St. Mary's was not off-limits to Muslims, who could apparently visit it freely; see *The Travels of Ibn Jubayr,* trans. R.J.C. Broadhurst (London, 1952), 349, concerning the author's Christmas visit to the church.

[41] The fact that the image of the Pantokrator was present in the chapel in the dome of the choir and thus manifestly "above" the king should also be stressed. Two other images of the Pantokrator occur in the eastern portion of the chapel: one is located in the lunette at the top of the eastern wall above the southern apse (Kitzinger, *I mosaici,* fasc. 1, fig. 253); the other is located in the conch of the main apse (ibid., fig. 130).

[42] Wolfgang Krönig, "Zur Transfiguration der Cappella Palatina in Palermo," *ZKunstg* 19 (1956), 162 ff; Ćurčić, "Some Palatine Aspects," 127 ff.

[43] Another case in which a balcony or loge in an ecclesiastical context is located directly across from a representation of the Transfiguration is the church of the Holy Cross at Aght 'Amar; see Sirarpie Der Nersessian, *Aght 'Amar: Church of the Holy Cross* (Cambridge, Mass., 1965), 7 ff, figs. 63 ff; eadem and Hermann Vahramian, *Aght 'Amar* (Venice, 1974), figs. 55 and 56 with general views of the interior; J. G. Davies, *Medieval Armenian Art and Architecture: The Church of the Holy Cross Aght 'Amar* (London, 1991), 154 ff, fig. 14 (diagram of narrative scenes); and Catherine Jolivet-Lévy, "Présence et figures du souverain à Sainte-Sophie de Constantinople et à l'église de la Sainte-Croix d'Aghtamar," in this present volume. The decoration is interesting because of the length and elaborateness of the christological cycle, but it is important to bear in mind that it differs from the presumed arrange-

and one indication of the split personality of the edifice.[44] As with the east end, the nave too presents archaeological problems, although less well known. They have been the subject of a study of mine, but rather than going through this complicated material in detail, I would simply like to sketch some of the main conclusions of my research.[45] In its present-day manifestation, the nave is an odd mix of Latin and Arabic forms, with some rather unseemly juxtapositions, such as the Old Testament cycle of the nave walls directly underneath the most forthright portrayal of the joys of the flesh on the numerous facets of the nave ceiling, and in what was for the Christian twelfth century their most pagan form. Originally, this was not the case. The nave of the Cappella Palatina was constructed under Roger II without any Christian images whatsoever—neither Old Testament cycle, nor series of scenes from the lives of Peter and Paul, nor majestic image of Christ flanked by Peter and Paul over the throne platform at the west end of the nave. These elements were all added later under Roger's successors, William I and William II. What covered nave and aisles to begin with was probably a purely ornamental decoration, and then on top of that, tapestries, at least on special occasions.[46] One result of the first arrangement would have been to bring into even greater prominence the nave ceiling. The nave also contained a balcony to the northeast, now completely gone, where some eighteenth-century mosaics presently stand.[47] The throne platform to the west was a much less intrusive affair. It lacked the mosaic above it, as well as the *fastigium,* which now turns it into an enormous, oversized throne. Originally it was just the platform—five steps up from the floor of the nave—and bounded north and south by low, openwork walls. The great slabs of marble and porphyry that now make up the throne sides came from the chancel barrier in the seventeenth century, where they formed a most decisive boundary between sanctuary and nave.[48] Missing too from the original scheme was the pulpit in the south aisle and its accompanying paschal candelabrum, and the monumental bronze doors in the two openings beside the platform to the west.[49]

---

ment in the Cappella Palatina in two critical ways: on the one hand, the scene of the Transfiguration was not located in the same zone as the figure of the ruler as he would have presented himself in the gallery on the wall opposite, but above him; on the other hand, the scenes from Christ's life did not serve to frame the ruler's loge. The 12th-century Episcopal Chapel at Schwarzrheindorf has also been compared to the Cappella Palatina in this regard; see Albert Verbeek, *Die Doppelkirche und Ihre Wandgemälde* (Düsseldorf, 1953), xxxxv, lxv, fig. 38; Krönig, "Zur Transfiguration," 162 ff, fig. 4.

[44] Kitzinger, "Cappella Palatina," 284; Ćurčić, "Some Palatine Aspects," 140 ff; Tronzo, "Cappella Palatina," 221 ff.

[45] For what follows, see also Tronzo, "Cappella Palatina," 197 ff.

[46] In the proemium of his sermon on the feast of Sts. Peter and Paul, Philagathos makes reference to multicolored textiles which may have hung on the walls of the nave and aisles; Taibbi, ed., 175 (as in note 38 above).

[47] "Un palchetto per i vicere" is mentioned by Cesare Pasca as having been located in the clerestory zone of the north wall of the nave near its eastern end; see Pasca, *Descrizione della Imperiale e Regale Cappella Palatina di Palermo,* 98, and the discussion of Tronzo, "Cappella Palatina," 215 ff. The 18th-century mosaics are discussed by Demus, *Norman Mosaics,* 34 f. I shall argue for the existence of a balcony in the nave of the chapel in Norman times in my forthcoming monograph.

[48] Tronzo, "Cappella Palatina," 212 f.

[49] Tronzo, "Cappella Palatina," 218 f. For the bronze doors, see Ursula Mende, *Die Bronzetüren des Mittelalters, 800–1200* (Munich, 1983), 53 ff, 145 f, figs. 35 f; Antonio Cadei, "La prima commitenza normanna," in *Le porte di bronzo dall'antichità al secolo XIII,* ed. S. Salomi (Rome, 1990), 367 ff, 21 ff. For the paschal candelabrum, see Josef Deér, *The Dynastic Porphyry Tombs of the Norman Period in Sicily* (Cambridge, Mass., 1959), 157 ff; Michael

The sum total of all of these additions was to transform the nave, to make it symmetrical with images and facing forward to the east, as the nave of a church should. Indeed it was to normalize in a Christian sense what before could only be described as an idiosyncratic space. What were the main ingredients of this space? Mention has already been made of the nave balcony. For a variety of reasons I believe that this balcony was a viewing platform, not for the king, but for members of his court—probably women. The space behind the balcony, over the north aisle, may also have given access to another viewing point, in the west wall of the north transept, thus allowing the women from within essentially the same environment to see the king in both of his places—in the sanctuary and in the nave.[50] The original main entrance to the chapel was the door to the southwest, where we encounter one additional and important piece of evidence.[51] The pavement of the Cappella Palatina is virtually intact and one of the most beautiful opus sectile floors from the twelfth century (Fig. 13).[52] As a design, it is arranged essentially symmetrically in square and rectangular panels with large motifs, with only one serious departure from the norm: in the first two bays of the south aisle to the west, at the foot of the main entrance. There we find a different kind of pattern—with parallel bands—which I have argued elsewhere was derived from a type well known for use at thresholds in antiquity and the Middle Ages.[53] As with other patterns in ancient and medieval floors, the threshold pavement type implied a movement through the area, and thus it is interesting to note that it was used twice in the Cappella Palatina—first in the first bay of the south aisle (facing the main door) and then again in the second. I have understood this duplication in terms of an implied movement first *into* the chapel and then from the south aisle *into* the nave, in other words, from the entrance into a direct encounter with the occupant of the platform, the king. Such a movement—which I think might best be understood in terms of *proskynesis*—goes some way toward explaining what use the nave of the Cappella Palatina was originally designed to serve.

As I have also argued elsewhere, I think that the Cappella Palatina was originally designed to serve a dual function consisting of parallel performances of sacred liturgies and royal receptions, much in the manner of the imperial liturgy of Constantinople as it may be reconstructed from the *Book of Ceremonies* or Pseudo-Kodinos.[54] But perhaps more to the point in the present context is that these two spaces, sanctuary and nave, were decorated in much more sharply constrasting styles in Roger's time than they would now appear to be, Byzantine and Islamic. The affiliation of the east end of the chapel to the Middle Byzantine church has already been discussed. With its viewing balcony and low, wide throne platform, *muqarnas* vault and tapestry-lined walls, on the

---

Schneider-Flagmeyer, *Der mittelalterliche Osterleuchter in Süditalien* (Frankfurt, 1986), 221 ff. On the restoration of the pulpit, see Trizzino, "*La Palatina*," 8.

[50] Tronzo, "Cappella Palatina," 215 ff.

[51] See, for instance, the hypothetical reconstruction of Valenti, "Era normanna," fig. 102. Tronzo, "Cappella Palatina," 223 ff.

[52] There are no adequate published photographs of the pavement in the Cappella Palatina. There is only one illustration of the design of the pavement, a schematic diagram made in the 19th century; see Hiltrud Kier, *Der mittelalterliche Schmuckfussboden* (Düsseldorf, 1970), 29, fig. 337; Tronzo, "Cappella Palatina," 223 f, fig. 23.

[53] See, for instance, the pavement from Pompeii illustrated in Kier, *Schmuckfussboden*, fig. 270.

[54] Tronzo, "Cappella Palatina," 225 ff.

other hand, the nave of the Cappella Palatina must have resembled the noble reception hall of a Fatimid palace more than anything else. The case is far too involved to argue here in detail. It depends on reconstructing the Fatimid situation from a number of different sources ranging from literary descriptions to extant monuments, like the fragments of eleventh-century *muqarnas* from the Bath of Abu'l-Su'ud in Fustat, which bear an extraordinary resemblance to the *muqarnas* of the Cappella Palatina in both form and decoration (Figs. 14, 15).[55] Suffice it to say that the ceiling itself, which is one of the main documents of the first phase of the nave, was the product of Islamic craftsmen (in the capacities of both architect and painter), as a comparison with the related ceiling in the cathedral of Cefalù, which was not, helps to demonstrate.[56]

Given the complexity of the subject, and the fact that there is still so much to be known, generalizations about Norman patronage are rather risky at best, but let me offer one observation that may help us to understand the stylistic logic of the Rogerian phase of the chapel. Byzantine art—that is to say, Byzantine style, technique, and decorative schemes—had its greatest success in Roger's kingdom in churches like the cathedral of Cefalù and St. Mary's of the Admiral, where it served to define the liturgical space, the place of the Allruler, the place of God on earth (Fig. 16). Conversely, Islamic forms had their greatest impact on the Norman scene in the palaces and villas of the earthly ruler, Roger himself, in places like the Torre Pisana, which was a component of the royal palace, the Zisa, and the Cuba, with their beautiful *muqarnas* vaults (Fig. 17).[57] I would argue that the two styles were more than merely a casual choice—that they defined the places of the two rulers visually, and when, *mutatis mutandis,* they were employed in the context of the king's own images of himself, they also functioned in a closely related way. Roger appeared in Byzantine garb when he himself stood in the realm of the Allruler, as in the image of the king in the Martorana (Fig. 11), and when he stood in the realm of his own court, he was enveloped in the imagery and style of Islam. The latter at least is implied by the design of the magnificent mantle of the king dated to the early 1130s, composed of a Tiraz fabric and ornamented with an elaborate kufic inscription (Fig. 18).[58] It is in this sense, I believe, that the juxtaposition of the two spaces of the Cappella Palatina should be understood—as the juxtaposition, or perhaps more accurately, the comparison of the heavenly and earthly realms, the one a sacred liturgical

[55] Jacques Sourdel-Thomine and Bertold Spuler, *Die Kunst des Islam* (Berlin, 1973), 262, pl. 34. Among surviving examples, the *muqarnas* of the Cappella Palatina also resembles that of the double bay vault in the nave of the al-Qarawiyyan mosque in Fez; see Henri Terrasse, "La mosquée d'al-Qarawiyin à Fès et l'art des Almoravids," *Ars Orientalis* 2 (1957), 135 ff; idem, *La mosquée al-Qaraouiyin à Fès* (Paris, 1968), 31 ff, figs. 21 f, pls. 28 ff.

[56] For the paintings in the nave of the cathedral at Cefalù, see Mirjam Gelfer-Jørgensen, *Medieval Islamic Symbolism and the Paintings in the Cefalù Cathedral* (Leiden, 1986).

[57] For the *muqarnas* vault in the Torre Pisana, see Valenti, "Palazzo reale," fig. 9. For the Zisa, see Ursula Staacke, *Un palazzo normanno a Palermo, La Zisa. La cultura musulmana negli edifici dei Re* (Palermo, 1991). For the Cuba, see Giuseppe Caronia and Vittorio Noto, *La Cuba di Palermo (Arabi e normanni nel XII secolo)* (Palermo, 1988).

[58] On the mantle of the king, see Erwin Margulies, "Le Manteau impérial du trésor de Vienne et sa doublure," *GBA,* ser. 6, 9 (1933), 360 ff; Ugo Monneret de Villard, *La tessitura palermitana sotto i normanni e i suoi rapporti con l'arte bizantina* (Rome, 1946); Hermann Fillitz, *Die Insignien und Kleinodien des Heiligen Römischen Reiches* (Vienna, 1954), 23 f, 57 f, figs. 23 ff; Deér, *Porphyry Tombs,* 40 ff; F. al Samman, "Arabische Inschriften auf den Krönungsgewandern des Heiligen Römischen Reiches," *JbKSWien* 78 (1982), 7 ff.

space, presided over by the Pantokrator, to whom the king, on his balcony, came closer than any other mortal man; the other a space for royal greetings and receptions, where the king stood only slightly elevated above his court, beneath the images of the perfect earthly kingdom, the pleasures and perfections of King Roger's own Sicily in the dancers, drinkers, and musicians that were strewn across the nave ceiling (Fig. 19).

The use of these two styles in Norman Sicily, in this particular moment of Roger's reign, approaches the systematic, for which there would appear, at least to me, nothing comparable in Byzantium. This is not to say that the Byzantines did not cultivate nonindigenous art forms and styles. Quite the contrary. From the Bryas Palace of Theophilos to that infamous twelfth-century pavilion in the Great Palace, the Mouchroutas, not to mention scores of objects of the so-called minor arts, we have evidence of the Byzantine recognition of and appreciation for—in this case—Islamic art.[59] But I do not know of a single situation in Byzantium where the "Islamic" and "Byzantine" were brought into a juxtaposition that created a meaningful comparison of the two, as I have argued was the case in Roger's Sicily. I would venture to characterize the Byzantine reception of the visual culture of their eastern and southern neighbors as contingent, based more on a love of ornament and luxury, and on the aesthetic appeal of the object, which brings me to my final point.[60]

Given the history of medieval Sicily, it would seem logical to expect to find an artistic tradition in both a Byzantine and an Islamic mode that would help to explain the extraordinary efflorescence of these arts under Roger. But the fact is that none exists. We can only assume that both craftsmen and designs were sought out from the indigenous cultures in which they were produced and imported into Sicily by the king for the express purpose of creating something new, which was nothing less than the visual culture of his kingdom, which itself was something new. One wonders, in the end, how Roger's expenditures in this regard—building and decoration—compared to those of other rulers—the Byzantine or the Fatimid, for instance.[61] It is difficult to gauge. But one suspects that these expenditures represented a truly extraordinary effort, and that Roger's interests more than usually ran to the visual, to which I return. In the *regnum* of Sicily in which many languages were yoked in various degrees of mediation, only one primary medium, the visual, provided a single basis for all to understand. It was the singular genius of the first of the Sicilian kings to have recognized this fact and to have

---

[59] A number of examples have been collected and discussed by André Grabar, "Le succès des arts orientaux à la cour byzantine sous les macédoins," *MünchJb*, ser. 3, 2 (1951), 32 ff. See also David Talbot Rice, "Iranian Elements in Byzantine Art," in *Memoirs of the International Congress of Iranian Art and Archaeology, Leningrad, 1935* (Leningrad, 1939), 203 ff; Oleg Grabar, "Islamic Art and Byzantium," *DOP* 18 (1964), 69 ff; Cyril Mango, "Discontinuity with the Classical Past in Byzantium," in *Byzantium and the Classical Tradition*, ed. Margaret Mullett and Roger Scott (Birmingham, 1981), 48 ff; Robert S. Nelson, "An Icon at Mt. Sinai and Christian Painting in Muslim Egypt during the Thirteenth and Fourteenth Centuries," *ArtB* 65 (1983), 201 ff; idem, "Palaeologan Illuminated Ornament and the Arabesque," *Wiener Jahrbuch für Kunstgeschichte* 41 (1988), 7 ff.

[60] See, for instance, the remarks of Emperor Constantine VII Porphyrogennetos on the gift of an Arab cup; Ioli Kalavrezou-Maxeiner, "The Cup of San Marco and the 'Classical' in Byzantium," in *Studien zur mittelalterlichen Kunst, 800–1250: Festschrift für Florentine Mütherich* (Munich, 1985), 173.

[61] Art patronage in the Middle Ages has yet to be the subject of an economic study, but see the incisive remarks of Richard Goldthwaite, *Wealth and the Demand for Art in Italy, 1300–1600* (Baltimore, 1993), esp. 150 ff.

exploited it, in both imagery and style, for the purposes of forging his kingdom. But perhaps then it might also be said that it was the singular urgency of the visual in mid-twelfth-century Sicily that gave the art produced there its extraordinary clarity of program-in-form.

As a coda to this interpretation, let me simply evoke the cathedral of Monreale, the great project of Roger's grandson, William II, with its Byzantine, Western, and Islamic motifs, now blended so that they cannot be so easily separated out, to stand as an image of how much Sicilian art—and by implication the conditions in which it was produced—had changed since the time of Roger's death in mid-century, with the completion of the first phase of the Cappella Palatina (Fig. 20).[62] One suspects that an even broader view of the interrelationships of the visual cultures of the Mediterranean world in the later Middle Ages would bring out more sharply the moment of Roger's reign and the originality of the first solution of the Cappella Palatina.

Williams College

---

[62] See Krönig, *Il Duomo di Monreale* for a discussion of the architecture; for the sculpture, see Roberto Salvini, *Il chiostro di Monreale e la scultura romanica in Sicilia* (Palermo, 1962). A more recent survey is provided by Krönig et al., *L'anno di Guglielmo, 1189–1989: Monreale, percorsi tra arte e cultura* (Palermo, 1989).

The Shared Culture of Objects

Oleg Grabar

In 1959 the distinguished philologist Muhammad Hamidullah published a text entitled *The Book of Treasures and Gifts*.[1] The manuscript of the text, preserved in the public library of Afyonkarahisar in Turkey, is, insofar as we know, unique and it contains a number of oddities and misunderstandings introduced by later copyists. However, Hamidullah established that the original author of the text was one al-Qadi al-Rashid Ibn al-Zubayr, probably an official of the Fatimid court or an administrator of some sort in Cairo, who had been, among other things, an eyewitness to the dramatic events that shook the Fatimid regime after 1060 and that included, in 1067–68, the looting of the imperial palace in order to pay the army. No dated or datable event recorded in the text is later than 1071.

The book consists of 414 separate accounts, some quite short, others going on for several pages, of treasures kept, found, looted, or inherited by, mostly, Muslim rulers and of gifts exchanged within ruling circles of the Muslim world on the occasion of marriages, convalescences, circumcisions, and other social or personal events, as well as between Muslim and other rulers. These accounts are organized into uneven sections dealing with the functions around which objects were exchanged or acquired. The book is not a work of *belles-lettres,* as it is poorly composed and makes little effort at literary effects, in spite of several quotations from poetry. It is in reality a sort of digest, with information restricted to the relatively limited topic of gifts and treasures.[2] It does not claim completeness (in fact, the copy we possess may well have been a summary from some larger opus), but there is a curious coherence in the book, a coherence of tidbits strung together, akin to the coherence of the "living" or "home" sections of today's newspapers and magazines. The book does not include moral judgments about the evils of wealth, a common theme of medieval writing in Arabic or Persian. It is not a "Mirror of Princes" proposing patterns of behavior for rulers, nor is it an account of marvelous and odd things from remote lands. In short, there is something unclear about the genre to which the book belonged or the exact medieval audience to which it was destined.

Some of the accounts in Ibn al-Zubayr's book are clearly legends and fancy stories

---

[1] Muhammad Hamidullah, ed., *Kitab al-Dhakha'ir wa al-Tuhaf* (Kuwait, 1959).

[2] The exact literary genre to which it belongs is unclear to me, and the book is not mentioned in the great encyclopedias such as C. Brockelmann, *Geschichte der arabischen Literatur,* 5 vols. (Leiden, 1936–42), or F. Sezgin, *Arabische Schrifttum* (Leiden, 1975 ff), 11 vols.

dealing with exotica like the treasures of the kings of China and the peculiarities of Tibetan and Hindu rulers. But an unusually large number of his stories are verified or verifiable through other sources, plausible for a variety of reasons, or actual eyewitness accounts. It is the latter, more particularly the reports about the looting of the Fatimid palace, that brought attention to this text when it was first published.[3] A number of the stories pertaining to relations between Muslim and non-Muslim courts were already noted some thirty years ago, but were not often used by scholars of medieval art whose reading habits do not usually include *Arabica* or *The Journal of the Pakistan Historical Society*.[4] The recent completion of a translation of the text with various commentaries, which one hopes will soon be published,[5] is an occasion for me to return to this source and to explore the topic of Byzantine court culture from the very special point of view of the information found in a book on past and present gifts and treasures for readers from the Arab, primarily Muslim, world.

Regardless, however, of the audience to which it was directed, this text contributes to something I would like to call the anthropology of the object. What I mean by that is an understanding or an appreciation of the thousands of items, which we usually exhibit or publish in terms of technique, time and place of manufacture, and decoration, as active ingredients in the fabric of daily or ceremonial life or as carriers of real or contrived memories. But this fabric of common or ceremonial behavior and these memories are not, most of the time, provided directly by the objects, but indirectly through their appearance in a written text. The difficult question is always to define the boundaries between a written document meant to be read or heard and images or objects meant to be seen or used. The problem is a well-known one for sculpture and painting, where a one-to-one relationship can be established between a text and an existing or destroyed work of art.[6] It is a more difficult one for objects, since texts are related to classes and types of objects rather than to individual ones. A full discussion of this particular and more theoretical topics should include those accounts in Ibn al-Zubayr's book which deal with lands other than Byzantium. However, that discussion will not be pursued in this essay, even though it is probably the most interesting contribution of this book to the history of the arts.

I shall begin by providing all the examples from the *Kitab al-Dhakha'ir* which deal with Byzantium. Most of them had already been translated into French over thirty years

[3] Although not the last word on the subject, O. Grabar, "Imperial and Urban Art in Islam," *Colloque International sur l'Histoire du Caire* (Gräfen, 1972; repr. in *Studies in Islamic Art* [London, 1976]), 183–85, contains most of the operative bibliography with respect to the arts. It is sad that the evidence from this event has not been picked up, to my knowledge at least, for further discussions of the arts available in Cairo in the 11th century.

[4] Muhammad Hamidullah, "Embassy of Queen Bertha of Rome to Caliph al-Muktafi billah in Baghdad, 293H/906," *Journal of the Pakistan Historical Society* 1 (1953); idem, "Nouveaux documents sur les rapports de l'Europe avec l'Orient musulman au moyen âge," *Arabica* 7.3 (1960), 281–300.

[5] Ghada H. Qaddumi, *A Medieval Islamic Book of Gifts and Treasures,* Ph.D. diss. (Harvard University, 1990).

[6] Without going back to Pausanias or to Pliny, the issue has been raised, among others, by H. Maguire, *Art and Eloquence in Byzantium* (Princeton, 1981); Paul Magdalino, "The Bath of Leo the Wise and the 'Macedonian Renaissance' Revisited: Topography, Iconography, Ceremonial, Ideology," *DOP* 42 (1988), 97–118, and M. Baxandall, *Patterns of Intention* (New Haven, Conn., 1985).

ago by Hamidullah himself, but he did not attempt to go beyond the identification of their historical circumstances. Some of them are known in part or as a whole from other Arabic, Muslim or Christian, sources as well, but I have not sought such parallels as may exist in Greek sources nor have I culled anew classical Arabic texts.[7] With one or two exceptions, all the examples will be between 900 and 1070. The closing date is obviously such because the source stops around 1072. It is also a legitimate one, because the twelfth century introduces, at least within the context of Seljuq domination in the Muslim world and as a result of the Crusades, a largely different configuration in the anthropology of courtly objects.[8] I shall suggest at the end that the tenth and eleventh centuries set the stage for that configuration in more interesting ways than those of merely preceding it.

A more curious point is the relative absence of examples before 900. The four that exist are remarkably short and imprecise: a present of silver, gold, precious stones, and silk (all raw materials) given to Emperor Maurice by Khosro Parviz in the sixth century (account 5); the gold and mosaics (again raw materials) given to al-Walīd for the mosque of Damascus (account 9); musk and sables added by al-Ma'mun for a present to the Byzantine emperor, probably Theophilos, in order to outbid the latter in a munificence which is not otherwise specified (account 31); fancy silk cloth and an equally fancy belt given by a Byzantine king to a governor of Azerbayjan who, in turn, gave it to Caliph al-Mu'tadid between 892 and 902 (account 62). There is not much to garner for the historian in these accounts, and all they evoke is within the standard statement of known and obvious facts or of perfectly trite minor events. Both the tone of the texts and the character of the information change drastically as we move into the tenth century.

After presenting Ibn al-Zubayr's stories, I will discuss briefly where possible visual illustrations for his accounts can be found. There is not a single instance where I (or anyone else so far) have been able to match a textual reference with a specific remaining object. All that can be done is to identify types and classes of things that existed in the past and that have at times been preserved through accidents of history. Then a series of additional observations derived from the texts will lead me to wider issues of interpretation and to some comments on objects of courtly art between the tenth to twelfth centuries.

(1) Accounts 73 and 74 deal with an event recorded otherwise in several Arabic chronicles but not in the detailed fashion of Ibn al-Zubayr.[9] The event is the arrival in Baghdad of a Byzantine embassy with gifts sent to Caliph al-Radi by Romanos Lekapenos, together with Constantine and Stephen ("leaders, of the Byzantines," the Arabic

---

[7] A. A. Vasiliev and M. Canard, *Byzance et les Arabes*, 2 vols. (Brussels, 1935; repr. 1968), vol. II, pp. 278–79, mentions Ibn al-Zubayr's recently published book and contains the only comparative sources I used systematically.

[8] Much has been written about the artistic changes that characterize architecture from the late 11th century on and the other arts from the middle of the 12th century. See R. Ettinghausen and O. Grabar, *Islamic Art, 650–1250* (London, 1987), 328 ff.

[9] Vasiliev and Canard, *Byzance et les Arabes*, II, 278–79.

being *ra'is,* "head"),[10] presumably his children.[11] What is given is the text of the Arabic translation of the letter allegedly sent from Constantinople which accompanied the gifts. The Greek text was written in gold and the Arabic translation in silver, thereby indicating that the letter was written down in both languages in Constantinople. The indicative value of the letter is complicated by the following words found at the end of the presumed translation, as reported in the eleventh century: "I, the translator, ask you to excuse my description of the gifts since I have not seen them with my own eyes so that I could describe them properly." The interpreter of today has even further difficulties in that he cannot understand or translate appropriately into English many technical terms that may have been clearer to the tenth-century writer or the eleventh-century copyist.[12] For the purposes of this paper, I shall skip these technical issues which are not central to this volume's concerns with the Byzantine court, but rather with techniques of manufacture, although at some point the latter must receive full scholarly attention by gathering together practicing artisans from different lands as well as classical Hellenists and Arabists.

The formal letter is addressed from Romanos, Stephen, and Constantine, highest placed (*al-'usama'*) in Byzantium and "believers in God" to "the honorable and magnificent sovereign of the Muslims" and avoids references to Christ or the Prophet which could create friction. After wishes for peace and for characteristic ransom and truce settlements, it continues:[13]

> we have sent . . . some fine articles which reveal the deep-rooted affection and sincere sympathy we have for your brethren [presumably the Muslims]. The articles are:
>
> three gold beakers inlaid with precious stones;
>
> a rock crystal flask encased in gilded silver, decorated and studded with precious stones and pearls; on top of its lid there is a rock crystal lion;
>
> another rock crystal flask which was on one side encased with gilded silver latticework studded with precious stones, in the center of which there are roundels; on the other side there were four silver threads overlaid with gold;
>
> a silver gilded vessel in the shape of a gourd and a tankard, both inlaid with precious stones;
>
> a gilded bucket-like jar inlaid with precious stones and studded with precious stones and pearls; it is inscribed at the mouth with [the statement]: "God's voice over waters (or over life)";[14]

---

[10] Since we are dealing with a translation from the Greek, it is curious that the relationship of Constantine and Stephen to Romanos is not more explicit. This may have something to do with the assumed Greek original.

[11] There was around that time a patriarch named Stephen, but his dates (925–928) do not quite fit and the Constantine is unlikely to have been Romanos' predecessor.

[12] Qaddumi's thesis is the first attempt to find appropriate contemporary equivalents for these technical terms, but some of her interpretations are only first steps in what should become a major investigation of the vocabulary for manufacturing in classical Arabic.

[13] What follows is a simplified translation that avoids almost all problematic terms and does not provide the Arabic equivalents, which can be found in Qaddumi's work.

[14] Hamidullah edited the text with "life" (*al-hayat*) and suggested "water" (*al-miyah*) as an alternative, but preferred the latter in his translation because it correctly identifies a passage from the Psalms (29:3) which was in fact used on objects, as was pointed out by I. Ševčenko, and therefore serves to authenticate the text of the letter.

another two-handled jar of gilded silver studded with pearls and various kinds of gems; on its lid is mounted the sculpture of a peacock;

a gilded silver bucket inlaid with precious stones and studded with pearls and precious stones;

another gilded bucket studded with precious stones;

a small three-handled gilded silver jar inlaid with precious stones and engraved with representations of small birds and of narcissi, and inscribed at the mouth;[15]

a small eight-sided gilded silver casket inlaid with precious stones, its oblong lid studded with pearls and precious stones; inside the box are three narrow scarves (?) of linen decorated with gold and large gilt roses, three narrow scarves decorated with gold and small roses; three raw-silk turbans, the edges of which are decorated with gold;

a silver case for several large goblets, inlaid with precious stones and inscribed at the mouth: "O God, strengthen king Romanos";

a small gilded silver jar with two small handles studded with precious stones and pearls; on its handle and rim there are three figurines of peacocks;

a case containing two knives whose handles are of bezoar encased with gold wires and inlaid with precious stones; on top of the handles are profusely ornate emeralds decorated with gold;

two other knives with handles decorated with small pearls and other stones; their case is studded with rubies, pearls, and black stones, and their scabbards are of gold profusely adorned with pearls;

a heavy battle-axe with a head made of gilded silver inlaid with precious stones and studded with pearls; on its shaft there is silver latticework profusely adorned with gilded silver;

three knives, one of which is profusely decorated with gold; the other two are of silver, and one of them has a gilded handle;

seven brocade covers, one with a design of eagles in two colors, another with a floral design in three colors, another with three-colored stripes, a red one with colored foliate design, the design of yet another one consisting of trees on a white ground, two with the design of a hunter set in a roundel on a white ground, two with crouching lions on a yellow ground, two with eagles set in roundels;

ten pieces of red *siqlatun* fabric;[16] ten more pieces of violet cloth; five pieces of multicolored *siqlatun,* five pieces of white *siqlatun*; twenty pieces of striped cloth;

four pelts, one of which is called *kabak* (with sable collar), the second of white fox, the third is *balis,* and the fourth is called *baks*;[17]

as to covers, two are of velvet with a design on a violet ground representing an eagle in a roundel and horse riders above;

two more wrappers with a similar design but without velvet pile;

---

[15] Qaddumi's translation here differs from Hamidullah's, but seems to reflect the text more accurately.

[16] For the various uses of this term which also means "scarlet," see R. B. Serjeant, "Material for the Study of Islamic Textiles," *Ars Islamica* 15–16 (1951), 301, for further references.

[17] These terms are all unclear, and there has been no attempt to elucidate them further.

another one with a palm tree design and a green background;

ten pieces of thin brocade, one with the representation of a riding king with a flag in his hand, another with a bird fighting a lion with its two wings. Two others with a winged beast, another with an eagle seizing an onager, one with a unicorn, another one with wild goats in six roundels, another one with fifteen roundels on a white ground; one more with a rhinoceros seizing a leopard, another with a winged quadruped with small eagles in the four corners;

ten large velvet outer garments, one of emerald green *siqlatun* cloth with elephants within its stripes; the other had within its borders rosettes, in the center of which there are ducks and other birds;

a *siqlatun* cloth with birds within its borders, another one with unicorns, while the borders of another one are decorated with a yellow lion; another one has lion heads with wide-open mouths and a tree in the center;

another has inside its borders figures of riding kings and a unicorn and inside a winged quadruped;

ten colored pieces with borders decorated in the *barmaniyah* (?) way; ten green hooded mantles with borders with ten protomes of beasts of burden;

ten kerchiefs with images.[18]

Such is a slightly simplified English version of a presumed translation into Arabic of a Greek text accompanying gifts brought from Byzantium to Baghdad. Most of these objects are plausible in the sense that, except perhaps for a certain extravaganza of precious stones, verbal descriptions agree with types of objects, techniques, and decoration known otherwise. At this stage of presenting the accounts in Ibn al-Zubayr's text, however, the response of Caliph al-Radi to the "three leaders of the Byzantine people" is particularly interesting: "the Commander of the Faithful has complied with what you have anticipated from your gift and has provided the envoy with what manifests his respect for you, instead of exposing you to shame and loss of pride, so as to prove yourself to be above [mere] opportunism. A list of this gift [i.e., the one al-Radi sends back with the Byzantine envoy] will be attached to this letter." The meaning is, I believe, that a comparable set of presents were sent to Romanos, so as not to humiliate the Byzantine emperor by appearing to treat his gift as a sort of bribe. Unfortunately we do not possess, at least to my knowledge, an Arabic or Greek list of the other half of the exchange.

This long passage also suggests a remarkably extensive cast of characters involved in the making of the text we possess: in Constantinople, some official gathering the gifts and making a list in Greek, having it translated into Arabic by someone who has not seen the gifts, which were presumably already packed; then in Baghdad, a process of administrative and ceremonial acknowledgment of reception and eventually the copying of the text put together in Constantinople into a work for the general public. Even larger numbers of people must have been involved in the packaging, protecting, delivering, and

---

[18] Other translations are possible, such as "borders" or "representations." The point seems to me that identifiable items were shown, whatever they were.

eventually storing of the objects. The budgetary implications of this text are quite staggering, above and beyond the value of the items it describes. It may well be possible to identify within the service structure of the Byzantine as well as Abbasid courts the individuals or at least positions involved in the transactions suggested by this gift and the spaces needed for the successful enactment of these transactions.

(2) Account 82. In 1046 Constantine IX Monomachos sent a gift to the Fatimid caliph al-Mustansir on the occasion of the signing of a treaty renewing for ten years the armistices at the frontier between the two realms. The mercantile attitude of a contemporary observer establishes first that the value of the gift was 216,000 Rumi (i.e., Byzantine) gold coins plus 300,000 Arabic dinars. Perhaps economic historians can establish the value involved in the gifts, which included one hundred fifty beautiful mules and selected horses, each of them covered with a brocaded saddle cloth, and fifty mules carrying fifty pairs of boxes covered with fifty pieces of floss-thin silk brocade. The animals were led by two hundred Muslim prisoners of war who had been held in captivity, and the boxes contained one thousand pieces of different kinds of brocade, three hundred pieces of thin brocade, red Rumi belts bordered with gold, high turbans embroidered with gold, drapes for curtains, and brocade kerchiefs in which clothes were wrapped.

(3) Accounts 84 and 85. In 1053 Michael VI sent a gift to al-Mustansir which included: Turkish slave boys and girls; partridges, peacocks, cranes, aquatic birds, ravens, and starlings, all of whom were white; huge bears that played musical instruments; Saluqi hounds and guard dogs; boxes and chests that numbered over seven thousand and contained "fine things," unfortunately not described. Two boats were used to transport all of this. The more interesting part of this story is that, after delivering the gifts in Cairo, the Byzantine messenger sailed to Jaffa, accompanied by Fatimid sailors, whence he went to pray in the church of the Holy Sepulcher in Jerusalem and to deliver gifts from the Byzantine emperor to the church rebuilt about a generation earlier. The list of these gifts is provided: a gold short sleeveless waistcoat studded with all kinds of splendid precious stones; two gold crosses, the length as well as the width of each being three and a half cubits weighing one whole *qintar* (around 45 kg)[19] and adorned with rubies and other precious stones; many gold trays adorned with precious stones; two gold ewers, the capacity of each being twenty Baghdadi *ratls* of wine; several gold chandeliers with gold chains and in their center small birds of rock crystal; many long drapes or curtains of thick embroidery with an abundance of gold threads and precious stones; and other such church equipment. All of this was exhibited on Easter day.[20]

(4) Account 91. In 1057 the Seljuq ruler Tughrilbek sent to the Byzantine emperor, presumably Michael VII, a pearl-encrusted vest on the front of which was sewn or

[19] These and subsequent evaluations of weight and length measures are approximate guesses based on Walther Hinz, *Islamische Masse und Gewichte* (Leiden, 1970).

[20] The events that led to the sending of this gift have been discussed by R. Ousterhout, "Rebuilding the Temple," *Journal of the Society of Architectural Historians* 48 (1989), 66 ff.

otherwise affixed the seal of Solomon in red rubies and weighing 45 *mithqals* (ca. 20 grams); a hundred silver candlesticks with large ceremonial candles; one hundred and fifty apricot-colored Chinese[21] porcelain dishes; one hundred garments, each composed of two pieces of cloth interwoven with gold; two hundred pieces of *siqlatun* cloth; two hundred pieces of black and white striped cloth; ten drum-shaped scent baskets lined with leather and filled with camphor and aloeswood. All of this, reports our author, was valued at 2,400 dinars, which seems rather cheap by comparison with what the Byzantine emperor sent to Cairo, but then the text adds that he (emperor or ambassador) also "was paid 50,000 dinars in cash."

(5) Accounts 97 to 99. Our author goes back in time and recalled that the Byzantine emperor Michael, probably the same Michael VII, had offered to the mother of al-Mustansir five bracelets of jewelry inlaid with glass of five colors: deep red, snow white, jet black, sky blue, and deep azure. It was beautifully fashioned, and its inlaid design was of the finest craftsmanship. The same emperor is also supposed to have sent to al-Mustansir three heavy saddles of enamel inlaid with gold. He mentioned that they were from among the saddles of Alexander the Great. But in the following account a saddle is described in great detail and, tells our author's informant, on the saddle there was a piece of paper with the handwriting of al-Mu'izz, the Fatimid caliph who established Cairo in 969, saying: "the Byzantine emperor offered us this saddle and the bridle after we entered Egypt." And the minister of the time added that it was one of the saddles that had belonged to Alexander the Great and had been transferred by the latter to the Byzantine treasury.

(6) Account 101. In 1062 our author hears from a freed slave of the governor of Sicily that Basil, the Byzantine king (in this story probably a generic Basil), had given to the former slave's master a casket in which there was medium-sized stone that could be used to cure dropsy.

(7) Account 105. In 1071 the Hamdanid Nasir al-Dawlah gave to Emperor Romanos IV Diogenes a gift worth 40,000 dinars. It included: two long sticks of aloeswood; five unique rock crystal objects with characteristics that are difficult to understand; a large tapering bucket with enormous capacity; brocade cloth with representations of wine-colored eagles on white ground, weighing 4,000 *mithqals* (168 kg) and valued at 1,000 dinars; cloth embroidered with gold and heavily encrusted; all sorts of pieces of cloth cut for a variety of purposes; beautiful jewelry, and all sorts of utensils. In exchange the Byzantine emperor sent to Nasir al-Dawlah gifts that included a compact embroidery with gold threads that was so heavy it was all a single mule could carry.

(8) Account 105. The felt cloak of Romanos IV that had been taken from him when he besieged Aleppo in 1031 was given to the new governor of Aleppo by the daughter

---

[21] The term used is *sīnī*, which could either mean "Chinese" or refer to a fancy technique of ceramic manufacture such as one of several varieties of luster wares.

of the previous one. "Its trails, sleeves, and openings were adorned with pearls of great weight. At the back and front of the cloak were gold crosses adorned with rubies."

(9) Accounts 161 to 164. This is another version of the celebrated story of the Byzantine embassy that went to Baghdad in 917.[22] It does not bear directly on the present subject, except for being a striking illustration of the display throughout the whole city of Baghdad of practically every person, animal, and object controlled by the caliph. Such showy displays existed also on a more modest scale. Thus, according to account 173, when a certain Basil was sent as an envoy to Caliph al-Hakim, fairly early in Fatimid times, the latter "wished to furnish the throne room with unusual furnishings and to hang up extraordinary wall hangings. He ordered that the storerooms of furniture be searched, and twenty-one bags of such things were found, which had been carried by caravan from Qayrawan in Tunisia to Cairo." Each piece had a slip attached to it which identified its technique and the time of its manufacture. In the foreground of the throne room a shield was hung which was adorned with all sorts of costly precious stones, illuminating its surroundings. "When sunlight fell on it, the eyes could not look at it, as they became tired and dazzled." Aside from its rare reference to the visual impact made by objects, this account offers a glimpse into what may be called the curatorial world of court treasuries, with identifying cards attached to every object.

(10) Account 229. When Marwan was captured by the Abbasids in Egypt in 750, there was in his treasury a table of onyx with a white background and black and red stripes. It had gold legs. There was also a goblet of Pharaonic glass with an image in high relief representing a lion and a man kneeling in front of him while fixing an arrow on his bow. These particular objects, the second one of which was certainly some late antique gem, were kept by the Abbasids and eventually given to a king of India. The interest of this story is that, like several other accounts (none, however, involving Byzantine objects from the period under consideration), it indicates a double mobility of objects. There was an internal mobility, whereby the imperial households used for practical purposes or played with things found in the treasury and passed them on to children, slave girls, or convalescing spouses. A precious object with a known pedigree was once found as a door stopper in Cairo or Baghdad, and many a wondrous item was destroyed as children's toys. And then there was an external mobility, as the gifts found in one place or belonging to one person were sent to someone else, in a continuous exchange of expensive white elephants.

(11) Account 263 is a curious passage that is like a moment from the *Book of Ceremonies* seen by a Muslim Liutprand, but without the venom of the bishop of Cremona. In 1071 one Ibrahim b. Ali al-Kafartabi, who had been in Constantinople, related that he saw

---

[22] Vasiliev and Canard, *Byzance et les Arabes,* II, 239–43; O. Grabar, *The Formation of Islamic Art,* 2d ed. (New Haven, Conn., 1987), 159–64.

Emperor Romanos Diogenes on the day of their (the Christians') great feast, probably Easter.[23]

> He was wearing a garment of the kind their emperors wear with great difficulty, as they are neither able to bear it properly nor to sit with it, because of its heavy weight and because they are too weak. The garment contained thirty thousand pearls, each of which weighed about one *mithqal* (this makes something like 126 kg, which is certainly too much); it is priceless, nothing comparable being known on earth. Al-Kafartabi told me that the emperor was accustomed to wear, during his travels, casual garments adorned with precious stones and large pearls of various kinds. Each garment was worth 200,000 dinars, some more, some less. He saw Emperor Michael frequently wearing some of these clothes, in different styles, on his military expeditions. He also informed me that the Byzantine emperors had crowns for different occasions that were suspended over their heads. One was the "largest crown," which was of gold adorned with various rubies, together with a variety of other jewels. The crown was usually suspended over the emperor's head when he sat in his audience room to receive the natives of his empire and the envoys of kings. Another was the crested crown, which he set on his head when he returned from a campaign in which he had vanquished his enemy. This crown was studded with precious stones, and its crest which protrudes over his face had pieces of ruby in it. The emperor sat on his gold throne studded with precious stones or on a studded gold *salin* [probably a rendering in Arabic of the Greek *sellion*]. He always let his legs come down from the throne or the *salin* to rest them on a footstool upholstered with heavily embroidered brocade. He had two red boots on his feet. A complete pair was worn only by the emperor. Those inferior to him wore one boot in red and the other in black. He also told me that he saw there [presumably the Byzantine palace] a piece of ambergris that looked like a huge camel kneeling in the center of a large platform.

This text is a wonderfully contemporary one, as it exhibits the ignorant curiosity so characteristic of most of our own press of today.

(12) Account 340. A very short one and a very peculiar one, which I will quote in its entire brevity.

> When Basil, son of Romanos, the emperor of Byzantium, died in the year 410 [1019–20], he left 6,000 baghdadi *qintars* of gold coins and jewels worth 54 million dinars.

Such are the stories and accounts in the *Kitab al-Dhakha'ir* which pertain to Byzantium. I have left out only the indirect references found in the description of the Fatimid

---

[23] Although not an important point for our purposes, it should be noted that at Easter time of 1071, the fateful year of Mantzikert, the emperor was campaigning in Armenia. Al-Kafartabi must have been relating something he had seen earlier.

treasures, but these texts are, relatively speaking, better known and would not add much substance to my argument.

Before turning to a number of concluding statements, I would like, however, to bring out one last account, which is only tangentially pertinent to Byzantium, but which can serve as a sort of foil for my conclusions. It is account 69 dealing with the gifts sent in 906 by Bertha, the Frankish queen, to al-Muktafi in Samarra.[24] The gifts involved are: fifty swords, fifty shields, fifty Frankish spears; twenty pieces of cloth woven with gold threads; twenty Slavic eunuchs; twenty pretty and gentle Slavic slave girls; ten huge dogs that even lions and other beasts of prey cannot withstand; seven falcons; seven hawks; a silk tent with all its furnishings; twenty pieces of cloth, much of a special wool that is in an oyster from the bottom of the sea and assumes different colors according to the hours of the day; three Frankish birds which, when they see poisoned food or drinks, utter horrible screams and clap their wings until the message gets across; beads that extract arrowheads and spear tips painlessly, even after flesh had built around them. The letter that accompanied the gift was on white silk in a script that "was similar to the Rumi (i.e., Greek) script, but more harmonious." Among its more bizarre features, the letter contained a proposal of marriage.

The problem was that no one at al-Muktafi's court could read Latin. Finally a Frank was found in the department of fancy garments who read the letter and translated it into Greek. Then Ishaq b. Hunayn, the well-known figure in translations from Greek into Arabic and in early Abbasid science, was summoned, who translated the Greek into Arabic. The plausibility, if not veracity, of this account seemed assured until the appearance of Ishaq b. Hunayn, which is a bit as though Shakespeare was called to translate some missive received by Queen Elizabeth from the doge in Venice. But, of course, it is precisely this sort of mediation by a well-known figure in cross-cultural connections which gave the seal of authenticity in the eleventh century to an account that would have remained a hearsay story without it.

What sort of conclusions or hypotheses can one draw from these accounts which vary in tone, verisimilitude, and objectivity and whose complete understanding *as texts* would also require comparison with stories in the same book involving Central Asia, China, Tibet, and India? I will only pick up a few specific threads from the stories and then elaborate a number of wider considerations.

The first specific point is that there exists a body of artifacts from the tenth, eleventh, and twelfth centuries which is typologically and functionally related to the items listed or described by Ibn al-Zubayr.[25] In the absence of specific identifications of described objects, the examples that can be proposed have the peculiarity that they come from both Byzantine and Islamic sources, or in reality alleged sources, as in many cases several places of manufacture can be proposed for the objects involved. What is more important

---

[24] This is the passage translated by M. Hamidullah in the *Journal of the Pakistan Historical Society* 1 (1953).

[25] A simple list can be made from catalogues of exhibitions such as: *Arts de l'Islam* (Orangerie, Paris, 1971), nos. 127, 129, 227–30, 271, 273, 294; Musée du Louvre, *Byzance* (Paris, 1992), esp. pp. 208–407; and H. R. Hahnloser, *Il Tesoro di San Marco* (Florence, 1971), pls. LXXXIX ff.

than the place of origin of the objects and even than their date is that their utilization and appreciation was shared by all courts, Christian or Muslim, once exclusively Christian signs and images are removed or avoided altogether.[26]

Three examples of objects associated with courts which are at times later than the texts I have quoted but which are very much within the period considered by this volume can help in elaborating the point of a shared culture. The first one is the celebrated cup in the San Marco treasury, presumably made in Constantinople, with perfectly clear but meaningless Arabic letters and perfectly clear but iconographically senseless classical figures.[27] The other one is the mantle of Roger II with a legible Arabic inscription different in content from any known inscription on an object and with a perfectly understandable imagery which cannot be easily explained, if at all, and with a shape and a lining that make it Latin European.[28] The third one is the Innsbrück cup with its nearly illiterate princely inscriptions in Arabic and Persian, its images which are at the same time quite clear and too numerous to make sense, its almost vulgar covering of every side of the cup, and its technique for which a Georgian source has recently been proposed but which is not associated with the northern Mesopotamian area of its patron.[29] In these instances, three different patrons used simultaneously Arabic letters, classical, and mythological motifs for objects that do not fit within the narrow boundaries imposed by religious art or within the art sponsored by the faiths involved, but which belongs to a common court art of luxury comparable to the art of couturiers and cooks today.[30]

None of these impressive creations has in fact a geographical or historical, probably not even a temporal, home. They reflect a culture of objects shared by all those who could afford them and transformed by their owners or users into evocations of sensory pleasures. The visual effects of the objects were then transferred into written form, in Ibn al-Zubayr's text, with two additional components. One is the almost vulgar physicality of objects identified in medieval texts or modern descriptions as large, heavy, shiny, expensive, and covered with precious stones or gold threads or with striking images or magic inscriptions. The second one is the awareness of technical and functional distinctions in the sociological sense of the word, that is to say, as statements of quality and worthiness rather than of ways of manufacture. This awareness is expressed in the pres-

---

[26] In fact, one of the examples I gave mentions the crosses found on an imperial robe.

[27] A. Cutler, "The Mythological Bowl in the Treasury of San Marco in Venice," in D. K. Kouymjian, ed., *Studies in Honor of George C. Miles* (Beirut, 1974), for an early interpretation, and I. Kalavrezou-Maxeiner, "The Cup of San Marco and the 'Classical' in Byzantium," *Studien zur mittelalterlichen Kunst, 800–1250: Festschrift für Florentine Mütherich* (Munich, 1985), for a more recent one that moves toward the explanation I am proposing here.

[28] The mantle is often illustrated, as in J. Soudel-Thomine and Bertold Spuler, *Die Kunst des Islam* (Berlin, 1973), fig. 199 and p. 265, with a brief bibliography. For recent work see T. Al Samman, "Arabische Inschriften," *JbKSWien* 78 (1982), 114 ff. The lining is now dated in the 13th century: Arne E. Wardell, "Panni Tartarici," *Islamic Art* 3 (1988–89), 110, with references.

[29] See now Scott Redford, "The Innsbrück Plate and Its Setting," *Muqarnas* 7 (1990), 119 ff, with references to earlier publications.

[30] H. Belting, "Kunst oder Objekt-Stil," in *Byzanz und der Westen* (Vienna, 1984), for a general statement about this common art; G. T. Beech, "The Eleanor of Aquitaine Vase," *Gesta* 32 (1993), for a rock crystal belonging to the common arts. There are many comparable examples.

ence of a specific vocabulary of verbs and nouns which are often impossible to translate and for which my own competence, at least, is limited both as an Arabist and as a technologist. The importance of this linguistic differentiation lies in its implication that the reading of words elicited some form of recognition or wonderment on the part of readers who were probably no more competent than I am, because the differentiation itself was important regardless of what it meant. The further elaboration of this particular point would take me away from the more immediately significant conclusion I propose, which is that a culture of shared objects implies a certain commonality of court behavior and of court practices. This commonality seems to me more appropriate than the "influences" from the East which had, in the past, identified the tenth century.[31]

A second specific point is that there are several concurrent hierarchies in the items listed in Ibn al-Zubayr's text. For instance, there are raw materials among them (I include in this category animals and slaves), semi-manufactured products like a piece of cloth, and fully manufactured objects ready to be used. The first category, that of raw materials, is relatively rarely ever mentioned in exchanges between Muslims and Byzantines, just as it is rare for China and India, also centers of old civilizations. But raw materials dominate in things coming from western Europe, North Africa, steppic Eurasia, and eventually Africa and southeast Asia. Semi-manufactured products are mostly textiles (and, curiously, medical or pseudo-medical items like aphrodisiacs), and they are more frequent among items sent from Cairo or Baghdad to Constantinople than the other way around, but the evidence from this single source is too thin to secure the conclusion that the Byzantine court imported more semi-manufactured items than it exported.

A more interesting point concerning hierarchies of objects and of their use may be that all but one of the examples above deal with exchanges between the highest-ranking authorities, the Byzantine emperor and the caliphal courts of Byzantium, Cairo, and Cordoba (there are no examples of Cordoba-Byzantine exchanges in Ibn al-Zubayr, but these exist elsewhere).[32] The one major exception occurs in 1071–72, when a Hamdanid *amir,* a second-rank ruler, sends a present to the Byzantine emperor, who, admittedly, was camping nearby. When we turn to the twelfth century, however, the loci of exchanges increase enormously, as the whole of Spain, Sicily, Anatolia, the Caucasus, Syria, and Mesopotamia all develop centers involved in exchanges of gifts with each other and with Byzantium, in fitting response to the multiplication of centers of authority.[33] In the ninth century, booty and very limited local exchanges predominated, as Abbasid or Byzantine rulers apparently dealt with each other only for the exchange of prisoners.[34] Should one attribute an apparent change, some time early in the tenth century, in the climate of the relationship between Byzantine and Muslim courts to changed politics or to economic and technological changes? Is it in fact valid to conclude that there occurred a change in the behavior between courts?

---

[31] A. Grabar, "Le succès des arts orientaux," *MünchJb* 2 (1951), for example.

[32] Vasiliev and Canard, *Byzance et les Arabes,* II, 324–28, among many other places.

[33] Lucy-Anne Hunt, "Comnenian Aristocratic Palace Decoration," in M. Angold, ed., *The Byzantine Aristocracy IX to XIII Centuries* (London, 1984), for examples.

[34] See Vasiliev and Canard, *Byzance et les Arabes,* I, for a list of these meetings.

A third factual detail is the paucity of mythical or unusual objects in these accounts involving Byzantium and the Muslims, the saddles of Alexander the Great being the only exception. This contrasts with other accounts in Ibn al-Zubayr's book and in many other sources of the same times which are full of fantastic stories about the tables of Solomon, David, the Prophet Qarun, and Constantine, strange animals, gigantic women, roaring lions, singing birds, and many other imaginary or mythical fixtures. *Mirabilia* came from the East, strange animals from the East and from North Africa, prophetic or imperial souvenirs from the Mediterranean with occasional detours elsewhere.[35] The speculative conclusion that emerges is once again that the objects shared by the Byzantine and Muslim courts were used as expressions of a competition, but one that, like the sporting events of today, involved the same functions, forms, and values. And in Cordoba, Aght'Amar, or Palermo, smaller but not always poorer or cheaper versions of the same games occurred. But these games were not shown in quite the same way everywhere, as Muslim courts enjoyed the pageantry of enormous displays like the 917 one in Baghdad, which was repeated on a smaller scale elsewhere.[36] I do not quite know what the Byzantine court did with its treasures and with the gifts it received.

Before concluding, one nagging difficulty should be mentioned in these interpretations of passages in an eleventh-century written text. A whole century before Ibn al-Zubayr, the great historian al-Mas'udi used the very same descriptive terms (but without Ibn al-Zubayr's technological precision) to refer to the gifts given or received by Khosro Anushirvan in the sixth century from China and India and especially to the gifts exchanged by the Byzantine emperor Maurice and the Persian grandee Bahram Chobin.[37] And so the skeptical historian may wonder whether his eleventh-century text is a conventional rather than specific description of expensive things. The lovingly listed beautiful things which can be identified through remaining types of objects may just be empty verbal formulas. Or perhaps, since Mas'udi wrote in the tenth century, that is to say, the very century when exchanges increased between Byzantium and the Muslim world, it is the reality of a new art of fancy objects which created in Mas'udi's time a new vocabulary for the description of objects and this vocabulary was artificially used for earlier times, but artificially continued for the following two centuries.

On the whole, I prefer, therefore, to assume the authenticity of Ibn al-Zubayr's text and to argue that we are not yet at the next stage, the one that grows in the twelfth century and commercializes both the making of objects and the memories associated with them. This later stage is symbolized by a celebrated aquamanile in the Louvre with two inscriptions on the breast of the bird. One, in Arabic, says *'amal' abd al-malik al-Nasrani,* which could mean "the work of the slave of the Christian king," or "the work of Abd al-Malik the Christian." The other inscription, preceded by a Maltese cross, is in Latin, and says *opus Solomonis erat,* which could be translated as "this was the work of

---

[35] Ibid., 366 ff; C.J.F. Dowsett, trans., *The History of the Caucasian Albanians* (London, 1961), 129. And there are many examples in Ibn-al-Zubayr. An anthology of such sources would be a most welcome enterprise.

[36] See above.

[37] Mas'udi, *Tanbih,* trans. B. Carra de Vaux (Paris, 1897), 236, for an early example of Byzantine merchants in Cairo.

Sulayman (a Muslim or Jewish or Christian artisan somewhere in the Mediterranean area), or this was a terrific job, or of Solomon (the Hebrew king, as a souvenir sold to an unsuspecting Crusader or merchant)."[38] If we put it together with so many silver bowls found in Ukraine and published by Darkevich,[39] or with the numerous inlaid or simply chased candleholders, ewers, and kettles all over the Near East, we have, I believe, the massively multiplied, feudal or urban, reflection, at times handsome and impressive, at other times, vulgar and clearly imitative, of the court art of objects in the tenth and eleventh centuries. What had been created in the latter can be summed up in the words Peter Brown has used recently for the fourth century: "the vigorous flowering of a public culture that Christians and non-Christians [I would add Muslims and non-Muslims] alike could share."[40]

But, obviously enough, these objects did not represent *the* culture of the Byzantine court with its icons, church visits, and prayers, with a visual as well as literary Christianity overwhelming everything. They did, on the other hand, represent much more of the culture of Muslim courts, whose piety was not expressed as much in visual terms and whose rulers were not accompanied by an organized ecclesiastical system and by a highly developed and precise liturgical practice. Where, then, did these objects operate within Byzantine court culture, if icons were brought to cure the sick, to promote victories or happy births, to celebrate weddings, or to crown emperors? They appeared, I submit, *after* the event. Once cured, wedded, crowned, or victorious, the emperor and his entourage sought a pleasure they rarely wrote about, as in the exceptional case of Constantine VII admiring the Arabian cup from which he drank before going to bed,[41] or in the materials used for the making of the official clothes in which princes were represented in something like the Skylitzes manuscript.[42] My contention is that this culture of sensory pleasure was much more widely shared than the religiously specific one of the church and the icon, the mosque and the Holy Book, which, then as now, separated people from each other while winning for all of them eternal life.

Institute for Advanced Study

---

[38] The object has often been illustrated and used in exhibition catalogues, as in *Arabesques et jardins de paradis* (Paris, 1989), no. 119, p. 148. The only in-depth study is still the one by A. de Longpérier, "Vase Arabo-Sicilien," *Revue archéologique* 6 (1865), 356–67, repr. in *Oeuvres,* vol. I (Paris, 1883), 442 ff.

[39] V. P. Darkevich, *Svetskoe iskusstvo Vizantii* (Moscow, 1975), all of whose interpretations I do not share, but whose groups of objects are quite accurate.

[40] P. Brown, "The Problems of Christianization," *Proceedings of the British Academy* 82 (1993), 96.

[41] Quoted in Kalavrezou-Maxeiner, "The Cup of San Marco," 173, on the basis of an indication by I. Ševčenko.

[42] A. Grabar and M. Manoussacas, *L'Illustration du manuscrit de Skylitzes* (Venice, 1979), color pl. II, figs. 42, 72, 75, etc., as just one set of examples of clothes that could have come from either culture.

Imperial Panegyric:
Rhetoric and Reality

George T. Dennis

Above all else the people we call Byzantines prized orthodoxy, correct doctrine, correct thinking, which they—and we—generally think of in a theological context. But there was another kind of orthodoxy, political orthodoxy, as some have termed it.[1] This involves correct thinking about the civil and institutional life of the empire, the whole imperial ideology. These orthodoxies, inseparable and sacred as they were, found expression in ways that were also sacred for the Byzantines. Theological orthodoxy found its expression largely in the divine liturgy and was there made known to the faithful. Political orthodoxy, in turn, was articulated by a literary elite and communicated to the citizens of the empire through rhetoric.

The use of rhetoric as an instrument of politics has ancient roots. In the fourth century B.C. Isokrates endeavored to influence Athenian foreign policy in favor of Philip of Macedonia, whom he compared to Herakles, the benefactor of mankind, just as Byzantine orators, a thousand years later, would compare their rulers to Christ, the lover of mankind, *philanthropos*.[2] In fact, many of the rhetorical clichés formulated by Isokrates would be heard over and over again throughout the Byzantine period. The imperial government, from Diocletian on, couched its decrees in rhetorical style to render them more solemn and memorable.[3] To its final days the Byzantine administration continued this practice, the most notable example being the preambles to imperial chrysobulls.[4] In its most prosperous days, as well as in its most penurious, in victory and in defeat, the Byzantine upper classes never gave up the study and practice of classical rhetoric. The basic handbooks by Hermogenes and Aphthonios were copied and commented on throughout the Byzantine centuries.[5] The medieval dictionary, the Suda, in its entry on Hermogenes, notes that "everyone has a copy" of his rhetorical manual.[6] As late as the fifteenth century, John Chortasmenos prefaced an encomium of Manuel II with the declaration that he was explicitly following Hermogenes, and that his oration should be

---

[1] See H.-G. Beck, *Das byzantinische Jahrtausend* (Munich, 1978), 87–108.

[2] H. Hunger, *Die hochsprachliche profane Literatur der Byzantiner*, 2 vols. (Munich, 1978), vol. I, 72.

[3] Hunger, *Literatur*, I, 71.

[4] H. Hunger, *Prooimion. Elemente der byzantinischen Kaiseridee in den Arengen der Urkunden* (Vienna, 1964).

[5] Hunger, *Literatur*, I, 76.

[6] *Suidae Lexicon*, ed. A. Adler, 5 vols. (Leipzig, 1928–38; repr. 1971), E 3046.

judged, not on its content, but on how closely it observed the rules of rhetoric.[7] While formal epideictic orations go back several centuries, it was Menander the Rhetorician, in about A.D. 300, who was credited with setting down the rules governing them.[8]

The fourth and fifth centuries saw a great flowering of Greek rhetoric in which both pagans and Christians participated. Names that immediately come to mind are Libanios, Themistios, Eusebios of Caesarea, Gregory of Nazianzos, Prokopios of Gaza. It was Eusebios, in his orations on Constantine the Great, who christianized the imperial ideology and articulated the political orthodoxy that would prevail until the death of the last Constantine. The speeches and letters of Libanios served as models of fine writing for rhetoricians, such as Psellos, and for emperors, such as Manuel II. Gregory of Nazianzos and others added biblical and Christian motifs and *topoi* to those of classical antiquity.

Even during the dark ages that followed, it is obvious that men continued the study and, presumably, the practice of rhetoric, for when, in the ninth century, the sources become more abundant, we find them engaged in their literary activities with renewed vigor. From then until the end of the empire, the teaching and practice of rhetoric underwent very few changes. Teachers of rhetoric attracted students; they taught them to imitate classical models, and, in due time, some, such as Psellos, Italikos, and Basilakes, were themselves held up as models.[9] Byzantium was never without rhetoricians.

Who were these rhetoricians, and why was rhetoric so very important to them? First of all, they were not very numerous. They formed a special class, a literary elite, which included emperors and empresses, ordinary laymen, secular clergy, bishops, and monks. The bond that held them together was rhetoric, the "communion of letters" as they termed it.[10] For one thing, it distinguished them from the ignorant tribes outside their borders. Manuel II felt obliged to continue his literary activity to set an example for his subjects, "so that as they mingle so much with barbarians they might not become completely barbarized."[11] And inside, it separated them, as Nikephoros Gregoras claimed, from ditch diggers and tavern keepers.[12] By maintaining classical rhetoric, with all its peculiarities, this class experienced continuity with the greatness of Rome and with Greek culture. In a world of change it gave security, stability, and meaning to their lives. In addition, proficiency in the art could lead to advancement and material rewards.

---

[7] *Johannes Chortasmenos (ca. 1370–ca. 1436/37). Briefe, Gedichte und kleine Schriften,* ed. H. Hunger (Vienna, 1969), 225.

[8] *Menander Rhetor,* ed. and trans. D. A. Russell and N. G. Wilson (Oxford, 1981); cf. Hunger, *Literatur,* I, 88.

[9] Cf. P. Wendland, *Commentaria in Aristotelem Graeca,* III, 1 (Berlin, 1901), appendix; J. Duffy, "Some Observations on a Byzantine Author and Title List," *Sixteenth BSCAbstr* (Baltimore, 1990), 81.

On Byzantine rhetoric one must begin with Hunger, *Literatur,* vol. I, 63–196, with detailed bibliography, 189–96. Also see G. Kustas, *Studies in Byzantine Rhetoric* (Thessalonica, 1973); S. Averintsev, "Vizantijskaja ritorika," in *Problemy literaturnoj teorii v Vizantii i Latinskom srednevekovje,* ed. M. Gasparov (Moscow, 1986), 19–90; G. Kennedy, *Greek Rhetoric under Christian Emperors* (Princeton, 1983), although this is less than satisfactory for the Byzantine period; Averil Cameron, *Christianity and the Rhetoric of Empire: The Development of Christian Discourse* (Berkeley, 1991).

[10] E.g., *Démétrius Cydonès Correspondance,* ed. R. J. Loenertz, 2 vols., ST 186, 208 (Vatican City, 1956, 1960), vol. II, ep. 270, p. 188, l. 47.

[11] *The Letters of Manuel II Palaeologus,* ed. G. T. Dennis (Washington, D.C., 1977), ep. 52, p. 150.

[12] S. Bezdeki, "Nicephori Gregorae epistulae XC," *Ephemeris Dacoromana* 2 (1924), 239–377; ep. 7, p. 340; ep. 50, p. 250.

Most rhetorical compositions were intended to be read aloud in a circle of one's friends or before the emperor and his court. Such readings were likened to a performance in the theater and were critically evaluated. Orations, which by their nature were meant to be delivered aloud, might be composed on the anniversary of a battle or some other significant event, for example, the reconciliation of Leo VI with his father.[13] Some pleaded certain causes; others were occasioned by the death of a prominent person; still others were meant to praise an individual, especially the emperor. It is with this last that this paper is concerned, the imperial encomium or panegyric, the *basilikos logos*. I limit the discussion here to compositions in prose, from the ninth to the fifteenth centuries, simply noting that much panegyric was in verse or in ceremonial acclamations.

Speeches in praise of a ruler go far back in human history, but the classical encomium took shape about the fifth century B.C. and by the fourth century A.D. had attained its definitive form, as codified by Menander and others. It shared the characteristics of all Byzantine rhetoric, that is, it tended to omit concrete details, especially names of persons and places. Psellos, for example, states that he does not need to give the name of a certain rebel, since he is addressing people who know what has been happening.[14] Reference is made to the Persians, Scythians, and others, rather than to the Turks and the Pechenegs. Some panegyrics were simply stylistic exercises and never pronounced in public.

The basic format for an official encomium of the emperor, as laid out in the rhetorical manuals, was fairly simple. The orator was to recall the emperor's place of origin, his birth, his parents, his education and physical appearance, his deeds in peace and war; he was to portray him as a shining example of the virtues, especially wisdom, courage, justice, and moderation. He should stress his philanthropy and piety. Within this framework, of course, a great many variations were possible. One or more of the standard topics could be omitted. In one oration, for example, Psellos does not mention Monomachos' family and fatherland, "even though the rules of the art call for it."[15] Other topics could be dealt with in greater detail than expected, while others could be more nuanced. The orator could include praise for the empress, other members of the imperial family, the patriarch, or others. While the Byzantines expected a panegyric to have the classical characteristics of the genre, they also delighted in little literary surprises, a play on words, a new twist on an old proverb, a subtle allusion to scripture or classical literature. Although Byzantine rhetoricians placed great importance on observing the standard format, their orations are more varied than one might expect.

What other elements characterized Byzantine imperial panegyrics? The modern reader, perhaps, is most struck by the extreme, almost sickening, flattery in these ora-

---

[13] This was commemorated on 20 July 901 or 902: *Arethae archiepiscopi Caesariensis Scripta minora*, ed. L. G. Westerink, vol. II (Leipzig, 1972), or. 65; also R. Jenkins, B. Laourdas, and C. Mango, "Nine Orations of Arethas from Cod. Marc. gr. 524," *BZ* 47 (1954), 1–40, or. 9.

[14] *Michael Psellus Orationes Panegyricae*, ed. G. T. Dennis (Stuttgart-Leipzig, 1994), 4, 293.

[15] *Or. Panegyrica* 2, 451–52. In addition to works on rhetoric, see L. Previale, "Teoria e prassi del panegirico bizantino," *Emerita* 17 (1949), 72–105, 340–66; C. Chamberlain, "The Theory and Practice of Imperial Panegyric in Michael Psellos," *Byzantion* 56 (1986), 16–27. Although focusing on the reign of only one emperor, the best discussion of imperial panegyric is by P. Magdalino, *The Empire of Manuel I Komnenos, 1143–1180* (Cambridge, 1993), 413–70.

tions, which reminds one of the personality cult accorded to certain dictators in this century. The ever recurring image of the emperor as the sun who brings warmth and light to the whole world is a prime example. Psellos addressed Constantine Mono-machos: "O Sun Emperor. Could anyone fault me for invoking you by this title, which fits you so perfectly? By your circle of virtues, your quickness of intellect, your natural magnificence, and your radiant beauty, do you not shine upon the whole earth?"[16] The empress, of course, is compared to the moon. According to Timarion, the souls in Hades called Psellos the sun-king because of his excessive use of that metaphor.[17] Psellos goes on: the emperor's speech is likened to that of Demosthenes, Isokrates, and Lysias. He charms his audience as much as do the odes of Pindar and the lyre of Sappho. And for his deeds, it would take another Homer to recount them. The emperor is lavishly praised for his benefactions, his piety, his martial valor, and a vast array of other virtues. The orator marvels at his handsome features, impressive stature, and generally superhuman qualities.

One wonders how the person so honored could sit and listen to such unabashed flattery without feeling some embarrassment. But, as far as we know, only one emperor, Manuel II, reprimanded his panegyrist, Demetrios Chrysoloras, and ordered him to curtail his extravagant praise.[18] His ancestor, Michael VIII, however, apparently found a *basilikos logos* by George Akropolites so annoying that he simply walked out while the orator was still speaking and went off to dinner.[19]

One could also question the sincerity of these orators. One could, for example, contrast Psellos' effusive praise of Constantine Monomachos in his panegyrics with his decidedly less complimentary comments in his *Chronography*. Manuel Holobolos was mutilated, imprisoned, and exiled by order of Michael VIII, whose ecclesiastical policy he openly detested, yet, in a Christmas oration, he praised him as an ocean of graces, a river of gold, and as the sun rising in the East.[20] And in an Epiphany oration, probably in 1273, he lauded Michael, who had attained the throne by treachery and murder, as the supreme model of virtue.[21] Perhaps, though, we should not be too harsh in judging these speakers. They were, in one sense, "just doing their job." While so much of it may seem to us shameless adulation at the expense of truth, we must keep in mind that the speakers and their audience firmly believed that, whatever they might think about the individual, the position of the emperor was sacred and worthy of all praise. In Michael's case, moreover, he was the New Constantine who had liberated the imperial city, and this overshadowed his faults. Finally, today I think we can mute our criticism of Byzantine oratory when we listen to, say, nominating speeches at a political convention or those accompanying the conferral of an honorary degree.

---

[16] *Or. Panegyrica* 1, 3–7.

[17] Ed. R. Romano, *Timarione* (Naples, 1974), 45; cf. trans. with notes by B. Baldwin, *Timarion* (Detroit, 1984), 74, 136–37.

[18] *Letters of Manuel Palaeologus*, pp. 137–39: epp. 46, l. 10; 47, ll. 10–11; 48, ll. 11–15.

[19] *Georgii Acropolitae Opera*, ed. A. Heisenberg, 2 vols. (Leipzig, 1903); repr. P. Wirth (Stuttgart, 1978), 89, vol. I, p. 188.

[20] M. Treu, *Manuelis Holoboli Orationes. Programma Victoria Gymnasium* (Potsdam, 1906), 30–50; (1907), 51–98, esp. 51–52.

[21] L. Previale, "Un panegirico inedito per Michele VIII Paleologo," *BZ* 42 (1943–49), 1–40, esp. 30.

One cannot help but note that imperial panegyric, at least as it has come down to us—and we have only a fraction of the orations actually composed—seems to flourish as the empire declines. Only one oration is extant from the reign of Basil II, and the largest number, by far, date from the reign of Manuel I; then there are quite a few right up to the disaster of 1204. Again, there was a final flowering in the last days of the empire, to Manuel II and his sons, John VIII and Constantine XI; these orations continue to heap extravagant praise upon the rulers and the imperial city with no hint of trouble or impending catastrophe.[22] It was, one suspects, one way of closing one's eyes to reality and living an illusion.

Another thing that impresses the reader is the extraordinary amount of liquid. Rivers of blood are shed by the empire's enemies; John Komnenos returns from campaigning in the East "swimming in a veritable ocean of barbarian blood."[23] The emperors shed vast quantities of tears in pleading with God on behalf of their subjects; among these, Leo VI seems to have been particularly productive.[24] But most abundant of all are the immense buckets of sweat poured forth by the emperors as they toil for their subjects in both peace and war. We read of the sweat of virtue, bloody sweat, and rivers of sweat.[25] There are very few imperial panegyrics that do not dwell on imperial perspiration.

Another characteristic comes from Christianity. The emperor is eulogized as the ideal Christian ruler, as God's representative on earth. He is compared with biblical paradigms, David and Solomon, and with the idealized Christian emperor Constantine. His piety averts God's anger, gains victories over the foe, and, in the case of Leo VI, brings rain to relieve a drought.[26] The emperor is commended for his zeal for orthodoxy, his philanthropy, his reverence for the patriarch, and his love of monks.

The panegyrics of the eleventh century that have come down to us generally praise the peaceful accomplishments of the emperor and less so his martial exploits. Constantine Monomachos, for example, was lauded for his support of learning, his generosity toward monasteries and philanthropic institutions, and his construction of aqueducts, fountains, and gardens. When rebels are defeated or foreign foes subdued, it is usually not the emperor himself who engages in combat. Toward the end of the century, though, as emperors such as Romanos Diogenes and Isaac Komnenos personally took the field, one notices a change in the rhetoric. Especially with Alexios Komnenos and his successors, the orators focus more on personal bravery and military strategy.[27]

Formal panegyrics were delivered in the presence of the emperor and his court by prominent rhetoricians, although it is not always clear how they were selected. The encomiast of Leo VI, about 901–902, was Arethas, a deacon at the time, who seems to

---

[22] See Isidore on Manuel II and John VIII, ed. S. Lampros, *Palaiologeia kai Peloponnesiaka,* vol. III (Athens, 1926), 132–221; John Dokeianos on Constantine XI, ibid., vol. I (Athens, 1912), 221–35.

[23] *Nicephori Basilacae Orationes et epistolae,* ed. A. Garzya (Leipzig, 1984), or. 3, p. 49, l. 20.

[24] *Arethae Scripta minora,* or. 58, p. 7, ll. 11–14; or. 59, p. 13, l. 17; or. 63, p. 38, l. 15.

[25] In the orations to Manuel I, allusion is sometimes made to the "sweat of virtue," as in Hesiod, *Opera et Dies,* 289, by Eustathios of Thessalonica: *Fontes rerum byzantinarum. Rhetorum saeculi XII orationes politicae,* fascs. 1–2, ed. W. Regel (St. Petersburg, 1892–1917; repr. Leipzig, 1982 = *FRB*), or. 1, p. 2, l. 30; or. 6, p. 124, ll. 24–26; bloody sweat, by Gregory of Antioch, *FRB,* or. 11, p. 201, l. 7; rivers of sweat, by Eustathios, or. 6, p. 124, l. 24; by Michael Rhetor, *FRB,* or. 10, p. 169, l. 21.

[26] *Arethae Scripta minora,* or. 61; Jenkins et al., "Nine Orations," or. 5.

[27] Cf. Magdalino, *Manuel I,* 418–25.

have been the official palace orator, although no specific title is given. Psellos bore the title of consul of the philosophers. But a contemporary of his, whose name we do not know, had held the title of master of the rhetoricians; he "had sat upon the throne of rhetoric and revealed the secrets of the art" to his students.[28] The same title was held by a disciple of Psellos, Theophylaktos, who lauded Alexios I in formal orations.[29] One also encounters the title "teacher of the rhetoricians." Praise of Michael Palaiologos was offered by Manuel Holobolos, "rhetorician of the rhetoricians and teacher of the teachers."[30]

Orations to honor the emperor were given on a number of special occasions and anniversaries. Fairly soon, however, Epiphany, the Feast of Lights, became the preferred date for an annual solemn oration in praise of the emperor. The first such that we know of was delivered by Arethas in honor of Leo VI, most probably on 6 January 901 and in connection with a banquet.[31] It then became a regular part of the court ceremonial for Epiphany.[32] It also provided an opportunity for the chosen rhetorician to present his students to the emperor, as Michael Psellos did on an Epiphany between 1045 and 1050. "O most sacred emperor, you see this holy and philosophical gathering; they are all the fruits of my planting and have all drunk from my springs, and they have whetted their tongues for rhetoric."[33] Some years later, his own student, Theophylaktos, concluded his Epiphany oration in 1088 before Alexios I by inviting his pupils to continue the praise of the emperor.[34] Euthymios Tornikes called upon his students to offer their praise of Alexios III on Epiphany 1201.[35]

What did these orators hope to gain from their lavish praise of the emperor? For one thing, they wanted to be recognized as an important segment of Byzantine society to which the emperor should listen. Panegyric orations provided an opportunity to lobby the emperor in furtherance of their collective and individual interests. To this end they sought public funding for the support of rhetoric and for themselves. "Be generous, o emperor," pleaded Theophylaktos to Alexios I, "as were the emperors of old, to the sophistic, and with public funds support the sophistic tongue."[36] Some orators, such as Psellos, were quite blunt about seeking personal reward.[37] Others went about it more

---

[28] P. Gautier, "Quelques lettres de Psellos inédites ou déjà éditées," *REB* 44 (1986), 111–97, esp. 162, 166.

[29] P. Gautier, "Le discours de Théophylact de Bulgarie à l'autocrator Alexis Ier Comnène (6 janvier 1088)," *REB* 20 (1962), 93–103.

[30] Treu, *Manuelis Holoboli*, 78.

[31] *Arethae Scripta minora*, or. 63, pp. 35–38; Jenkins et al., "Nine Orations," pp. 34–36.

[32] This is described in *Constantin Porphyrogénète, Le livre des cérémonies*, ed. A. Vogt, 2 vols. (Paris, 1935–39), 34–35; vol. I, pp. 130–36. After the processions and the liturgy, the emperor and the patriarch, with others, are seated at table in the Hall of the Nineteen Couches and have a drink. A banquet follows, concluded by the emperor and the patriarch having another drink. After everyone leaves, they have still another drink before departing. The Epiphany oration by Arethas, just mentioned, apparently took place at a banquet in the presence of the emperor and patriarch. The ceremony of the *prokypsis* (manifestation of the emperor) developed later: *Pseudo-Kodinos, Traité des Offices*, ed. J. Verpeaux (Paris, 1966), 195–98.

[33] *Or. Panegyrica* 6, 261–92.

[34] Gautier, "Le discours de Théophylacte," 120.

[35] J. Darrouzès, "Les discours d'Euthyme Tornikès (1200–1205)," *REB* 26 (1968), 49–121, esp. 56–57.

[36] Theophylaktos to Alexis I: Gautier, "Le discours de Théophylacte," 119; Michael Rhetor to Manuel I, *FRB*, or. 10, p. 167, ll. 18–21.

[37] *Or. Panegyrica* 2, 798–825; *Or. Panegyrica* 12, 45–53; Manuel Straboromanos to Alexis I: P. Gautier, "Le dossier d'un haut fonctionnaire d'Alexis Ier Comnène, Manuel Straboromanos," *REB* 23 (1965), 168–204, esp. 191.

subtly by praising the literary and rhetorical abilities of the emperor and his interest in those endeavors. Some hoped to advance their careers in state or church. Leo VI rewarded Arethas by naming him archbishop of Caesarea. Theophylaktos gave a speech in honor of Alexios I, on 6 January 1088, which marked the high point of his career, after which he was appointed archbishop of Ohrid.[38] Michael Italikos gave an oration for Manuel I, in 1143, which clearly demonstrated his right to the throne and the endorsement of him by the church; not long after he was named bishop of Philippopolis.[39] Finally, of course, the orators wanted applause. They performed before an audience composed not only of the emperor and his courtiers, but also of their colleagues, their intellectual and literary peers. Impressing them with their verbal wizardry was most important for their reputation and, perhaps, for the recruiting of students.

It is very difficult to evaluate these panegyrics as rhetoric and as literature. These were speeches, and, unless we hear them delivered orally and in the language in which they were composed, accompanied by the appropriate gestures, we miss their full impact. Were they any better or worse than the baroque orations of, say, the sixteenth and seventeenth centuries given at royal and pontifical courts? We dislike much about their speeches, but they clearly seem to have liked them. Certainly the emperors liked them; at any rate, they kept inviting the speakers back to give yet another speech, as Constantine Monomachos did at least seven times with Psellos.[40] All we can do is judge them, not by our standards, but by what we can understand of theirs. Did they follow the rhetorical manuals, and did they deviate from them just enough to please their colleagues? As mentioned above, Psellos, Italikos, Basilakes, and others were pointed out as models to subsequent orators, and thus must have met the standards of their contemporaries.

Do these orations have any value as historical sources? Are they merely empty bombast, or do they provide information about real people and events? Obviously, the orators did not intend to compose historical documents, as we know them, and we cannot stretch that point too far. Still, it is legitimate to ask whether we can use these speeches to learn more about the history of the times. Unlike a narrative source, which may have been written some thirty or forty years after the events recorded therein, these orations were generally delivered within a year of two of the events they described, and many can be accurately dated. People in the audience had participated in those events, and the orator, while permitting himself some embellishment, could not present a total fabrication. True, unpleasant events such as military defeats may be glossed over, but, in general, these panegyrics are more reliable as historical sources than has been recognized. Some authors, such as Choniates, even used their orations in compiling their histories. We can ask what the orator adds to the information given in the narrative sources, more facts, or perhaps certain details or nuances we might otherwise miss.

In his book on Manuel Komnenos, P. Magdalino has made exemplary historical use of the orations addressed to Manuel I, and there is no need to repeat that here. A few other examples might also be illustrative. Some of the orations of Psellos on Constantine Monomachos provide historical information not found in other sources. For example,

---

[38] Gautier, "Le discours de Théophylacte," 93.

[39] *Michel Italikos, Lettres et discours,* ed. P. Gautier (Paris, 1972), 26.

[40] *Or. Panegyrica* 1–7.

from a panegyric we learn that his father's home was near a large city to which he moved and in which the future emperor was born.[41] Psellos, of course, does not name the city, but simply refers to it as "the city of God," *Theou polis,* which his audience knew—and we know—is a common epithet of Antioch in Syria. In his second panegyric, Psellos informs us that Constantine performed military service under Basil II, and then fell into disfavor, therefore before 1025, when Basil died, thus setting a date for Constantine's birth sometime before the year 1000. While the *Chronography* of Psellos tells us that Constantine's father, Theodosios, had been imprisoned for conspiring against Basil, the panegyric implies that he was executed or at least died in prison.

Within a year of his accession to the throne, Constantine had to deal with a major rebellion in southern Italy. This is recounted in three narrative sources and in one oration.[42] Among the forces making up the rebel army, Psellos notes in his speech, were infantry and cavalry from Old Rome, as well as the large army of the East and, in particular, a Russian detachment, a detail not found elsewhere.[43]

Other sources mention Constantine's building activity, but provide few details. Psellos, though, in his orations, informs us that this emperor had constructed, perhaps also repaired, canals, aqueducts, and fountains in and around the capital. "He has diverted entire rivers, made them flow up and then flow down again."[44] "You have drawn rivers together, elevated waters, and linked seas, so that you might assuage our drought in the summer and give drink to your thirsty people. . . . The water is forced into a constricted space, shoots up to a great height; it cools the air and seems to be a new sort of rain coming down from the clouds."[45] Allowing for some exaggeration, he is clearly describing fairly elaborate hydraulic engineering projects.

The historian Attaleiates writes that Constantine liked to entertain his subjects by displaying exotic animals. Psellos, in an oration delivered in the spring of 1043, speaks of such animals as gifts from foreign potentates. An elephant, with its driver seated on top, was paraded around the hippodrome, as was also a giraffe.[46] An elephant was trained to kneel before the emperor's throne and touch its forehead to the ground.[47]

A century later, in an encomium on John Komnenos, Nikephoros Basilakes provides a detailed description of the emperor's itinerary and campaign in Asia Minor, which corroborates and adds to the information in the narrative sources. The orator also describes the emperor's innovative way of protecting his stone-throwing machines at the siege of Anazarba.[48] In fact, the orator has a number of interesting things to say about

---

[41] *Or. Panegyrica* 6, 45–54.

[42] *Chronographia,* 6, 76–88; ed. E. Renauld, *Michel Psellos Chronographie,* 2 vols. (Paris, 1926–28), vol. II, 1–18; ed. S. Impellizzeri, *Imperatori di Bisanzio (Cronografia),* 2 vols. (Milan, 1984), vol. II, 8–22; *Ioannis Scylitzae Synopsis Historiarum,* ed. I. Thurn (Berlin, 1973), 427–28; *Michaelis Attaliotae Historia,* ed. I. Bekker (Bonn, 1853), 18–20; *Or. Panegyrica* 2, 715–49.

[43] *Or. Panegyrica* 2, 719.

[44] *Or. Panegyrica* 1, 241–43.

[45] *Or. Panegyrica* 4, 406–14.

[46] *Or. Panegyrica* 1, 267–87.

[47] *Or. Panegyrica* 4, 156–65.

[48] *Nicephori Basilacae Orationes,* 61; cf. *Ioannis Cinnami epitome rerum ab Ioanne et Alexio Comnenis gestarum,* ed. A. Meineke (Bonn, 1836), bk. 1, par. 7, pp. 17–18; *Nicetae Choniatae Historia,* ed. J. L. van Dieten, 2 pts., CFHB 11 (Berlin, 1975), I, 26; *Michel Italikos,* no. 43, p. 254, ll. 8–12.

the stone-throwing machines.[49] One hurled a very large number of stones in rapid succession, while another shot a stone the size of a wagon. Is this rhetorical exaggeration? Not necessarily. Twenty years later it is almost certain that the Byzantines were making use of the counterweight trebuchet, the heavy artillery of the middle ages; perhaps a slightly earlier date could be postulated for its invention, quite possibly by the Byzantines.[50] A traction trebuchet transported by the Byzantine army in 1071, which required a pulling crew of twelve hundred men, is reported to have fired a stone weighing 96.21 kg (212.10 lbs.).[51] Using smaller stones, a traction trebuchet could get off more than four shots a minute.[52] A counterweight trebuchet employed by the Crusaders at Damietta hurled stones weighing 185 kg (407.84 lbs.), and Arab machines are reported to have shot stones of 259 kg (570.98 lbs.).[53] Closer examination of accounts of siege warfare and other military matters in these orations should prove fruitful.

These panegyrics, then, often provide unexpected factual information for the historian. Study of them will also tell us a great deal about how the Byzantines looked upon themselves and upon other peoples. In his second panegyric, Psellos gives a lengthy account of the emperors from Basil II to Monomachos, most of which is also in his *Chronography*, but here with different emphases, showing how he expected his fellow citizens to view their past. Several orations also give expression to the Byzantine dislike, if not contempt, of foreigners.[54]

These panegyric orations, which were so important to the Byzantines, served several purposes. They provided a forum for the literary elite to present their concerns directly to the emperor, as well as the opportunity to influence, in varying degrees, the direction of policy, although this had to be done with extreme subtlety and caution. But they were primarily expected to talk, not so much about themselves and their agenda—although they did much of that—but about the emperor and his agenda. Praise of the emperor was praise of the system, and from the time of Eusebios of Caesarea the transcendent theory of empire held sway. The emperor was God's vicar on earth, and all had to obey him. While the Christian people endured temporary setbacks, the emperor, with God's favor, would eventually subject the entire world to his dominion. A sure promise that this will indeed come about is provided by the submission of foreign rulers, manifested even by gifts of elephants and giraffes, and by the victories of the emperor over the barbarians of the day. Whether the emperor is praised for building aqueducts or for slaughtering barbarians, the intent was the same: to portray the emperor toiling

[49] *Nicephori Basilacae Orationes*, 57–59.

[50] The first recorded use of the counterweight trebuchet was at the siege of Zeugminon in 1165: *Nicetae Choniatae Historia*, I, 134. C. Foss argues that the counterweight trebuchet reached Byzantium by the middle of the 12th century: *Survey of Medieval Castles of Anatolia, I: Kütahya* (Oxford, 1985), 77–84, but see review of Foss by R. W. Edwards in *Speculum* 62 (1987), 678–79.

[51] Al-Fath ibn 'Ali al-Bundari in M. Houtsma, *Recueil de textes relatifs à l'histoire des Seljoucides*, vol. II (Leiden, 1889), 42.

[52] At the Crusader siege of Lisbon in 1147: *De expugnatione Lyxbonensi*, ed. and trans. C. W. David (New York, 1936), 142–43.

[53] See Ibn al-Muqaffa, *History of the Patriarchs of the Egyptian Church*, ed. and trans. Y. 'Abd al-Masih and O. Burmester, 4 vols. (Cairo, 1942–74), vol. III, pt. 2, p. 218; A. Melkonian, *Die Jahre 1287/1291 in der Chronik al Yuninis* (Freiburg, 1975), 86. A few years ago, in England, medieval enthusiasts constructed a counterweight trebuchet that hurled an Austin Mini automobile a considerable distance: *Mechanical Engineering* (January 1994).

[54] See, e.g., the speech of Eustathios to Manuel I, *FRB*, or. 6, pp. 94–95.

for the well-being of his subjects and, in return, demanding their unquestioning allegiance. Some orations were designed as propaganda for specific imperial policies or for generating desired attitudes among the populace, regarding a rebel leader, say, or a military defeat. It would seem, although there is not much concrete evidence, that these panegyrics, or at least their message, based largely on the reputation of the speakers, were widely disseminated throughout the empire, certainly in other major cities, such as Thessalonica. Although the imperial portrait may not have been carried about from city to city, as in Roman times, the imperial image and message, unchanging but ever variable, was conveyed by means of these panegyrics throughout the empire, and eventually down the ages to us.

Catholic University of America

In Search of the Byzantine Courtier:
Leo Choirosphaktes and Constantine Manasses

Paul Magdalino

Between 829 and 1204, the Byzantine imperial court was the most ancient, wealthy, and splendid in the Christian world. Within the empire, all social advancement and most cultural production depended on court patronage; the only way out of the system led into another court, that of the heavenly king. Here, it would seem, was the medieval court society par excellence. Why, then, was the 1994 Dumbarton Oaks Symposium the first serious attempt to examine the phenomenon in all its aspects? Why has the parvenu court culture of the medieval and early modern West received so much more attention? Why is there no equivalent for Byzantium of Huizinga's *Waning of the Middle Ages*, or of Norbert Elias' *Die höfische Gesellschaft*,[1] not to mention the fine recent studies by Stephen Jaeger,[2] Joachim Bumke,[3] and Aldo Scaglione?[4] The answer cannot lie solely in the loss of source material, or in the backwardness of Byzantine studies, or even in the miraculous ability of most western medievalists to exclude Byzantium from their field of vision. It has, I think, much more to do with the fact that the Byzantines themselves did not isolate the court as a social and cultural phenomenon worthy of literary attention. Like diplomacy—the subject of another recent symposium[5]—court culture was a fact of Byzantine life which those who lived it did not feel the need to articulate. The Greeks did not really have a word for it. In medieval Greek literature, αὐλή and its derivatives lack the resonance of the Latin and vernacular vocabulary which has given us the words "courtly," "courteous," "courtier" and "courtesan." Αὐλή is freqeuntly used, mostly in the plural, to designate the palace building, but less often to describe the court as an institution.[6] The adjectival form αὐλικός, which Modern Greek has bor-

---

[1] N. Elias, trans. E. Jephcott, *The Court Society* (Oxford, 1983).

[2] C. Stephen Jaeger, *The Origins of Courtliness: Civilizing Trends and the Formation of Courtly Ideals, 939–1210* (Philadelphia, 1985).

[3] J. Bumke, *Courtly Culture: Literature and Society in the High Middle Ages*, trans. T. Dunlap (Berkeley, 1991).

[4] A. Scaglione, *Knights at Court: Courtliness, Chivalry and Courtesy from Ottonian Germany to the Renaissance* (Berkeley, 1991).

[5] J. Shepard and S. Franklin, eds., *Byzantine Diplomacy* (Aldershot, 1992).

[6] For one example, see A. Maiuri, "Una nuova poesia di Teodoro Prodromo in greco volgare," *BZ* 23 (1920), 399:

οὐδ' εἰς αὐλὰς ἐσέβηκα τοῦ δεῖνος καὶ τοῦ δεῖνος . . .
ἀλλ' ἀπ' αὐτῆς τῆς βρεφικῆς καὶ πρώτης ἡλικίας
μίαν αὐλὴν ἐγνώρισα καὶ ἕνα αὐθέντην ἔσχον.

rowed from ancient Greek to translate the western European words for "courtly" and "courtier," occurs very rarely[7]—in interesting contrast to medieval Latin, which used *aulicus* as well as *curialis*.[8] The abstract noun αὐλικότης—the notional equivalent of *curialitas* or *courtoisie*—does not occur at all.

The Byzantines failed to develop not only a vocabulary of courtliness but also an ethos of courtliness comparable to that which took root in Germany and France around the year 1000 and matured five centuries later in Baldassare Castiglione's *Libro del Cortegiano*. It was the West, and not Byzantium, which formed the image of the court as the ideal milieu for the cultivation of social grace, aesthetic appreciation, intellectual elegance, martial arts, blood sports, and amorous sentiments, and which idealized the role of the courtier in combining all these qualities. Correspondingly, Byzantium never properly articulated the negative image of courts and courtiers which runs through western literature from Boethius through John of Salisbury and Aeneas Sylvius Piccolomini to Sir Walter Raleigh. Kekaumenos, in his guide to survival in the imperial system, certainly implies that the imperial court was a highly dangerous part of it, where "you should have your denunciation and your fall before your eyes every day," but he does not pass moral judgment on the system as such, and he does not see the dangers as being confined to the palace; he envisages no alternative, and no retreat, except for the toparch with a power base beyond the frontier.[9] It is pointless to speculate as to whether the picture might be different had more treatises like that of Kekaumenos survived. The fact is that neither Kekaumenos in the late eleventh century, nor the anonymous author of the slightly later *Timarion*, a trenchant and witty satire on the whole Byzantine establishment,[10] come anywhere near the western—mainly English—critique of the court as a nest of flattery, intrigue, slander, and vice; a place of frivolous trifles, shattered dreams, and capricious reversals of fortune which the man of integrity must shun if he knows what is good for him.[11]

None of this means, of course, that we should necessarily privilege the western model as if it were normative, when it can just as easily be regarded as eccentric. It is important to emphasize the traits that are common to all court societies: the acute sense of hierarchy, rank, and proximity to the ruler; the ethos of attendance, service, and reward; the cult of luxury, exoticism, delightfulness, and play; the fascination with unlocking the hidden and forbidden secrets of nature and the future. It is also important to note the affinities that existed between Byzantine and western courts, especially toward the end

---

[7] As in the "Bagoas" of Nikephoros Basilakes, ed. A. Garzya, *Nicephori Basilacae orationes et epistolae* (Leipzig, 1984), 101.33: reference to monks who were αὐλικοὺς καὶ οἰκότριβας.

[8] See, notably, Dante, *De vulgari eloquentia*, I.18.

[9] Ed. B. Wassiliewsky and V. Jernstedt, *Cecaumeni Strategicon* (St. Petersburg, 1896; repr. Amsterdam, 1965), esp. 3 ff, 76 [= ed. G. G. Litavrin, *Sovety i rasskazy Kekavmena* (Moscow, 1972), 122 ff, 298].

[10] Ed. R. Romano, *Pseudo-Luciano, Timarione* (Naples, 1974), Eng. trans. B. Baldwin (Detroit, 1984). On the date, see E. Tsolakis, Τιμαρίων· μία νέα ἀνάγνωση, in *Μνήμη Σταμάτη Καρατζᾶ* (Thessalonike, 1990), 109–17.

[11] In addition to the studies by Jaeger and Scaglione cited above, see E. Türk, *Nugae curialium: Le règne d'Henri II Plantagenet (1145–1189) et l'éthique politique* (Geneva, 1977); J. Fleckenstein, ed., *Curialitas: Studien zu Grundfragen der höfisch-ritterlichen Kultur* (Göttingen, 1990); R. V. Turner, "Towards a Definition of the *Curialis*: Educated Court Cleric, Courtier, Administrator, or 'New Man'?" *Medieval Prosopography* 15 (1994), 3–35.

of the period under review. Crusaders were undoubtedly impressed by the brilliance of the imperial court of the Komnenoi.[12] In the same period, Byzantine court culture came close to looking courtly in a western sense. It is in the twelfth century that one finds the words αὐλὴ and αὐλικὸς occasionally being used to refer to the court as opposed to the palace. Emperor Manuel I was a universal man who hunted, jousted, womanized, chaired rhetorical contests, engaged in theological debates, and dabbled in astrology.[13] Writers celebrated his prowess in all these areas while underlining their dependence on his favor, in ways reminiscent of intellectuals at the contemporary courts of Frederick Barbarossa and Henry Plantagenet.[14] Some of them even wrote in the vernacular and composed romances. At the same time, other writers took a negative view of court life—and not simply, as in earlier centuries, as being the antithesis of the monastic life.[15] John Tzetzes and Michael Choniates ostentatiously and rhetorically declined to prostitute their learning in the search for imperial or magnate patronage.[16] The *History* by Michael's brother Niketas is largely an indictment of the moral corruption and emptiness of the imperial court under Manuel Komnenos and his successors.[17]

Yet in the final analysis the structural similarities merely point up the conceptual differences. Whether Byzantine authors write to celebrate or deplore, the focus of their attention is the individual emperor or society and the world in general, not the court as a social and cultural milieu. This difference in emphasis is all the more significant in view of the fact that the twelfth-century imperial court was exposed to western fashions and ideas. The exposure is most obvious in the case of Manuel I and his jousting; it may also, perhaps, have stimulated the revival of Greek romantic fiction. If so, however, the romances are remarkable for being distinctly uncourtly in that they depict courts as alien, disruptive elements in the lives of their heroes and heroines, whose parents are not kings and queens but respectable citizens in a vaguely evoked ancient polis.[18] With the excep-

---

[12] See R. Hiestand, "Kreuzzug und höfisches Leben," in G. Kaiser and J.-D. Miller, eds., *Höfische Literatur, Hofgesellschaft, höfische Lebensformen um 1200: Kolloquium am Zentrum für interdisziplinäre Forschung der Universität Bielefeld (3. bis 5. November 1983)*, Studia Humaniora, Düsseldorfer Studien zu Mittelalter und Renaissance 6 (Düsseldorf, 1986), 192–97, 203–9, esp. 194: "Was Konstantinopel zeigte, war ein Hof, der höfisches Leben in fast allen seinen Facetten vorführte, große Gastmähler, feierliche Aufzüge, musische Darbietungen ebenso wie Gaukler und Akrobaten, ein Hofstaat, wo den Herrscher ein zahlreiches Gefolge von Höflingen umgab, Aufstieg in die Gunst und in der Gunst ebenso rasch in ihren Entzug und den Sturz in die Tiefe umschlagen konnte."

[13] See, in general, P. Magdalino, *The Empire of Manuel I Komnenos, 1143–1180* (Cambridge, 1993), esp. chaps. 1, 5, 6.

[14] See F. Cairns, "The Archpoet's Confession: Sources, Interpretation and Historical Context," *Mittellateinisches Jahrbuch* 15 (1980), 35–103; idem, "The Archpoet's 'Jonah Confession' (Poem II): Literary, Exegetical and Historical Aspects," *Mittellateinisches Jahrbuch* 18 (1983), 168–93; C. H. Haskins, "Henry II as a Patron of Literature," in A. G. Little and F. M. Powicke, eds., *Essays in Medieval History Presented to T. F. Tout* (Manchester, 1925), 71–77.

[15] As, e.g., in the Life of St. Stephen the Younger: see M.-F. Rouan, "Une lecture 'iconoclaste' de la Vie d'Étienne le Jeune," *TM* 8 (1981), 425–28.

[16] See *Ioannis Tzetzae historiae*, ed. P.A.M. Leone (Naples, 1968), no. XI.13 ff; *Ioannis Tzetzae epistulae*, ed. P.A.M. Leone (Leipzig, 1972), 35–36; Μιχαὴλ Ἀκομινάτου τοῦ Χωνιάτου τὰ σωζόμενα, ed Sp. P. Lampros, vol. I (Athens, 1879), 7–23; cf. Magdalino, *Empire*, 337 ff.

[17] Ed. J.-L. van Dieten (Berlin-New York, 1975); cf. Magdalino, *Empire*, 5–14.

[18] See R. Macrides and P. Magdalino, "The Fourth Kingdom and the Rhetoric of Hellenism," in P. Magdalino, ed., *The Perception of the Past in Twelfth-Century Europe* (London, 1994), 148–52; idem, "Eros the King and the King of *Amours*: Some Observations on *Hysmine and Hysminias*," *DOP* 46 (1992), 199–204, esp. 204.

tion of wedding songs and one or two allusions to Eros in poems addressed to Manuel I,[19] love at court is a distinctly unromantic business in Byzantine literature, the stuff of prurient disapproval rather than sublime inspiration.

It does appear, therefore, that Byzantine court culture was considerably more reticent about its courtliness than was the case in the medieval West, and it is worth asking why this was so. Without attempting to give a proper answer, I shall merely list, in brief, some points that seem to me relevant. First, learning and civilized behavior in Byzantium were associated with Constantinople rather than specifically with the palace—except, notably, in the posthumous reputation of Constantine Porphyrogennetos.[20] Second, the sacred functions of the emperor, the integration of church and state, and the close geographical proximity of the patriarchate meant that imperial court culture could never be characterized as purely secular or profane. Third, there was no internal competition between courts until the new imperial system of the Komnenoi led to the proliferation of large princely households, which was perhaps the major reason for the greater courtliness of Byzantine court culture in the twelfth century. Fourth, Byzantine society, at least in Constantinople, was not conducive to the male bonding between lord and knight, and between companions in arms, which was so vital to the growth of chivalry in the West. The imperial court was too vast, and protocol too elaborate, for that kind of intimacy. Most uncastrated males who attended on the emperor returned at night to their own homes, to domestic bliss or, as in the comic scenes portrayed by Ptochoprodromos, to a nagging wife.[21] The absence of primogeniture and the social acceptance of castration meant that there was not a large pool of landless younger sons seeking a cause to fight for; on the other hand, there were many eunuchs.[22] All this may also help to explain why the bonding between male and female in the imperial palace was not the stuff of romantic fiction.

Basic to all these points is the fact that the imperial court of Byzantium was an integral part of a large capital city. The quality and the scale of urban life are matters of ongoing debate, and it is arguable that without the court the city would have been insignificant. But Constantine's city, the New Rome, was vital not only to the material support but also to the legitimate identity of the court in ways which comparisons with other capital cities can only dimly illustrate. The proof lies above all in the sheer amount of "coming and going" between the palace and the city.[23] However much some emperors may have tried to distance the court from the city by going on campaign, by fortifying the palace, or by retreating to the suburbs, it remained tied by a dense and intricate network of bureaucracy, ceremonial, and commerce to the Hippodrome, the fora and porticoes, the

[19] Ibid., 200–203.

[20] Theophanes Continuatus, ed. I. Bekker, CSHB (Bonn, 1838), 446; cf I. Ševčenko, "Rereading Constantine Porphyrogenitus," in Shepard and Franklin, eds., *Byzantine Diplomacy* (as in note 5 above), 167–95.

[21] Ed. H. Eideneier, *Ptochoprodromos* (Cologne, 1991), nos. I and II.

[22] Fulcher of Chartres estimated that there were 20,000 in Constantinople at the time of the First Crusade—clearly an exaggeration, but a revealing one: *Historia Hierosolymitana*, ed. H. Hagenmeyer (Heidelberg, 1913), 217.

[23] This is well brought out by J. Herrin, "Byzance: Le palais et la ville," *Byzantion* 61 (1991), 215–30.

great public churches, and the evergrowing number of urban monasteries. The enduring and decisive importance of the urban environment is reflected in the continuing use of the words ἀστεῖος and ἀστειότης ("urbane" and "urbanity") to describe the package of social graces which medieval Latin referred to, from the eleventh century, as *curialitas*. *Urbanitas* did remain in use, in place of *curialitas* or conjointly with it, and it should not be overlooked that a *curia* had in ancient times been a town council. Yet it is surely significant that the early medieval West did need to develop a substitute for, or an alternative to, *urbanitas*, for which it coined no vernacular form.[24] It is also significant that the vernacular equivalent of *curialitas—cortesia/courtoisie*—derived from Medieval Latin *curtis*, itself a derivative of classical *cohors*.[25] As the term *curia* became assimilated to this meaning, *curialitas* was effectively stripped of any urban associations. The idea that the Roman Senate survived in the papal Curia was not enough to halt the trend. This again makes an interesting contrast to the East, where the terms βουλή, γερουσία, and σύγκλητος, when applied to the imperial court, usually exclude the imperial household and are inevitably used in a Constantinopolitan context.

Ten years ago, in the conclusion to a study of Byzantine snobbery, I stated that the words ἀστειότης and *courtoisie* "reflect a world of cultural difference."[26] I would reiterate that statement today, and I would go on to suggest that it poses a real methodological problem: how do you apply the very concept of court culture, which derives from the western tradition of courtliness, to a society which did not isolate courtliness as a cultural phenomenon? To limit the scope of the problem, how do you go about identifying the figure of the Byzantine courtier? Was it anyone who attended the court, or was it a specific category of person? The task is vitiated by the absence of treatises on monarchical government of the kind which some other nonwestern cultures provide, and which in the Persian and Arab world, for example, clearly identify the *nadim*, the "boon companions" of the ruler, as a group fulfilling the range of functions which Castiglione expected of the Renaissance courtier.[27]

There being no such obvious category, and no such literature, in Byzantium, I see two ways forward. One is to sift laboriously through all references to court personnel in the hope of isolating a promising cluster of recurrent labels and value judgments. The other is to look at the writings of individuals associated with the court in an attempt to pinpoint the types of person, and the types of writing, that came closest to representing a court mentality or a court ideology. I have no doubt that the former alternative is the more worthy and the more scientific; I also have a strong suspicion that its value lies more in the labor of sifting than in the interest of what will be left in the sieve at the

[24] See T. Zotz, "Urbanitas: Zur Bedeutung und Funktion einer antiken Wertvorstellung innerhalb der höfischen Kultur des hohen Mittelalters," in Fleckenstein, ed., *Curialitas* (as in note 11 above), 392–451.

[25] See the articles by P. G. Schmidt and U. Mölk, ibid., 15–38.

[26] P. Magdalino, "Byzantine Snobbery," *The Byzantine Aristocracy, IX to XIII Centuries*, ed. M. Angold, British Archaeological Reports, International Series 221 (Oxford, 1984), 70; repr. in idem, *Tradition and Transformation in Medieval Byzantium* (Aldershot, 1991).

[27] See Masudi, *The Meadows of Gold. The Abbasids*, trans. P. Lunde and C. Stone (London, 1989), 325–26; Nizam al-Mulk, *The Book of Government or Rules for Kings*, trans. H. Drake (London, 1960), chap. 17, pp. 92–94.

end of the day. The "sociology" of the Byzantine court is in any case discussed in another contribution to this volume.[28] I shall therefore take the less worthy course of shortlisting courtier writers, and this not being a monograph, I shall cut short the selection procedure by nominating two figures who seem to me to be particularly eligible. In case anyone is wondering why Michael Psellos is not among them, I have excluded him for several reasons. A significant proportion, perhaps the bulk, of his literary production is not concerned with the court. That part of his oeuvre which is concerned with the court is being dealt with by George Dennis in this volume. In any case, as I have made clear elsewhere, I do not accept that imperial panegyric was primarily a court as opposed to a civic genre: it celebrates the emperor on behalf of, and as the head of, the whole *politeia*.[29]

Leo Choirosphaktes and Constantine Manasses recommend themselves in three particulars. They represent, respectively, the beginning and the end of the period under review; the one belongs to the "Macedonian renaissance," the other to the "twelfth-century renaissance." The emperors under whom they wrote, Leo VI and Manuel I, were both remarkable for their extremely lofty conception of the imperial office. They perhaps went further than any other rulers of the Middle Byzantine period in asserting the divinity of their role. Choirosphaktes and Manasses both remained laymen throughout their literary careers, at least as far as these are known to us, and both were dependent on imperial favor, although Manasses was less exclusively so because of his lower status and the structure of the Komnenian regime. A mark of their secularity is the fact that both believed in astrology, which was condemned by the church and needed court patronage to survive. Both men went on diplomatic missions. Both complained of being the victims of Phthonos (Envy). Finally, and most crucially, both composed *ekphraseis*—descriptive celebrations—of the court environment. Such pieces are much less numerous than one might imagine. Apart from the descriptions of palace buildings in the *Vita Basilii*,[30] I can think of only two other examples in Middle Byzantine literature, one being the *ekphrasis* of a park by John Geometres[31] and the other the anonymous twelfth-century *ekphrasis* of an imperial joust.[32] Yet this was court literature at its most unequivocal. The writers who produced it thus deserve special attention, as indeed does the rarity of the phenomenon.

Leo Choirosphaktes flourished in the late ninth and early tenth centuries;[33] the idea that he was born in the 820s is, as we shall see, without foundation. He was *mystikos* under Basil I, the first to hold this office, which he combined with the dignity of *spatharo-*

---

[28] See A. P. Kazhdan and M. McCormick in this volume.

[29] Magdalino, *Empire*, chap. 6.

[30] Theoph. Cont., 327–38.

[31] Ed. J. A. Cramer, *Anecdota graeca e codd. manuscriptis regiae parisiensis Bibliothecae*, vol. IV (Oxford, 1841), 276–78; cf. H. Maguire, "A Description of the Aretai Palace and Its Garden," *Journal of Garden History* 10 (1990), 209–13.

[32] Ed. Sp. P. Lampros, Ἔκφρασις τῶν ξυλοκονταριῶν τοῦ κραταίου καὶ ἁγίου ἡμῶν βασιλέως, *Νέος Ἑλλ.* 5 (1908), 3–18.

[33] See, in general, G. Kolias, *Léon Choerosphactès, magistre, proconsul et patrice*, Texte und Forschungen zur byzantinisch-neugriechischen Philologie 31 (Athens, 1939).

kandidatos.[34] It was almost certainly Leo VI who granted him the three higher dignities of *anthypatos, patrikios,* and *magistros* which he held by 896. All his surviving writings can be dated to Leo's reign or to the minority of Constantine VII. He led embassies to Symeon of Bulgaria in 896,[35] and to Baghdad in 906.[36] Some time after this he fell from favor, accused, apparently, of having exceeded his brief, and was banished to a place in the provinces called Petra.[37] During his disgrace, he was subject to a virulent attack by the metropolitan of Caesarea, Arethas.[38] He was at least partially rehabilitated either by Leo or by Alexander, for at Alexander's death in 913 he was residing in Constantinople with the title of *patrikios.* Implicated in the failed coup d'état of Constantine Doukas against the regency government of Constantine VII, he was forced to enter the Stoudios monastery, where he presumably remained until his death some time after 920.

Apart from his well-known correspondence with Symeon of Bulgaria, Emperor Leo, and various imperial officials, Choirosphaktes wrote five works which can be classified as court literature. One, which we shall consider shortly, is a theological treatise in twelve-syllable verse, dedicated to an emperor or an imperial heir. The other four are anacreontic poems written to celebrate court occasions: two on one of Leo VI's four marriages, probably the second; one on the opening of a palace bath built by Leo; and one on the marriage of Constantine VII to Helen Lekapene in 920.[39] The wedding songs need not detain us, since their purpose is to evoke, in fairly predictable and super-ficial terms, the festive mood of the occasion, the sex appeal of the bride, and the splen-dor of the nuptial chamber—though we may note an allusion to Leo as a "divine statue of wisdom" (σοφίης ἄγαλμα θεῖον).

The poem on the bath is altogether more interesting, since it effectively takes the form of an *ekphrasis* of part of the court environment. Having discussed the probable appearance of this building in two previous publications,[40] and having been corrected once by Cyril Mango,[41] I do not need to say any more on this subject. It is sufficient to recall the following points: that the building incorporated substantial remains of an early fifth-century structure belonging to the House of Marina; that it featured ancient statues and relief sculptures, a mosaic cycle of aquatic scenes, and some bird and animal figures, possibly in the form of water spouts; and that the whole thing struck contemporaries as being wonderfully exotic and antique. What interests us here is the way in which the author uses the building to praise the emperor. First, the bath is celebrated as a work of the

---

[34] G. Schlumberger, "Sceaux byzantins inédits (cinquième série)," *Revue numismatique,* 4th ser., 9 (1905), 347; cf. N. Oikonomidès, *Les listes de préséance byzantines des IXe et Xe siècles* (Paris, 1972), 324.

[35] Letters 1–14, ed. and trans. Kolias, 76–91.

[36] Letters 15–19, ibid., 90–97.

[37] Letters 20–27, ibid., 96–129; see below, note 54.

[38] See below, p. 151.

[39] Ed. P. Matranga, *Anecdota graeca* (Rome, 1850), vol. II, 561–68; ed. T. Bergk, *Poetae lyrici graeci,* vol. III (Leipzig, 1882), 356–62.

[40] P. Magdalino, "The Bath of Leo the Wise," in *Maistor: Classical, Byzantine and Renaissance Studies for Robert Browning,* ed. A. Moffatt, Byzantina Australiensia 5 (Canberra, 1984), 225–40; idem, "The Bath of Leo the Wise and the 'Macedonian Renaissance' Revisited: Topography, Iconography, Ceremonial, Ideology," *DOP* 42 (1988), 97–118 (text and translation, based on Bergk's ed., on pp. 116–18).

[41] C. Mango, "The Palace of Marina, the Poet Palladas and the Bath of Leo VI," Εὐφρόσυνον: Ἀφιέρωμα στόν Μανόλη Χατζηδάκη, vol. I (Athens, 1991), 321–30.

emperor's creative genius—he has "surpassed the imagination of Daedalus" in creating a place of manifold beauty and great healing. Second, certain features of the bath—the opening doors and the flowing waters—are imagined to be singing a hymn of praise to the emperor, so that the poem ascribes its own function to the emperor's creation. Third, the iconography of the decoration of the main bath chambers is treated as an image of the emperor's cosmic kingship and special virtues. I accept Mango's point that the royal figures, who dominate the aquatic cycle of river gods, fishing scenes, fish banquets, and spring nymphs are more likely to represent Poseidon and Amphitrite than the emperor and empress. He is also no doubt right that Leo did not commission the whole decorative program from scratch. I nevertheless persist in believing that even if the palace officials and the artists who carried out the restoration work for Leo did not rephrase the iconography in a religious sense and with reference to the emperor,[42] Choirosphaktes does read the decoration in this way. The poem is too carefully constructed, and the hints it drops are too broad, to admit of any other interpretation. The description of the aquatic cycle dovetails subtly with the metaphor of the hymn of praise to the emperor, by concluding with a mention of a warbling songbird at the feet of the male ruler figure, here called *despotes*; the mention is inserted between the evocation of the singing doors and that of the singing waters. The praise (αἶνος) sung by the waters picks up the earlier reference to "metrical praises" inscribed beside the river gods. The poem then takes us through a sequence of four images—a serpent, a lion, a crane, a tree—which evoke the elements of earth and air and thus mediate between the water of the aquatic cycle and the fire exhaled by the griffin, the next and final figure to be mentioned. The last two strophes of the poem then celebrate the union of these two opposite elements which is effected in the healing hot water of the bath.

It is of course left up to the reader to discover this and other layers of symbolic meaning, and there is a danger of discovering too many. However, the text does put down some markers. The serpent is said to creep up "in wisdom" (σοφίη), and wisdom was Leo VI's special quality,[43] celebrated as such not only in other writings of the period but in the same poem, in the *koukoulia* or refrains which act as a sort of antiphonal running commentary on the description. The first one refers to the emperor's reputation for *sophia*. The third one, coming right after the mention of the "metrical praises" inscribed beside the river gods, reads as follows: "Write divine doctrines (θειολόγα δόγματα), O youths; rain descends from godlike mouths." It is these words, above all, which persuade me that the iconography was meant to be read as a Christian allegory, and that the inscriptions at least may have been added in Leo's day. The fourth *koukoulion* comes between the description of the songbird at the ruler's feet and the image of the singing bathwater; it reads: "Reject all babble of false words; Leo has now gathered all rhetorical

---

[42] If, as seems likely, the restoration by Leo was the first since the 6th century, it must have entailed some replacement of dilapidated fabric. This is confirmed by the 10th-century chronicle reference, which also attributes the construction to Leo, and indicates that further restoration work was necessary after only a generation of neglect following Leo's death: Theoph. Cont., 460–61; Magdalino, "Revisited," 99–101; Mango, "The Palace of Marina," 323. Of course, if the mosaic cycle was on the floor, as Mango suggests (p. 327), it could easily have survived intact, but the phrase ἐπὶ τὸν πρόκογχον (line 34) suggests wall or ceiling level.

[43] See Shaun F. Tougher, "The Wisdom of Leo VI," in P. Magdalino, ed., *New Constantines: The Rhythm of Imperial Renewal in Byzantium, 4th–13th Centuries* (Aldershot, 1994), 171–79.

writings (τεχνικῶν λογίων)." The next refrain celebrates a different aspect of Leo's wisdom: "Let the revolving axis of heaven rejoice that Leo perceives the unalterable threads (ἄτροπα νήματα) of the bearers of light." This is remarkable for the claim that is made not only for the emperor but also for the science of astrology. In the context of the poem, the statement, coming just before the mention of the fiery griffin, serves to indicate that our contemplation of the microcosm in the bath has now risen to the heavens from the watery depths of the sea, and that Leo's wisdom has guided us there. The *koukoulion* which concludes the poem returns to the literary aspect of that wisdom with the remark that "The guardian of rhetoric has reached the summit; begone, O forgers of artless words."

It was nothing new for panegyric to celebrate a ruler's buildings as products of divinely inspired genius, and to this extent Choirosphaktes' poem appears to follow the sixth-century *ekphraseis* of St. Sophia, or Photios' more recent *ekphrasis* of the Pharos church.[44] Yet Choirosphaktes innovates in several ways: he uses a lyric verse form, he celebrates a completely secular building, and, if Mango is right, he appropriates for Leo a building which had existed for nearly five centuries. Furthermore, if I am right, the poem represents the emperor in terms of a set of allegorical images with religious overtones. I would therefore reiterate my earlier conclusion that the text employs a language of symbolic representation such as Byzantine religious art had rejected when it adopted icons.[45] The important difference is that I would now emphasize the input of Choirosphaktes in encoding the pictorial vocabulary with references to Leo VI which the artists themselves, or whoever commissioned them, may not have intended.

What I suggest, in fact, is that Choirosphaktes was using the celebration of Leo's palace bath to expound an ideology, or indeed a *theology,* of rulership which in style, and even in substance, was at variance with the mainstream of post-iconoclastic Orthodoxy. The clearest proof of this is the explicit association of the ruler with astrology. We now need to satisfy ourselves that this linkage is not a "one-off," and that the poem itself is not merely a virtuoso extravaganza. Can we discover the same ideas and intellectual preoccupations in other works by the same author?

The obvious place to turn is to what was undoubtedly the most ambitious of the author's surviving works, his *Thousand-Line Theology* (χιλιόστιχος θεολογία). Unfortunately, this is still unpublished, and the full text survives only in Vaticanus graecus 1257, not the most user-friendly of manuscripts.[46] What follows is a somewhat tentative review based on an imperfect working transcription.[47] The work consists of forty chapters, the initial letters of which form an acrostic identifying the poem as the work of Leo *magistros,*

---

[44] For discussion and bibliography, see R. Macrides and P. Magdalino, "The Architecture of Ekphrasis: Construction and Context of Paul the Silentiary's Poem on Hagia Sophia," *BMGS* 12 (1988), 47–82.

[45] H. Maguire, *Earth and Ocean: The Terrestrial World in Early Byzantine Art* (University Park, Pa.-London, 1987), 83–84.

[46] The script is illegible in places, at least in photographs. Although it seems to be of the 10th century, there are numerous scribal errors due to the copyist's frequent (but inconsistent) failure to understand what he was copying.

[47] I cite extensively from the text in order to give the reader an idea of the language and style. For reasons of space, and because I do not regard my emendations as final, I have not signaled them; they are not, however, such as to affect the overall sense. A critical edition of the text is being prepared by Dr. Ioannis Vassis of the University of Crete, to whom I am grateful for help with some problematic readings.

anthypatos, and *patrikios.* While there can be little doubt that Choirosphaktes is the author, the date of composition poses a problem. The work is ostensibly addressed to a person referred to as "the glory of the palace,"[48] and the didactic tone suggests that the addressee is younger than the author. Some of the verses are transmitted, under Leo's name, in another manuscript (Oxford, Barocc. gr. 76, fol. 381r), with the information that they were composed under Michael III and Bardas. But this, as L. G. Westerink has pointed out, would have made Choirosphaktes close to one hundred years old at the time of his death.[49] Although he refers to his advanced years in his letters from exile,[50] the words used (γέρων, γῆρας) could indicate any age from forty-seven to sixty-eight.[51] Besides, as we have seen, it seems very unlikely that he could have held the three titles named in the acrostic before Leo's reign. The addressee can most plausibly be identified with Leo himself or with the young Constantine VII.

The theology of the poem consists of a demonstration of the transcendent oneness of God, the omnipresence of his providence in time and space, and the threefold manifestation of his glory. The demonstration is accompanied by a point-for-point refutation of pantheism, polytheism, dualism, and the idea that the material world is uncreated, uncontrolled, or infinite. In essence, the content of the work boils down to a philosophical argument, in Neoplatonic terms, for a monotheistic Christian cosmology.[52] Whatever Choirosphaktes' patristic sources—they include Origen, St. Athanasios, and Pseudo-Dionysios, and the work may owe more than its metrical form to the inspiration of George of Pisidia's *Hexaemeron*[53]—he was fighting a cause that had been fought and won more than three centuries earlier. We may well wonder what was the point of returning to the fray around the year 900. The denial of dualism could have been aimed at the Paulicians, but it occupies only one chapter of the work.[54] Was this perhaps written as a pedagogical exercise? This would fit in with Paul Speck's idea that the various books on government produced at the behest of Leo VI and Constantine VII were for the instruction of the heir to the throne.[55] Certainly, the work is something of a rhetorical exercise. Its verse form and its acrostic arrangement reflect a certain striving for technical effect. The refutation of the "adversary" is conducted with a colorful invective which displays

---

[48] XLV. 1–2 (fol. 56v):

   Ἄκουσον οὖν ἔνθεν δὲ μικρὸν ἐν τέλει
   τί δογματίζω, τῶν ἀνακτόρων κλέος

[49] L. G. Westerink, *Michaelis Pselli poemata* (Leipzig-Stuttgart, 1992), xxxiv.

[50] Ed. Kolias, *Léon Choerosphactès,* 101, 117, 121.

[51] See J.A.H. Tittman, *Iohannis Zonarae lexicon* (Leipzig, 1808; repr. Amsterdam, 1967), vol. I, 434: γηραιός. ἀπὸ ἐτῶν μ̅ζ̅ ἕως ἐτῶν ξ̅η̅.

[52] I would respectfully disagree with the statement by a leading Neoplatonic scholar that the *Theologia* "keinerlei Vertrautheit mit dem Neuplatonismus verrät": L. G. Westerink, "Das Rätsel des untergründigen Neuplatonismus," in D. Harlfinger, ed., *Φιλοφρόνημα: Festschrift für Martin Sicherl zum 75. Geburtstag* (Paderborn, 1990), 105–23, at p. 120. The work's Neoplatonism lies not in any explicit reference to ancient authority, or in use of technical vocabulary, neither of which is to be expected in a theological work of the Middle Ages, but in its indifference to Orthodox Christian soteriology and its advocacy of an elitist *gnosis.*

[53] PG 92:1425–1578, esp. lines 60 ff for invective against Proklos and other pagan philosophers; cf. F. Gonnelli, "Le parole del cosmo: Osservazioni sull'*Esamerone* di Giorgio Pisida," *BZ* 83 (1990), 411–22.

[54] XII–XIII (fols. 43v–45r).

[55] In P. Speck et al., *Varia III* (Bonn, 1991), 267, 269–306, 326–27.

great ingenuity and erudition while contributing absolutely nothing to the argument. Thus, to quote only the first of numerous examples, the addressee is urged to "flee the dark throaty cyclopean wolves, monstrous corrupting tomb demons, profane undisciplined boasters who turn everything upside down by guile."[56] Yet only one passing reference to the "mob of the Hellenes" gives any hint as to who the much-abused enemies of the truth might actually be.[57]

The very implausibility of the invective, however, provides a clue to the deeper purpose of the work. It suggests that the enemy is being conjured up as a smokescreen to obscure the controversial nature of the author's own propositions. He himself was accused of Hellenism and impiety by Arethas in the latter's *Choirosphaktes or Wizard-Hater* (Χοιροσφάκτης ἢ μισογόης).[58] According to this, Choirosphaktes made a show of honoring and imitating the church fathers, although in fact he was as opposed to them as Julian the Apostate, of whom he was a great admirer. Many godly people, says Arethas, had denounced Choirosphaktes' "ungodliness" (ἀθεΐαν). Particularly revealing is the following comment: "Is this man so shameless as to engage in theology, who has unlearned and abjured his native faith, but relearned and admired the teachings of the Hellenes, even though he now faithlessly and deceitfully betrays them?"[59] Of course, accusations of Hellenizing—like accusations of Judaizing—were part of the stock-in-trade of Byzantine religious polemic, and we should not take them too literally, especially when they flow from the pen of a churchman who was himself a classical scholar with an interest in Plato, and had also faced accusations of "impiety."[60] It is also clear that Arethas' complaints were not directly occasioned by the *Thousand-Line Theology* but by some other work which we have lost. Even so, on careful reading of the *Theology,* it is not hard to see how this could have scandalized Orthodox opinion in post-iconoclastic Byzantium and laid Choirosphaktes open to denunciation. To begin with, its very lack of reference to any contemporary controversy, notably Iconoclasm, might have aroused suspicions. These suspicions would have been amply confirmed by the poem's minimal and essentially cosmetic references to the basic framework of scriptural and patristic authority. There is a fleeting allusion to the Gospels in the preface,[61] the fathers appear equally fleetingly under the designation of θεήγοροι,[62] the prophets are cited in connec-

---

[56] II.25–28 (fol. 40r):

φεύγων ζοφώδεις λαιμοκύκλωπας λύκους
γιγαντιῶντας τυμβοδαίμονας φθόρους
φυσιῶντας δὲ παμβεβήλους ἀτάκτους
ἄνω κάτω τὰ πάντα ποιοῦντας δόλῳ

[57] XII.26 (fol. 44r): καὶ δογματίζειν ὡς πανελλήνων ὄχλος.

[58] Ed. L. G. Westerink, *Arethae scripta minora,* 2 vols. (Leipzig, 1968–72), vol. I, 200–212, esp. 205–8, 212; trans. (based on the older edition by Compernass) P. Karlin-Hayter, "Arethas, Choirosphactes and the Saracen Vizir," *Byzantion* 35 (1965), 468–81, repr. in eadem, *Studies in Byzantine Political History* (London, 1981).

[59] Ed. Westerink, *Scripta minora,* I, 207.12–15.

[60] Ibid., II, 49–55; Westerink, "Das Rätsel," 116–19. For the "symmetry" of Judaism and paganism as enemy religions, see G. Dagron, "Judaiser," *TM* 11 (1991), 359–60.

[61] Lines 5–6 (fol. 39r):

ἡ τετράδελτος τὴν τρίφωτον οὐσίαν
αἰνεῖ, γεραίρει ῥυθμικαῖς εὐγλωττίαις

[62] XIII.9 (fol. 44v), XXIX.1 (fol. 52r).

tion with the symbolic names of God,[63] and three lines toward the end sweepingly invoke Christ, the apostles, the fathers, and the church;[64] but that is all. There is little mention of angels, which is doubly interesting—first, because Arethas implies that Choirosphaktes had no time for them,[65] and second, because it seems to reflect a divergence from the Christian Neoplatonism of Pseudo-Dionysios.[66] This essentially sacramental theology of a union with God mediated by the hierarchy of the church who image the liturgy of the heavenly host finds no echo with Choirosphaktes. Similarly, in reproducing St. Athanasios' argument that the harmony of the universe demonstrates that there is only one Creator, he omits Athanasios' discussion of the relationship between the Father and the Logos in the process of creation.[67] While he devotes a few final chapters to the doctrine of the Trinity, his allusions to the Incarnation are brief and perfunctory compared with his insistence on the immateriality of the Divine, and no more prominent than his allusions to number symbolism.[68] This leaves a big void at the center of his Orthodoxy—a void which he fills with a depersonalized and intellectualized conception of the knowledge and revelation of the Divine. From three basically unexceptionable propositions—that God is unknowable, that he makes himself partially known to the initiate, and that his providence is revealed in the beauty and order of his creation—Choirosphaktes arrives at the dubious conclusion that the knowledge of God is accessible only to those who can contemplate creation and read it with the eyes of *logos*. This elitism is reminiscent of the mystical tradition of Orthodox asceticism, and at the beginning Choirosphaktes says that by prayer and asceticism the initiate can see as in a mirror the shadow of reality.[69] Throughout the rest of the work, however, the repeated emphasis is on *logos* as the key to enlightenment, and by *logos* Choirosphaktes means above all the science of understanding the principles behind the construction of the cosmos. The key chapters are those where he argues that creation itself is the evidence for the unity and the providence of the divine mind.

---

[63] XXX.2 (fol. 52v).

[64] XXXVII.21–23 (fol. 55v):

οὕτως νοοῦσιν εὐσεβῶν ἀνδρῶν τέκνα
καὶ Χριστὸς καὶ φέριστον ἕρκος κηρύκων
ἐκκλησίαι τε καὶ βίβλοι μυστοπόλων

[65] Ed. Westerink, *Scripta minora*, I, 211.13–21.

[66] See A. Louth, *Denys the Areopagite* (London, 1989).

[67] See Athanasios, *Contra gentes*, 35–47, ed. and trans. P. T. Camelot, *Athanase d'Alexandrie, Contre les païens*, SC 18bis (Paris, 1977), 166–211.

[68] See, above all, I.13–18. These lines were transmitted anonymously in other manuscripts, and Theodore Prodromos, commenting on them in the 12th century, attributed them to Maximos Confessor: ed. I. D. Polemis, "An Unknown Treatise of Theodore Prodromos," *Byzantion* 62 (1992), 414–23.

[69] I.22–28 (fol. 39v):

τὸ κρεῖττον ἴθι εὐκτικῇ λειτουργίᾳ
τήξας τὼ χεῖρε ἐγκρατεῖ χαμευνίᾳ
εἴσω φρενῶν φάνηθι καὶ χαίρειν φράσας,
ἴδοις ἐσόπτρῳ τὰς σκιὰς τῶν πραγμάτων
κενεμβατῶν ἄβυσσον εἰς αἰνιγμάτων
θεὸν ἑαυτὸν δογμάτων ἐξ ἐνθέων
ἀγνωσίᾳ νοῦ γνώσεως ὑπερτέρα

Sense perception of the cosmic systems provides us with the breadth of good Experience; this introduces the benefit of Art, which in its turn sets up the methods of Science which leads to perfection of Knowledge, by which it is that contemplative men can see. Therefore the world is good as being from Good, bringing me to a good destiny by way of sense-perceived objects.[70]

[If there were several deities] matter, shaken and confused, would be scattered and unfinished. But it is not shown to be so, and creation is witness, being united in firm coordination. Thus there is one exalted Monad, good, just, all-powerful and most wise. Being good, it produced the world incorruptibly; justly, it gave good order; being supreme, it manifests power; as all-wise, it blends opposites, and supervising salvific minds, it wards off the rebels as soul destroyers.[71]

The first mind, utterly supreme . . . bearing everything within itself in manifold ways, manifests the wide, well-choreographed heaven of the stars. It produces it by the first stroke, like a musician, imparting the mind of knowledge, in a seven-stringed and most psalmodic lyre. Its strength is not unprovided for, for it is not by an instrument without an artist. Whoever heard of a house, a chariot, a ship, a band of instruments, without someone to fit it together by exact calculation (*logos*)? But you will say he set up the heaven out of matter. Where did this come from? . . . The heaven would not have remained in many uncorrupted years if it had not observed the leader's command. The God of Gods set it up as a book, prescribing many things in ether-turning cycles . . .[72]

[70] XII.14–21 (fol. 44r):

αἴσθησις ἡμῖν κοσμικῶν συστημάτων
πείρας παρέσχε πλάτος εὐκλεεστάτης,
αὕτη δὲ τέχνης εἰσάγει προμηθείαν·
ἡ δ'αὖ συνιστᾷ τοὺς ἐπιστήμης λόγους,
ἢ πρὸς τελειότητα γνώσεως ἄγει,
ἐξ ἧς θεωροὺς ἐστὶν ἀνθρώπους βλέπειν·
ὁ κόσμος οὖν κάλλιστος ὡς καλοῦ παρὰ
φέρων δι'αἰσθητῶν με πρὸς καλὸν πέρας.

[71] XIV.15–25 (fol. 45r):

ὕλη δονουμένη τε καὶ πεφυρμένη,
ἦν ὡς ἀσυντέλεστος ἐσκεδασμένη·
ἀλλ'οὐ δέδεικται τοῦτο καὶ μάρτυς κτίσις
εἰς εὐσταθῆ σύνταξιν ἑνουμένη.
Τοίνυν μονὰς πέφυκεν ἐξηρημένη·
ὡς οὖν καλὴ παρῆξε κόσμον ἀφθόνως,
ὡς ἐνδίκως δέδωκε τὴν εὐταξίαν,
ὡς ἀρκτικὴ δείκνυσι τὴν ἐξουσίαν,
ὡς πάνσοφος κίρνησι καταναντία
καὶ ἐπιστατήσασα σωτήρας νόας,
ἀποστάτας τρέπουσα ὡς ψυχοφθόρους.

[72] XV.1–23 (fol. 45v):

Ὁ νοῦς ὁ πρῶτος ὡς ὑπερτελὴς μέγα,
†ῶ μερμελέχα† τῶν ἄνω θεαμάτων,
ἐντὸς φέρων τὰ πάντα ποικίλῳ τρόπῳ
ἔναστρον εὐρὺν εὐχόρευτον δεικνύει,
ἄγει δὲ ῥιπῆς τοῦτον ἐκ πρώτης ἄγει,

What I propose concerning the light-bearers is as follows. . . . In their moving course these are an excellent agency in life, whose lights by their emanations are there to provide strength for us . . .[73] And this you should ascribe to forethought, that the world is a wonder to beholders. A road is given to it, in regular courses, which is above expression (*logos*), wonder of wonders, that of the seven-mouthed trumpet.[74]

For us the lovers of learning (*logos*) God measures the movement of time and the limit of the sphere. Whence [the stars] are providers of great gifts not, you should know, by their motions, but as foretellers of secret revelations . . .[75]

ὡς μουσοποιὸς νοῦν ἐπιστήμης νέμων
ἐν ἑπταχόρδῳ ψαλμικοτάτῃ λύρᾳ.
Οὐκ ἀπρόμηθές ἐστιν αὐτοῦ τὸ σθένος,
οὐ γὰρ δι'ὀργάνου τοῦ τεχνίτου δίχα.
Τίς οἶκον οἶδεν, ἄρμα, ναῦν, στίφος νάβλων,
ἐκτὸς συναρμόζοντος ἀκριβῆ λόγῳ;
ἀλλὰ φράσεις, ἔστησεν ἐξ ὕλης πόλον·
πόθεν δὲ ταύτην, ὦ φρενῶν ἡττημένε;
σόφισμα ψευδὲς οὖσαν ὡς ἐνεισάγεις,
ἄναρχον, αὐτόχρημα τῆς ἀβουλίας·
ἢ τίς παρῆξεν ἄλλος αὐτὴν εἰς τόδε;
ἢ ποῦ παροῦσα, ποῦ μέτεστι καὶ πόσον,
τόπου σαφῶς οὐκ ὄντος, ὦ ληρωδίας,
ἀνθρωπίνης, ἄνθρωπε, χειρὸς καὶ τέχνης;
δός τι πλέον τῷ πάντα ποιοῦντι πράτος·
οὐκ ἐν χρόνοις ἔμεινε πολλοῖς ἀφθόροις
σημάντορος πρόσταγμα μὴ κεχρημένος·
Θεὸς Θεῶν ἔστησε τοῦτον ὡς βίβλον,
πολλὰ προγράψας αἰθεροστρόφοις κύκλοις·

[73] XVII.1–7 (fol. 46v):
Ἅπερ προτείνω φωσφόρων εἰσὶν περὶ
—καὶ δὴ ταλαίφρων πάντα κωφὲ καὶ λάλε,
νῦν ὦτ' ἀκουστεῖν τῆς ἀληθείας πρέπον—
κινητικὴν ἔχοντες οὗτοι γὰρ τρίβον
ἔργον τε καὶ ἄριστον εἰσὶν εἰς βίον,
ὧν καὶ τὰ φῶτα ταῖς ἀπορροίαις μόνον
πάρεισιν ἡμῖν εἰς σθένους χορηγίαν.

[74] XVII.19–23 (fol. 46v):
Καὶ τοῦτο δή σοι γραπτέον προμηθείᾳ
ὡς κόσμος ἐστι θαῦμα τοῖς ὁρωμένοις,
ὁδὸς δέδοται τούτῳ τακτικαῖς τρίβοις,
ὑπὲρ λόγον πέφυκε θαῦμα θαυμάτων,
ἑπταστόμου σάλπιγγος ἡ πολυφθόγγου·

[75] XVIII.10–14 (fol. 47r):
Μετρῶν χρόνου κίνημα καὶ σφαίρας πέρας
Θεὸς παρ'ἡμῖν ἐστι τοῖς λόγου φίλοις,
ὅθεν χορηγοὶ πλουσίων δωρημάτων
οὐκ εἰσὶν εἴπερ οἶδας ἐκ κινημάτων
ἀλλὰ προλέκται μυστικῶν δηλωμάτων

The sting is drawn out of the last line by the continuation (XVIII.15 ff):
Εἰ δ' ἐκ φαïνῶν ἀστέρων ἁμαρτίαι
ὡς οἱ πάλαι λέγουσιν λοξίαι, φεῦ μοι,
ἐξοίχεται νοῦς καὶ φρόνησις καὶ νόμος
ἐξοίχεται παίδευμα, σεμνείων τόπος,

Understand that God, before eternal years, bore all things in mystical contemplation . . . The leader of musicians in concert, the builder of a ship, the architect of a house, though he may not actually be directing his intention to specific tasks, though he may not be applying his judgment to works, possesses in himself the principles (*logous*) of science, possesses in intellect the arrangements which are in progress . . .[76]

But the Greatest does not have irrational impulses. How can the simple nature need fulfillment, when it is understood to have no share of emptiness? The sovereign monarchy does everything, when it can be useful to the things it has made, when created things have need of it. . . .[77]

To conceive of the cause above mind, O initiate beloved child, is indeed a strange thing and great to behold. For how can you comprehend something so great in a limited mind? And if you do not comprehend it, how can you articulate it in language (*logos*)? And if you do not have reason (*logos*), how can you behold? You have no way to do this, however much you learn. You cannot conceive of the created as uncreated. It provides just a small ghost to feed the soul, enlivened by which you will not understand creation to be self-produced. Say, then, with friendly candor. Who constructed the dazzling heavens, I mean the gold-gleaming and revolving ones, in seven-circled star-written lights? Although he assigns motion, he does not fail to receive conspicuous mobility, and as artist he is not just a patron. And what artist who bears knowledge of things which have been combined in proper substantiation will not then thoughtfully contribute what is missing? Bold is the man who wishes to grasp the universe with his mind, and he is to be forgiven who does not clearly succeed, but the man who merely believes is full of nonsense, and he who does not desire it shows that he has no mind. . . .[78]

προαίρεσις, βούλησις, ἀρχείων φόβος,
καὶ σωφρονοῦσαι μυρίων τῷδε βίβλων

[76] XIX.1–9 (fol. 47v):
Θεὸν νόει μοι πρὸ χρόνων αἰωνίων
φέρειν τὰ πάντα μυστικῇ θεωρίᾳ,
ᾧ ψυχρὰ πλάττων θρηνοποιὸν εἰς σέβας,
καὶ γὰρ λυρῳδῶν ὄρχαμος συμφωνίας·
νεὼς τεχνίτης, ἀρχιτέκτων οἰκίας,
κἂν μὴ προτείνῃ τὸν σκοπὸν πρὸς πρακτέα,
κἂν μὴ πρὸς ἔργα τὴν κρίσιν καταρτίσει,
πλουτεῖ παρ'αὐτοῦ τοὺς ἐπιστήμης λόγους,
πλουτεῖ νοήσει τὰς ἐν ἐκβάσει θέσεις.

[77] XIX.20–25 (fol. 47v):
Ἀλλ' οὐ τὸ κρεῖττον ἀκρίτους ὁρμὰς ἔχει·
πληρώσεως δὲ πῶς ἁπλῆ δεῖται φύσις
κενώσεως ἄμοιρος ἐννοουμένη;
Ποιεῖ δὲ τὰ πάντα κυρία μοναρχία,
ὅταν συνοίσειν οἶδε τοῖς ποιουμένοις,
ὅταν δέον πάρεστιν τοῖς ἐκτισμένοις.

[78] XXII.1–25 (fol. 49rv):
Ἄγειν λογισμῷ τὴν ὑπὲρ νοῦν αἰτίαν
ὦ μύστα, μύστα, τέκνον ἠγαπημένον,
ὄντως ξένον σοι καὶ θεάσασθαι μέγα.

The nature of the *kosmos* bears providence, although we do not know all its ways completely. It should be evident, even to those who are blind in learning, that providence is accompanied by foreknowledge, and foreknowledge is not without providence.[79]

The decorum of the earth also works providentially in harmony with the divine brightness of the heavens. For what else causes the soul to break out of its earth-bound cycle, to shed its earthly nature by good deeds, and to reach the ether by immateriality? And who grants to the five senses perception of the four elements, "and causes the circumscribed mind to see beyond, as if giving it eyes and teaching it to seek itself at the summit"?[80] Two later passages confirm that this extrasensory perception, this rising

---

Πῶς γὰρ τοσοῦτον πρᾶγμα νῷ βραχεῖ λάβοις;
ἢ μὴ λαβὼν πῶς διαρθρώσει λόγῳ;
λόγον δὲ μὴ σχὼν πῶς ἰδεῖν ἐξαρκέσαις;
Ἀμήχανόν σοι τοῦτο κἂν μάθει τόσα,
τὸ κτιστὸν οὐκ ἄκτιστον ἐννοεῖν σθένει,
φάντασμα μικρὸν προξενεῖ ψυχοτρόφον,
ᾧ ζωοπορηθεὶς ἐκ πολυστόργου θέας,
αὐτουργότευκτον οὐ νοήσει τὴν κτίσιν·.
Εἴποι δὲ ταῦτα σὺν φίλῃ παρρησίᾳ.
Τίς τοὺς καταυγάζοντας ἤγειρεν πόλους
τοὺς χρυσολαμπεῖς καὶ περιδρόμους λέγω,
ἐν ἑπτακύκλοις φωσὶν ἀστερογράφοις;
καὶ τὴν ἀειπρόσεκτον εὐκινησίαν
οὐχ ὡς νέμει κίνησιν οὐ δεδεγμένος
οὐχ ὡς τεχνίτης προστάτης ἐστὶν μόνος.
Καὶ τίς τεχνίτης οὐχ ὁ τὴν γνῶσιν φέρων
τῶν συγκριθέντων οὐσιώσει κοσμίῳ
εἶτα προσοίσει καὶ τὸ λεῖπον ἐμφρόνως;
Τολμηρός ἐστιν ὃς τὸ πᾶν νοεῖν θέλοι,
σύγγνωστός ἐστιν ὃς σαφῶς οὐ τυγχάνει, |
ἁπλῶς ὁ πιστεύων δὲ ληρεῖ πλουσίως,
ὁ μὴ ποθῶν ἔδειξεν ὡς νοῦν οὐκ ἔχων·

[79] XXIII.18–22 (fol. 49v):
τοίνυν φέρει πρόνοιαν ἡ κόσμου φύσις
κἂν τοὺς τρόπους ἔγνωμεν οὐδόλως ὅλων,
ὡς δῆλον εἶναι καὶ τυφλοῖς τὰ τοῦ λόγου,
ὅτι προνοίᾳ καὶ πρόγνωσις συντρέχει,
πρόγνωσις οὐ προνοίας ἔξω δ᾽αὖ μένει

[80] XXIV.1–26 (fol. 50r):
Ὁδῷ διδάσκου γῆς νοῶν εὐκοσμίαν
ἁπλὴν διαυγῆ τῷ νοήματι κτήσας·
ἄναστρον αὐτὴ καὶ πόλον καὶ φῶς νέμει
καταρτίσασα φθόγγον εἰς ὑμνῳδίαν,
τρυφὴν ἔχουσα τὴν ἄνω θεαυγίαν
ὁμοφρονοῦσαν εἰς καλοῦ συνουσίαν,
ἄγουσαν, ἰθύνουσαν εἰς σωτηρίαν
ἔθνη τὰ δυσμάθητα ταῖς ὁδηγίαις,
μὴ πανταχοῦ παροῦσαν εἰς λειτουργίαν,
ἀλλ᾽ οὐσιωδῶς, οὐ ῥοπῇ θεωρίας,
τελοῦσαν ἢ τυποῦσαν ἔργα καὶ φρένας·
περιγραπτὴ γὰρ ἐστὶν καιρῷ καὶ τόπῳ.
Τὸ θεῖον εἴπερ χρῆμα τὴν ψυχὴν λέγω,

above matter, is the affair of an intellectual elite: "We love his revered light, and he loves those who are honored with *logos* . . ."[81] He draws all who are honored with *logos* to heaven and to the intelligible essences."[82]

The message is clear: mere faith is not enough;[83] only those with *logos* can rise toward God, and *logos* is the science of reading the codes which God has written into the book of creation. Particular emphasis is given to the messages encoded in the heavenly spheres. The subtext of Choirosphaktes' theology is thus nothing less than a subtle apologia for the science of astrology. He takes the Orthodox patristic line that the stars are not causes but signs of earthly events much further than any church father had been prepared to go.[84] The general patristic consensus was that the significance of the heavenly bodies was meteorological. Only Origen—a father of far from impeccable credentials—had, somewhat reluctantly, conceded that their movements and configurations might be prophetic, and the image of the heavens as a book inscribed by God seems to derive ultimately from his *Commentary on Genesis.*[85] But whereas in Origen's view the divine writing was for angelic eyes only, Choirosphaktes considered it a legitimate matter for human expertise. In this he combined the basically negative Origenist tradition with more positive arguments in defense of astrology which may have been formulated in late antiquity but which first surfaced in Byzantium in the 790s in a treatise attributed to a certain Stephen the Philosopher.[86] "Stephen" describes himself as an immigrant

---

ἀνόλεθρον θέαμα, χρηστὴν εἰκόνα,
τίς μηχανουργεῖ συμβιάζων τῇ εἰκόνι
κινήσεως πρόνοιαν αὐτὴν εἰσάγων;
Καὶ τίς παρέσχε ὡς ἐπιστήμη κράτος
αὐτὴν πρὸς αὑτῆς ἐν κύκλῳ δινουμένην
τὸν χοῦν καταβάλουσαν ἐξ εὐπραξίας,
τὸν αἰθέρα φθάνουσαν ἐξ ἀϋλίας,
τὸ κρεῖττον ἐκζητοῦσαν ἐξ εὐβουλίας;
Καὶ τίς βραβεύει τῶν ὁπῶν τῇ πεντάδι
τὰς ἀντιλήψεις τῆσδε τῆς τετρακτύος,
τὸν νοῦν περίγραπτον δὲ καὶ πόρρω βλέπειν,
ὡς ὄμμα ταύτῃ τίς δίδωσίν εἰπέ μοι,
ζητεῖν ἑαυτὴν ἐκδιδάξας εἰς ἄκρον;

[81] XXVI.20–21 (fol. 51r):
ἐρῶμεν αὐτοῦ τοῦ σεβασμίου φάους
ἐρᾷ δὲ κ'αὐτὸς τῶν λόγῳ τιμωμένων

[82] XXXVIII.9–10 (fol. 55v):
ἕλκει δὲ πάντας τοὺς λόγῳ τιμωμένους
πρὸς οὐρανόν τε καὶ νοητὰς οὐσίας

[83] XXII.24 (above, note 78); see also XXIII.8.

[84] See in general P. Hildebrand Beck, *Vorsehung und Vorherbestimmung in der theologischen Literatur der Byzantiner,* OCA 114 (Rome, 1937), 65 ff; U. Riedinger, *Die heilige Schrift im Kampf der griechischen Kirche gegen die Astrologie, von Origenes bis Johannes von Damaskos* (Innsbruck, 1956).

[85] *Philocalia,* 23: ed. F. Junod, *Philocalie 21–27, Sur le libre arbitre,* SC 226 (Paris, 1976), 130–211, esp. 200–202, with introduction, 24–65; cf. L. Koep, *Das himmlische Buch in Antike und Christentum* (Bonn, 1952), 42–45. In the Origenist controversy of the late 4th and early 5th centuries, Origen was misrepresented by his detractors as having claimed that Christ's foreknowledge was based on the movement of the stars: Theophilos of Alexandria, *Synodica 2 in Sancti Eusebii Hieronymi epistulae,* ed. I. Hilberg, CSEL 55 (Leipzig, 1910–18), II, ep. 92, 149–50.

[86] Ed. F. Boll et al., in *Catalogus codicum astrologorum graecorum,* vol. II (Brussels, 1900), 181–86; cf. Beck, *Vorsehung,* 68–69; see D. Pingree, "Classical and Byzantine Astrology in Sassanian Persia," *DOP* 43 (1989), 238–39. It has recently been suggested, without reference to Pingree, that Stephen was a literary invention inspired by the

from Persia (i.e., the Abbasid caliphate) to Constantinople, where, finding astrology to be "extinguished," he saw it as his duty to revive this most "useful science" among the Romans. His justification for astrology is in part epistemological—demonstrating its superiority to all other arts, and its similarity to medicine as a science of "expert guess-work"—and in part theological, arguing that if the heavenly bodies are divine creations it is not merely permissible to contemplate them as evidence of divine wisdom, but blasphemous not to do so. Two passages of this argument read like a summary of the central section of Choirosphaktes' *Theology*:

> astronomy when used with pious reflection for the comprehension of the heavenly movements and positions and configurations, and also of good and bad things that are about to happen, arouses to glorification of the Creator and raises the mind on the wings of divine contemplation to the brightness above . . .
>
> Man, unfold your mind on creation and behold the sense-perceived creatures of God and understand each one with reason. So when you hear the names of the zodiac and the planets, do not think that they have souls or feelings, or that they are makers of things, as some have imagined, being led astray by error. For they are not makers but made by the thrice-hypostate God who is without beginning. Thus he created them for his glorification and set them as signs to be of benefit to men just like the other elements which are on the earth, that is, air, fire, water, and the various plants, for the use and energy of the animals.[87]

It does not follow, of course, that Choirosphaktes read "Stephen" or approved of everything he wrote; at one point "Stephen" says that it is through the activity (ἐνέργειαν) of the heavens that "this world goes on in birth and destruction—animals are born, plants germinate, the weather changes, rain precipitates, kingdoms arise, and wars flare up."[88] But it does seem fair to conclude that Choirosphaktes was the heir to, and an exponent of, the attempt to reconcile astrology with Christianity which "Stephen" had imported or restored to Constantinople at the end of the eighth century. It is also reasonable to suppose that the link between the two men was formed by the enigmatic and controversial figure of Leo the Mathematician, who certainly had astrological interests, and who drew praise from Choirosphaktes as well as accusations of impiety from others.[89] Thus the *Thousand-Line Theology* belongs to the third generation in a revival of Neoplatonizing, astrologizing philosophy running parallel to the more Orthodox, and

---

7th-century Stephen of Alexandria: G. Dagron, "Les diseurs d'événements: Réflexions sur un 'thème astrolog-ique' byzantin," in *Mélanges offerts à Georges Duby*, vol. IV (Aix-en-Provence, 1992), 57–65; idem, "Formes et fonctions du pluralisme linguistique à Byzance," *TM* 12 (1994), 235.

[87] Ed. Boll et al., 185.

[88] Ibid., 183.

[89] Kolias, *Léon Choerosphactès*, 132; Constantine the Sicilian, ed. P. Matranga, *Anecdota graeca* (Rome, 1850), vol. II, 555–57; P. Lemerle, *Byzantine Humanism: The First Phase* (Canberra, 1986), 171–204; N. G. Wilson, *Scholars of Byzantium* (London, 1983), 79–84; L. G. Westerink, "Leo the Philosopher: *Job* and Other Poems," *Illinois Classical Studies* 11 (1986), 193–222.

better known, revival of learning represented by Patriarch Nikephoros and others of his generation, followed by Photios and Arethas.[90]

At all events, the *Theology* certainly provides the firm link which we are seeking with the astrological couplet in the poem on the bath of Leo VI. With that link established, other similarities emerge. The theological poem describes itself as a work of praise (αἶ-νος) for the creator,[91] and it describes the earth as "tuning notes in hymnody."[92] In both poems, praise is punctuated with denunciation of falsehood. Central to both poems is the theme of wise and provident artistic design by an all-powerful and all-discerning monarch. Furthermore, the theological poem confirms the symbolic interpretation of the *ekphrasis*. It shows that Choirosphaktes saw *logos* as having an anagogical function. It also shows that he believes firmly in the use of dissimilar symbols to express the transcendent, immaterial unknowability of God. This, it seems to me, is the thrust of those chapters where he does seem to echo the Neoplatonism of Pseudo-Dionysios.[93] In particular, it is worth citing the passage where he discusses the symbolic language used by the Old Testament prophets: "They reject all images (*eikonas*) of apparitions, since he in no way wants an apparition. They fittingly (εἰκότως) describe by association; giving discordant, well-chosen names, they assign words *without coloration*."[94] At the end of the poem, Choirosphaktes advises his addressee to follow the same practice: "If you avoid explicit nomenclature, you will not go wrong . . . for you will not find any impressions of a footprint."[95] This was diametrically opposed to the Orthodox iconophile understanding of the Dionysian doctrine of signs.[96]

The *Theology* thus celebrates God as the architect of the Kosmos much as the *ekphrasis*

---

[90] It is thus clear that the Neoplatonic revival of the 11th and 12th centuries, represented by Psellos, Italos, Italikos, the *sebastokrator* Isaac, and others, was based to some extent on work of the 9th and 10th centuries: for other indications, see L. G. Westerink, "Das Rätsel"; cf. also E.-A. Leemans, "Michel Psellos et les Δόξαι περὶ ψυχῆς," *L'antiquité classique* 1 (1932), 203–11, and Wilson, *Scholars of Byzantium,* 87, 140.

[91] VIII.1 (fol. 42r): Μεγιστόλεκτον αἶνον ἄλλον προσφέρω.

[92] XXIV.4 (above, note 80).

[93] XXIX–XXX (fol. 52rv); cf. particularly Dionysius, *Divine Names* and *Celestial Hierarchy*: PG 3: 120 ff, 585 ff; trans. C. Liubheid, *Pseudo-Dionysius* (New York, 1987), 49–191.

[94] XXX.12–16 (fol. 52v):
φαντασμάτων ῥίπτουσι πάσας εἰκόνας
φάντασμα μὴ θέλοντος αὐτοῦ μηδόλως
διαγράφουσιν εἰκότως μετουσία,
κλήσεις τιθέντες ἀντιφώνους εὐλόγους
λόγους κατευνάζουσι τῆς χροίας ἄτερ

[95] XLV.8–12 (fol. 56v):
σαφῆ δὲ φεύγων κλῆσιν οὐ παραπέσεις
ἔστιν δὲ φύσις οὐδόλως ἐγνωσμένη,
ἰδεῖν δὲ σῶμα, σχῆμα μὴ μάτην ποθεῖν
εὑρεῖν δὲ τέρμα τῆσδε μὴ ζητεῖν φίλει·
ἴχνους δὲ αὐτῆς οὐδαμῶς εὕροις τύπους
Cf. also VII.23–24 (fol. 41v):
φεῦ μορφοποιεῖς τὴν τύπου ἀνωτέραν
καὶ σωματουργεῖς τὴν ἁπλοῦς ἁπλουστέραν

[96] See Averil Cameron, "The Language of Images: The Rise of Icons and Christian Representation," *Studies in Church History* 28 (1992), 1–42, esp. 24–29.

celebrates Leo as the architect of his palace bathhouse. The parallel between the two texts is confirmed and completed by a third poem, a long anacreontic piece on the thermal springs at Pythia across the Sea of Marmara.[97] S. G. Mercati demonstrated convincingly that Choirosphaktes wrote this poem for the young Constantine VII.[98] The objection raised by R. Anastasi, that the poem shows an iconoclast tendency,[99] far from disproving the attribution, in fact only goes to strengthen it, because this tendency is one of several themes that link the poem to the other two. It is a celebration of a bathhouse built by God. A long description of the natural operation of the hot springs concludes with the statement that "From another opening are forced water and fire mixed, and this friendly mixture of opposites confirms the foursome [of elements]." This is unmistakably reminiscent of the climax to the *ekphrasis* of Leo's bath. The text then goes on:

> Thus the Lord of all creates, leads, directs, blends and weaves as he knows best. He clearly raises up natural phenomena for wonder and worship. Him call your God, imprinting nothing in the way of form, if you don't want to err. He is an unknown spirit, an ineffable fact, an interminable wonder, bearing worlds and lives in an all-wise dance, in just Providence.

The similarities with the *Thousand-Line Theology* are too obvious to need comment.[100]

The trilogy of poems by Leo Choirosphaktes states a coherent and programmatic ideology. It is first of all an ideology of science, which advocates spiritual and intellectual fulfillment through contemplation and knowledge of the laws of nature, notably the principles of astrology. At the same time it is an ideology of absolute monarchy: Leo in the *ekphrasis*, like God in the *Theology*, is described as king of kings.[101] On both counts, it is a court ideology in that it marginalizes the church; most seriously, it pointedly refuses to endorse the theory of images to which the church had recently committed itself.[102] No wonder Arethas was upset. Leo Choirosphaktes was in effect advocating a monopoly of power and learning by the emperor and a small secular elite of court philos-

---

[97] Text in PG 86: 2263–68; supplemented and corrected by Mercati (see following note) on the basis of London, British Library, add. MS 36749.

[98] S. G. Mercati, "Intorno all'autore del carme εἰς τὰ ἐν Πυθίοις θερμά (Leone Magistro Choirosphaktes)," *Rivista degli studi orientali* 10 (1923–25), 212–48; repr. in S. G. Mercati, *Collectanea Byzantina* (Bari, 1970), vol. I, 270–309.

[99] R. Anastasi, "Quando fu composto il carme εἰς τὰ ἐν Πυθίοις θερμά?" *Siculorum Gymnasium*, n.s., 17 (1964), 1–7.

[100] Note also that in the fuller text of the London manuscript, the poem ends by addressing Constantine VII as γαιοῦχε, the word used of the ruler figure depicted in the bath.

[101] VIII.14 (fol. 42r): ἄναξ ἀνάκτων εὐσθενὴς θεαρχία; *Ekphrasis*, line 62: . . . ἄναξ μεδόντων.

[102] It is also remarkably close to the western conception of symbolism, as described by G. Ladner, "The Concept of the Image in the Greek Fathers and the Byzantine Iconoclastic Controversy," *DOP* 7 (1953), 9–10 (repr. in idem, *Images and Ideas in the Middle Ages: Selected Studies in History and Art* [Rome, 1983], 84): "For the Christian East, not only angels and men but also their symbols and images had gradually come to be incomparably more important than mere things of nature—and the victory of the orthodox image doctrine in the Iconoclastic Controversy completed this development. Contrary to the Augustinian and, generally speaking, the Western idea of knowing God even through his vestiges in non-human nature, the Byzantines saw the things of nature only as accompanying symbols within a vast cosmic liturgy performed by Christ and by hierarchies of angels and men, and represented by the sacred icons."

ophers. He was idealizing those very aspects of Leo VI's regime which threatened the Photian concept of church-state relations. Whether the emperor went along with all this is another matter; however, he did nothing to condemn it, and there is no evidence that Choirosphaktes fell from grace on a charge of impiety.[103] Three key concepts in his theology—*kosmos, taxis,* and *harmonia*—are key words in the program of codification undertaken by Leo and completed by Constantine VII.[104] Leo Choirosphaktes worked as hard as any Byzantine writer—including Eusebius—to make the Christian world picture conform to the priorities of the earthly ruler, and this is his claim to be regarded as the ultimate Byzantine courtier.

Our other candidate, Constantine Manasses, lived almost three centuries later. The events and persons mentioned in his extant writings place these firmly in the third quarter of the twelfth century. Nothing is known of his family background. His surname is rare, which makes it very likely that he was related to the contemporary Orthodox patriarch of Antioch Athanasios Manasses.[105] He no doubt came from the "bourgeois gentry" of middle-ranking property owners who educated their sons for high religious or bureaucratic careers.[106] As far as we know, however, Constantine Manasses never held office and never took any kind of holy orders. O. Lampsides has convincingly disproved the opinion that he became metropolitan of Naupaktos.[107] There is not even any hint that he received a pension of the kind which kept his contemporaries John Tzetzes, Theodore Prodromos, and "Manganeios Prodromos" in semi-monastic retirement. He seems to have been a professional parasite who spent all his time frequenting the houses and soliciting the favors of the magnates of the extended imperial family. He dedicated his verse chronicle to the *sebastokratorissa* Irene, widowed sister-in-law of Manuel I and patron of several contemporary literati.[108] He was clearly dependent in some way on the *sebastos* John Kontostephanos.[109] He composed two orations on the death of John's wife Theodora,[110] and he formed part of the retinue which John took with him on an imperial embassy to the court of Tripoli in 1160. Manasses described his experience of the journey in his famous *Hodoiporikon.*[111] When he fell seriously ill at Tyre, Kontostephanos arranged for him to go and recuperate in the healthier air of Cyprus, where the local

---

[103] The sources quoted by Kolias, *Léon Choerosphactès,* 54 ff, do not support his conclusion. Both Arethas (*Scripta minora,* ed. Westerink, I, 203.10 ff) and Choirosphaktes himself (ed. Kolias, 121ff) indicate that he was accused of misconduct in his embassy to Baghdad.

[104] See P. Magdalino, "The Non-Juridical Legislation of Leo VI," *Fontes minores (Athener Reihe)* 1 (1996), 73–86. All three concepts are also prominent in St. Athanasios, *Contra gentes.*

[105] See A. Failler, "Le patriarche d'Antioche Athanase Ier Manasses (1157–1170)," *REB* 51 (1993), 63–75.

[106] Magdalino, *Empire,* 339 ff.

[107] O. Lampsides, "Zur Biographie von Konstantinos Manasses und zu seiner Chronike Synopsis," *Byzantion* 58 (1988), 97–111.

[108] Σύνοψις χρονική, ed. I. Bekker, *Constantini Manassis Breviarium historiae metricum* (Bonn, 1837), pp. 3–4, lines 1–17; cf. O. Lampsidis, "Zur Sebastokratorissa Eirene," *JÖB* 34 (1984), 91–105; K. Varzos,ʹΗ Γενεαλογία τῶν Κομνηνῶν (Thessalonike, 1984), no. 76.

[109] Ibid., no. 104.

[110] Ed. E. Kurtz, "Dva proizvedeniya Konstantina Manassi," *VizVrem* 7 (1900), 630–45.

[111] Ed. K. Horna, "Das Hodoiporikon des Konstantinos Manasses," *BZ* 13 (1904), 313–55. Cf. M. Markovich, "The *Itinerary* of Constantine Manasses," *Illinois Classical Studies* 12 (1987), 277–91.

governor, Alexios Doukas, took very good care of him.[112] Manasses thus gained, or rediscovered, another aristocratic benefactor. Alexios Doukas was a grandson of Anna Komnene, who befriended several men of letters, and Manasses was among the orators who lamented the death of another of her grandsons, Nikephoros Komnenos.[113] He was also, as he tells us, one of several literati made welcome at the home of a certain Palaiologos, probably to be identified with the *megas hetaireiarches* George Palaiologos.[114] Naturally he looked for benefits to the emperor himself, whom he praised in several writings, notably in an oration written in 1173.[115] At some time before this, he lost the emperor's favor on account of certain rumors that reached the emperor's ear. To combat these malicious slanders, he wrote a eulogy of the emperor's chief minister, the logothete of the drome Michael Hagiotheodorites, asking him to mediate.[116] To make sure that the logothete, then on campaign with the emperor, received the text, Manasses sent it via the *sebastos* George, who, unless he is to be identified with George Palaiologos, was evidently yet another aristocratic patron.[117]

The overall impression is of a man who was remarkably single-minded in attaching himself to his social superiors—an impression reinforced by Manasses' almost total lack of reference to his social equals. In this he was not untypical of his age, but he seems to have taken the phenomenon to an extreme. The same can be said of his literary interests, which, while showing much in common with the work of his contemporaries, lack the academic dimension—the interest in philological, philosophical, legal, or theological commentary—which is evinced by other writers of the period. Manasses is neither scholarly nor scholastic. He writes only to entertain or to instruct on a very basic level. He likes to moralize and he likes to describe, and in both he is clearly court-oriented. In his moralizing, he is obsessed with the power of impersonal forces which he personifies as supernatural beings: Envy (Φθόνος), Fortune (Τύχη), Love ("Ερως), and Gold. These are the forces which govern his world, and they do so not only in the fictional, antique setting of his romance *Aristandros and Kallithea*[118] but also in the real, historical Christian world of his verse chronicle.[119] Throughout this work, Envy and Fortune loom

---

[112] Horna, "Hodoiporikon," 335 ff.

[113] See Varzos, Γενεαλογία, nos. 32, 115, 119; E. Kurtz, "Evstathiya Thessaloniiskogo i Konstantina Manassi monodii na konchinu Nikifora Komnina," *VizVrem* 17 (1910), 302–22.

[114] Ed. L. Sternbach, "Beiträge zur Kunstgeschichte," *Jahreshefte des Österreichischen Archäologischen Instituts* 5 (1902), Beiblatt, col. 83: . . . ὁ τὸ γένος περίοπτος καὶ τὴν ψυχὴν μεγαλοπρεπής, οὗ καὶ παλαιοῖς λόγοις ἡ ῥίζα τοῦ γένους ἀνάγραπτος . . . Ἐγὼ τοίνυν περὶ τὸν ἄνδρα τοῦτον θαμίζων, ὅτι καὶ χαίρει λόγοις καὶ οἰκειοῦται τοὺς λόγων τροφίμους.

[115] Ed. E. Kurtz, "Eshche dva neizdannykh proizvedeniya Konstantina Manassi," *VizVrem* 12 (1905), 88–98.

[116] Ed. K. Horna, "Eine unedierte Rede des Konstantin Manasses," *Wiener Studien* 28 (1906), 173–84 (eulogy), 185 (covering letter).

[117] Ibid., 185–86.

[118] Ed. O. Mazal, *Der Roman des Konstantinos Manasses* (Vienna, 1967); also ed. E. Tsolakis, Συμβολὴ στὴ μελέτη τοῦ ποιητικοῦ ἔργου τοῦ Κωνσταντίνου Μανασσῆ καὶ κριτικὴ ἔκδοση τοῦ μυθιστορήματος τοῦ Τὰ κατ᾽ Ἀρίστανδρον καὶ Καλλιθέαν (Thessalonike, 1967). References here are to the edition by Mazal. Envy: fragments 26, 31, 48, 76, 87, 129, 169; Fortune: nos. 49, 54, 57, 59, 68, 137, 159; Eros and physical attraction: nos. 1, 6, 11, 21–22, 24, 41, 64, 89, 95–96, 116–18, 165; Gold: nos. 23, 84, 133.

[119] References are to page and line nos. of the CSHB text, ed. Bekker. Envy: 56.1277–79, 58.1325, 77.1773, 114–16.2640–2701, 139–40.3229–59, 151.3514, 242.5686 ff, 279–81.6582–6618. Fortune, and the image of the Wheel: 91.2088–89, 116.2688–89, 124.2876 ff, 195.4548, 235.5526–27, 237.5581–82, 252–53.5941 ff,

much larger than Divine Providence, which he mentions but twice—once to explain why Romulus and Remus were nurtured by the she-wolf,[120] and once to point out that it was futile for the emperor Zeno to try to avert a prediction made by an astrologer.[121] This is one of four passages where, by recording astrological forecasts that proved correct, Manasses implicitly defends astrology against its critics.[122] He thus clearly identifies with the court party in the contemporary debate about the compatibility of astrology with Christian belief which had been set off by the personal interests of Manuel Komnenos.[123]

Manasses' preoccupation with the power of Envy and the Wheel of Fortune is courtly not only in the sense that it reveals a secular, semi-pagan outlook on life, but also, and primarily, because he almost always expresses it in connection with court situations. It is, moreover, a preoccupation which he shares with Latin narrators of court affairs, notably with those who chronicled the turbulent history of the Sicilian royal court in the later twelfth century.[124] Whether he was in any way influenced by western writing is just one part of another question which cannot be considered here.[125] He was certainly influenced by his own personal experience of Envy at the court of Manuel I,[126] and that experience surely lies behind his bitter comments on eunuchs, both in his history and in his romance, where, in one of the surviving fragments, he observes that once upon a time, "they say," when a viper bit a eunuch, it was the viper that died.[127]

Manasses' penchant for description is striking even in his narrative works, where his evocations of people and places are loaded with adjectives, and his account of the creation of the world at the beginning of his chronicle is in effect an *ekphrasis* of the beauties of nature celebrating the artistry of the creator.[128] However, what marks him out as an author with an exceptional urge to describe are the five freestanding pieces of *ekphrasis* which have come down to us under his name. Of these, only one, a description of the snaring of small birds on the Asiatic shore of the Bosporos, does not explicitly deal with an aspect of the court milieu.[129] Two *ekphraseis* concern works of art located, respectively,

---

262.6164, 276.6495. Gold: 126–27.2916–34, 152–53.3550–68, 170.3952–56, 195.4552 ff, 208.4859–60. Eros: 51.1152–54. Cf. Macrides and Magdalino, "Fourth Kingdom," 124–26.

[120] Ed. Bekker, Σύνοψις χρονική, 69–70.1584 ff.

[121] Ibid., 129.2999 ff.

[122] See also 80–81.1836–50, 89.2047–51.

[123] See Ph. Evangelatou-Notara, Ὁποῖόν ἐστι μέρος τῆς ἀστρολογίας κακιζόμενόν τε καὶ ἀποτρόπαιον (Ἀστρολογία-Ἀστρονομία καὶ οἱ σχετικές ἀντιλήψεις κατά τον ΙΒ´ αἰώνα), in N. Oikonomides, ed., *Byzantium in the 12th Century: Canon Law, State and Society* (Athens, 1991), 447–63; Magdalino, *Empire*, 377 ff.

[124] Hugo Falcandus, *Liber de regno Sicilie*, ed. G. B. Siragusa (Rome, 1897); Peter of Eboli, *Liber ad honorem Augusti*, ed. E. Rota (Città di Castello, 1904).

[125] On the theme of Fortune in medieval Greek literature, see most recently C. Cupane, "Κατέλαβες τὰ ἀμφίβολα τῆς τυφλῆς δαίμονος πρόσωπα: il Λόγος περὶ δυστυχίας καὶ εὐτυχίας e la figura di Fortuna nella letteratura greca medievale," in *Origini della letteratura neogreca*, ed. N. M. Panagiotakis (Venice, 1993), vol. I, 413–37. As is pointed out by P. A. Agapitos and O. Smith, *The Study of Medieval Greek Romance: A Reassessment of Recent Work* (Copenhagen, 1992), 39 note 79, the image of the Wheel of Fortune was used in ancient Greek literature, but this in itself does not explain Manasses' preoccupation.

[126] See Horna, "Eine unedierte Rede," 184–85; ed. Bekker, Σύνοψις χρονική, 140.3258–61.

[127] Ibid., 93.2134–37, 119.2758–59, 240.5648–49, 243–44.5727–31, 260.6130 ff; Mazal, no. 80.

[128] Ed. Bekker, Σύνοψις χρονική, 4–15.

[129] Ed. L. Sternbach, *Analecta Manassea* (Krakow, 1902).

in the imperial palace and in the house of a certain Palaiologos.[130] Another is devoted to a crane hunt featuring Emperor Manuel and his veteran falcon from the Caucasus.[131] The fifth text describes a dwarf who was brought from Chios to be displayed in the imperial palace.[132] Between them, these texts evoke the beauty and antiquity of the court environment, the princely sport of falconry, and the court as a museum of exotica. More generally, all Manasses' descriptions can be thought of as catering to a court society's taste for literature that was refined but not too rarefied, a pleasing mixture of sensual evocation and intellectual reflection. The freestanding *ekphraseis* were probably composed to be delivered at *theatra,* literary gatherings convened by the emperor or some other magnate. The *ekphrasis* of nature at the beginning of the chronicle may well have been written to please the *sebastokratorissa* Irene, to whom the work was dedicated. Several of the poems written for this lady by another author in her entourage, the so-called Manganeios Prodromos, make extensive use of garden imagery.[133]

We have now looked separately at two Middle Byzantine authors whom we have selected for their extreme dependence on, and orientation toward, secular court society. Let us now look at them side by side and see what patterns emerge from the juxtaposition of their writings. The striking feature that sets Choirosphaktes and Manasses apart from nearly all other Byzantine writers is their discreet but unmistakable endorsement of astrology. Less unusual, but nevertheless still striking, is their fascination with the artistry of the natural world. We have already quoted Choirosphaktes on the subject; here we may note that Manasses, in his opening *ekphrasis* of Creation, refers to God as the artist (καλλιτέχνης), the craftsman (τεχνίτης), the wise architect of the universe (ὁ παντοτέκτων ὁ σοφὸς), the universal workman (παντεργάτης).[134] It is thus no coincidence that these two authors produced two of the three surviving Middle Byzantine *ekphraseis* of palace buildings. For Manasses' *ekphrasis* of a palace mosaic depicting the earth, just like Choirosphaktes' *ekphrasis* of Leo's palace bath, celebrated an artificial microcosm created by man in imitation of God.[135] Both authors were clearly exercised by the relationship between human creativity and the "world-creating Word" (κοσμοκτίστωρ Λόγος).[136]

I refrain from concluding that the typical Byzantine courtier was an astrologer who wrote *ekphraseis*. There may be a case for concluding that the essence of courtliness in Byzantine literature was the celebration of the court as the image of the cosmos. But we

---

[130] Both ed. L. Sternbach, "Beiträge zur Kunstgeschichte," *Jahreshefte des Österreichischen Archäologischen Instituts* 5 (1902), Beiblatt, cols. 74–79, 83–85; see above, note 114. A new and more complete edition of the first of these *ekphraseis,* describing a mosaic of Earth in the imperial palace, has now been published by O. Lampsidis, "Der vollständige Text der Ἔκφρασις γῆς des Konstantinos Manasses," *JÖB* 41 (1991), 189–205.

[131] Ed. Kurtz, "Eshche dva neizdannych proizvedeniya" (above, note 115), 79–88.

[132] Ed. L. Sternbach, "Constantini Manassae ecphrasis inedita," in *Symbolae in Honorem Prof. Dr. L. Cwilinski* (Lemberg, 1902), 6 ff: Τοιοῦτόν τινα μικρὸν ἀνθρωπίσκον καὶ ἡ νῆσος ἤνεγκε Χίος καὶ ἠνέχθη τὸ τέρας ἐπὶ τὴν Βύζαντος καὶ διῆγεν ἐν βασιλείοις (p. 7).

[133] See in general Magdalino, *Empire,* 336–56.

[134] Ed. Bekker, Σύνοψις χρονική, 5.41, 49–50; 6.63.

[135] See Maguire, *Earth and Ocean,* 76–77.

[136] Ed. Bekker, Σύνοψις χρονική, 4.27.

still have to look at the differences between our authors, and to attempt to grade them in order of courtliness. At first sight, the twelfth-century Constantine Manasses emerges as the clear winner. He *looks* more like a courtier. He works harder to be noticed and liked, not only by the emperor but by a variety of other lords. He writes more entertainingly and covers a greater variety of court situations. His descriptive style is more concrete, and he is interested in the material world for its own sake, not as the dim manifestation of a higher reality. In his insistence on Envy and Fortune, he is distinctly reminiscent of the western court culture where the idea of courtliness was born.

Yet in the final analysis Manasses lacks the ideology, which we encountered in Choirosphaktes, of an absolute monarchy informed by the science of stargazing. Just as he does not look for mind beyond matter, so he does not listen for the music of the spheres in the court of the earthly king. He praises the handiwork of God's Creation, and he praises the emperor, but he does not connect the two. In his scheme of things, they are separated by a world of human chaos in which Fortune and Envy reign supreme. Thus Manasses does not idealize the court or his dependence on it. He loves trees and birds—especially birds[137]—more than gold, silk, and marble. When he is far from home, in Palestine and Cyprus, it is Constantinople for which he pines, not the imperial palace.[138] It is instructive, in closing, to look at his "cosmic" *ekphrasis* of a palace mosaic,[139] and to note three significant differences between this and Choirosphaktes' poem on the bath of Leo VI. First, although both authors are describing late antique or early Byzantine works of art, only Manasses acknowledges the fact—and thus, here as in his other *ekphrasis* of a piece of ancient sculpture, implicitly suggests that artistry of this quality is a thing of the past. Second, whereas Choirosphaktes gives all the credit to the emperor who commissioned the work, Manasses praises the skill of the artist. Third, while both authors set up a dialogue between the art of the work described and their own art of rhetoric, Manasses makes this dialogue much more personal, and even, by styling his work an ἀντιγραφὴ to the γραφὴ presented by the mosaic, hints that he is trying to emulate or surpass the visual artist.[140] Like so much of twelfth-century Byzantine literature, the *ekphrasis* is a manifesto for the professional skill of the rhetor in recapturing the antique past. Lords and courts provided the framework, the funding, and much of the subject matter. As in the ninth and tenth centuries, the rhetor had to be something of a courtier. Now, however, he was not much interested in celebrating any genius but his own.

University of St. Andrews

---

[137] This is evident both from two of his *ekphraseis* (above, notes 129, 131) and from his frequent references to small birds in his other works: see Horna, "Das Hodoiporikon," 339; Mazal, *Der Roman,* no. 60; ed. Bekker, Σύνοψις χρονική, 199.4665, 205.4800, 212.4973 ff, 216.5073, 222.5208, 225.5269, 228.5341–57, 248.5849, 253.5958, 275.6472–74, 279.6569–70.

[138] Horna, "Das Hodoiporikon," 328, 331, 334–35, 337, 338–39, 342, 343; cf. C. Galatariotou, "Travel and Perception in Byzantium," *DOP* 47 (1993), 225 ff.

[139] Ed. Lampsidis, "Der vollständige Text" (above, note 130).

[140] See E. Mitsi and P. A. Agapitos, Εἰκὼν καὶ λόγος; ἡ περιγραφὴ ἔργων τέχνης στὴ Βυζαντινὴ γραμματεία, *Χρονικὰ Αἰσθητικῆς/Annales d'esthétique* 29–30 (1990–91), 116–18.

The Social World of the Byzantine Court

Alexander P. Kazhdan† and Michael McCormick

To study the social world of the Byzantine court is to examine how monarchy and aristocracy intersected to form the upper reaches of Byzantine society. Yet, for all the ink that has flowed about the summit of a society that seems almost emblematically identified with a court, little previous research has focused on the broader issue of the court as a social phenomenon. Our picture can therefore be only a beginning, a provisional sketch of some salient points of Byzantine court society, particularly in the ninth and tenth centuries, before, that is, the sweeping changes that attended the Komnenian revolution.

From the outset, we must be clear on what we are looking for. We will use a set of concepts that sometimes overlap: aristocracy, the ruling class, elite, and courtiers. We take *aristocracy* to mean a legally defined, theoretically hereditary stratum of society which bears certain privileges. *Ruling class* designates a legally and economically diverse group wielding actual power; *elite* refers to the upper crust of the aristocracy or ruling class. A courtier is a person directly connected with service to the ruler or the ruler's household.

The essential figure in defining the court is the emperor himself. In one of his marvelous examples, Symeon the Theologian asked, "Who is in service (δουλεύειν) to the emperor? Those who stay in their own homes? Or those who are everywhere by his side?"[1] The answer is obvious for us no less than for his tenth-century audience. The court was the human group physically closest to the emperor, a social world in which the emperor's household and his government overlapped, and a social world structured by the emperor's decisions.

We begin by examining the Byzantines' understanding of the ruling class—the main recruiting ground for courtiers—and the problem of vertical mobility, before turning to the Byzantines' own words for what we call *court*. We then seek to uncover the court's key features as an overall social entity: its size, the physical location of its members, and some significant subgroups within the court, including the important but ignored

---

[1] Symeon the "New" Theologian, *Book of Ethics*, 7, 133–35, ed. J. Darrouzès, *Traités théologiques et éthiques,* vol. II, SC 129 (Paris, 1967), 166. See in general A. P. Kazhdan, "Das System der Bilder und Metaphern in den Werken Symeons des 'Neuen' Theologen," in *Unser ganzes Leben Christus unserm Gott überantworten* (Göttingen, 1982), 221–39.

phenomenon of the *sekreton ton gynaikon,* "the court of women." The material basis for courtiers' existence leads us again to the problem of vertical mobility and to the patterns by which individuals entered the court, and what they reveal about the role of household and service in court life. We conclude with a few reflections on the court ethos and its role as the ideological center of gravity of the Byzantine world.

1. The Ruling Class

In tenth-century Byzantium, aristocracy in the strict, technical sense of the word was only in the making. The ruling class was constitutionally vague and not without features of a meritocracy. Formed and recruited by its relation with the emperor, it wielded its authority via the machinery of state, whereas those who possessed private or economic power often stood on the outskirts of the official rankings. The elite was unstable. It consisted of high-ranking military commanders, state bureaucrats, and courtiers, among whom the distinctions were blurred. Courtiers of different ranks—including a substantial number of eunuchs—pervaded a state apparatus in which the modern distinction between public and private had little place. Family names were just beginning to crystallize.

A clear indicator of how late tenth-century Byzantines construed their meritocratic aristocracy comes from the novel issued by Basil II in 996: the legislator expressed indignation that some families had been occupying outstanding positions in society for as long as seventy or even a hundred years.[2] Eleventh-century writers did not invariably include blood origin in their notion of aristocracy. It was only from the middle or even late eleventh century that noble origin began to feature as a necessary element of aristocracy in the public mind.[3]

This process of the aristocratization of society and mentality springs into relief when we compare the contrasting roles of family names in the ninth and the twelfth centuries. It has long been observed that surnames appear only rarely on the lead seals issued by Byzantine officials between the eighth and tenth centuries. In the eleventh and twelfth centuries, on the other hand, family names became a regular part of the nomenclature of seals.[4] Although it has been asserted that a good many surnames were already established or in the process of becoming so in the eighth and ninth centuries, closer scrutiny may reveal a more complex picture in which sobriquets and various epithets are beginning to distinguish individuals, but have not yet come universally to characterize trans-

---

[2] Zepos, *Jus,* I, 264.17–18; the scholiast who commented on the novel expanded the period to 120 years.

[3] A. P. Kazhdan, *Social'nyj sostav gospodstvujuščego klassa Vizantii XI–XII vv.* (The Social Composition of the Byzantine Ruling Class in the Eleventh and Twelfth Centuries) (Moscow, 1974), 37–55.

[4] A. P. Kazhdan, "Ob aristokratizacii vizantijskogo obščestva VIII–XII vv." (On the Emergence of an Aristocracy in Byzantine Society from the Eighth to the Twelfth Century), *ZRVI* 11 (1968), 52–53; cf. his *Social'nyj sostav,* 223–25. See also V. Laurent, *Les sceaux byzantins du Médaillier Vatican* (Vatican City, 1962), 198.

generational patrilineal lineages.[5] For instance, the substantial ninth-century letter collections of Theodore of Stoudios, Ignatios the Deacon, and Photios yield few unambiguous cases of family names.[6] Historians such as Patriarch Nikephoros I and Theophanes tend to use sobriquets introduced by qualifiers such as *(to) epiklen, (epi)legomenos,* and *onomati.* The sobriquets seem to be individual: in Theophanes there are only two cases (Serantopechoi and Triphyllioi) when two indubitable relatives bear one and the same surname.[7] In other words, the situation differs drastically from historians' usage in the twelfth century, when a writer such as Niketas Choniates applied family names systematically.

In any case, the process of family name formation was under way by the tenth century. This coincides with the chronology of family prominence bewailed by Basil II. By the end of the century, the habit of bearing a family name appears to have become well established, although the modes of transmission remained flexible. For instance, a tenth-century writer commenting on the ninth century suggests that the surname of Kontomytai could be transmitted to a son-in-law.[8] And not everyone flaunted an unambiguous ancestral surname: sobriquets, often less than flattering, continue to crop up among high officials. Thus Theophanes Continuatus claims that the patrician Himerios was called Choiros ("The Pig") because of "his wild look," an idea that appealed to the author of the Life of Basil I, who adds that the man's lifestyle fit such an appellation (πρόσρησις).[9] By the very end of the tenth century Leo the Deacon supplies family names with some regularity, despite his classicizing affectations. Qualifiers such as *epiklesis* or *eponymon* are sometimes applied and sometimes omitted with regard to the same person. And yet Leo still explains Emperor John I's surname "Tzimiskes" as a personal sobriquet deriving from the Armenian word for "short."[10] Taken as a whole, the general pattern of the formation of family names illuminates and reflects that of the aristocracy and underscores the dynamic—and therefore unstable and sometimes conflicting—characteristics of the social group that would furnish so many of the emperor's associates.

---

[5] "Many" surnames ("eine Anzahl"): F. Winkelmann, *Quellenstudien zur herrschenden Klasse von Byzanz im 8. und 9. Jahrhundert* (Berlin, 1987), 147. See in general the thoughtful reflections of E. Patlagean, "Les débuts d'une aristocratie byzantine et le témoignage de l'historiographie: Système de noms et liens de parenté aux IXe–Xe siècles," in *The Byzantine Aristocracy, IX–XIII Centuries,* ed. M. Angold (Oxford, 1984), 23–43.

[6] Among the 564 letters of *Theodori Studitae Epistulae,* ed. G. Fatouros (Berlin, 1992), ep. 112.32–33 mentions a κληρικός, Gregory, οὗ ἐπίκλην Kentroukoukouros, and a certain Peximenites, both of which usages look like sobriquets. Litoios (Fatouros, index, 982) is also unclear. Mithanes in epp. 260–61 may be a family name, but Fatouros considers it a common noun describing the men's profession, *Leinenhändler* (1.307*–308*). Ignatios, ed. M. Gedeon, Ἀρχεῖον ἐκκλησιαστικῆς ἱστορίας (Constantinople, 1914), 1–64, reveals no obvious cases except for Demochares, in epp. 21–24. Among the 299 letters of Photios, a handful may conceal family names: Lalakon (epp. 147 and 151); Angourios (epp. 50, 74, 87, 130); Democharis (ep. 49; cf. Ignatios!); Chrysocheres (ep. 134, cf. ep. 33); Drakon (ep. 29); and Madiam (ep. 44).

[7] Theophanes, *Chronographia,* ed. C. de Boor (Leipzig, 1883–85) (hereafter Theoph.), 474.3 and 476.9–10; 476.7–9, cf. 479.10–11; Triphylles: 491.6–7.

[8] *Theophanes Continuatus,* ed. I. Bekker (Bonn, 1837) (hereafter Th.C.), 175.8–10.

[9] Th.C. 172.15–16; 253.17–19.

[10] *Leonis Diaconi Caloënsis Historiae,* ed. C. B. Hase (Bonn, 1828) (hereafter Leo Diak.), e.g., 173.24–25 and 174.4; "Tzimiskes": 92.2–5.

Another significant contrast between the ninth and twelfth centuries can be found in the role of the imperial kin. The elite of this aristocracy in the making included but was not dominated by the imperial kin.[11] In this, the ninth- and tenth-century situation differed fundamentally from the Komnenian period, when writers perceived the relatives of the dynasty as a specific social group holding a particular place in the life of society and in state ceremonial. In the mid-twelfth century, for instance, the Komnenoi and lineages related to them by affinity held almost 90 percent of the highest military appointments. Three hundred years earlier, only the relations of Empress Theodora, her brothers Bardas and Petronas, Bardas' son Antigonos, and the son-in-law Symbatios/ Sabbatios, formed a comparably thick kinship constellation which wielded administrative power. And this was in the unusual, precarious circumstances of a regency for a minor emperor.[12] A convergent pattern emerges from the attitude of "Genesios" toward personal identifications. The chronicler names fourteen generals plus Thomas the Slav and three of his supporters in the ninth century. None is identified by the tenth-century historian as the emperor's relative.[13] At the end of the tenth century, when aristocratic lineages like that of the Phokas were already crystallizing, the imperial minors Basil II and Constantine VIII seem to have had no relatives to support them except Basil the Nothos, and he was the castrated bastard of a female slave and Romanos I. As late as the end of the eleventh century, the caesar John Doukas advised Nikephoros III to marry the Georgian princess Maria precisely because she was a foreigner and had no local relations to bother the emperor.[14] Alexios I took just the opposite approach and used his relatives as the mainstays of his political regime.[15]

The terminology that designated the ruling class casts further light on the nature of this aristocracy in the making, and the vertical mobility that characterized it in this period. Thus Irene's novel on judicial oaths specifies the various social groups that supplied suitable witnesses in a Constantinopolitan lawyer's mind around the year 800: priests, archons, *strateuomenoi*, *politeuomenoi*, the well-to-do, and pious people. The language of the law, which should normally be the most rigorous in its use, here betrays no general concept or term for aristocracy.[16] Less rigorous but no less interesting, the

---

[11] See on this P. Schreiner, "Réflexions sur la famille impériale à Byzance (VIIIᵉ–Xᵉ siècles)," *Byzantion* 61 (1991), 181–93.

[12] On the imperial kinship in the 12th century, see Kazhdan, *Social'nyj sostav*, 170–71, etc. On the kinship constellation of Empress Theodora's family during Michael III's regency, see the table in Winkelmann, *Quellenstudien*, 189.

[13] *Iosephi Genesii regum libri quattuor*, ed. A. Lesmüller-Werner and I. Thurn (Berlin, 1978) (hereafter Genes.): the index yields the following generals whom the text of "Genesios" does not explicitly identify as imperial kinsmen: Adrianos, Andrew, Bardanios, Theoktistos, Theophobos, Katakylas, Krateros, Constantine Tessarakontapechys, Leo V before the throne; Manuel; Michael II before the purple, patrician Nasar, Olbianos, Christopher. Cf. ibid., Thomas the Slav, Anastasios, Gregory, and Constantine, who was Thomas' adopted son.

[14] *Anne Comnène, Alexiade*, ed. B. Leib with index by P. Gautier (Paris, 1937–76) (hereafter An. Komn.), 1, 107.25–26.

[15] E.g., Kazhdan, *Social'nyj sostav*, 174–76.

[16] F. Dölger and P. Wirth, *Regesten der Kaiserurkunden des oströmischen Reiches* (Munich-Berlin, 1924–77) (hereafter *Reg.*), I, no. 358, ed. L. Burgmann, "Die Novellen der Kaiserin Eirene," *Fontes minores* 4 (1981), 20.54–56; well-to-do: εὐπορίαν ἢ ἐπιτήδευμα ἔχοντες. Cf. A. Guillou, *Saint Nicolas de Donnoso* (Vatican City, 1967), 12, 39, and Kazhdan, *Social'nyj sostav*, 29.

contemporary segments of Theophanes yield some insight into how society was structured by his lights. Thus Nikephoros I's vexations affected the whole population of the capital: *hoi en telei kai mesoi kai euteleis*: "the authorities, the middling people, and the poor." Here government position is the antonym of poverty; later versions of similar formulas will replace officialdom with economic wealth.[17]

The situation appears substantially the same a century and a half later: Theophanes Continuatus views senators and *hoi en telei* as the upper echelon of society. To the common people (*asemos, idiotes*) he opposes neither rich nor noble but an officer—a *droungarios* or tourmarch.[18] A similar mental schema also occurs in contemporary hagiography. One example from many: when the author of the Miracles of the Virgin at Pegai wished to emphasize that all ranks of society benefited from the Virgin's miraculous power, he enumerated them as *basileis kai archontes kai idiotai kai penetes*: "emperors and officials and private citizens and the poor."[19]

This upper echelon was open to vertical mobility. Constantine Porphyrogennetos, in almost as many words, says that Constantinople particularly fostered social mobility.[20] For instance, as a youth, so his biographer tells us, the well-educated future patriarch Methodios left his native Syracuse for the capital, loaded with money and thirsting for court titles and fame.[21] Career descriptions sometimes stress the need for a certain level of education. In the eleventh century, Michael Psellos, a man of mediocre origin, scaled the ladder of offices and dignities primarily due to his exceptional talent and literary culture.[22] The impact of education on the ethos of officialdom perhaps explains the fact that more than one manuscript has survived because it was copied or commissioned by court dignitaries.[23] But education was not indispensable. Neither Theophylaktos Abaktistos, nor Basil I—educated by his father—nor probably the young Symeon the Theologian, owed their positions to their book learning.[24] Even though the case of Podaron, *protospatharios* of the Phiale, who was an experienced warrior but illiterate (ἀγράμματος) and who needed a judge of the Hippodrome to assist him when he heard legal cases, appears to be exceptional, we hear nothing about examinations for candidates for imperial service.[25]

---

[17] Theoph. 487.22; cf. οἱ ἐν τέλει (454.14, 467.18–19, 480.22); and combined with archons (475.24); the expression is contrasted with the common people (467.33–468.1). For a clear, later instance of the opposition rich-poor see, e.g., I. Ševčenko, "Alexios Makrembolites and His 'Dialogue between the Rich and the Poor,'" *ZRVI* 6 (1960), 187–228, here 203.

[18] Th.C. 149.19–20; 89.17–18.

[19] *De sacris aedibus deque miraculis Deiparae ad Fontem* (BHG 1072), 42, *ActaSS,* Nov. 3 (1910), 878–89 (hereafter *Mir.Deip.*), here 889A.

[20] *Vita Basilii I,* in Th.C., 211–353 (hereafter *V. Bas.*), here 221.6–9.

[21] *Vita Methodii* (BHG 1278), 2, PG 100:1245B.

[22] On his career, see Ja. N. Ljubarskij, *Michail Psell: Ličnost' i tvorčestvo* (Michael Psellos: The Man and His Works) (Moscow, 1978), 23–24.

[23] R. Browning, *History, Language and Literacy in the Byzantine World* (Northampton, 1989), pt. VII, 42–45. On literacy in Byzantium see H. Hunger, *Schreiben und Lesen in Byzanz* (Munich, 1989); N. Oikonomides, "Mount Athos: Levels of Literacy," *DOP* 42 (1988), 167–78; R. Browning, "Further Reflections on Literacy in Byzantium," in *Studies in Honor of Speros Vryonis,* vol. I (New Rochelle, N.Y., 1993), 253–65.

[24] On Basil I's education: *V. Bas.* 220.1. For Abaktistos and Symeon the Theologian, see below, section 7.

[25] Constantine Porphyrogenitus, *De administrando imperio,* ed., trans., and comm. G. Moravcsik and R. Jenkins (Washington, D.C., 1962–67) (hereafter *De adm.*), 51, 250.100–102.

The principle of vertical mobility was emphasized over birth in Leo VI's *Taktika*. "In the same manner," says the Byzantine tactician, "that we divide beasts into noble (εὐγενῆ) and ignoble on the basis of their own actions and habits, we must evaluate the nobility of men, taking into consideration their own actions and exploits, not their ancestors." And then he specifies: "Would it not be improper and ignorant . . . to choose as *strategoi* [those who have good] ancestors even though the men [themselves] are incompetent?" He even goes so far as to state that *strategoi* who have no ancestors to boast of will make better commanders, since many generals who inherit fame (εὔκλεια) behave negligently and irresponsibly.[26] This kind of approach was by no means exceptional. A hundred years later, Symeon the Theologian used the metaphor of the emperor raising a man from "abject poverty" to wealth and glorious titles in order to concretize the idea of the true monk summoned to the face of Christ.[27] And if we may believe Skylitzes, Michael VI, in the mid-eleventh century, thought likewise, when he praised Kekaumenos Katakalon for having won high office by his own deeds and not thanks to his ancestors or some partiality (ἐκ προσπαθείας τινός).[28] There were of course those who disapproved of vertical mobility. Symeon Logothete criticizes Disinios, *magistros* and *strategos* of Melitene, because, in his youth, this prosperous magnate had earned a living by administering enemas to the sick. Christopher of Mitylene seems to reflect a similar attitude when he vituperates the arrival of janitors, vine growers, shepherds, woodcutters, bread and vegetable sellers, cobblers, and used sandal salesmen in the ranks of the clergy; these ignoramuses would mix up both their priestly attire and their prayers. But the reproving remarks of Symeon and Christopher only underscore the reality of mobility.[29]

In sum, governmental position supplies the very terms in which these writers imagined the ruling class; the absence of official appointments characterizes the lower classes. Vertical mobility was a factor real enough to elicit both positive and negative reactions from contemporary observers. It meant that the elite was not sealed off from below. The composition of the social group that supplied the court with its most distinguished members was, between the ninth and eleventh centuries, varied and open.

2. The Byzantine Court: Terminology

Our own word "court" comes from the medieval West. "Court" entered English from Latin via French: classical *cohors, cohortis* meant a "pen" or "enclosure." By exten-

---

[26] *Taktika* 2, 22–24, PG 107:688A–B, derived from Onasander. Cf. G. Ostrogorsky, "Observations on the Aristocracy in Byzantium," *DOP* 25 (1971), 4–5, with I. A. Antonopoulou, "The 'Aristocracy' in Byzantium: Evidence from the *Tactica* of Leo VI the Wise," *Byzantiaka* 13 (1993), 151–53, and A. Kazhdan, "The Aristocracy and the Imperial Ideal," in *The Byzantine Aristocracy, IX to XIII Centuries*, ed. M. Angold (Oxford, 1984), 43–44.

[27] *Syméon le Nouveau Théologien, Chapitres théologiques, gnostiques et pratiques*, ed. J. Darrouzès, SC 51 (Paris, 1957), 2, 8, 73.

[28] *Ioannes Scylitzes Synopsis historiarum*, ed. I. Thurn (Berlin, 1973) (hereafter Skyl.), 483.13–17.

[29] V. G. Vasil'evskij, "Dva nadgrobnych stichotvorenija Simeona Logofeta," *VizVrem* 3 (1896), 578.1–2; Christopher Mitylenaios, *Die Gedichte*, ed. E. Kurtz (Leipzig, 1903), no. 63.6–10.

sion the word came to mean a segment of a camp, and the troops encamped there, as well as beasts or people crowded into a pen or other space.[30] In the rural world that was the early medieval West, the popular Latin form *cortis* came to mean as well a farmyard and by extension the king's farmyard or country residence, especially in northern Italy. From the mid-ninth century, it occurs unambiguously as the place or human group associated with the king. The Byzantines borrowed the vulgar Latin form *cortis,* and at least one ninth-century source connects the word with Italy. Nonetheless, the way the Byzantines used the loanword *korte,* as in *komes tes kortes,* appears, at first blush, to owe more to the bureaucratic lingo of late Roman administration than to contemporary Italian kings.[31]

There is no single Byzantine term that exactly corresponds to our word "court." Perhaps the word that best circumscribes the specific reality of the tenth-century court is *to palation,* "the palace." Prayers were proffered for the emperor and for the palace, not in the sense of the building of course, but as the "establishment surrounding the emperor" or "court."[32] The more special sense of court underlies Nicholas Mystikos' criticism of Leo VI's marital misconduct, which had never been displayed before by any previous emperor "nor," says he, "by anyone holding the lowest rank in the government nor by anyone merely enrolled in the palace." So too he speaks of the chamberlain "and the other glorious officials of the sacred palace."[33] In like fashion, a tenth-century hagiographer refers to a holy man who became "a familiar of the emperor and of the palace people."[34] The identification reaches an extreme in a version of the Life of St. Andrew the Fool, whose author speaks of the "emperor of the palaces" (βασιλεὺς τῶν παλατίων).[35]

In internal documents of court life such as the *Book of Ceremonies,* the trees—the various institutions and subgroups—tend to crowd out the forest of the court. In the few places where he articulates a vision of the whole, Constantine VII refers to the "imperial office and . . . senatorial corps" (βασίλειος ἀρχὴ καὶ συγκλητικὸν σύστημα). Perhaps most revealingly, he contrasts "the imperial community" (τὸ βασιλικὸν πολίτευμα) with "the private and unfree state of life."[36] In the protocols of actual ceremo-

---

[30] A. Ernout and E. Meillet, *Dictionnaire étymologique de la langue latine* (Paris, 1967), 131; *Thesaurus linguae latinae,* vol. III (Leipzig, 1906–12), 1549–59.

[31] J. F. Niermeyer and C. Van de Kieft, *Mediae latinitatis lexicon minus* (Leiden, 1954–76), 295, s.v. *curtis* for a general orientation; on the Byzantine word, A. Kazhdan, "Hagiographical Notes," *Byzantion* 56 (1986), 148–49. On the lexical complexity of this problem, see H. and R. Kahane, "Abendland und Byzanz," *RB,* I (1970–76), 345–640, here 510.

[32] See, e.g., M. McCormick, *Eternal Victory: Triumphal Rulership in Late Antiquity, Byzantium, and the Early Medieval West,* 2d ed. (Cambridge, 1990), 189 note 2.

[33] Nicholas I, Patriarch of Constantinople, *Letters,* ed. and trans. R.J.H. Jenkins and L. G. Westerink (Washington, D.C., 1973) (hereafter Nik.Myst.*Ep.*), here ep. 32, 216.25–27: μηδεὶς τῶν πρὸ αὐτοῦ μὴ ὅτι γε βασιλέων, ἀλλ᾽ οὐδὲ τῶν εἰς ἐσχάτην τελούντων ἀρχῆς τάξιν ἢ ἁπλῶς τῶν εἰς παλάτιον κατειλεγμένων. Officials: ep. 67, 312.2–3.

[34] καὶ βασιλεῖ γνώριμος . . . καὶ τοῖς ἐν παλατίῳ. *Mir.Deip.* 884B.

[35] *Vita Andreae Sali* (*BHG* 117). There is no παλατίων in the text as published by L. Rydén, *The Life of St. Andrew the Fool,* vol. II (Uppsala, 1995), 24.178, but it comes up in PG 111:644C.

[36] *De cer.* 1, *praef.* Vogt I, 1.5; τὸ βασιλικὸν πολίτευμα opposed to ἡ ἰδιωτικὴ καὶ ἀνελεύθερος διαγωγή, ibid., 1.16–2.1. The term πολίτευμα might reward further study in this regard. In Th.C. 239.4–8, for instance, it is opposed to the Senate. Cf. Philotheos, *Kletorologion,* ed. and trans. N. Oikonomidès, in *Les listes de préséance*

nies, we find terms like *sekreton,* or, more obviously, *synkletos.* "Senate" and related terms are essential, but the range of meanings may be wider and more ambivalent than is commonly realized.[37]

A thorough study of Byzantine terminology would rely on concordances, which are still few and far between. A manuscript concordance of the *History* of Niketas Choniates has been prepared by Alexander Kazhdan and is stored at Dumbarton Oaks. Although Choniates is obviously later than the period treated here, it is useful to peruse his vocabulary of the court. Choniates speaks of *archeion* (in the singular and in the plural, 49 times); *anaktoron* (38 times, only once in the singular); *basileion* (34 occurrences, mostly in the plural); *palation,* mostly *mega palation* (23 times); and *aule* (11 times). The rare word *tyranneion* occurs thrice, including an instance where it means an independent principality.[38] Most of these terms denote the palace as a building; occasionally they can be used to refer to the patriarchal palace, especially *archeion* (6 times). But only in a few instances are the terms used metaphorically to designate the court, or court life, or even secular affairs.[39] "The select of the palace" (οἱ τοῦ παλατίου ἔκκριτοι) occurs once to designate the elite group among courtiers.[40] The use of *aule* is distinctive in that it tends to occur in contexts that refer to the body of courtiers rather than the palace buildings.[41] Using various verbs, Choniates speaks about those "who dwell in the imperial *aule*"(54.83, 107.8, 421.62); he uses it especially in prepositional phrases: *hoi peri* (293.92, 508.93), *apo* (411.88) or *ek* (214.73, 321.28, 479.40), that is, those who are "in" or "from" the *basileios aule.* He also uses *aule* once in a figurative sense to mean the "courtiers" of Christ (338.5). Whether this fondness for *aule* is specific to Choniates is an open question. But it is interesting that the word is semantically the closest to the western "court." As a general matter, with the exception of *tyranneion,* these word frequencies look to be roughly the opposite of the same words' currency in medieval demotic Greek, as mapped by E. Kriaras.[42] But it is noteworthy that these synonyms mostly share an association with a place, a physical structure. In other words, even the recherché wording of Choniates confirms our initial deduction. His rich and varied diction focuses

byzantines des IXe et Xe siècles (Paris, 1972), 65–235 (hereafter *Klet.*), here 165.12: αἱ τοῦ οἰκείου πολιτεύματος ἀξίαι.

[37] Ἡ σύγκλητος, οἱ συγκλητικοί seem sometimes to encompass all ranking members of court; at others they seem to designate nonmilitary officials: see, for instance, ἡ ὑπὸ καμπάγιν σύγκλητος: *Klet.* 169.2–3; cf. the contrast in *De cer.* 1, 56 (47), Vogt II, 49.11–12, between a συγκλητικὸς πατρίκιος and one ἀπὸ σπαθίου. Does the distinction implicit in this contrast carry over into the definition of the group πᾶσα ἡ σύγκλητος which is convoked for the ceremony? Ibid., 44.3–4. The answer is unclear at this point.

[38] Nicetas Choniates, *Historia,* ed. J. L. van Dieten (Berlin, 1975) (hereafter N.Ch.), 502.13.

[39] E.g., ἀρχεῖον: N.Ch. 490.67; τὰ βασίλεια: 225.59, 227.21, 441.20. Secular affairs: τὰ κατὰ τὰ ἀνάκτορα: 490.81.

[40] N.Ch. 407.79.

[41] It also is used once to designate a sheepfold: N.Ch. 378.74.

[42] These statistics are based on the unpublished thematic concordance of the works of Choniates compiled by A. Kazhdan. For the boundaries of the demotic lexicon surveyed by E. Kriaras, see Λεξικὸ τῆς μεσαιωνικῆς ἑλληνικῆς δημαδοῦς γραμματείας, *1100–1669,* vol. I (Thessalonica, 1968), ι′–ιγ′. Ἀρχεῖον is completely absent; ἀνάκτορον (II [1971], 91); αὐλή (III [1973], 342); βασίλειο(ν) (IV [1975], 54). The volume for Π has not yet reached us.

on the place to refer to the human group of the court. The role of the palace in shaping the Byzantine court appears primordial, and we shall return to it more than once.

3. An Order of Magnitude

To grasp the social nature of the overall phenomenon of the court which these terms described, the first question we need to address is size. How large was the human group that constituted the Byzantine court? Did this group comprise dozens of people, hundreds, or possibly thousands? The only direct statement of size known to us is imprecise, yet it yields a valuable clue. In the eleventh century, Michael Attaleiates referred to the "whole Senate" which "numbers more than myriads of men."[43] Though we may doubt that court society really numbered in the tens of thousands, Attaleiates does suggest that this human group numbered considerably more than several dozen.[44] Recent calculations about the imperial budget ca. 842 have resulted, indirectly, in an effort to quantify the court. These calculations seem to suggest, in fact, a group of just over two thousand men.[45]

Another approach is to measure the space in which the court congregated, much as R. Janin tested what Byzantines said about the numbers of a monastic community against the size of their church.[46] We know that, in certain circumstances, the court assembled in the galleries of the Hagia Sophia. A few years ago, the late Robert L. Van Nice kindly calculated for one of us the total usable space in the galleries at 2,867 square meters. Allowing a generous square meter for each person, we arrive at a theoretical maximum of ca. 2,900 persons. This, of course, supplies merely a possible upper limit: there is no evidence that the space was completely filled.[47]

At first glance, the known seating capacity of the imperial banquet halls seems to contradict this hypothetical maximum as well as Attaleiates' statement. The biggest banquet hall was unquestionably the Triklinos of the Nineteen Couches; in fact, in the parlance of the palace, it was simply "The Big Banquet Hall" (ὁ μέγας τρίκλινος).

---

[43] Michael Attaleiates, *Historia*, ed. I. Bekker (Bonn, 1853) (hereafter Attal.), 275.12–13: . . . πᾶσα γὰρ ἡ σύγκλητος, ὑπὲρ μυριάδας ἀνδρῶν παραμετρουμένη. . . . Cf. P. Lemerle, *Cinq études sur le XI* siècle byzantin* (Paris, 1977), 291.

[44] N. Skabalonovič, *Vizantijskoe gosudarstvo i cerkov' v XI veke* (The Byzantine State and Church in the Eleventh Century) (St. Petersburg, 1884), 157, who was probably the first to interpret the passage, took this to mean "no less than a thousand."

[45] W. Treadgold, *The Byzantine State Finances in the Eighth and Ninth Centuries* (Boulder, Colo., 1982), tables III–VI (members of the *tagmata* have been counted down to the *mandatores*) and 47, for his estimate of court officials who do not appear in those tables, which seems to imply ca. 300 more officials.

[46] R. Janin, "Le monachisme byzantin au moyen âge: Commende et typica (X^e–XIVe siècle)," *REB* 22 (1964), 5–44, here 29.

[47] McCormick, *Eternal Victory*, 194 note 27. For the court in the galleries, see C. Delvoye, "Empore," *RBK*, II (1971), 129–44, here 131–33, and, for the movements of the emperor and empress, C. Strube, *Die westliche Eingangsseite der Kirchen von Konstantinopel in justinianischer Zeit* (Wiesbaden, 1973), 72–75 and 79–96, along with the observations of R. Taft, in his review: *OCP* 42 (1976), 296–303, here 301–2.

Under normal circumstances, it could accommodate 228 guests.[48] Does this suggest that the maximal hypothesis from the galleries of the Hagia Sophia supplies the wrong order of magnitude?

The historian of the Byzantine court has the extraordinary privilege of examining the emperor's typical guest lists. The banquet cycle of the twelve days of Christmas provides the most comprehensive account, and indicates that more than 2,500 invitations were issued for state dinners between Christmas and Epiphany. When, however, we discount guests who received repeated invitations or who, like the 216 indigents, clearly did not belong to the court, we are left with a total guest list of about 1,600 persons.[49] So we may surmise that the male courtiers—like everything else at court, the banquets were gender-segregated—numbered between one and two thousand persons. The figure is less than that deduced from the Hagia Sophia. But the order of magnitude is not out of keeping with that figure, nor with Attaleiates' description of myriads of senators, nor with recent hypotheses deriving from Byzantine state expenditures. And we have not even begun to take into account wives and other socially invisible types.

4. Some Subgroups at Court

Any social group this large surely comprised various smaller groups and subcultures. In theory, nothing should be easier to distinguish, given the zest with which officials ranked every conceivable dignitary in the imperial hierarchy. In fact, however, this Byzantine love of ranking complicates the task: it is so easy to see where on the vast ladder of state an individual officeholder fits that one hardly notices that he cannot be assigned to a distinct social, as opposed to institutional, group. But perhaps, for the rulers, this was an advantage of a social world dominated by court precedence. For other forms of social grouping surely existed at court: kinship structures may have been changing, but they were undeniably present and, as will be seen shortly, played a significant role in court life. It would, moreover, be no less misleading to lose sight of the fact that the court's social world included lower echelons. Though stewards and porters stood well below the upper crust of patricians and generals, their daily contributions to court life were recognized, for instance, in annual banquets.

---

[48] *De cer.* 1, 9, Vogt I, 57.16; 1, 81 (72), 2, 161.13–14; cf. 162.17–181; 2, 15, Reiske 594.4–5; and *Klet.* 164 note 136.

[49] *Klet.* 165–89, calculated as follows: 11 banquets × 228 guests = 2,508 invitations. From this we must subtract 864 invitations, which makes a total of 1,644 guests from the court. The subtractions can be calculated as follows. A total of 312 indigents were invited to join imperial banquets (12 indigents × 8 banquets—they are explicitly attested in six banquets and implicitly in two others, when the total of ranking guests in the hall comes to 204, i.e., the *atriklines* implicitly leaves one table of twelve for the customary indigents: *Klet.* 173.30 and 179.16—as well as the banquet of the eighth day when 216 indigents were invited); we must also subtract the 216 monks invited on day six, the 204 guests of the ninth banquet (essentially the same guest list as banquet one), and the 24 Arab prisoners invited on Christmas. Furthermore, the twelve invitations to share the emperor's high table for ten of the banquets presumably went more or less repeatedly to the same people, the emperor's closest associates and friends, so that some 108 should be subtracted from these 120 invitations as probable repeats. Obviously these calculations have no claim to quantify precisely and rigorously the number of (male) Byzantine courtiers in A.D. 899. But it seems clear that they furnish a useful approximation.

Ethnicity must have featured in patterns of association in so cosmopolitan a court. Why else should Symeon Logothete specify how, in the dangerous hours following Michael III's assassination, as Basil and his co-conspirators stood outside the locked entrance to the Great Palace, they had a Persian associate explain "in his own tongue" to the commander of the palace guards that Michael was dead and that the new emperor demanded entry. The Persian-speaking *hetaireiarches* Artavasdos responded by seizing the keys from the *papias,* and opened the gates to the palace and the empire for Basil.[50] No group has received more attention in this respect than the Armenians, but at various times other ethnic groups, such as the Varangians or the "Latins," were thick at court.[51]

Alongside such obvious forms of social grouping there are hints of more elusive subcultures. Communities of taste, for instance, should interest art historians no less than historians of Byzantine society. In a social group this large, fashions in ideas or things may have spread among subgroups in ways that are revealing. For instance, how individuals responded to varying trends may be detected in changing attachments to saints' cults, or in styles of artistic expression on objects closely identified with known individuals, such as the tens of thousands of surviving lead seals, or even in changing preferences in personal naming. Traces of the social underpinnings of fashions perhaps lie in the circumstance, for example, that several very prominent women at court developed a cult for the shrine of the Virgin at Pegai early in our period. The story of the miracles that occurred there names several ladies: Empress Irene, whose benefactions were commemorated in votive mosaic portraits; Thecla, the sister of Michael III, whose mother, Empress Theodora, granted chrysobulls in gratitude; not to mention Helen Artavasdina, a *magistrissa,* or Maria *magistrissa,* mother of the patrician Tarasios.[52] Future research may uncover other such communities of taste and explore their connections with social subgroups. But, as tantalizing as such traces are, they cannot obscure the fact that at court such groupings remained submerged under the institutional structures of offices, dignity, and precedence, the key to which, promotion, remained firmly in the emperor's hands.

It seems typical of Byzantine civilization in this era that those subgroups that do stand out at court are, first and foremost, institutional in nature rather than social or economic. Again the imperial banquet invitations provide an easy approach to them. One essential group apparent from the banquet invitations was the elite, the emperor's closest associates. The emperor's friends, his *philoi,* rank among the few privileged mortals who were

---

[50] *Leonis Grammatici Chronographia,* ed. I. Bekker (Bonn, 1842) (hereafter Sym.Log.), 251.23–252.11. Cf. *Reg.,* no. 422 on the incorporation of a large Persian force into the imperial army ca. 830 and, additionally, the *Vita Athanasiae Aeginae,* ed. F. Halkin, *Six inédits d'hagiologie byzantine* (Brussels, 1987), 181.7–9 and *Synaxarium CP* 611.51–52. The *Vita Methodii,* 7, PG 100:1249c-d puns on Theophilos' name, calling him ἐθνόφιλος.

[51] See, respectively, A. P. Kazhdan, *Armjane v sostave gospodstvujuščego klassa Vizantijskoj imperii v xi–xii vv.* (Armenians in the Composition of the Ruling Class of the Byzantine Empire in the Eleventh and Twelfth Centuries) (Erevan, 1975); S. Blöndal and S. Benedikz, *The Varangians of Byzantium* (Cambridge, 1978); A. P. Kazhdan and A. Wharton Epstein, *Change in Byzantine Culture in the Eleventh and Twelfth Centuries* (Berkeley, 1985), 172–80.

[52] On lead seals in this context, see W. Seibt, "Die Darstellung der Theotokos auf byzantinischen Bleisiegeln, besonders im 11. Jahrhundert," in *Studies in Byzantine Sigillography,* ed. N. Oikonomides (Washington, D.C., 1987), 35–56, who speaks repeatedly of "fashion trends." Women of the court and the Pegai shrine: *Mir.Deip.* 880c, 880c-d, 882d–883d, 884c–885c. On female donors of the shrine of Pegai in the 14th century, see A.-M. Talbot, "Epigrams of Manuel Philes on the Theotokos tes Peges and Its Art," *DOP* 48 (1994), 151–58.

consistently by his side in public. They were there, at the imperial high table during banquets and when the emperor breakfasted in church on great feasts, or when he boarded the imperial yacht. A ninth-century biographer found no detail more revealing of the prestige of his hero's father-in-law than the fact that the patrician Leo daily shared the emperor's table.[53] Ca. 900, the imperial table mates typically held the rank of *magistroi, anthypatoi,* or patricians.[54] We may suspect that some were in fact imperial kinsmen, although there was no institutional recognition of that fact. This elite group numbered at least a dozen or two, and can perhaps be identified prosopographically in the ranking laymen named at major church councils.[55]

Another very high ranking and more sharply circumscribed socio-institutional group was the *koubouklion,* the corps of palace eunuchs.[56] Court eunuchs had been around since the Roman Empire, but those of the tenth century differed in several respects. Although some, like Samonas, were still foreign-born, now native Byzantines were also castrated more commonly. The chief reason lay in the unique career opportunities open to eunuchs.[57] Nothing makes this clearer than the edifying story of a Paphlagonian farmer named Metrios, who, seeing the success of his neighbors whose eunuch children were making careers in the capital, prayed for the birth of a son. He hoped to emasculate the child and have someone to support him in his old age. After a remarkable good deed, his wish was granted by an angel; the boy entered the service of the empress, who placed him with the emperor. Ultimately the boy Constantine climbed the eunuch ladder to wind up as Leo VI's patrician and *parakoimomenos.* As his father had hoped, the eunuch son brought innumerable benefits to his entire *genos.*[58] A little later, a castrated imperial bastard, Basil the Nothos, outlasted his own lineage at the center of power, came to head the *koubouklion,* and even to steer the ship of state.[59]

Notwithstanding their ambivalent gender and sometimes base origins, local eunuchs

---

[53] ὁμοτράπεζος τῷ βασιλεῖ καθ' ἑκάστην ὑπῆρχε καὶ φίλος περιδέξιος, *Vita Theophanis (BHG* 1789), Theoph. 2, 4.31–32.

[54] E.g., *Klet.* 167.3–5 (μεγιστᾶνες ἐκ τῆς βασιλικῆς συγκλήτου), or 185.14–18, breakfast in the Hagia Sophia for the emperor and fourteen such guests; twelve φίλοι at the emperor's high table: ibid., 167.10–14; they are repeatedly called φίλοι in the section on the Easter banquets: 201.21, 203.7, etc. *De adm.* 51, 246.22–26.

[55] Perhaps, but not certainly. Thus one might think that, if Sym.Log. is to be believed, the persons he identifies as Basil I's principal co-conspirators in the assassinations of Bardas and Michael III might have appeared in this group. But the longest list at the fourth ecumenical Council of Constantinople, which attests the leading *magistroi* and patricians who attended the tenth session of council barely three years after the coup, yields a possible overlap of only three or four names, and they are so common as to support no firm conclusion: cf. Winkelmann, *Quellenstudien,* 87–94 and *Concilium Constantinopolitanum IV, actio 10,* Mansi, XVI, 157E–158B. The most promising is probably "Marinus magnificus patricius et logotheta militaris," who may be identical to Basil I's brother Marianos, *patrikios, logothetes ton agelon,* and *domestikos ton scholon;* cf. Winkelmann, 89–90. Anastasius Bibliothecarius, who was responsible for this Latin text of the council, seems elsewhere to substitute "Marinus," a name well known at Rome, for "Marianos," which was less familiar to Romans: Mansi, XVI, 151E with marginal note.

[56] Oikonomidès, *Listes,* 299–301; and, in general, R. Guilland, *Recherches sur les institutions byzantines,* vol. I (Berlin, 1967), 165–97.

[57] Samonas' Arab birth: A. Kazhdan and A. Cutler, *ODB,* III, 1835–36; cf. in the 11th century, the story of John Orphanotrophos and his four brothers: three of the five had been castrated, Skyl. 390.71–76.

[58] *Narratio de Metrio (BHG* 2272), *Synaxarium CP* 721–24. Cf. *V. Davidis, Symeonis et Georgii Mytilenae (BHG* 494), ed. [J. Van den Gheyn], "Acta graeca SS. Davidis, Symeonis et Georgii," *AnalBoll* 18 (1899), 209–59, here 240.11–14.

[59] A. Kazhdan and A. Cutler, *ODB,* I, 270.

were now more fully integrated into Byzantine society, as these stories suggest and as the appearance of eunuch patriarchs confirms.[60] Leo VI in fact recognized eunuchs' social position and ambition by allowing them to form kinship groups through adoption. And Basil II who knew their influence from firsthand experience, notably of Basil the Nothos, reacted against the extent of their assimilation when he acted to curtail their inheritance rights.[61]

Nothing shows better the social integration of this group than the fact that by ca. 800 a eunuch was scheming to win the purple for his own family and that, two centuries later, another eunuch, John Orphanotrophos, actually realized this objective.[62] And there is no more typical indicator of their influence than the conclusion that, by the ninth-century, they controlled the details of imperial ceremonial. Indeed, the punctilious attention of the *Book of Ceremonies* to the special perks of eunuchs hints at their role in compiling or revising that bible of Byzantine court life, a hint that may find confirmation in the manuscripts themselves.[63] Practically alone among Byzantine men of the court, their peculiar sexual status allowed them to cross the gender boundaries at court, which also helps explain their success. And of course, palace eunuchs made signal contributions to imperial administration and military enterprises. But for all their influence, the eunuchs never completely shed their social ambivalence. How else can we explain that during the Christmas banquet that feted the court's top twelve eunuchs, the rest of the hall was filled with indigents?

As in matters of lineage and the aristocratization of society, the Komnenian period witnessed profound change in both the position of and attitudes toward eunuchs. In the eleventh century, eunuchs still held critical appointments and some of them, like John Orphanotrophos, the logothete John, Nikephoritzes or John of Side came to head the state apparatus. Eunuchs held military posts, for instance, as *domestikos* of the *scholai, stratopedarches, doux,* and security positions such as great *hetaireiarches* and *droungarios* of the Vigla. Of a group of fifty-five eunuchs attested in the twenty decades of the eleventh and twelfth centuries, 52 percent were active in the six decades between 1025 and 1081. The four decades of Alexios I's reign (1081–1118) mark a transition: 21 percent of the total group were his contemporaries, but only one of them, Leo Nikerites, belonged to the military elite. Besides him, one eunuch was patriarch and two, great *droungarioi.*

---

[60] For example, Niketas I (766–780): Theoph. 440.12–13; Ignatios is a well-known 9th-century example. The case of Methodios I is less clear.

[61] Leo VI, *Novella* 26, ed. P. Noailles and A. Dain (Paris, 1944), 101–5; cf. M. T. Fögen, "Legislation und Kodifikation des Kaisers Leon VI.," *Subseciva Groningana: Studies in Roman and Byzantine Law,* ed. J.H.A. Lokin et al. (Groningen 1989), 23–35, here 28 note 18 and 29–33. Basil II invalidates bequests to eunuchs: *Peira* 31,1, ed. Zepos, *Jus,* 4:137.

[62] Under Irene, the eunuch Aetios sought to have his brother Leo proclaimed emperor: Theoph. 475.20–32 and 476.12–17. Orphanotrophos: G. Ostrogorsky, *History of the Byzantine State,* trans. J. M. Hussey, 2d ed. (New Brunswick, N.J., 1969), 323–24.

[63] On the shift of ceremonial control to the eunuchs, see McCormick, *Eternal Victory,* 222–26. Contents hint at eunuchs: for example, the first book of *De cer.* concludes with the protocol for the promotion of the *proedros* of the Senate (*De cer.* 1, 97, Reiske 440–43), a title which, according to Skyl. 284.2–5, was created especially for Basil the Nothos. J. Haldon, ed., Constantine Porphyrogenitus, *Three Treatises on Imperial Military Expeditions* (Vienna, 1990), 37 note 8, reports the results of a forthcoming study by O. Kresten which will show that the Leipzig manuscript of the *De cer.* was produced "under the supervision" of Basil the Nothos, ca. 963–969.

The other eunuchs of Alexios' reign held no major offices. The most radical change characterizes the six decades in which John II and Manuel I reigned (1118–80). Only 9 percent of eunuchs attested over the two-hundred-year period lived in these decades, and none held an important function. In particular, none of them commanded military units. The final years of the twelfth century seem, on the other hand, to have witnessed a restoration of the pre-Komnenian pattern: 18 percent of the whole group flourished then, and at least four eunuchs were military commanders.[64]

In the year 900, several subgroups of the capital's religious personnel appeared on the imperial guest lists. In addition to the patriarchal staff and various metropolitans—the *synodos endemousa* played a significant role in the life of the capital—the palace clergy, then numbering at least twelve priests and many deacons, subdeacons, readers and *psaltai*, figured prominently at court banquets.[65] Although no study has yet been devoted to the palace clergy as a social or even institutional group, one may suspect that their privileged position and proximity to power made for remarkable careers. Some stray evidence seems to confirm this. Its members' duties went beyond the liturgy. For instance, Damianos, *basilikos klerikos,* interpreted Latin during the Council of Constantinople in 869. The patriarch John VII (834–843) began his spectacular rise in the ranks of the palace clergy: he caught the attention of Michael II, who selected him as Theophilos' tutor. His imperial pupil later made him *synkellos* and ultimately patriarch.[66]

The middle-ranking bureaucrats of the "Sandaled Senate" (ἡ ὑπὸ καμπάγιν σύγκλη-τος), the civil servants with their distinctive sandals, were particularly favored at Christmas banquets.[67] With them we approach a social group that reached below the nascent aristocracy and extended beyond the ruling class as we defined it earlier. The lower-ranking bureaucrats dined with others who might well be considered courtiers, although they did not belong to the upper reaches of Byzantine society. The members of the Sandal Senate were invited twice over Christmas and perhaps numbered fewer than 168, since the remaining tables of the Triklinos of the Nineteen Couches were filled out, mainly, with lower officers of the four *tagmata,* the shock troops stationed around Constantinople.[68] Another celebration honored city officials, along with officers of the impe-

---

[64] A. P. Kazhdan, "Sostav gospodstvujuščego klassa v Vizantii XI–XII vv. Anketa i častnye vyvody, VI: Evnuchi" (The Composition of the Byzantine Ruling Class in the Eleventh and Twelfth Centuries: Questionnaire and Particular Conclusions: VI: Eunuchs), *Antičnaja drevnost' i srednie veka* 10 (1973), 184–94.

[65] *Klet.* 185.26–29.

[66] On Damianos, see *Concilium CP. IV,* Mansi, XVI, 20c, 27c, 98b, and 122b; cf. 357d. For John VII: Th.C. 154.18–155.3.

[67] Uncritical use of Latin dictionaries perhaps explains that the Latin loanword καμπάγια is frequently translated as "boots." See the very detailed description of this footgear given by John Lydus, *De magistratibus,* 1, 17, ed. A. C. Bandy, *Ioannes Lydus On Powers* (Philadelphia, 1983), 30.22–32.5; cf. E. Saglio, "Campagus," *Dictionnaire des antiquités grecques et romaines,* ed. C. Daremberg and E. Saglio, vol. I.2 (Paris, 1887), 862–63, and Oikonomidès, *Listes,* 167 note 145.

[68] From the rank of spatharocandidate on down, i.e., everyone except for the highest class of dignities (the latter extending from *magistros* to *protospatharios*). See esp. day nine, where the ranks are spelled out more fully than in day one: *Klet.* 169.1–8 and 181.11–32. Oikonomides warns against assuming that, in the case of the *scholai,* ἅπαντες οἱ ἄρχοντες τοῦ τάγματος τῶν σχολῶν (*Klet.* 171.23), means literally all of the officers. This may be true, but it need not preclude an effort merely to ascertain the order of magnitude of the human population of the court.

rial fleet. Near the end of the Christmas cycle, a banquet brought together the officers of the palace security forces, the heads of city welfare institutions, the archdoctors in their two-toned blue uniforms, and the *diaitarioi,* that is, the service personnel who actually ran the palace.

This last group of stewards, housemen, and porters were the people who raised the curtains at imperial audiences, heated the palace baths, and opened or closed doors, both literally and figuratively. They were headed by the eunuch *papias,* a kind of supreme concierge, and they were attached to specific buildings, offices, or functions. The same group included the *domestikos* of each palace, the imperial goldsmiths, the men who set up the benches in the Hippodrome, the lamplighters, gong strikers, and clock attendants.[69] Next to them we might place the servants of the tables of the emperor and the empress.[70] Modest though their social and economic status might have been, these men enjoyed a measure of the gratifications that reached to the summit of the Byzantine hierarchy: indeed, the best lists we have of them derive precisely from their perks and invitations to imperial banquets. The imperial tailors and goldsmiths marched in some imperial processions and received a tip for their trouble.[71] The *diaitarioi* of the Great Palace and of the Daphne Palace figured next to archdoctors, *gerokomoi,* and *xenodochoi* at the state banquet on the tenth day of Christmas.[72] They occasionally worked themselves into the Byzantine cultural pantheon in other ways: thus an ascetic saint of the capital region was the daughter of John *diaitarios* of the Blachernai shrine in the eighth century.[73] One wonders whether family names like Dekanos or Palatinos might owe their origin to particularly successful members of this social world.[74] And one might well suspect that many of these palace personnel were recruited locally, from the greater capital region, in contrast to the broader geographic horizons of other members of the court.

This enumeration of institutionally defined social groups at court confirms and deepens the implication of the narrative sources that government officials and ruling class overlapped. It shows, moreover, that military men outweigh all other groups, since they constitute more than half of all guests in the Christmas cycle, even though the theme

---

[69] *De cer.* 2, 55, Reiske 800.8–20; cf. 802.17–803.9 and 805.4–15. Cf. *Klet.* 131.5–11 with comments of Oikonomidès, 131 notes 91–94. It would appear that these *diaitarioi* were identical to the *hebdomadarioi* of which the palace counted six groups, subordinated to the *papias* in 899. If *hebdomadarioi* really means that they alternated weeks of service, one wonders what they did in their spare time. For an empress' servant in charge of heating a bath, see *V. Lucae Stylitae* (*BHG* 2239), ed. H. Delehaye, *Les saints stylites* (Brussels, 1923), 195–237, here 214.10–11.

[70] *Klet.* 229.4–5; cf. W. Seibt, "Über das Verhältnis von κηνάριος bzw. δομέστικος τῆς τραπέζης zu den anderen Funktionären der βασιλικὴ τράπεζα in mittelbyzantinischer Zeit," *BZ* 72 (1979), 34–38. Cyril κινάριος, the earliest holder of this title and mentioned in Eustratios' *Vita Eutychii* (*BHG* 657), ed. C. Laga, CCSG 25 (Turnhout, 1992), 76.2377–78, should be added to this list.

[71] *Klet.* 133.5–13.

[72] *Klet.* 183.9–18.

[73] St. Anne: *Synaxarium CP* 170.18–20; cf. ibid., 174.16–178.46, whose variant version identifies the father as *diakonos* of Blachernai 174.17–18; *diaitarios* is the *lectio difficilior* and therefore more probable reading.

[74] Dekanos: see Kazhdan, *Social'nyj sostav,* 188; Palatinos: 138–39; Kazhdan, 212, suspects they may have been Latins because of the name. He classifies both as military groups. For δεκανοί in the palace: A. Kazhdan and A. Cutler, *ODB,* I, 601. The family names Hikanatos and Chrysoberges are further possibilities.

armies are not represented as such. Even more important in light of later developments is the fact that the two career streams of military and civil service do not yet seem to have become the distinct social worlds they would form by the twelfth century. Thus, although the first and ninth banquets of Christmas were primarily given over to the civilian Sandaled Senate, these bureaucrats nonetheless shared the hall with several tables filled by lower-ranking military officers of the *tagmata*.[75] The same social contacts might be implied by the grouping of the palace stewards with the lower officers of the palace security forces.[76] Finally, the guest lists reach very far down into the hierarchy, in both the military and civilian ranks.[77]

Just as they submerge ethnicity and kinship under the institutional structures of empire, the banquet lists risk blindfolding us to the institutionally invisible people, the people who eluded or were ignored by ceremonial managers. Where, for instance, are the court jesters (σκηνικοί) like Titlevakios and Lampoudios, whom Zaoutzes suborned to mock the patriarch during entertainment at an imperial banquet?[78] Slavery was part of the contemporary Byzantine social fabric, but it is not easy to see the slaves who must have been attached to the court and courtiers. The historian's difficulties are not lessened by the ambivalence of the term *doulos,* which might mean slave but, as we shall see, could also take on quite an honorable meaning. The "Scythian" slave who gave birth to the illegitimate son of Romanos I, the future Basil the Nothos, was presumably in palace service.[79] And where in fact are the women? Females of all ranks are almost totally absent from court treatises. Clearly the institutional units discerned by ceremonial managers do not exhaust the social groupings, or even individuals, present at court.

This glaring absence is particularly acute for the most powerful woman at court, the Byzantine empress, who remains enveloped in even more obscurity than the gender segregation of her times warrants. We lack even a basic list: the most recent catalogue of Byzantine empresses that we know of dates from the ninth century.[80]

Notwithstanding Charles Diehl's protestations to the contrary, empresses' public life in the ninth century was largely separate from that of their husbands.[81] In this they

---

[75] *Klet.* 167.10–169.9 and 181.20–30. Cf. Winkelmann, *Quellenstudien,* 227–28 and Kazhdan, *Social'nyj sostav,* 244–58.

[76] *Klet.* 183.9–18.

[77] μικροὶ ἄρχοντες: *Klet.* 181.27.

[78] *Vita Euthymii patriarchae CP,* ed., trans., and comm. P. Karlin-Hayter (Brussels, 1970) (hereafter *V. Euth.*), 43.25–27.

[79] Skyl. 244.9–10; cf. Leo Diak. 94.3–4. We hear occasionally of "imperial slaves" whose circumstances hint that they may have been attached to the palace, for instance, in Pseudo-Symeon, in Th.C. 673.13–18. Cf. Leo VI, *Nov.* 38, Noailles and Dain 153.5–14, and Attal. 317.13–23. Much of the evidence on Byzantine slavery in this period is collected and appraised in A. P. Kazhdan, "Raby i mistii v Vizantii IX–XI vekov" (Slaves and *Misthioi* in Byzantium, Ninth to Eleventh Centuries), *Učenye zapiski. Tul'skij gosudarstvennyj pedagogičeskij institut* 2 (Tula, 1951), 63–84.

[80] See the catalogue of empresses from Theodora and Helen, wives of Constantius I, to Theophano, wife of Leo VI, ed. C. de Boor, *Nicephori archiepiscopi Constantinopolitani opuscula historica* (Leipzig, 1880), 104–6. Schreiner, "La famille," 188–90, produces a list for the 8th through 10th centuries. Reiske collected some interesting material for all periods: *De cer.* 2, 373–75. Cf. the sketch in M. McCormick, "L'imperatore," in *L'uomo bizantino,* ed. G. Cavallo (Bari, 1992; Eng. trans. in press), 341–79, here 363–69.

[81] C. Diehl, *Byzantine Portraits,* trans. H. Bell (New York, 1927), 5–7.

reflected a general tendency of Byzantium's upper classes toward sexual segregation. Thus the empress was the pinnacle of a distinctive social and institutional group, the women of the court, or rather, as the *Book of Ceremonies* calls it, "the court of the women."[82] Even a cursory glance at Theodore of Stoudios' correspondents reveals an interesting range and number of female addressees, bearing the feminine form of the usual court dignities: *patrikia, protospatharia, spatharia, kandidatissa,* and the like.[83] The grandees of Michael II, a widower, are supposed to have complained: "It is not proper for an emperor to live without a wife, nor for our wives to be deprived of a mistress and empress."[84] As their words suggest, the empresses presided over their own autonomous social and ceremonial sphere formed by the wives of the ranking members of the state hierarchy, the "court of the women." Thus, during the Easter liturgy at the Hagia Sophia, the empress, surrounded by eunuch *koubikoularioi* and *spatharioi,* granted a solemn audience to the wives of the imperial dignitaries, in which each rank of court women was admitted to receive the kiss of peace from her.[85] A little before our period, a foreign observer witnessed a great ceremony of the adoration of the Cross which began on Holy Thursday, when the emperor and his court venerated the relic in the Hagia Sophia by order of precedence. On Good Friday it was the turn of the empress, the women of the court, and those of the city, who also worshiped in order of precedence.[86] So too in the tenth century, when Princess Olga of Kiev was presented to the empress, the seven *vela* or raisings of the curtain, which marked the ceremonial entrées, differentiated the women of the court according to precise precedence, beginning with the *zostai patrikiai,* followed by the *magistrissai, patrikiai,* and so on, down to the *kandidatissai.* The emperor appeared for Olga's private audience with the empress and imperial children in the imperial chamber, and two state banquets were held, apparently simultaneously: one for women and one for men.[87] We catch a rare glimpse of the social life of women of the court when, for instance, a hagiographer mentions how grandees' wives congregated at the house of the *patrikia zoste* to spend time with a certain holy man.[88]

Of course there were occasions when certain women, particularly empresses or *patrikiai zostai,* might overstep the gender strictures separating the court of women from that of men. An anti-Amorian anecdote related by a tenth-century chronicler describes how Emperor Michael III summoned his mother, the dowager empress Theodora, to what may have been a riotous evening of entertainment in which Grylos, the emperor's boon companion, impersonated the patriarch. The empress appeared *"met' eulabeias kai aidous"*

---

[82] Τὸ σέκρετον τῶν γυναικῶν: *De cer.* 1, 49 (40), Vogt II, 12.12.

[83] On women in the correspondence of Theodore of Stoudios, see A. P. Kazhdan and A. M. Talbot, "Women and Iconoclasm," *BZ* 84–85 (1991–92), 391–408, here 396–400. Cf., on women's seals, G. Schlumberger, *Sigillographie de l'empire byzantin* (Paris, 1884), 78.

[84] Th.C. 78.14–16.

[85] *De cer.* 1, 9, Vogt I, 61.10–62.1.

[86] Adomnan, *De locis sanctis,* ed. L. Bieler, CCSL 175 (1965), 228.29–32.

[87] *De cer.* 2, 15, Reiske 595.20–598.12.

[88] Gregory, *Vita Basilii iunioris* (*BHG* 263), ed. A. N. Veselovskij, "Razyskanija v oblasti russkogo duchovnogo sticha," *Sbornik otdelenija russkogo jazyka i slovesnosti imperatorskoj Akademii nauk* 46 (1889–90), suppl. 3–89, here 301.18 and 27–29.

and by mistake venerated the pseudo-patriarch; the case is cited by the pro-Macedonian author as evidence of Michael III's unworthiness.[89]

Significantly, the women of the court did not generally enjoy personal promotion ceremonies; rather, they seem to have held their titles through their husbands. The *Book of Ceremonies* specifies female promotions in only the most exceptional cases, such as that of the empress. True to form, two separate ceremonies paid homage to the new empress: one by male dignitaries and another by "the court of women."[90] The promotion of a female cubiculary involved a ceremony in which a woman was temporarily brought into the male sphere of the emperor; after her promotion she returned to the empress' chambers.[91] The wife of a newly promoted patrician was not even allowed to witness her husband's investiture. She awaited his return at home: a parade, headed by a *silentiarios* displaying to all passersby the diptychs of appointment (τὰ κωδικέλλια), escorted the new patrician to his house. There the silentiary gave the *kodikellia* to the new *patrikia*, who rewarded him with a substantial tip.[92]

How long did this separate "court of women" continue? It may have been eroding under the Komnenoi. We hear that Alexios I was accompanied by the empress and the *gynaikonitis* on his expeditions.[93] Two episodes recounted by Niketas Choniates point in the same direction, suggesting that in the twelfth century women participated in palace banquets and accompanied the court on its movements outside the capital. In the first case, Choniates depicts a drunken revelry (δεῖπνος) at the court of Isaac II. The emperor innocently asked for salt (Greek *halas*). Now in the medieval pronunciation, the word sounded exactly like *allas* ("other [women]"). Hearing the emperor's request, the mime Chaliboures pointed to the crowd of concubines and imperial kinswomen and exclaimed "Let's try these women first, before we order other ones to be brought in!"[94] The joke implies that the emperor's mistresses and female relatives were present at the banquet.

The second episode occurred in the imperial camp at Pelagonia. Andronikos Komnenos was having an affair with his niece Eudokia and spent the night with her inside a tent. Eudokia's relatives—her brother John, *protosebastos* and *protovestiarios,* and her brother-in-law John Kantakouzenos—assembled a crowd of armed followers and waited for Andronikos to emerge so they could cut him down.[95] Leaving aside the ruse Andronikos used to outwit the outraged relatives, what matters for us is that the noble lady, a young widow by this time, was in a camp with other members of the court. We do not know whether the court had come to Pelagonia on campaign or simply to hunt, but it

---

[89] Th.C. 201.13–202.4. On Michael III's "anti-ceremonial" see Ja. Ljubarskij, "Der Kaiser als Mime," *JÖB* 37 (1987), 39–50; P. Karlin-Hayter, "Imperial Charioteers Seen by the Senate or by the Plebs," *Byzantion* 57 (1987), 326–35; E. Kislinger, "Michael III—Image und Realität," *Eos* 75 (1987), 389–400.

[90] *De cer.* 1, 49 (40), Vogt II, 12.16–23.1.

[91] *De cer.* 2, 24, Reiske 622–24.

[92] Diptychs of appointment (κωδικέλλια, also called πλάκες): *De cer.* 1, 57 (48), Vogt II, 54.20, etc. *De cer.* 1, 56 (47), Vogt II, 47.32–48.5; cf. 1, 57 (48), 2, 56.27–31.

[93] *Ioannes Zonaras Epitome historiarum,* vol. III, ed. T. Büttner-Wobst (Bonn, 1897) (hereafter Zon.), 18.26.9, 373.12–15.

[94] N.Ch. 441.23–27.

[95] N.Ch. 104.49–52.

is clear that in this case male aristocrats shared their space with their female counterparts. Only further research can confirm what appears to be yet another significant social shift under the Komnenoi and elucidate its causes, and in particular whether this apparent retreat of gender segregation offers a further instance of imitation of a western European lifestyle.

5. Locating the Court

So we now have an idea of the overall size and some salient subgroups of the court. But where normally was the court? Obviously at Constantinople. And at Constantinople, the Great Palace was the structure that defined the court in a physical way. Although the chronology of its walls remains unclear, it was not an open building. We hear of its defensive wall no later than the reign of Justinian II, and Nikephoros II fortified the central part of the palace.[96] As the encounter of Basil I and his co-conspirators with Artavasdos has already revealed, the palace was locked up at night. It also closed for the siesta hours, and the routine with which the *hetaireiarches* and *papias* opened it twice daily was described in the *Book of Ceremonies*.[97] We have seen that *palace* and related terms loom large in the terminology of the court, and the ability to enter this structure defined in a very practical way court society. The Life of Basil I underscored this when it justified describing the palatine church, the Nea Ekklesia, on the grounds that tenth-century readers who were forbidden from entering the palace might nonetheless imagine its marvelous art.[98]

In relation to the Great Palace, the topographical pattern of courtiers' residences may have changed since late antiquity, when great officials' houses had tended to cluster in the shadow of the palace.[99] By the ninth century, courtiers' residences seem to have become more decentralized. So far, the closest ones to the palace we have found are the mansion of the Phokas clan on the Sophian Port and the house of one of their supporters in the vicinity of the Forum of Constantine. Other courtiers are found north of the palace "*en tais Arkadianais.*"[100] Romanos I the Elder, when he was a high-ranking naval officer, had resided in a mansion at the Myrelaion. In the tenth century, two *praipositoi* lived in a house on the Harbor of Eleutherios. Leo Katakoilas, *droungarios tes Viglas,* owned a fine residential property by the Stoudios monastery. And when the rioting supporters of Nikephoros Phokas torched the homes of "many senators," they had fanned out "across many quarters of the city" (κατὰ πολλὰ μέρη τῆς πόλεως).[101]

---

[96] Theoph. 367.13–14; W. Müller-Wiener, *Bildlexikon zur Topographie Istanbuls* (Tübingen, 1977), 225; C. Mango, *ODB*, II, 870.

[97] *De cer.* 2, 1, Reiske 518–22.

[98] *V. Bas.* 329.14–19.

[99] M. McCormick, "Emperor and Court," in *Cambridge Ancient History*, 3d ed., XIV (Cambridge, in press).

[100] The houses of Constantine and of Anastasia πατρικία καὶ ζωστή: *V. Basil. iun.* 300.16–17, 27–28 and 301.16–18. On the Arkadianai, cf., e.g., C. Mango, *Le développement urbain de Constantinople* (Paris, 1985), 52.

[101] Leo Diak. 83.22–84.1 and 146.21–22. Romanos I's apparent pre-imperial residence at the Myrelaion: Th.C. 402.8–11; cf. Müller-Wiener, *Bildlexikon,* 402.8–11. Katakoilas: *V. Euth.* 27.19–22 and 29.26–33; cf. 11.14–18 and Winkelmann, *Quellenstudien,* 171–72; for the house of the two eunuch brothers, the Gongylioi,

At the same time, however, that some of the court society may have been dispersing across the now more sylvan city, a new and opposite phenomenon was afoot. Another segment of the elite took up residence inside the Great Palace. Thus, when Constantine VI married Philaretos the Merciful's granddaughter, virtually the entire clan of the old man seems to have left the village of Amnia and received from the emperor large houses close to or actually inside the palace.[102] A half century later, key figures in the regency of Michael III were living inside the palace complex. The patrician and domestic of the *scholai* Antigonos, the caesar Bardas' son, built a reception hall within the imperial residences (ἐν ταῖς βασιλικαῖς οἰκίαις), near the imperial court, *aule*. The regent and logothete Theoktistos also built a mansion with a garden and private baths inside the palace; when he clashed with his fellow regent Manuel, who equally resided in the palace, Manuel decided to live "farther from the palace." He moved to a mansion he had near the cistern of Aspar, about 1,500 meters from the palace, but it might as well have been 1,500 miles. From there Manuel "commuted" every day to the palace and participated in the deliberation of state affairs, but he was effectively "out of the loop" and his influence and power dwindled.[103] The establishment of major officials with their own households inside the imperial complex opened palace doors for a new group of people, as we will see.

More than just the highest officials resided in the Great Palace. We have already encountered the imperial clergy as a distinct institutional group within court society. Leo V's assassins had been smuggled into the palace in the guise of the emperor's clergy who came in every morning to perform the office in the imperial chapel. Whether because of this breach in security, or because of a more general trend for certain courtiers to reside inside the palace, by the tenth century the emperor's clergy no longer slept outside the palace.[104] When a sudden change in imperial disposition delivered the future patriarch Methodios from his lengthy incarceration, Theophilos commanded that the iconophile priest, whose scholarship he apparently appreciated, take up residence in the palace.[105]

Manuel's story suggests that more than convenience brought some of the elite to residences inside the palace complex. Was there a hierarchy of space in Byzantium? The Life of Basil I allows us to suspect that the Byzantines were sensitive about their residential topography. The author describes an expedition against the Cretan Arabs in 866 that

---

who were *praipositoi*: *V. Basil. iun.* 57–58; homes of the σύγκλητος: *De cer.* 1, 96, Reiske 437.3–15; in different quarters of the city: Skyl. 258.37–43.

[102] Niketas, *Vita Philareti* (*BHG* 1511z), ed. M. H. Fourmy and M. Leroy, "La Vie de S. Philarète," *Byzantion* 9 (1934), 85–170, here 145.4–5; 151.8 and 18. For Niketas' autobiography: ibid., 165.19–23; cf. 161.29–31.

[103] Antigonos: Th.C. 229.1–6. Manuel's move: Th.C. 168.5–169.4; cf. Genes. 61.5–16 and Müller-Wiener, *Bildlexikon*, 279. Theoktistos' mansion inside the palace: Georgius Continuatus, ed. Th.C. 816.1–2: . . . οἰκήματα καὶ λουτρὰ καὶ παράδεισον ἐν τῇ νῦν καλουμένῃ Ἀψίδα πεποίηκεν πρὸς τὸ πλησίον αὐτὸν εἶναι τοῦ παλατίου, where the last word apparently means the part of the palace in which the empress resided, since the Apse seems to have been inside the complex, between the Daphne palace and the Great Palace, according to R. Guilland, *Études de topographie de Constantinople byzantine*, vol. I (Berlin, 1969), 95–96.

[104] Th.C. 38.15–18, contrasted with ὡς νῦν. Cf. Genes. 18.49–52. No later than the 10th century, the palace clergy seem to have lodged in the upper story of a dining hall constructed by Theophilos a century before: Th.C. 143.5–7.

[105] *V. Methodii*, PG 100:1252B–C. Ps.-Symeon, in Th.C. 644.8–645.7.

halted at a place called Kepoi, in the estuary of the Meander River. When camp was pitched, it happened—"either by chance or by intention"—that the tent of Emperor Michael III was erected in a low place, whereas that of the caesar Bardas stood high on a hill. This incongruence produced rumors hostile to Bardas. The author then repeats this statement or rather interprets it by saying that the emperor's tent was "close to the ground and humble" and that of Bardas "brilliant and lofty."[106] This particular case is obvious: even an arrogant politician and elder kinsman like Bardas was not supposed to pitch his tent in a higher place than the emperor's. This concrete "topographical" conflict shows that in general the location of a dwelling could resonate with social rank.

6. Courtiers and Wealth

A fuller analysis of the material basis for the court's existence and functioning is an important task. But we shall be satisfied here simply to emphasize a few fundamental features. Land was essential to wealth, and courtiers certainly owned land. Early in his career, the future emperor Basil received money (χρήματα) from the rich widow Danielis, which he used to buy property (κτήματα) in Macedonia. When Symbatios and Peganes rioted against Basil, they set fire to numerous fields (ἀγροί) located around Constantinople that belonged to the great and powerful.[107] Courtiers perhaps tended to become involved in real estate transactions with one another. Thus in 865/866, the swiftly rising Basil, now *parakoimomenos,* purchased an estate on the Black Sea from the patrician Arsavir, brother of Patriarch John VII.[108] Examples of courtiers' landed holdings could easily be multiplied. The problem is that the data usually do not allow us to calculate the relative weight of courtiers' income derived from their land, on the one hand, and, on the other, that which came from the salaries, grants, kickbacks, or gifts associated with court life and which formed a substantial component of their revenues. The Life of Basil I lists several kinds of emoluments available to imperial officials: annual salaries (ῥόγαι), rations (σιτηρέσια), and gifts (φιλοτιμιῶν παροχαί), which one is sometimes hard put to distinguish.[109]

Only in the late eleventh century do we find a few texts, especially wills, that have allowed some scholars to emphasize the apparent discrepancy between the limited income deriving from landed properties and the abundance of liquid assets in the hands of several aristocrats. This has led to the conclusion that Byzantine aristocrats earned a relatively limited proportion of their income from their estates, in an era when the Byzantine economy seems to have been expanding rapidly.[110] If the special circumstances

---

[106] Th.C. 236.1–9; cf. A. Vasiliev, *Byzance et les Arabes,* vol. I (Brussels, 1935), 261–62.

[107] *V. Bas.* 228.17–20 and 240.16, respectively.

[108] Th.C. 157.9–14.

[109] *V. Bas.* 259.15–16.

[110] G. Litavrin, "Otnositel'nye razmery i sostav imuščestva provincial'noj vizantijskoj aristokratii vo vtoroj polovine XI v." (The Relative Size and Composition of the Wealth of the Byzantine Provincial Aristocracy in the Second Half of the Eleventh Century) in *Vizantijskie očerki* (Moscow, 1971), 152–68 with G. Weiss' review in *Byzantina* 6 (1974), 472–74. Cf. Litavrin, *Vizantijskoe obščestvo i gosudarstvo v X–XI vv.* (Byzantine Society and State in the Tenth and Eleventh Centuries) (Moscow, 1977), 96–102; G. Weiss, "Vermögungsbildung der Byzantiner

do not explain its pattern, the marriage of Manuel I's niece Theodora to Baldwin III of Jerusalem described by William of Tyre may confirm that the nature of the Byzantine elite's wealth contrasted with that of western feudal lords. Theodora's dowry consisted of 100,000 gold coins, plus 10,000 more for the wedding expenses, as well as clothing, jewelry, rugs, silks, and precious objects evaluated at another 40,000 gold pieces. No mention is made of any immovables in her wealth, and this particularity of her possessions seems only to be underscored by the fact that her bridegroom presented her with a territory, the town of Akko (St. Jean d'Acre).[111]

Whatever the relative proportion of land and cash revenues, it is clear that the salaries and pensions attached to court titles added financial substance to the social prestige of precedence. Further bonanzas occurred sporadically when the emperor celebrated important political events such as coronations, marriages, or triumphs with cash handouts, which could be large.[112]

"Handouts" is the right word. Wealth was not transferred in an impersonal, abstract act, like the electronic deposit of salaries today. High officials came to the court literally to drag their salaries away from an audience with the emperor or his leading officials. Liutprand of Cremona has painted a brilliant picture of how the leading officials filed into the imperial presence for their pay—in order of precedence. Through Liutprand's eyes we see the *raiktor* heaving his salary in moneybags and robes over his shoulders, or the *domestikos* of the *scholai* and his helpers dragging his moneybags out of the audience chamber. The physicality of the act of receiving payment is not diminished by its being performed before envious onlookers who presumably included more than just Liutprand.[113]

This was only the most obvious transfer of wealth at the court. Court society's complex structure of personal and institutional allegiances was cemented by tips and gratifications.[114] If the emperor bound his servants to him with payments, pensions, and perks, his chief servants in turn reinforced the links binding them to the rest of the court through their own largesse. It occasions little surprise that a new empress should lavishly distribute cash to the patriarch, clergy, and Senate.[115] But other dignitaries did likewise.

The schedule of gratifications required from newly promoted patricians shows that a broad range of palace personnel had tangible reasons to rejoice at each new honor. With

---

in Privathand: Methodische Fragen einer quantitativen Analyse," *Byzantina* 11 (1982), 75–92; cf. the more reserved position of M. Hendy, *Studies in the Byzantine Monetary Economy, c. 300–1450* (Cambridge, 1985), 201–20.

[111] William of Tyre, *Chronicon,* ed. R.B.C. Huyghens, CCSL *Continuatio mediaevalis* 63A (1986), 843.22–34.

[112] On revenues from appointments, see P. Lemerle, "*Roga* et rente d'État aux Xᵉ–XIᵉ siècles," *REB* 25 (1967), 77–100; cf. N. Oikonomides in this volume, and Hendy, *Studies,* 195–201; on the changing targeting of such munificence, see McCormick, *Eternal Victory,* 228–30.

[113] *Antapodosis,* ed. J. Becker, MGH, *ScriptRerGerm* (Hannover, 1915), 157.29–158.34. Cf. Lemerle, "*Roga,*" 78–79.

[114] See in general on this theme of "corruption" in the empire's earlier centuries R. MacMullen, *Corruption and the Decline of Rome* (New Haven, Conn., 1988), 122–70; cf. G. Kolias, *Ämter und Würdenkauf im früh- und mittelbyzantinischen Reich* (Athens, 1939).

[115] *Vita Theodorae imperatricis* (*BHG* 1731), ed. W. [=V. E.] Regel, *Analecta Byzantino-Russica* (St. Petersburg, 1891), 5.19–25.

each promotion, the emperor did more than reward service, bequeath status, and bestow income on one member of his court. For the new patrician was expected to share his success with court personnel by giving the eunuch *praipositoi,* that is, the ceremonial managers, the gratification of 8 pounds of gold. The *praipositoi,* in turn, reinforced their empire within the court by making, at no expense to themselves, a lengthy series of sub-gratifications extending from the imperial maître d's down to the palace bath attendants and through the personnel of the Hagia Sophia. Everyone in fact who participated in the promotion ceremony honoring the new patrician, and then some, received a share of the loot. Small wonder that the *Book of Ceremonies* refers to "the emperor who makes us rich" (ὁ πλουτοποιὸς ἡμῶν βασιλεύς)![116] This reveals another insufficiently appreciated dimension of court ceremonial: not only did it impose and project order, dignity, and symbolic message onto public moments in the life of the Byzantine aristocracy, but performances of some ceremonies helped finance the functioning of that court by subsidizing its personnel above and beyond their regular salaries.

In a sense, then, Zonaras' striking image of the Komnenoi's packing up the wealth of the state "by the wagonload" and carting it off represents not a contradiction or aberration from previous practice, but the ultimate expression of the state as the source of private wealth. But closer scrutiny reveals interesting changes with respect to the earlier period. Zonaras describes how Alexios I distributed public wealth among his relatives and servants (θεράποντες) and granted them annual distributions (χορηγίαι), so that they collected royal wealth and acquired estates (οἶκοι) as big as cities.[117] In Zonaras' eyes, the Komnenian practice was limited to a narrow group of imperial kinsmen and retainers; it is public funds (δημόσια χρήματα) and not the private payments of tenth-century fellow officials which are distributed. And he emphasizes that the final result of this transfer of wealth was the acquisition of immense estates owned by members of the Komnenian clan. In other words, both the direction and the nature of the flow of wealth at court seem to have changed under the Komnenoi.

7. Processes of Integration into the Court

How people entered the court opens doors for the historian. Processes of integration into court society uncover new facets of its life, even as they underscore once again the extraordinary powers of the emperor in orchestrating the composition of this milieu and the tenor of its activities.

Probably the most celebrated way of entering the Byzantine court was simply to buy your way in by purchasing a court dignity. More than one scholar has commented on the case of the cleric Ktenas who, for a lavish price, managed to obtain from Leo VI the dignity of *protospatharios* and a substantial increase in his precedence, even though he

---

[116] *De cer.* 1, 57 (48), Vogt II, 57.8.
[117] Zon. 18, 29, 24, 767.2–10.

was already a member of court, since he belonged to the palace clergy. But there were other ways.[118]

One could also enter the court through distinguished military service. As we saw above, some emperors encouraged this form of vertical mobility. Thus the Phokas family rose from tourmarch to vying for the purple within three generations.[119] Another example of even swifter ascension is the family of Theophylaktos Abaktistos who saved Basil I's life during a campaign against the Arabs in 872. He was rewarded with an estate and, it would appear, a position at court, since we find his son Romanos I among the leading dignitaries at the court of the child emperor Constantine VII.[120]

It is characteristic of the system that a snap decision by the emperor could raise a man from the dust to the pinnacle of court. Michael III pointedly reminded his own protégé of this one drunken evening, and thereby sealed his own doom.[121] The emperor's awesome power was amplified, if we understand the *Book of Ceremonies* correctly, by the fact that the decision to promote a man to the patriciate might be communicated to the court—and, apparently, to the beneficiary himself—only minutes before the ceremony began.[122] It is not difficult to imagine how charged with tension ceremonial assemblies may have become when the issue was so uncertain.

But before an emperor could stun you and your peers with your elevation, you had to come to his attention, you had already to have entered the court. A few case histories from the eighth to the eleventh century suggest a pattern that turns on four principles: attractive youth, kinship, *oikia* (or household structure), and *douleia* (service). Let us examine in some detail the cases of entry into the court of Constantine-Cyril, Apostle of the Slavs, and Basil I, and supplement them with data drawn from the less fully documented careers of Sts. Theophanes Confessor, Evarestos, Symeon the Theologian, and Emperor Michael IV.

The excellence of the Old Church Slavonic Life of Constantine-Cyril as a historical source needs little emphasizing today. And even if Symeon Logothete's rather hostile story of Basil's rise might appear less sincere, nonetheless the account had to preserve verisimilitude in the eyes of court readers. In the case of Sts. Theophanes and Symeon, the court was an obstacle to their sanctity; their stories are nonetheless revealing for the court's peripheral place in them.

According to his Old Church Slavonic Life, Constantine-Cyril, the son of a *droungarios,* came to the attention of the powerful logothete and regent Theoktistos for his physi-

---

[118] *De adm.* 50, 244.235–56; cf. Lemerle, "*Roga,*" 79–80.

[119] A. Kazhdan, *ODB,* III, 1665–66.

[120] J. L. van Dieten, *RB,* I.2 (1969), 1–2.

[121] Sym.Log. 249.16–19.

[122] We deduce this from the fact that the emperor sends ὁ ἐπὶ τῆς καταστάσεως to speak with the man about to be promoted right before the entry of the *vela* in the solemn audience of promotion; as the various dignitaries are about to enter the imperial presence by entrées, or *vela,* the ἐπὶ τῆς καταστάσεως goes off to tell the name to the factions who then start composing acclamations tailored to his name (κατὰ τὸ ὄνομα) on the spot. *De cer.* 1, 56 (47), Vogt II, 45.5–9; cf. ibid., 47.5–13. The next chapter is even clearer: *De cer.* 1, 57 (48), Vogt II, 54.3–17: the future patrician may already be standing in his old rank in the audience, when the emperor communicates (λέγει, γνωρίζει) his name to the *praipositos,* who communicates it to the ἐπὶ τῆς καταστάσεως, who goes off and suddenly (ἐξαίφνης) brings him forward.

cal beauty, wisdom, and diligent study.[123] Young Constantine—he was in his teens or twenties—presumably came to the capital to further his education; his biographer claims he studied with Photios. Though some have doubted this detail, around this time Photios may already have begun the court career that culminated with him as a *protospatharios* and *protoasekretis* in 858. Given Photios' brilliant family connections, as a relative of the late patriarch Tarasios and, more to the point, as the nephew of the reigning empress' sister-in-law, this would explain perfectly how the bright young man from the provinces came to Theoktistos' notice.[124] The logothete incorporated the promising young fellow into his own household, taking him into some form of service, since he gave Constantine authority over his own house.[125] Now, as we have already seen, Theoktistos resided in the Great Palace. This meant Constantine was henceforth himself, *ipso facto,* a member of court society: service in a great courtier's house opened the palace to Constantine.

Theoktistos was so delighted with his protégé's "good looks and wisdom" that he decided to take young Constantine one final step into his entourage: he proposed that the young man marry his goddaughter, who was "beautiful, rich, of good and great birth." "And at the same time," the logothete continued, "[you will] receive a dignity and office from the emperor, and expect greater things, since you will soon be a *strategos*."[126] On the eve of launching his protégé's career of government service, in other words, the mentor wishes to incorporate the young man permanently into his own family. Although the eunuch could not produce a biological clan, he had nonetheless expanded his family network through spiritual kinship, and it was into his spiritual family that he wished to integrate Constantine. Of course Constantine refused the offer in order to pursue a religious vocation. So the logothete merely adjusted his sights and adopted a parallel strategy for advancing his protégé's career within the church. With the support of the empress, Theoktistos had him tonsured as a priest—in disregard for the canonical age—and appointed to a high office in the patriarchal administration of the Hagia Sophia.[127]

---

[123] ". . . ot krasote bo jego i moudrosti i prileznem oučenii," he summoned him to study with the emperor. *Vita Constantini-Cyrilli palaeoslavonica,* ed. F. Grivec and F. Tomšič, *Constantinus et Methodius Thessalonicenses, Fontes,* Radovi staroslavenskog instituta 4 (Zagreb, 1960) (hereafter *V. Const. slav.*), 98. On Constantine's early life, see I. Ševčenko, *Byzantium and the Slavs* (Cambridge, 1991), 479–92.

[124] *V. Const. slav.* 98 and 99, which seems to have the Logothete summoning the boy from Thessalonica. It may be more likely that he was sent to the capital to pursue higher education and attracted attention once there. Cf. C. Mango, "The Liquidation of Iconoclasm and the Patriarch Photius," in *Iconoclasm,* ed. A. Bryer and J. Herrin (Birmingham, 1977), 133–40. P. Lemerle, *Le premier humanisme byzantin* (Paris, 1971), 160–65, has rightly questioned F. Dvornik's excessive interpretation of this passage; he nonetheless admits the possibility (p. 164) of Constantine's relations with Photios' intellectual circle; and it is hard to understand what Lemerle then makes of the word "nauči" (*V. Const. slav.* 99). Photios as *protospatharios* and *protoasekretis*: Niketas, *Vita Ignatii* (*BHG* 817), PG 105:509A.

[125] *V. Const. slav.* 99: "logofet dast' jemou vlast' nad' svoim' domom' i v carevou polatou s dr'znoveniem' vŭchoditi."

[126] *V. Const. slav.* 100: Constantine's qualities: "krasota i moudrost'" (cf. ibid., 99, cited above); quotation: ". . . krasnou i bogatou i roda dobra i velika; ašte chošteši. podrouziju siju ti dam; ot cara že nynja veliju č'st' i knežie priim' i bol'šuju čai, vŭ'skore bo stratig' boudeši."

[127] *V. Const. slav.* 100. The special pleading of F. Dvornik, *Les légendes de Constantin et Méthode vues de Byzance* (Prague, 1933), 49–66, about Constantine's ordination is of no avail against the words of the text itself. Cf. V.

The story of the young Theophanes parallels elements of the pattern apparent in that of Constantine-Cyril. The son of a *strategos,* Theophanes married the daughter of an influential courtier. But the couple decided to lead a chaste life and, eventually, to enter monasteries. However, Theophanes' father-in-law, a patrician, had other plans, and he went to the emperor to complain of his son-in-law's behavior which was leading his daughter into poverty. The result was that Leo IV appointed the *strator* Theophanes to administer "some public (or fiscal) business" (δημόσια πράγματα) in Kyzikos. Here, then, a wealthy young man enters the family of a high-ranking courtier via marriage and begins his court career as a low-ranking courtier (ὑπηρέτης). The biographer emphasizes that Theophanes did not start out with a leading position, one of *hoi en telei,* but was involved with the imperial horses as a *strator.* As a direct result of his father-in-law's petition, emperor Leo IV appointed him to an office at Kyzikos. At only a slightly more advanced stage than Constantine-Cyril, Theophanes opted out of a secular career to become a monk.[128]

Around the same time that Constantine-Cyril's career was getting under way, another newcomer to the capital was treading a no less momentous path into the court. Whatever the part of legend in Basil I's meteoric rise from obscurity, the story had to be believable at court. Around the age of twenty-five, Basil entered the service (δουλεύειν) of the *strategos* of his home region.[129] Dissatisfied with the opportunities, he headed for Constantinople. He camped outside of the church of St. Diomedes, by the Golden Gate, where the *prosmonarios* (sacristan) was miraculously led to befriend the strapping young man. They became adoptive brothers via the custom of *adelphopoiia.*[130] Now the *prosmonarios'* brother was a doctor in service (ἐδούλευεν) to a prominent member of the court and relative of the emperor, Theophilitzes.[131] At a dinner—another banquet?—at which the doctor was seated near his lord, Theophilitzes happened to say he needed a groom: the doctor mentioned Basil, who was summoned and who amazed Theophilitzes by his size. He got the job and so entered the household service of a prominent courtier.[132] One day when Michael III was having trouble with a high-spirited horse, Theophilitzes suggested his personal groom be summoned: Basil performed his job ably, breaking the horse and winning the emperor's admiration. At Michael's order, Basil was enrolled in the imperial guards and left Theophilitzes' household for service in the emperor's stable.[133] We know that Michael was fond of horses and racing, and Basil used this to ingratiate himself into the emperor's intimacy. The rest is history, as they say. We note finally that Basil's new protector also arranged a suitable marriage, even though by now Basil was already married.

Grumel, "Byzance et Photius dans les légendes slavonnes des saints Cyrille et Méthode," *EO* 37 (1934), 341–53, here 351–52.

[128] *Vita Theophanis* (*BHG* 1789), Theoph. 2, 7.2–29.

[129] Sym.Log. 233.8–9: ἐν τῇ ἰδίᾳ χώρᾳ προσεκολλήθη δουλεύειν στρατηγῷ Μακεδονίας. Cf. the insightful analysis of H. G. Beck, *Ideen und Realitäten in Byzanz* (London, 1972), XI, 6 ff.

[130] Sym.Log. 233.10–234.3. R. J. Macrides, *ODB,* I, 19–20 and 22.

[131] ἐδούλευεν τὸν Θεοφιλίτζην, Sym.Log. 234.4. Cf. *V. Bas.* 224.18–20.

[132] Sym.Log. 234.4–17.

[133] δουλεύειν ἐν τοῖς ἵπποις αὐτοῦ, Sym.Log. 230.6–22.

St. Evarestos showed signs of being a very promising young man in his native Galatia, and so was taken to Constantinople by his father when he was around twenty-three years old. There they stayed in the household of "one of the men who are officials and who are well off."[134] Not coincidentally, this man, a member of the Bryennios clan who would one day rise to patrician, was related: his wife was the future saint's kinswoman.[135] The Constantinopolitan relative was so pleased by the young man's character and intelligence that he kept him in his household when Evarestos' father returned to Galatia a few days later. Evarestos was enrolled among his kinsman's leading servants.[136] Evarestos' entry into Bryennios' household brought with it court service: when Empress Theodora thereafter sent Bryennios on an embassy to the Bulgarians, Evarestos went with him.[137] Early on in the embassy, Evarestos decided on a monastic life and ended the promising beginning of another court career.

Two final cases underscore that some elements at least of this pattern continued into the late tenth and eleventh centuries. Symeon, the future Theologian, was sent from his native Paphlagonian village to Constantinople, where his kin dwelt. He attended school and, according to his biographer Niketas Stethatos, received only an elementary education. Nonetheless, his paternal uncle, who was a eunuch courtier (κοιτωνίτης) and enjoyed some influence with the young emperors Basil II and Constantine VIII, was struck by the young man's physical beauty, and obtained for his nephew the position of *spatharokouboukoularios*. Before abandoning the world, Symeon was even enrolled in the Senate.[138] Some two generations later, Emperor Michael IV came, apparently, from a Constantinopolitan family and was, like his brother, a moneychanger. He owed his rise to the fact that his brother, the eunuch John Orphanotrophos, was in service to Romanos Argyros, eparch of Constantinople, and that John followed his master into the palace when he ascended the throne. John introduced his handsome young brother, along with his other relatives, into imperial service and arranged for him to meet the empress, fostering a relationship that would bring Michael the purple. Again the scenario is similar: presence in Constantinople, youth and good looks, and a relative already in service to a high official.[139]

Presence at Constantinople was the *sine qua non* for all these careers. In several cases,

---

[134] παρὰ οἰκίαν ξενίζονταί τινος τῶν ἐν τέλει καὶ τῶν εὖ γεγονότων, *V. Evaresti* (*BHG* 2153), ed. C. Van de Vorst, "La Vie de S. Évariste, higoumène à Constantinople," *AnalBoll* 41 (1923), 288–325, here 300.9–20; age: ibid., 288.

[135] *V. Evaresti*, 300.22–23: ἐξαδελφιδοῦς γὰρ ἦν ὁ Εὐάρεστος τῆς γυναικὸς Βρυαινίου. The first word is in the nominative case: cf. the accusative ἀδελφιδοῦν in *Inventio et miracula S. Photinae* (*BHG* 1541m), ed. F. Halkin, CCSG 21 (1989), 118.216. On the problem of this relative's identity with Theoktistos Bryennios, see Winkelmann, *Quellenstudien*, 165–66.

[136] *V. Evaresti*, 300.23–31: . . . τοῖς πρώτοις ἑαυτοῦ τοῦτον ὑπηρέταις ἐγκαταλέγει. Cf. ibid.: ὑπηρεσία.

[137] Ibid., 301.10–15.

[138] *Vita Symeonis Theologi* (*BHG* 1692), ed. I. Hausherr, *Vie de Syméon le Nouveau Théologien par Nicétas Stéthatos*, Orientalia christiana 12 (Rome, 1928), 2–6.

[139] Psellos, *Chronographia*, Romanos III, 18.8–21, ed. S. Impellizzeri and S. Ronchey (Florence, 1984), 96–98; cf. E. Renauld, ed., vol. I (Paris, 1926), 44.5–45.23. The phrase τὸν μὲν πρὸ τῆς βασιλείας χρόνον ἔτι μειράκιον is ambivalent: Renauld and Ronchey translate it to mean that the βασιλεία in question was that of Romanos III; it could as well refer to that of Michael himself. In either case, the sentence means Michael was still young when he entered imperial service. Cf. Skyl. 390.71–90.

physical appearance allied with talent to provide the tools for entry into the court milieu. All our courtiers on the make were young, in their teens or twenties. But the key for many a young man was kinship or marital affinity with someone already at court. When it was lacking, adoption into a family that itself was in service to a courtier or directly at court served a similar purpose. With his new kin's introduction, Basil I was able to enter the household of a courtier at a level that looks a lot humbler than the palace stewards we examined above. Constantine and Evarestos also entered the households of powerful men at court, whereas Michael IV, Symeon, and Theophanes had kin who held the ear of the emperor or empress. Marriage cemented relations of power and patronage. Kinship, both spiritual and biological, good looks, talent, households (οἰκίαι), and personal service (δουλεία) are the essential elements of this story.

The last two factors in particular would reward further research. Households and service were essential ingredients in the processes of integration into the Byzantine court. The author of the Life of Basil I even summarizes entry into the court in so many words.[140] Because he had authority within the logothete's household, young Constantine-Cyril had already taken an essential step into public life. His story underscores how our modern understanding of the boundary between private and public domains differs from that of Byzantium. Thus, in the wake of the revolt of Thomas the Slav, Stephen *ho epi ton deeseon* was charged with investigating illegal confiscations. In this connection he transferred a former vice-governor of the Kibyrrheotai theme into his own mansion at Constantinople, where he had him interrogated and beaten in the *triklinion* and then imprisoned in a cell there.[141] So too, about a century later, the *praipositos* summoned the factions into his own house, where he examined the service records which he kept at home and where he paid them their salaries from public funds.[142] In much the same way, the positive concept of *douleia*, "service" applies equally to public and private life. The term recurs constantly in works describing the court, government, and households. The concept echoes through acclamations chanted by courtiers at public events: "We are the *douloi* of the emperors."[143] The word occurs at least twenty-seven times, for instance, in Kekaumenos, where it shifts indifferently between service of the emperor or the state and service of other men.[144]

So a preliminary investigation of the social world of the Byzantine court has turned up some broader trends as well as new problems. After a first effort to track the terminology of the court, the issue was broached of the court's place within the wider patterns of Byzantine social history. Some light has fallen on the surprisingly substantial size and

---

[140] *V. Bas.* 224.20–225.1: δι᾽ αὐτοῦ ἀξιοῦντος εἰσοικισθῆναι καὶ πρὸς δουλείαν δοθῆναι τῶν ἐμφανεστέρων τινί. On the problem of the household and this society, see P. Magdalino, "The Byzantine Aristocratic *Oikos,*" in *The Byzantine Aristocracy,* 92–111.

[141] *Vita Antonii iunioris* (*BHG* 142), ed. A. I. Papadopoulos-Kerameus, Συλλογὴ Παλαιστινῆς καὶ Συριακῆς ἁγιολογίας, *Pravoslavnij palestinskij sbornik* 19.3 [57] (St. Petersburg, 1907), 209.27–210.28.

[142] *De cer.* 2, 56, Reiske 807.1–33; cf. McCormick, *Eternal Victory,* 223–25.

[143] E.g., *De cer.* 1, 52 (43) and 78 (60), Vogt II, 32.10–11 and 128.30–31.

[144] Ed. G. Litavrin, *Sovety i rasskazy Kekavmena* (Admonitions and Anecdotes of Kekaumenos) (Moscow, 1972), 319, s.v. On the varying meanings and connotations of δουλεία in this period, see A. P. Kazhdan, "The Concept of Freedom (*eleutheria*) and Slavery (*douleia*) in Byzantium," in *La notion de liberté au Moyen Age: Islam, Byzance, Occident* (Paris, 1985), 215–26, esp. 219–22.

the spatial configuration of this human group. Certain of its institutional and social sub-groups and subcultures have emerged with clarity; the existence of others has at least been detected. Problems connected with its members' wealth have surfaced. The ways in which people entered this milieu have illuminated the court's submerged microstructures of household and service and their interaction with ties of kinship, patronage, and power in shaping the social world of the Byzantine courtier. Enunciating these points along our itinerary prompts a final question: how might these realities have contributed toward the ethos of the Byzantine court?

8. A Court Ethos: Ideology, Social Psychology, and Ceremonial

Paradoxically, it is the very concrete buildings of the court, the Great Palace complex, that invite a few final reflections on ideas. We cannot underestimate the power of cultural continuity embodied by so great a set of buildings. Western medievalists have noted the correlation between the presence of a large cathedral and the topographical continuity of cities in an era of deurbanization. As Cyril Mango has observed, the tenth-century court was, in some ways, a living archaism right down to its old-fashioned Roman dining couches or *akkoubitoi* and the obsolete elements of its costume, like the Roman-style sandals.[145] Five hundred years before, the court of the Roman Empire had settled into a permanently sedentary mode in the very building complex in which tenth-century emperors and their advisors still lived. That this palace had never been substantially disturbed over the intervening centuries had important consequences simply in terms of the accumulation of archives and objects. Art historians have stressed how Constantinople functioned as a kind of perpetual font of artistic Hellenism.[146] Given that more recent historical research has uncovered dramatic discontinuities in the urban life of the imperial city, might we not prefer to seek that reservoir of late antique artistic Hellenism in the sumptuary arts of the Great Palace itself? Through countless changes of regimes, remodelings, and historic upheavals, the palace had accumulated and protected precious objects for half a millennium, like a kind of medieval Vatican Museum. And those precious *objets d'art* were regularly brought out of the imperial vaults to adorn ceremonies in a manner reminiscent of a spectacular art exhibition.[147] We know for certain that tenth-century courtiers could thus admire five-hundred-year-old thrones commissioned by Arcadius and Maurice, or a great silver platter bearing the name of Licinius, while Constantine VII could consult a Justinianic work on protocol.[148] The function of the

[145] Cf. C. Mango, "Daily Life in Byzantium," *JÖB* 31.1 (1981), 338–53.

[146] See, e.g., A. Grabar, "L'asymétrie des relations de Byzance et de l'Occident dans le domaine des arts au moyen âge," *Byzanz und der Westen,* ed. I. Hutter, Sitzungsberichte der Österreichischen Akademie der Wissenschaften 432 (Vienna, 1984), 9–24, esp. 19–23.

[147] See, for instance, the inventory of objects used to adorn a 10th-century audience: *De cer.* 2, 15, Reiske 570.16–575.21.

[148] Throne of Arcadius, *De cer.* 2, 15, Reiske 587.5; throne of Maurice and platter named ὁ Λικίνιος: *Oikonomides Taktikon,* ed. Oikonomidès, in *Listes,* 275.10 and 17. For an overview of the late Roman sources of *De cer.,* see M. McCormick, *ODB,* I, 596–97.

Great Palace itself as a dam against the river of change underscores the profound significance of the shift, when the Komnenoi physically relocated the court to the Blachernai palace.

By way of conclusion to this preliminary exploration of a large and complex social world, we would like to evoke the ever-changing rituals that recurred in those ancient halls and choreographed the court's public life. These ceremonies have been analyzed for the rich insights they yield into so many different facets of Byzantium, from the symbolism of power to the complicated institutions of the empire and their development. Their performance variations have indicated social change and revealed ephemeral political calculations.

Insofar as the emperor was able to manipulate them effectively, hoisting one supporter up past another, blocking a family's aspirations at a lower level, or promoting a whole class of dignitaries in honor of some recent success, the ceremonial apparatus of the Byzantine court looks like a magnificent tool for the social and political control of an ambitious and changing ruling class. The social psychology of the court lent itself to this function, for, in a general way, court life was conducive to a peculiarly dependent way of life. One key characteristic of the court's lifestyle was leisure, or, perhaps more accurately, a life largely geared to and commanded by the functions of the palace. How else can we explain the striking fact that, over and over again, the ceremonial protocols of the empire foresaw less than twenty-four hours notice when members of court were convoked for one or another function? Usually the orders went out in the afternoon or evening for the next morning.[149] These functions were not scheduled at "dead" times of the day, but during prime business hours; and attendance was not optional for members of the court resident at Constantinople.[150] In terms of daily life, this must mean that courtiers expected the unexpected, arranging their lives to attend the emperor not only on predictable, recurring occasions like religious feast days or coronation anniversaries, but also unexpectedly and at short notice. The experience of large numbers of officials being convoked at the drop of a hat must have powerfully reinforced a social psychology of dependence and imperial omnipotence. And when the courtiers were convoked to appear at a ceremony, they might not know what awaited them: the exaltation of their own success or the quiet humiliation of watching their rival's promotion.

It may well be that the vertical mobility of the Byzantine ruling class and its court allied with this social psychology of uncertain dependency to foster the great need for precedence in this large and disparate social group, for the carefully codified rankings of an ever-changing elite, which was elaborated, memorized, revised, and enforced by the specialized corps of professionally marginal men, the court eunuchs. The desire for unchanging stability was perhaps exacerbated, in ideology and aesthetics alike, by the very precariousness of each person's perch in an unstable society. For it is clear that even

---

[149] See, e.g., the evidence collected by D. Th. Beljaev, "Ežednevnye priemy vizantijskich carej i prazdničnye vychody ich v chram sv. Sofii v IX–XI vv." (Daily Receptions of the Byzantine Emperors and Their Processions on Feastdays to St. Sophia in the Ninth to Eleventh Centuries), *Zapiski imperatorskogo russkogo archeologičeskogo obščestva*, n.s., 6 (1893), i–xlvii and 1–199, here 22 note 2.

[150] McCormick, *Eternal Victory*, 198 and 200–202.

ceremonial order was sometimes threatened by pushing and shoving, by men struggling for recognition at the imperial banquets and processions. Constantine VII complains about *ataxia*; Philotheos castigates the disgraceful confusion that results from errors in precedence, even as he carefully and physically steers each rank-holder to his proper seat, and no other.[151] Subtle threats to precedence only emphasize its importance for defining the glamour and celebrity of public life for all beholders, in the words of Philotheos. For precedence, and the ceremonies in which it was enshrined, gave structure and stability to a Byzantine court, whose social composition and configuration were perhaps more open and fluid than we sometimes think. And it is perhaps no accident that precedence lists disappear from the Byzantine court in the century that saw the emergence of a new, different, and, in some respects, less open hierarchy of power based on kinship ties, even as the power of the eunuchs who had enforced the old system declined.

Dumbarton Oaks and Harvard University

Postscriptum. The order in which the names of the authors of this article would appear was the subject of amiable controversy between Alexander Kazhdan and myself. Physical proximity to the publisher had allowed him to gain the upper hand. His sudden death on 29 May 1997 changed that. Wherever he is, I hope my friend is smiling at the fact that I have finally managed to have the last word in one of the many animated discussions in which we both rejoiced.

M. McC.

---

[151] On disorder and ceremonies, see M. McCormick, "Analyzing Imperial Ceremonies," *JÖB* 35 (1985), 5; *Klet.* 83.7–9 and 21–24; 135.21–23.

Title and Income at the Byzantine Court

Nicolas Oikonomides

When speaking of titles, one thinks automatically of the aristocracy, if not of the nobility. But any distinguished social position should normally be accompanied by wealth and all its external signs: an adequate mansion, the appropriate dress, servants, lifestyle, and power. All members of the imperial court needed a large income, but the nature of this income, and the way in which it was obtained, changed radically from the time of the Macedonian dynasty of the ninth to tenth century to that of the Komnenoi of the twelfth, together with the mentality and the social structure. This study outlines these changes and proposes an interpretation,[1] a monetarist interpretation, thus inevitably a partial one. The basic premise is that in the eleventh century Byzantium underwent a period of shortage of precious metal because its needs increased while the supply remained practically unchanged.

(a) In spite of what Psellos says about the wealth accumulated by Basil II in 1025 (14.5 million gold coins), and in spite of the information concerning massive hoarding on the part of some ecclesiastical authorities,[2] Byzantium was then coming out of a thirty-five-year war with Bulgaria and had annexed that country, which had not yet known a monetized economy (the entire treasure of the Bulgarian tsar is said to have amounted to no more than 720,000 coins).[3] The new territories had been left to function on a financial system based on barter, but when, in the 1030s, taxes were required to be paid in cash, the Bulgarians joined the revolt of Peter Deljan.[4] It is clear that, with the conquest, the population of the empire had increased considerably, that the money economy prevailing elsewhere had started making inroads into the new territories, but that these were not monetized as fast as the Byzantine administration would have liked them to be.

(b) On the other hand, the eleventh and the twelfth centuries were periods of remarkable economic expansion, in Byzantium[5] as well as in the rest of Europe. This tendency was not seriously affected by the fall of Asia Minor to the Turks as, after the First Crusade, Byzantium recovered the control of the economically significant lowlands and

---

[1] I am grateful to Professor Angeliki Laiou for reading a draft of this paper and for commenting on it.

[2] Ioannes Skylitzes, ed. I. Thurn (Berlin, 1973), 402, 429: 231,000 nomismata hoarded by the metropolitan of Thessalonica, and 180,000 by Patriarch Alexios Stoudites.

[3] M. Hendy, *Studies in the Byzantine Monetary Economy, c. 300–1450* (Cambridge, 1985), 225.

[4] Skylitzes, 412.

[5] A. Harvey, *Economic Expansion in the Byzantine Empire, 900–1200* (Cambridge, 1989).

shores, limiting the invaders to parts of the Anatolian plateau. This expansion would automatically mean the necessity for higher levels of liquidity, in order to avoid resorting to the less flexible and more cumbersome process of barter and the inevitable reduction of the volume of exchanges.

Now, an increase in population and an increase in the volume of transactions not accompanied by any change in the credit and banking system inevitably creates the need for larger quantities of coined money to operate an economy such as the Byzantine one. And, as far as we can tell, there were no substantial new sources of precious metal—or, even if there was some new gold, it was certainly not enough for the ever-developing economy.[6] The Byzantine state had to face this reality and, being a very centralized organization, had to propose solutions, without necessarily having achieved high levels of economic thinking.

In what follows, and because of the nature of our sources, I focus on public finances and not on the economy as a whole, except to the degree in which it was affected by financial and monetary policies. Moreover, Byzantium was a centralized state, exercising control over all aspects of life, and its finances could not but reflect other, more general economic trends. The imperial finances largely regulated the circulation of coined money through the dialectical process of levying the state's share at the same time as compensating for services to the state. Public expenditure is thus at the center of our attention here.

In a medieval state, the two main consumers of public funds are the administration and the army, both headed by members of the aristocracy. Consequently the income of this aristocracy, although a relatively small percentage of the overall budget, is significant for our purposes, as it indicates the basic trends of the financial policies of the state. Moreover, we have some sources to study it and to evaluate its importance and repercussions on the economy and on society in general. The upper class was the model: some of its members and some who aspired to become its members certainly thought, already in these times, that what was good for the upper class was good for the whole empire.

The Macedonian aristocracy was financed by the emperor mainly through salaries in cash, the famous *roga*. On 24 March 950, Palm Sunday, Liutprand, the bishop of Cremona, attended the distribution of the yearly salaries to imperial officials in Constantinople.[7] In the large dining hall of the Nineteen Tables in the Great Palace, which normally seated 228 guests, Emperor Constantine VII Porphyrogennetos took his place behind an enormous head table covered with bags of gold coins and heaps of precious silk garments called *skaramangia*. Then the officials who filled the hall were invited to

---

[6] Charles Brand kindly draws my attention to the fact that new African gold is said to have been brought into Byzantium by the end of the 11th century, allowing the coinage reform of Alexios I Komnenos (P. Spufford, *Money and Its Use in Medieval Europe* [Cambridge, 1988], 168). But one has to keep in mind that the economic expansion persisted in the 12th century, constantly increasing the need of coined money.

[7] Liutprand, *Antapodosis*, VI, 10.

the table according to their rank, and received their yearly salary from the emperor's hand. First came the rector, the top official not belonging to the imperial family;[8] he received four *skaramangia* and an unspecified quantity of gold, the total being so heavy that he had to carry it on his shoulders, not in his hands. Then came the *domestikos* of the Schools (the general in chief of the Byzantine army) and the *droungarios* of the *ploimoi* (the chief admiral); they received even more, so much so that they had to get some help in order to drag the bags with their salaries behind them out of the room. Then, following the hierarchical order, came the *magistroi,* each of whom received 24 pounds of gold coins[9] (1,728 pieces of gold, weighing 7.68 kg) and two *skaramangia.* Then came the *patrikioi* with half of the above, then officials of lower grade who received smaller amounts, down to those who were limited to one pound of gold (72 pieces, of a total weight of 320 grams of gold).

This was what the emperor himself distributed. Those entitled to less than one pound received their salaries from a palatine official, the *parakoimomenos,* on subsequent days. The whole distribution was completed before Easter Sunday.

It is probable that what Liutprand writes contains inaccuracies, that he may not have understood all the intricacies of the Byzantine court system and the criteria according to which the amounts of the salaries were established. But the basic description is certainly very vivid and essentially correct: more important, the figures he quotes may be inaccurate but are not exaggerated.

Several Byzantine texts[10] confirm that the yearly salaries were distributed by the emperor himself, "with his own hands," in an act that stressed the personal relationship between the sovereign and his officials, and the complete dependency of the latter on the former. The emperor seems to have had full powers over the *roga*: he had to find ways to meet this yearly obligation (including, if necessary, melting gold objects from the palace);[11] he could lessen its amount[12] or arbitrarily withhold it altogether;[13] he could also increase it in order to please his officials or to please a specific individual.[14] The

---

[8] It seems, though, that the rector of the year 950 was Michael Lakapenos, the son of the deceased emperor Romanos Lakapenos. See R. Guilland, *Recherches sur les institutions de Byzance,* vol. II (Berlin-Amsterdam, 1967), 214.

[9] In spite of the existing uncertainties (Hendy, *Studies,* 337–38), I consider that the Byzantine pound (litra) weighed 320 grams.

[10] *Ecloga,* ed. L. Burgmann (Frankfurt, 1983), 224; Theophanes Continuatus, Bonn ed., 173, 259, 265; Zepos, *Jus,* I, 227, 623: Νέος Ἑλλ. 19 (1925), 154, 159; Leo the Deacon, Bonn ed., 100; Ioannes Scylitzes, 390, 483; E. Kurtz, *Die Gedichte des Christophoros Mitylenaios* (Leipzig, 1903), no. 8; Michael Attaliates, Bonn ed., 122, 142; Skylitzes Continuatus, ed. E. Tsolakes (Thessalonike, 1968), 133, 142; Anna Comnena, *Alexiade,* ed. B. Leib (Paris, 1937–76), I, 133–34.

[11] Theophanes Continuatus, 173.

[12] Michael Attaleiates, 60–61; Skylitzes Continuatus, 104; cf. Zepos, *Jus,* I, 638 (a diminished *roga* of 24 [instead of 72] nom. paid together with the *protospatharioi*); Nicephoros Bryennios, ed. P. Gautier, 258–59; Ioannes Zonaras, Bonn ed., 732–33.

[13] *Peira* of Eustathios Romaios (in Zepos, *Jus,* IV), 17.14.

[14] Leo the Deacon, 100: προῖκα τὴν ῥόγαν ἐπηύξησεν; Nicholas I, Patriarch of Constantinople, *Letters,* ed. R.J.H. Jenkins and L. G. Westerink (Washington, D.C., 1973), 362; Kekaumenos, *Sovety i rasskazy,* ed. G. G. Litavrin (Moscow, 1972), 266.

distribution of cash and precious garments (that were as good and as prestigious as cash, and interchangeable with it)[15] regularly occurred during the week before Easter.

In the Macedonian court system, salaries were paid to the top public servants as well as to holders of honorific titles. Public service provided a salary for as long as the individual held an office; honorific titles and their salaries were for life. As we shall see, there was more to these salaries than simply buying services and favors for the emperor. They had an important economic function and considerable repercussions on the social structure.

Salaries Paid for Services to the State

We shall ignore here the way in which some civil servants were paid—directly from the citizens who used their services. This practice is constantly attested throughout the Middle Ages and guaranteed substantial incomes; but these were low-level positions that had to be bought for a considerable price.[16]

In order to control corruption, the Isaurian emperors' puritanical reforms introduced, in the eighth century, the general principle that the top officials in each service were expected to receive from the imperial treasury a very important salary, so that they would be completely immune to external influence and able to inspire proper behavior in their subordinates.[17] This system of salaried top officials survived intact from the eighth through the eleventh century.

We know with relative precision which elements constituted the salary of a Macedonian high official thanks to the law (novel) of Constantine IX Monomachos issued ca. 1047 for the creation of the position of *nomophylax* (the law professor at Constantinople). After defining his position in the Senate and in the court hierarchy ("he will sit right after the *epi ton kriseon*," ἕξει δὲ καθέδραν εὐθὺς μετὰ τὸν ἐπὶ τῶν κρίσεων), and his right to visit the palace on specific days, the emperor added: "he will receive every year from my hand a salary of 4 pounds and one silk garment and one *baïon,* and he will have such and such food supplies" (καὶ ῥόγαν ἀνὰ πᾶν ἔτος λήψεται ἐκ ἡμετέρων χειρῶν λίτρας τέσσαρας καὶ βλαττίον καὶ βαῖον, σιτηρεσίων δὲ χάριν ἕξει τάδε καὶ τάδε).[18]

The income is divided into two parts: (a) the salary and the other high value objects

---

[15] Silk garments were added to the *roga* when the emperor was short of gold. Cf. Skylitzes Continuatus, ed. Tsolakes, 142: οὐ διὰ χρυσίου πᾶσαν, ἀλλὰ τὸ ἐνδέον σηρικοῖς ὑφάσμασιν ἀναπληρωσάμενος; or gold was added to cover a deficiency in silk garments: *De Cerimoniis aulae byzantine,* Bonn ed., 668–69.

[16] P. Lemerle, "*Roga* et rente d'état," *REB* 25 (1967), 81: the payments varied from 20 (notary of the *stratiotikon*) to 64 pounds (chartulary of the *genikon*); if we suppose that these officials had a yearly income of 300 nomismata (and in fact they probably had much more, as they were fiscal officials), this would represent an annual yield of 6–20 percent of the invested capital.

[17] *Ecloga,* ed. Burgmann, 166.

[18] Zepos, *Jus,* I, 623 = A. Salač, *Novella Constitutio saec. XI medii* (Prague, 1954), 25.

that accompany it, which are given to the official by the emperor himself, and (b) the food supplies, which he received from someone else, no doubt the fisc. The same division appears in a tenth-century novel saying that the judges received (a salary) "from the emperor's hand" and a *prosodion* (a subsistence allowance in kind).[19] It seems that this compensation in kind was relatively unimportant: for example, the imperial secretaries (*asekretai*), were entitled to 2 modioi (i.e., ca. 25 kg) of wheat per month or ca. 833 grams per day, a quantity sufficient to feed one person, and which corresponded to an additional revenue of not more than 2 gold coins per year.[20]

The main revenue of the *nomophylax* was what he received from the emperor's hand: 4 pounds of gold, 288 gold coins weighing ca. 1,280 grams; only one silk garment; and a *baïon*, literally a "palm branch," an object the nature of which Theodore Balsamon did not know in the late twelfth century.[21] Balsamon supposed that it might have been a palm branch made of a precious metal such as gold or silver. At any rate, we know that in the ninth to tenth century the emperor distributed on Palm Sunday to his officials real palm branches decorated with flowers and accompanied, according to the rank, by precious silver crosses or crosslets. Thus the *baïon* was a symbolic gift of a certain value.[22]

What other figures do we know relevant to the salaries of high court officials? There is a famous text, the tariff of the salaries of the *strategoi* and *kleisourarchai*, that is, of all high provincial commanders, which dates from the year 911–912.[23] Those of Asia Minor and of Thrace and Macedonia (the provinces that traditionally had belonged to the Late Roman *praefectura praetorio per Orientem*) received salaries that varied from 40 pounds for the *strategoi* of the Anatolikoi, Armeniakoi, and Thrakesioi, to 30 pounds for those of Opsikion, Boukellarioi, and Macedonia, to 20 for most of the others, except for those of the maritime themes who received 10 pounds and the *kleisourarchai* who received 5 pounds. It is interesting to note that the amounts of the salaries do not always follow the hierarchical order of their recipients.

There is no reason to doubt the veracity of these figures because they compare well with some other scarce information that we have. For example, the position of *strategos* of Taron, newly created in the early tenth century, was endowed with an annual salary of 20 pounds.[24] Also we know that the *roga* of the *hypertimos* in 1082 amounted to 20 pounds of (debased?) gold,[25] and that the salaries of judges under Andronikos I (1183–

[19] Zepos, *Jus*, I, 227 (945–959).

[20] Symeon Magister, Bonn ed., 673. I assume that we have here the *thalassios modios* (12.8 kg) and not the Constantinopolitan one (234 kg), which would yield unrealistically high quantities of grain to feed one household.

[21] Theodore Balsamon in G. Rhalles and M. Potles, Σύνταγμα τῶν θείων καὶ ἱερῶν κανόνων, vol. IV (Athens, 1854), 523–29.

[22] *De cer.*, 170; N. Oikonomidès, *Les listes de préséance byzantines des IXe et Xe s.* (Paris, 1972), 197, cf. 217.

[23] *De cer.*, 696–97.

[24] Constantine Porphyrogenitus, *De administrando imperio*, ed. G. Moravcsik and R.J.H. Jenkins, chap. 43, lines 68–69. It must be noted, though, that as the *strategos* was also a *magistros*, it is not clear whether the 20 litrai were the salary corresponding to the position of *strategos* or to the title of *magistros*. The latter point of view in Lemerle, "*Roga*," 83–84.

[25] Zepos, *Jus*, I, 369.

85) amounted to 40 or 80 pounds of "silver" (a gold/silver alloy?), an amount said to correspond to 13–26 pounds of gold.[26]

The salaries of the *strategoi* represent very considerable amounts, ranging from 12,800 grams to 1,600 grams of gold, which, together with the information about the *nomophylax* (being a professor, he was naturally paid less), confirms that Liutprand's figures were not exaggerated: after all, almost 13 kg of gold plus some very heavy garments constituted a considerable weight and anyone might need some help carrying them around.

This was not the only kind of income that the *strategoi* had. One of them, the *strategos* of Mesopotamia, did not receive any salary because he collected all the *kommerkion* of his province, while another one, the *strategos* of Chaldia, who lived in Trebizond, received only 10 litrai from the emperor "because he received another 10 litrai from the *kommerkion* [of his province]." Those were the two main entrances for oriental trade by land into the empire. For Mesopotamia we know that already in the ninth century there was a *strategos,* who had a seal of the same type as those of the *kommerkiarioi*[27]—a detail that shows that the administrative unit was from the beginning conceived as a fiscal unit.

Lastly, the *strategoi* of the Balkan themes to the west of the Strymon did not receive any salary, because they collected gratuities (*synetheiai*) from their own themes. We have no idea of the cumulative importance of these gratuities, but we assume that the western *strategoi* collected sums similar to those of their eastern colleagues. And, more important, they collected them directly from the taxpayer, without burdening the imperial budget. These were an extra burden for the Balkan populations, but undoubtedly not a very significant one.[28]

The *strategoi* received high salaries but also incurred heavy expenses.[29] They had to provide for their personal guard and for their personal administrative office, which were clearly distinguished from the military and administrative organization of the province. In 949 the personal suite (*proeleusis*) of the *strategos* of the Thrakesion (one of the best paid, according to the tariff) included at least two administrative assistants (*protomandator, protokankellarios*), his personal standard-bearer (*protobandophoros*), twelve [mounted] non-commissioned officers (*protodomestikoi, protokentarchoi*), and a hundred foot soldiers.[30] The salaries of these men would presumably eat up half the *strategos'* income. To this, one should add his numerous servants and the maintenance of his mansion. The *strategos*

---

[26] Nicetas Choniates, *Historia,* ed. J. van Dieten (Berlin-New York, 1975), 330; cf. J.-C. Cheynet, E. Malamut, and C. Morrisson, "Prix et salaires à Byzance," in *Hommes et richesses dans l'empire byzantin,* vol. II (Paris, 1991), 370.

[27] W. Brandes, "Überlegungen zur Vorgeschichte des Thema Mesopotamien," *Byzantinoslavica* 44.2 (1983), 171–77.

[28] We have no figures for the Byzantine population. But we can assume with some certainty that in the 10th century the Peloponnesos had approximately 1,500 military households (*De administrando imperio,* chap. 52; N. Oikonomides, "The Social Structure of the Byzantine Countryside in the First Half of the Xth Century," *Symmeikta* 10 [1996], 114–15, and, with a different estimate, A. Bon, *Le Péloponnèse byzantin jusqu'en 1204* [Paris, 1951], 115). It is not impossible that the nonmilitary population was several times that figure. Consequently, putting together an amount of, say, 20 pounds (1,440 nom.) would need less than 1/10 of a nomisma per household.

[29] Cf. Cheynet et al., "Prix et salaires," 367.

[30] *De cer.,* 663.

was quite an important lord inside his territories, with a retinue more important than that of other aristocrats, who all seem to have been surrounded by "their men."[31]

Salaries Paid to High Dignitaries

The honorific titles that defined one's place in society and one's degree of familiarity with the emperor also brought a yearly income, a salary or pension often related to an investment. The system has been studied by Paul Lemerle.[32] By investing a considerable amount of money in the state, an individual, approved by the emperor, could obtain a title with a yearly salary (*roga*) proportionate to his payment, with an annual yield of 2.31–3.47 percent of the invested capital, well below the usual interest rate of 6 percent. The yield was very poor, the more so because the capital paid was lost forever to the profit of the state—and became even worse when emperors such as Nikephoros Phokas temporarily diminished the amounts distributed to the senators.[33] Consequently this investment, at least at the moment when it was agreed upon, should not be studied as an economic venture; but it was accompanied by the acquisition of a title and eventually with participation in the Senate. This not only flattered one's vanity but also provided one with substantial social advantages that cannot be evaluated in money. What was closer to an economic venture was the possibility, under certain conditions, to increase the *roga* by supplementary payments at the rate of 9.72 percent, which was higher than the normal interest rate. But here again, the capital was lost forever, and consequently the economic profitability of the scheme could be questioned, although we know that many Byzantines subscribed to it. The economic arrangement would become more palatable with time and with the promotions or *roga* increases that the emperor distributed on festive days.

What is certain is that with this system the state was collecting back from its aristocrats part of their income. It must be stressed, though, that these payments to the state are attested only for certain titles, those called "imperial" and designating initially personal servants or bodyguards of the emperor: *mandator* (courier), *strator* (squire), *kandidatos*, *spatharios*, *spatharokandidatos*, *protospatharios* (bodyguards), the last of which opened to the individual the prestigious doors of the Senate. No such payment is attested for the higher dignities of *patrikios*, *anthypatos*, *magistros*, *vestes*, *vestarches*, and *proedros*, which might mean that these dignities were either given without initial investment, "for free," or after specific negotiation. Be that as it may, they were also accompanied by even higher salaries, the actual payment of which is clearly and repeatedly attested by the sources,[34] but

---

[31] H. G. Beck, *Byzantinisches Gefolgschaftswesen*, Sitzungsberichte der bayer. Akademie der Wissenschaften, Phil-hist. Klasse (1965).

[32] Lemerle, "*Roga*."

[33] Skylitzes, 274; Zonaras, 504–5.

[34] Apart from Liutprand, who speaks of the salaries of the *magistroi* and the *patrikioi*, cf. the following notes as well as the texts mentioning the loss of the *roga* of a *magistros* and of a *kouropalates* because the individual entered the monastery and lost the title and the *roga* (*Νέος Ἑλλ.* 19 [1925], 159; Michaelis Pselli, *Scripta minora*, ed. G. Kurtz and F. Drexl, vol. II [Milan, 1941], 92).

the amount of which is not: the *magistros* Niketas (10th century) received a *roga* because someone intervened in his favor with the emperor,[35] and Psellos speaks of a "poor" *patrikios*,[36] no doubt one who had not negotiated a substantial *roga* at the time of his nomination. In other words, I think that efforts to guess the exact amounts of the salaries of the higher dignities are futile.

The System

As is normal, the top administrative positions were usually occupied by individuals who already had high honorific titles; high titles were bestowed upon successful administrators and officers. The two salaries could be cumulated. And the result could be people (and, after them, families) with a very high yearly revenue in ready cash.

One should add that this revenue increased thanks to all kinds of tips and gratuities to which imperial officials were entitled: for example, they regularly received a gratuity from any new colleague—but as they also had paid such gratuities at their nomination, this revenue could be considered as a compensation for an already incurred expense. They benefited more substantially from the promotions or the increases of salary that the emperor usually distributed on festive occasions (almost always at his coronation) or in order to reward acts of valor. They also benefited from the ritual gifts the emperor made to his officials in order to increase their motivation before an important operation such as a military campaign: the *Book of Ceremonies* mentions the cash carried by the emperor while on campaign in order to make gifts to distinguished soldiers as well as the detailed description of the precious or less precious garments that an emperor should distribute, according to rank, to the officers of the thematic army when they prepared for a campaign.[37] Such gifts were called φιλοτιμίαι, gifts destined to kindle the officials' ambitions. Their amount was not fixed in advance, and consequently they were not part of the regular pay of the officials. But they were repeated with some regularity and thus constituted a substantial addition to one's regular income.

Emperor Basil II speaks of those who become wealthy and powerful in these terms:[38] the powerful man will keep his wealth for a long time and transmit it to his successors. If perchance he is a *patrikios*, he will transmit his power to his descendants; if perchance he is a *magistros* and *domestikos* of the Schools, his successors will be powerful, will enter the imperial entourage, and will extend their well-being for seventy or a hundred years. It is clear that in the eyes of this emperor material wealth was above all the result of high titles and high administrative positions.

It is a characteristic of Byzantium that in all times—and in the Macedonian period more than in others—extreme wealth came mainly from service to the state, not from business. In other words, wealth was intricately bound up with titles and imperial sala-

---

[35] *Νέος Ἑλλ.* 19 (1925), 154.

[36] K. Sathas, *Μεσαιωνικὴ Βιβλιοθήκη*, vol. V (Venice, 1876), 38.

[37] *De cer.*, I, 417, 486.

[38] Zepos, *Jus*, I, 264.

ries. And there were specific rules concerning the ways in which wealth could be used or invested on the part of an aristocrat: he was not allowed to participate in trades and crafts; he was not allowed any interest rate beyond 4 percent. Consequently aristocrats were obliged to invest their surplus in real estate, that is, houses in town or fields in the countryside. The return on such investments seems to have hovered above 5–6 percent every year.[39] Thus imperial salaries ended up by creating an aristocracy of landowners—the same aristocracy that the tenth-century emperors tried to contain with the well-known rural legislation.

In this tenth-century system, the state, by distributing titles and salaries, was providing the emperor's men membership in the aristocracy and the necessary material means. It was creating a clientele relationship between the emperor and the official (who received his salary from the emperor's hand), and between the official and his men, who benefited from the further distribution of this salary: a pyramidal structure, the kernel of significant further developments. But all was under the direct control of the emperor, and salaries were guaranteed only for a certain time or, at best, for life.

The state appears as the main motor that puts money into circulation and collects it back through taxation. This system could function only if considerable quantities of coined money were accumulated and kept inactive for long periods, from the time of tax collection (September and March) to the distribution of salaries (Easter for the officials and summer for the campaigning armies). This would be called, by some, a command economy.

The Eleventh-Century Crisis

The eleventh century experienced an acute economic and social crisis, one expression of which was a manifest shortage of gold: the Byzantine nomisma was devalued several times, beginning in the reign of Michael IV in the 1030s. According to the tempting—but not universally accepted—interpretation of Cécile Morrisson, initially these were devaluations of expansion due to the increase of the volume of exchanges. The same phenomenon appears in Italy at the same time. Later, in the 1070s, we have crisis devaluations that will cause the collapse of the Middle Byzantine numismatic system.[40]

The first manifestation of what I take to be the gold shortage appeared in the early

---

[39] Cf. the calculations proposed in my article Ἡ ἐπένδυση σὲ ἀκίνητα γύρω στὸ ἔτος 1000, *Τὰ Ἱστορικά* 7 (1987), 15–26. Another calculation can be made, based on the fact that (a) the rent (*pakton*) of first-class land was 1 nomisma per 10 modioi, while (b) its price was 1 modios per nomisma, and (c) the whole tax should correspond to 1/24 of the landowner's revenue: a land of, say, 240 modioi of the first class, worth 240 nomismata, provides its owner with a gross revenue of 24 nom. per year as *pakton*; minus 10 nom. for his taxes, he is left with 14 nom. of profit, which corresponds to 5.83 percent of the invested capital.

[40] C. Morrisson, "La dévaluation de la monnaie byzantine au XIe siècle: Essai d'interprétation," *TM* 6 (1976), 3–48; cf. P. Lemerle, *Cinq études sur le XIe siècle byzantin* (Paris, 1977), 285, 307 ff. This interpretation has been challenged by Hendy, *Studies*, 236, who thinks that both devaluations are due to the same reason (budgetary imbalance), and that the difference between them is "one of degree and not of nature." See also C. Morrisson, "Monnaie et finances dans l'empire byzantin, Xe–XIVe s.," in *Hommes et richesses* (as in note 26 above), II, 291–315, and the comment of J. Day, pp. 317–19.

eleventh century. The maximum allowed rates of interest increased by almost 39 percent in Byzantium, the basic one passing from 6 percent to 8.33 percent, the others following proportionately. In a revived, active money economy, interest rates may have fluctuated and certainly increased because of increased demand for cash, a situation echoed by other sources of the time, including Kekaumenos.[41]

Then the rates of selling *rogai* of honorific titles changed. This is clearly attested for the preferential rate in the *Peira*: for each pound of gold paid to the state, the beneficiary would now receive an annual salary of 6 (instead of 7) nomismata,[42] that is, he would receive an 8.33 percent return instead of 9.72 percent. There are other texts that show that this change was applied across the board in the system of titles, and was not a unique or exceptional phenomenon.[43] So the state, being presumably assured of the irresistible attraction of these titles, felt that it could "sell" them at a lower compensation rate, thus considerably increasing its own benefits. This effort to fill the treasury may also be at the origin of the special measures taken by two eleventh-century emperors, Constantine IX Monomachos and Constantine X Doukas, who for the first time in history opened participation in the Senate (i.e., gave high honorific titles) to some Byzantines to whom this had previously been forbidden: Lemerle proposes that Constantine IX opened the Senate to the administrators and Constantine X to the businessmen of Constantinople.[44] Whoever these new senators may have been, it is certain that most, if not all, of them had to acquire dignities and consequently boost the emperor's finances in exchange for their new titles and social position. In other words, these measures, which deeply affected the upper society, may have also had a fiscal motive, to attract to the state treasury the capital accumulated by these *nouveaux riches,* a capital that, until then, remained completely outside the *roga* system.

The crisis also affected the salaries of offices. We learn that under Isaac Komnenos (1057–59) the *rogai* of the *offikia* were curtailed for the first time.[45] Later Nikephoros III Botaneiates will be forced to interrupt payment of all dignitaries' and administrators' salaries.[46] This happened because this populist emperor distributed titles and offices *gratis* (προῖκα), with the result that the "expenses [of the state] outgrew manyfold its income" (πολλαπλασίους τὰς ἐξόδους τῆς εἰσόδου γενέσθαι). In other words, the whole system went bankrupt. Later Alexios I Komnenos will definitely abolish the yearly salaries that were traditionally paid to the holders of honorific titles.[47]

---

[41] Angeliki Laiou, "God and Mammon: Credit, Trade, Profit and the Canonists," in *Byzantium in the 12th Century,* ed. N. Oikonomides (Athens, 1991), 266–85.

[42] *Peira* 38.74; cf. Lemerle, *"Roga,"* 89–90.

[43] In the 10th century the payment necessary for a *spatharios* to become *protospatharios* was 18 pounds of gold (6 to become *spatharokandidatos* and 12 to become *protospatharios,* or 18 if he became *protospatharios* directly: *De cer.,* 692). In the 11th century (ca. 1056) this promotion was evaluated at 20 pounds (Μεσαιωνικὴ Βιβλιοθήκη, V, 210; cf. Lemerle, *"Roga,"* 84–88). This increase is roughly proportionate to the change in the price of the *roga* mentioned above: an investment of 18 pounds at the rate of 7 would give a revenue of 126; an investment of 20 pounds at the rate of 6 would give 120.

[44] Lemerle, *Cinq études,* 287 ff.

[45] Attaleiates, 61; Skylitzes Continuatus, 104: τὰς τῶν ὀφφικίων δὲ δόσεις αὐτὸς πρῶτος περιέτεμεν.

[46] Bryennios, ed. Gautier, 258–59: ἀξιώμασι καὶ τοῖς ὀφφικίοις ἐκ βασιλέως ἀνήκουσαι δωρεαὶ διὰ τῶν χρημάτων σπάνιν ὑπεκρούοντο.

[47] Zonaras, 732–33.

There are two new and interesting elements that appear in this text concerning the administrators: first, they also had to pay something in order to obtain their position; second, they could survive without receiving a complete salary. Obviously the administrative positions provided an income other than the salary. It seems that this practice was imposing itself from the second quarter of the eleventh century on, when the first signs of economic strain appear in Byzantium.

During the reign of Michael IV (1034–41) when finances were administered by his uncle, John the Orphanotrophos, the necessity to increase the revenues of the state is manifested by the measures taken in order to assure their quick collection. The Orphan-otrophos, according to the historians, "invented all roads to injustice"; "by selling the administrative positions and by giving to all a free hand to commit injustices, he filled the world with thousands of misfortunes, as the judges feared nothing when taxing the peasants, and no one controlled what they were doing."[48] It is clear from this text that the sale of offices was linked to arbitrarily increased fiscal charges on the part of those who collected it, the provincial judges.

Tax farming was not an innovation of the eleventh century; it is well attested until the seventh. But it seems that with the eighth century and the Isaurians, tax farming was severely limited if not altogether abolished. It took more than two centuries to come back. It is said that during the sole reign of Constantine VII (944–959), corruption had crept into the court and the wrong people were appointed to important positions, particularly because of Empress Helen and the *parakoimomenos* Basil who "provided that administrative positions be put up for sale,"[49] but this is clearly something done against the rules and sounds more like kickbacks than like farming out the positions. In the early eleventh century, the author of the *Peira* (8.14) specifies that all judges, tax collectors, *strategoi,* or those exercising any public office undertake service because they want it and "also give something" (παρέχοντες καί τινα)—that is, either some legal *sportulae* or some illegal kickbacks. What is certain, though, is that the author of the *Peira* does not envisage real selling of the top administrative positions.

The situation changed under John the Orphanotrophos, who practiced office farming at the highest level. Even though Empress Zoe decreed in 1042 that nominations to administrative positions should be made without purchase money,[50] the sale of top administrative offices is attested again in later times with specific examples that show how it was done. For example, at the time of Constantine X Doukas, an Armenian proposed to govern the fortress of Ani as *doux* of the theme without collecting the salary (σιτηρέσιον) that his position entailed; so he was appointed *doux.*[51] He made such savings in public spending (and, presumably, he kept a good part of the public income for himself) that the whole administration and defense of the province were wrecked and it became

---

[48] Skylitzes, 408–9: ὤνιον προτιθέμενος τὰς ἀρχάς, καὶ πᾶσι χαλινὸν ἐνδιδοὺς ἀδικίας, μυρίων συμφορῶν ἐνέπλησε τὴν οἰκουμένην, ἀδεῶς τῶν κριτῶν φορολογούντων τοὺς ἐντοπίους καὶ μηδενὸς ἐπιστροφὴν τιθεμένου τῶν γινομένων.

[49] Skylitzes, 237: ὠνίους τὰς ἀρχὰς ποιεῖν παρασκευαζόντων.

[50] Skylitzes, 422: ἀπριάτην τε τὰς ἀρχὰς γίνεσθαι καὶ μὴ ὠνίους, ὡς πρότερον.

[51] Attaleiates, 80–81.

easy prey to the Turks. From other texts we learn of the famous Nikephoritzes who was appointed judge of Peloponnesos and Hellas because he promised money—but his administration does not seem to have left any scars on the province.[52] To make up for any payments to the state, the provincial administrators naturally relied on the collection of taxes, usually done through subcontractors, who, according to Kekaumenos, "undertook the obligation to give to the governors what they collected from the poor, and who earned only sins while the others earned money."[53] The aristocrat at the top did not participate personally in the menial task of pressuring the taxpayer, but he made sure that others would do it for him.

Taking over other financial business for the state was always very lucrative but also entailed some risk. Kekaumenos describes how it was general belief in the eleventh century that all the major mansions in Constantinople were built with money gained by people who undertook the administration of state finances; but he also mentions the case of a *strategos* who tried an enterprise of the sort (managing the imperial domain [*episkepsis*] at Arabissos) and ended up with a deficit of 60 pounds of gold, with having his house confiscated, and with a prison term for himself.[54] This is business at a different scale than the tenth-century salaries. Compare the *deficit* of 60 pounds from one domain to the 40 pounds for the salary of the *strategos ton Anatolikon*. If a rather limited enterprise allowed one to envisage such a scale of business, much more could presumably be expected from the administration of a whole province. In the eleventh century, farming of offices was becoming extremely lucrative and went up to the top echelon of the administration: the old *roga* system was obviously getting outmoded.

The New System of the Komnenoi

The restoration of the empire came with the reign of Alexios I Komnenos (1081). The new regime renovated the administration as well as the title system in an effort to favor the already established aristocratic families or clans. The new hierarchy of titles was strictly reserved to individuals of high birth; the important administrative positions, to relatives of the emperor. Komnenian Byzantium looked very much like a big clan enterprise and differed sharply from the Macedonian empire, where administrators were selected according to the ruler's good pleasure but without any significant family requirements, often among the palace eunuchs. The personal relationship with the emperor was replaced by the family relationship.

The coinage system was also reformed. A new gold nomisma of a high degree of fineness was struck, the *hyperpyron*, that remained stable for quite some time. But the state continued to issue many divisionary coins.[55] At the same time, any significant dis-

---

[52] Attaleiates, 182; Skylitzes Continuatus, 155.

[53] Kekaumenos, 238: πακτονάριον καὶ πακτόνειν σεαυτὸν εἰς τὸ διδόναι τοῖς ἄρχουσιν, ἃ λαμβάνεις ἀπὸ τῶν πενήτων, καὶ σὲ μὲν κερδαίνειν ἁμαρτίας, τοὺς δὲ λαμβάνοντας ἀπὸ σοῦ κερδαίνειν χρήματα.

[54] Kekaumenos, 196.

[55] Cf. C. Morrisson, "La *logarikè*: Réforme monétaire et réforme fiscale sous Alexis Ier Comnène," *TM* 7 (1979), 419–64, esp. 462; Hendy, *Studies*, 513 ff. For the possible influx of gold from Africa, see above, note 6. See also the publications of C. Morrisson cited above, note 40.

cussion about the salaries either of the honorific titles or of the administrative positions disappears from the sources, at least after Alexios Komnenos' very early years: he abolished all salaries. Farming remained active for tax collection, and allowed enormous profits, and unbelievable excesses.[56] In this first phase of the Komnenian state, services were rewarded by donations of land or fiscal revenues or both. Let us take some well-known examples.

In 1084 Alexios I's brother, the *protosebastos* Adrianos Komnenos, had been given the right to collect directly and for his own profit all the taxes paid by the whole peninsula of Kassandra.[57] In fact, this was the application of a known fiscal technique, attested since the late ninth century, providing for the cession to an individual of the taxes due from a property, usually his own. The essential difference in 1084 was the size of the donation (a whole peninsula) and the fact that the tax-producing units probably did not belong to the beneficiary of the donation at all. This was a clear case of devolution of fiscal revenues. In other words, (instead of a salary?) the *protosebastos* was given the right to directly collect the fiscal revenues of a vast province. A similar apanage in the region of Stroumitza was given in the mid-twelfth century to the caesar John Rogerios.[58]

Another case, not very different but known with more details:[59] Nikephoros Melissenos, after having attempted to take the throne in 1081, reached an agreement with Alexios Komnenos and abandoned his ambitious plan in exchange for the title of caesar and for "the city of Thessalonica." In fact, after Alexios' coronation, Nikephoros was named caesar and was given the fiscal income of Thessalonica and its region. This income was made up of the taxes and of some domains that belonged to the state. In order to create his own clientele, Melissenos, with the approval of the emperor, ceded part of the domains to some of his friends and followers, such as a certain Samuel Bourtzes, who was his relative and who had probably lost his properties in Asia Minor to the Turks. In other words, the emperor provided his caesar with a vast domain and with important fiscal income, and the latter used this source of wealth in order to support his own men, thus creating a social pyramid of mutually depending interests. This is the time when a similar and rare pyramid at the social level appears: under Alexios I we find state officials who declare themselves to be the servants of another high official, who in turn is qualified as the servant of the emperor.[60]

Another very well known case is the one of Leo Kephalas: a high official, he obtained from successive emperors the property rights over several domains with partial tax exemption; in 1086, after having successfully defended Larissa against the Normans, he obtained a whole village, Chostiane, with a complete tax exemption; and in 1089, the

---

[56] E.g., in 1082, we learn that from a land that paid a basic tax of 19 nomismata, the judge collected another 20 for his *antikaniskon* (Ἐπ.Ἐτ.Βυζ.Σπ. 3 [1926], 125), i.e., for the *adaeratio* of the traditional food basket to which he was entitled and which, half a century earlier, would have consisted of one loaf of bread, one chicken, half a measure of wine, and some fodder for his horse (*Actes de Saint-Pantéléèmon*, ed. P. Lemerle, G. Dagron, and S. Ćirković [Paris, 1982], no. 3, line 31). Another case: in 1104, an aristocrat, Demetrios Kamateros, farmed out the taxes of Thrace and Macedonia, having promised to double their fiscal revenue (Zepos, *Jus*, I, 334).

[57] *Actes de Lavra*, ed. P. Lemerle, A. Guillou, N. Svoronos, and D. Papachryssanthou (Paris, 1970), no. 46.

[58] B. Ferjančić, "Апанажни посед кесара Јована Рогерија," *ZRVI* 12 (1970), 193–201.

[59] *Actes de Docheiariou*, ed. N. Oikonomidès (Paris, 1984), no. 4.

[60] N. Oikonomides, Οἱ αὐθένται τῶν Κρητικῶν τὸ 1118, in Πεπραγμένα τοῦ Δ' Διεθνοῦς Κρητολογικοῦ Συνεδρίου, vol. II (Athens, 1981), 308–17.

right to transmit this property and privileges to his children and descendants.[61] While this happened, Kephalas was also mounting in grade: from *vestarches* (1082) to *magistros* (1083) to *proedros* (1086, 1089). On the other hand, Kephalas also exercised military functions, from *primikerios ton vestiariton* (1082) to governor of Larissa, to *katepano* of Abydos (1086). One forms the impression that these donations were meant to boost his revenue in a way befitting his social status.

Finally, a few words about the properties of Gregory Pakourianos, the chief general of Alexios I Komnenos' armies, described in the typikon that he issued in 1083 for his monastery at Petritzos. Most originate from imperial donations, a few are his own acquisitions, but most were previously properties of the state. The state donated to Pakourianos the right to collect from his properties the fiscal revenue that was defined at the time of the donation, but reserved to itself the right to collect any further revenue that might be created if Pakourianos improved them.[62] In other words, the state donated to Pakourianos specific amounts of fiscal revenue—something very similar to a salary, with a fundamental difference in the way in which it was collected.

This whole concept of society and of economic compensation is based on a scheme close to the feudal one and differing in substance from the *roga* system: it is based on concessions of land or of state revenue either for life or forever. Of course, as in all Byzantine institutions, this was not a complete novelty; these forms of donation existed well before the arrival of the Komnenoi to power. They are the various kinds of λογίσιμα and σολέμνια, that is, concessions, one way or the other, of fiscal revenues to private individuals or institutions, described in detail in the Fiscal Treatise of the Marciana; these existed already before the reign of Leo VI (886–912), who tried to control and organize them.[63] What changed was the extent and frequency with which they appear: what used to be a special favor became part of the system; what was mainly done to benefit ecclesiastical institutions became massively accessible to lay aristocrats; what used to be an exception became the norm of the twelfth century. From the social point of view, this served the important aristocratic families and clans well, whose predominant position received further economic confirmation. From the economic point of view, we have a new set of rules affecting the circulation of money, or at least part of it.

The regular distribution of precious garments seems also to have stopped—it is not mentioned in the sources, as far as I know. In the eleventh and twelfth centuries, silk production had greatly proliferated, especially in the western provinces,[64] and high-quality silks were presumably less of an imperial monopoly. The precious garments are mentioned as gifts. Gregory Pakourianos had received several such presents (that he finally bequeathed to his monastery at Petritzos) from Alexios I Komnenos and from the *sebastokrator* Isaac Komnenos, usually upon his return from an important military victory; these garments are called "imperial" and of "highest value" (βασιλικὰ τιμαλ-

[61] *Actes de Lavra*, nos. 44, 45, 48, 49.

[62] Lemerle, *Cinq études*, 181–83.

[63] F. Dölger, *Beiträge zur Geschichte der byzantinischen Finanzverwaltung*, Byzantinisches Archiv 9 (Leipzig, 1927), 117–18.

[64] D. Jacoby, "Silk in Western Byzantium before the Fourth Crusade," *BZ* 84–85 (1991–92), 452–500.

φέστατα), thus showing that the emperor still disposed of top-quality silks; some of them the emperor was wearing himself and gave them to Pakourianos, who was very much flattered by the gesture.[65]

The period of Alexios I Komnenos was an intermediary one and presented some feudalizing features that will disappear later. In the twelfth century state there are substantial changes in the pay of the armed forces, especially in the financing of the reservists of the provinces.[66] The Komnenoi applied the system of *pronoia/oikonomia* for maintaining a provincial cavalry. The system appears already under Alexios I Komnenos and is generalized by Manuel I (1141–80). It is based on the lifelong concession to the soldier of a revenue of the state, usually a number of taxpayers and a quantity of land, whence the soldier will extract all revenues that the state would otherwise have extracted, usually taxes and land rents. These lands return to the state after the soldier's death. In normal circumstances, the *pronoiarios* serves in the army with no salary at all. His income is expressed by a fixed amount of gold coins, the *posotes,* but in fact most of it comes in kind, in the form of a part of each year's crop.[67] The procedure is only partially monetized.

This system of conditional donations of fiscal revenue to individuals in lieu of a salary came to replace, to a large extent, the system of the *roga* in ensuring the functioning of the state: first, in the late eleventh century and under Alexios I Komnenos, in the form of permanent donations of lands and tax exemptions to the few of the upper level; then, already under Alexios I but mainly under Manuel I, it took the form of the *pronoia* and became accessible to larger numbers, including the few of the upper level, with the essential difference that now the donation was not made forever but only for a lifetime and was under the constant control of the emperor. Thus the centralized character of the government was asserted once again.

At the same time, part of what used to be "big government" passed to private or semi-private hands. Some imperial domains, which used to produce a revenue directly for the state coffers, were transformed to *pronoiai,*[68] thus skipping the cumbersome administration and bringing the user of the revenue, the soldier, in direct contact with the producer, the taxpayer.

One must stress here that these changes affected only part of the public finances. For the rest, taxation was still collected in cash. The Komnenian state appeared to be wealthy for its times, disposed of large quantities of ready cash, and was able to finance its external policies lavishly and to hire, when necessary, large mercenary armies.

[65] L. Petit, "Le typikon de Grégoire Pakourianos," *VizVrem* 11 (1904), Priloženie 1, 14, cf. 53.

[66] The standing army of mercenaries is attested in both time periods that we are studying: they were professional, fully equipped soldiers, who received a salary in order to be constantly ready to participate in military operations. As they make no difference from one period to the other, we shall ignore them in what follows.

[67] I have discussed this problem in *TM* 8 (1981), 354. Recently it has been reexamined with overoptimistic conclusions by M. Bartusis, *The Late Byzantine Army: Arms and Society, 1204–1453* (Philadelphia, 1992), 172–73.

[68] N. Oikonomides, Ἡ διανομὴ τῶν βασιλικῶν ἐπισκέψεων τῆς Κρήτης (1170–1171) καὶ ἡ δημοσιονο-μικὴ πολιτικὴ τοῦ Μανουὴλ Α΄ Κομνηνοῦ, *Πεπραγμένα τοῦ Β΄ Διεθνοῦς Κρητολογικοῦ Συνεδρίου,* vol. III (Athens, 1968), 195–201.

An Attempt to Compare and to Understand

In the Macedonian system, the state is ever present; it functions as a pump that puts into circulation the coined money and collects it back in the form of taxes. The system of the *rogai* distributed to the high dignitaries and, to a certain degree, to the provincial army is almost completely monetized,[69] and its functioning requires the use of large amounts of coins, especially gold coins: each nomisma goes from the taxpayer to the tax collector, to the treasury, and from the treasury to the dignitary or to the state official or to the soldier in the form of a *roga*; part of it will in turn be distributed to subordinates, and the rest will be spent for the purchase of goods. This circulation, operated at the slow rhythm of public administration, condemns huge amounts of money to long periods of immobility.

In the Komnenian system this role of the state in the economy is phased down. Part (only *part*) of the public finances is demonetized. The state always controls taxation, fixes its amount on paper, and tries to enforce its collection in a spirit of equity and in cash. But large chunks of the state's financial activity now seem to be outside this process. The state is no longer the motor for all money circulation. A substantial part, at least of the tax money, does not follow the slow itinerary that kept it unproductive for the better part of the year.

The dignitary, the public official, or the soldier collects his revenue directly from the taxpayer. In this process, cash is used less than in Macedonian times, when the tax collector insisted on the *charagma*. A private person who is entitled to collect directly from the peasants can always collect part of his income in kind, either in order to feed his household and servants and, eventually, his private militia, or because he finds that the rent in kind, the *morte*, is more profitable than the rent in cash (*pakton*). This automatically entails a more intensive exploitation of the resources and a better marketing of the agricultural surplus, which is now available in larger concentrations than in the time of the small landowners. Moreover, officials or soldiers can start spending their income right away, without any administrative delays. This is a considerable increase in the efficiency of money. Neither officials nor soldiers require any salary from the state.

Let me conclude after repeating that this is an attempt to propose a partial explanation of phenomena that are by nature extremely complex, and that while the limited supply of precious metal was not the only problem of eleventh-century Byzantium, it was one of the problems.

I believe that already in the ninth and tenth centuries Byzantium had a vastly monetized economy and public finances, as can be seen in the lives of saints of the period, in

---

[69] I mean the salaries that were paid by the state to all thematic soldiers who participated in campaigns; and the obligation to pay the *strateia* for the holders of *stratiotika ktemata* who, for some reason, did not participate in military operations. For the rest, it is known that the subsistence of the thematic soldiers was financed by partial tax exemptions granted to their own lands. I have described my understanding of the system in "Middle Byzantine Provincial Recruits: Salary and Armament," in *Gonimos: Neoplatonic and Byzantine Studies Presented to L. G. Westerink at 75* (Buffalo, N.Y., 1988), 121–36.

which almost all attested exchanges are described as being done with cash,[70] and from the very clear cases of tax collecting and of salary paying that we know. But the efficiency of money, that is, the speed with which it circulated, was relatively limited. This was possible in a relatively slow economy.

In a context of economic expansion, further needs were created and a more versatile usage of cash was necessary. Faced in the eleventh century with the inadequacy of its precious metal reserves, the Byzantine state tried several solutions. The traditional *roga* of the tenth century was replaced by other forms of compensation meant to stabilize the economy while stepping aside from part of the money circulation—by demonetizing a sector of the public finances, and by ceding to aristocrats and to the military reservists properties and/or privileges and *pronoia* grants. On the one hand, the volume of cash pinned down by the taxes/salaries system diminished; on the other, the efficiency of cash and its availability for other economic functions not related to the state increased. Some would say that this was less of a command economy but not quite a market economy.

University of Athens

---

[70] I have put together the relevant texts in Σὲ ποιὸ βαθμὸ ἦταν ἐκχρηματισμένη ἡ μεσοβυζαντινὴ κοινωνία, in *Ροδωνιά: Τιμὴ στὸν Μ. Ι. Μανούσακα*, vol. II (Rethymnon, 1994), 363–70.

Daedalus and the Nightingale:
Art and Technology in the Myth of the Byzantine Court

James Trilling

Traditional absolute monarchy has a double nature. There is the acquisition and exercise of power, and there are the physical and intellectual trappings of power. The court is where they come together, the place where symbol and reality are most densely intertwined. The courtly art par excellence is the ceremony, a kind of theater in which every spectator is also a performer, and the performer is inseparable from the role. With worldly success and sometimes life itself at stake, the role-playing extends far beyond ceremony in the restricted sense. In the endless game of precedence, even the most trivial words and actions reverberate.

Every court creates its own legend. The elements are refinement, sycophancy, intrigue, splendor, complacency, learning and patronage, bureaucracy, debauchery, and fear. The permutations are endless. In some cases historical records balance and correct the legend. For Byzantium they do not. In art, especially, the legend will always be more compelling than any reality we can reconstruct. Contemporary texts evoke a world of mechanical singing birds and levitating lion-thrones whose quality of workmanship and distinctive artistic "flavor" we can never know.

Assuming that secular court art is a meaningful category in Byzantine terms, and that some of it still survives, how can we identify it? What, for that matter, do *we* mean by court art? Should we limit the term to art that depicts the imperial family, or that clearly asserts or buttresses some aspect of imperial ideology or the internal structure of the court? Or shall we use it more loosely, to mean any art commissioned by, or presented to, the emperor? a member of the imperial family? or anyone holding a title or position at court? Subject matter and patronage aside, can we simply equate court art with whatever we judge to be the best of Byzantine secular art? Or does court art differ in some fundamental (though not necessarily obvious) visual way from the much broader category of luxury art? The chronicler Theophanes was born to great wealth. How did the luxury goods he enjoyed on his family estate differ from the ones he enjoyed as a courtier? How did those, in turn, differ from goods reserved for the emperor's own use? And how can we hope to answer these questions from the pitiful remnant of such objects still in existence?

The obvious answer is to look for other sources of evidence. Court art tends to be exquisite and self-referential, reflecting the idea of the court as a world unto itself. This "courtly" stereotype, found in many unconnected traditions, goes along with a very high degree of pictorial inclusiveness. Even things unconnected with what we all too easily call the "real" subject are thought worth recording in meticulous detail. As a result we know exactly what the courts of the Safavids or the Tudors or the Duc de Berry looked like, or at the very least, what their members wanted to think (and wanted other people to think) they looked like (Fig. 1).[1] By this principle, we might expect the political and religious art of the Byzantine court to contain a good deal of "incidental" detail about the courtly environment, including the objects in daily and ceremonial use there. Unfortunately it does not. Byzantine art abounds with representations of emperors and empresses, shown either semi-allegorically with heavenly figures or realistically in an earthly setting. Yet it would not be much of an exaggeration to say that the entire surviving body of Byzantine pictorial art tells us less about the material culture of the Byzantine court than one well-chosen Persian miniature tells us about the Persian court.

Not only are we left in ignorance of Byzantine imperial taste in precious weapons, drinking vessels, musical instruments, and the like, we are not even given a setting in which to imagine them. Deprived of the setting, we remain ignorant of whole categories of things that might have embellished it: furniture, rugs, curtains; decorative painting, mosaic, and stonework. It is enough to make us look back to Justinian and Theodora in San Vitale as a model of inclusiveness. The one exception is imperial costume, jewelry, and other personal regalia. Here the Middle Byzantine documentation is ample; the portrait of Nikephoros III (1078–81) in the Paris Chrysostom manuscript includes eight or nine different textile patterns (Fig. 2).[2] Still, what the painter leaves out is as important as what he includes. There is one example of a medallion silk, but from the pictorial record alone we could not know that these were the Byzantines' greatest contribution to the history of textile design.[3] Many other Byzantine textile patterns, masterpieces of the silk weaver's art, are unrepresented in painting or mosaic and would be lost to us if a few precious fragments had not survived (Figs. 3, 4).[4]

Another approach is to extrapolate from religious or political to secular art on the basis of style. The Romanos ivory in the Cabinet des Médailles (Fig. 5) virtually defines the religious side of the Middle Byzantine courtly ideal, with its precision and elegance, fusion of heavenly and earthly authority, and emphasis on detail in the depiction of regalia.[5] The casket in the treasury of Troyes cathedral (Fig. 6) comes closest to capturing these qualities in secular form.[6] In execution it appears somewhat simpler and more static, but the comparison is hardly fair. The Romanos plaque is static in its very nature—style and content fuse perfectly—while in the casket there is a clear attempt to

---

[1] Fogg Art Museum, 1958.76. See Stuart Cary Welch, *Wonders of the Age: Masterpieces of Early Safavid Painting, 1501–1576* (Cambridge, 1979), 181.

[2] Paris, Bibliothèque Nationale, Coislin 79, fol. 2. Ioannis Spatharakis, *Corpus of Dated Illuminated Greek Manuscripts to the Year 1453* (Leiden, 1981), no. 94.

[3] J. Trilling, *The Medallion Style* (New York, 1985).

[4] Otto von Falke, *Kunstgeschichte der Seidenweberei* (Berlin, 1913).

[5] Adolf Goldschmidt and Kurt Weitzmann, *Die byzantinischen Elfenbeinskulpturen* (Berlin, 1934), vol. II, no. 34.

[6] Ibid., vol. I, no. 122.

1 Nighttime in a palace. Attributed to Mir Sayyid-'Ali. Miniature from a manuscript of the *Khamsa* of Nizami, Persian, 1539–43. Cambridge, Mass., Fogg Art Museum, 1958.76. Gift of John Goelet

2　Emperor Nikephoros III Botaneiates enthroned. Miniature from a manuscript of the
homilies of St. John Chrysostom, 1078–81. Paris, Bibliothèque Nationale, Coislin 79, fol. 2

3   Silk textile with lions, late tenth or early eleventh century.
Cologne, Diocesan Museum, inv. no. p392

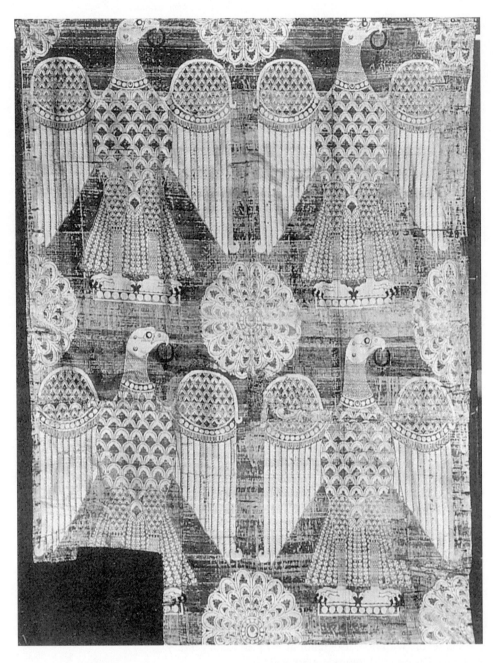

4   Silk textile with eagles (the "Shroud of St. Germain"), probably late tenth century. Auxerre, Musée Saint–Germain (photo: Giraudon Art Resource)

5 Christ crowning Emperor Romanos and Empress Eudokia, ivory, mid–tenth century.
Paris, Cabinet des Médailles (photo: Hirmer Fotoarchiv)

6 Lion hunt (front panel of a casket), ivory, probably tenth century. Troyes, cathedral treasury (photo: Hirmer Fotoarchiv)

7   The Rape of Europa (detail from the lid of the Veroli casket), ivory, tenth century. London, Victoria and Albert Museum, no. 216–1865

8   Istanbul, Hagia Sophia, northwest bay, arcading above the gallery with decoration in opus sectile, sixth century

9   Istanbul, Hagia Sophia, nave, southwest face of northwest pier,
sixth century

10 Sardonyx cup, tenth century? Venice, Treasury of San Marco
(photo: Fondazione Giorgio Cini)

adapt a static tone to dynamic themes. Given the basic contradiction, the artist has succeeded very well.

These works are impressive, but they are not fun. They depict an airless, hieratic world of balance and dignity, restraint and repetition, in which individuality is meaningless, spontaneity unthinkable, and life is lived in the stately rhythms of imperial ceremony. Their real-life counterpart is the ceremonies themselves, which we are told derived a great part of their power from blocks of single colors: rank upon rank of courtiers, each wearing the same costume.[7] We should nonetheless be careful not to exaggerate the aesthetic element in Byzantine ceremony, or the ceremonial element in Byzantine aesthetics. The temptation is strong because so much of the surviving Byzantine court art corresponds to our idea of ceremony. But because we encounter ceremony so rarely in our daily lives, it is easy to invest it with more glamour than the reality can bear.

Except in the military and certain religious traditions, the closest we come to ceremony on a regular basis is probably an academic procession. At the same time, we may absorb an idea of ceremony that is filtered through the performing arts. For sheer drama, what actual church service can compete with the end of the first act of Puccini's *Tosca?* As a procession fills the church to the sound of a *Te Deum,* Scarpia, dreaded leader of the secret police, dispatches his henchmen on their sinister errands; then, with the words, "Tosca, you make me forget God!" turns and joins the ever-stately procession as the music swells to a climax. It is not a *real* ceremony, but that is just my point. Artists are free to imitate, co-opt, and reshape ceremony in any way they like, as an end in itself or a counterpoint to something else. A team of highly specialized professionals can turn a "ceremony" into a spectacle of extraordinary power. In the few cases where an actual ceremony has this kind of power, it is almost certain to be strictly limited in scope, duration, and number of participants. And with good reason. The uncannily precise drill performed by the guard at the Tomb of the Unknown Soldier is as far beyond the reach of courtiers as an Olympic performance is beyond the reach of a weekend figure skater. We should seek our models for Byzantine ceremony elsewhere: in church services, academic processions, and for more spectacular occasions the pageantry surrounding the Sienese Palio.

In a recent article on the *Book of Ceremonies,* Averil Cameron gives, as one of the basic elements of Byzantine ceremony, "movement, whether real or symbolic, between sacred and profane contexts."[8] It would be hard to overstate the importance of symbolic movement for the aesthetics of Byzantine court ceremony, yet this importance is largely negative. It governs what a ceremony looks like, because it governs what a ceremony *does not have to look like.* So long as the emperor and his entourage get from place A to place

---

[7] Constantin VII Porphyrogénète, *Le livre des cérémonies,* trans. and ed. Albert Vogt (Paris, 1935), vol. I, 19, 73, 119, 169; vol. II, 2, 48, 94, 112, 160. For an overview of Byzantine court costume, its uses and impact, see Adele La Barre Starensier, *An Art Historical Study of the Byzantine Silk Industry,* Ph.D. diss. (Columbia University, 1982), esp. chap. 6.

[8] Averil Cameron, "The Construction of Court Ritual: The Byzantine *Book of Ceremonies,*" in David Cannadine and Simon Price, eds., *Rituals of Royalty: Power and Ceremonial in Traditional Societies* (Cambridge, 1987), 106–36.

B, the symbolic connection is made, and the ceremony is complete and successful. This does not mean that a disorganized rout would have been just as impressive as a carefully coordinated procession. A certain basic level of stateliness was required, and we can assume that it was maintained. But such enactments are bound to leave a gap between ideal and actual, and that is what allowed Liutprand of Cremona to write his bitterly mocking description of an imperial procession.[9] Allowing for his well-exercised powers of exaggeration, I have no trouble believing that he did find it somewhat slack, if not downright shabby. My own response to the Palio was the same.

There is more to court life than ceremony, and even Byzantine courtiers were people. It is true that Byzantine art offers nothing like the lively vision of Figure 1: the court as a place of fashion and fantasy, where each courtier shows off his own sense of style within a set of constantly evolving rules, shaped by tradition, by the sovereign's personal tastes, and by the composition of the court at any given time. Yet we can be sure that Byzantine courtiers were capable, at the very least, of laughing at their own conventions.

Only this explains a work like the Veroli casket.[10] The astonishing finish of the carving does not sit easily with the kewpie-doll figures. This is not the only awkwardness. Many of the scenes or combinations of scenes make no apparent sense. The best-known example is the Rape of Europa (Fig. 7). Europa, her two female attendants, and the bull are familiar and consistent. Not so the six scowling men who are about to pelt the bull (and Europa?) with stones. According to John Beckwith, "This group is copied from a scene depicting the stoning of Achan . . . in the Joshua Roll (Vatican, gr. 431, IX)."[11] In fact, it is *not* a copy, since it differs in every detail from the putative "model" and is far more dynamic, but the images are similar enough that anyone who had seen the Joshua Roll would have made the connection.

For Beckwith this is "additional evidence that the Byzantine ivory carver was acquainted with manuscripts executed in the Great Palace in Constantinople." Are we really to believe that so skilled an artist, working in a rare and precious material, incorporated an unrelated scene simply because it was there? Or that a patron would have accepted such a pastiche? It would be like explaining the black-humored cartoon *Bambi Meets Godzilla* by the fact that the film-maker had seen both *Bambi* and *Godzilla* and combined them without thought to the implications. Anthony Cutler has a better explanation. The composite scene is ludicrous because it is meant to be. The stone-throwers represent an "actual" response to the mythical event, a plausibly foolish expression of startled, impotent rage. As Cutler shows, there is nothing out of character in this deflation of high drama. The Byzantines had a long tradition of irreverent, sometimes blasphemous skits, in which emperors themselves were known to participate.[12] But the fact that the stone-throwers have leaped straight into the scene from another, far more serious tradition, carries the humor beyond farce, to a bizarre comedy of dislocation—Monty Python for courtiers.

[9] Liutprand of Cremona, *Relatio de Legatione Constantinopolitana,* IX–X.

[10] Goldschmidt and Weitzmann, *Die byzantinischen Elfenbeinskulpturen,* vol. I, no. 21.

[11] John Beckwith, *The Veroli Casket* (London, 1962), 3.

[12] Anthony Cutler, "On Byzantine Boxes," *Journal of the Walters Art Gallery* 42–43 (1984–85), 32–47, esp. 42 ff.

Even the liveliest court art can be difficult for us to appreciate on its own terms. The quality that I called airlessness may actually make the Romanos plaque and its kin easier to accept than the Veroli casket. They are so detached, and so beautiful in their detachment, that we relate them to a spiritual, not a human, world. Moving to the casket and its pedantic parodies, and suggesting that this is the *human* side of Byzantine court art, threatens to bring that bugbear of court culture, the accusation of *artificiality,* down on us with a vengeance.

Not long ago, I read Hans Christian Andersen's story "The Nightingale" for the first time since childhood. It is a parable of the nature of art and the role of the artist; above all, a devastating attack on the artificiality of court art as the antithesis of "true" art. An emperor (Andersen places him in China, but it scarcely matters) hears tell of a nightingale whose song is more beautiful than any other sound. His ministers summon the bird to perform before the emperor, and it does. The emperor weeps at the beauty of the song and insists that the nightingale remain. "It was now to remain at court and have its own cage, and liberty to take exercise out of doors twice in the day time and once at night. It had twelve attendants, each of whom had a silken thread attached to its leg, which they held tight."[13] One day, the emperor receives a package from his opposite number in Japan, containing an exquisitely constructed *mechanical* nightingale. This jeweled music box is an immediate success: "For observe, your lordships, and the emperor above all, with the real Nightingale one can never calculate what will come next, but with the artificial bird all is definite; it is thus, and not otherwise. It can be accounted for; one can open it up and show the human contrivance, how the waltzes are set, how they go, and how one follows on another." The real nightingale is banished.

Eventually the emperor falls deathly ill. He calls for music, but his attendants have all run away; no one is left to wind the mechanical nightingale, which by this times does not work very well anyway. Miraculously, the real nightingale appears and revives the emperor with its song. The emperor asks the nightingale to return to court and to name its reward. The bird refuses any payment: the emperor's tears when he first heard it are still enough. It also refuses to live at court but agrees to return, at times of its own choosing, to sing for the emperor, on condition that the emperor permit it to sing about whatever it has seen *away* from court, the bad as well as the good, the lives of fishermen and laborers as well as courtiers.

Certain points stand out. During its term as an "official" court artist, the nightingale is no better than a slave. Then comes sudden disgrace and banishment at the emperor's whim. Not only does the mechanical nightingale dazzle with gold and jewels, while the real one is plain, but the mechanical bird has the virtue of predictability: one knows exactly how it works and what it will do. When the real nightingale returns, it refuses the offer of a reward: for a true artist, to have one's art appreciated is reward enough. Finally, the artist agrees to serve the ruler—if we can even call it service—on terms of freedom, almost of equality. Freedom to come and go as it pleases. Freedom to choose the songs it will sing. And above all, freedom to carry out the artist's real responsibility,

---

[13] Hans Christian Andersen, "The Nightingale," in Andersen, *Forty-Two Stories,* trans. M. R. James (London, 1930), 157–66.

which is not just to entertain but to instruct; in this case, to be the emperor's social conscience.

Andersen has stacked his deck with great skill. Who would have a good word to say for a milieu and a mind-set that prized the repetition of a glittering machine over the truth and spontaneity of art?[14] Perhaps the closest anyone has come to it is William Butler Yeats, whose poem "Sailing to Byzantium" transposes the mechanical bird to the Byzantine court:

> Once out of nature I shall never take
> My bodily form from any natural thing,
> But such a form as Grecian goldsmiths make
> Of hammered gold and gold enamelling
> To keep a drowsy Emperor awake;
> Or set upon a golden bough to sing
> To lords and ladies of Byzantium
> Of what is past, or passing, or to come.

Here the artifact has the power of speech, even prophecy, and a redemptive power as a symbol of an old man's escape from mortality. It remains, however, an ambivalent symbol because it is also an escape from life.

The image of the mechanical bird has more than this contrived and tangential relation to Byzantium. In his account of a visit to the court of Constantine Porphyrogennetos, Liutprand describes how "Before the emperor's seat stood a tree, made of bronze gilded over, whose branches were filled with birds, also made of gilded bronze, which uttered different cries, each according to its various species."[15] Thanks in part to its use by Andersen and Yeats, this artifact, of which no physical trace survives, is central to the modern myth of the Byzantine court. It is a compelling image of strangeness and splendor. Yet if we try, prosaically, to imagine how it actually looked and sounded, we hardly need Andersen's dismissive tale to feel that the very existence of this object, together with the levitating throne that Liutprand describes in the same passage, defines the culture of the Byzantine court as shallow and tawdry. This is a serious misreading of the role of artifice in court culture.

Automata—artifacts programmed to move, as distinct from puppets that require constant direct manipulation—have a special place in western culture, at the intersection of art, myth, and technology. Myth came first. Already in Homer we hear of self-moving

---

[14] Sometimes reality leaves satire gasping in the dust. During the 18th century it was fashionable to teach canaries to sing recognizable tunes. This was a time-consuming process: each tune had to be played over and over on a special set of pipes. Hence the invention, around 1760, of the serinette (from the French word *serin*, canary), a music box powered by compressed air. The serinette was not a substitute for trained songbirds, it was a tool for training them. Within a few years, however, the mechanism was refined, miniaturized, and incorporated into automata which not only sang but moved about their cages, turned their heads, and flapped their wings. In a craft that had begun with the attempt to make birds imitate human music, the ultimate test of skill was now the accurate recreation of birdsong. Yet many of the best examples were programmed to alternate songs of avian and human origin (A. Chapuis and E. Gélis, *Le monde des automates* [Paris, 1928], chap. 18).

[15] Liutprand of Cremona, *Antapodosis*, 6.v, in F. A. Wright, trans., *The Works of Liudprand of Cremona* (London, 1930), 207.

tripods and robot serving maids, the work of Hephaestus.[16] Although completely fanciful, these are true automata: Homer presents them as creations of divine *skill* rather than magic. Among mortals, the great craftsman of Greek myth is Daedalus, whose statues were said to run away if their owners forgot to tie them down.[17] These statues are not automata; there is nothing mechanical in their capacity for self-movement. The two versions of the "moving statue" theme represent different ways of attacking the barrier between artifice and life. Although Homer never tries to explain how Hephaestus' automata might actually work, they embody an ideal of workmanship that humans could and did emulate. In contrast, the self-movement of Daedalus' statues cannot be attempted directly. It is a metaphor for the animation that great art confers on an image.[18]

In modern terms, the difference is between craft and art. We make this a radical distinction, to the detriment of craft and the impoverishment of art. Although we tend to disdain naturalism as an end in itself, we have no trouble distinguishing between an image so skillfully made that it appears capable of movement and one that actually moves. The former remains a work of art, while the latter is no more than a gimmick— at best, in the right setting, a special effect. For the Greeks the distinction was not so clear-cut.[19] In the technological flowering of the Hellenistic world, some of the most innovative engineers—notably Ctesibius in the early third century B.C. and Hero of Alexandria in the first century A.D.—gave automata their serious attention.[20]

More was involved than moving figures. Work on automata went hand in hand with the construction of self-regulating fountains, trick vessels that held several liquids without mixing them, or maintained a constant level no matter how much liquid was taken out, mechanical theaters, singing birds (the pipe organ was a product of the same technology), astronomical computing devices, and elaborate water clocks. All are aspects of what is known as *fine technology*. Behind the often frivolous artifacts, historians of technology recognize the beginning of a rich and continuous tradition leading to the invention of the mechanical clock movement in the fourteenth century, and from there to the precision mechanisms of modern science and industry.[21]

---

[16] *Iliad*, 18.373–77, 417–21.

[17] Plato, *Meno*, 97.

[18] For an extended study of the myth and mystique of Daedalus, see Sarah P. Morris, *Daidalos and the Origins of Greek Art* (Princeton, 1992). Chapter 8, "Magic and Sculpture," is especially enlightening; it shows how easily the Greeks could move between the "living" statue as a metaphor and as a literal fantasy. In view of the Greek veneration of Daedalus as a creator of *lifelike* art, it is unfortunate that "daedalic" as an art historical term refers to an early archaic style which in modern eyes is anything but lifelike.

[19] For a different approach to the relation of art and craft in ancient Greece, see Christopher Janaway, "Arts and Crafts in Plato and Collingwood," *Journal of Aesthetics and Art Criticism* 50 (1992), 45–54. Janaway focuses on poetry rather than the visual arts, but emphasizes the modern elevation of art over craft.

[20] The best brief account of early automata and related technologies is Donald R. Hill, *A History of Engineering in Classical and Medieval Times* (La Salle, 1984). For more detail see B. Woodcroft, *The Pneumatics of Hero of Alexandria* (London, 1851); Victor Prou, "Les théâtres d'automates en Grèce au IIe siècle avant l'ère chrétienne," *Mémoires présentés par divers savants à l'Académie des inscriptions et belles-lettres* 9.2 (1884), 117–274; A. G. Drachmann, *Ktesibios Philon and Heron: A Study in Ancient Pneumatics* (Copenhagen, 1948). On automata in Hellenistic culture see Henner von Hesberg, "Mechanische Kunstwerke und ihre Bedeutung für die höfische Kunst des frühen Hellenismus," *Marburger Winckelmann-Programm* (1987), 47–72.

[21] Silvio A. Bedini, "The Role of Automata in the History of Technology," *Technology and Culture* 5 (1964), 24–42; Derek de Solla Price, *Science since Babylon*, enlarged ed. (New Haven, Conn.-London, 1975), chap. 2. By

Whereas the artistic imitation of nature is primarily a statement about art, the mechanical imitation of nature is in some degree a statement about nature. It implies that nature operates mechanically and thus can be explored, described, and at least symbolically claimed or mastered mechanically. The most explicit examples are the earliest mechanical clocks and the water clocks that preceded them by well over a thousand years. Tours de force of design and craft, the best of these were not just timekeepers but working models of the cosmos. Like art and craft, the mechanical understanding of nature and the technical skill to embody it are inseparable. It is no accident that the visual trappings of ancient and medieval clocks often included automata.[22]

Fine technology was not confined to the Greek world. India had a similar tradition.[23] The Chinese, at almost exactly the same time as the Greeks, developed an elaborate technology of hydrostatics and gearing, which they too applied to automata, astronomical calculation and simulation, and time measurement.[24] Closer to home, the Arabs studied and improved on the work of Hero and his colleagues, raising hydrostatic technology, especially, to unequalled heights.[25] In Byzantium the best-known examples of fine technology are those described by Liutprand, but an earlier tree with singing birds is known to have existed.[26] Earlier and less familiar is Prokopios of Gaza's *ekphrasis* of a water clock depicting the labors of Herakles.[27] Only in the Latin West are automata and related objects unattested, at least before the thirteenth century.[28] In partial compensa-

---

far the most detailed history of automata in the West is Chapuis and Gélis, *Le monde des automates*. A later work by A. Chapuis and E. Droz, *Automata: A Historical and Technological Study* (New York, 1958), supplements but does not supplant the earlier study. For related technologies see Derek de Solla Price, *Gears from the Greeks* (New York, 1975), and Henry C. King with John R. Millburn, *Geared to the Stars: The Evolution of Planetariums, Orreries and Astronomical Clocks* (Toronto, 1978). The career of Jacques Vaucanson provides the best corrective to the belief that traditional automaton technology is without practical application. Vaucanson, the most famous builder of automata in 18th-century Europe, went on to become a pioneer of industrial technology. Among his achievements was a device for mechanizing the weaving of patterns in silk, which anticipated and made possible the so-called Jacquard loom; see André Doyon and Lucien Liaigre, *Jacques Vaucanson, mécanicien de génie* (Paris, 1967). For the enormous cultural significance of clockwork, see Otto Mayr, *Authority, Liberty and Automatic Machinery in Early Modern Europe* (Baltimore-London, 1986).

[22] Price, *Science since Babylon*, chap. 3.

[23] V. Raghaven, "Yantras or Mechanical Contrivances in Ancient India," *Transactions*, Indian Institute of Culture (Bangalore) 10 (1952), 1–31.

[24] Price, *Science since Babylon*, chap. 2; Joseph Needham, Wang Ling, and Derek J. de Solla Price, *Heavenly Clockwork: The Great Astronomical Clocks of Medieval China* (Cambridge, 1960); J. Needham, *Science and Civilization in China*, vol. IV, pt. 2 (Cambridge, 1970), 156–65, 435–546. The historical connections between Chinese and western technology, both Greco-Roman and medieval, are still under investigation.

[25] For a summary see Donald R. Hill, "Hiyal," *Encyclopedia of Islam*, supplement, fasc. 5–6 (Leiden, 1982), 371–74. The work of the Banū Mūsa in the 9th century, and of al-Jazarī in the 13th, are the high points of the Arab achievement in this area. See Muhammad ibn Mūsa ibn Shākir (Donald R. Hill, trans. and annot.), *The Book of Ingenious Devices* (Dordrecht-Boston-London, 1979); Ibn al-Razzāz al-Jazarī (Donald R. Hill, trans. and annot.), *The Book of Knowledge of Ingenious Mechanical Devices* (Dordrecht-Boston-London, 1974); René R. Khawam, "Les statues animées dans les Mille et Une Nuits," *Annales* 30.5 (1975), 1084–1104; Ahmad Yusuf Hassan and Donald R. Hill, *Islamic Technology: An Illustrated History* (Cambridge-Paris, 1986).

[26] G. Brett, "The Automata in the Byzantine 'Throne of Solomon,'" *Speculum* 29 (1954), 477–87.

[27] H. Diels, "Über die von Prokop beschriebene Kunstuhr von Gaza," *Abhandlungen der königlich preussischen Akademie der Wissenschaften* (1917), Philosophisch-historische Klasse 7.

[28] Charlemagne had an elaborate water clock, but it was a gift from Harun al-Rashid. See *Annales regni Francorum*, ed. F. Kurze, MGH, *ScriptRerGerm* 43 (Hannover, 1895), 114, 123–24.

tion there is a wealth of legendary material: even in this form, the idea of fine technology had the power to fascinate, not least because it was so easily conflated with magic.[29]

Although fine technology has never been an official court monopoly, in practice it ranks second only to ceremony as the expression of a courtly ethos transcending cultural boundaries. This has been true across Eurasia from Hellenistic times almost to the present. A recent book by the anthropologist Mary W. Helms, *Craft and the Kingly Ideal,* explores the links between material culture and ideology at court.[30] Although she does not mention automata, her study leaves no doubt as to why rulers and courtiers have found the combination of craftsmanship, novelty, humor, mystery, exclusivity, scientific investigation, cosmic symbolism, and control over the forces of nature irresistible.

Helms connects traditional political authority with what she calls skilled crafting. This is not craftsmanship in the familiar sense, the ability to make useful and beautiful things. It implies a degree of virtuosity beyond even the best utilitarian work. Helms extends the concept to include music, poetry and oratory, as well as long-distance trade and the skills associated with it, such as navigation and diplomacy. What they have in common is this:

> Skilled crafting associated with public figures is itself public rather than private. Skilled crafting of this sort is also non-utilitarian and non-pragmatic, being ideological in meaning and moral or honorable in quality rather than being strictly materially or economically useful. Stated another way, skilled crafting is metaphoric and ritualistic in significance rather than literal or inconsequential. Skilled crafting for political-ideological leaders is also grander and more ostentatious than ordinary; it is an explicit and substantial index of the intangible prestige, worth, and valor of the leadership itself. Skilled crafting of this sort helps to *over*-communicate the characteristics of political status and roles as opposed to crafting that has no or little status-related significance.[31]

While retaining Helms' definition of this important phenomenon, I would substitute the term *conspicuous virtuosity* for *skilled crafting.* Many words have a technical sense quite different from the common one, but it is dangerous simply to graft a new meaning onto a familiar word. Art historians, who take skill in craft for granted, will balk at Helms' use of skilled for something extraordinary. As for crafting, to most people it means making *things.* We sometimes extend it, half metaphorically, to intangible artifacts such as poems. If we extend it even further, to skills and activities like diplomacy, which often produce no artifact at all, the word's familiarity ceases to be a guide and becomes a source of confusion. *Virtuosity* is a better term for extraordinary skill; it is highly inclusive and already has connotations of display and performance which crafting lacks. The addition of *conspicuous* further emphasizes the element of public prestige, especially since it evokes the closely related idea of conspicuous consumption.[32]

---

[29] Merriam Sherwood, "Magic and Mechanics in Medieval Fiction," *Studies in Philology* 44 (1947), 567–92.

[30] Mary W. Helms, *Craft and the Kingly Ideal: Art, Trade and Power* (Austin, 1993).

[31] Ibid., 14.

[32] Thorstein Veblen, *The Theory of the Leisure Class* (New York, 1899).

Ideologically speaking, artistic creation is an essential part of rulership because it enables the ruler to take on the role of culture hero, reshaping and renewing the whole human environment.[33] Daedalus epitomizes conspicuous virtuosity in its most intimate association with royalty. His almost magical creations, inconceivable without royal patronage, confirm the ruler's status as artificer-by-proxy. In Leo Choirosphaktes' poetic *ekphrasis* of the bath built and decorated by Leo VI, it is the emperor, not the artist, who "has surpassed the imagination of Daedalus."[34] Its decorative program wove together the themes of imperial wisdom, mastery over the cosmos, renewal, and paradise. As the Byzantines still knew very well, Daedalus didn't just make great things, he made great kings.

Choirosphaktes' poem, though highly condensed and therefore weak in detail, admits at least the possibility that several elements of the decoration were automata.[35] In one case it is a virtual certainty. "The noise of the doors with artful contrivance sends out a musical song; the song says, 'Glory of rulers, O Basileus, King!'" (lines 59–62). Hero of Alexandria tells how to make a device—a very simple one as such things go—that sounds a trumpet when a door is opened.[36] Since there is no suggestion that it could imitate human speech, the "words" of the song may be poetic license, or perhaps a reference to an actual song whose opening notes the apparatus played. Of the living creatures mentioned in the poem—songbird, snake, lion, griffin—only one, the snake, actually moves. Three emit their characteristic sounds, a cliché of Heronic technology (we know from Liutprand that a few decades later Leo's son Constantine Porphyrogennetos had a throne equipped with roaring lions). As for the griffin, it breathes out fire, "terrifying the mortal nature of those present." Finally, there is a tree with tinkling golden leaves, though without the familiar birds.

Any or all of these *could* be automata. We have no way of knowing, and this in itself is significant. Whether the Byzantine poet is describing pictorial images or automata, he dwells on their convincing naturalism. Middle Byzantine art is not naturalistic by modern standards, and it is hard to believe that Middle Byzantine automata were any different. It is tempting to invoke convention, and assume that art had to be described as naturalistic no matter how it was perceived. But convention is a distillation of experience, not a denial of it.[37] Few art forms have contributed as much to our understanding of the human condition as ancient Greek drama, where convention governed everything from poetic form to music and staging, including elaborate special effects. These devices were susceptible to parody from the start, but parody is not rejection. The longevity of Greek stagecraft proves that there was no fundamental incompatibility between conven-

---

[33] Helms, *Craft and the Kingly Ideal*, chap. 5.

[34] Paul Magdalino, "The Bath of Leo the Wise and the 'Macedonian Renaissance' Revisited: Topography, Iconography, Ceremonial, Ideology," *DOP* 42 (1988), 97–118; text and translation on 116–18.

[35] Paul Magdalino, "The Bath of Leo the Wise," in Ann Moffat, ed., *Maistor: Classical, Byzantine and Renaissance Studies for Robert Browning* (Canberra, 1984), 225–40. On p. 237 Magdalino raises the possibility that some of the images mentioned in the poem were automata.

[36] Drachmann, *Ktesibios Philon and Heron*, 143–44.

[37] A case in point is Photios' response to the mosaic of the Virgin and Child in the apse of Hagia Sophia; see J. Trilling, "Medieval Art without Style? Plato's Loophole and a Modern Detour," *Gesta* 34 (1995), 57–62.

tion and human insight, or between mechanical contrivance and the "pure" art of dramatic poetry.

With the help of this example, we should recognize that automata were not some kind of anti-art, nor even a decadent form of art. They do not imply contempt for life or nature, but the desire to recreate it in much the same way that the theater recreates it. They are symbols of power, not just in the economic sense. As an attempt to carry art to the point where it simulates as well as represents life, they symbolize the power to understand and control the physical world. In this respect they reflect the idiosyncratic love of nature which is a hallmark of the Byzantine elite.

There is plenty of evidence for the love of nature in Byzantium; all we have to do is take it seriously. Paul the Silentiary rhapsodizes over the decoration of Hagia Sophia: "connected arcs laden with fruit, baskets and leaves . . . birds perched on boughs. The twining vine with shoots like golden ringlets winds its curving path and weaves a spiral chain of clusters" (Fig. 8).[38] To us the actuality seems far removed from nature, but then we are unlikely to think of a row of columns as "blooming like a grove with bright flowers."[39] Nature was present for the Byzantines in ways that we can hardly credit. Only with this recognition does their fascination with colored marble make sense: not just their connoisseurship of different varieties, or the language of meadows and flowers in which they praised them, but the distinctively Byzantine art of book-matched marble slabs (Fig. 9). Of these, Paul the Silentiary says: "you may see the veins of the square and octagonal stones meeting so as to form devices; connected in this way, the stones imitate the glories of painting."[40] This does not just mean that marble, like painting, is beautiful and deserving of recognition as an art in its own right. Since we know that the Byzantines considered their pictorial art naturalistic, the comparison of marblework to painting reflects not only delight in the beauty of the material, but a belief that, modulated by the artist's hand, the natural colors of the stone create an image. Not a direct representation of nature, but an image abstracted from nature, analogous to an ornamental vine motif, in which the pleasure of artifice is inseparable from its ability to evoke the natural world.[41]

[38] Paul the Silentiary, *Description of H. Sophia,* in Cyril Mango, *The Art of the Byzantine Empire, 312–1453: Sources and Documents* (Englewood Cliffs, N.J., 1972), 86.

[39] Ibid., 84.

[40] Ibid., 85. For comparable descriptions of stonework by Khorikios and Prokopios, see ibid., 61, 70, 76.

[41] Cf. John Onians, "Abstraction and Imagination in Late Antiquity," *Art History* 3 (1980), 1–23. From the rhetorical descriptions, Onians argues that the Byzantines saw actual figures, landscapes, etc. in their marble. Whether or not this is literally true, it is clear that the Byzantines "saw" far more in marble than their Roman predecessors did. History never repeats itself, but the early 20th century offers an interesting and perhaps helpful parallel. Under the leadership of Adolf Loos, architects and designers succeeded in replacing traditional figure- and pattern-based ornament with variegated stone and other natural materials. The ability to take natural effects seriously as "art"—in effect, to make natural and artistic effects interchangeable—was crucial to the rapid evolution of modern architecture and design. See J. Trilling, "Modernism and the Rejection of Ornament: The Revolution That Never Happened," *Common Knowledge* 3.2 (1994), 79–110.

Gardens provide yet another example of the Byzantine enthusiasm for nature tempered by artifice. In addition to Anthony Littlewood's paper in this volume, see Henry Maguire, "Imperial Gardens and the Rhetoric of Renewal," in Paul Magdalino, ed., *New Constantines: The Rhythm of Imperial Renewal in Byzantium, 4th–13th Centuries* (Aldershot, 1994), 181–98. Helms, *Craft and the Kingly Ideal,* chap. 5, sheds light on the association of imperial power with "natural" as well as artistic renewal.

Not only does the Byzantine love of nature and "naturalistic" art put the meaning of the singing-bird automaton on a new footing, it also sheds light on another aspect of Byzantine court art, the making of cups and bowls in decorative, often semiprecious stones. Compared to contemporary Muslim work, Byzantine precious vessels appear almost clumsy; were it not for the mounts in which we often find them, we might assume that they represent a level of craft below the courtly level (Fig. 10).[42] One explanation is that the Byzantines were simply not very skillful in this area. However, their enthusiasm for the beauty of stone provides a more fruitful explanation. Whereas carvers in other societies have struggled to assert their absolute control over even the most difficult materials, the Byzantines, placing a special value on the inherent beauty of the stone, may have done no more than they considered necessary to let this beauty speak for itself.

I have tried to stand conventional wisdom on its head by separating the art of the Byzantine court from the ideas of ceremony and rigid order. As a symbol of court taste, the tree of singing birds is bivalent. It points to the Byzantine court as nature-loving if not exactly spontaneous, but at the same time it shows that Byzantine ideas of nature and of the imitation and love of nature are very different from ours. But the automata that Liutprand saw at the Byzantine court served another purpose than decoration, or even the display of conspicuous virtuosity. According to Liutprand, the tree stood next to the emperor's throne.

> The throne itself was so marvelously fashioned that at one moment it seemed a low structure, and at another it rose high into the air. It was of immense size and was guarded by lions, made either of bronze or of wood covered over with gold, who beat the ground with their tails and gave a dreadful roar with open mouth and quivering tongue. . . . At my approach the lions began to roar and the birds to cry out, each according to its kind; but I was neither terrified nor surprised, for I had previously made enquiry about all these things from people who were well acquainted with them. So after I had three times made obeisance to the emperor with my face upon the ground, I lifted my head and behold! the man whom just before I had seen sitting on a moderately elevated seat had now changed his raiment and was sitting on the level of the ceiling. How it was done I could not imagine, unless perhaps he was lifted up by some such sort of device as we use for raising the timbers of a wine press.[43]

Several interesting things emerge from this account. We can infer that a visitor might well have been surprised or terrified by the spectacle. Otherwise Liutprand would not have gone out of his way to say that he was not. Terror must have depended on surprise; Liutprand was forewarned and thus forearmed. It is probably also fair to assume that startling or frightening their official guests was not the Byzantine authorities' main goal. The people who told Liutprand what to expect may have been members of the court

---

[42] David Buckton, ed., *The Treasury of San Marco Venice* (Milan, 1984); for Islamic examples see 216 ff.

[43] Liutprand, *Antapodosis*, 6.v.

or previous visitors, but it does not really matter: the existence of such spectacular machinery could hardly have stayed a secret. Although the whole performance seems faintly (or not so faintly) ridiculous today, Liutprand did not make fun of it. Dare we infer that he was actually impressed? There is no question of his being deceived: birds, lions, and levitating throne are all recognized as machines. Yet he admits to ignorance of how it was done.

This ignorance is crucial. Over and above their conspicuous virtuosity, and their suggestion of near-magical power over nature, the Byzantine automata carry a very practical if not sinister message. It concerns the so-called Greek fire, whose invention in the late seventh century gave the Byzantine navy an advantage comparable to that of long-range artillery against an enemy ignorant of its nature and armed with hand weapons alone. The endless debate on its composition—whether it was or contained an early form of gunpowder, what ingredient(s) enabled it to burn on water, whether it was launched by explosive detonation or by some other means—is beyond my skills or the scope of this paper. It is enough to know that Greek fire was not just an incendiary mixture but an elaborate launching mechanism. No modern reconstruction has been accepted as definitive, but the mechanism was clearly a product of Heronic fine technology.[44] This is the same technology that powered courtly automata. One need not have understood the technology to make the connection. On the contrary, it was the mystery of both the

[44] See, for example, Hero, *Pneumatics*, no. 9. On Greek fire as a weapons system in something like the modern sense, see Alex Roland, "Secrecy, Technology and War: Greek Fire and the Defense of Byzantium, 678–1204," *Technology and Culture* 33 (1992), 655–76. Roland argues that by compartmentalizing the secret, the Byzantines made sure that the system as a usable whole would not fall into enemy hands. Since parts of the system, up to and including whole ships, did fall into enemy hands at various times without the secret being compromised, attention shifts from construction to operation as the key: "Hero's *Pneumatica* and Vitruvius' *De architectura* would have provided enough information to design the caldron, pipes and siphon. The technique itself would have been a secret of almost as much sophistication as the formula, for without pressure gauges and safety valves it was surely a delicate task to heat and pressurize a highly volatile liquid in dark and cramped quarters below deck in combat without accidents" (p. 663). It is also possible "that the formula might have entailed an early version of modern binary munitions, which are activated only when two components are allowed to combine" (p. 663, note 30): a promising suggestion, in view of the Heronic fascination with vessels that held two or more liquids without allowing them to mix.

Roland believes that the secret was known to so few people that it could not long survive the vicissitudes of Byzantine politics. He goes so far as to suggest that "the complete secret of Kallinikos fire was lost long before 1204, perhaps even as early as the tenth century, the testimony of Constantine VII Porphyrogenitus and Anna Comnena notwithstanding" (p. 678). The real danger, it seems to me, was too little secrecy, not too much. The Arabs had exactly the same technology. Not only were they well versed in the chemistry of incendiary substances (Hassan and Hill, *Islamic Technology*, 108), but Hero's *Pneumatics* was well known to them, and by the 9th century, at least, the Banū Mūsa (above, note 25) show a greater mastery of Heronic fine technology than anything recorded in Byzantium. Furthermore, there was nothing intrinsically startling in the adaptation of fine technology to military use. Writers on fine technology often worked on military projects. Greek fire was a new and instantly successful fusion of chemistry and fine technology, and it caught the Arabs flat-footed, but in a life-or-death struggle they would have had no trouble duplicating anything they captured. In these circumstances it is hard to understand how Greek fire remained a secret for so long. The simplest answer is that it probably did not. The Arabs' failure to fight fire with fire may have been a matter of technological and military style, not ignorance: they favored hand-thrown grenades as a delivery system for their combustibles (Hassan and Hill, *Islamic Technology*, 106 ff). Needless to say, these considerations apply only to the Arabs. Byzantium's rivals or potential rivals to the north and west during the middle period had no comparable background in fine technology.

lion throne and Greek fire that would have driven home their similarity. Few things put a rival more effectively at a disadvantage than a display of qualitatively superior technology, and there is no better test of qualitative superiority than its ability to baffle.

Liutprand, a learned and worldly man, was baffled by the emperor's throne. This in itself would have been no small achievement in diplomacy, where psychological advantage weighed heavily. But behind the courtly display was a more threatening message. Not only did the Byzantines have a secret technology, but they knew how to use it in less fanciful ways. Nor should we underestimate the value of internal propaganda. Impressing one's own people can be as important as impressing a potential enemy. If Leo's griffin was indeed a fire-breathing automaton, the terror it inspired was not just a poet's flourish but a practical demonstration of the emperor's power.

The relation between the courtly and military aspects of fine technology was reciprocal. Just as Greek fire provided a deadly serious subtext for courtly special effects and diplomatic one-upmanship, the same special effects had their place in war. Here is Anna Komnene describing the preparations for a sea battle:

> As he [Alexios I] knew that the Pisans were skilled in sea-warfare and dreaded a battle with them, on the prow of each ship he had a head fixed of a lion or other land-animal, made in brass or iron with the mouth open and then gilded over, so that their mere aspect was terrifying. And the fire which was to be directed against the enemy through tubes he made to pass through the mouths of the beasts, so that it seemed as if the lions and the other similar monsters were vomiting the fire.[45]

It is a reminder that beneath the ceremony and symbolism, an imperial court is concerned above all with the reality of power.

Providence, R.I.

---

[45] *The Alexiad of the Princess Anna Comnena*, trans. Elizabeth A. S. Dawes (London, 1928), bk. XI.10, 292.

Présence et figures du souverain à Sainte-Sophie de Constantinople et à l'église de la Sainte-Croix d'Aghtamar

Catherine Jolivet-Lévy

L'étude des portraits impériaux (ou royaux) monumentaux, envisagés dans leur contexte iconographique et fonctionnel, se heurte, pour la période des IXe–XIIe s., à la relative pauvreté du matériel conservé se prêtant à une telle approche. En outre, les quelques ensembles qui viennent immédiatement à l'esprit ont tous déjà fait l'objet de plusieurs recherches en ce sens, qu'il s'agisse de l'église cappadocienne dite de Nicéphore Phocas à Çavuşin,[1] des mosaïques de Sicile[2] ou des fresques des églises géorgiennes.[3] Les deux ensembles qui ont retenu mon attention ne sont pas moins célèbres ni moins étudiés que les précédents, mais peut-être permettent-ils de proposer quelques hypothèses nouvelles. Éloignés dans l'espace, ils sont proches dans le temps, puisqu'il s'agit des mosaïques disparues des tribunes de Sainte-Sophie de Constantinople (en particulier de la tribune sud) et des sculptures et peintures de la Sainte-Croix d'Aghtamar, église située dans une région reculée n'appartenant pas à cette époque au territoire de l'Empire, mais partiellement tributaire du répertoire de l'art aulique de Byzance.

La tribune sud de Sainte-Sophie présente un cas particulier. Outre les mosaïques conservées (panneaux impériaux et Déisis), nous ne connaissons en effet que le décor des voûtes de la travée centrale et celui-ci peut être attribué à la fin du IXe ou au début du

---

[1] N. Thierry, *Haut Moyen Age en Cappadoce. Les églises de la région de Çavuşin* (Paris, 1983), 43–57.

[2] Bibliographie sélective: E. Kitzinger, "The Mosaics of the Cappella Palatina in Palermo: An Essay on the Choice and Arrangement of Subjects," *ArtB* 31 (1949), 269–92, repr. dans idem, *The Art of Byzantium and the Medieval West: Selected Studies,* éd. W. E. Kleinbauer (Bloomington-Londres, 1976), X, 290–319, 394; I. Beck, "The First Mosaics of the Cappella Palatina in Palermo," *Byzantion* 40 (1970), 119–64; N. Nercessian, *The Cappella Palatina of Roger II: The Relationship of Its Imagery to Its Political Function,* Ph.D. diss. (Université de California, Los Angeles, 1981); M. J. Johnson, "The Royal View at Cefalu: A Note on the Choice of Subjects and Their Arrangement in the Mosaics of Norman Sicily," *BSCAbstr* 9 (1983), 12–13 (développé sous le titre "The Episcopal and Royal Views at Cefalu," *Gesta* 33.2 [1994], 118–31); S. Ćurčić, "Some Palatine Aspects of the Cappella Palatina in Palermo," *DOP* 41 (1987), 125–44; E. Kitzinger et S. Ćurčić, *The Mosaics of St. Mary's of the Admiral in Palermo,* DOS 27 (Washington, D.C., 1990) et le compte rendu de ce livre par J. Albani, *JÖB* 43 (1993), 476–79; E. Borsook, *Messages in Mosaic: The Royal Programmes of Norman Sicily (1130–1187)* (Oxford, 1990).

[3] N. Thierry, "Le souverain dans les programmes d'églises en Cappadoce et en Géorgie du Xe au XIIIe siècles," *Revue des études géorgiennes et caucasiennes* 4 (1988), 127–70; A. Deyman Eastmond, *Royal Imagery in the Medieval Kingdom of Georgia,* Ph.D. diss. (Courtauld Institute, Londres, 1992).

Xe s.:[4] il n'y a donc ni contemporanéité, ni proximité physique réelle entre les thèmes religieux représentés dans cette tribune et les portraits impériaux qui sont situés sur le mur est et qui remontent aux XIe (Constantin IX et Zoé) et XIIe siècles (Jean II Comnène, Irène et Alexios) (Fig. 1). Ici, c'est la présence de l'empereur lui-même, non de son image—encore que des portraits, aujourd'hui disparus, aient pu exister dans cette travée centrale, comme le suggère le témoignage d'Antoine de Novgorod[5]—qui nous permettra d'interpréter le programme iconographique. La partie centrale de la tribune sud, où se trouvaient les mosaïques qui nous intéressent, constituait avec la travée orientale un espace réservé, isolé vers l'ouest par une clôture,[6] relié au Patriarcat comme au Palais impérial et directement accessible au clergé et à l'empereur (Fig. 2). Ce dernier prenait place dans cet oratoire, quand il était présent à Sainte-Sophie sans prendre une part active à la liturgie; il y suivait tout ou partie de l'office liturgique lors de certaines fêtes (Dimanche après Pâques, Exaltation de la croix, Dimanche de l'Orthodoxie) et y rencontrait à certaines occasions le patriarche.[7]

Le décor, aujourd'hui disparu, des deux voûtes qui couvrent la travée centrale nous est connu par les descriptions et dessins anciens dus à l'artiste suédois Loos (1710), à l'architecte suisse Fossati (1847–49) et au prussien Salzenberg (1848), tous documents publiés par C. Mango.[8] A l'est, le buste du Christ Pantocrator s'inscrivait dans un médaillon à bordure irisée, au sommet de la voûte (Fig. 3). Il était entouré de chérubins (au-dessus des pendentifs sud-ouest et nord-ouest), de séraphins (au-dessus des pendentifs sud-est et nord-est) et de roues de feu dans une mer de flammes qui remplissait entièrement les pendentifs (occidentaux et sans doute orientaux) (Fig. 4). A l'ouest était représentée la Pentecôte, dont, malgré les divergences entre les dessins conservés, on peut restituer la composition ainsi: au centre, le trône de l'Hétimasie (dessins de Fossati), plutôt que l'image du Christ (Salzenberg et Loos),[9] d'où partaient les rayons descendant sur les têtes nimbées des apôtres, assis sur un banc continu à haut dossier et surmontés des langues de feu; les figures des nations, tribus et langues étaient représentées dans les pendentifs (Fig. 5).

---

[4] C. Mango, *Materials for the Study of the Mosaics of St. Sophia*, DOS 8 (Washington, D.C., 1962), 33–34, 98.

[5] C. Mango, *The Art of the Byzantine Empire, 312–1453: Sources and Documents* (Englewoods Cliffs, N.J., 1972), 237.

[6] Clôture que l'on s'accorde à considérer comme primitive: T. F. Mathews, *The Early Churches of Constantinople: Architecture and Liturgy* (University Park, Pa.-Londres, 1971), 95; R. J. Mainstone, *Hagia Sophia: Architecture, Structure and Liturgy of Justinian's Great Church* (Londres, 1988), 225.

[7] Mathews, *Early Churches*, 132; Constantin VII Porphyrogénète, *Le livre des cérémonies*, éd. A. Vogt, I (Paris, 1935), 90–91, 116–17, 147–48; pour la consécration d'un patriarche: *De Ceremoniis*, éd. J. J. Reiske, Bonn éd. (1829), II, 566. On considère en général que la place de l'empereur était dans la partie orientale, mais l'ensemble formé par les travées centrale et orientale constituait bien un espace réservé à l'empereur et à sa cour, ainsi qu'au patriarche.

[8] Mango, *Materials*, 29–38.

[9] La représentation du Christ dans la scène de la Pentecôte est attestée par certaines images paléochrétiennes d'"Ascension-Pentecôte" (ampoules de Monza), la fresque d'Aghtamar (N. Thierry, "Survivance d'une iconographie palestinienne de la Pentecôte au Vaspourakan," *Atti del primo simposio internazionale di arte armena, Bergame 1975* [Venise, 1978], 709–16), ou encore un coffret d'ivoire fait au Mont Cassin(?) vers 1070 et conservé au Trésor de l'abbaye de Farfa (E. Leesti, "The Pentecost Illustration in the Drogo Sacramentary," *Gesta* 28 [1989], 207), mais à Sainte-Sophie, la restitution du symbole trinitaire du trône vide est plus vraisemblable.

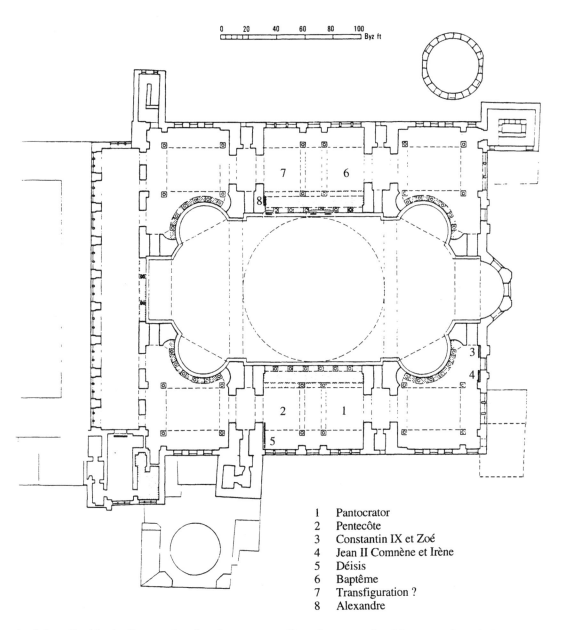

1 Pantocrator
2 Pentecôte
3 Constantin IX et Zoé
4 Jean II Comnène et Irène
5 Déisis
6 Baptême
7 Transfiguration ?
8 Alexandre

1   Sainte-Sophie de Constantinople: plan montrant l'emplacement des thèmes représentés dans les tribunes (d'après Mainstone, *Hagia Sophia,* p. 281)

2   Sainte-Sophie de Constantinople: travée centrale de la tribune sud, vue vers l'ouest
(d'après Mainstone, *Hagia Sophia,* fig. 67)

3   Sainte-Sophie de Constantinople, tribune sud: buste du Christ Pantocrator
(Fossati, d'après Mango, *Materials,* fig. 23)

4   Sainte-Sophie de Constantinople, tribune sud: travée centrale vue vers l'ouest
(Loos, d'après Mango, *Materials,* fig. 22)

5   Sainte-Sophie de Constantinople, tribune sud: voûte de la Pentecôte
(Loos, d'après Mango, *Materials,* fig. 29)

6   Sainte-Sophie de Constantinople: tribune nord
(Loos, d'après Mango, *Materials,* fig. 55)

7 Sainte-Croix d'Aghtamar, vue générale de la façade sud (d'après M. S. İpşiroğlu, *Die Kirche von Achtamar. Bauplastik im Leben des Lichtes* [Mainz, 1963], fig. 23)

8 Sainte-Croix d'Aghtamar, façade
ouest: Gagik présente le modèle de
l'église au Christ (d'après Ipşiroğlu,
Die Kirche von Achtamar, fig. 48)

9   Sainte-Croix d'Aghtamar, façade ouest, partie supérieure: les
frises animales et végétales (d'après Ipşiroğlu, *Die Kirche von Achtamar,*
fig. 49)

10   Sainte-Croix d'Aghtamar: la frise principale, détail (d'après Ipşiroğlu, *Die Kirche von Achtamar,* fig. 41)

11 Sainte-Croix d'Aghtamar, façade orientale: roi trônant
(d'après Thierry, *Monuments arméniens,* pl. XXXII, 2)

12 Sainte-Croix d'Aghtamar, façade orientale: Adam surmonté du roi trônant
(d'après Ipşiroğlu, *Die Kirche von Achtamar,* fig. 20)

13   Sainte-Croix d'Aghtamar, façade orientale: vue générale (d'après Ipşiroğlu, *Die Kirche von Achtamar,* fig. 2)

14 Sainte-Croix d'Aghtamar, façade sud: les princes Sahak et Hamazasp (d'après Der Nersessian et Vahramian, *Aght'amar,* fig. 38)

15   Sainte-Croix d'Aghtamar, façade sud: l'histoire de Jonas (d'après Ipşiroğlu, *Die Kirche von Achtamar,* fig. 33)

16   Sainte-Croix d'Aghtamar, façade sud: David et Goliath

17   Sainte-Croix d'Aghtamar, fresque dans le tambour
de la coupole: Adam dans le jardin d'Éden
(schéma N. Thierry)

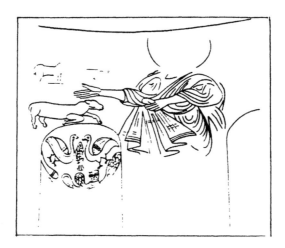

18   Sainte-Croix d'Aghtamar, fresque dans le
tambour de la coupole: détail de la scène du
Seigneur présentant les animaux à Adam
(schéma N. Thierry)

19   Sainte-Croix d'Aghtamar, conque sud: la tribune royale (d'après I. A. Orbeli, *Iz istorii
kul'tury i iskusstva Armenii X-XIII vv.,* vol. I [Moscow, 1968], pl. VII)

Conque sud **Conque nord**

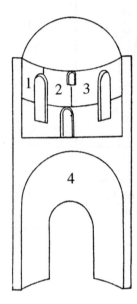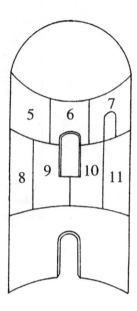

1 Annonciation   2 Visitation   3 Nativité
4 Seconde Venue ?

5 Baptéme   6 Transfiguration   7 Noces de Cana
8 Crucifixion   9 Myrophores au sépulcre
10 Anastasis   11 Apparition aux Saintes Femmes

20   Sainte-Croix d'Aghtamar, programme iconographique des conques sud et nord
(d'après Thierry, *Monuments arméniens,* fig. 67)

21 Sainte-Croix d'Aghtamar, conque sud: Seconde venue?
(d'après Der Nersessian et Vahramian, *Aght'amar,* fig. 65)

22   Sainte-Croix d'Aghtamar, conque nord: vue générale
(d'après Der Nersessian, *Aght'amar: Church of the Holy Cross,* fig. 67)

23   Palerme, Chapelle Palatine: mur sud, face à la loge royale
(d'après Ćurčić, "Some Palatine Aspects of the Cappella Palatina," fig. 7)

Ces deux compositions étaient orientées, comme l'a noté C. Mango, pour être vues de l'est et donc conçues en relation avec les utilisateurs de cette tribune: l'empereur et la cour, dont les processions se dirigeaient toujours d'est en ouest. Malgré cette constatation importante, elles n'ont été interprétées jusqu'à présent que comme des théophanies, dont le choix aurait été déterminé par l'importance des visions divines dans l'iconographie post-iconoclaste. Or, la fonction de la tribune sud n'explique pas seulement l'orientation des sujets, elle en justifie la présence même en ce lieu et en éclaire la signification.

Le décor de la voûte orientale—le Christ entouré de figures célestes—correspond au thème habituel, après le Triomphe de l'Orthodoxie, pour la coupole centrale de l'église[10] et est attesté, à peu près à la même époque, dans plusieurs églises de la capitale: Sainte-Sophie,[11] la Théotokos du Phare[12] (v. 864), l'église du monastère de Kauléas[13] ou celle de Stylianos Zaoutzès (v. 890), où Léon VI décrit le Christ en buste entouré de ses serviteurs, les anges, parmi lesquels il mentionne les *polyommata* (chérubins) et les *hexapteryga* (séraphins).[14] Le déplacement d'un thème de coupole centrale à une voûte secondaire de l'église confirme l'utilisation de cette partie de la tribune comme un sanctuaire privé à l'intérieur de la Grande Église. Courante est à cette époque l'interprétation qui met en relation l'image du Pantocrator entouré d'anges et l'empereur entouré de ses dignitaires et, qu'il y ait eu dans la travée centrale un trône[15] ou un portrait, le Pantocrator représenté dans la voûte surmontait l'empereur et la cour, physiquement présents à plusieurs occasions, en une composition hiérarchisée, évoquant celle du Chrysotriclinos[16] et exprimant visuellement le rapport entre la cour céleste et la cour terrestre.

La présence de la Pentecôte dans la voûte voisine confirme, me semble-t-il, cette interprétation "impériale" du décor. Textes et images montrent clairement le parallélisme établi entre la descente de l'Esprit Saint qui donna autorité aux apôtres pour conduire le peuple chrétien et la mission de l'empereur, investi par la Sagesse divine pour poursuivre l'œuvre des apôtres, guider le nouveau peuple élu dans la foi droite et détruire l'impiété des nations non chrétiennes. L'ampleur du mouvement missionnaire—encouragé par les empereurs—à l'époque macédonienne ne pouvait que favoriser le

---

[10] En accord avec la signification symbolique de celle-ci. En l'absence de coupole, il peut être transféré dans la conque de l'abside, comme on le voit au Xe s. dans les églises de Cappadoce, où les ordres célestes représentés à Sainte-Sophie (chérubins, séraphins, roues de feu) sont figurés autour du Christ, également de type Pantocrator, mais trônant. Le témoignage des fresques cappadociennes, ainsi que celui de l'Homélie de Léon VI sur l'église de Stylianos Zaoutzès, confirment la datation proposée par C. Mango—et généralement acceptée—pour les mosaïques de la tribune sud de Sainte-Sophie.

[11] Mango, *Materials*, 87 (type iconographique incertain).

[12] D'après l'homélie X de Photios: C. Mango, *The Homilies of Photius, Patriarch of Constantinople*, DOS 3 (Cambridge, Mass., 1958), 187–88.

[13] Homélie 28 de l'empereur Léon VI: Mango, *Art*, 202–3.

[14] Homélie 34: Mango, *Art*, 203–4.

[15] Mathews, *Early Churches*, 133–34, a proposé de situer au rez-de-chaussée l'emplacement du trône dans cette travée centrale, mais cette restitution reste fragile (cf. le compte rendu de C. Strube, *BZ* 67 [1974], 412).

[16] La décoration en mosaïque exécutée sous Michel III (856–866) montrait l'image du Christ au-dessus du trône impérial: Mango, *Art*, 184; S. Der Nersessian, "Le décor des églises byzantines du IXe siècle," *Actes du VIe Congrès International des Études byzantines*, II (Paris, 1951), 317–18, repr. dans *Études byzantines et arméniennes*, I (Louvain, 1973), 38–39.

succès d'un tel rapprochement.[17] Lors de la fête de la Pentecôte, hymnes et acclamations répètent avec insistance la même idée: le souverain a bénéficié, lors de son couronnement, comme les apôtres à la Pentecôte, de la venue de l'Esprit Saint, et celui-ci lui permet d'œuvrer pour la défense et la propagation de la foi chrétienne.[18] Citons par exemple ce chant des Bleus (troisième réception): "Dieu, par ses illuminations en forme de langues, ayant détruit les impiétés des nations, entreprend de vaincre et de détruire, par vous, souverains pleins de courage, les impiétés des nations. Qu'il entraîne ceux qui parlent des langues étrangères à parler la même langue de la foi, un tel et un tel, joie et orgueil des Romains."[19] L'Euchologe insiste de même, lors du couronnement, sur l'obligation qu'a l'empereur de soumettre les nations barbares à son autorité et de faire triompher le christianisme.[20] Du reste, parmi les thèmes de glorification de l'empereur, celui de la propagande religieuse, condition de l'unité de l'Empire en-deçà des frontières et de sa suprématie en dehors, est un des plus importants.

La représentation de la Pentecôte dans la tribune sud rappelait ce devoir religieux du *basileus,* primordial aux yeux du patriarche, dont Sainte-Sophie était aussi l'église. L'une des rares fêtes importantes à l'occasion de laquelle l'empereur monte dans la tribune sud pour écouter la lecture de l'évangile et la litanie est d'ailleurs le Dimanche de l'Orthodoxie, qui commémore la défaite des Iconoclastes, événement considéré comme le triomphe définitif de la vraie foi, grâce à l'action des empereurs.

L'iconographie de la scène à Sainte-Sophie s'accordait avec cette interprétation, puisqu'elle offrait, avec la miniature du manuscrit des Homélies de Grégoire de Nazianze exécuté pour Basile 1er (Paris. gr. 510),[21] l'un des plus anciens exemples de la représentation des nations, tribus et langues. A raison de quatre figures dans chaque pendentif, on avait seize représentants des peuples, ce qui correspond au nombre des nations nommées dans les Actes des Apôtres. L'universalité de la prédication apostolique ainsi rappelée faisait allusion—dans un contexte aulique—à l'action de l'empereur, isapostolique, œuvrant pour l'universalité de l'Empire chrétien. Bientôt, la présence d'un personnage désigné par ses vêtements comme un empereur byzantin, à la tête des peuples, des tribus et des langues, explicitera cette référence et les prétentions universalistes des empereurs de Byzance.[22]

[17] A. Grabar, "L'art religieux de l'Empire byzantin à l'époque des Macédoniens," *L'art de la fin de l'Antiquité et du Moyen Age,* I (Paris, 1968), 160–63; Z. A. Gavrilović, "The Humiliation of Leo VI the Wise (The Mosaic of the Narthex at Saint Sophia, Istanbul)," *CahArch* 28 (1979), 91–93.

[18] O. Treitinger, *Die Oströmische Kaiser- und Reichsidee nach ihrer Gestaltung im höfischer Zeremoniell vom Oströmischen Staats- und Reichsgedanken* (Darmstadt, 1956), 37.

[19] Vogt, *Cérémonies,* I, 9 (pour la fête de la Pentecôte), 54–55; et aussi ibid.: "La présence de l'Esprit Saint a illuminé ceux qui sont sur terre de science divine," "L'esprit qui est Dieu, aujourd'hui a été manifesté aux apôtres en forme de langues de feu et vous, bienfaiteurs couronnés, vous ayant honorés de la pourpre et de la couronne, Il a jugé juste, en son divin vouloir, que vous régniez dignement sur les Romains."

[20] *Euchologion sive rituale Graecorum,* éd. Fr. I. Goar (Paris, 1647), 925. On peut citer aussi ici l'homélie XVIII de Photios (867), qui, célébrant la victoire sur toutes les hérésies, glorifie l'orthodoxie des pieux empereurs Michel III et Basile 1er: Mango, *Homilies,* 297–315.

[21] Fol. 301: H. Omont, *Miniatures des plus anciens manuscrits grecs de la Bibliothèque Nationale du VIe au XIVe siècle* (Paris, 1929), pl. XLIV.

[22] Le premier exemple est peut-être celui de l'église cappadocienne de Göreme, Tokalı kilise 2, vers le milieu du Xe s.: C. Jolivet-Lévy, "L'image du pouvoir dans l'art byzantin à l'époque de la dynastie macédonienne (867–

La signification politique que l'on peut attribuer à la Pentecôte de Sainte-Sophie est confortée par le témoignage d'œuvres approximativement contemporaines. Ainsi, K. Corrigan avait-t-elle proposé de mettre en relation l'ivoire de Berlin représentant le couronnement d'un empereur Léon (V ou VI) par la Vierge, et le Christ entre Pierre et Paul, avec la liturgie de la fête de la Pentecôte à Sainte-Sophie, interprétation aujourd'hui contestée.[23] L'analogie des schémas iconographiques utilisés pour la Pentecôte (fol. 301) et le second concile œcuménique (fol. 355), dans le manuscrit des Homélies de Grégoire de Nazianze, Paris. gr. 510, a souvent été relevée et mise en relation avec le destinataire impérial du codex;[24] l'introduction, un peu plus loin, d'une miniature représentant l'envoi des apôtres en mission et le baptême des peuples païens (fol. 426v°), sans rapport direct avec le texte de l'homélie illustrée, relève probablement des mêmes préoccupations.[25] Est-ce un hasard, enfin, si le thème de la Pentecôte manque rarement dans le décor des fondations impériales? Aux Saints-Apôtres de Constantinople, restaurée sous Basile 1er, la Pentecôte dans la coupole ouest (avec probablement les nations dans les pendentifs) était complétée, d'après Nicolas Mésaritès,[26] par des scènes de prédication des apôtres, enseignant les nations, sujets certes à leur place dans une église dédiée aux apôtres, mais qui devaient apparaître aussi comme la préfiguration de l'œuvre missionnaire de Byzance. On notera, en outre, que l'association Pantocrator/Pentecôte de la tribune de Sainte-Sophie reflète, en réduction, le programme des coupoles centrale et occidentale des Saints-Apôtres. La présence de la Pentecôte est attestée aussi dans l'église de la Théotokos de la Source,[27] restaurée par Basile 1er, et à Saint-Georges des Manganes, fondation de Constantin IX Monomaque;[28] Jean Mauropous dans le discours qu'il prononce en 1047 pour l'inauguration de l'église des Manganes,[29] en présence de

---

1056)," *Byzantion* 57 (1987), 459–60; la formule sera souvent reprise par la suite, même quand les représentants des peuples sont réduits au minimum: D. Mouriki, *The Mosaics of Nea Moni on Chios* (Athènes, 1985), 190–91.

[23] K. Corrigan, "The Ivory Scepter of Leo VI: A Statement of Post-Iconoclastic Imperial Ideology," *ArtB* 60 (1978), 407–16, interprétation critiquée par A. Arnulf, "Eine Perle für das Haupt Leons VI.: Epigraphische und ikonographische Untersuchungen zum sogenannten Szepter Leons VI.," *Jahrbuch der Berliner Museen* 32 (1990), 69–84.

[24] Au trône de l'Hétimasie répond le trône portant le livre des évangiles, source de la Sagesse divine qui inspire le concile, présidé par Théodose, pour juger les hérétiques. Le parallélisme des images vise à souligner le rapport entre la mission confiée aux apôtres et celle de l'empereur, successeur des apôtres et gardien de l'Orthodoxie: Gavrilović, "The Humiliation of Leo VI," 91; Jolivet-Lévy, "L'image du pouvoir," 459–60.

[25] S. Der Nersessian, "The Illustrations of the Homilies of Gregory of Nazianzus, Paris gr. 510: A Study of the Connections between Text and Images," *DOP* 16 (1962), 221.

[26] T. Baseu-Barabas, *Zwischen Wort und Bild: Nikolaos Mesarites und seine Beschreibung des Mosaikschmucks der Apostelkirche in Konstantinopel (Ende 12. Jh.)* (Wien, 1992), 60–73, 174–78.

[27] Mango, *Art,* 202.

[28] Mango, *Art,* 219–20. D'autres exemples, plus tardifs, pourraient être cités comme la Chapelle Palatine de Palerme, dont la Pentecôte a été mise en relation avec les tentatives de conversion des Juifs menées par Roger II (Kitzinger, "Cappella Palatina," 277–78; voir aussi Borsook, *Messages,* 22–24) ou l'église de la Nativité à Bethléem (v. 1169), où la Pentecôte et la Dormition sur le mur nord du sanctuaire répondaient à la Présentation au temple et vraisemblablement au portrait de l'empereur Manuel, sur le mur sud; présidant symboliquement les conciles représentés dans la nef, l'empereur était ainsi présenté en successeur des apôtres et en arbitre de l'Orthodoxie: L.-A. Hunt, "Art and Colonialism: The Mosaics of the Church of the Nativity in Bethlehem (1169) and the Problem of 'Crusader' Art," *DOP* 45 (1991), 78.

[29] Il compare l'église à la nouvelle Jérusalem et dit qu'"elle est si grande qu'elle peut accueillir aujourd'hui tous ses sujets, des myriades d'hommes venus à lui des extrémités de l'univers, les tribus innombrables des na-

l'empereur, de l'impératrice, des dignitaires de l'Église et de l'État et des étrangers, développe d'ailleurs ce thème de la mission universaliste de l'empereur.

Les mosaïques à sujets religieux—Pantocrator, Pentecôte—qui décoraient les voûtes de la tribune sud, étaient donc liées, sinon à des portraits, du moins à la présence impériale en ce lieu, illustrant la hiérarchie des pouvoirs du monarque céleste et du *basileus* et glorifiant le rôle de l'empereur pour la défense et la propagation de la foi chrétienne.[30]

On sait que la tribune sud de Sainte-Sophie servait aussi de lieu de réunion pour des synodes, mais cet usage, rarement attesté avant le XIe s.,[31] ne fut probablement pas déterminant dans le choix du programme iconographique. Pourtant, l'image de la Pentecôte s'accordait aussi parfaitement à cette fonction, les participants des saints synodes étant censés être inspirés, comme l'avaient été les apôtres, par l'Esprit Saint.[32]

Le décor symétrique de la travée centrale de la tribune nord est incomplétement restituable et de datation incertaine.[33] Un dessin de Loos montre qu'à l'est était représenté le Baptême du Christ,[34] tandis qu'à l'ouest, où le thème n'est pas reconnaissable, C. Mango propose de restituer la Transfiguration (Fig. 6). L'analogie entre l'épiphanie du Christ dans le Jourdain et l'épiphanie de l'empereur,[35] surtout évoquée lors de son couronnement, et l'influence sur l'iconographie de l'idéologie liant les thèmes de la Sagesse divine, du Baptême et de la Royauté ont été souvent étudiées.[36] Le Baptême du Christ

---

tions, et le peuple élu, avec ses dignitaires, peuple heureux dont la vie, grâce à la philanthropie impériale, est une fête": J. Lefort, "Rhétorique et politique chez Jean Mauropous en 1047," *TM* 6 (1976), 265–303.

[30] Sur l'iconographie reflétant l'idéologie impériale et l'essor missionnaire à l'époque macédonienne: Grabar, "L'art religieux," 151–68.

[31] La plus ancienne mention, à notre connaissance, de cette utilisation de la tribune sud concerne le concile de 869: Mansi, XVI (Graz, 1960), col. 309c; je remercie Michael McCormick d'avoir attiré mon attention sur cette référence; cf. aussi C. Walter, *L'iconographie des conciles dans la tradition byzantine* (Paris, 1970), 146. Pour le XIe s.: V. Grumel, *Les Regestes du Patriarcat de Constantinople: vol. I. Les actes des patriarches: fasc. 2 et 3. Les Regestes de 715 à 1206* (Paris, 1989), n° 826 (1019), 844 (1038), 869 (1054), 896 (1066), etc.

[32] Le parallélisme traditionnellement établi par l'iconographie entre Pentecôte et concile a été rappelé plus haut, à propos des miniatures du Paris. gr. 510.

[33] Mango, *Materials*, 47–48, 98.

[34] Les deux théophanies représentées dans les tribunes, Pentecôte et Baptême, sont théologiquement liées, ces deux événements étant marqués par la descente de l'Esprit Saint et associés par les témoignages de Jean-Baptiste (Mt. 3,11) et du Christ (Actes des Apôtres 1,5). Ce parallélisme a été parfois exprimé par l'iconographie, comme le montre l'analogie entre l'Ascension-Pentecôte de l'ampoule 10 de Monza (Main de Dieu, colombe du Saint Esprit, rayons) et le Baptême tel qu'il apparaît par exemple à la même époque sur le médaillon en or trouvé à Chypre et conservé à Dumbarton Oaks (M. C. Ross, *Catalogue of the Byzantine and Early Medieval Antiquities,* II [Washington, D.C., 1965], 33–35, n° 36). Rappelons aussi que la Pentecôte était l'une des principales fêtes au cours desquelles le baptême était administré.

[35] Treitinger, *Die Oströmische Kaiser- und Reichsidee*, 35; cf. aussi A. Wenger, "Notes inédites sur les empereurs," *REB* 10 (1952), 51–54; P. Grierson, "The Date of the Dumbarton Oaks Epiphany Medaillon," *DOP* 15 (1961), 221–24; K. Hoffmann, *Taufsymbolik im Mittelalterlichen Herrscherbild* (Düsseldorf, 1968); H. Maguire, "The Mosaics of Nea Moni: An Imperial Reading," *DOP* 46 (1992), 210–11. Pour les acclamations de l'empereur le jour de la fête des Lumières: Vogt, *Cérémonies*, I (3), 35–37. C'est aussi le jour de l'Épiphanie (6 janvier 870) que Léon VI fut couronné par son père: V. Grumel, "Notes de chronologie byzantine," *EO* 35 (1936), 331–33.

[36] S. Ćurčić, "The Original Baptismal Font of Gračanica and Its Iconographic Setting," *Zbornik narodnog muzeja* 9–10 (1979), 313–23; Z. Gavrilović, "Divine Wisdom as Part of Byzantine Imperial Ideology," *Zograf* 11 (1980), 44–52; eadem, "The Forty Martyrs of Sebaste in the Painted Programm of Žiča Vestibule," *JÖB* 32.5 (1982), 185–93; eadem, "Kingship and Baptism in the Iconography of Dečani and Lesnovo," *Dečani et l'art byzantin au milieu du XIVe siècle* (Belgrade, 1989), 297–304; eadem, "The Archbishop Danilo II and the Themes of

est l'antétype de l'investiture divine de l'empereur, qui reçoit avec le pouvoir suprême l'Esprit Saint et la Sagesse divine. Les paroles du Père entendues à l'occasion du Baptême—"Celui-ci est mon fils bien-aimé qui a toute ma faveur"—sont reprises et appliquées à l'empereur, en particulier lors de son couronnement. L'un des textes exprimant le mieux cette idée est le poème de Théodore Prodromos assimilant l'empereur victorieux Jean II Comnène, élu de Dieu, au Christ baptisé: "Je crois entendre une seconde voix venue du ciel qui s'écrie dans les nuages: 'Celui-ci est mon empereur, celui en qui j'ai mis toute ma complaisance.'"[37] L'iconographie de l'époque macédonienne reflète ce rapprochement. Citons le *solidus* d'Alexandre, couronné par saint Jean-Baptiste[38]—coïncidence sans doute, Alexandre est précisément représenté dans la tribune nord de Sainte-Sophie—ou la célèbre miniature du Psautier de Paris qui montre la descente de l'Esprit Saint sous la forme d'une colombe au-dessus de la tête de David, représenté en empereur byzantin.[39] Le Baptême est représenté face à la tribune royale dans l'église d'Aghtamar et, plus tard, à la Chapelle Palatine de Palerme;[40] dans l'église de Çavuşin, en Cappadoce, le Baptême, hors cycle, fait face à l'absidiole nord, où sont peints, comme dans une loge, Nicéphore Phocas et Théophano,[41] et dans les églises serbes du XIVe s., il est rapproché des portraits des souverains.[42]

Si la composition associée au Baptême dans la travée centrale de la tribune nord de Sainte-Sophie était bien, comme on l'a supposé, la Transfiguration, elle pouvait avoir une signification analogue: comme pour le Baptême, les paroles du Père ("Celui-ci est mon fils bien-aimé . . .") entendues lors de la Transfiguration ont été appliquées au souverain. C'est sans doute pour cette raison que la scène figure—avec le Baptême—face aux tribunes royales d'Aghtamar et de la Chapelle Palatine de Palerme,[43] et que dans l'église du Sauveur de Macxvariši (Svanétie), en 1140, elle surmonte, déployée sur toute la hauteur de la voûte, l'image du triomphe du roi Demetre 1er, rappelant l'élection divine dont se réclamait le Roi des Rois de Géorgie.[44]

Le décor disparu des tribunes de Sainte-Sophie avait donc, selon toute vraisemblance, une signification politico-religieuse, en accord avec la fonction de ces tribunes et avec les seules images qui y sont conservées: les portraits impériaux.

Kingship and Baptism in 14th Century Serbian Painting," *L'archevêque Danilo et son époque* (Belgrade, 1991), 471–79.

[37] W. Hörandner, éd., *Theodoros Prodromos, historische Gedichte* (Wien, 1974), 249.

[38] C. Jolivet-Lévy, "L'image du pouvoir," 447–48; N. Thierry, "Le Baptiste sur le solidus d'Alexandre (912–913)," *Revue numismatique* 34 (1992), 237–41.

[39] A. Cutler, *The Aristocratic Psalters in Byzantium* (Paris, 1984), fig. 251. Un poème anonyme du Marcianus gr. Z. 524 (vers 1166) décrit également une représentation de l'empereur avec la colombe de l'Esprit Saint descendant du ciel: P. Magdalino et R. Nelson, "The Emperor in Byzantine Art of the Twelfth Century," *ByzF* 8 (1982), 148–49.

[40] Voir infra.

[41] C. Jolivet-Lévy, *Les églises byzantines de Cappadoce. Le programme iconographique de l'abside et de ses abords* (Paris, 1991), 14 n. 6, 20–21.

[42] Voir la bibliographie indiquée supra, note 36.

[43] Ćurčić, "Some Palatine Aspects of the Cappella Palatina," 127–28, 138.

[44] N. Thierry, "Le souverain dans les programmes d'églises en Cappadoce et en Géorgie du Xe au XIIIe siècles," *Revue des études géorgiennes et caucasiennes* 4 (1988), 134–37.

Au sud-est du lac de Van, dans l'ancienne province arménienne du Vaspurakan, roy-aume vassal de Bagdad, Aghtamar fut l'une des principales résidences du roi Gagik Ar-cruni qui avait fortifié l'île et y avait fait construire un somptueux palais et une église dédiée à la Sainte-Croix, dont la date généralement admise se situe entre 915 et 921 (Fig. 7).

Cette église palatine, monument de prestige aux façades extérieures tapissées de sculp-tures et à l'intérieur richement décoré de peintures, a été très souvent décrite et analysée, l'accent étant mis tantôt sur ses liens avec l'art princier du monde musulman, tantôt sur le contenu religieux du décor, ou encore sur sa signification politique.[45] La complexité de cet ensemble, dans lequel les sujets sont souvent liés entre eux d'une façade à l'autre et/ou sur une même paroi par tout un jeu de correspondances, se prête en effet à plu-sieurs niveaux d'interprétation. Je ne m'attacherai qu'à certains des aspects du pro-gramme iconographique, qui peuvent être mis en relation avec l'exaltation du souverain et avec la fonction palatine du monument.

La composition du donateur, sur la façade ouest, légitime le statut du roi Gagik (nimbé, richement vêtu) en le représentant en compagnie du Christ, auquel il offre le modèle de l'église[46] (Fig. 8). Inspirée d'une formule traditionnelle à Byzance, la compo-sition se distingue cependant des images byzantines contemporaines par l'absence de hiérarchie établie entre le Christ et Gagik. Ils sont tous deux debout, de face,[47] au même niveau, et si la taille supérieure du roi ne s'explique probablement que parce que les blocs étaient sculptés avant leur mise en place, on ne peut qu'être frappé par l'absence de tout attribut honorifique—trône, marche-pieds, tapis—pour le Christ, dont la pré-séance n'est suggérée que par l'inscription gravée sur son codex—"Je suis la lumière du monde" (Jn. 8,12)—et par le geste de bénédiction qu'il adresse à Gagik. Entre eux, deux anges, à plus petite échelle, tiennent l'image de la croix, à laquelle l'église est dédiée, et deux grands séraphins encadrent la scène.

Plusieurs frises, animales et végétales, entourent cette composition et se poursuivent tout autour de l'église,[48] associées à des figures humaines et à des animaux réels ou

---

[45] Bibliographie sélective, dans l'ordre de parution: S. Der Nersessian, *Aght'amar: Church of the Holy Cross* (Cambridge, Mass., 1965); S. Der Nersessian et H. Vahramian, *Aght'amar,* Documenti di architettura armena 8 (Milan, 1974); C. Jolivet, "L'idéologie princière dans les sculptures d'Aghtamar," *Second International Symposium on Armenian Art, Erevan 1978* (Erevan, 1981), III, 86–94; S. Mnac'akanyan, *Alt'amar* (Erevan, 1985) (compte rendu de N. Thierry, *REArm* 22 [1990–91], 408–11); J. M. Thierry, *Monuments arméniens du Vaspurakan* (Paris, 1989), 271–86; J. G. Davies, *Medieval Art and Architecture: The Church of the Holy Cross Aght'amar* (Londres, 1991). Je n'ai pas eu accès au résumé de la communication de Lynn Jones, "The Decorative Program of the Church of the Holy Cross, Aghtamar," *BSCAbstr* 18 (1992), développé dans "The Church of the Holy Cross and the Ico-nography of Kingship," *Gesta* 33.2 (1994), 104–17, paru après la rédaction de mon article.

[46] Gagik avait reçu la couronne royale de l'émir Yusuf en 908 (Thomas Artsruni, *History of the House of the Arts-runik,* trad. et comm. R. W. Thomson [Detroit, 1985], 347–48), dignité bientôt entérinée par Byzance qui con-fère à Gagik le titre d'archonte des archontes (*De Ceremoniis,* II, 48, éd. Bonn [1829], I, 687, l.4–5); F. Dölger, *Corpus der griechischen Urkunden des Mittelalters und der neueren Zeit, Reihe A, Regesten,* I (Munich-Berlin, 1924), 78 (n° 630, 631).

[47] Seuls les pieds de Gagik sont tournés vers le Christ.

[48] Frises d'animaux sous le toit conique de la coupole, sous ceux des exèdres et des niches. Sous les figures, une frise étroite à entrelacs, raisins et palmettes; au-dessus, des animaux intercalés entre les figures, et, plus haut, un large rinceau de vigne habité.

fantastiques, disséminés entre elles ou au-dessus. Le plus important de ces motifs est le large rinceau de vigne qui ceinture tout l'édifice: les ceps s'entrelacent en rinceaux couverts de grappes de raisin auxquelles se mêlent des grenades et ce rinceau est peuplé d'animaux et de scènes profanes, principalement agrestes (Figs. 9, 10). Toute cette imagerie se prête—et se prêtait sans doute dès sa création—à plusieurs niveaux de lecture, mais mon propos n'est pas de reprendre ici le problème, toujours controversé, des différentes significations symboliques possibles de ce type de programme ornemental, dont l'origine remonte à l'époque hellénistique.[49] Constatons seulement qu'on est à Aghtamar en présence d'un type de décor d'église plutôt inhabituel pour l'époque médiobyzantine—exception faite, justement, des fondations princières[50]—et qui se rattache aux traditions palatines.[51] La décoration de la toute proche résidence de Gagik, à Aghtamar, évoquée avec émerveillement par le Continuateur de T'ovma Arcruni,[52] devait être comparable; certains des sujets mentionnés—le roi trônant majestueusement entre de jeunes serviteurs, les scènes de combat, les lions et autres bêtes sauvages, les oiseaux—sont d'ailleurs communs à l'église et au palais, qui devaient former un ensemble décoratif homogène.[53] Ces thèmes faisaient partie du répertoire de l'art aulique du monde islamique,[54] et Gagik avait probablement la prétention d'égaler à Aghtamar la magnificence des demeures califales abbassides.

Les pampres de vigne, auxquels se mêlent des grenadiers, évoquant une terre fertile, les petites scènes qui leur sont associées—images de la vie rurale, de la chasse ou des plaisirs de la cour—exprimaient, dans ce contexte palatin, la richesse de la création, la prospérité et la paix apportées par le gouvernement de Gagik, garant de la fécondité du Vaspurakan et de ses habitants. Le thème est habituel chez les panégyristes,[55] et T'ovma Arcruni et son Continuateur ne manquent pas de célébrer ce premier devoir du prince.[56]

Mais l'association des motifs profanes à des figures bibliques (ou historiques) suggère

[49] Voir récemment H. Maguire, *Earth and Ocean: The Terrestrial World in Early Byzantine Art* (University Park, Pa.-Londres, 1987); H. Maguire, "Imperial Gardens and the Rhetoric of Renewal," dans *New Constantines: The Rhythm of Imperial Renewal in Byzantium, 4th–13th Centuries,* éd. P. Magdalino (Aldershot, 1994), 181–97; P. Magdalino, "The Bath of Leo the Wise and the 'Macedonian Renaissance' Revisited: Topography, Iconography, Ceremonial, Theology," *DOP* 42 (1988), 107–9; et pour Aghtamar: Davies, *Medieval Art and Architecture,* passim.

[50] Où sujets religieux et profanes se mêlent; cf. Der Nersessian, *Aght'amar,* 27–28 (Sainte-Sophie de Kiev, la Chapelle Palatine de Palerme).

[51] Plantations diverses, vignobles, parcs d'animaux destinés aux divertissements du prince étaient attachés aux palais, en Arménie comme à Byzance: Artsruni, *History,* 117, 316, 353; dans sa description d'Aghtamar, le Continuateur de T'ovma souligne le rôle du roi dans la création de parcs, de jardins fleuris et dans la plantation d'arbres variés arrosés par une source intarissable qui, grâce à la providence divine, coulait au milieu de la cité (Artsruni, *History,* 356); cf. aussi H. Maguire, "A Description of the Aretai Palace and Its Garden," *Journal of Garden History* 10 (1990), 209–13.

[52] Artsruni, *History,* 357–58.

[53] Le décor du palais et celui de l'église pouvaient aussi avoir en commun figures et scènes religieuses, comme le suggère par exemple la description du palais de Digénis Akritas; cf. A. Bryer, "Achthamar and Digenis Akritas," *Antiquity* 34 (1960), 195–297; repr. dans *Peoples and Settlements in Anatolia and the Caucasus* (London, 1988), I.

[54] Cf. Der Nersessian, *Aght'amar,* 25.

[55] Des exemples dans H. Maguire, "Style and Ideology in Byzantine Imperial Art," *Gesta* 28 (1989), 218–21; voir aussi Magdalino, "The Emperor in Byzantine Art," 146.

[56] Artsruni, *History,* 52–54, 295, 313–15, 317, 340–41, 350–51, 352–53.

un autre niveau d'interprétation. Sur la façade orientale, opposée à celle de la composition du donateur, le rinceau de pampres comporte en son centre l'image d'un roi anonyme, couronné et nimbé, assis en tailleur sur un coussin, une coupe de vin à la main (Fig. 11). Non nommé, il est souvent identifié à Gagik, ou encore au roi Trdat (Tiridate), responsable au IIIe s. de la christianisation de l'Arménie, mais plutôt que du portrait d'un personnage précis, il s'agit d'une figure symbolique du prince festoyant, selon une formule traditionnelle dans l'art aulique sassanide et reprise par l'art musulman. Or, cette représentation est alignée sur une figure en buste inscrite dans un médaillon, celle d'Adam (Fig. 12). L'analogie formelle entre les deux images—l'enroulement du rinceau décrit autour du roi un médaillon—confirme le caractère intentionnel de leur rapprochement, destiné à établir une comparaison entre le roi terrestre et Adam, mais Adam racheté, puisque figuré vêtu et sous les traits du Christ, qui est le "nouvel Adam."[57] L'inscription qui accompagne l'image—"et Adam donna leur nom à tous les animaux et bêtes sauvages" (cf. Genèse 2,19–20)—évoque le moment où Dieu donne autorité à l'homme sur toute la création, ce qui confirme notre interprétation. On retrouve ici un thème—celui de la royauté d'Adam, souverain de la création—bien connu depuis Philon d'Alexandrie dans l'exégèse biblique[58] et que développe aussi le chroniqueur T'ovma Arcruni: retraçant les vicissitudes de la famille Arcruni depuis Adam et Eve, il s'arrête longuement sur le don fait à l'homme des délices du Paradis; il célèbre "la splendeur infinie, la grandeur et la gloire dont Il (Dieu) avait couronné l'homme, jouissant en monarque des délices du Paradis."[59] L'iconographie a traduit cette idée dès l'époque paléochrétienne, dans les mosaïques de Syrie (Huarte, Copenhague et Hama);[60] plus tard, les miniaturistes des psautiers grecs médiobyzantins illustrent le Ps. 8,5–6, sur l'homme "couronné de gloire et d'honneur," "ayant toutes choses sous ses pieds," par l'image d'Adam entre les animaux.[61] La scène apparaît ensuite en Russie, où elle semble, comme à Aghtamar, mise en relation avec le pouvoir princier.[62]

---

[57] Cf. I Cor. 15,22; Rom. 5,12–20. La thématique de la façade orientale répond ainsi à celle de la façade occidentale, où le roi, en donateur, est associé au Christ.

[58] Philon d'Alexandrie, *De Opificio Mundi*, éd. R. Arnaldez (Paris, 1967), 196–201 (§§83–88); notons que les œuvres de Philon, qui étaient disponibles en traduction arménienne, sont souvent utilisées par les historiens arméniens et que T'ovma Arcruni lui fait plusieurs emprunts (Artsruni, *History*, 39–40, 73, 75, 81); Grégoire de Nysse, PG 44:144; cf. M. T. D'Alverny, "L'homme comme symbole. Le microcosme," *Settimane di studio* 23 (1976), 137–39; X. Muratova, "'Adam donne leurs noms aux animaux.' L'iconographie de la scène dans l'art du Moyen Age: les manuscrits des bestiaires enluminés du XIIe et du XIIIe siècles," *Studi medievali* 18.2 (1977), 380; H. Maguire, "Adam and the Animals: Allegory and the Literal Sense in Early Christian Art," *DOP* 41 (1987), 368 note 33.

[59] *Collection des Historiens arméniens, I. Th. Ardzrouni, Xe s., Histoire des Ardzrouni*, trad. M. Brosset (St.-Pétersbourg, 1874), 9 (= Artsruni, *History*, 72).

[60] D'Alverny, "L'homme comme symbole," 143–44; Muratova, "Adam donne leurs noms aux animaux," 380; Maguire, "Adam and the Animals," 367–68. Le thème est naturellement à rapprocher de celui d'Orphée charmant les animaux, dont la comparaison avec l'empereur est un *topos* des panégyriques impériaux: Magdalino, "The Bath of Leo the Wise," 104–7.

[61] Muratova, "Adam donne leurs noms aux animaux," 370 note 15 (Vat. gr. 1927, fol. 10v; British Library 40 731, fol. 16r; British Library Add. 19 352, fol. 6v).

[62] Muratova, "Adam donne leurs noms aux animaux," 379 (Saint-Démétrius à Vladimir, cathédrale de Souzdal).

Destiné à régner comme vice-régent de Dieu, Adam, *typos* du Christ, est donc aussi la préfigure du roi terrestre, sculpté au-dessus, et un hommage au pouvoir de Gagik, la glorification du prince passant, selon un procédé analogique traditionnel, par son affinité avec une figure biblique.[63] De façon significative, le thème d'Adam, maître de la création, a d'ailleurs été repris à l'intérieur de l'église dans le cadre du cycle de la Genèse peint à la base de la coupole: j'y reviendrai.

La présence d'Adam confère une connotation paradisiaque aux motifs animaliers et végétaux environnants: il est encadré par les têtes saillantes du bœuf et du lion, allusion probable à la vision paradisiaque d'Isaïe ("Le lion comme le bœuf mangera de la paille," Is. 11,7) tandis qu'au registre inférieur, quatre animaux paisibles (lions affrontés, panthère et capridé) évoquent eux aussi le Paradis (Is. 11,6). La décoration de la façade orientale de l'église (Fig. 13), à la composition harmonieuse et équilibrée, faisait ainsi allusion au jardin d'Éden, planté à l'Orient, et au Paradis reconquis, grâce à l'œuvre rédemptrice du Christ;[64] mais elle célébrait en même temps le rôle du roi créant sur terre un paradis pour ses sujets, qu'il mène vers le "nouvel Éden," thème souvent développé par les panégyristes byzantins.[65] A peu près contemporaine d'Aghtamar, la description du décor du bain de Léon VI à Constantinople par Léon Choirosphaktès est ainsi prétexte à l'éloge du *basileus,* créé à l'image de Dieu pour gouverner la création.[66]

Les autres figures de la façade orientale ont été déjà maintes fois commentées: à Jean-Baptiste et Élie, s'ajoutent les évangélisateurs et fondateurs de l'église arménienne: Grégoire l'Illuminateur, auquel fait pendant probablement Thaddée, apôtre par excellence de l'Arménie,[67] Bartholomée(?) et Jacques de Nisibe(?). Ces figures se rattachent au thème de la diffusion et de la défense de la vraie foi, thème indissociable de l'exaltation du souverain—auquel elles sont ici visuellement associées—et particulièrement d'actualité après de longues années de domination arabe et de persécutions religieuses. Elles s'inscrivent ici dans un programme plus vaste, comportant l'évocation de la propagation universelle de l'évangile (les quatre évangélistes dans les frontons, aux quatre points cardinaux), et l'exaltation des martyrs locaux. Saint Sargis (Serge), en cavalier vainqueur du mal, sur la façade nord, peut être considéré comme tel, en raison de sa grande popularité dans la région,[68] tandis que sur la façade sud, près de l'accès royal à l'église, les princes Sahak et Hamazasp Arcruni, ancêtres de Gagik, martyrisés par les Arabes au

[63] Souvent c'est au créateur lui-même, Dieu, qu'est associé l'empereur, qui gouverne à l'imitation du souverain du cosmos: Maguire, *Earth and Ocean,* 73–80.

[64] Interprétation en accord avec le symbolisme ancien de l'église comme Paradis; cf. F. C. Conybeare, *Rituale Armenorum* (Oxford, 1905), 20, 23, 32, 13; Der Nersessian, *Aght'amar,* 42; Kitzinger, *Mosaics of St. Mary's of the Admiral,* 215–17.

[65] Magdalino, "The Bath of Leo the Wise," 97–118 (oraison funèbre de Léon VI pour son père Basile ler, poème de Jean Géomètres, *ekphrasis* d'un bain impérial par Léon Choirosphaktès); voir aussi Maguire, "Imperial Gardens," 190–91.

[66] Même si les mosaïques en question, créées à l'époque théodosienne, n'avaient pas à l'origine de connotation impériale particulière, comme le soutient C. Mango, "The Palace of Marina, the Poet Palladas and the Bath of Leo VI," *Euphrosynon* (Athènes, 1991), I, 321–30.

[67] T'ovma Arcruni raconte qu'à l'époque du roi Abgar, un prince Arcruni, Khuran, fut le premier à recevoir le baptême de l'apôtre Thaddée: Artsruni, *History,* 111.

[68] Davies, *Medieval Art and Architecture,* 101.

VIIIe s., témoignaient du rôle de héros défenseurs de la foi chrétienne de la famille Arcruni (Fig. 14).

Il y a une quinzaine d'années, lors du Second Symposium d'Art arménien d'Erevan, j'avais attiré l'attention sur l'interprétation particulière du cycle de Jonas (façade sud), qui comporte un épisode rare—la prédication au roi de Ninive, qui appelle les habitants à faire pénitence (Jon. 3,5–6)[69] (Fig. 15)—allusion possible à Gagik, dont le chroniqueur fait remonter la généalogie à Sennachérib et, au-delà, à Assour, fondateur de Ninive;[70] le rappel de l'ancienneté de la race est un autre des lieux communs destinés à consolider le pouvoir du prince. Portant le même type de couronne que Gagik, sur la façade ouest, assis à l'orientale comme le souverain de la façade est, le roi est présenté ici en guide spirituel de son peuple. En dessous, Jonas repose non pas sous le traditionnel ricin (Jon. 4,6), mais sous un grenadier chargé de fruits, symbole d'immortalité et de résurrection, qui nous renvoie au thème paradisiaque déjà évoqué. Ainsi, l'image de paix et de joie célestes—Jonas reposant sous le grenadier—est visuellement associée à la représentation du roi, qui conduit son peuple vers le salut.

Plus banales sont les images qui exaltent les héros bibliques auxquels il était d'usage d'identifier les princes pour légitimer leur pouvoir: David, dont Gagik prétendait descendre par sa mère (princesse bagratide),[71] et dont l'affrontement avec Goliath occupe une place particulièrement importante sur la façade sud[72] (Fig. 16), mais aussi Samson,[73] Moïse, Ézéchias (vêtu comme le prince Hamazasp), roi pieux exemplaire, qui lutta contre l'idolâtrie et libéra Israël de la domination assyrienne, ou même Daniel.[74] A travers ces figures bibliques, attestées dans d'autres cycles palatins,[75] c'est encore le roi du Vaspurakan que l'on glorifiait et dont on affirmait la légitimité tout en exprimant son espérance de salut: choisi par Dieu pour guider son peuple, il était assimilé aux chefs et aux rois d'Israël, célébré pour sa piété et sa vaillance, et l'on demandait pour lui l'assistance divine.

L'usage de réserver à l'extérieur de l'église des images à résonance princière est tradi-

---

[69] Le thème de la prédication de Jonas à Ninive, inconnu des images paléochrétiennes, comme des miniatures arméniennes, apparaît en revanche dans les manuscrits impériaux byzantins, Paris. gr. 510 (fol. 3: Omont, *Miniatures*, pl. xx) et Paris. gr. 139 (fol. 431v: Cutler, *Aristocratic Psalters*, fig. 256)—dans ce dernier, le roi n'est pas représenté—ainsi que dans le Psautier de Vatopédi, cod. 760 (fol. 283r: ibid., fig. 390).

[70] Artsruni, *History,* 68–69, 82, 313, 369, 370.

[71] Artsruni, *History,* 313.

[72] Goliath étant désigné d'un terme qui en arménien signifie à la fois le Philistin et l'étranger (I Samuel 17,38–51). La formule iconographique suivie est proche de celle de la miniature du Psautier de Basile II, Venise, Bibl. Marc. gr. 17 (Cutler, *Aristocratic Psalters,* fig. 413).

[73] Ouvrant la gueule d'un lion (Juges 14,6) et assommant un Philistin avec une mâchoire d'âne (Juges 15,15).

[74] L'iconographie de Daniel entre les lions est caractérisée par l'attitude de soumission des animaux; la fin du récit est particulièrement appropriée au contexte, cf. Dan. 5,29: "Alors Daniel fut vêtu de pourpre par ordre du roi; on lui mit au cou un collier d'or et on fit publier qu'il aurait la puissance dans le royaume comme en étant la troisième personne"; cf. L. Zakarian, "Iconographie des sculptures du monastère Surb-Stepanos Aljoc," *REArm* 23 (1992), 495–503.

[75] J. Mavrogordato, *Digenis Akritas* (Oxford, 1956), 217–23; A. Grabar, *L'empereur dans l'art byzantin* (Strasbourg, 1936), 95–97 et idem, "Les cycles d'images byzantins tirés de l'histoire biblique et leur symbolisme princier," *Starinar* 20 (1969), 135–37.

tionnel—dans le domaine byzantin les exemples conservés sont cependant plus tardifs[76]—et il me paraît indéniable que tel était le cas à Aghtamar, même si dans sa description de l'église, le Continuateur de T'ovma Arcruni ne relève nullement cet aspect.[77] Il s'attache, en revanche, à présenter Gagik comme un monarque idéal, rempli par la Sagesse divine et l'Esprit Saint, successeur des grands chefs du peuple élu et régnant sur un nouvel Israël.[78] Outre sa signification religieuse, le décor sculpté de l'église de la Sainte-Croix, créé sous le règne d'un roi qui avait su, malgré la menace arabe et les rivalités internes, rétablir la paix et la prospérité,[79] avait donc un contenu politique reflétant l'idéologie princière contemporaine, en accord avec la fonction palatine du monument.

On peut se demander si le programme iconographique mis en place à l'intérieur de l'église[80] ne contribuait pas, lui aussi, à l'exaltation royale. On y retrouve tout d'abord— et le doublet est en lui-même révélateur—le thème paradisiaque évoqué sur la façade orientale. A la base de la coupole, entre les fenêtres du tambour, se développe un cycle de la Genèse, très mal conservé,[81] qui se déroulait de gauche à droite, en débutant avec la création d'Adam (Gen. 2,7), à peu près à l'aplomb du sanctuaire (à l'est-nord-est), suivie par Adam (qui a les traits du Christ) dans le jardin d'Éden (Gen. 2,15 ff), la création d'Ève (Gen. 2,21 f), le Seigneur établissant la souveraineté d'Adam sur tous les animaux (sud-sud-est; Gen. 1,27 f); puis, après une lacune de trois ou quatre sujets, les reproches de Dieu (nord-ouest; Gen. 3,10–19), l'expulsion (Gen. 3,23) et, au nord-est, le chérubin gardant la porte du Paradis (Gen. 3,24). Ce cycle paradisiaque, évoquant les premiers temps de l'histoire du salut, sert de prélude au récit (peint plus bas) de l'Incarnation du Christ et de la Rédemption, opposant la vie du Christ à la faute originelle et le second Adam au premier. Ce contenu théologique du programme se double peut-être d'une signification autre, en accord avec l'interprétation proposée plus haut de l'association entre Adam régnant sur la création au Paradis et le roi établi par Dieu pour gouver-

---

[76] Cf. L. Hadermann-Misguich, "Une longue tradition byzantine. La décoration extérieure des églises," *Zograf* 7 (1977), 5–10; exemples: Saint-Georges de Kurbinovo, Mavriotissa de Castoria, Sainte-Sophie de Trébizonde, églises de la région de Vladimir Souzdal, Église de la Vierge Péribleptos (= Sulu Manastir) à Constantinople, Saint-Nicolas de Manastir, Saint-Nicolas Bolnički d'Ohrid, églises moldaves du XVIe s., etc.

[77] Il mentionne seulement "les portraits parfaitement exacts, d'Abraham à David et à Notre-Seigneur Jésus Christ, la série des prophètes et des apôtres . . . , des masses d'animaux sauvages et d'oiseaux, sangliers et lions, taureaux et ours, affrontés, figurant les oppositions de leurs natures, ce qui plaît fort aux penseurs, . . . des ceps chargés de raisins, des vignerons, des réunions d'animaux et reptiles, dont les représentations, variées suivant les espèces, amusaient le regard": Brosset, *Collection des Historiens,* 240 (= Artsruni, *History,* 360).

[78] Voir en particulier Artsruni, *History,* 334–35, 341, 348, 359, 365–66.

[79] L'abondance des constructions, tant religieuses que profanes, en témoigne: Thierry, *Monuments arméniens,* 54.

[80] Sur les peintures: N. Thierry, "Les peintures de l'église de la Sainte-Croix d'Aghtamar (915–921)," *Second International Symposium on Armenian Art, Erevan 1978* (Erevan, 1981), III, 182–90; T. F. Mathews, "The Genesis Frescoes of Alt'amar," *REArm* 16 (1982), 245–57; N. Thierry, "Le cycle de la création et de la faute d'Adam à Alt'amar," *REArm* 17 (1983), 289–329; A. D. Grishin, "The Aght'amar Wall Paintings: Some New Observations," *Parergon,* n.s., 3 (1985), 39–51. Contrairement à Grishin, nous pensons que la plupart des peintures, contemporaines des sculptures, datent du règne de Gagik.

[81] O. Demus, *The Mosaics of San Marco in Venice,* II (Chicago-Londres, 1984), 144, pense que le cycle de la création commençait aux registres supérieurs de la coupole, reconstruite vers 1280, après un effondrement.

ner sur terre. Un premier indice en faveur de cette hypothèse est la présence de l'image d'Adam dans le jardin d'Éden[82] (Fig. 17), thème rarement illustré dans les cycles courts (comme celui d'Aghtamar) et peu retenu par les auteurs arméniens,[83] à l'exception, comme nous l'avons relevé plus haut, de T'ovma Arcruni, qui développe ce passage.[84] Peut-on en déduire qu'il a été représenté ici en raison de sa signification comme archétype du monarque jouissant des dons de Dieu? Second indice: la présence, après la création d'Ève, de la scène d'Adam auquel le Seigneur présente les animaux (Fig. 18), établissant ainsi sa souveraineté sur la création, épisode que le récit de la Genèse place avant la création d'Ève. Bien que l'extension de la composition vers la droite ne puisse plus, en raison de son état de conservation, être précisée, on constate que l'inversion chronologique des deux épisodes a permis de peindre Adam, maître des animaux, à peu près à l'aplomb de la loge royale aménagée pour Gagik dans l'exèdre sud de l'église. Comme à l'extérieur de l'église, Adam est présenté, à l'intérieur, en archétype du souverain, rapprochement destiné à glorifier la royauté de Gagik.

Située à mi-hauteur, au-dessus d'une voûte en cul-de-four, et accessible par un escalier extérieur détruit au XIXe s. (quand on ajouta un clocher devant l'entrée sud), la tribune royale[85] était fermée par une balustrade d'environ 1,50 m de haut, percée de cinq ouvertures cintrées et décorée vers la nef de branches de grenadiers et de six protomes d'animaux, comme on en voit sur les façades extérieures de l'église. Cette balustrade à claire-voie, détruite, est connue par des photographies antérieures à l'abandon de l'église en 1917 (Fig. 19).

Au-dessus de la loge royale débute le cycle christologique avec les scènes évoquant la Première Venue du Christ (Annonciation, Visitation, Nativité), tandis qu'au-dessous, dans la conque surmontant la porte, une composition montrait le Christ au-dessus d'une double rangée d'une quinzaine de saints alignés frontalement (Fig. 20). Peu lisible, en raison de son médiocre état de conservation et de la présence d'un important repeint (Fig. 21), la scène est habituellement identifiée comme la Seconde Venue, en raison de son analogie, d'ailleurs relative, avec des images comme la miniature du manuscrit de Cosmas Indicopleustès, au Vatican (cod. gr. 699, fol. 89).[86] Quelle qu'ait été son iconographie précise, elle évoquait la domination universelle du Christ et, probablement, le salut final pour les justes, en une composition solennelle et hiérarchisée, et elle avait vraisemblablement été conçue en fonction de la présence, au-dessus, de la tribune royale et de celle, au-dessous, de la porte menant au palais de Gagik.

[82] Jardin planté d'arbres au feuillage épais; la main gauche levée vers l'oreille, Adam écoute les prescriptions de Dieu et leur obéit.

[83] Qui suivent plutôt le premier récit de la Genèse (1,28–30); ni l'*Apocryphe de la Création et de la Faute*, ni le livre de *la Pénitence* n'en font mention: Thierry, "Le cycle de la création," 296.

[84] Cf. supra, note 59.

[85] Mentionnée par le Continuateur de T'ovma Arcruni: Artsruni, *History*, 361.

[86] Miniature qui représente la structure de l'univers par la superposition de trois registres (anges, hommes, morts) sous le Christ trônant: C. Stornajolo, *Le miniature della Topografia cristiana di Cosma Indicopleuste. Codice Vaticano greco 699*, Codices e Vaticani selecti 10 (Milan, 1908), pl. 45, 49. On l'a également comparée à la représentation du Jugement dernier dans le manuscrit des *Sacra Parallela* (Paris. gr. 923), fol. 68v: K. Weitzmann, *The Miniatures of the Sacra Parallela, Parisinus graecus 923*, Studies in Manuscript Illumination 8 (Princeton, 1979), pl. XCVI, 441.

Dans l'exèdre nord (Figs. 20, 22), face à la tribune, on remarque la mise en valeur, au registre supérieur, de trois compositions: Baptême, Transfiguration, Noces de Cana, trois sujets théologiquement liés. Aux deux grandes théophanies s'ajoute le premier miracle du Christ, autre signe qui manifesta aux disciples sa gloire et sa divinité. Les exégètes n'ont pas seulement souligné la signification sacramentaire du miracle de Cana, figure de l'Eucharistie, ils l'ont aussi expliqué comme une illumination et une figure du Baptême,[87] sujet qui lui fait pendant à Aghtamar, et comme une révélation de sa divinité. Ces trois scènes peuvent être ainsi mises en relation avec la présence, en face, du roi siégeant dans sa tribune. Il est significatif, à cet égard, que le Baptême et la Transfiguration, dont j'ai rappelé à propos de Sainte-Sophie la signification particulière dans un contexte aulique, soient semblablement représentés face à la loge royale dans la Chapelle Palatine de Palerme[88] (Fig. 23). Quant aux Noces de Cana, elles présentent à Aghtamar une iconographie inhabituelle, inspirée de l'art palatin, qui s'accorde avec cette interprétation; elles constituent, en effet, "une charmante scène de la vie quotidienne en Orient, conçue de façon étagée; le Christ en haut et à droite est assis bénissant, prié par Marie; plus bas, assis en tailleur, les deux jeunes époux tiennent des gobelets de vin, petit sujet habituel aux scènes de festin d'Asie centrale et du monde arabe; face à eux, une foule de serviteurs en perspective surhaussée emplissent les urnes et circulent avec des carafes et des verres."[89] Le choix et la disposition des trois sujets peints dans l'exèdre nord, ainsi que l'iconographie particulière des Noces, ont été, à mon avis, déterminés par la présence, en face, de la loge royale: établissant une comparaison entre la vie du Christ et celle du souverain, ils rappelaient l'origine divine du pouvoir de celui-ci, conformément au *topos*—l'empereur image du Christ.[90] Pourtant, c'est moins le "point de vue royal" (ces sujets étaient-ils bien visibles de la tribune?)—invoqué par exemple pour le programme de la Chapelle Palatine de Palerme—qui explique l'emplacement des trois thèmes, que le désir d'établir un parallélisme entre le roi et les scènes christologiques.[91] Physiquement présent dans l'église, Gagik se trouvait intégré au programme iconographique[92] et prenait ainsi place dans l'histoire du salut.

---

[87] J. Daniélou, *Bible et liturgie* (Paris, 1951), 296–99.

[88] Cf. supra, note 43.

[89] Thierry, "Les peintures de l'église de la Sainte-Croix," 185. Rappelons aussi les acclamations prononcées lors du mariage et du couronnement nuptial d'un empereur, dans le *De Ceremoniis*: "Que Celui qui, à Cana, assista aux noces et, à ces noces, bénit l'eau par amour pour les hommes, et fit du vin pour donner jouissance aux hommes, que Celui-là vous bénisse, avec votre épouse": Vogt, *Cérémonies*, II, 6–7; cf. aussi ibid., 181.

[90] L'analogie entre iconographie impériale et iconographie chrétienne est développée par exemple par Euthymios Malakès, dans son discours à Manuel Comnène (Magdalino, "The Emperor in Byzantine Art," 133). Pour l'éloge du prince image du Christ chez Tʻovma Arcruni: Artsruni, *History,* 257, 264 (pour le prince Gurgen, fils d'Apulpech).

[91] En dessous, au registre médian de l'exèdre nord, sont peintes, conformément au déroulement narratif du récit christologique, les scènes de la mort, de la sépulture et de la résurrection du Christ, thèmes qui sont parfois associés au portrait du donateur (éventuellement un souverain) et/ou à son tombeau, pour évoquer son salut: S. Ćurčić, "Medieval Royal Tombs in the Balkans: An Aspect of the 'East or West' Question," *Greek Orthodox Theological Review* 29 (1984), 177–78; N. Teteriatnikov, "Private Salvation Programs and Their Effect on Byzantine Church Decoration," *Arte medievale* 7 (1993), 47–62.

[92] L'espace royal est au cœur d'un réseau d'images, articulé selon un axe horizontal (sujets peints face à la tribune, dans l'exèdre nord) et selon un axe vertical, marqué de haut en bas par l'image d'Adam au Paradis, la Première Venue du Christ et, sous la loge royale, la Seconde Venue(?).

Œuvre exceptionnelle, supervisée par le roi Gagik, qui, nous dit le chroniqueur, fit appel pour les constructions d'Aghtamar aux meilleurs artistes, "rassemblés de toutes les nations de la terre,"[93] la décoration de l'église Sainte-Croix est composite: en partie redevable de l'art palatin du monde islamique environnant (en particulier pour la partie ornementale du programme), comme cela a été souvent souligné, elle doit aussi beaucoup aux traditions de l'art aulique et à l'idéologie princière de Byzance, ce qui s'accorde avec ce que l'on sait par ailleurs de l'influence de l'Empire en Arménie au Xe s.[94]

A travers les décors des tribunes de Sainte-Sophie de Constantinople et de la Sainte-Croix d'Aghtamar, nous avons entrevu deux types de programmes iconographiques déterminés par la fonction aulique d'un espace religieux. Associés à la présence du souverain, réelle ou en image, ils instauraient par le biais des analogies bibliques—procédé bien connu en rhétorique—une relation de *mimèsis* entre l'histoire du salut et la réalité contemporaine, destinée à mettre en évidence la participation de celle-ci au monde du sacré.

Université de Paris 1

---

[93] Artsruni, *History,* 357.

[94] Cf. V. A. Arutjunova-Fidanjan, "L'image de Byzance dans l'historiographie arménienne du Xe s.," *VizVrem* 52 (1991), 113–26, et le résumé français d'I. Sorlin, "Bulletin des publications en langues slaves," *TM* 12 (1994), 523–524; la lettre du katholikos Jean de Drashanakert (897–925) à Constantin Porphyrogénète—véritable miroir du prince—est à cet égard éloquente.

The Heavenly Court

Henry Maguire

The Byzantines created for themselves two courts, a real court centered on Constantinople and an imaginary one in heaven. This paper examines the complex interactions between these two courts, material and spiritual, especially as revealed in art.

It is generally accepted that the Byzantines visualized the emperor's court as a reflection of the one above;[1] the relationship was expressed succinctly by Theophylaktos of Ohrid, in a letter addressed to Nikephoros Melissenos: "every emperor," he said, "is an image of God, . . . just as the archetype is higher than all [creation], so the likeness will be above all [others]."[2] Of course, the heavenly capital was more splendid than the one on earth; the Life of Basil the Younger specified that it was one hundred times larger than Constantinople.[3] This model of the two courts, one mirroring the other, seems at first sight to correspond well with such Byzantine works as the enamels now adorning the Holy Crown of Hungary, which were originally part of a gift sent to King Géza I of Hungary by Emperor Michael VII. At the front of the present crown (Fig. 1) there is an arched plaque portraying Christ elevated on his throne, flanked by six square plaques containing his archangels Michael and Gabriel, his soldier saints, George and Demetrios, and the doctor saints Kosmas and Damian. The angels and the saints recognize the suzerainty of their master by turning their heads or their eyes toward him. On the back of the crown (Fig. 2), it is Emperor Michael VII who takes the central position in an arched plaque, flanked by his son Constantine on the left and by King Géza on the right, both framed by squares. Like the saints in heaven, the Hungarian king indicates his submission to his earthly overlord by turning his eyes toward the center. Whatever was the character of the Byzantine object originally decorated by these enamels, it is plain

---

[1] See, for example, C. Mango, *Byzantium: The Empire of New Rome* (London, 1980), 151: "The Byzantines imagined God and the Heavenly Kingdom as a vastly enlarged replica of the imperial court at Constantinople. . . . their mutual resemblance was taken for granted."

[2] Ed. P. Gautier, *Théophylacte d'Achrida, Lettres* (Thessalonica, 1986), 157.14–17. Compare Psellos in an oration addressing Constantine Monomachos: "What the Creator is in relation to you, this you may be in relation to us (your subjects)." Ed. E. Kurtz and F. Drexl, *Michaelis Pselli scripta minora*, vol. I (Milan, 1936), 31.1–3.

[3] Ed. A. N. Veselovskij, *Sbornik Otdelenija russkogo jazyka i slovesnosti Imperatorskoj Akademii nauk* 46 (St. Petersburg, 1889–90), 39. For a detailed description of the architecture of the heavenly palace, having the same features as its earthly counterpart in Constantinople, see the vision of the 10th-century monk Kosmas, ed. H. Delehaye, *Synaxarium CP* 107–14, and C. Angelidi, "La version longue de la Vision du moine Cosmas," *AnalBoll* 101 (1983), 73–99. The text is summarized in Mango, *Byzantium*, 151–53.

that they always formed two groups, centered respectively on Christ flanked by his angels and on the emperor flanked by his co-emperor and the subordinate king.[4]

However, there are also significant differences between the enamels on the two faces of the crown. In the first place, only Christ is enthroned (Fig. 1). Emperor Michael, like the other figures subservient to Christ, is in bust form (Fig. 2). And second, it is not Christ who wears the imperial costume, but his angels; Michael and Gabriel wear jeweled collars similar to that of the co-emperor Constantine. So the one court is not an exact reflection of the other.

A better way to visualize the relationship is to take our cue from Lewis Carroll's *Alice through the Looking Glass*. One court *was* an image of the other, but the mirror that did the reflecting was permeable; as in the case of Alice's mirror, it was possible for characters to pass through and come out on the other side. That is, members of the earthly court, the living as well as the dead, entered the heavenly court, while members of the heavenly court entered the earthly realm and took up roles there. These looking-glass worlds existed in the Byzantines' imaginations, but were made concrete by their art. It is this interchange of characters from one setting to the other that is explored here: first some visualizations of the emperor's court in which heavenly beings are present, and then images of the divine court in which the emperor plays a role. Along the way I hope to suggest solutions to two puzzles: first, why do archangels and some nonimperial saints appear in imperial dress, and, second, why do emperors have wings?

Occasionally in Byzantine panegyrics heavenly beings are found assisting at the court on earth. Either the companions of the emperor are metaphorically described as angels, who escort the ruler as if he were Christ, or, more daringly, the angels themselves take up residence at the imperial palace, no longer being impersonated by courtiers. Thus a twelfth-century oration addressed by Gregory Antiochos to the *sebastokrator* Constantine Angelos, the brother of Isaac II, asks that the *sebastokrator* intercede with the emperor on the speaker's behalf, just as angels and martyrs mediate between men and God.[5] In a poem by the eleventh-century court rhetorician John Mauropous, we find the angels themselves guarding the palace and throne of Michael IV.[6] The orator says that the emperor seems to him to be "by nature some kind of God." He trembles at the sight of the emperor's immaterial servants, the winged angels that guard the vestibule of the palace. He has to appeal to the emperor himself for assistance in getting past them. Once John Mauropous has crossed the threshold of the palace, and has come close to the imperial throne, he fears the cherubim who are stationed there with their flaming swords and who would strike and burn him were it not for the goodwill of the emperor.

A visual counterpart to this poem is provided by the famous portrait miniatures that were painted, perhaps in 1072, as frontispieces to a collection of homilies of John Chry-

---

[4] J. Deér, *Die heilige Krone Ungarns* (Vienna, 1966); K. Wessel, *Byzantine Enamels* (Recklinghausen, 1967), 111–15, pl. 37; E. Kovács and Z. Lovag, *The Hungarian Crown and Other Regalia* (Budapest, 1980). On the problem of the original arrangement of the enamels, see especially Deér, *Die heilige Krone,* 81–88.

[5] Ed. M. Bachmann and F. Dölger, "Die Rede des μέγας δρουγγάριος Gregorios Antiochos auf den Sebastokrator Konstantinos Angelos," *BZ* 40 (1940), 400.15–401.2

[6] Ed. P. de Lagarde, *Iohannis Euchaitorum metropolitae quae in codice Vaticano graeco 676 supersunt* (Göttingen, 1882), 28–32, no. 54. See also Mango, *Byzantium,* 153.

1   Budapest, National Museum, the Holy Crown of Hungary. Christ and his court
(photo: Bildarchiv Foto Marburg)

2 Budapest, National Museum, the Holy Crown of Hungary. Michael VII Doukas and his court (photo: Bildarchiv Foto Marburg)

3   Paris, Bibliothèque Nationale, Coislin 79, fol. 2. Nikephoros III Botaneiates between court officials

4   Paris, Bibliothèque Nationale, Coislin 79, fol. 2v. Nikephoros III Botaneiates between the Archangel Michael and St. John Chrysostom

5   Berlin, Dahlem Museum, ivory. Christ between Sts. Peter and Paul (photo: Hirmer Fotoarchiv)

6   Berlin, Dahlem Museum, ivory. The Virgin between the Archangel Gabriel and Leo VI (photo: Hirmer Fotoarchiv)

7   Constantinople, St. Sophia, looking east (photo: Byzantine Photograph and Fieldwork Archives, Dumbarton Oaks)

8 Constantinople, St. Sophia, vault of sanctuary. Mosaic of the Virgin between Archangels (photo: Byzantine Photograph and Fieldwork Archives, Dumbarton Oaks)

9 Gold coin of Isaac II, mint of Constantinople, reverse. The emperor and the Archangel Michael (photo: Dumbarton Oaks)

10 Chapitre de Sion, silk. Addorsed griffins (photo: Musées Cantonaux, Sion)

11   London, British Library, Add. 39627, fol. 3. Tsar Ivan Alexander and his family

12 Copper coin of John Komnenos-Doukas, mint
of Thessalonica, reverse. Winged emperor
(after Bertelè, *L'imperatore alato,* pl. 1.1)

13 Copper coin of Michael VIII, mint of Thessalonica, reverse.
Winged emperor (photo: Bertelè, *L'imperatore alato,* pl. 1.4)

14 Nicaea, church of the Koimesis, bema, destroyed mosaics. Archangels flanking the
Hetoimasia (after Schmit, *Die Koimesis-Kirche von Nikaia,* pl. 13)

15   Constantinople, St. Sophia, mosaic in the north gallery. Emperor
Alexander (photo: Byzantine Photograph and Fieldwork Archives,
Dumbarton Oaks)

16   Gold coin of Constantine VII with Christopher,
mint of Constantinople, reverse (photo: Dumbarton Oaks)

17   Kastoria, Hagios Athanasios tou Mouzaki, fresco. Deesis with Christ and the Virgin in
imperial costumes

sostom, now Coislin 79 in the Bibliothèque Nationale.[7] It is possible that these paintings originally portrayed Emperor Michael VII Doukas but were subsequently retouched for presentation to Michael's successor, Nikephoros III Botaneiates, whose name they now bear. The miniature now on folio 2 shows the emperor on his throne, which is flanked by two imperial virtues above and by four officials below (Fig. 3). On the back of the same leaf is another miniature, which depicts the emperor standing in the center upon an ornate cushion, flanked on the right by the Archangel Michael and on the left by St. John Chrysostom, who offers the ruler a book (Fig. 4). Below the feet of the emperor, at the bottom right, is a tiny kneeling figure. Thus, on one side of the page, the emperor is flanked by his courtiers, and on the other by a saint and an archangel. The position of the archangel and the saint vis-à-vis the emperor suggests they bear the rank of courtiers. The poem inscribed above the miniature on the verso says that both St. Michael and St. John Chrysostom are asking the emperor for his goodwill toward the supplicant, who is identified as either the scribe or the painter.[8] We can, then, almost read the image as a kind of imperial deesis, with the subject asking the saint and the angel to intercede on his behalf with the emperor.[9] Here, as in the rhetoric of Gregory Antiochos and John Mauropous, access to the emperor is mediated by heavenly powers.

These, then, are visual and verbal portrayals of the emperor's court in which the emperor, in effect, plays the part of God, supported by angels and other supernatural beings. On the other hand, in Byzantine visualizations of *God's* court, the emperor is present in a subservient capacity. Nevertheless, the rhetoric of word and image assigned to him a very high rank at the heavenly court, on a par with the angels. The emperor has acquired this exalted status already on an ivory in Berlin, which depicts Leo VI. The original function of this piece is uncertain, although it has often been interpreted as the tip of a scepter (Figs. 5, 6).[10] As Kathleen Corrigan has pointed out, the design of each side of the ivory echoes the architecture of St. Sophia in Constantinople: we see the great eastern arch that supports the dome, beneath which opens the semi-dome of the central apse, flanked by the two semi-domes of the lateral niches. As in St. Sophia, the upper tier of the central apse has three windows (Fig. 7).[11] Beneath this earthly frame, appear half-length images of members of the heavenly court. In the center of the front side of the ivory is Christ flanked by Sts. Peter and Paul (Fig. 5). On the two narrow sides of the object are Sts. Kosmas and Damian, while the back displays the Virgin in the center, flanked by the Archangel Gabriel on the right (Fig. 6). The figure on the left

[7] I. Spatharakis, *The Portrait in Byzantine Illuminated Manuscripts* (Leiden, 1976), 107–18, figs. 69–76; C. L. Dumitrescu, "Remarques en marge du Coislin 79: Les trois eunuques et le problème du donateur," *Byzantion* 57 (1987), 32–45; *Byzance: L'art byzantin dans les collections publiques françaises,* exh. cat., Musée du Louvre (Paris, 1992), 360–61, no. 271 (with color reproductions of fols. 2 and 2v).

[8] Text in Spatharakis, *The Portrait in Byzantine Illuminated Manuscripts,* 112.

[9] This observation was made by Dumitrescu, "Remarques," 40–41.

[10] K. Corrigan, "The Ivory Scepter of Leo VI: A Statement of Post-Iconoclastic Imperial Ideology," *ArtB* 60 (1978), 407–16, interprets the ivory as a scepter. This identification is doubted by A. Arnulf, "Eine Perle für das Haupt Leons VI.: Epigraphische und ikonographische Untersuchungen zum sogennanten Szepter Leons VI.," *Jahrbuch der Berliner Museen* 32 (1990), 69–84, and by A. Cutler, *The Hand of the Master: Craftsmanship, Ivory, and Society in Byzantium* (Princeton, 1994), 200–201.

[11] "The Ivory Scepter of Leo VI," 413.

of the Virgin, however, is not another archangel, but the mortal emperor Leo VI, identified by an inscription, whose head the Virgin crowns, or possibly adorns with a jewel
or pearl.[12] The emperor's costume mirrors that of the archangel on the right, for, like
Leo VI, Gabriel both carries an orb and wears the imperial *loros,* the long jeweled scarf
that makes a "V" at the neck and drapes over the left forearm. The angel and the emperor even hold their staffs at identical angles. We might say that the images on the back
of the ivory echo, but also significantly change, the somewhat earlier mosaics that appeared at the east end of St. Sophia (Fig. 8). In the church the Virgin was portrayed in
the central apse, with two archangels originally flanking her, one on each side of the
barrel vault in front of the apse. In the mosaics the archangels did not wear the *loros* but
were dressed in tunic and *chlamys.* In the ivory the Virgin again appears in the center,
but the emperor has taken the place of the angel who was depicted to the left of the
Virgin in the vault of St. Sophia, while the remaining angel has been given the *loros* and
made to resemble the emperor. The ivory, then, both shows the earthly church of St.
Sophia and implies that it has been peopled by the heavenly court, in which the emperor
has been given the rank of an archangel. It is at the same time a statement of the emper-
or's present political power and a prayer for his reception into the court of heaven. Such
a double message is conveyed by the inscription on the front and back arches of the
scepter, which adapts the second verse of Psalm 20: "Lord, in your power Emperor Leo
will rejoice, and in your salvation he will exult exceedingly."[13]

The imagery of the ivory, with its mixture of heavenly and earthly beings, and its
setting in a real building in Constantinople, has parallels in some texts of the ninth
century which describe visions of the heavenly court sitting in judgment. The most vivid
of these accounts is in the late ninth-century *Absolution of Theophilos,*[14] which provides a
fascinating mixture of a specific earthly location and supernatural proceedings. The de-
fendant, the Iconoclast emperor Theophilos, is deceased; his advocate, Empress Theodora, is living; the trial judge and the court officers are from heaven; and the setting is
the Chalke gate of the Great Palace, which by the late ninth century was functioning in
real life as a law court.[15] We are told that the empress had a dream in which she saw
herself standing in the Forum, when a crowd of noisy angels came down the street,
carrying various unpleasant instruments of torture. In their midst they were dragging
Theophilos, who was naked and had his hands bound behind his back.[16] Theodora followed the procession, and when they reached the Chalke, she saw there "a huge and
fearsome man sitting on a throne, in front of the fearful and holy icon of our lord Jesus
Christ."[17] The latter was evidently the mosaic that had been placed over the Chalke gate

[12] Arnulf, "Eine Perle für das Haupt Leons VI.," 82–83.

[13] Ibid., 73.

[14] Ed. W. Regel, *Analecta byzantino-russica* (St. Petersburg, 1891), 33–35. The text is discussed by C. Mango,
The Brazen House (Copenhagen, 1959), 131–32.

[15] Theophanes Continuatus, ed. I Bekker (Bonn, 1838), 259.18–260.2. See Mango, *Brazen House,* 34.

[16] The scene can be visualized through a miniature from the 9th-century Khludov Psalter, showing an angel
pulling a sinner by the hair, with his hands bound behind him: Moscow, Historical Museum, MS gr. 129D, fol.
156; M. V. Shchepkina, *Miniatiury Khludovskoi psaltyri* (Moscow, 1977).

[17] Ed. Regel, 34.11–17.

after the end of Iconoclasm.[18] The text relates that Theodora fell in tears before the fearful and glorious emperor, and beseeched him with tears to spare Theophilos. Eventually the judge responded, "O woman, great is your faith," and her husband was pardoned and returned to her.

Another heavenly trial, described in the Life of Ignatios by Niketas David Paphlagon, actually took place in the church of St. Sophia, like the scene portrayed on the ivory of Leo VI. In this case the dreamer was the caesar Bardas, who saw himself being condemned to death before a tribunal headed by St. Peter, who was enthroned in the sanctuary of the church and flanked by two archangels standing beside him and "exhibiting the rank of *praipositoi*."[19] In the case of the vision presented on the ivory, however, the emperor is evidently in a better situation, for here he is crowned by the Virgin beneath the apse, as a colleague of the angels, not as one who is rejected by them (Fig. 6).

A similar interplay of earth and heaven, with a favorable promotion of the emperor, can be found in Leo VI's funerary oration for Basil I. Addressing his departed predecessor, Leo declares: "Now, in return for your humility without measure, you are exalted, having become lofty beside God; . . . in return for having founded temples to God, you now walk in divine palaces; in return for establishing the singing of sacred choirs, you now glory in the chants of angels."[20] Here, as on the ivory, earthly churches are linked with the court of heaven, and the emperor with the angels.

The association of emperors and angels was elaborated and made more explicit in the verbal and visual rhetoric of later centuries. For example, the eleventh-century scholar and court official Michael Psellos made use of this comparison on several occasions. In one of his panegyrics of Constantine IX Monomachos, Psellos compared his task of adequately describing the emperor's great virtues to that of Jacob struggling with the angel: even to make the attempt was to win a victory.[21] In another oration, Psellos spoke of "the angelic way of life that the emperor embraced in the palace."[22] Here the rhetor expressed a certain hesitation, for in an aside he termed his simile "a daring expression," but in another speech addressed to Constantine Monomachos he allowed himself to be yet more daring: "Shall I, then, compare you to someone? But whoever could make you a subject of comparison, you who are so great and above compare? . . . For you have outdone nature, and have become closest to the ranks of the spiritual beings . . . How, therefore, shall we complete your portrait . . . ? For you are to some extent a being with a body and without a body, both above nature and better than nature. We compare you, therefore, to the finest of bodies and to the more immeasurable of those

[18] On the icon of Christ Chalkites, see Mango, *Brazen House*, 108–42; A. Frolow, "Le Christ de la Chalcé," *Byzantion* 33 (1963), 107–20.

[19] PG 105:533D–536C (I am indebted to Alice-Mary Talbot for this reference).

[20] Ed. A. Vogt and I. Hausherr, "Oraison funèbre de Basile I," *Orientalia christiana* 26.1 (1932), 76.22–28. For an analysis of the prefatory miniatures of the Paris Gregory manuscript (Bibliothèque Nationale, MS gr. 510, fols. A–C), which associate Basil I visually with the Archangel Gabriel, see H. Maguire, "A Murderer among the Angels: The Frontispiece Miniatures of Paris. Gr. 510 and the Iconography of the Archangels in Byzantine Art," in R. Ousterhout and L. Brubaker, eds., *The Sacred Image East and West*, Illinois Byzantine Studies 4 (Urbana, 1995), 63–71.

[21] *Scripta minora*, ed. Kurtz and Drexl, I, 13.10–12.

[22] Ibid., 34.26–35.1.

without bodies."[23] We may note here that Psellos does not merely associate and rank the emperor with the bodiless angels, but he implies that the emperor's very nature partakes of the superhuman immateriality of the heavenly powers. Twelfth-century Byzantine orators also termed the emperor an angel. Michael Italikos, for example, in an oration delivered to John II Komnenos, termed him "an angel of God, sent by him to prepare the road against the enemy."[24]

The idea became even more of a commonplace at the end of the twelfth century, when the dynasty of the Angeloi came into power, for the name invited the Byzantine device of punning. It should be emphasized, however, that the panegyrists of the Angeloi were only exploiting a convention that had already become well established in Byzantine verbal and visual rhetoric. A typical example is an epigram by Theodore Balsamon, which describes a painting of Emperor Isaac II Angelos shown on horseback and wielding a sword: "As you see the angelic flood of light poured into a bodily nature, think of the salvation of the Lord. For, as the presence of God in the flesh put an end to the deadly work of Satan, so by (divine) wisdom the grace of an angel, having taken on a bodily nature, stopped the tyrannical homicide" [the reference here is to the fall of Isaac's predecessor, Andronikos I]. The poem continues, "So, seeing Angelos carrying his sword, and, indeed, Angelos wearing his crown, praise him for his sword and his crown."[25]

A visual parallel to this passage was a new type of gold coin minted by Isaac II (Fig. 9). On these nomismata, the emperor and the Archangel Michael appear paired, standing side by side and holding between them a large sword.[26] In another poem, describing the restoration of a bathing pool at the Hodegetria monastery by Isaac II, Balsamon refers to the emperor as an "angelic grace," an "angelic protection," and "chief of the angels."[27] It is, perhaps, not surprising that the western Crusaders took objection to the letters of Isaac II in which, they claimed, he "proudly and arrogantly named himself an angel of God."[28]

In the thirteenth century, the emperor finally acquired the specific iconographic attri-

[23] Ibid., 31.8–19.

[24] Ed. P. Gautier, *Michel Italikos, lettres et discours,* Archives de l'Orient chrétien 14 (Paris, 1972), 249.8–10. Compare Christ's words in reference to John the Baptist, in Matt. 11:10.

[25] Ed. K. Horna, "Die Epigramme des Theodoros Balsamon," *Wiener Studien* 25 (1903), 200, no. 43; trans. and comm. P. Magdalino and R. Nelson, "The Emperor in Byzantine Art of the Twelfth Century," *ByzF* 8 (1982), 154–60.

[26] M. F. Hendy, *Coinage and Money in the Byzantine Empire, 1081–1261* (Washington, D.C., 1969), 143, pl. 20.1–4; Magdalino and Nelson, "The Emperor in Byzantine Art," 159, fig. 13. On some bronze coins of Isaac II, a half-figure of St. Michael appears on the obverse, in imperial dress and holding a scepter in his right hand, while a similar representation of the emperor appears on the reverse, also holding a scepter; Hendy, ibid., 145, pl. 21.10 and 11.

[27] Ed. Horna, 190–91, no. 27; trans. and comm. Magdalino and Nelson, "The Emperor in Byzantine Art," 153–54. See also Balsamon's poem on an icon of the bishop of Sidon together with the emperor and the patriarch: ed. Horna, 184–85, no. 17; trans. and comm. Magdalino and Nelson, "The Emperor," 152–53.

[28] "Predictus itaque rex superbe et arroganter angelum dei et originem nostrae fidei et Romanorum imperatorem se nominans." Letter of Bishop Dietpold of Passau, in *Chronicon Magni Presbiteri,* MGH, *SS* 17 (Leipzig, 1925), 510.2–5. See T. Bertelè, *L'imperatore alato nella numismatica bizantina* (Rome, 1951), 102 note 97; E. Nau, "Der geflügelte Kaiser," *Schweizer Münzenblätter* 35 (1985), 64–69, esp. 69 note 18 (I am indebted to Philip Grierson for this reference).

butes of an angel, namely, the wings. Here it is necessary to digress briefly on the symbolism of wings in Byzantium. Angels, of course, were provided with wings to represent their powers of heavenly ascent and descent; this idea was spelled out explicitly by several Byzantine writers. For example, Ignatios, in his Life of Patriarch Nikephoros I, posed the question of why artists devised for angels the appendage of wings. He answered as follows: "In order that the angels not be perceived as men, by the addition (of wings) the artists showed the distinction . . . , hinting at their airborne nature, and their abode in heaven with God, and their rushing descents from there to us and ready ascents from us to heaven."[29] Likewise, Michael Psellos, in a treatise on the iconography of angels, explains that "their being winged hints at their exalting and heavenly ascent."[30] For emperors, before the thirteenth century, the concept of heavenward flight was symbolized by winged creatures, either by eagles,[31] which had been associated with the ascent of the emperor since Roman times, or by mythical griffins, which were associated with the flight of Alexander.[32] Eagles and griffins were depicted on the emperor's costume, as we learn, for example, from an anonymous *ekphrasis* of the jousts of an emperor who was probably Manuel I Komnenos.[33] One of the garments worn by the ruler at that tournament evidently displayed a red medallion containing golden addorsed griffins, perhaps similar to the ones on a Byzantine silk now preserved at Sion in Switzerland (Fig. 10).[34] The *ekphrasis* gives us a rare statement of the imperial symbolism of such animal motifs: "Around the shoulders in a red circle griffins spread their wings in different directions. They were golden and adorned with many pearls, intimating altogether by the circles, by the wings, and by the color that the emperor is on high and elevated; and thundering, as it were, from heaven, he performs great and wonderful deeds."[35] The emperor also had white eagles depicted in pearls on his red shoes, so that "through the whiteness of the pearls and the high flying of the birds the total elevation of the emperor might be depicted. For the emperor is spotless like a pearl and high flying like the eagles."[36] There are no extant portrayals of Byzantine emperors wearing shoes with

[29] Ed. C. de Boor, *Nicephori archiepiscopi constantinopolitani opuscula historica* (Leipzig, 1880), 184.30–185.7. I thank Alice-Mary Talbot for this reference.

[30] Ed. K. Snipes, "An Unedited Treatise of Michael Psellos on the Iconography of Angels," in *Gonimos: Neoplatonic and Byzantine Studies Presented to Leendert G. Westerink at 75*, ed. J. Duffy and J. Peradotto (Buffalo, 1988), 200.4–5.

[31] J.M.C. Toynbee, *Animals in Roman Life and Art* (London, 1973), 242; S. G. MacCormack, *Art and Ceremony in Late Antiquity* (Berkeley, 1981), 99–100, 317 note 30.

[32] See especially C. Settis Frugoni, *Historia Alexandri elevati per griphos ad aeram. Origine, iconographia e fortuna di un tema*, Istituto storico italiano per il medio evo, Studi storici, fasc. 80–82 (Rome, 1973), esp. 147–207; V. P. Darkevich, *Svetskoe iskusstvo Vizantii* (Moscow, 1975), 154–58; L. Bouras, *The Griffin through the Ages* (Athens, 1983); S. Ćurčić, "Some Uses (and Re-uses) of Griffins in Late Byzantine Art," in *Byzantine East, Latin West: Art-Historical Studies in Honor of Kurt Weitzmann*, ed. D. Mouriki et al. (Princeton, 1995), 597–601.

[33] Ed. S. P. Lambros, *Neos Ellenomnemon* 5 (1908), 3–18.

[34] W. F. Volbach, *Il tessuto nell'arte antica* (Milan, 1966), 148, fig. 69. Compare also two silks preserved in Berlin, illustrated in O. von Falke, *Kunstgeschichte der Seidenweberei*, vol. II (Berlin, 1913), pls. 247–48. A depiction of a figure labeled as Alexios V and wearing a garment woven with griffins in medallions appears on fol. 291v of Vienna, National Library, MS hist. gr. 53 (chronicle of Niketas Choniates): Spatharakis, *The Portrait in Byzantine Illuminated Manuscripts*, 155–58, fig. 99.

[35] Ed. Lambros, 17.27–31. The text of Lambros reads γύπες, but the correct reading must surely be γρῦπες.

[36] Ibid., 18.6–8.

eagles depicted on them, but this type of footgear is worn by the Bulgarian tsar Ivan Alexander as he is portrayed in his Gospel book in London (Fig. 11).[37] Moreover, there are several surviving portraits of Byzantine emperors with their feet resting on red cushions decorated with eagles, as may be seen, for example, in a chrysobull of Andronikos II dated 1301.[38]

The convergence of these two traditions, the comparison of the emperor to an angel, and his association with winged creatures, made the next step logical: the emperor himself had to be given wings. Already in an oration of Constantine Manasses, Manuel I Komnenos was called "winged" (πτερωτός) in the context of military pursuit,[39] but it was not until the thirteenth century that the emperor specifically acquired wings in visual imagery. The earliest appearance of this motif occurred in the coinage of the Empire of Thessalonica, where certain copper issues of John Komnenos-Doukas (1237–44) showed a full-length figure of a winged emperor wearing a jeweled crown and *loros* (Fig. 12).[40] This imagery was continued at Thessalonica on coins of Michael VIII, which clearly show the emperor standing between two large wings that extend to the ground (Fig. 13).[41] A similar winged portrait occurred on some coins of Andronikos II.[42] Here, too, there were close parallels between verbal and visual oratory, as may be demonstrated by a juxtaposition of the coins minted by Michael VIII with some verses composed by Manuel Holobolos in praise of the same emperor, who, since he was related to the Angeloi, was in name doubly an angel.[43] The title of one of the poems specifies that it was written for the *prokypsis* ceremony, during which the emperor together with his sons appeared on a curtained dais, or stage, flanked by lights. In this poem, we find that Michael VIII does not simply associate with angels, as Basil I did in the rhetoric of his time, but the Palaiologan emperor and his sons *become* the three angels who were entertained by Abraham: "Like an intelligible tent bearing three angels, this bright eminence bears the emperor with his children."[44]

Another of the poems of Holobolos echoes a passage in an oration of Themistios comparing the emperor's virtues to the wings of statues and paintings of Eros and Nike.[45]

[37] British Library, MS add. 39627, fol. 3; Spatharakis, *The Portrait in Byzantine Illuminated Manuscripts,* 69–70, fig. 39; color illustration in L. Shivkova, *Das Tetraevangeliar des Zaren Ivan Alexandar* (Recklinghausen, 1977), 85. I am grateful to Slobodan Ćurčić for this reference.

[38] Athens, Byzantine Museum, MS 80: Spartharakis, *The Portrait in Byzantine Illuminated Manuscripts,* 184–85, fig. 134. See also, among others, the portraits of John VI Kantakouzenos in Paris, Bibliothèque Nationale, MS gr. 1242, fols. 5v and 123v: Spatharakis, *The Portrait in Byzantine Illuminated Manuscripts,* 129–39, figs. 86–87; color reproductions in *Byzance* (as in note 7 above), pp. 419, 461.

[39] Ed. E. Kurtz, "Dva neisdannyh proizvedenija Konstantina Manassi," *VizVrem* 12 (1906), 91.108.

[40] Bertelè, *L'imperatore alato,* 19, pl. 1.1; Hendy, *Coinage and Money,* 285, pl. 41.17–18; P. Grierson, *Byzantine Coins* (Berkeley, 1982), 242–43.

[41] Bertelè, *L'imperatore alato,* 19–20, pl. 1.2–7. The most conspicuous monument associating Michael VIII with his angelic namesake was the great bronze statue group of the emperor kneeling before the archangel that was placed, before 1280, on top of a column in front of the church of the Holy Apostles in Constantinople; see A.-M. Talbot, "The Restoration of Constantinople under Michael VIII," *DOP* 47 (1993), 243–61, esp. 258–60.

[42] Bertelè, *L'imperatore alato,* 21–24, pls. 1.8–2.25.

[43] These passages are noted by Bertelè, *L'imperatore alato,* 50, and discussed by A. Heisenberg, *Aus der Geschichte und Literatur der Palaiologenzeit* (Munich, 1920), 112–32.

[44] Ed. J. F. Boissonade, *Anecdota graeca,* V (Paris, 1833), 167, no. 7.

[45] Ed. G. Downey, *Themistii orationes,* vol. I (Leipzig, 1965), 227.27–228.1.

Here Holobolos describes the emperor's two sons as his two wings: "O crown-bearing Angel, let your wings be said to be the great Andronikos, the victor over all men, the wondrous emperor, the image of your glory, and the famous and wondrous scion of the purple. . . . Therefore, with these, O emperor, rule for many suns, cherishing the race of the Romans, O powerful one, with your wings."[46]

It is now time to turn to the problem of why archangels appear in imperial dress in Byzantine art. The imperially costumed archangel already appeared at an early period, as can be seen in the sixth-century mosaics of Sant' Apollinare in Classe in Ravenna, where Gabriel and Michael wear the same red shoes and purple cloak as Emperor Justinian in the mosaic in San Vitale.[47] In post-Iconoclastic Byzantine art, archangels were frequently shown in the costume of contemporary emperors, that is, draped in the narrow *loros,* wearing red pearl-studded shoes and carrying orbs, as could be seen, for example, in the mosaics restored after 843 in the bema of the Koimesis church at Nicaea (Fig. 14).[48] The angelic costume here resembles that of Emperor Alexander as he is shown in his mosaic portrait in St. Sophia (Fig. 15).[49] As a general rule, the archangels assume these imperial vestments in Byzantine art only when they accompany Christ or the Virgin in images of the *heavenly* court, such as the Vision of Ezekiel, the Christ "Pantokrator," the Hetoimasia or "Prepared Throne" (Fig. 14), the Deesis, the Last Judgment, and the Virgin enthroned or being assumed into heaven. As we have seen, the Archangel Gabriel also assumes this imperial costume on the ivory of Leo VI, where he accompanies Christ and the Virgin, even though the heavenly court is framed here by St. Sophia (Fig. 6). In Byzantine art, however, when the same archangels appear in *earthly* contexts where they are no longer part of the heavenly retinue, they usually change their attire, appearing in the antique tunic and *himation,* as when Gabriel announces the incarnation of Christ to Mary, or in military dress, as when St. Michael appears to Joshua, or in either of these costumes, as when the same angel performs the miracle at Chonae. While it is true that the archangels may, on occasion, retain their red shoes for these terrestrial visits, they almost invariably put aside the imperial *loros* and globe.[50] In Byzantine texts, also, angels and archangels do not appear on earth dressed

---

[46] Ed. Boissonade, *Anecdota graeca,* 173–74, no. 12. See also ibid., 168–69, no. 8.

[47] F. W. Deichmann, *Frühchristliche Bauten und Mosaiken von Ravenna* (Baden-Baden, 1958), figs. 370, 402–3; idem, *Ravenna: Hauptstadt des spätantiken Abendlandes,* vol. II.2 (Wiesbaden, 1976), 245.

[48] T. Schmit, *Die Koimesis-Kirche von Nikaia* (Berlin, 1927), 23–28, pls. 13–14.

[49] P. A. Underwood and E.J.W. Hawkins, "The Mosaics of Hagia Sophia at Istanbul: The Portrait of the Emperor Alexander," *DOP* 15 (1961), 187–217. See also C. Mango, "St. Michael and Attis," Δελτ.Χριστ.Ἀρχ.Ἑτ., 4th ser., 12 (1984), 39–62, esp. 43.

[50] The exceptions to the rule that archangels only appear with globe and *loros* when they are participating in scenes of the heavenly court tend to be late, and on the margins of the Byzantine empire. They include the 14th-century paintings of the Annunciation at Staro Nagoričino (G. Millet, *La peinture du moyen âge en Yougoslavie,* vol. III [Paris, 1962], pl. 79.3–4), and Dečani (V. R. Petković and D. Bošković, *Dečani,* vol. II [Belgrade, 1941], pl. 171). For a discussion of this iconography, see G. Millet, *Recherches sur l'iconographie de l'Évangile* (Paris, 1916), 87. On one object only, a silver cross fragment at Dumbarton Oaks, does St. Michael assume full imperial dress in a depiction of the Miracle of Chonae; see S. Gabelić, "The Iconography of the Miracle at Chonae, an Unusual Example from Cyprus," *Zograf* 20 (1989), 95–103, esp. 98, fig. 1, and J. A. Cotsonis, *Byzantine Figural Processional Crosses,* exh. cat., Dumbarton Oaks (Washington, D.C., 1994), 81–83, fig. 29. On the costuming of angels, see in general D. I. Pallas, "Himmelsmächte, Erzengel und Engel," *RBK,* III, 13–119, esp. 26–31; Mango, "St. Michael and Attis," esp. 39–44.

as emperors but as court eunuchs. For example, a text of the Miracles of St. Michael contained in an eleventh-century manuscript speaks of the archangel making a nocturnal appearance in a church while clad in the garments of a *praipositos,* that is, the chief of the eunuchs.[51] In the legendary *Narratio de S. Sophia,* the angel who guards the church of St. Sophia is described as "a eunuch dressed in bright clothing, beautiful in appearance, as if in truth sent from the palace."[52] Paul of Monemvasia tells a story of a sick man who had a near-death vision of a eunuch from the palace who appeared with a glorious retinue to call him to account for his sins.[53] Finally, the *Dream-Book* of Achmet says that if someone dreams of a beautiful eunuch, the eunuch should be interpreted as an angel.[54]

While it may seem logical for angels to appear in the guise of eunuchs on earth, at first sight it is puzzling that Byzantine artists portrayed the archangels in imperial dress at the court of Christ; this iconography has, indeed, been seen as an anomaly by modern scholars.[55] Although Byzantine writers spoke of the archangels' command over the heavenly hosts,[56] both early Christian and Byzantine authors concurred that Christ was the *basileus,* or "despot," while the angels were his servants.[57] The portrayal of Michael and Gabriel in imperial costume was even attacked as an idolatrous image of pagan derivation by Severus, the sixth-century patriarch of Antioch,[58] in a text that was subsequently cited at the Second Council of Nicaea.[59] Why, in view of this history, was the iconography of imperial archangels preserved in post-Iconoclastic Byzantine art, and why was it even brought up to date vis-à-vis contemporary imperial costume, with the addition of the narrow *loros* or scarf? The answer lies in the interconnections between the earthly and the heavenly courts. It would have made no sense to dress the archangels in the imperial insignia if the two courts were parallel but completely separate, that is, perfect mirror

[51] Ed. F. Halkin, *Inédits byzantins d'Ochrida, Candie et Moscou* (Brussels, 1963), 150; cited by Mango, *Byzantium,* 155. See also the passage from the Life of St. Ignatios by Niketas Paphlagon, cited in note 19 above.

[52] Ed. T. Preger, *Scriptores originum Constantinopolitanarum,* vol. I (Leipzig, 1901), 86.9–11; cited by Mango, *Byzantium,* 155. See also G. Dagron, *Constantinople imaginaire* (Paris, 1984), 201 and 292.

[53] Ed. J. Wortley, *Les récits édifiants de Paul, évêque de Monembasie, et d'autres auteurs* (Paris, 1987), 38.46–51.

[54] Ed. F. Drexl, *Achmetis oneirocriticon* (Leipzig, 1925), 6.7–11. An exception to these appearances of angels as court eunuchs is a tale in the *Narratio de S. Sophiae* concerning an angel appearing to the master builder of St. Sophia in the guise of Justinian, but this is perhaps a special case, as the point of the story is that the angel was impersonating the patron; ed. Preger, I, 90.18–19. On the earthly appearances of angels, see also Mango, "St. Michael and Attis," 44, and idem, *Byzantium,* 155.

[55] Mango, "St. Michael and Attis," 39.

[56] For example, Psellos wrote in an encomium of St. Michael: "For he, having from the beginning been entrusted with the rule and power over the angels, watches over their ranks." Ed. Kurtz and Drexl (as in note 2 above), 121.9–11.

[57] Thus Eusebios stated that Christians, like Jews, consider angels to be "powers subject to and ministering the all imperial God"; *Praeparatio evangelica,* 7.5.18, ed. K. Mras, GCS 8.1 (Berlin, 1954), 394; cited by Mango, "St. Michael and Attis," 39. Constantine VII spoke of "Christ the despot, and Gabriel the first of the angelic powers"; *Vita Basilii,* 83; ed. Bekker, 325.12–13.

[58] *Homiliae cathedrales,* ed. and trans M. Brière, PO 12.1 (1919), 83–84.

[59] Mansi, XIII, 184c. C. Mango proposed that the iconography of the imperially dressed archangel may have originated outside the official church, being associated with the winged *Kosmokrator* Attis, whose cult was strong in western Asia Minor; "St. Michael and Attis," 55–62.

images, but it was perfectly logical if the two courts were interpenetrating, with each incorporating members of the other. Until the fourteenth century, in Byzantine depictions of the *heavenly* court, imperial dress was a costume of the second rank, assumed by both emperors and archangels, and even occasionally by nonimperial saints. In the *earthly* court, on the other hand, the *loros,* the pearly red shoes, and the orb was the costume of the first rank, as can be seen in the mosaic of Emperor Alexander in St. Sophia (Fig. 15). Archangels in their visits to earth, if they did not wear the antique tunic and *himation,* generally changed into appropriate second-rank costumes, appearing in the guise of generals or court eunuchs, as we have seen. In the heavenly court, however, archangels wore imperial costume because they were ranked by political ideology with the earthly emperors, who were definitely not emperors in heaven. For this reason, Michael Psellos, in his treatise on the iconography of archangels, does not interpret the spheres they carry as symbols of imperial power, as they would be on earth. Instead he says that they convey the quickness of the angels' movement.[60]

In Byzantine literary descriptions of heaven, it is not Christ who appears dressed in imperial costume, but his subordinates, such as saints arrayed in their glory. For example, in the Life of St. Andrew the Fool we read how Epiphanios, a disciple of the holy man, prayed that St. Andrew's status in heaven should be revealed to him. He was rewarded that night with a splendid vision in which he saw God on an elevated throne, flanked by a host of angels. Although Christ is termed by the text *basileus,* and his appearance is said to be of indescribable brilliance, he does not wear an imperial costume.[61] It is St. Andrew himself who carries the imperial insignia, specifically a scepter and a crown decorated with jewels and pearls; the text says that the latter had "the cross of the imperial crown" at the front.[62] Such crosses appear prominently on imperial crowns depicted on coins, as can be seen in the images of Constantine VII and Christopher on the reverse of the nomisma illustrated in Figure 16.[63] Another vision of this kind concerns St. Athanasia of Aegina. According to her ninth-century biography, forty days after her death she revisited her nunnery, where she appeared in her heavenly costume. Two of the nuns were surprised to see her standing before the sanctuary of the church being dressed by angels in the attire of an empress, in a purple robe adorned with pearls and precious stones, and being crowned with a crown having crosses at the front and back.[64] These stories from the saints' lives confirm that, as far as the *heavenly* court was concerned, the imperial dress was the costume of honored servants of God, worn by archangels, saints, and emperors alike. Only in the fourteenth century, and only outside of Byzantine territory, as the emperors in Constantinople became increasingly weak and powerless, was it possible for artists to introduce a new iconography which gave the

[60] Ed. Snipes (as in note 30 above), 200.5–8.

[61] PG 111:736B–D.

[62] Ibid., 737B–C.

[63] On this feature of the imperial crown, see P. Grierson, *Catalogue of the Byzantine Coins in the Dumbarton Oaks Collection,* vol. III.1 (Washington, D.C., 1993), 127–30, table 13.

[64] Ed. F. Halkin, "Vie de sainte Athanasie d'Égine," in *Six inédits d'hagiologie byzantine,* SubsHag 74 (Brussels, 1987), 191. Alice-Mary Talbot kindly brought this passage to my attention.

imperial costume to Christ, as King of Kings.[65] When it was no longer feasible to imagine that the reigning Byzantine emperor was playing an important role at the court of Christ, *then* it was possible without confusion to clothe Christ himself in imperial costume, as can be seen at Hagios Athanasios tou Mouzaki at Kastoria, which preserves one of the finest examples of the new iconography (Fig. 17).[66] In these frescoes, which date to 1384/5, on the eve of the Ottoman conquest of Kastoria from the Albanian Musachi family, we see Christ wearing a *loros* and a domed crown with *prependoulia,* attended by the Virgin, also with an imperial crown, and by saints dressed as contemporary courtiers.[67] Here, finally, we have a depiction of the heavenly court that truly mirrors the earthly court, but only when the court at Constantinople is on the brink of extinction.

In our consideration of the heavenly court, we have traced the slow development of an idea, through several centuries of Byzantine verbal and visual rhetoric. The angelic emperor was a *topos,* but not an unchanging one. At the beginning of our period, in the oratory and art addressed to Basil I and Leo VI, the emperor was only an associate of the angels, sharing their space at the heavenly court and similar in costume and pose. Then, in the eleventh and twelfth centuries, the rhetoric of the comparison began to pass from association to identification. The emperor did not merely join the ranks of the angels, but his very nature became angelic. Finally, in the thirteenth century the emperor was explicitly given wings, and the identification was complete.

For the Byzantines the heavenly and the earthly courts were not discrete entities, one mirroring the other, but they were overlapping. This intermingling of the two courts helps to explain some iconographic features that have puzzled present-day historians, such as the archangels in imperial dress. Both angels and emperors were courtiers in heaven. The intermingling of the courts also set the angels and saints in a curious double role. In the heavenly court they served Christ and interceded with Christ on behalf of the emperor. In the earthly court they on occasion served the emperor, and interceded with him on behalf of his subjects. Many of these imperial texts and images, therefore, had a double function, for their rhetoric was addressed to both courts at the same time. In the earthly court their function was to elevate the status of the emperor by means of hyperbole and high-flown associations with heaven. But in the heavenly court their function was to address the medieval ruler's fears and anxiety, to which the hyperbole of both images and texts responded. The other side of flattery was insecurity. Like everyone else, the emperors had need of safety from the dangers of both this world and the next. If the emperors had a special status among supernatural beings, this was certainly an advantage they were eager to exploit, not just to impress their subjects, but also to reassure themselves of the security that came from powerful associates.

University of Illinois, Urbana-Champaign

---

[65] On the iconography, see L. Grigoriadou, "L'image de la Déesis Royale dans une fresque du XIVe siècle à Castoria," *Actes du XIV Congrès International des Études byzantines,* vol. II (Bucharest, 1975), 47–52.

[66] Ibid., figs. 1–2; S. Pelekanidis, M. Chatzidakis, *Kastoria* (Athens, 1985), 106, figs. 12–13.

[67] For parallels to the costumes in 14th-century depictions of Byzantine rulers and officials, see Grigoriadou, "L'image de la Déesis Royale," 48–51.

Index